THE MAKING
OF A COUNTRY
LAWYER

ST. MARTIN'S PRESS ❦ NEW YORK

THE MAKING

OF A COUNTRY

LAWYER

GERRY SPENCE

Production Editor: David Stanford Burr
Book Design by Gretchen Achilles

ISBN 0-312-14673-6

CONTENTS

———

ACKNOWLEDGMENTS

WITH GREAT LOVE and gratitude I think of the many who have contributed important parts of their lives to me. Some were not mentioned in this book or were given short shrift because, from the standpoint of the book's structure, their great contributions to me could not be adequately told. I think, of course, of Ann Fidelia Wilson, the mother of my children. We were married twenty-one years and her gifts to me were immense and selfless. I think also of the women who worked for me as assistants and secretaries, Kathleen McMillen, Cleo Arguello, Dee Kleppinger, and, of course, Rosemary McIntosh whose loyal contributions to my journey are uncountable. These rare and wonderful years I have lived with Imaging and the transformation her life has worked on mine is a magical story in itself and will, perhaps, someday be adequately chronicled.

My dear friend, John Johnson, who died during the writing of this book, is responsible for much of my growth as a person. I have often said, he introduced me to Gerry Spence. Bob Rose took me in when I needed a friend and has remained my closest and dearest friend and brother these many years. I think of my partners in the law, the incomparable Ed Moriarity, as loyal and decent a friend as a man ever had, and I think of my other longtime partners, Bob Schuster and Gary Shockey who, with Skip Jacobson and Doug McCalla are the best examples I know of both men and lawyers. They have stood by me and my family when more timid souls would have fled, and when I asked, they have taken the load from me.

My children, Kip, Kerry, Kent, Katy, Brents and Christopher, have made me proud, and have taught me to be a parent as we, their mothers and I, have attempted to lead them in such ways that they might discover themselves. I have been richly gifted with many other friends, both living and dead. I remember this one last time Tommy Vass, and Jack Hohnholtz my hunting partners, who I loved and who died too early.

If this book should prove to have ultimate merit it is in great part due to the vision, the work and the meticulous caring of Bob Weil, my editor and close friend. The book was his idea. D. J. Bassett, the photographer, and also my friend, is responsible for much of the photographic content. I must acknowledge the family I enjoy at St. Martin's Press. There are few such houses left anymore where an author can find such closeness and attention. I thank Tom McCormack, Sally Richardson, Roy Gainsburg, and Michael Pratt for their faith in the book. I thank John Mooney, John Murphy, Becky Koh, Mark Kohut, Barbara Andrews, Lisa Bianchi, and the wonderful staff of marketers and salespersons who have brought this book to the readers of America, and my agent, Peter Lampack, Sandra Blanton, and the rest of their powerful staff. Without all of these people I would have been talking to myself.

PROLOGUE

—

Esther Sophie Spence, mother of Gerry Spence.

SHE WAS A woman you'd look at, all right, a woman you wouldn't mind people seeing you with, but up close you knew something was awry. Her dark hair, burnt umber, was graying slightly, but in inconsequential places. You suspected that she had had the face messed with, put the money out to some surgeon who does the same procedure on six hundred different women a year at five thousand dollars a throw. He could do one in his sleep. You know how they look, those kinds of faces, smooth, especially under the eyes, the eyes not left with any tracks of life, not one. Each side of the nose pulled down, tight, the skin translucent, even through the powder, like rawhide on a drum. Back up a little, say three feet, and it was all right. The woman's eyes were ordinary blue and tired, but it was hard to see much more there. Still, in the dream, I could tell she was my mother, and she had come home.

I had recognized her before she saw me. And I had called out to her, and I had grabbed both of her hands and pulled her to me. "Mother!" I cried. She shied back to focus on me. Then she pulled a hand free, and she covered part of her face, as if in horror. I was so old. I was an old man. The last time she had seen me I was a boy of twenty, blond, thin, and tall as a lodgepole pine grows in the shade. She looked younger than I had remembered her; the face-lift, I suppose. The last time I'd seen her she'd been sitting silently across from me in that small, forest green living room, my mother, distant, cool, held back as she had been.

"Mother, you have come home!" I was crying. An old man crying. "You have come home."

She stared at me.

"I'm your son. I'm Gerry. Don't you remember me?"

She stared as if in disbelief.

"I'm old, now, Mother. On the outside, old," I tried to lighten it up, "but on the inside I'm still your boy. Your boy, Mother. Aren't you glad to see me?"

"Oh, yes, of course," she said, politely. Her hand came down from her face as if she had finally recognized me.

"But you look so young," I said. "How can that be?"

"I am not young," she said. She lifted up a foot, and she slipped off her shoe for me to see. The top of her foot was decrepit, bulging with ugly varicosities, the flesh old and crinkled up like bleached tripe.

And then the music began, and we walked over to where the people were dancing, and I said, "Would you care to dance?" and she didn't reply, just stood there, equivocal, off somewhere else. I took her in my arms, and I told her how glad I was that she had come home, and she said nothing in response, and we danced—I can't remember the music, nothing special—and at that moment before I awakened from my dream, I was very happy.

PART ONE

THE BOY

———

CHAPTER 1

Gerald M. Spence, father of Gerry Spence, at age ninety-two.

IN WYOMING, ON the endless prairies, the meadowlarks attack the world with song. You can hear the war in every direction, the joyous warbling born of new life, pounding in high, melodious trills against the thin air of spring, and the war-bling back, like great cannons of rapture exploding across the countryside.

I thought how we had walked together across those blithe lands, my father, and I as a child. We were silent as churchgoers, silent in the presence of the music. Neither my father nor I spoke, for no one would sully the sound of the singing with words. Now in another landscape as cold and brittle as a hospital room the old man lay waiting for the nurses to bring in the gurney. Gurneys haul off the dead, or those about to die. They also transport the desperate to desper-ate places. Soon the nurses would take my father to the operating room. His lung was cancerous. Had to come out. He was eighty-two, but if he were a meadowlark he would have been singing.

The family had gathered at his bedside. If you listened to the sounds of the people talking, you would be put in mind of parishioners gathered in the church basement for a covered-dish supper. Tom, my brother, twelve years younger than I, and my father were telling stories about their hunting trips, the "do-you-remember-whens," while Mae, my stepmother, poised and proper and sweet as fresh-picked chrysanthemums, was adding her smallish laugh. My sister Barbara, two years older than Tom, joined in, and Imaging, my wife, sat silently, mostly watching me, a small worried smile on her face.

I sat back, thinking: The nurses are going to come in here any minute with that gurney, and they're going to haul my father off, and I'm never going to see him again. He'd already had a half-dozen heart attacks of one kind or another. This old man is going to die, I thought, and the last words from his lips are going to be this, this meaningless chatter, like squirrels in the woods "chip-chip-chipping" away about Lord knows what, while the hunter is taking aim on one of them.

I pulled my chair up close to the old man's bed and held his soft, bony old hand. He squeezed my hand back to say he was still strong. Then he looked at me, smiled, and gave me one of his winks, as if the wink would take care of everything.

"Dad," I began, "this is a pretty serious operation, as you know, and I've been wondering if there's anything we ought to be talking about before the nurses come."

"Why, I don't think so. Everything's taken care of. We got our wills and things."

"Well, just in case things don't come out as we figure they will, have you made—you know—arrangements?"

"Yes," he said, slightly annoyed. "Mae and I bought one of those prepaid plans a few years back. They take care of everything, come get ya, take ya to the crematory, and deliver back the ashes. It's all fixed up." I remembered how he used to make jokes about the ashes. A person could never be sure whose they were. "Maybe an alley cat's," he'd say, "and the whole family getting all teared up over an old alley cat's ashes." Then that smile of his would spread itself from one big ear to the other, and his ears would move backward with the smile when it had reached its maximum, and his old faded blue eyes would laugh, too. "The way I look at it, ashes are ashes," he said. "It doesn't make a whole lot of difference."

"Well, Dad, sometimes a man has some unfinished business, and I was wondering if you had any."

He thought a long time, to make sure. "I guess we do have some unfinished business," he said at last.

"What's that?" I asked, mindful of my duty as the eldest child.

"Well, there's a bunch a skunks under the house. I been trying to trap 'em with that box trap I made. You remember how I made one of those box traps for you when you were a kid? You tie a piece of meat on the trigger and when the old skunk takes a yank on it," he slapped the palm of one hand with the other, "down comes the lid! Well, I'd appreciate it, son, if you got the skunks out from under the house. Mae has lived with a skunk all these years, and after I go she

shouldn't have to live with any others."
That smile again, the ears moving
back with it.

Now I was making conversation.
"What do you do with the skunks that
you catch, Dad?"

"Well, you just throw the trap,
skunk and all, into the back of the
pickup and haul it down the road
about twenty miles, and open up the
trap and turn the little fellow loose,
careful as to which end of the skunk

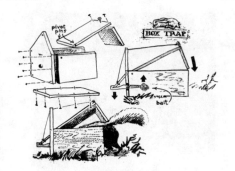

Box trap.

comes out first. He's too far away to get home again." He thought for a moment.
"But once in a blue moon the trap comes down too quick and the lid falls on the
skunk, and then you have to get out the old .22 and shoot it—you remember,
the old .22 you and I used to shoot rabbits with. You can bury the skunk in the
roses."

"In the roses?"

"Why, yes," he said. "That way, the skunk comes up in the spring as a rose.
Now that's something, isn't it?" His smile again.

"That is something," I said. "Which brings up the question, where do you
want your ashes spread if it should ever come to that?"

"Well, in that event," he said, his smile coming well ahead of his words, "you
can just take the ashes, whosever they are, and bury them in the roses with the
skunk."

Then the nurses came with the gurney, and he lifted himself up and on it
like a condemned man happy to get it over, and when he saw the worried look
on my face he said. "Well now, son, don't you worry. There's a lot worse ways of
dyin' than on the operating table." Then he added quickly, "I'll be back."

I reached down and kissed him on the lips. Spence men kiss each other.
Then he gave me that wink again, which meant that the subject was closed, and
everything would be all right, and the nurses wheeled him away.

We walked fast alongside the gurney, keeping up with the nurses, and when
they pushed him through the door, we all said, "See you soon, Dad," and, "Love
you." Nobody said, "Good luck," because nobody wanted to admit there might
be bad luck, and nobody said, "Good-bye," because nobody wanted to believe
that this might be the last good-bye.

Suddenly I felt the same feeling of fear and the same shame of my fear that
I had felt many times when, as a boy hunting with my father, he had left me
alone deep in the Big Horn Mountains.

"There's nothing to be afraid of here, son," he'd say. But I was afraid, nothing or not. "Good tracking snow today. I'm just going to keep on this old elk's
trail for a while, see where he's goin', see if he's gonna stop somewhere for a

Boy alone in the woods.

breather, long enough to get us a little elk steak."

"I want to go with you," I'd say.

"You can't keep up in this deep snow, sonny. You just stay right there. I'll be back. And remember: There's nothing to hurt you out here. Only thing a man ever needs to be afraid of in the woods is another man. Bad men never come up here. Only good men love the mountains."

"What happens if you don't come back?" I wanted to say. And I wanted to cry. But a ten-year-old boy wasn't going to let his father know he was afraid. I wanted to ask, "What would happen to me if I got lost up here?" But I knew. He'd told me many times. You go down. Always go downstream and you'll finally hit civilization.

Probably never make it down. Probably perish in the wilderness, freeze to death. Besides, if he didn't come by dark I would go looking for him. Maybe he'd be struggling in the snow, his leg broken, or maybe I'd find him under a huge boulder that had fallen on him. But one thing I instinctively knew. My father never got lost. Not my father, the hunter.

After the door on the operating room closed, we all walked back to my father's room and sat down to wait. He'd never failed to keep his promise. "I'll be back," he said, grinning up from the gurney. I looked at Mae with that stoic smile on her face, her hair, cotton white, her hands folded across her lap. She'd be alone in this world without my father. She must have known the terror I felt as a child. I looked at my brother and sister. They would lose a man who had been both father and mother to them if he didn't come back from that cold, bright-lighted place where masked men told jokes to each other while an old heart struggled against the assaults of scalpels and saws. Yet neither Mae nor my brother nor my sister wept nor trembled nor said they were afraid.

As I waited for the nurses to return our father, either his bony corpse or a gasping, racked old body with but a single lung, I thought how we are still too afraid of fear to speak of it. What if I began to weep in front of my sister and my brother? What if I began to cry out like a child lost in the woods? Even as a child I knew I could not survive the sound of my own terror cutting through the silence of the forest. We are not brave. We are too frightened of fear to give in to it. Oh, I wished then, as I have always wished, as I wish even now, that I could be fearless like my father.

When they brought the old man out of the operating room he was as still as death, and gray. His cheeks were sunken and the bones of his skull were plain to see. His lips were purple, his eyes half open. But not seeing. He looked worse than death, for those we see in death have been remade, fluffed up, puffed up, stuffed into pretty, silk-lined caskets. But my father was breathing. He had tubes in his nose, and his mouth was open and the drool of the unconscious collected at the corners. I wiped his mouth with a piece of tissue by the side of the bed and then we waited.

Pretty soon he stirred. Then he looked at me as if he didn't see me. His old blue eyes, like glassy blue marbles hidden deep inside the lids, held no expression. He made no sound except the sound of labored breathing. Then I heard him call my name in a far-off whisper, like a wraith crying from the firmament.

"Gerry."

"I'm here, Dad."

"Bring me a glass of water." Of course. The old man was thirsty. He had lost a lot of blood and a whole lung. I saw the fluids dripping down the long plastic tube into his arm. But he needed more. I stepped over to the sink, quickly filled a glass and brought it to him. He took it in his left hand, and before I could stop him he reached up with his right hand, pulled the oxygen tube out of his nose and stuck it into the glass of water. Then seeing that bubbles were being made, confirming that a flow of oxygen was being maintained, he nodded his approval, stuck the tube back into his nose and dozed off.

Within a few weeks he was out in the garden tending to the roses. He got rid of the skunks himself.

CHAPTER 2

Gerry and Little Peggy at Christmas.

"IT WAS A COLD night in hell the night that kid was born," my father liked to say. "Twenty below and blowin'." The wind always blew in Laramie. "You could hear the window glass in the old house a rattlin', and that boy's been rattlin' ever since." I was the first born to Gerald and Esther Spence, born at home with the help of a midwife shortly after midnight on January 8, 1929, in that small rented house at 600 South Fourteenth Street, Laramie, Wyoming.

My father was a country boy, a "hillbilly kid," as, in his later years, he liked to call himself. You could see him coming a mile off, the way he walked, his hands in his pockets with that towheaded chubby-faced fat-kneed little kid between him and that farm girl in her homemade dress, the hem in the back crooked, the stitches all askew, that innocent look on her face. The carneys caught him right away. Breathing sucker. Showed him how to play the shell game.

"Ya got me that time, Mac." And my father wins a couple. Easy. Wins a couple more. The carney is crying. "My God, the boss is going to fire me. Fifty cents a throw. Give me a chance to win a little back." Carney loses again. You can see the farm girl tugging at her husband's sleeve. That's my mother. "Come on, Gerald," she says to my father. "Let's go. Gerry wants to ride on the Ferris wheel, and there's the loop-o-plane if you really want to be brave and all. Come on." Her voice is soft.

"I want to ride in the bumper cars," I holler. Six years old—something like that.

"The kid can ride in the bumper cars all night, lady, but don't go yet. This guy has took me for four dollars,

Gerry at three months.

and four dollars is a week's work at this carnival. I tell you one thing, mister. I am in a peck of trouble. Have a heart. I'm just a workin' stiff too, and these are hard Hoover times. Give me a chance to get even. Which shell? You seen it. That one? Well, I'll be damned. Where the hell did that pea go to? I woulda swore you was right. But here it is! Well, let's try 'er again. You musta been distracted. Pretty girl go by there just when you was supposed to be lookin' here? Wouldn't want the little lady to think you was lookin' at the wrong place now, would you?"

"Come on, honey. Gerry wants to ride the bumper cars. We could ride 'em, too. Ten cents a ride. We could spare a ride or two." Her voice isn't plaintive, exactly. But you can hear the "please" in it.

"Well, ya gonna quit just when you was about to win, I speck. Well, so long. They is suckers born every day. You want to play a free one? Well, which shell. This one? That there is right. See, ya woulda won. Want ta play another? Put down the money. An' watch close. The little lady can watch too. Four eyes is better'n two. Two dollars is the minimum bet. Two little dollars. Well, I never thought ya would have the nerve to put yer money down there. Thought ya was a chump fer sure. Well, now which shell? You think that one too, lady? You in agreement? Well, let's us take a little look here. I'll be damned. Somethin' wrong here. I damn sure thought it was there too. Well let's try one more time. Double up and get even. Four dollars. Well, lady, I'm the only game in town.

"No, it's not gambling. And it's not against the will of God. Everybody knows that. This is just lookin' and thinkin.' You want to try it one more time? Four dollars. No. The bumper cars will be going all night. One last shot. Well, I'll be damned. Somethin' went wrong again." That smirk on the carney's face when my parents walk away, my father looking down, his hands still in his pockets.

We watch the Ferris wheel go around and around, and the people screaming with excitement, and I want to ride it too, but as my mother says, "Your father lost all of our money gambling." All four dollars. She never spoke of it again. She wasn't the kind.

In 1938, the country lay still deep in the Depression, and the insurance salesmen came to our house like leopards in the night. My room was above the living room, and I could hear them through the floor register, which opened to allow the warm ceiling air to drift to up from the room below. I pressed my ear next to the register listening to the salesmen. "Why just last week a fellow working on the railroad was killed in a train wreck. You might have known him." I knew Burton Stockhouse—kid in my Sunday School class, skinny, smiley, sweet kid. My father had taken the family out to see the wreck—those huge old steam engines, barreling down the tracks, a head-on, scattering cars and steel for half a mile in each direction, and there was nothing left of Burton's dad except a smear up against the cab. My father helped me climb up on top of the steam engine, lying on its side, a terrible sight. And then afterward what should a boy say to another boy? "I saw where your dad was killed," or "It sure was a terrible wreck"? Kids don't know what to say to kids when one of their parents dies. Like if the kid lost an arm or something. You can't talk about it. And I didn't know what to say to Burton, and so I didn't say anything, and I always felt bad about that.

The leopards went on talking to my folks. "You say you belong to Ladies' Aid with Mrs. Stockhouse? Well, I will tell you one thing if it is strictly confidential. The man didn't have a nickel's worth of insurance to his name. And I'll tell you something else. She and those three kids of theirs are going to be out on the street. I mean they didn't have enough to even bury the man. Soon as the neighbors quit feeding 'em they're gonna come a beggin'. You can bet on that."

My parents were silent. "It was a sin for that man to leave his family like that," the insurance men said. "Must not a cared for her or the kids much. But some men are like that. I know for a fact that he went to every movie that come ta town. Twenty-five cents a show. Coulda bought a good policy for his wife and kids. But no. He must not give a good hoot in hell. Pardon my French. But I'll tell ya one thing: I tried to sell him just like I'm tryin' ta sell you. Dangerous work you do down there, Mr. Spence." I learned years later that none of what the legends said about the Stockhouses was accurate, but legends do not fiddle with the truth. Legends kill.

For days after, I heard my mother talking in her soft frightened voice to my father about whatever would happen to her and little Gerry if something should happen to him. "You know, Gerald," as she called my father, "there are people getting hurt all the time at the plant. How about the time that man fell into the creosote tank, and when they finally drug him up, they couldn't even open the casket because he was dyed brown as an Indian? What about his wife and his children? And remember the Stockhouses."

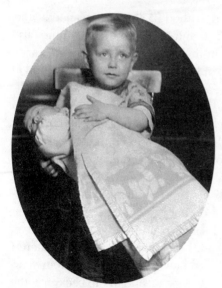

Gerry and Little Peggy, ages two years and three months.

Gerry and Little Peggy, ages four years and almost three years.

And the bums kept coming to our door, ragged, dirty, blank-eyed, homeless men. Could she spare a hungry man a meal? She always answered the door, but she would only feed them on the back porch. I watched them through the kitchen window. They ate silently in large gulps like hungry curs, and they wouldn't look up from their eating, and when they had finished the last morsel from their plates, they thanked my mother with a quiet "Thank ya, ma'am," and left. Probably the children of a father who died without insurance, I thought.

My father claimed the bums had marked our house in some way because my mother would always feed them—a piece of antelope steak and some fresh lamb's-quarter she had me pick out of the alley, or some fresh eggs from the hen house and some homemade biscuits and gravy. And after my father came home from work she'd launch into it again. How would it be if she and little Gerry had to go house to house asking for food and a place to sleep? She'd probably have to go back to her father's farm in Colorado, and everyone knew how her father was—a regular tyrant, no patience for little kids, a hard man like all those dry-land German farmers. And, remember, she had a bad back from that back-breaking work on the farm when she was a girl. That's why she had to wear her Spencer corset, a frightful piece of armor made of canvas and stays that came up over her rib cage and laced down the front, and in the back it extended down around her buttocks. Said she couldn't work without it, her back pained her so. They had saved six months to buy the corset, and if she went back to the farm with her father he would put her to work in the fields hoeing beans and carrying in the milk, and that would be the end of her, and Lord knows what kind of man's labor her father would have little Gerry doing.

And, of course, all of us were afraid because Little Peggy had died. I remembered every detail. She'd gotten sick that summer morning and by night she was dead. Cerebral meningitis. Her ghost was with us all the time. But she was not often spoken of because the memory brought instant pain to my mother and father. Still she was an indelible presence. My first memories were of this small angel, she barely three and I four, her eyes as luminous as fire, her happiness, it seemed, an inexhaustible flame. I do not remember ever hearing her cry. But memories edit. And it was hard for me to understand how a perfect angel could die. She had been my first friend. I took her with me everywhere I went. I remember her small chubby hand and how it felt. I, the big four-year-old brother, took her to find the candy Easter eggs outside in the backyard; the eggs wet from the dew of the night made our hands stick together and we laughed. And then she died.

The funeral: I can see the green canvas awning that provided the shade against the hot bright day, and under it the small closed casket, the pink roses on either side and a wreath of pink roses on top. I remembered sitting next to my parents, their faces contorted so they were no longer my parents. I could touch the casket. But I could not touch her. They said she was sleeping inside. And that she would be with God. Then they shipped her body to Colorado where my father's parents would be buried, and where my parents said they would be buried too, and there they buried the little angel. So it became very clear to me at an early age that God was not trustworthy. God could take you any time. And if God could take Little Peggy, he could take our father. Just like that.

I heard the preachers every Sunday: "If you accept Jesus Christ as your Lord and Savior, you will know the unspeakable bliss of eternal salvation. If you don't, hell awaits." The insurance salesmen argued the same: "Buy our insurance and you will enjoy security. Fail to buy it—well, can you see your family huddled under a bridge someplace? We're here to provide peace of mind, ma'am. Blessed security." It's easy to sell salvation and insurance. Were it otherwise, the insurance industry and the churches wouldn't control the major wealth of the world.

Years later as a lawyer, I viewed the insurance companies with their pay-on-death policies and the carnival crooks with their shell games and the Mafia chiefs with their protection scams as all kindred under the skin. They all peddled the same thing—the placation of fear. All understand the dominant motivations of the species—fear and greed. In the end, fear wins out.

My gentle father seemed fearless to me except when it came to the insurance companies. He never ran from a soul. He never hid. He never locked a door. As if he had never encountered it, he never spoke of fear. He was unafraid of nature, of the endless miles of dark, down-timbered jungles where the elk hid, and where, when you walked, the trees walked as well. My father wasn't even afraid of dying. But he was afraid of leaving his wife and his child penniless. Love fueled his fear, and when he couldn't defend against the arguments of the insurance salesmen he bought $10,000 worth of life insurance, more than he could afford—a fortune in those days—enough, the leopards said, to take care of the wife and little Gerry for a whole lot of years.

Every month my father cashed his paycheck at the bank and brought the cash home. Then he and my mother counted it out on the kitchen table. The church's share came off the top. Looked to me as if they were playing both ends against the middle. If God took my father, we had the insurance. If He didn't, we had my father and the insurance company had our money. Seemed like God and the insurance companies were in cahoots. Anybody could see that.

My mother was a handsome woman, tall for her time, with dark hair and blue eyes that seemed less tired behind her rimless glasses. A red triangular birthmark on her right cheek marked where, as my father held, she had been kissed by an angel. My Grandfather Pfleeger, that old-country monarch, had not been able to keep her down, neither down in spirit nor down on the farm. Education wasn't for women, Grandpa Pfleeger argued. Women were already too smart. But when she finished grade school, this renegade daughter left the farm to attend "prep school," as they called high school in the early 1920s. She worked her way doing the hard jobs she knew how to do. She cooked and waited tables and washed dishes at a broardinghouse operated by an old woman named Mrs. Weed who became her surrogate mother, and there she met my father, who boarded there as well. She was a bright student and her teachers encouraged her to attend college at Colorado A and M where, still working for Mrs. Weed, she took a bachelor of science degree, majoring in home economics. After she graduated she bravely traipsed off to the Navajo country for a job at a boarding school in Hesperus, Colorado. The school was some twelve miles west of Durango, Colorado, which my father later stated was "far enough away from Durango, with its whorehouses, gambling joints and saloons, so that the students had difficulty getting contaminated." Then in 1927 she and my father were married, at the old Pfleeger farm at Limon, Colorado.

My mother made most of our clothing, my father's and mine, on her Montgomery Ward electric sewing machine. She made our shirts and our pajamas—both our heavy flannel pajamas of winter and our light, short-sleeved cottons of summer. Like animals shedding their winter coats, our change of pajamas marked the two principal seasons in Wyoming. Oh, the joy of discarding those hot, heavy flannels for the balmy, light cottons of summer, and the welcome comfort of the flannels when the frost came leaving the lawn looking like the short white hair on an old man's head.

She sewed our coats out of the deer and elk hides skinned from the game my father had killed. He sent the hides, rolled up and salted down, the hair still on them, to Jonas Brothers in Denver. Months later, by parcel post, came this small, flat, heavy box. Inside lay the beautiful hides, tanned, as soft as Grandma's hand, and with that wondrous smell of leather. Even now I see my father gently lifting up a piece of the leather from the box and examining it carefully.

"Yep. This is from the right front quarter of that old bull elk I shot last fall."

"Let me see the bullet hole, Daddy," I would say. And sure enough, there it was, a tiny entry hole behind which the heart had hidden. Then my father would hold up the corresponding piece from the other side of the animal.

"And here's where the bullet came out," a hole as big as a man's fist. "Mushroom bullet. Knocks 'em down, and they stay down"—my father's constant concern, for of all the mortal sins a man could commit, to wound an animal, to let it suffer and die, to waste its life was a crime right up there with the worst of them. My mother would have to cut around the hole to make our coats.

My mother's sewing stitches were never straight. Straight stitches were not the issue—a seam that would hold was. Some of the neighbor kids would laugh at the shirts and the coats she made—"Your mamma makes 'em" they would taunt. They, and anyone else who looked, could see the stitches.

I watched her lay out the hides and cut out the patterns from old newspapers. I saw her happy at her work, attacking the hides with her precious scissors that neither my father nor I was permitted to touch. I can see her bent over the old sewing machine, urging it on, sometimes a stitch at a time, the tired electric motor stalling and whining, my mother spinning the wheel with her right hand to add more power to the struggling motor, and all the while holding the leather in place with her left. Reluctantly the needle punched through the hide in small jumps and spurts. She hacked at the leather, attacked it with gritted teeth, punched it, pulled and jerked on it, her mouth twisted this way and that in sympathy. She patted it, bunched it up, held it up, examined it, talked to it, talked to herself, bit her lower lip, wiped her forehead and attacked it again until, at last, she formed it into my coat, and a coat just like it that my father proudly wore. But her stitches, even through the precious leather, were as crooked as the trail of a drunk. Yet, despite the crooked stitches, there was something wonderful about wearing something close to one's heart that had been fashioned by the caring hands of one's mother. I daresay that the knights of old went into battle wearing under their armor those soft cotton garments fashioned by their mothers. Today when people ask why I wear a fringed leather jacket designed and sewn by my own love, Imaging, it is hard for me to explain that the small boy, now a man of serious years, still needs to wear into battle the protective garment of love.

Outside, my mother worked in the garden we grew in the backyard. My father spaded it by hand. In the springtime he would come riding home from work on his old rusty bicycle with its skinny tires and its high hard seat, and, still in his working clothes, take up the spade. He would turn over the sod, spade at a time, across the full width of the garden, and then back again. As he spaded he dumped in chicken manure and the coal ashes from the furnace in the basement and the wood ashes from the fireplace, and always the rotted leaves that, during the fall before, he had piled up against the fence. And thus the soil was magically enriched and by his labor and sweat made ready to produce yet another year's bounteous crop.

After the spading my father would attack the ground with a rake, breaking the clods and leveling the ground. I helped. And then we planted. My mother would start at one end of the row and I at the other, and we would meet in the middle. We planted the round black radish seeds and the long, thin seeds of the carrots. "Don't plant them so close together," she warned. "It only wastes the seeds and we will have to thin them later." We planted parsnips and beets and lettuce and chard. We planted spinach and squash and beans and peas and cucumbers. It was as if we were in charge of the universe. Mother ordered the seed from Burpee's catalog. Cheaper. And better seed, she claimed, seed grown for a mountain climate. She grew our starter tomato plants in a small wooden box on the sill of the kitchen's south window. And we transplanted the scrawny, sun-hungry plants when we planted the rest of the garden, covering them carefully with brown paper sacks against the frost at night. We also grew the perennials—rhubarb and asparagus and dill, and in the far corner of the yard a very large and friendly chokecherry tree flourished.

Every spring mother planted flowers: snapdragons and phlox, and pinks that were mostly red, not pink, and she loved her gaillardia, a yellow daisy with a red face, and the petunias of red and white and deep blue. And she planted sweetpeas that grew up a six-foot-high chicken wire fence that divided the garden in two. Then we watered the garden, my mother and I, and on our hands and knees we thinned the beets and the carrots. We stretched thin strips of chicken wire held in place by wooden stakes for the peas and beans to climb, and we tied the tomato plants to stakes. I thought gardens were magical and, when they demanded weeding, the invention of the devil.

My father worked in his garden until he was past ninety. I think of all the very old and beautiful men I have known, and most have been gardeners. Yes, if you see a very old man walking sprightly down the street swinging his cane and smiling at people as he passes by, and if you stop to talk to him and ask how he grew so wonderfully old, he will tell you that it was not a matter of fortunate genes. He inherited, instead, a love of a garden.

To understand very much of anything at all, one must believe in magic, and there is magic in a garden, the magic of growth, the same magic that nourishes the plants, that fills the gardener's nostrils with their pungent smells and his lungs with their earthy power and his hands with the clean feel of dirt. And the magic is also in the gardener. Man, like the dandelion, like any living thing, cannot rest until he has bloomed and seeded and the magical mechanism that abides in every molecule of plant and person alike knows when the organism has ripened and seeded and when therefore, its work is done. But the gardener, ah, the gardener—his work is not yet complete. Must he not survive the winter like the tulip? For he is inextricably attached to the act of living, and, therefore, gardeners live approximately forever.

Like my father, my mother was content at home. She appeared happy and the suffragette movement had not touched her life. Her role was as important as that of my father, who showed her great respect. I thought they loved each other a good deal. Only once did I hear them quarrel.

I'd fallen on the radiator in the dentist's office and opened a large cut in my scalp just above the hair line. My father brought me home, but he was afraid that the cut required stitches.

"It will heal just fine," my mother said.

"Well, I think it needs some stitches and that we should call Dr. Carr. He can come over and sew it up right."

"No need to spend good money on a doctor," my mother said. "I'll shave it and put a bandage on it and it will be just fine."

"Well, you remember about old Shantz down at the plant?" my father said. I knew about old Shantz. He caught the largest brown trout in the history of Wyoming fish. It reached from his chest to the ground. One day old Shantz got a terrible bellyache and he went home. He never called a doctor and he died. Died of a ruptured appendix.

"Well," my father continued, "old Shantz was too cheap to call a doctor."

"This boy doesn't need a doctor," my mother replied.

Then my father said the one thing that he had never said before and that likely he would have given his tongue to take back. "That's what you said about Little Peggy."

My mother burst into tears. "Are you blaming me for Peggy's death? That was a rotten, unchristian thing to say."

My father said he wasn't blaming her.

"Well, the doctor said there was nothing anybody could have done no matter when he had been called. You know there is no cure for meningitis."

My father said he knew that.

"Well, why did you say that then?"

He didn't know. He was sorry.

"Well, how could you ever, ever say such a thing?"

And then the hurt that they both felt from the terrible loss, which they had hidden from themselves and from each other, came tumbling out in great sobs, and finally my father was crying as well. I sat, stunned.

Finally I asked, "Are you going to get a divorce?"

"No," my father said. "We are not going to get a divorce." Then he got up from the table and he walked around to where my mother sat, and he bent down and put his arms around her and held her to his chest, and she sobbed for a very long time until his blue work shirt was wet in front. When my father saw me staring at them, my face frozen in horror, he said, "You better go outside and play. It will all be all right."

But I didn't believe it would all be all right. And, indeed, it was never all right again. Even in the face of Christ's admonition to forgive, it would never be all right again. Although my mother often proclaimed the old saw that "sticks and stones can break your bones but words can never harm you," I learned early on that words could be as dangerous, yes, as injurious as a knife. Words could kill. Words left wounds, and if the wounds ever healed, scars were left in their place. Often when my mouth went on automatic my mother would say, "Gerry, you know a person the minute he opens his mouth. Taste your words before you speak them." Still, in the days that followed, my mother seemed happy enough. She laughed often, laughing by sucking in air which sounded as much like sobbing as laughter, a laugh that had never been given permission to come bursting forth to release the sound of unrestrained human joy.

CHAPTER 3

Gerry and Nanny.

FALL WAS THE SEASON of beginnings, a new hunting season, a new grade in school, and, most of all, fall was when the family went chokecherry picking. To Piney Creek. Chokecherries, I thought, must be God's favorite tree, for not only did the berries make the best jelly in the universe, but the trees always grew best next to a good trout stream. When we went berry picking we had a picnic with friends, and we fished, and once I remember my father captured a young magpie that I took home to raise. Sometimes we shared chokecherry groves with black bears, who never made their appearance on Sunday, which was our day, but were surely present the rest of the week. This we knew because we would come onto their leavings, and we knew it was the scat of bear because man didn't eat chokecherries seeds and all.

Chokecherry time! We stripped the bushes and dumped the full pails into bushel baskets and hauled them home. And as I picked the berries, I ate the fullest, juiciest ones by the handfuls. Sometimes I would hold a seed between my teeth and shoot the seed out with a smart snap from my tongue, and the seed would go sailing, six feet maybe, maybe farther, maybe hit a pal on the back of the head. The taste of the rich ripe berries caused the mouth to pucker and turned a person's tongue as purple as liver, and the taste of chokecherry jelly on hot homemade bread—well, chokecherries had to be God's favorite tree. And therefore mine as well.

Sometimes in the fall when there were extra berries, I would hitch up old Pat, my brown and white, wiggly-tailed, half-spaniel, half–fox terrier dog, to the dog cart my father had made. And I would fill the cart with several gallons of chokecherries and down the street Pat and I would go, Pat strapped to the cart by a harness of rawhide, also fashioned by my father. Then I would go knocking on the doors. "Wanna buy some fresh-picked chokecherries? Ten cents a gallon." Sometimes I sold them. But usually not. Most folks didn't want to take the time to make chokecherry jelly, or didn't know how. I didn't care if I couldn't sell them. Before the day was over, my mother would convert the excess berries into syrup and we could eat them on our Sunday pancakes the rest of the year.

One clear, fall Sunday we drove the Model A north of town to a dilapidated old farm out on the prairies near Lodge Grass where a falling-down shack housed a funny-looking old man with a dirty hat and dirty overalls and a long, white beard. The place was overflowing with goats of various sizes and colors. I had never seen a live goat before, the kids running and hopping stiff-legged all over the place. One small kid came up and nibbled at my finger. I picked him up and held him on my lap, and then he nibbled on my ear. I thought the old man who came out of the shack must surely be Heidi's grandfather. He and my father carried on for some time passing the time of day, as was my father's way. But at last they got down to business. My father wanted a good milking goat, and finally he bought what the old man said was his best nanny for ten dollars. She was already bred back and ready to kid in a few months, and the man threw in an old blackened leather goat collar to boot. Then we loaded Nanny into the backseat of the Model A with me, and we headed for home.

The poor nanny bleated pitifully as we bounced along, her yellow eyes bulging with fear, her poor body trembling. Then, suddenly, up went her tail and down she squatted.

"Dad! Dad! She's peeing back here," I cried.

"Well, we can't stop and put a diaper on her."

Gerry and Pat with dog cart.

"Dad, she's doing the 'back door' now! Number two!" Her marbles hit the floorboards.

"We'll be home soon."

"Dad! It's on my shoes."

"It won't kill you."

"It stinks."

"Open the window," my father said.

When we got old Nanny home I learned I had a new job: to take care of Nanny; my father's job was to milk her and Mother's to strain and refrigerate the milk and skim off the rich white cream. Goat's milk was said to be healthy, especially for children. But we needed to understand something about goat's milk, my father warned. If the nanny eats dandelions or milkweed, the milk will taste, and the taste is very bad—something just short of drinking turpentine. "No human being has ever been known to drink a full glass of goat's milk after the nanny has been feeding on dandelions or milkweed," my father said. "Even her kids would rather starve than drink the stuff." Yet, strangely, I was to discover, there's nothing a goat would rather eat than dandelions and milkweed.

Nanny was a smart, sweet goat, and I was soon able to break her to lead. In a short while she would follow me like a pup. Fulfilling my duties, I took Nanny up and down the alley behind the house to graze. Free pasture. And I could also pasture her on the vacant lot and on the creek bank, where, while she ate, I picked wild asparagus and lamb's-quarter for supper. Then I would tie her to a stake on a long cotton rope and go about my business playing Hopalong Cassidy with Buddy Taylor and Bob Lott. In choosing our movie idols, we thought Tom Mix was a sissy. Nobody wanted to be him. But Hoppy, well, he had that deep voice and that fast trigger finger. And he never smiled. And he killed a lot of people. I'd seen him in a movie once, the second movie of a matinee double feature my mother allowed me to see since the main attraction was some sweet little crybaby thing with Shirley Temple and all of her disgusting curls and her pouting lower lip. I stayed late to see Hoppy.

But while we were playing cowboys, and despite my careful staking, Nanny got into the dandelions. That night her milk—you could smell it through every room in the house—was unfit for consumption by any living thing.

"Did you let Nanny get into the dandelions?" my father asked.

"No, I didn't."

"Well, she must have pulled one over on you. Suppose that goat's smarter than you are? Taste this milk," my father said. He handed me a glass.

"I don't wanna."

"Well, just take a little sip so you know what dandelions taste like when they get turned into goat's milk."

I brought the glass up to my mouth, but the nose preceded. I pushed it away. Then my father took the glass and poured it down the sink. Even the chickens wouldn't eat their mash with the milk poured over it.

When Nanny came fresh, she had twins, little brown kids with yellow eyes and white stockings and a white streak down their faces on each side. They had pink noses and their bleat was high and quivery and sounded like a baby crying. They played teeter-totter on the seesaw my father had made me, and they chased each other in circles and climbed everything and chewed on everything. They jumped on top of the chicken house. They ate paper. They chased the chickens. I fed them out of a bottle so we could milk Nanny. Then one day one of the kids was gone, and for supper we had the best and sweetest meat I had ever eaten. It wasn't antelope or deer or elk. It wasn't rabbit. It wasn't sage chicken.

"What's this meat?" I asked at the supper table.

No one answered. I got up from the table and looked out the kitchen window into the backyard.

"Where is Jupiter?" I asked, referring to the missing kid.

"We couldn't keep Jupiter," my father said.

"Are we eating Jupiter?" I asked.

My father appeared horror-stricken. He looked at my mother. Finally he said in his quiet voice, "Yep. We're eating Jupiter."

"Are you eating Jupiter, Mom?"

"Yes, I'm eating Jupiter," my mother said. "Remember son, God put goats on the earth for man's health and for his sustenance. We mustn't forget that." On that day, at that moment, there at that kitchen table in the presence of my father and my mother, both of whom were chewing hunks of Jupiter, and me with a bite of Jupiter in my own mouth, I began the irreversible slide out of innocence. How could you eat your friends and be a Christian?

Fall can have a heart attack in Wyoming and die in one day. The heavy snows came, often before we had our flannels on. In the winter, which could come as early as October, we went sledding on Tank Hill, where the town's water tank rose up like a great windowless castle: the half-hour trek up the hill for the minute down, no more, the head stuck out, the aviator's helmet buckled under the chin, the teeth gritted against the danger, the eyes squinted against the wind, the breath held, the heart high and out of place. Then down the hill without a cry, silently into the jaws of hell, to hell with it, we said. Here we go like the bravest of aviators in a power dive, their scarves flying straight behind them. At the bottom we staggered to our feet, breathing again. We stood there grinning, and when we grinned, the snow on our snow-packed faces cracked off, our noses running, we boys, immersed in the euphoria that soaks the heart when, once more, we had survived the run down Tank Hill.

At home, that night, we made chocolate fudge. Licking the pan was among the ten greatest experiences a boy could have, even up there with flying kites and eating turkey on Christmas, right up there with fishing. Yes, it was even better sometimes than fishing.

❀ ❀ ❀

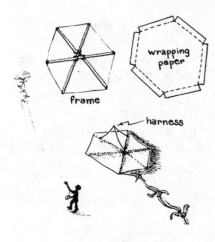

Drawing of kite.

In Wyoming, spring fought birth like a child who dreads its fate. Yet finally it came bursting, in song, in smell, in the fuzzy touch of buds, in the primal, deep hug of life. In the springtime, my father taught me how to make a splendid kite of sticks and brown wrapping paper.

And stilts: They were easy to make. Just nail a couple of blocks to two-by-twos six feet long with leather straps to hold the feet in, and you could become a giant as quickly as you could climb aboard.

Among the many the things my father taught me was how to make willow or chokecherry whistles. In the springtime when the sap is running you take a live piece of chokecherry branch about five inches long—chokecherry is slightly better than willow. The branch would be without any sub-branches erupting from the selected piece. Then you cut one end of the branch horizontally, and the other at a slant. At the horizontally cut end, you cut through and around the bark the entire circumference of the branch in one neat slice. Then cut a V notch in the top of the branch.

Now take your pocket knife and with the handle tap the bark lightly, but smartly, but not hard enough to break the bark. Keep tapping and tapping. Then twist the bark loose. It will come off in a single piece, leaving behind a green slick stick. At last, cut out the thin air channel on the branch, deepen the notch slightly, and slip the bark back on. Blow. You have a wonderful, magical whistle to call to all of your tribal members hiding in the woods. There, my dear father—as the Indian says, the gift is not complete until it is passed on.

Although my father was a great whistle maker, he taught me to use whistles sparingly. He had an eternal respect for the sanctity of the woods, which he felt could be polluted as easily by sound as by physical trash. To him it was as bad to talk out loud when walking through the woods as it was for picnickers to scatter their garbage. Noise showed the woods disrespect and spoiled the experience. When he was separated from my mother as they walked through the timber, they would keep in touch with each other by an occasional soft, low whistle that, if put to words, sounded like "Sweetheart." "Sweetheart," my mother, forever afraid of being lost, would whistle back. Soon my father could be heard whistling, low and sweet, "Sweetheart," and if I was with my mother I knew we were not lost. We would never be lost, not if Daddy was within whistling distance leading the way.

Besides building kites and whistles, we raised chickens in springtime—in fact, in the backyard at 226 West Seventh Street in Sheridan. We bought the baby chicks at the Sheridan Chicken Hatchery out by the Flour Mill, six cents a chick, little yellow fuzzy peeping balls that ran around on match sticks for legs. We brought them home in a cardboard box with air holes cut in the sides, and in the cold of the early spring, we put the box on the dining room floor register, and at night, when the furnace was mostly off, we hung a light bulb over the box and covered the box to keep the baby chicks warm. We fed the chicks ground corn and chick meal, and we put water for them in an empty tuna fish can, and the chicks grew, nearly overnight.

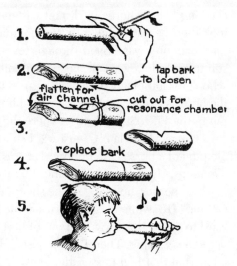

Chokecherry or willow whistle.

Then one day the first red feather in the chick's tail would come bursting through. And the chicks became ungainly and long-legged and awkward. We moved them to a small pen we built on the back porch, and laid newspapers on the porch floor to catch their droppings. Soon they graduated to the chicken house and soon after that they grew to fryer size. Off came their heads, and we dunked the fryers into a pail of scalding water, dunked them once and again, and out steamed the rank smell of hot, wet chicken feathers. My mother and I plucked the chickens, she fried a couple for Sunday dinner, but the rest went into the Mason jars for winter. The young pullets were spared, those Rhode Island Reds who laid their first dainty pullet eggs in the nests my father built on the south wall of the hen house. And soon, sooner than one could believe, the pullets grew into large fat red hens with fat legs and yellow skin, and they laid brown eggs, not white. When they quit laying and wanted to sit on their eggs, out came the ax again and out came the pressure cooker, and Mother made chicken and dumplings and chicken with noodles she cut with the noodle cutter her mother had brought over from Germany and had given her as a wedding present.

The eggs we didn't eat we stored for winter's use in the basement in a ten-gallon crock filled with water glass, a soupy silicon jelly that sealed the pores of the eggs so they were slow to rot. And in the same basement in a moist sand box, we stored the carrots and the parsnips and the turnips and the onions dug from the garden.

I knew that summer had finally come when, sleeping next to the window in my upstairs bedroom, I was awakened by a thumping on the bridge planks and a clanking like a chorus of distant castanets. In the early summer the ranchers took their herds of sheep to the mountains. A band of sheep, perhaps a thousand or more, was driven through town while most of the householders were still in bed, the ewes, all bleating simultaneously, some baaing high as singing schoolgirls, others moaning low as gravely-voiced crones, and their lambs lost in the herd, whimpering their mournful little trilly cries. I jerked on my pants and ran to the Fifth Street bridge where the herd was crossing Goose Creek.

"Got any bum lambs, mister?" I shouted to the Mexican herder. He rode an old plug of a horse with hoofs as large as plates below hairy fetlocks that looked like mops. "If ya got a bum lamb, I'll take good care of it."

The herder, hollering at the sheep, paid no attention. "Haw! Haw! Get on! Get on!" He swung his gunny sack at the sheep, and they scattered, running forward to escape his fury. "Get out of here, keed," the Mexican herder said without looking at me. Then I saw Cousin. He was a tired, toddling little lamb with a long tail that had missed the docking knife, and his head was hanging down and, but for the fact that he was being pushed forward by the herd, he would not have walked another step. I was up alongside the herder's big-footed horse.

"See that bum," I said. "Can I have him? He's gonna die anyway."

"Take that foking lamb, keed, and get the fok outta here!"

I grabbed Cousin and ran home. Mother got out the bottle with the big nipple, with which we had fed Jupiter and Juno, and we fed Cousin good warm milk from Nanny. My father even made a collar for him, and then I taught Cousin to lead and I took care of him all summer, and he grew. I took him to the draw with me to play, and there I picked lamb's-quarter for supper and Cousin would eat at the same patch of tender leaves, and Cousin and I were friends. Then, one day, again without knowing it, I was eating Cousin.

"Lambs grow up to be eaten, Gerry," my mother said.

"Not Cousin," I cried. "Cousin wasn't a lamb. He was my friend." And I thought anew that it would be better to starve than to eat one's friend. And I thought, if it is all right to eat your friends just because they grow up, whatever would happen to me when I grew up?

My mother cut my hair twice a month, but in the summer, she cut it as short as the rancher sheared his sheep. Our neighbor across the street was a barber and his son, Buddy Taylor, was my constant playmate. Buddy and his mother made cutting remarks, as it were,

Gerry with his lamb, Cousin, and his dog, Pat.

about my haircuts. "Only cost

two-bits to have a real barber cut your hair," Buddy's mother would say. "Wouldn't think your mother would want to cheat a man out of a living by cutting your hair like that." She half-whispered it under her breath. I often passed Grover Taylor's barber shop on the way uptown. And when I looked in, as I always did, Grover Taylor was usually slumped in his own barber's chair waiting, waiting, the sleeves of his white shirt rolled halfway to his elbows exposing the solid tattoos that, according to Buddy, covered his entire body—snakes and dragons and naked women, all of which my mother said was a very wicked thing for the man to have done—to desecrate God's temple, one's body, with such evil graffiti. Wicked or not, when I passed his shop and his chair was empty, I felt guilty, for my mother and I were surely cheating a poor man out of his chance to make an honest living.

Buddy said his father ran a union shop. The scabs, some doing haircuts for a dime, were driving union men out of business. I hated the scabs. But what about my mother? She cut hair for nothing.

The torture took place in the kitchen. First my mother put some toilet paper around my neck to substitute for the barber's tissue. Then she pinned an old oilcloth table covering over that, and she pulled out the old Montgomery Ward hand clippers, oiled them up with sewing machine oil, put a board across the old wooden arm chair, sat me on it and took after me. It was a merciless attack. She held my head with one hand and whacked away with the other. The clippers pulled whole bunches of hair at a time from the back of my neck and I would jump out of the chair and holler.

"Yer pullin' me, Mom! Yer pullin'." I couldn't swear, not in front of my mother and, with God watching and listening all the time, not ever. My only defense was to jump out of the chair, put my hands on my hips, look my mother in the eye and holler, "You're pullin' my hair out by the roots." Didn't do any good.

"Gerald Leonard Spence, you get back here. The clippers just slipped a little. I won't pull anymore. I'll be careful."

"Promise?"

"Well, a person shouldn't promise if the promise can't be kept. But I'll try. Now come back here. You don't want me to turn you out on the street looking like a half-sheared sheep, do you?"

She had me—the groove up the middle of the back of the neck. Had to finish it.

"Why can't I get a regular haircut from a real barber?"

"They charge too much," my mother replied.

"Only a quarter," I said. "Besides, you're a scab."

"Whatever are you talking about?" my mother scolded. "I am not a scab. I am your mother. Now sit still or you'll get pulled again."

"You're getting the hair down my neck and it itches. And you are too a scab. You don't belong to the barbers' union."

"Mothers don't have to belong to unions to cut their own children's hair. Now sit still!"

"Well, how can Buddy's father make a living if we scab on him?"

"He must have plenty of money. At least he has enough to buy beer. And don't forget," she would admonish, "a quarter will buy three loaves of day-old bread at Bondi's Market and leave a penny over for a sucker for you."

When the torture was over she would stand back and look at me. Then she'd turn to my father. "Doesn't he just look sweet enough to kiss?" And my father would reckon as how she was right. I was sweet enough to kiss, and so they both kissed me, and that was supposed to be full compensation for the torture I had endured.

In the summer the family rented the two spare bedrooms as well as my room to the tourists. My father painted two signs on plywood and framed them with quarter-round. One sign, black on white, read TOURIST ROOMS. The other read the same, except it included an arrow pointing up the street in the direction of our house with the words THREE BLOCKS. My father made arrangements with the owner of the property at Seventh and Main to put up the sign. Probably paid him a dollar, which in those days was a day's pay. Now tourists looking for a cheap room could see the sign there on Main Street as they drove into Sheridan, and, turning up Seventh, in three blocks they would come to this big white house with a similar sign, TOURIST ROOMS, on the front porch, and cars of tourists often stopped.

I remember how we would see them drive up, and instead of answering the door we would wait until they rang the doorbell, one of those mechanical kind you turned with a vengeance to the right to ring the bell. My mother would take off her apron, put on her most friendly smile and answer the door. Then she would show them the room—the downstairs guest room first.

"Nice. Where is the bathroom?"

"Right handy here, right next to your room," she'd say, leading them to our only bathroom, which was screened off from the kitchen with a homemade folding screen my father had fashioned, also out of plywood. We got fifty cents a night for a room. My room rented last because it was upstairs and the renter had to climb up and down the stairs to get to the bathroom. In the summer I slept on an army cot in the backyard in our old hunting tent which my father pitched under the chokecherry tree. In the mornings of late summer I was awakened by the blackbirds who gathered in that tree to peck away at the ripening chokecherries. The birds spit out the seeds, which, in turn, dropped onto the tent and came rolling down its sides—bump, bump, bump—like the sound of tennis balls bouncing off the roof of a house. Then I walked barefooted through the dew to the house, my feet soaking wet by the time I got to the kitchen, and there I had breakfast with the family, corn flakes—you got more for your money with Kellogg's Corn Flakes, according to my mother, than with Wheaties, which came in a smaller box. After such a breakfast, my mother and I would wash the tourist sheets of the night before, and I would hang them out to dry.

Mother, of course, did not use Ivory Flakes. She used White King bar soap instead. She cut it into small slivers with the kitchen paring knife and dumped the slivers into the wash water with the old beater going back and forth, back and forth. White King was cheaper by about half, and she claimed it washed just as well. She did the washing on the back porch, and then I helped hang out the clothes in the backyard, and when they were dry I brought them in by the armful, the smell of the cottons made fresh and clean from the hanging, and then we folded the clothes, and rolled and stuffed the socks into round balls. We slept on unpressed sheets made fragrant from the open air, and we changed to summer sheets when we changed to our summer pajamas. In the winter we slept on unpressed flannel sheets and in flannel pajamas. If I were designing heaven, all the angels would sleep on unpressed sheets, flannel in the winter, cotton in the summer, which would, for eternity, mark the change of seasons.

The next day I ironed the sheets on the kitchen ironing board—ironed them with those old cast-irons we heated on the gas burners of the kitchen range. Cheaper to heat the iron with gas than with electricity, which was, for most uses, still a luxury. I learned to iron my Sunday trousers, and I knew how to sprinkle and iron my shirt, starting first with the yoke, and then to the collar and then the rest of the shirt.

After the tourists had gone I made up the beds with clean pressed linens, and, to the horror of my mother, some of the tourists smoked in the rooms. She would open the windows and complain strongly about such people, who fouled not only God's temple, but our home as well. If she had known she wouldn't have rented them the room in the first place, she said. Yet I never heard her inquire if the tourist was a smoker. Instead, she left ashtrays on the dresser, and once I heard her tell my father that she prayed they wouldn't burn our house down.

When I had earned several dollars from the rentals of my room, I rode my bike down Main Street to the First National Bank of Sheridan, pedaling, of course, past Taylor's Barbershop, the money and my little green savings deposit book tucked safely in my overalls. I walked up as big as any man to the teller's cage to "put the money away" in what was known as my "College Fund," for the promise was that if I studied hard and behaved myself, I would grow up and go off to college and, with God's help, I might thereafter make something of myself.

For a long time I remained mortified by the fact that our family had to take in lodgers, embarrassed beyond words when people came to our house and were greeted by the black and white hand-painted TOURIST ROOMS sign nailed to the front of the porch. While the other kids slept in their own rooms, I camped in a tent in the backyard. While other families had their homes to them-

selves, we shared ours for fifty cents a room with strangers, and our one bathroom as well.

The neighbor kids made fun of me. "Get yer room rented out yet, tonight,
Gerry?" Or, "Whatcha running over at yer house, Spence? One of them flop-
houses er somethin'?" Or, "I hear yer ol' man ain't doin' so hot, having to take
in tourists and all."

I complained to my mother. "Well, the Taylors across the street don't own
their own home," she replied. "They rent. Don't forget that. And their landlord
can make them move whenever they don't pay their rent. And their car isn't
paid for either. They live from hand to mouth. If something happened to their
daddy, they would be on relief. They don't have any insurance. If something
happened to our daddy, we would at least have our insurance and we could rent
out our rooms and we could get by. And when you get old enough, you can go
to college."

Late summer was canning time. I can hear the sound of the old pressure
cooker sitting on the gas range, spitting, spitting, the escaping steam filling the
room with the smell of cooking vegetables. A person had to be careful of a pressure cooker as a person has to be mindful of a gun. It could blow up. We heard
stories about how some poor soul's release valve had gotten stuck and the
cooker exploded and took out half a wall in the kitchen along with the woman
of the house. My mother canned everything in Mason jars with the two-piece
brass Kerr lids. And by fall one side of the basement was lined with shelves
brimming with jars of the fruits and vegetables she canned.

In the late summer when the canning specials were on at Piggly Wiggly, she
bought peaches and apricots by the bushels, plums and cherries by the wooden
boxes full, and sugar by the hundred-pound sack, hauled them all home in the
back seat of the old Model A Ford, and canned them. She canned up pickles,
sweet and dill, and relishes of various kinds. She canned the beets, the string
beans, and peas and tomatoes from the garden. I helped shell the peas, and I
pulled the strings from the long backs of the string beans with a paring knife.
She canned spinach and chard that I had first washed, and then washed again.
"Get the grit out. Nobody likes to eat the grit." I thought the grit was the iron
that made Popeye so strong. But after it was canned I didn't like the spinach—
it had a vaguely nasty taste to it. I husked the corn on the kitchen floor and
hauled the husks out to the garden, and after that Mother boiled the corn
("blanched it," she called it), and then when the corn was half cooked we sliced
off the tender kernels with long strokes of the paring knife, and, with the blade
of the knife perpendicular to the ear, we scraped off the rest of the leavings,
which, mixed with the kernels, made the canned corn creamy and sweet.

Then it was hunting season again, and we knew it was fall. She canned elk
and deer and antelope, and the canning process somehow removed the wild
taste from the meat. She canned the trout that weren't eaten at the time they
were caught. They tasted like canned salmon. I thought my mother was the can-

ningest woman who ever lived. I thought she would have canned salvation in pickle juice and holiness in salt brine if she had half a chance.

I thought my mother's bargain with life was a pretty good one. She made as much money for the family by her work at home as she could have made had she worked at the dime store for ten cents an hour, as Bill Sare's mother did, and she got to stay at home and raise her family, and Bill Sare's mother had those painfully swollen legs from varicose veins, which left her in constant pain from having stood all those years behind the counter.

Besides, we didn't need to be a family with two working parents. In those days we didn't have to buy automatic washing machines and dryers, and we didn't have to own a dishwasher, and two cars and a motorboat and a couple of television sets. Instead, we listened to FDR's fireside chats over KOA, Denver, and on the same radio we heard the blow-by-blow as Joe Louis destroyed Max Schmeling in the first seconds of the first round to preserve our nation's pride, and to regain the world's heavyweight championship when that damned Nazi, whom Hitler loved, tried to keep it from us. In those days we didn't have deep freezes and TV dinners. Once in a while we bought a sack of nickel hamburgers at Castle Hamburgers with "everything on them"—mustard and onions and dill pickles. We'd never heard of pizza, and today's franchised restaurants hadn't yet been invented. My mother owned two Sunday dresses, one black and one red, and her clothes and my father's one navy blue Sunday suit all fit into one small closet. My father wore a white shirt, the collar points of which, no matter what, always turned toward heaven, and he wore the same blue tie he'd had for Lord knows how many years. Such were all the clothes anyone needed, the excess of which would have been sin and vanity.

As for me, I owned one pair of Sunday shoes and one pair of school boots, the lace-up kind with the knife pocket on the side. I wore to school my one pair of knickers with their deerhide patches at the knees. I had one itchy wool Sunday suit, and a Sunday hat. My mother and father also each had hats. My mother's was a blue straw contraption with blue feathers on the side that looked like some molting blue fowl had chosen to nest on her head. My father's was a snap-brim hat that sat down low on his large ears as if, but for the ears, nothing would have stopped it from sinking over his face. We wore our hats to church, mostly, I thought, so that the men could have something to take off when they went inside and the women something to leave on, thereby permitting the preacher, at a glance, to tell the men from the women in that otherwise colorless congregation who came to endure, as their penance, and as good Christians must, the pain of his equally colorless sermons.

I thought my mother was more free than many mothers today. She never had to go to work and never had to trade her motherhood for another car or another TV. She never had to give up her role as mother to a day-care center or to baby-sitters. She never had to surrender to the demands of "the good life," because, to her, in her innocence, she had a good life, a loving husband, and a son whom she had secretly given to God. She was her own boss. She was the boss of the house as well. She ran things. And she was good at it. She made do and she was proud of her skills. She paid the bills and what little credit we had was good. We owed no money to the banks. In those days in the twilight of the Great Depression my parents were solvent. They were employed, and they had a family and a family life, and they had "a little put away for a rainy day."

But in the end, the value of my mother's labor did not inure to the benefit of the family. Any excess over and above the bare necessities my father provided out of his paycheck also did not accrue to the family's betterment. My father and mother invested the best part of my father's savings and my mother's home labor in that very dear insurance policy, and years later when he needed it, it proved inadequate to pay a week's stay in the hospital much less enough to take care of his widow for even part of a year. Yet over the years I evened the score against that industry, evened the score not once but hundreds of times. When a case against an insurance company came up for settlement, I, representing the widows or orphans or the horribly maimed, would set a just goal in dollars. Then, at the last minute, my settlement offer would go up. Not much, maybe only ten thousand dollars—like the ten-thousand-dollar policy my parents labored most of their lifetimes to pay for, bitter dollar at a time, out of fear, out of love, out of their wonderful innocence.

CHAPTER 4

Grandpa Leonard Pfleeger at the Pfleeger farm,
and Gerry, age four.

MY ANNUAL VISIT to my grandparents in Colorado was like a trek to a foreign land. It was my mother's job to take me. My father, who worked six days a week, stayed home, for how could he use up precious vacation days visiting his parents when he had committed the time to the most important of all human endeavors—hunting? Hunters cannot go home again, not when they have but ten vacation days a year.

My mother boasted that her son had already been in a dozen states or more when most children grew up in one town, spent their lives there and died without having seen any other part of the world. Buddy Taylor had never been out of Sheridan County so far as my mother knew, but my mother's son had already been to Illinois, where my father had been working for the CB&Q Railroad as a chemist in the railroad's tie treating plant at Galesburg when Little Peggy died. And when my parents fled Illinois the day following Peggy's funeral, as if fleeing the plague, I traveled with them through Nebraska and Colorado, and all the states westward to California, to Lompoc, where my father took any job he could find. Luckily, he had a friend who pulled strings. He found work as a laborer at the Celite Products Company. All day he pushed a hand truck carrying four eighty-pound sacks of Celite from the packers to the stackers in the warehouse. At night he ached so badly he could scarcely undress.

After three or four months I traveled with my parents back through all of the states between California and Wyoming, where my father took the chemist's job at the tie plant at Sheridan, again for the same railroad, the CB&Q. Traveling was not new to the family. Even before Little Peggy's death, my father had worked a short while in Nashua, New Hampshire, following which I had been in all the states between New Hampshire and Illinois. By the time I was five years old I was well traveled, but knew little beyond the inside of the Model A Ford. But traveling on the train with my mother to my grandparents' was a powerful primary experience for me, and the magic that took us there from Sheridan each summer was the free railroad pass, one of the few comps provided by the railroad for the families of its employees.

The free pass, of course, was not good for anything but the chair car. Rich people rode the Pullman. Rich people ate in the dining car served by black waiters in starched, white uniforms. Poor people with passes rode the chair cars and carried their own lunches. The conductors were not a friendly lot. You first met the conductor when the train was already half an hour on its way.

"Ticket," the conductor demanded, gazing out the window with a deadly bored look on his face, and, as my mother rummaged through her purse for our pass, he tapped his foot and cleared his throat. She knew the conductor was going to ask for the ticket. Why had she buried it in that purse of hers full of all that junk? And it wasn't "Ticket, please." It was just plain hard "Ticket!" When she finally produced the pass the conductor punched the pass, not once, but a lot of times, and put a stub of his own up in the ticket holder above our seat, a little piece of cardboard the size of a movie ticket, and then he punched this ticket menacingly as well, not once, but punch, punch, punch, and sometimes, punch again to make sure it had enough holes in it, punched it with his shiny puncher that hung from a chain affixed to his belt. Each conductor had his own punch. Sometimes the holes were round, sometimes they were patterned. They were all different shapes. Then I noticed it.

The conductor punched our ticket more than he punched the paying passengers' tickets, and our ticket was white while theirs was red. We were the only ones in the whole car who had a white ticket stuck up in the ticket holder. Therefore, everyone who cared to pay the slightest attention, which was probably everyone, knew that we were freeloaders riding on a free pass. And that was why the conductor was rude and never said "please" and never said "thank you" either.

"How come the conductor punches our ticket more times than he punches the others?" I asked my mother.

"Well, we don't pay for our ride as other people do," my mother whispered, as if my father's hard-earned comp was something akin to receiving charity from the railroad. And it was shameful to accept charity, all the people on relief and all.

Sometime around noon the porter from the dining room came walking through the chair car where we freeloaders rode. As soon as he entered the car he started hollering, "Sandwiches, drinks, sandwiches, drinks." My mother stopped him.

"Sandwich, ma'am?"

"A bottle of milk, please, for my son," she said.

"Ten cents, ma'am."

Our lunch in a brown paper bag consisted of the usual peanut butter, butter and lettuce sandwiches my mother made and wrapped in waxed paper, and maybe she had held back a ripe plum from her canning and included it. Sometimes she made deer meat and salad dressing sandwiches—we didn't buy mayonnaise, it cost five cents a quart more. The fat in cold deer meat sticks to the roof of your mouth—a person could scrape the fat off his palate with his fingernail. I hated deer meat sandwiches. But oh, the milk! The milk came in small bottles that contained one glass, and the milk was pasteurized. Pasteurized, think of it! Pasteurization changes the flavor of raw milk, and it was delicious, this cold pasteurized milk that rich people drank every day. And I could drink it too, with a straw on the train on the way to visit my grandparents.

Chair cars are among the most marvelous inventions of man. At each end of the chair car stood a water dispenser furnished with white conical cups. You could pull down a cup and drink, and then you could pull another cup and drink, and then, if you had to go, there was also a bathroom at each end of the car—one for men and one for women. In some of the chair cars the men's bathroom was inside the smoking room, and if you had to go, you had to brave it through the smoke.

"You hold your breath, Gerry, when you walk through that room," my mother admonished. "And don't talk to the men in there. If men will desecrate their bodies, which are the Lord's temples, with tobacco smoke, and if they will become addicted to such a horrid habit, and do so voluntarily, and against God's will, they are not the kind of men a boy should know or talk to." She had warned me before about such noxious places. When, in the summer, I walked in downtown Sheridan and had to pass the several Main Street bars, their doors flung open against the heat, the Indians from the Crow Reservation, despite the swelter, sitting on the sidewalk wrapped up in their heavy blankets and wearing their old black stove-pipe hats, she would warn me in the same fashion.

"When you walk by those bars, Gerry, you hold your breath. You shouldn't let the smell of alcohol enter your body. You wouldn't let such smells into church and you shouldn't let such smells into your body."

But, once inside the men's toilet, having already held my breath as I fought my way through the smoke, and having securely locked the door behind me in that small closet of a toilet, wildly fascinating things were there to behold. When I flushed the toilet, the throat of the toilet opened up, exposing the tracks below. So there we were, rushing across the land at sixty miles an hour, and when I flushed and held down the lever, I could see the ground between the tracks flashing by, and hear the sound of the train come rushing up through the flush-hole. I stood there for many a minute looking down at the speeding ground, listening to the roar of the train, and, from time to time, hearing its long, plaintive whistle announcing to the world that we were coming, freeloaders or not. When I got home I bragged about my trip to Buddy Taylor and Bill Sare, whose father was a tie-hack on the railroad, and a friend of my father's.

"I peed on three states—on Wyoming, Nebraska and Colorado—and I peed on 'em coming home, too."

"That ain't nothin'," Buddy Taylor said.

"Big deal!" Bill Sare said. But I knew they wished they'd been where I'd been and done what I'd done.

The backs of the seats of the chair car could be reversed so a person could face either direction, a feature that permitted the porter to turn all of the seats in the direction the car was moving in order to prevent the passengers from riding backward. If the chair car was nearly empty, my mother would search out four empty seats on the same side of the aisle, the seats being two abreast. Then she would reverse two of the seat-backs so that those two now faced the other two. After that she lifted the footrests from both seats so they touched, thus forming a platform between the seats, after which she lifted a cushion from still another vacant seat and set it on this platform. Now she had a bed which, for each of us, had used up three seats.

"I hope the conductor doesn't make us put these seats back," my mother would say. We both knew that sitting up all night on a noisy, swaying chair car would be an abominable torture.

After nine o'clock the conductor turned off the lights. If a person wanted to read he had to go to the smoking car. Even before the lights went out I would lie down on this jury-rigged bed, close my eyes and listen. The sound of the steel wheels on the rails cried out in a hypnotic clickety-click, clickety-click, clickety-click, on into the night, the sound of the train's long whistle far ahead, clearing the tracks, the insistent ding, ding, ding of the crossing bell sounding louder and louder as we approached, and, passing, the same ding, ding, ding fading into the distance. The old chair car, at full speed, swayed bravely back and forth like a boat over heavy waves, which required the conductor to hold on to the luggage rack above the seats as he made his way up and down the aisle. I lay there next to the window, stretched out on that makeshift bed, enraptured by the sounds and the motions. I hear them and feel them today, and, should I ever be awarded a ticket to heaven, I hope it would be on a train speeding through the night, and I would listen to that clickety-click, and sway onto the edge of eternal sleep on the old CB&Q. But make the bed a Pullman.

One night when the train was somewhere between Upton, Wyoming (the BEST TOWN ON EARTH—the sign along the railroad tracks said so), and Alliance, Nebraska, I wet my makeshift bed on the chair car. Maybe God had ignored my prayers, which, after the Lord's Prayer, went as follows:

Now I lay me down to sleep
I pray the Lord my soul to keep
Watch over me through the night
And wake me up in the morning bright.

To which I added:

And please, Dear Lord, may I not have bad dreams,
Or wet the bed.

This prayer, as usually taught to children, ends:

If I should *die* before I wake
I pray the Lord my soul to take.

But my mother had changed the wording, for she had taught me to think of the *meaning* of the words I said in my prayers. She argued that if I merely recited the words without thinking about their meaning, then the words would come through meaningless to God as well. She illustrated her point one night when we were listening to the radio. The words of the announcer were garbled with static. "That's how God hears your prayers when you don't think about what you're saying to God in your prayers," she said. "It all comes through staticky like that."

I remember her criticizing the standard prayer. "A child should not go to bed thinking about death and afraid he will die while he sleeps," she said. I suspect that a proper study might reveal that most insomniacs as children prayed, "If I should die before I wake, I pray the Lord my soul to take," leaving them terrified, even as adults, to go to sleep for fear they would die in their sleep. A power grew out of the words my mother had substituted, for, indeed, didn't I awaken every morning just as I had prayed? And since I had prayed that I might be awakened, were not my prayers answered, and therefore did that not prove the existence of a loving God? Besides, since I had vigorously prayed not to wet the bed, my prayers had usually been answered, it being quite likely that on the rare occasions when I did wet the bed I had loosed my prayer into the firmament without having thought of what, exactly, I was praying for, and my prayer had gotten to God all garbled and staticky.

On the night in question, I probably went to sleep somewhere between Upton, Wyoming, and Alliance, Nebraska, without saying my prayers, lulled by the lullaby of the rails and the soft rocking of the train. Now I had to pay the price.

Worse, the *center* cushion was wet—one of the cushions my mother had taken from another seat across the way, and the conductor, who barely tolerated this felonious use of his chair car seats in the first place, would probably throw us off, or at least he might take out his chrome-plated puncher, and Lord knows how many more times he might punch our ticket, which would signal to the next conductor a secret message about us, and especially me. "This boy is a bedwetter. He has wet the cushion over there, and he is not even paying for this trip. He is a freeloading, bed-wetting, low-down rapscallion," which was the worst set of words I could think of all at once. "Pass the word along."

I could not fathom what to do in this life-or-death predicament. Suddenly my mother proved her mettle in an emergency. She threw a blanket over me, took a fresh pair of overalls out of the suitcase, and told me to change under the blanket. Then she wrapped the wet overalls in some newspapers some passenger had left behind, and stuffed the package into our suitcase. At last she laid newspapers on the wet cushion, and told me to say my prayers again and go back to sleep. "And think about what you are saying to God."

"But what if this cushion starts to stinking and the conductor smells it and throws us off?"

"The conductor spends all of his time back in the smoking room. He's one of those smokers, Gerry. He can't smell anything. *He's* the one who smells! Pee-*yew!* I hope you never smell like that!" she said. "Now say your prayers and go to sleep."

When I awakened the train was pulling into Alliance, Nebraska. It was one o'clock in the morning. I was stuck to the newspapers.

We had to wait three hours for our connection at Alliance. We carried our bags into the depot—one huge, cheap black metal suitcase with riveted seams and another black leather two-handled handbag about the size of a hundred-pound bag of flour. I grappled with the latter while my mother lifted the metal suitcase, staggered and struggled with it, a few feet at a time, sat it down, caught her breath and started all over again until we finally got into the depot. I was worried about her back, the Spencer corset and all. Inside the depot the benches were those old blond oak monsters about six feet high with curved backs. I slept on one, my mother next to me sitting up as proper as if she were in church. When our connecting train was about to arrive, once more she staggered out with the big metal suitcase to where the train would be pulling up, and there the porter, seeing her pitifully trying to get the suitcase on board, came to her rescue. When the train came roaring up, the porter jumped off, even before the train had come to a complete stop, and he lifted the suitcase on board as if it were no heavier than a lunch pail.

He was a black man, very polite, and he smiled at me and patted me on the head. I mention this because there were no black people in Sheridan. Not one I ever saw. But one thing I knew: Jesus loved black people, because my mother told me so, and so did my father, and we sang about it in Sunday School.

Red and yellow, black and white,
All are perfect in His sight,
Jesus loves the little children of the world.

Moreover, in the basement of the Methodist church I saw a picture on the wall that proved that Jesus loved all the children of all the races: a picture of a white Christ, a golden halo surrounding his head, his face radiating love, and a black child, an Indian child, and a Chinese child sitting on his lap, and the other children gathered at his feet. And Jesus was touching the children with loving, open hands.

In Sheridan, Wyoming, the only black man I had ever seen was Paul Robeson, who had come to Sheridan as a young singer during those Depression times when struggling artists took to the road and visited the backwoods places as part of the Community Concert Series. The concerts had become large social events for the town, and the townspeople turned out in large numbers and filled the theater to overflowing. My mother had somehow scraped the money together for our tickets, a penny and a nickel at a time, squeezed from already strained and impoverished sources in order that she might take her son to the concerts, so that he might be exposed to good music, and absorb some culture. In the year's preceding concerts I had sat with my mother in the old Fox Theater listening to the harpsichords and French horns and violins play those dissonant descants she called "parlor music." The concerts didn't start until eight o'clock, which was my bedtime. I wanted to sleep. But the strange stridency of the strings, the woeful, laborious sounds, kept me twisting in my seat, my rough wool Sunday trousers sweating and itching and generating in my heart not a love of classical music, but a need to avoid, at nearly any cost, such cruel late-night cacophony.

Yet how wonderfully different it had been when Paul Robeson stood on the stage of the Fox Theater, this giant of a black man with his powerful, godly bass voice that filled the theater without the aid of any electronics. The great young singer stood in the center of the stage like Goliath, his legs spread over huge feet, his massive right hand cupped to his ear as if to better hear the vibrations of his vocal cords. And he thundered the arias, like God hollering at the people, and the walls shook and the singing left me breathless. At the last, when he sang "Old Man River," "the sillies" shivered up my spine, and I wanted to run up and grab hold of the tree trunks that were the legs of this giant, and I wanted to look up into his huge black sweating face and say, "I love you Paul Robeson, and Jesus loves you too."

In our house I had never heard disrespectful words spoken about black people or about foreigners. I was told that Grandpa Pfleeger was a foreigner who had come to America from Germany as a young man to escape the Kaiser's draft. But Grandpa Pfleeger was proud to be an American; so proud, in fact, that he wouldn't allow his German wife, who at first could speak no English, to speak to him in their native tongue, not even when alone—not even, he claimed, in their conjugal bed. "We are Americans," he would thunder. "And Americans don't speak no German."

In those days black people were called "Negroes," both in polite society and in the history books. Negroes lived in the South. They were poor and picked cotton, except George Washington Carver, who was a famous agricultural scientist and knew a lot about peanuts and sweet potatoes. And there was "Way Down Upon the Swanee River," and *Uncle Tom's Cabin,* and that was about the extent of my education about race except that everybody knew Negroes were not treated like other people, even though Lincoln had freed them. To me, Abraham Lincoln, whose picture hung high up on the wall of my schoolroom in the J. S. Taylor School, was a major deity, right up there next to Christ. He had freed the slaves, I would boast, because they were people, even though they were black, and Lincoln loved them and Jesus loved them and so I loved them too.

In those days people often used the word "nigger," but as for me the word escaped from innocent lips. A "nigger-shooter" was made from a willow crotch in the form of a *Y* and strips cut from a rubber inner tube. The rubber strips were attached to each shaft of the fork and then the other ends of the strips were fastened to a leather pouch that held the rock. We boys shot blackbirds with our "nigger-shooters." In those days all blackbirds were bad. All sparrows were bad, especially English sparrows. All hawks were bad because they killed songbirds. Owls, spotted or otherwise, could be shot for their feathers. "Nigger-shooter" was just a name, not a derogatory word back then, a name like "BB gun" or "slingshot." But a slingshot was different from a nigger-shooter. A slingshot was a leather pouch tied to two long leather thongs. My father once made me one, and I would swing it around and around, faster and faster, and then, just at the exact right time, I would let loose of one of the thongs and the stone would go flying out, Lord knows in what direction, and Lord knows what it would hit, but it was a slingshot, not a "nigger-shooter." A slingshot was what David killed Goliath with. The racist origins of the word "nigger-shooter" never touched my conscious mind as a boy. Words have only the power we give them.

In the same way, Brazil nuts were "nigger-toes" even to my angel mother, even to my father, who told me I should be like Lincoln and fight for the rights of all people. "Nigger-toes" was merely a word that identified a brown nut that was hard to crack and that we were treated to, sometimes, on Christmas. No one in that far north little town had reason to think about racism. No one understood that that ugly word hurt people. In Sheridan, Wyoming, the collective conscience still slumbered. And we were supposed to love the Chinese, too. For as long as I could remember my mother made me clean my plate at every meal out of respect for "the starving Chinese."

"Gerry," my mother would admonish. "Remember the starving Chinese. Clean your plate. 'Waste not, want not.' " It escaped

"Nigger-shooter."

me how gorging myself with food I didn't like would save a starving person in China. Once my parents actually invited a missionary who had worked in China to come to our house after church for Sunday supper. She was a great lady, on a par with Lincoln. She loved people and devoted her life to people. Her name was Miss Abel, and she talked in a high flat twangy voice. "She's been so long in China she sounds like a Chinese," my father said.

After supper Miss Abel told the family about the poor Chinese peasants who worked a year to make as much as my father made in a day, and how they bound the feet of their baby girls, and how little girls were taken from their parents and sold into slavery, and I cried at the Sunday supper table, even in front of the great missionary.

Soon my mother launched her program of caring for the Chinese. The week following Miss Abel's visit, she baked a batch of fresh cinnamon rolls and sent me out to sell them door-to-door so that the proceeds from her labor and my developing skills as a salesman could go to Miss Abel's mission.

When we were finally aboard the train at Alliance, Nebraska, after an interminable wait, the porter in his white coat and his black trousers and his shiny black shoes and his black cap, which looked like a policeman's cap with a very shiny patent leather bill, slid our big black tin suitcase behind the first seat in the chair car. He smiled at my mother, and my mother thanked him, but not with a tip. Once more we were on our way to Grandpa's, we free-pass passengers, on the CB&Q Railroad.

At Denver we changed trains yet again. Denver—the largest city in the world, so far as I knew. It even had a Woolworth's store with an escalator. It had the Daniel and Fisher Tower, which was higher, according to my mother, than the Leaning Tower of Pisa, and besides that, the Daniel and Fisher Tower did not lean. The Union Depot, as it was called, provided a women's rest room with black marble walls and white marble floors—I knew because my mother took me in there to wash my face and hands. Denver was the place! I wore the cowboy hat my parents had bought me the Christmas before, and I was quite the little rage among the people who smiled or tipped their own hats and greeted me with, "Howdy, Cowboy," and things like that.

We had an even longer layover in Denver, about five or six hours. We checked the big metal suitcase in at the depot checkstand. Ten cents. But we carried the handbag to save the extra dime. My mother reasoned that if I could carry it a little way, the two of us could carry it a long way and thereby end up a dime ahead. My goal was to get to Woolworth's, fifteen or twenty blocks up from the depot. I carried the suitcase a block. She carried it two. When we finally got to Woolworth's I dragged it on the floor as I walked along the open counters that stood at about my eye level. I gawked at the beautiful glass marbles in netted bags of twenty, and I stared at the cheap black-painted tin revolvers that clicked inside— "Click, click, you're dead"—when you pulled the trigger.

I'd saved my allowance—ten cents a week as long as I did the dishes once a day. I bought a bag of marbles for a dime and the clicker gun and holster for thirty cents. Then I lost my mother. The horrid panic. What had happened to her? I began running up and down the aisles dragging our suitcase and crying, "Mother! Mother!" like a lost bawling calf. But no answer. People looked at me and walked on by. Surely I would perish in that frightening urban wilderness.

Then, like the sound of an angel, I heard her whistle, the one she and my father called out to each other in the deep woods of Wyoming. "Sweetheart. Sweetheart," the sound came, and once more I was snatched back, barely— either by God or my mother, it made no difference—from the great and ghastly abyss of abandonment in the F. W. Woolworth's in downtown Denver.

We looked in other windows, and I dragged the suitcase through the stores, but my mother bought nothing. Not one thing. Then suddenly it was time to go—the fairy tale was ending, the magic trance in its last afterglow. And then she said those words that will ring in my ears until I die:

"Whatever will we do if we miss the train?" It was the most dreadful of all possible abominations. That another train might come along was never a consideration as an alternative to the certain disaster that surely would befall us if we missed the train. I looked at my mother's face for a clue as to how serious the horror. Her face was grim, her eyes consumed with fear. We ran as fast as we could go, considering the suitcase. I was panting. She was panting. "Whatever will we do?" We would probably die in the streets, I thought. We would be captured by the gypsies and become their slaves. To this day my mother's transferred fear, still deeply tainting every cell plunges me into the most unrelenting anxiety whenever I am about to catch a plane. "Whatever will I do if I miss the plane?" As the years pass we take on the outward appearance of adults, but it is only a large, noisy, hairy-chested façade that obscures the child within. Like the tree, we have grown from the inside out.

We caught the train with plenty of time to spare, and when it pulled into that desolate place called Limon, Colorado, Grandpa and Grandma Pfleeger were standing there to meet us. We were saved. Grandpa held on to his hat while the wind blew Grandma's flowered cotton Sunday dress tight up against her little round legs. The town looked as if the people had long ago abandoned it. Newspapers blew up against the sides of the buildings, and empty cans rolled in the wind down Main Street. The few men who dared brave the day marched into the wind like one-armed soldiers, one hand on their hats, and the women scurried into the doorways like refugees under fire. The wind in Limon, Colorado, never stopped, and the dry land farmers, deep into the Depression, struggled to survive in those desperate dust-bowl days of *The Grapes of Wrath*.

Grandpa lifted out our large tin suitcase with one hand and flung it into the trunk of his old black Buick. Then, aiming the car down the yellow center line of the road, he drove the old wreck back to the farm with his oldest daughter, Esther Sophie Pfleeger, and his only grandchild, this boy, Gerald Leonard Spence, who bore his given name as a middle name, aboard. The highway, yes, the whole world belonged to Leonard Pfleeger. When we met a car, only reluctantly and at the last possible moment did he pull over to his own side of the road.

"Why don't you drive on your own side of the road?" this plucky daughter of his demanded.

"I know how to drive the car," he answered in his heavy German accent. "I don't need no help from you." He spoke in a way that there would be no more discussion about it. He would not brook such questions. All creatures, man or beast, got out of his way. He was not in awe of preachers; he had no insurance, because the devil himself was afraid of Grandpa Pfleeger. He had no respect for bankers, and he wasn't afraid of the Depression. He wasn't even afraid of God. He gave ten cents, no more, to the church on Sunday morning. If that wasn't enough, well, God could go to hell. Tithing—well, ten cents was 10 percent of a dollar and that was about all the cash he had, or that was all he would admit to, and it was nobody's business, including God's, if he had a little stashed away somewhere.

The story was often told how, during the First World War when the U.S. government was selling Liberty Bonds to finance the allied effort, Leonard Pfleeger came upon a neighboring farmer in the bank, where the neighbor had just bought a Liberty Bond.

"I suppose Leonard Pfleeger, being German and all, won't be buying any Liberty Bonds," the neighbor said within purposeful earshot of Grandpa.

The story insists that Leonard Pfleeger grabbed the man by his overall straps, lifted him off the floor and hollered, "By damn, I'll match you bond for bond," and slammed the man down. The duel was on. When his cash was gone, Grandpa borrowed more money from the bank and so did the neighbor, until finally Grandpa Pfleeger offered to put a mortgage on next year's bean crop. The neighbor wouldn't go that far, and walked out of the bank a beaten man. Leonard Pfleeger would never be beaten, not by any man, not by the weather, not by hard luck or God. When nearly every man was penniless in those piteous days of the Great Depression, Grandpa Pfleeger was the only farmer around who still had a dollar. He cashed his bonds and ended up owning his neighbor's farm, and the farms of several other neighbors as well.

Leonard Pfleeger had fled to this country from Germany to escape the Kaiser's draft. One of the brighter students in his village, he had been slated to become a teacher, but he wanted to be a farmer. America had plenty of cheap land and he came for it. He worked like an indentured servant, saved every penny he earned and, after five years, returned to Germany with enough to buy passage to America for his mother and two brothers. On his voyage back he met Barbara Lang, my grandmother.

The Pfleegers were strong, square-made people: Grandfather with that broad, powerful chest and strong arms and a large square head and dark hair with a bald spot in the back; and Grandmother, short, with hardly any figure at all, scurrying around the kitchen from first morning light and into the night like a busy, frightened country mouse. She wore a plain cotton dress that tied in the back and she smiled at me with soft, dark eyes that seemed happy when Grandpa wasn't around. Her once-black hair was graying and done up neatly in a bun. She was a gentle-spoken woman with a heavy German accent who never raised her voice against anyone and who never, not once, spoke back to my grandfather. When he hollered she would sometimes dare look at him quickly with her plaintive, wearied eyes, and sometimes she would look down as if in shame.

I remember how he soundly scolded that dear little woman. As if she had committed some egregious sin, he hollered, "Barp" (which we all knew to mean Bar*b*), "you left the salt out of the oatmeal!" His eyes were bright and terrible. I had never heard a man shout at a woman before.

"I just forgot, Leonard," she whispered.

"How can you forget?" he shouted back. The salt must have been a matter of life or death. "I don't forget to take the harnesses off of the horses at night, do I?"

"No, Leonard," she said and looked down again.

Leonard and Barbara Pfleeger had first settled in Pipestone County, Minnesota, before the turn of the century. They were farmers, of course, laboring at whatever honest work they could find. There, in the year 1901, my mother was born, their second child. Soon after, the Pfleegers moved to Zion, Illinois, where Leonard Pfleeger encountered a religious order, the members of which, although Protestant, followed zealously the literal pronouncements of the Old Testament. They called themselves Zionists and believed, truly believed, believed to the heart, to the bone, to the marrow and beyond, that the second coming of Christ was at hand. They knew the day. They knew the hour. They knew the place, and they, with the faith that moved mountains, walked up Peach Tree Hill to meet their Redeemer. None doubted that He would appear. None doubted that they would be taken to Paradise with Him. After that exalted moment arrived, all believed that none would ever return for another moment of earthly existence, not ever. All believed that in that moment they would never again be with their friends or the nonbelieving members of their families. They were leaving their possessions behind because in the Kingdom they would have no need for them. But it was also said that before Leonard Pfleeger trekked up Peach Tree Hill to leave it all behind and to meet his Savior, he locked the house up good and tight, just in case something went wrong up there.

When Leonard Pfleeger made up his mind, his decision was as irrevocable as death. By this time he was reading the Old Testament, which insisted that it was a mortal sin to eat the flesh of any beast that did not possess a cloven hoof and that did not chew its cud. Pig did not meet the test. Although pigs had cloven hooves, they did not chew a cud. Pig meat! Before that time he had bragged to all who could hear him, and you could hear Leonard Pfleeger if he was within a country mile, that he could raise more pigs than Grandma could raise chickens.

But suddenly one day in response to the biblical injunction, Leonard Pfleeger took out his rifle and shot every boar, every nutless shoat, every sow, every poor little piglet on the place, after which he hooked onto their carcasses with a team of horses and hauled them to a gully where, be damned with the caveat "Waste not, want not," he left them to rot away in the Illinois sun as a sacrifice to the God of Zion. And whiskey was out as well. Drinking whiskey was a mortal sin. Even good German beer was out, and, of course, tobacco. No person dared smoke in the house of Leonard Pfleeger. Not one puff had ever been exhaled in Leonard Pfleeger's house. By God, he was a man of God, this Leonard Pfleeger, who did nothing by the halves except, of course, tithing, which was nobody's business.

Several years later, in about 1907, Leonard Pfleeger, along with the rest of America, caught the go-West itch. He was going West to homestead in Colorado—going to be a big-time farmer. He was going to own half the county by the time he was ready to retire, when he would move to a nice quiet town with shade trees and live in a pretty brick house with a rich, green lawn and a lilac bush. The railroad offered to haul those who could pay the price of passage to the plains of Colorado, and Leonard Pfleeger had the price. Onto four boxcars he loaded the cows, the draft horses, even the chickens, the plows, the discs, the harrows and the buggy, the furniture, the bedding, the cooking utensils, and, of course, the Holy Bible, and at last he stuffed in the wife, the kids and the dogs. They unloaded at Limon, Colorado.

Twenty-five years later I first laid eyes on Grandpa's farm. He and his three sons had built a large red barn, but the paint on the siding by that time had been mostly sandblasted by the wind. They had built a sternly upright two-story white house with no porch—no need for a porch, no time to swing on porch swings or to engage in any porch-place foolishness. And around the small hard dirt yard in front of the house he erected a galvanized wire fence to keep the cows out of Grandmother's moss roses—the only concession I ever knew the man to make on her behalf. In silent gratitude, every day she watered her moss roses along the narrow concrete walk with the rinse water from her dishes. Looking up from the small red and yellow blossoms along that desperate concrete walk, one could see nothing but dirt and blowing dust for as far as the eye could focus.

Next to the barn a windmill rattled and banged, complaining against the constant prairie gale, and across from the barn stood a dilapidated toolshed, an old shack of a brooder house for the turkeys, a board and tarpaper chicken house, and an outdoor privy through the roof of which one could count the stars at night.

By July the beans had already dried to the ground in the relentless drought. Sometimes a tumbleweed from another county came bouncing across the landscape, racing just ahead of the wind. The grass, the little that had not been worn away, was short, brown, dust-covered and hard. The cottonwood trees that once shaded the farm had long since died, their bark blown off, their trunks polished by the wind so that they stood silvery and stark on the flat prairies.

I thought of my Grandfather Pfleeger's as a place of death. Nothing wanted to grow there, and all living things soon gave up their lives. The prairies died and lay down to be covered by the blowing dust. The head of the vealed calf, dropped behind the barn where it had been slaughtered, lay gazing up at the sun, its tongue rotted out, the flies picking away at its eyes. The cancer-eyed cows, too sick to make it to market, were also butchered and their meat fed to the dogs and the chickens. If we ate the meat, it was a secret no one spoke of.

The calves at branding were thrown down in the dusty manured corral where my uncles held them down, one uncle on the head of the calf, and two others stretching the bawling little creature out flat, dusty boots up against flank and neck, the hot branding iron searing its tender sides. The smoke of burning hair and hide enveloped the men's hard, brown, serious faces, the smell of burning flesh causing small noses to recoil. I wept at the calves' piteous bawling when the hot iron touched them. The old cows came looking, wanting to charge those who were torturing their bawling young, but they were afraid of the men and the fire and the iron. And then my grandfather stepped up with the knife, and with his hard hand he stretched out the calf's small wrinkled white sac, slit it neatly across the top and exposed the tender pink testicles within. He tossed the severed top of the sac into the dirt, and, with an instrument that looked like a kind of pliers, he reached in and, one at a time, pulled out the testicles and their long attached cord. Then he milked each cord several times, and when the cord was fully exposed, sometimes a foot or more, as if pulling the cord out of my pajama bottoms, he neatly cut the cord free from each testicle and dumped the testicles into a pail of saltwater.

"Want some Rocky Mountain oysters, Swede?" my Uncle Clarence, the oldest son, hollered. He called me "Swede" because my hair was so blond it was almost white. I didn't answer. When my uncles released the calf, it staggered to its feet, wobbled, and stood for a moment wild-eyed and looking for its mother. Then the calf ran stiff-legged here and there in the corral, not knowing where it was or where its mother was among the cows huddled together in the far end of the corral. And I, who had been lost from my mother, knew how the calf felt.

Some nights my grandfather started up the old Buick, with Uncle Clarence on one fender and Uncle Harold, my mother's younger brother—they called him "Heck"—on the other, and sometimes my youngest uncle, Uncle Fred, came along, and off my grandfather would drive, my uncles like gunners in an old bomber, one on each fender, shooting the jackrabbits with their shotguns as the rabbits bounded across the road in front of the car, confused, as they often were, by the headlights. The men filled the backseat of the Buick to the ceiling with dead rabbit carcasses. I helped unload them, jackrabbits as big as spaniels, their eyes glazed and staring, their hairy bodies dripping in their blood and the blood of their kin, their long hind legs loose and floppy. I held a jackrabbit up by the ears and he extended from my armpits to the ground. The dogs, black-

and-white mongrel collie-shepherd crosses, sniffed at the carcasses, lapped at the blood, and nipped at the entrails.

"Get out of there!" my grandfather hollered, and gave a dog a kick.

"Get!" my uncles echoed, and the dogs slunk away, tails between their legs, their jowls dripping, a hungry look on their faces.

We hauled the carcasses into Grandma's kitchen and piled the rabbits on the floor, and then that very night Grandmother cooked them in her ever-ready pressure cooker. Later the meat, hair, bones, entrails, and all, was fed to the chickens. And they stunk. But the chickens prospered, and dutifully laid their eggs, and the fryers provided Sunday dinner for the family, as well as a small cash crop when my grandfather took fresh fryers to the Limon market early on a Saturday morning.

I once witnessed the execution of a flock of innocent turkeys at Grandpa Pfleeger's farm. First, by a loop of binder's twine, the men hung the live turkeys upside down from a nail in the brooder house. Vainly the turkeys struggled, flapping their great gray wings and squawking, their mouths open, their tongues as pointed as daggers, exposed, their eyes bulging in terror awaiting the knife. Then the executioner—one of my uncles—grabbed hold of the turkey's neck just behind the head and jammed a long, narrow, razor-sharp blade down the turkey's throat, and with an evil slashing he cut the turkey's jugular. I can see the blood gushing from the bird's mouth, its voice box also severed so that it bled to death in silence except for the sound of its desperate flailing wings, which made a small

The Pfleegers: Back: (left to right) Harold, Clarence, Fred.
Margaret, standing left. Esther, Gerry's mother, standing, right.
Leonard Pfleeger and Barbara Pfleeger, Gerry's grandparents, in front.

high cry through the air, a cry that must have pierced eternity. And after the turkey wings fell limp there followed a terrible quivering that shook the bird's body until the rafters in the old roof rattled. After a day of killing, the blood of the turkeys, saved in the collecting tub below, was also fed to the chickens.

Then the turkey carcasses were dunked into tubs full of boiling water and picked—by my grandmother's dear cracked, callused, crooked fingers. I sat silently watching. Finally I began to help her. The wing feathers came out hard. I would wrap my fist around a single feather and sometimes I was not strong enough to pull it out. The feathers were ugly and wet and they reeked, and my fingers shriveled at their tips from soaking so long in the hot water. The water in which the bodies of the turkeys had been dunked turned a nasty gray, and my hands grew tired and at last I pulled back. But never once did my grandmother stop, and never once did she look up from her work, not until the last turkey was completely plucked.

Today I go to the lunch counter, and I hear somebody holler, "Gimme a turkey san. Lettuce and tomato. No mayo. Turkey's good for you, right? No fat. Right?"

Sometimes I see the turkeys giving up their bloodless bodies in terror. But where did the terror go? Every cell must be laced with it.

Feast on the turkey's terror. What will terror nourish? Sometimes I think of things like that. I have eaten many a turkey sandwich with and without the mayonnaise. My mother would have argued that turkeys were created by God to feed mankind. Always at Christmastime Grandma Pfleeger sent us a turkey by parcel post. Even though it must have taken more than a week for it to travel the distance by train, and although it was not packed in ice, it nevertheless arrived unspoiled and perfectly delicious.

One day Grandpa Pfleeger sent the boys out to round up the cattle. They returned with a hundred head or more of skinny Hereford cows and their bawling calves. They were a pitiful bunch, skin and bone, their ribs protruding as if death had already come and gone without the cows having recognized it.

"Look those cows over good," Grandpa told the boys. "Cut out a dozen with the biggest calves." He always shouted with that deep, foreboding Moses voice. "The ones with the biggest calves are givin' the most milk." Then the boys weaned the calves and began to milk the cows. They were wild range cows, but Grandpa Pfleeger made milk cows of them, sold their scanty cream for cash, and fed the curdled skim milk, with the flies it captured, to the chickens.

My parents were married in the summer of 1927 at this same Pfleeger farm. It was a big affair on the prairie, this dry land farmer's oldest daughter getting married—she, the first college graduate in the family. Grandpa Pfleeger didn't think Gerald Milner Spence was worthy of his daughter. No man really was. Not Leonard Pfleeger's daughter. And as for this young Spence, what did he have? One of those degrees was all he had. A piece of paper. Nobody'd give you a dime for the paper. This young Spence was just a farmer's son himself, without a farm. And although he had a job and the two had been courting all through high school and college, Grandpa didn't approve of his daughter marrying a man who was not a landed man, who was not a businessman, and who was not a German. But the marriage would go on. He knew that. He couldn't stop her. His daughter had stood right up to him and told him plain out that she was either going to run away and marry Gerald Spence or she was going to marry him at the farm. He could take his choice.

"Well, by *Gott,* I can't stop ya. But I don't have ta agree ta it." But he finally relented a little. They could be married at the farm and he would attend the wedding, but his protest would be apparent to everyone. He would not give his daughter away to that Spence fellow.

My mother wore a white satin dress that extended half a foot below her knees, one that she and her mother had made. A long skirt would have dragged in the dust and caught in the weeds growing in front of the house. She carried a bouquet of long-stemmed white roses that had been shipped in all the way from Denver. And my father, his hair trimmed short and his ears sticking out, then standing his full six feet tall, wore his navy blue suit. All of my mother's brothers and her younger sister, Margaret, who was her bridesmaid, and my father's youngest brother, Hunter, who stood as his best man, wore their Sunday best. The relatives came, my grandmother's brother, Fred Lang, and his family and the few neighbors who were still friendly. But my mother would not be cowed by this man, Leonard Pfleeger. If he didn't want to give her away she would have her uncle, Fred Lang, give her away.

Then the wedding procession began down the short concrete walk in front of the house, my mother hanging on to her uncle's arm, with all the people gathered in front of that plain stark farmhouse. When she arrived at the front door where the preacher stood, my grandfather, wearing his brown suit and his bow tie and his rough, burned face below his white farmer's forehead, pushed Uncle Fred aside and took his place beside my mother, and when the preacher asked who gave the bride, Grandpa Pfleeger said in his loud voice, "I do." And that's all there was to it, and so they were duly married. After they married the newlyweds moved to Laramie, Wyoming, where my father took up his duties as assistant state chemist and where I was later born.

I was always afraid of Grandpa Pfleeger. Everyone around him was. He spoke in that loud voice through a large black mustache that covered his long upper lip. He talked to people as if they were a couple of blocks away instead of standing next to him. Even his pats hurt. His hands were so hard he could rasp with them, every one of his fingers had been broken and had healed crookedly, and their tips, covered with fingernails as thick as shoe leather, pointed in every which way.

Sometimes he didn't laugh when things were really funny. He had that German sense of humor, or lack of it, my father said. Moreover, Grandfather Pfleeger thought himself a poet. He made a poem up about me:

Gerald Leonard Spence
Sitting on a fence
Trying to make a dollar
Out of fifteen cents.

Grandpa Pfleeger possessed a handy and ready assortment of bastardized aphorisms. Instead of "If at first you don't succeed, try, try again," he'd say, "If at first you don't succeed, try and suck another seed." He thought that very funny and always laughed uproariously. "Enough is enough," he would shout, "and too much is aplenty already."

One evening I came into Grandma Pfleeger's kitchen, and, like Wild Bill Hickok, I was shooting everybody in sight. My new black tin clicker gun, my weapon, the one I had bought at Woolworth's in Denver the day I lost my mother. "Come 'ere, Gerry Leonard Spence. Lemme see yer new gun," Grandpa Pfleeger said. He was sitting at the far end of the kitchen waiting for his supper.

I walked over to the huge old man, as old and as big as God. His eyes were blue and bright and hard like the eyes of a blue-eyed hawk and he had all of his teeth, which were yellow and flat and worn down nearly to the gums.

"So this is yer gun," he said. I backed up. He took the gun and clicked it a couple of times. And laughed. Then he reached out for my new leather holster. And with his bare fingers he tore out a piece of the leather and held it up.

"Cheap leather they make nowadays," he said.

I began to cry. "Mother, Grandpa just ruined my holster."

My mother had been peeling the potatoes. She turned to see what was going on, and when she saw what her father had done she was suddenly transformed into a grizzly sow.

"How dare you do that!" she said. I had never seen my mother attack. "That boy saved his money for half a year to buy that toy, and you just ruined it for the fun of it? What kind of a man are you anyway?"

The old man shied back. Suddenly his eyes watered.

"How much did it cost?" he asked.

"It cost that boy thirty cents," she said, her hands still on her hips, her chin jutted out. The old man got up and left the kitchen. I thought he'd been insulted, and didn't know how to respond to my mother's wrath. In a minute he returned. "Here," he said, putting three shiny dimes in my hand. Then he reached in his pocket and pulled out one more. "And this one's for the wrong."

One day the weather changed at Grandpa Pfleeger's farm. In the distance we could see clouds beginning to form. Towering cumulus soon rose from the distant horizon, and began to march like an ominous army toward us. Already I could smell the rain. And the wind—the wind, as if in respect, had stopped its interminable blowing. It was noon. The men were in for the heavy meal of the day they all called dinner.

Nobody mentioned the impending storm around the table. If you said it might rain, well, the devil might come to prove you wrong. Don't mention it. Don't think about it even. It never rains in Colorado. "I will tell you one thing," Grandpa Pfleeger said, "we are here, and the devil is trying to dry us up and blow us out a here, and by *Gott*, I'm not a goin'. I'm stayin', I don't care if it don't rain fer a hundred more years, which it probably won't."

After dinner I walked outside. By then a small, eerie breeze had begun to blow from the south. The chickens had stopped their clucking, and the turkeys were silent, and the cows in the corral were as still as death. My mother stepped outside the front door to look. In her face I could see the desperation she had grown up with as a child. I could see it in her eyes. It never left her eyes.

"Come into the house," she said, grabbing hold of my hand. I didn't want to go in.

"Maybe it's gonna rain," I said. She looked at me as if I had broken the spell, and that surely now the clouds would dry up and blow away as they always did.

"Maybe it will, God willing," she said. "Pray to God for the rain, Gerry. God can hear you." I pull away from my mother and sat down on the ground next to the house. "Your Grandpa Pfleeger needs a crop, and a good rain could save him," she said. After she went in the house. I decided I would pray to help Grandpa Pfleeger. I prayed and I prayed. I thought about the meaning of the words so that they wouldn't come through to God all staticky. And pretty soon, sure enough, the towering clouds marched right up to the house, and it got as dark as night, and suddenly the wind started to blow very hard, harder than I had ever seen it blow before, and then the rain came. It came in huge cupsful as if God had had a change of heart and had decided to flood us out. I thought of Noah. But we had no ark.

My Uncle Clarence, the tallest of my uncles, who looked like an Indian and who had my grandmother's dark eyes, stepped out of the house. "Come on in, Swede, you're gonna get wet."

But I liked the rain. It was my rain. I made it. I mean, God and I made it. "I don't want to go in," I said. The rain was pelting down on me in drops so large as marbles. I was shivering. "It's hot," I said. "It's very hot."

My uncle started to laugh his high laughter that sounded like a coyote yapping. "This kid is really dumb," my uncle hollered through the beating rain. "He hasn't got enough sense to come in out of the rain." Then he let out that high loud laugh again and shook his head in disbelief. My mother glared at him.

"You leave him alone," she warned, and the big man moved back from her and went into the house.

It rained for the rest of the afternoon. That night the family gathered around the long table in the dining room for supper. The room was dimly lit by a kerosene lamp that flickered ghostlike shadows on the walls. The table was covered with a bright flowered oilcloth. No napkins. The men used their sleeves and wiped across their mouths in a hurry. Grandpa Pfleeger sat at the head of the table, the family around him, all but Grandma, whose fast little steps brought the food in from the kitchen. Boiled potatoes. Roast beef. Gravy. Biscuits. Butter from the cows they milked, and for dessert, her sugar cookies which she ruined, I thought, by sprinkling caraway seeds on top.

But before the family ate, my grandfather said a prayer. Nothing fancy like the preachers in church. Straight and to the point. He cleared his throat, and the room was silent and we all waited.

"We thank you for the rain, amen," he said. Then my dear little German grandmother, still standing at the door of the kitchen, bowed her tired head and said the blessing in her soft broken English. My mother reached under the table for my hand. Her hand was hard like the hands of her mother, hard from work, and yet it seemed gentle to me. As I listened to my grandmother's simple prayer of thanksgiving spoken out of her heart, something very tender broke inside of me, and I could feel whatever it was envelop me, and I knew then and there that I loved my dear little Grandma Pfleeger very much.

But now I had a secret, too: It was I who got God to bring the rain to save my grandfather's crop. It was I who, following my mother's teaching that "faith can move mountains," had believed, and the rain had come. They all thanked God. But nobody thanked me.

That night, I gave the whole matter of faith and prayer some further thought. Considering the fact that I had already saved my grandfather's crop, and since "faith can move mountains," I thought, well, it ought to be easy enough to pray myself into the bicycle I had always wanted. And so I began to pray. Oh, what supplications, what heartfelt beseechments I offered up. Did I believe? Oh, yes, how I believed! I believed clear to the bottom of my hungering soul. And since my faith was strong enough to move mountains, it would please me beyond words if God would simply deposit my new bicycle, a red one with balloon tires and steerhorn handlebars, if you please, at the foot of the stairs where it would be easy to find when I got up in the morning. Satisfied that my prayers were in order, and my faith adequate to do the trick, I slipped off into sleep.

When I awakened I rushed down the stairs like an excited child on Christmas morning. I looked around. There must be some mistake.

"Mother," I said. She was helping my grandmother make breakfast in the kitchen. "Did you see a bicycle around here?"

"No," my mother replied. "Why should there be a bicycle around here?"

"I prayed for one and I know it's around here someplace." When she saw the look on my face, she grabbed me and held me to her.

"Honey," she said softly, "your prayer to God was for the wrong thing. Pray to Him for the strength and the will to *earn* a bicycle, and see if that prayer isn't answered someday. God wants us to help ourselves whenever we can."

I thought that one over for some time. But why earn it if God can give it to you in response to a faith like mine that was so powerful it could make it rain? I prayed some more that night. But no bicycle. Maybe God didn't hear a young fellow's prayers after all. Or maybe someone else was praying louder and harder than I. But one thing I knew: Some of my prayers had been answered. I hadn't wet the bed since I got to my grandparents', and I did, I really *did,* make it rain at Grandpa Pfleeger's.

But I reasoned further: The fact that I was questioning God was proof that I had no faith at all. Yes, I was a bad and faithless child. On the other hand, maybe God wasn't all He had been made out to be. In the end I decided I would withhold my judgment on God, at least for a day or two more.

CHAPTER 5

John Henry Spence, Gerry's grandfather.

WHEN OUR VISIT was over at Grandpa Pfleeger's, my mother and I boarded the train once more, and traveled west and north for Loveland, Colorado, where Grandpa and Grandma Spence came to meet us in their own Dodge automobile. It had served the family well as the family car and, when the rear seats were removed, as the family truck.

I had never thought to ask when Grandfather Spence's ancestors came to America. Such a monumental figure as he was as much a permanent part of the earth as the mountains or the old spreading silver maple in the front yard. But my father had collected the family history and, after Grandfather Spence died, he forwarded the thin folder to me with the terse note: "Thought you might be interested some day."

The history revealed that the Spences were of Scottish origin, belonging to the MacDuff clan. But they had emigrated from Ireland and had landed in New York before the Revolutionary War. John Henry Spence, my great grandfather, was a regular in the Union Army and was wounded in the Civil War. My Grandfather Spence, who bore his father's name, recounted to me how the Rebels were running short of powder and were loading their rifles with half loads of powder and firing their rifles in a high arc in order to reach their targets. One such bullet hit his father between the eyes, but the arc of the bullet was such that the bullet's course penetrated down through the roof of his mouth. He recovered from the wound and rejoined the army only to be later discharged, again for medical reasons.

After the war my great grandfather married Margaret McCausland, also Scotch-Irish, whose ancestors had emigrated to Delaware from Ireland in 1796, but he died of tuberculosis a month before my grandfather was born in Carroll County, Ohio. Once in America, all the Spences were farmers. Grandpa Spence was raised by his mother's brother.

Grandfather Spence looked for all the world as I imagined Santa Claus would look if he shaved off his beard. He had a large round head with white thinning hair, a ruddy complexion and a prominent, rather handsome nose, and you could trace the course of his veins along the sides of his cheeks as one can follow the tricklets of melting snow down the side of a hill in the springtime. He seemed as broad at his hips as he was at his shoulders, but bib overalls, without a waist, do that to a man. He wore a silver-cased watch in the watch pocket of his overalls that was secured to a leather watch thong, and his shirt was light-weight blue denim. He wore long underwear summer and winter.

"How come you wear long underwear in the summer, Grandpa?" I asked one day. "Ain't ya hot?"

"I wear my longies for the same reason a squirrel wears his," he replied. "They keep me warm in the winter and cool in the summer," and his old squint-ing blue eyes would sparkle and get watery when he laughed. Then he'd pat me on the head, and say, "Come on, let's go milk old Bossy." And down we'd walk to the barn, Grandpa and me, me holding his rough old hand with his thick nails trimmed short, and his other hand swinging a shiny empty milk pail. His steps were short, and his legs crooked, and he limped on both legs. I tried to walk in step with Grandpa, because men who take the same steps together *are* together.

Something in all the cells of a boy begins to sing in a cow barn. Given the choice, I would likely choose Grandpa and the cow barn at milking time over heaven, for nothing fun ever happened in heaven so far as I could determine. At Grandpa's barn, the old man hobbled over to the door, threw it open and called in a long call, "Come, Boss. Come, Boss," and from the far end of the green meadow a brown Guernsey cow came trotting, her full bag swinging, her teats leaking small streams of milk, her black eyes bulging and as large as ripe plums. She ran past me, this miniature man who wore the same kind of bib overalls as the old man, and she looked me over good. Then, willing to make the bargain, her milk for Grandpa's oats, she stuck her head in the stanchion, whereupon Grandpa gave the latch a flip and she was stuck there with her wet nose in a generous helping of oats.

She watched me, on her left, with her left eye, and she chewed, and she cleaned her nostrils with her long gray tongue. She seemed very happy indeed, and so was I, and so was Grandpa. He reached down and brushed off her teats, and then, with his thumb and forefinger, he stripped out some milk in long squirts into a square, black, homemade iron dish for the cats that gathered at his feet in fulfillment of their bargain with Grandpa—a few squirts of milk, morning and night, in exchange for keeping the mice population down. Grandpa aimed a stream of milk at the yellow cat, and the cat opened its mouth, its small pink tongue lapping at the milk, and then it shook its head to clean away the excess. Grandpa would grin at me and then squirt a stream of milk at the black cat with the white paw, and it too would lap up the milk with its tongue. Then he slipped a loop of binder's twine around Bossy's tail, lifted it up and hooked the other end of the loop on a nail that had been pounded into the rafter.

"How come you're doin' that, Grandpa?" I asked.

"Keeps her tail out of the milk pail when she swats at the flies," he said. He took down a small hand pump with an enclosed glass cup at its end that held the fly spray, and he pumped a mist of fly spray over Bossy's back and legs, and at last he affixed a pair of "kickers" just above the elbows of her hind legs—two iron clamps connected with a short length of chain that Grandpa could shorten or lengthen.

"How come you're doin' that, Grandpa?" I asked.

"Keeps her from kickin' at the flies and knocking your old grandpa on his keester." Then he laughed and lifted a tin cup off a nail, milked the cup full, and handed the cup to me. The milk was warm and foamy and sweet. Finally Grandpa pulled up his one-legged, T-shaped milking stool, worn round on the bottom, and settled down to serious business.

He snuggled up to old Bossy, laid his head against her warm side, the brim of his old felt hat pushed flat against her belly. He half closed his eyes and began to milk, and his face became very peaceful and soft. The streams of milk rang out as they struck the bottom of the empty pail. Grandpa squeezed the milk out with his right hand, followed quickly by the milk squeezed out with his left, right and left, right and left, right and left, in a strong, steady rhythm, the stream from the right sounding higher when it hit the bottom of the pail than the sound of the left. And as the pail began to fill, you could hear milk streams squirting into milk, into foam, making more foam until at last the sounds were nearly smothered.

Other sounds filled the barn—of old Bossy chewing and chewing, the cats purring as they rubbed up against Grandpa's leg, the fluttering of barn swallows that had built their mud nests under the barn's eaves.

Next to the far wall under the barn's window, old Bossy's brown-and-white pinto calf began bawling in its pen. I went to it and I stuck my finger through the slats and felt the calf's cold wet nose. It nibbled at my finger. I jerked back.

"Grandpa," I cried. "The calf bit me."

He laughed. "He wants his supper. He wants to suck your finger."

"Suck my finger? How come the calf wants to suck my finger?"

"Because that is what calves do. They suck, just as boys like you ask questions." Then I gathered up my nerve, and this time I didn't jerk back, and sure enough, the calf sucked my finger, and it felt very strange and I thought it was better to be a talking boy than a sucking calf.

The small barn, with its low ceiling, was dark and cool, constructed of native lumber which had turned to rich hues of umber that had darkened over the years. The barn had been built close to the ground on a foundation of red sandstone. The rustic boards that made up the siding served also as the interior walls, and thus the wood framing of the barn was exposed. Dark streaks of rust ran below the nail holes, and on the far wall across from the stanchion hung an old set of harness Grandpa used to hitch up his mules, the leather blackened with oil and sweat, the hames of the harness capped with those traditional brass balls polished bright by many a year. The barn smelled of cows and of mules, of milk and of fresh alfalfa hay, and of the oats in the bin and the smell of Grandpa, which was good to the nose of a child.

When Grandpa had finished milking, when the careful stripping of each teat was complete, he untied Bossy's tail, unhooked her kickers, opened the stanchion, and out she came past us in a terrible rush.

"She's in a hurry," Grandpa said.

"How come?" I asked.

"Because cows have no place to go, and if you had no place to go you'd be in a hurry too." He laughed and I laughed back as if I understood, and because I laughed at his jokes, Grandpa thought I was very bright. Then he poured a quart of milk into a bucket wired to the side of the calves' pen, and the calf was already in the bucket even as Grandpa poured the milk, the milk dripping down its face, and I could hear the deep sucking sounds as the calf emptied the pail as fast as the old man poured it in.

After milking, we headed for the house with the full pail. I could tell it hurt the old man to walk up the hill, but he didn't complain and we talked all the way, I asking questions and he answering them. He was so very careful not to spill a drop from the bucket. Back at the house we climbed down the red flagstone steps into the cellar, where the smell of apples perfumed the air and where the milk separator waited like a half monster-man, half machine. Grandpa poured the milk into the large metal bowl at the top of the separator, and then he began slowly turning the handle of the beast, and the machine groaned like an old man continually turning over in bed. Grandpa turned the handle faster and faster and the groaning became a high-pitched hum as if the machine were singing an eerie tune, and I thought surely the machine would say something. But before it could say anything, the milk began to pour from its spout into a clean pail Grandpa had placed under it, and the cream, in a smaller stream, poured from another spout into a kettle, and when the machine was purring along, Grandpa let me take the handle, which was going faster than I could turn it.

The skim milk was left to sour on the back porch, and when it was ripe it was fed to the chickens. The cream went to Grandma for sweet butter, and some was set aside for Grandpa's cereal. Not a drop of milk was ever wasted, and many years later when I had grown into an older man, I began to see my own life as Grandpa's bucket of milk, and I began to think how precious the milk. I remembered how it fed the cats and the calf and the chickens and all of the family, and how it had been taken in a fair bargain from old Bossy, who, but for Grandpa and the work of his mules, would never have been treated to a pail full of fresh, tender, homegrown oats, morning and night. Yet something more precious grew out of the bargain: a noble connection between man and beast, one never spoken, but understood by both, and one I understood when I saw the peace flood over the old man's face as he milked his cow and felt the warmth of her body against his cheek. And old Bossy knew it as well.

In the morning after Grandpa finished his chores, he harnessed his mules in the barn, drove them out and, depending on the work of the day, hitched them to an old horse-drawn mower, or a sulky rake or a manure spreader.

"How come you have mules instead of horses, Grandpa?"

"Mules are better than horses," Grandpa said.

"How come?"

"Because mules are stronger than horses, and they eat less. And mules are a whole lot smarter than a horse. You can turn a mule and a horse loose in a granary full of oats and the horse will eat until it founders and dies, but not a mule. He knows when to quit. And if you walk into a barn, quietlike, and the horse doesn't know you're there, and suddenly you do something to startle the horse, he'll let fly with a kick. But not a mule. He'll just pull in his rump. And besides all of that, mules live longer than horses. Old Pete and Jim here are almost as old as your father and they're still going strong. Now, don't you wish you hadn't asked that question?" And he laughed, and I laughed too.

One morning Grandpa hitched his team to a ditcher—a two-handled V-shaped scoop with Grandpa walking behind guiding the handles like a plow. I walked along with Grandpa.

"Mother Nature doesn't like ditches," he said. "See how she grows 'em over? But if we can't keep water in the ditch we can't water the orchard, and if we can't water the orchard, we won't have any apples, and if we don't have any apples, Grandma can't make apple pie, and if Grandma can't make apple pie, then we'll be unhappy men, won't we? So we better clean the ditch."

Sometimes he would hand me the reins, and there I'd be, in control of those powerful beasts—a boy who didn't come up much past the mules' underbellies—making them turn by a small pull on the reins, a little to the right and then a little to the left, and, like Grandpa, causing the mules to go faster with a quick little slap on their backs.

When the work began Grandpa took over and called out their names, "Pete! Jim!" and the mules pulled in their rumps and hunkered down, and together they lunged forward, a mule on each side of the ditch, in their work, fulfilling their part of their own bargain. I could see the wrinkles in their old hides as they tugged at the ditcher. Jim was the darker mule, nearly black and the smaller of the pair, and Pete the color of waxed walnut with those sad, worn eyes.

"I had to change Pete's name," Grandpa said. "Name used to be Jack, but whenever I hollered 'Jack!' at him he'd stop and start to back up. Thought I was hollering 'Back!' Mules are smart, but they can't speak English very well." Then he looked at me. "But they don't ask questions," he said, and he grinned and I knew my grandpa liked me. After a while Grandpa rested the mules, and we took swigs of cool spring water out of a gallon-size crockery jug that was covered with wet burlap, my lips where his lips had been on the wet neck of the jug, and that was all right because Grandpa and I were a team.

At dinnertime, which at Grandpa Spence's was also at noon, we unhitched the mules, drove them to the shade of the barn, and in accordance with their bargain, fed them each a gallon of oats.

Grandpa Spence had been educated at what was then called "The Academy" in Carroll County, Ohio, an institution somewhat equivalent to our modern-day junior college. After graduation he had taught school for several years before he came West to seek his fortune. At Denver he was introduced to bicycle racing, became a professional bicycle racer riding for the Victor Bicycle Works of Denver, and in his races pedaled from Denver to Fort Collins past Masonville. But he was a teacher, and Masonville needed a teacher, so the school board hired John Henry Spence for the job. There he met Alice Melinda Smith, my grandmother.

"You will never be a bicycle racer," my grandfather said one day as we sat on the old leather daybed in the family room. He was holding my foot in one hand and examining my calf with the other. "You don't have a runner's calf. You have the legs of your Grandpa Pfleeger. Those are lifting legs, not running legs. But I'll tell you something: You are going to be a better man than any of us, better than your Grandpa Pfleeger, better than me, and even better than your father."

"How come?" I asked, surprised.

"Because when you mix pureblooded strains together you get a better, stronger offspring. If you cross a Hereford cow and a Black Angus cow, you come up with a black, white-faced calf. That calf is stronger, bigger, quicker, lives longer, and is more hardy than either of its parents. Now don't ask me why. I don't know. But it's so. So you may not be a great runner or a great bicycler, but you are going to be *something!* Something special." He gave me a little pat on the head and stretched out to take his afternoon nap. Then Grandpa closed his eyes and soon he was snoring, his false teeth rattling. That's why Grandma made him put them in a cup of water when they went to bed at night.

My little Grandmother Spence reminded me of a skinny, nervous sparrow. She weighed less than ninety pounds and her legs were as thin as toothpicks. She wore her waist-long brown hair done up in a bun behind her head. No curls,

no curlers. A very businesslike little lady without much
humor, who walked as fast as a mouse skitters. Her
family from her father's side, the Smiths, had emigrated from England, Jonathan Smith, one of
her lineal ancestors, having been born in
Rhode Island in 1750. My grandmother's
father, Edward Smith, a schoolteacher, was
also the first county clerk of Larimer
County, Territory of Colorado, and a member of Chivington's Constabulary, which
had slaughtered scores of helpless Indian
women, children, and old men at the Sand
Creek Massacre, an incident that haunted
and sickened him for the rest of his life. He
died, probably from tuberculosis, leaving
behind his wife, a hostelry business, debt and
three children, one of whom was my grandmother, the only daughter. My grandmother's
mother, Sarah Milner Smith, sold the hotel,
took the little cash she received from the
sale, and moved to Buckhorn Creek near
Masonville, where she homesteaded. There
she and her boys ran the ranch, and she taught
in a school in Loveland, Colorado, that today
bears her name, the Sarah Milner School.

*Alice Melinda Spence, Gerry's
grandmother.*

Every evening before bedtime, by the light
of their gasoline lantern, Grandma and
Grandpa played a game of either Chinese
checkers or regular checkers. Grandma
almost always won. It was humiliating to me
and, I thought, to Grandpa that this nervous
little sparrow of a woman could beat him like
that. After all, she had never read all of
Grandpa's history books and she knew nothing of Shakespeare and Longfellow. She
mostly had read only the Bible. She had never
written anything except her weekly letters to my
parents. Although never published, Grandpa himself had written a novel, and he knew all
about presidents and nature and rocks and
trees, and he also knew a lot about dogs
and mules and horses and cows and boys,
and yet she beat him at checkers.

*Gerald M. Spence holding Gerry
and Sarah Milner Spence, Gerry's
great-grandmother, who is over
ninety in this photograph.*

Grandma Spence could can with her pressure cooker, but not as well as my mother. She could sew on her old Singer pedal machine, but not as well as my mother. She could make those big white doughy sugar cookies, and they didn't have caraway seeds on top like Grandma Pfleeger's, but they weren't as good as my mother's "icebox cookies." She wore the same brown silk dress every Sunday to the old brownstone community church near Masonville, and she wore the same ridiculous hat, and she could sing with that trilly church voice of hers, higher and louder than anyone in the congregation, which was never more than ten or twelve of the local farmers anyway. Both before and after church, this group of bareheaded laboring men stood around grinning and nodding at each other with their hands in their suit pants pockets, and sometimes they mumbled a word or two about the weather, their wives looking as silly as my grandmother in their own ridiculous hats. And my Grandmother Spence was very good at praying. When she prayed her voice was as piercing and trilly as when she talked. She was no word waster. When she prayed or when she talked, a person knew she was in charge.

Grandma Spence, that spindly little nudge of a woman, bossed everyone. Grandpa usually kept a red bandanna handkerchief stuffed well down into the rear pocket of his faded denim bibs, for his eyes often watered and sometimes his nose would run. On this particular day, contravening one of Grandma's standard rules of civilized conduct, Grandpa had permitted his red bandanna handkerchief to show, it having crept out of his back pocket where it hung down like the tongue of a panting dog. Grandma attacked.

"Dad!" Grandma hollered as he was headed for the back porch. "Stuff your handkerchief back in!" I had always thought that Grandpa Spence, who was allegedly hard of hearing, was deaf mostly in defense. He never had trouble hearing me when we were out behind the mules. Now he paid no heed to Grandma's demands, as if the batteries in his hearing aid were dead.

"Dad!" she hollered even louder. "I said stuff your handkerchief in!"

Again he paid no heed as if he were totally deaf, but when he got to the porch door, he slammed it smartly, the red handkerchief dangling behind him as he went, which provided a most eloquent argument in response. I can't remember his ever having hollered back. I thought he was too smart for that.

One afternoon I was sitting in the dining room looking out to the red cliffs below the house that the folks called "the hogback." It was a hot day, too hot for movement of beast or boy. My mother was off to visit a neighbor. Old Chappie, Grandpa's black-and-white English shepherd whose job was to bring in the mules, lay under the silver maple that spread its shade in the front yard. The apples were green on the trees, and in the heat even the chickens lay panting on the shady side of the hen house. Grandpa was stretched out on the daybed absorbed in his after-dinner nap. Grandma, her wooden embroidery hoop stretched over a piece of linen, had snuggled down in her rocking chair. She had lined it with pillows to protect her brittle bones, which were mostly exposed and

unpadded. She was sewing quietly away at a flower design on a napkin. Without looking up from her work she began to speak to me.

"Gerry, your mother is a wonderful Christian woman. She is an example for
all of us to follow. I wish I could be as good a Christian as she."

I didn't say anything. I knew she was pretty perfect all right. I knew she was
like Christ, like Mrs. Christ, anyway, and I knew she hardly ever said a bad word
about anyone. "If you can't say something nice don't say anything at all," she
would admonish. I knew she never swore, not once—rarely even said "darn"—
and she said that liquor had never touched her lips, and that she had never
smoked, not once, and being faithful to one's husband was so much a given it
was never mentioned. I knew she prayed and had taught me to pray and that
she believed in God. But I never knew she was so good that my little Grandmother Spence, who was so pious she never even laughed, wanted to be like my
mother. It made me proud.

"You should cherish your mother," she said, using that old-fashioned word.

"I do," I said. But my grandmother made no reply.

After a while and a lot more rocking she said, "I do, I certainly do."

When I was ten my sister Barbara Jean was born, thus ending my life as an only
child. I was to discover that my parents had been trying to have another child
for all those years following Peggy's death. My mother's pregnancy with Barbara
Jean was interpreted as a miracle, and I dare speculate, my mother had done
much praying on the matter herself. If faith could move mountains, faith could
surely produce another child.

But medical science was also given credit. I overheard conversations
between my mother and her closest friend, Genivieve White. My mother had
been seeing a woman doctor who had prescribed packing the womb with Argyrol, a brown liquid that looked like the brown tobacco juice grasshoppers spit at
you when you caught them. In those days doctors dropped the same stuff in
newborn babies' eyes to combat infant blindness, and my folks flooded my eyes
with it when I would awaken in the morning, my eyes stuck shut from an eye
infection. Argyrol and God combined forces to render my mother pregnant. I
don't remember that my father received much credit in the matter.

Then Genivieve White, herself barren for ten years, undertook the same
treatment from the same doctor, and the miracle was repeated. She, too, soon
became pregnant, also with a baby girl. I write this account for whatever worth
it may have, for the treatment was mostly unknown in those days, and I have
not heard of it since. At times, the din and glitz of modern medicine obscure
simple remedies.

This new little angel, Barbara—how I loved her. How proud I was to carry
her about, this small doll with curly brown hair and large blue eyes and a tiny
nose, who was born of this miracle. Before she could walk I took her to the neighbors, to see Buddy Taylor, even to see his mother. I became adept at changing

Argyrol was the magic that produced this picture. (Left to right) Oola, father's Norwegian elkhound bitch, Gerry, Sharon White, Tom Spence as a baby, Ward White, Gerry's best friend, and Barbara Jean Spence.

diapers. I hung out the wash for my mother, brought the clothes in from the line, folded the diapers. Kept the diaper pail clean. The immense joy of this child was not only her beauty but her radiating happiness, which touched us all.

Two years later Thomas John Spence was born.

I named him myself. His name had to be Tom because then it would be Tom and Gerry, after the cartoon cat and mouse characters. Besides, I was going to become a veterinarian, because I loved animals, and when my little dog Pat had been run over by a car and I held him as he died, and I couldn't bring him back no matter how I prayed, I decided to become a veterinarian so that I could save little dogs myself. I walked around the neighborhood and at church holding this small chubby-cheeked little brother of mine, proclaiming that he and I were going to be partners. We would be veterinarians together. It would be "Tom and Gerry, 'Vetranary,' " I said.

A boy had to work. Boys who do not work are lazy, and it is sinful to be lazy. It is bad to play without first earning the right to play by working. "Just as well paint the picket fence your father built," my mother said. "The fence needs the paint and the boy needs the work." But everybody had already heard of Tom Sawyer and how he got his fence painted. I was left with no way out but to slosh at the fence with a concoction my father had invented consisting of green pigment and creosote—a paint that would render the fence green and preserve it at the same time. The creosote splattered on my bare summertime chest, and it stung. And there were thousands of pickets around that big yard, each of which had a top and four sides. You could grow old and rickety painting a picket fence by hand. I would rather weed the lawn. You could at least sit down weeding the lawn, and the grass was cool to sit on. Gradually I devised a plan that would provide the requisite work and at the same time save me from the picket fence.

Beautiful lawns without dandelions were weedless because, in those days— before chemical weed killers that later were to kill both weeds and man—kids, on their hands and knees, dug the weeds out one at a time—ten cents an hour.

Plantain weed was as bad as dandelion, the
roots deep and mean, and if you left a little root, the plant came sneaking up again,
this time twice as strong, and the owner
would say, "That Spence kid—you don't
want to hire him. He doesn't dig the roots
out. Look at that lawn! I paid him fifty
cents last week and it's full of weeds
again." At least, that's what my mother said
they would say.

I decided to organize "The Weed
Brigade," consisting of myself as the captain and five boys about my age, including
Buddy Taylor, who would be my sergeant. I
went to the other side of town where the
big-lawned, big-moneyed people lived and
offered to weed their lawns for ten cents
per hundred weeds dug—pay only for the
weeds with good roots. I agreed to pay my

*Gerry and his new baby sister,
Barbara Jean.*

weed soldiers a nickel a hundred. Old Henry Ford wasn't the only one to perform time and motion studies. I figured that a soldier could dig one weed with
good roots every ten seconds, a hundred in a thousand seconds. I therefore concluded that a weed soldier could gross thirty-six cents an hour before he paid me
my 50 percent commission. Each soldier could net for both himself and me eighteen cents an hour. I could get rich with five soldiers—ninety cents an hour. I
figured I'd be lucky to keep the troops working five hours a day, but that
would amount to $4.50 profit! I could end up making more than my father, just
digging weeds.

I found a big house with a big lawn and lots of blooming dandelions. The
lady of the house, a doctor's wife, answered the door, hands on hips.

"Would you like to get rid of the weeds in your front yard?" I pointed to the
disgusting sight. "I represent the Weed Brigade. We will dig your weeds out and
you only have to pay ten cents for every hundred weeds with good roots. You can
count 'em. How does that sound? We can clean this all up for you tomorrow."

She took her hands off her hips and looked at me a long time, thinking it
through. I helped her. "Now if we dug a couple hundred weeds out of that lawn
it would sure look a lot better, wouldn't it?" I spoke with my nose sort of wrinkled up at the sight we were looking at. A fine home with a lawn going to weeds?
I had her trapped in shame.

The next morning bright and early the Weed Brigade, all five of us, assembled at the doctor's house. It was a rich find. Scores of dandelions per square
yard populated our customer's yard, and the soldiers took the big easy ones. We
came in with bushel baskets full of dandelions. At day's end it looked as if the

lawn hadn't been touched, but the five of us had earned a little over ten dollars, my share, of course, being half.

I knocked on the door to collect our day's earnings. "Where have you boys been digging those dandelions?" the doctor's wife demanded, once more with her hands on her hips. "I can't see that you've made the slightest dent in my lawn. Are you digging those dandelions somewhere else?"

"No, ma'am," I said. "They all came out of your lawn," which they had. She slammed the door in my face. Pretty soon she came back with a ten-dollar bill. "Here, take this," she said, shoving the bill in my face, "but don't come back. I can't afford you." I started to tell her she couldn't afford to let her lawn go like that, but she slammed the door in my face again. I felt both bad and good. I had lost my first customer, but I'd already made a fortune.

The next day I was out again knocking on doors in the block up the street from the doctor's house. I chose another big house, and another large yard full of dandelions exhibited to the public, and once again I appealed to the house-holder's sense of shame. But two of my soldiers had already gone AWOL, the municipal swimming pool having opened, and only three of us remained to engage the enemy in this war on weeds. We didn't get to digging until after lunch, and by four o'clock, when my troops wanted to quit, the count for the three of us added up to fifteen dollars. I couldn't figure it out. Three of us had dug half again as many weeds as the five of us had the day before, and in half the time. Then I discovered the answer.

The day before some of the bundles had been wrapped with red yarn that I had brought from home, my mother's yarn being the only string I could find at the time. I called my two remaining troops over:

"Which one of you guys hauled the weeds over here from yesterday's job?" I asked.

"What difference does it make?" the kid said. He was from Tenth Street, three streets below where I lived. Tough neighborhood. They put rocks in their snowballs.

"We can't charge her for weeds we didn't dig in her lawn," I said.

"You tell and I'll kick the livin' Jesus outta ya," the Tenth Street kid said.

About then the lady came out of the house to settle up. She surveyed her yard for a long time. We all held our breaths. After a while she said, "Why, I can't see that you kids have even touched those weeds. Where did all these weeds come from?" She kicked in the direction of the bulging bushel baskets.

I looked down, trying to figure out what to say. "Well," she said, "I'm not going to pay you anything, not if you're going to cheat me like that. That should teach you a lesson." Then the tough kid gave me a hard shove and took off up the street, and I went home contemplating the risks of being an employer and doing business with the public. All the kids had quit. That left me back painting the picket fence.

It was time I gave my position in life new and serious thought. My mother had often insisted that I had important things to do, an admonition I had also received from Grandpa Spence. The gift of vision, when given to the child, opens wondrous doors. A child deprived of the gift is a child locked in. Yet I wondered how my mother could possibly know that I was going to amount to something. I knew the persistent legend that I had a "very high IQ." My mother let it slip one day when she was impressing on me my duty not to waste "the gifts God has given you," as she liked to say. "You had the highest score on your IQ test in the entire eighth grade. Miss Stolt told me so. Somewhere close to near genius," whatever that meant. But it meant nothing. If I was so smart, why did I have to work as hard in school as the others? I acted smart, all right. But I didn't feel smart. And I wasn't tough. And I scared easy. Yet I knew that mothers know certain things.

"You have a special talent," she would insist, "and God has a plan for you. You must never squander those precious gifts." Sometimes when I would say one of the neighborhood kids was dumb, "just dumber than chicken poop," she'd stop her work, take me gently by the arm and sit me down in a kitchen chair, and then she'd pull a chair up close to me, and knees to knees she would talk to me.

"God did not give everyone the same gifts, Gerry. Those he gave the greatest gifts to have the greatest duty to use them—in the service of God and in the service of others. That is why you were given such gifts. Do you understand?" I nodded. Then she said, "Well, now you better go paint the fence."

One thing I knew: It was easier to sell something, anything, than to paint that damnable fence. Business was better than labor. Besides, my mother had also told me that the world turns on selling. Her brothers had finally left the farm and become salesmen. Ended up with their own car agencies and my mother said they were rich. She claimed you could sell God's word just as easy as you could sell a car. "Preaching is mostly selling," she said once. Salesmanship is mostly asking. "Ask and ye shall receive," she quoted out of the Good Book. Thus, in my desperate desire to escape the misery of the fence I began to consider a career as a salesman. Indeed, I eventually became one, for successful trial lawyering is merely the sale of the truth and justice of one's case to the jury. But what did I have to sell in Sheridan, Wyoming? I thought again of the ditty of my Grandpa Pfleeger:

Gerald Leonard Spence
Sitting on a fence
Trying to make a dollar
Out of fifteen cents.

He knew me, all right. I walked into the garage looking for something to sell. I walked around the yard, looking. Then suddenly I saw them. The flowers, of course! People like flowers. If people were like me they loved to bury their faces in a bouquet of red and pink and purple and white sweetpea blossoms. Ah, to feel the soft, cool petals against your cheeks, to smell that sweet, delicate odor.

"How do you sell flowers?" I asked my mother.

"Here's the phone book," my mother replied. "You can call all of the cafés and the hotels in town and ask them if they would like to buy your flowers."

I sat down at the phone and began to call. "Would you like to buy some sweetpeas, two bunches for a quarter?"

"No, kid. We don't want none." Some just hung up without even saying no.

"I give up," I said. "People have their own flowers."

"That isn't the way you do it," my mother said. "You say, 'I have some very pretty, very fresh, very sweet-smelling sweetpeas here, and I can deliver them to you right away. And I only charge a quarter for two bunches. Can I bring them to you?' "

"I have to say all that?"

"You have to paint them a picture. They have to actually see the sweetpeas and smell them. Then they'll buy them. And don't forget what Grandpa Pfleeger says: 'If at first you don't succeed, try and suck another seed,' " and she laughed one of her rare sucking-in laughs and handed me the phone book back.

After a while I began to perfect my pitch. I sold my first sweetpeas to the Sheridan Inn, where Buffalo Bill used to stay. And I sold sweetpeas to Ann Newell's Café, the best restaurant in town.

I picked the sweetpeas from the six-foot-high chicken wire fence that separated the squash, cucumbers, and tomatoes from the rest of the vegetable garden. The blossoms on the sweetpeas were dew-covered in the morning, blossoms looking for all the world like a crowd of little old maids in their fresh, prim, brightly colored bonnets, and the more of them you picked, the more bloomed, as if there were a contest as to who would win, the sweetpeas or me.

Later in the summer I sold zinnias and snapdragons and phlox, and my mother showed me how to make the bouquets beautiful with asparagus fern. Then, after the phone sales had been made, I would trudge down the street in the heat of the day with the bouquets wrapped in newspaper, and where the stems gathered I soaked the paper in water to keep the bouquets fresh. When I delivered a bouquet, I smiled at the people and they paid me—fair and square. And, oh, the smell of roast beef in Ann Newell's Café! Wild meat never smelled like that.

Once I called Louie's Hamburgers.

"This is Gerry Spence. Would you like to buy some nice sweet-smelling, fresh, wonderful, beautiful sweetpeas that are all kinds of colors, and they will make your customers very happy and your restaurant very pretty, and they only cost two bouquets for a quarter?" I ran out of breath, but as long as you were talking they couldn't say no. Sometimes I feel that way in court when I'm pleading my case to a jury.

"Yeah, kid!" he hollered, and hung up. I didn't know if that meant, yeah, I want to buy them, or if it was a curt rejection. At Louie's, hamburgers were ten cents—but they were larger than the nickel kind at the Castle. And folks said a lot better. Louie was a bachelor who had put half a dozen kids from poor families in Sheridan through college while he shoveled hamburgers on his hot greasy grill and laughed and hollered with his customers in his broken Greek. We never bought hamburgers at Louie's. Even after Louie bought my sweetpeas we didn't reciprocate. Too expensive, my mother said, and too greasy.

Once I sold some sweetpeas by phone to the Rex Rooms, a walkup hotel on Main Street. Delivering the sweetpeas required me to pass by several bars, and in the summer their swinging doors were wide open. Once when I hadn't held my breath in time I caught a whiff of the pungent, musky smell of stale beer that wafted onto the sidewalk. I sneaked a frightened peek into one of those forbidden places as I walked by. It was dark in there and men were hanging over the bar, and there was music blaring out. As usual, a couple of Indians with their tall black hats were sitting by the door on the sidewalk sleeping. This was a house of sinners, sure enough, just as my mother had said. The men inside were probably robbers and murderers and kid killers. And they were partaking of the elixir of the devil. They would all probably be sentenced to death in Wyoming's gas chamber, and their evil souls would burn in hell! Then as my mother had commanded, I held my breath and walked on by.

At the Rex Rooms I climbed a long, narrow flight of wooden stairs. At the top I found a door with a peephole. I rang the bell. After a while a white woman wearing a flowered black silk bathrobe answered the door. Her black hair was done up in curlers, and she wore high-heeled slippers like some of the women in the Montgomery Ward catalog. She looked like she'd been sleeping, and the makeup around her eyes was smeared. She looked bad, but for reasons I wasn't sure of, I thought she looked good.

"Whaddya want?"

"I'm here with the flowers, ma'am."

"Who is it?" I heard another woman's voice from inside.

"Come on in, kid," she said. "So you got the flowers for Mazie, huh?" She stooped down to look me squarely in the eye. I tried not to look. My knees got shaky.

"Here's yer sweetpeas," I said. Her eyes looked like they were sort of clouded over, and she smelled good, better than lilacs, better than roses, even almost as good as my sweetpeas.

"Hey, Mazie, what do you have here—a towel boy?" a big blond woman hollered. She walked up to inspect me. She was also wearing a silk bathrobe.

I didn't mean to ask, but I was already considered a professional question-asker, a trait that was to serve me well. "What's a towel boy?"

Doorway to the old Rex Hotel.

The women broke out in hilarious laughter. "What's a towel boy?" the blonde mocked and slapped her legs with both hands. "What's a towel boy?" she cried, slapping her legs again.

"A towel boy is a boy who brings the ladies their towels," Mazie said. Then they both began to laugh. Mazie took the sweetpeas I was clutching and gave me the quarter. "Cute little fellow, isn't he?" Mazie said, giving me a very wet kiss on the back of my bare neck. My face got all flushed and hot and I couldn't think of what to say.

"Too bad they grow up," the blond woman said.

"Thank you for buying my flowers," I said. I fought to get the words out straight. Then I turned and opened the door with the peephole and started fast down the stairs, and, without meaning to, I heard myself asking another question. "Why do ladies need towels?"

And the women began to laugh again. "Good-bye, Sweetpea," they called to me, and then the door went shut, and I walked on down to the street and, on the way home, as I passed the bars with their doors open, I dutifully held my breath again.

CHAPTER 6

*Gerry Spence, age ten, ready to go
to Sunday School.*

WHEN HE WAS nearly eighty my father endured that medieval torture the medical profession labels a "transurethral prostatic resection." My father called it what it is: "It's a ream job," he said. "They go in through the only thing they can go in through and ream a fellow out. Sorta like a Roto-Rooter. This is the second time they did it to me." Then matter-of-factly he said, "Had to have it done."

My father was that way—did whatever he had to do, bearing an innocent faith in the medical profession and taking it all in stride like a man who had to clean the drain in the kitchen sink when it got plugged.

On this occasion he called me after the operation had been completed. We had talked about everything else, and just before he was ready to hang up he mentioned the operation very casually, as if it were but an afterthought. "Well, I had another one of those ream jobs last week." That's how he dealt with such a prodigious personal event, one that to me would have provided a monumental marker in my life—the day I had to enter a strange hospital, live through the fright of some stranger sticking those big needles in my spine for the spinal block, permit another stranger to penetrate a man's most vulnerable part and through its tender orifice have the prostate reamed out with those nasty little razor-sharp blades, a procedure that not only would have proven painful but that might also render one impotent.

A year or so later my father and I were talking about the myth of "the golden years."

"They aren't so golden, are they?" I said, already feeling the unwelcome intrusion of my own approaching years.

"They're all right," he said. "I have nary an ache nor a pain."

"Well, how old do you have to be before you can no longer—well, you know, as you used to say it, 'take care of your woman'?"

"Don't know," he said with his big grin. "You'll have to ask somebody older than me."

Once when I was inquiring about how couples communicate with each other I happened to ask Mae, when both she and my father were past eighty-five, "Do you ever talk about sex with Dad?"

"Of course," she said.

"What do you say when—you know—when you're in the mood?"

"I don't say anything. I just put my pillow on his side of the bed. He knows what that means."

My own mother struggled at being open about sex. She knew it was unhealthy for her son to have his sexual psyche imprisoned in the darkness of Christian repression. Indeed, I often saw my mother nude. She thought a mother ought not be secretive about the human body, it being a family tenet that the body was not innately shameful. I was permitted to run around the house naked as a wild urchin. But as open as everyone tried to be about the body, the reality that a boy might possess his own sexuality was flatly denied by my mother.

Early on my father explained to me how babies were made. He drew pictures. I understood tadpoles. And human spermatozoa looked like tadpoles. I knew how chickens were bred and born, a knowledge many adults do not possess, namely that all birds of either sex possess but *one* orifice through which both sexes perform the same functions that, in all mammals, require two such channels.

"How do they pee, Daddy?"

"Through the same place they do everything else."

"Do they have a penis?"

"No."

"Well Daddy, how do they do it without a penis?"

"The old rooster just mounts the hen, grabs hold of some feathers up along her neck, and he reaches down and rubs his on hers. That does the trick for a chicken. Glad I'm not a chicken," he added.

I saw the eggs in the bellies of butchered hens, the soft-shelled eggs about to be laid. It would turn hard the next day. I saw the full-sized yolk next in line, followed, like roe, in a progressively smaller string of yolks until they were as small as a pinhead and smaller.

My mother tried to cover her own sexuality as one might hide a crippled arm. She provided her child the presumption of innocence, namely that he possessed no sexual urges of his own. His little testes being white and hairless and his face as innocent as an angel's, how could he already be cursed with that sinful, libidinous plague? Heaven forbid if her male child were already gripped by sexual cravings. Might he not be expected to grow into some kind of dreadful fiend, like the child who tortures kittens will surely become a serial killer, or something like that?

My first sexual remembrance, at about age four, was lying on my back on the kitchen floor peering up the long calico skirt of a baby-sitter. And what of this childish erection?

"Why is your 'do-dad,'" as my parents chose to call it, "like *that*?" my mother's horror not well concealed.

I didn't know. How could I know? Yet, instinctively I knew something exciting emerged from my feelings, not my mind, and I knew she knew everything about it, too. I looked at the erect little soldier. Already I felt shame.

One day when I was five I had awakened early from my nap. My mother had taken the occasion to slip out of the house to visit a neighbor. Finding myself alone, I began to cry and to holler for my mother. I ran outside crying, "Mother, Mother," screaming at the top of my lungs. Soon a neighbor woman came over to the house, took me by the hand and walked me back through our own front door. Then she sat down in our old overstuffed chair and lifted me onto her lap. She was the fattest woman I had ever seen. Fascinated, I stared down the front of her dress at her huge unharnessed breasts. She saw where I was looking.

"Well, well," she said, patting me on the head, after which she began unbuttoning her front. "Do you want to nurse these?" I jumped off of her lap and ran, and then my mother came, and I heard the woman explaining that she had tried to comfort me. But the world was all right again. My mother was there.

As I grew older, strange rules began to damn my innocence and to prescribe the limits of propriety. I was to understand that playing with little girls was permissible if you were out in the open where everyone could see you. But if you were playing with the same little girls in the neighbor's garage you were presumed to be up to no good.

What power in the word *shame*. To the child, shame is the product of the parent's judgment. The child, by his dependence, vests in the parent the power to make judgments of the child's worth, and the parent is feared, for the parent may exercise that power at any moment. One could not imagine a worse condemnation than to be rejected by one's mother, to have her withhold her love, which would be tantamount to death. I would surmise that the child's shame before the parent and the parent's before God have identical origins. Be that as it may, Buddy Taylor and I played with the girls—at least twice—in Buddy Taylor's garage.

I was ten. Buddy was nine, the girls of similar ages. It was sex in one of its most aboriginal forms—we at one end of the garage and they at the other. Group exhibitionism! There in Buddy Taylor's garage I first learned the essence of contract law, an experience in quid pro quo—"I'll show you mine if you'll show me yours." Oh the shame of it, the wondrous shame!

Then just when we were about to fulfill the contract, my mother called. Of course! It was the Saturday before Easter, and it was egg-coloring time. She had saved a dozen brown eggs from our Rhode Island Reds, boiled them, prepared the dye, and was calling me to come home for the fun. At that precise moment I learned that a hierarchy of pleasure exists, and that the pleasure of *sex*—a word that was never spoken aloud—was at the very top. Still, as much as I had yearned to dye Easter eggs, and as much as I had daily pestered my mother to dye them *this very moment,* I had never before experienced this sex business with the girls in Buddy Taylor's garage, the experience of which had, in comparison, reduced Easter egg dying to the upper levels of boredom.

But the contract demanded fulfillment. A couple of weeks later Buddy and I once more invited the girls to come play with us in his garage.

"Ya wanna come over to Buddy's garage?"

"What for?"

"To play."

"Play what?"

"You know what." Then the girls laughed and ran off. But when Buddy and I went to his garage, the girls soon came knocking at the door.

I realized, of course, as I had realized before, that God was watching. Somehow this knowledge did not inhibit me. God watched everything. God was the great voyeur in the sky. He watched my mother and father do it (and by now I knew they did it). And He knew I was evil, as evil as if I *had* done *it,* because I had *thought* about doing *it,* and thinking about doing it, as everybody knew, was as bad as doing it. I was a ruined boy anyway. And since God knew, and since I was already ruined, what did I have to lose by meeting with the girls in Buddy Taylor's garage?

And so we were about to get on with the show, which is to say that my blue overalls were unbuttoned and down around my knees and so were Buddy's, and we were about to receive the quid pro quo from the girls when Mrs. Taylor suddenly opened the door.

"What are you doing?" she demanded, her hands on her round little hips. She was looking squarely at me. I was a year older than Buddy and therefore I was to blame for this shame.

Nobody answered. Nobody could. What was one to say? "We were shot by Buck Jones and Hopalong Cassidy, and these two nurses just happened along and . . . "

"I'm going to tell your mother, Gerry Spence," Mrs. Taylor said, her fat little jowls aquiver.

"You don't have to, ma'am," I said, jerking up my overalls. "I'm going to run home right now and tell her myself."

"You'd better or I will, for sure," she hollered after me. "I may anyway." Then I ran home, and I prayed to God all the way that Mrs. Taylor wouldn't tell my mother. Oh, the horrid shame of it. "Please do not let Mrs. Taylor tell," I prayed over and over. "Please dear wonderful God, do not let her tell! If you will only keep her from telling, I will never do *it* again."

But why could God hear me, this sinner of sinners who had committed this horrible crime? Besides I was not, I repeat *not,* going to tell my mother even though I had promised Mrs. Taylor I would. I would not tell her even to save my soul. No, nothing could make me tell her. And so, as I saw it, I was put between what my father called "a rock and a hard place." If I told my mother I could never bear the shame of it. But if I didn't keep my word with Mrs. Taylor, well, God would know I lied to her. Therefore, there was little doubt in my mind that He would have Mrs. Taylor spill her guts to my mother, and it was likely to happen any moment. But as slim as the chance was that Mrs. Taylor wouldn't tell, I would take the chance. Maybe God had been watching someone else do *it* at the time. He must like to watch that sort of stuff.

Day after miserable day I waited for Mrs. Taylor to come. Every time I heard a knock on the door, I knew it was that fat old witch across the street, Buddy Taylor's mother, who was about to do me in. I made it through one day. But she would surely come tomorrow. And then I waited the next day and the next. I didn't go to Buddy's house for several months, believing that to do so might only remind Mrs. Taylor of that which, hopefully, she had by now forgotten. And I never told my mother.

Maybe God loved me after all. But no. It was all recorded in some kind of ledger book He kept up there and, when the right time came, everything in the book would come tumbling down on me. That much I was pretty sure of. And as for the little girls, and their obligation to perform under the doctrine of quid pro quo—well, there is an exception under the law that relieved them of responsibility, namely, an intervening act of God—or of Mrs. Taylor, however one cares to argue the case.

CHAPTER 7

Ward White and Gerry Spence, about age six, at gravestone at Custer's Last Stand, Custer Battlefield, Little Big Horn, Montana.

J. S. TAYLOR SCHOOL was situated on the corner of West Seventh Street and Main, a square old tan two-story brick building with a hip roof bearing the school's goal over the front door, one I have thought of many times: ENTER HERE TO LEARN. GO OUT TO SERVE. We lived down Seventh Street a couple of blocks, on the block next to the banks of Goose Creek.

The schoolhouse held six grades, the first three grades on the ground floor, the fourth, fifth, and sixth on the top floor. The school board had moved two bungalows to the back of the school for an extra first and second grade. These bungalows stank. One child does not smell bad. A roomful of children does not necessarily smell bad. But children emit an odor peculiar to children. And that odor, layered month after month in those stuffy rooms, made us hold our noses when we stuck our heads in. Within were housed the slow kids. We felt sorry for them, to be sure, but we didn't play with them at recess, because they came from the "stinky rooms."

I first heard the *Nutcracker* suite in Miss Bagnell's first-grade class, where we read about Dick and Jane and Spot. I then skipped the second grade—a serious mistake, for when in later years the rest of the boys could point with pride to a newly sprouting pubic hair I had nothing to show, nothing whatsoever. When the boys in my class were developing deep voices, I was still singing soprano. When the boys went out for sports, I couldn't compete. My father tried to comfort me. "We Spences are always slow to develop," he'd say. "But we live a long time." Little comfort that was. At that age one's life goes on forever anyway.

Miss Stolt, the superintendent of public instruction, came by Taylor School a couple of times a year. It was a special time, for she was the most important person I had ever met other than the preacher. Our class was always prepared for her. Our teacher somehow knew when she was coming and would warn us, "Miss Stolt is coming today, and we must be very good and quiet children. We don't want her to make a bad report on us, do we?" Breathlessly we awaited her arrival. Whatever would happen to us if she made a bad report? Moreover, no one knew for sure what the superintendent of public instruction did to errant children, or what she did at all, for that matter.

Then came a knock at our classroom door, and when the teacher opened the door, there she stood, this mammoth woman as tall as my father wearing her black dress with its white collar, just like a Pilgrim. She had a nose on her that put one immediately in mind of a hippopotamus and, at the tip of her nose, as if on proud display, grew a huge brown mole the size of a pea with hair growing out of it. She was by all standards the most foreboding, the most humorless, the most unattractive woman I had ever seen. She talked to the class in her high-pitched nasal voice about our studies, and asked a few questions of the students, where upon our teacher turned to me.

"Stand up, Gerry," the teacher said, "and recite your poem for Miss Stolt." I was embarrassed but precocious. I strutted stiff-legged to the front of the room. I recited the poem by heart, for I had written it on the tablet of my mind. Still in bed of a fresh spring morning, the window thrown open, I had heard the robins singing, and I could smell the soft sweet smells and I felt joy, like the robin, and full of song, I stared at the ceiling and the poem came to me.

> Spring is coming along
> For I hear the robin's song.
> I know that spring is near
> Because the pussy willows are here.

"Gerry, you come with me," Miss Stolt said. I should follow her? Where? What was she going to do to me? I looked at the teacher, and she smiled and nodded, and so I went with the woman. For all I knew she was leading me to some dark, dangerous place where she would torture me. Maybe kill me. Instead, she took me into a small anteroom on the first floor and motioned me to a seat.

"You are a very bright young man," she said to me. "I expect a lot from you. Do you understand?"

I nodded. "That's fine," she said. "You may go now." And every time Miss

J. S. Taylor School.

Door to J. S. Taylor. The sign read,
ENTER HERE TO LEARN.
GO OUT TO SERVE.

Stolt came to visit it was always the same. I was asked to follow her to the same anteroom where she told me I was bright and that she expected a lot from me, and with nothing more, she sent me back to class.

"What did Miss Stolt want with you, Spence?" the kids would ask.

"Nothin'," I'd say.

"Nothin', I'll bet. Bet you done somethin'. What did you do, Spence?" Dick Shanor asked. He was the toughest kid in the third grade.

"Nothin'," I said.

Then Shanor said that was a lot of bullshit, that I was "lyin'," and he took me down and sat on my face until I almost suffocated.

Later we learned the multiplication tables from cards we took home, learned the tables raw and hard, the answers smashed into our brains without association. And after I had studied and my mother tested me, my father would reward me.

"Come over here," he'd say, real stern as if he were angry. I knew what was coming. And I'd run to him. "Get up here," he'd command, and I'd crawl up on his lap, and then he'd pull out the *Sheridan Press,* rolled up with a screen wire around it, and he'd break the wire, and without even looking at the headlines he'd turn directly to the funnies as if they contained all the wisdom of the day. He read me "Dick Tracy," and "Orphan Annie," "The Gumps," "Maggie and Jigs," "Blondie and Dagwood," "Red Ryder and Little Beaver," "Major Hoople," and "Alley Oop." Alley Oop was my favorite, this caveman who rode a dinosaur named Dinny, who had this beautiful girlfriend named Oola, for whom my father named his favorite dog, a Norwegian elkhound bitch. Oh, what a fortune I would give to return to childhood for just one evening, to curl up on my father's lap, to experience once more the pure joy I knew when my father read the funnies. Oh, to feel his warmth, and his strength, to savor the good man-smell, his own unique smell-print, by which every small animal can distinguish its parent from every other living creature on this earth.

In school, when the teacher's back was to us, we shot spit wads at our country's saints, George Washington and Abe Lincoln, whose portraits reverently hung from high on the classroom wall. If a fellow was a good shot and got his spit wad really juicy, it would stick to the nose of Lincoln or splat on the ear of Washington. As we learned the Palmer method of penmanship—move your whole hand, not the fingers (but everyone used their fingers)—we shot spit wads at each other. When we got permission to go to the pencil sharpener we tossed paper airplanes out the window. We scoured the *National Geographic* for pictures of bare-breasted African natives, which were the only pictures of bare breasts any of us had ever seen.

At my mother's insistence, I took my spelling lessons home, and she had me practice the words until I could spell them perfectly. I was good at drawing. I could write stories. Mr. Wright, the physical education teacher, came once a week, and we did exercises in the classroom. Kids could buy milk for three cents a bottle, but my mother saved the money. We had cheaper milk at home. If we brought a note from home, which I did, we could take a free chocolate iodine pill once a month that would save us from developing a goiter.

At recess we built snow forts and had snowball fights. We played a game where we ran from one side of the school yard to the other and the kids in the middle tried to tackle us when we came by. We played marbles in the spring, Cat's Eye and Big Circle. We lagged to a line scratched in the dirt, and whoever got closest got first shot. Some boys owned agate shooters cut of real stone, beautiful marbles half again the size of the regular glass marbles, and when the agate struck a marble squarely, it left a pretty half moon on the agate. I never owned an agate. They cost fifty cents, the bigger and prettier ones a dollar. I shot with a large marble instead, usually one with multicolored blue swirls in it, but such shooters weren't as heavy as agate shooters and didn't knock the marbles out of the ring as readily. Sometimes I shot with a "steely," which was a ball from a ball bearing that we boys found down at the Sheridan Iron Works, but they were usually too heavy. We used them mostly for lagging.

I was absolutely forbidden to play marbles for keeps. My mother held that shooting for keeps was gambling, and, therefore, evil. But all marble games at school were for keeps, and so a fellow played for keeps or he didn't play at all. Only sissies played "funzies." When I went to school, both pockets bulged with marbles. I won and I lost. Over the years I lost. But one day I invented a game where I won every time. I took a pint Mason jar, cut a hole in the lid the size of a marble, and put ten marbles in it.

"Wanna win ten marbles?" I'd ask a kid.

"Yeah, what's the catch?"

"Okay. You stand straight up over this jar with those ten marbles in it, see?

Take aim at the hole. And if you can drop your marble into the hole you get 'em all. If you don't, I get your marble, see?"

"Yeah. That's easy," the kid said. But no one ever dropped the marble into the hole, because the dropped marble would always hit slightly to one side or the other and bounce off. I won scores of marbles until my mother found out what I was doing and made me stop. That was gambling, too, maybe worse than gambling. It was sinful how I was taking the marbles from all of those poor boys, and I should return their marbles to them immediately. I knew in my heart she was right. Okay, I said, I would. But I didn't. And now I was a criminal. Sometimes I liked being a criminal.

To reinforce her position, my mother asked a simple question: "What would Miss Ives, the principal, do to you if she caught you gambling like that on the school grounds, taking the other boys' marbles like that?" I gave that some thought. Miss Ives had a rubber hose with which she supposedly beat bad boys, and, according to conventional wisdom, she was always watching out of her second-floor office window, watching as God watches, and if she didn't catch me and beat me with her rubber hose, well, God would probably get me anyway. The odds were always against the criminal, which I never thought quite fair. I quit the jar game, but I made a deal with myself—I'd keep the marbles I'd won.

The girls played on one side of the schoolhouse, the boys on the other. No one dared venture to the girls' side any more than one dared sneak into the girls' toilet. Moreover, I wouldn't go under the bridge with Eleanor Cornelius even though my pal Bill Sare and Eleanor were cousins, and both Bill and Eleanor begged me to go under the bridge with her. She was going to kiss me. I knew that, and I wasn't going under. Never! Eleanor had pretty little curls all around her head like Shirley Temple's, the kind you could stick your finger up. Sissies kissed girls. It was disgusting. But deep down where I felt certain things, I knew I wanted to go under the bridge with Eleanor.

The girls played jacks and skipped rope to the ditty:

Charlie Chaplin
Went to France
To see the ladies
Do their dance
First the heel
Then the toe
Then around and around you go.

Each year my parents invited my teacher to our house for supper and we suffered through a very polite and formal evening. I put on my Sunday best, my itchy wool tweed pants, my white shirt, and my clip-on brown tie. My parents put on their church clothes, and the teacher was all dressed up as well. What do you say at such stiff, hard times? We sat there in the living room, my teacher and my father and I. My father wasn't much of a conversationalist either. There were long spaces between exchanges, and a lot of throat clearing, and smiling, and looking at the hands. Finally my mother came in from the kitchen to tell us that supper was ready.

The dining room, between the kitchen and the living room, served many functions in our family. The dining room floor register was the warmest place in the house, and there we pulled up a chair, hung our wet clothes over the chair's back, and, in the morning, they would dry. The dining room register was the place we kept our baby chicks warm when we brought them home from the hatchery, and the dining room table was where my mother stretched out the cloth and laid the patterns down and cut out the pieces for our shirts or our coats or the pajamas she was making. I studied at the dining room table, and the dining room was where I sat watching the icicles melt on a sunny winter day and longed for spring, which would never come. The floors were oak, laid by my father over the old fir flooring. He bought the flooring out of the Montgomery Ward catalog. Good, clear two-inch oak. Then he sanded the floors with a rented sander and finished the floors with two coats of clear varnish.

When my mother called us for dinner, the elk roast was already steaming from its platter on the table. It was surrounded by new potatoes, their skins as brown as beans. My mother had baked a corn soufflé from the corn we had canned from the garden. She made a raspberry Jell-O salad with little pieces of fruit ensconced like butterflies in red plastic, and she dropped a teaspoon of salad dressing on top of the Jell-O. She served canned peas from the garden flavored with butter, and for dessert she brought in steaming mincemeat pie from the oven made from the mincemeat she had earlier canned from the leftovers of elk or deer.

The dinner talk was polite, mostly about the food, and our garden, and how my father had hunted the elk we were eating. I wondered if anybody but us would eat wild meat. I watched my teacher, but she picked at everything, even though she said the food was good. Then when eight o'clock came, my parents sent me off to bed. Once I was out of their presence they got the full report on their only son. I listened through the upstairs register.

"Frankly, he's a little show-off," I heard the teacher say.

"I know," my mother replied sadly.

"He wants all the attention on himself."

"Yes," my mother said quietly.

"He is very bright. He is ahead of all of the other children even though he's skipped a grade, and I don't know what to do with him." I felt sorry for my teacher.

"He is a problem," my mother said. "I try to keep him busy. I have told him, no one likes a smart aleck and no one will like you if you show off all the time."

"Well, I sent him to the hall one day. He was disturbing the other children, talking and cutting up."

"I know," my mother sighed.

"And his posture is terrible. He slumps down in his seat all of the time and his shoulders are getting round."

"We're a round-shouldered lot," my father said in his off-handed way.

"Well, you don't want your son to be round-shouldered, too, do you?"

My father didn't answer.

"I recommend that you take his suspenders off. I think they are pulling his shoulders down."

The next day my mother took the suspenders off my britches and took me aside. "You shouldn't be a smarty, Gerry. No one likes a smarty."

I tried not to be a smart aleck, but it was impossible. I was addicted to speech. Besides, how could one remain quiet when there was so much to say?

When I was nine I was operated on for a scrotal hernia that made me so weak I couldn't pull myself up when I tried to climb trees. My parents took me to the hospital where Dr. Carr, our family doctor, was to perform the surgery. I was terrified at staying in the hospital alone all night waiting for them to haul me into some operating room to cut me open, wide open, and Lord knew what they would do to me after that. I would probably die, or wish I were dead. By the next morning, when the operation was scheduled, I was running a fever.

"Probably the boy got too excited by his night in the hospital," the doctor said. "Sometimes kids get upset, and that causes the fever. But we can't take any chances. Take him home and we'll schedule him for another day." I was relieved, and within a few days forgot all about it. Then one day several weeks later my father said, "Come on, son, let's you and I take a ride."

"Where are we going?" I asked.

"Going for a ride," he said.

I liked to ride with my father. But in a little while I realized where we were going—to the hospital.

I remember the sweet smell of the gas, which I am told was followed by the ether. I remember the dreams that followed, frightful dreams, floating, crazy, horrid dreams, dreams of swirling and folding in and out again. When I came to, I was deathly sick. I began to vomit, and the pain of vomiting against the surgery was the worst pain I had ever felt. I was crying and gagging. Both my parents, doubtless haunted by visions of dead Little Peggy, hovered over my bed, but I wanted my father. He read me a Tarzan story between the heaving until at last the nausea faded. The next day I was home in a bed my parents set up in the dining room, handy for my mother, and in ten days the doctor said I could get up and go play, and after that I could, in fact, climb trees all right.

In those days if a child came down with chicken pox or measles, the law required the parents to immediately notify the county health officer, who came to the house and tacked up on the door an ugly red sign with huge letters: WARNING: COMMUNICABLE DISEASE WITHIN. The sign quarantined you until the same officer

certified you were over the disease. Members of the family were also forbidden
to frequent public places until the quarantine was removed. I got the measles and
our family was quarantined. It was humiliating—like being a leper. And even
when I got well and the sign was taken down, the kids wouldn't let you forget.

"Spence has somethin'."

"Yeah. Don't get near *him.*"

"I'm over it."

"How do we know?"

"Sign's down, ain't it?"

"Sign may be down, but you may not be over it. My dad said so." And after
that nobody would talk to me for another week. When I got over the measles
my mother took me to the rodeo.

In the summertime, Sheridan hosted the Sheridan, Wyoming Rodeo. The
biggest event of the year was launched with a parade down Main Street. Main
Street in Sheridan has changed little over the past half century. The same buildings, some with false fronts, are still pushed in together and face each other
from opposite sides of the street like combatants ready for the fight. The town's
most important businesses, including its two banks and its several bars, its clothing stores and hardware and furniture stores, are contained in five blocks, more
or less, the importance of the businesses increasing as Main Street approaches
the courthouse on the hill.

At parade time the townsfolk all turned out to see the Indians and the cowboys and the floats. We sat on the curbs, and some people brought folding canvas stools. We carried old copies of the *Sheridan Press,* and my mother sat on
them. The Indians, the Cheyennes and the Crows from nearby reservations in
Montana, rode their big-headed, U-necked ponies, some spotted, some not, all
skinny, all sleepy, their heads drooping like wilted posies. I thought then that the
Indians could never win a war against white men on poor horses like that. They
would take all day getting to the battle, and when they got there they would be
shot, because the ponies were awkward and had feet as big as a man's head and
couldn't run. The chiefs rode at the front of the tribe with flowing headdresses
of eagle feathers that trailed down their backs nearly to the ground. The braves
painted their bodies black, red, yellow, and white. And the men, especially the
chiefs, were fat, with breasts hanging down like the old African women we saw
in the *National Geographic.*

The women wore white buckskin dresses with pretty beading and rode the
scraggliest horses of all. Some women pulled travois behind the horses they
rode. The travois was a crude carrier fashioned with two poles nearly fifteen feet
long, one fastened on each side of the horse, the ends of which dragged on the
ground. The poles were bound together behind the horse with a frame the
width of the horse upon which the Indians carried their belongings, sometimes
their papooses as well. I felt bad for the Indians, those once brave and proud

warriors now slogging along in the white man's parade, for what or why, I could not say.

"Were those the Indians who killed Custer?" I asked. We'd been to Custer's battlefield.

"Some of them were probably there," my mother said, absently.

"Those Indians couldn't kill Custer," I said.

"We should have seen them before they began drinking alcohol," my mother said. "They were very beautiful and very brave before that. That's what alcohol does to you, Gerry." And then she wouldn't say any more. "Hush," she whispered. "People are listening."

The rodeo was held at the Sheridan County fairgrounds. The grandstand was for folks who could pay more than fifty cents for a ticket, and the bleachers, where people sat without a roof to protect them from the sun or rain, were for ordinary folks. My mother thought a boy should see the events of his community even if they were somewhat uncivilized. What if a child grew up in Sheridan, Wyoming, and never saw a rodeo?

We witnessed all the great events—the bucking horses, both bareback and saddle, the wild bull riding, calf and steer roping and bulldogging. There was wild cow milking where the cowboys had to rope a wild cow, tie her up and milk a cupful of milk into a tin cup and run to the finish line without spilling the milk. We laughed to see the bowlegged cowboys run. There were chuckwagon races, with four-horse teams running their hearts out, all four wheels of the wagons flying off the ground, the pots and pans bouncing and clanging, and the cowboys hollering at their horses and slapping them hard on their butts with the reins.

The Indians held races, some on skinny, long-legged Thoroughbreds that ran with their nostrils flared as wide as a man's fist, and the bodies of the riders were painted with yellow and white and black war paint, and they rode bareback. Maybe these were the horses the warriors rode into battle, I thought. The cowboys competed in wild horse races in which they had to first rope a wild horse, saddle him, mount him, and then ride him around the track to the finish line. Sometimes the horse would jump the fence and sometimes it would run in the wrong direction and the cowboy couldn't stop him. Sometimes the horse lay down, and sometimes the cowboys were thrown.

I thought I could never be a cowboy. I was even afraid of Old Coon, Grandpa Spence's black Morgan, and all he ever did was toss his head around and prance. But the horse was powerful beyond belief and so tall Grandpa had to lift me up, and he was so quick I had to hold on to the saddlehorn with both hands. And then what did a fellow do with the reins? "Only dudes hold on to the saddlehorn with both hands," Grandpa said. Then he laughed and tied the reins together and led Old Coon into the corral. Once the corral gate was closed he let loose of him, and the old horse knew what he was supposed to do—go round and round to give a kid a ride. Must have been humiliating to a real cow horse, I thought.

The most fun at the Sheridan, Wyoming Rodeo were the trick ropers, who sometimes performed even in front of the bleachers. The best ropers were the Monte Montana family, a father, a mother, and a son. They were dressed in matching black and red and silver shirts, their black riding pants tucked inside their high-topped, fancy inlaid boots. These boots, even the boy's, were trimmed at the toe and the heel with silver. Sometimes they roped two horses abreast standing up, and they spun their ropes overhead and up and down, and they danced over the ropes, and they danced through the ropes, even as they rode at a full gallop dancing on top of their saddles. They roped blindfolded, and they roped riding backward and sidesaddle, and they did somersaults and they jumped up and down off the rear end of their horses as they ran and the crowds whistled and cheered when they tipped their pure white hats at the end.

On the way home my mother and I walked through the Indian camp. The Rodeo Committee had enticed the Crows to come to the rodeo with the promise that they would be given the rodeo livestock that was wounded and had to be killed. Sometimes the bulldoggers broke a steer's neck, and sometimes a roper jerked a steer around so hard its neck was broken, too. Sometimes a roped calf's leg was broken, and occasionally a bucking horse was hurt and had to be shot, and the Indians were given the carcasses. They divided up the meat among their families, and as we walked through the dust of the camp we saw the thin strips of meat covered with flies hanging on wires like bloody icicles, drying in the sun for jerky.

The Indians glared at my mother and me as we walked by

ABOVE: *Wyoming Indian Chief.*

BELOW: *Wyoming Indian woman.*

their old faded white army tents. None spoke. None smiled. None nodded. The Indian children ran from tent to tent, barefoot and dirty and half-naked. Their hair was matted and gray with dust. Some had impetigo sores on their faces, but they were laughing, and they ran as wild as jackrabbits. My mother and I didn't brave going to the center of the camp. We skirted the edges so we were in plain sight of civilization, my mother holding on to my hand tightly, I supposed, so that I would not be kidnapped by the Crows.

I was afraid of the Indians. "Don't stare at them," my mother said. "It's not nice to stare at those poor people." I tried not to.

One day during the rodeo, an old Indian woman wrapped in her blanket walked slowly down the sidewalk in front of our house, headed to the fairgrounds. She walked in moccasins and her toes pointed in slightly. My mother had gone to town to shop, and without cause or reason or forethought Buddy Taylor and I began to taunt her. We walked backward in front of her making faces. We were horrid children who should have been thrashed, but no one was home to thrash us. We stuck our tongues out at the poor woman and taunted her with things like "Na, na, na-nah, na."

Suddenly the woman opened up her blanket to reveal a long butcher knife held menacingly in her brown hand. She started after us. Buddy ran across the street to his house, so she chose me. I ran for the front door of our house as fast as I could and slammed it in front of her and locked it. The woman stood outside silently beating on the door with her knife. After a while she left, but the marks of her knife on the front door remained. Sometimes I showed the tourists where an Indian woman tried to kill me, and they would look at me askance, and some would laugh and say, "Really?" I never told my mother.

Most of all, summertime was for fishing. I went to the slough down the street about ten blocks where the city fathers had planted truckloads of yellow striped perch seined from nearby Lake DeSmet. Caught 'em on worms and a bobber. Buddy Taylor had better worms in his garden than we did in ours. His father fed their worms with coffee grounds. I brought home long strings of fresh-caught perch and cleaned them in the kitchen sink: Slice along each side of the stickery dorsal fin and pull it out with the pliers. Then at the top, slice the fish its full length, take the pliers and pull off the skin from both sides. Open up the belly and take out the entrails. Cut off the head. Then right away dip the fillets in a batter of egg, flour, and cornmeal, and fry. Pretty close to perfect.

Summer was also for roller-skating on the sidewalks, and after we wore out the skates or lost one, we made roller-skate scooters. You began with an old clamp-on roller skate, took it apart and nailed the front two rollers on the front of a two-by-four about three feet long and the back two rollers on the back end of the two-by-four. Then at one end of the two-by-four you nailed an apple crate for the upright and across the top of the crate you nailed a strip of wood that stuck out over the edges of the crate and served as handle bars.

We made rubber guns, pistols fashioned out of a strip of one-inch wood about fourteen inches long with a handle nailed on at one end and a clothespin secured to the back of the handle for a trigger, the ammunition for which were rubber bands sliced from an old inner tube.

My uncle Fred Pfleeger, my mother's youngest brother, who lost his leg in the Second World War at the Anzio beachhead in Italy, bought me Christmas presents he thought might get me into trouble, or so my mother accused. One Christmas when I was nine or ten he sent me a Daisy air rifle with which I shot at every blackbird and sparrow that flew over the county—never killed a bird, but the intent was there, all right. Sometimes we played Joe Louis in the front yard and boxed with some kid's boxing gloves. I was always Joe Louis. The other kids got to be Two-Ton Tony Galento or Max Baer. The fight was over in a few minutes. Nobody won. The gloves were too heavy and our arms too small. We built tree houses in the trees up the draw across the Eighth Street Bridge, and we dug a cave into the creek bank where we hid from the cowboys if we were Indians, and vice versa.

"Somebody found our cave," Buddy Taylor announced one day.

"How do you know?" I asked.

" 'Cause, somebody shit in it, and it wasn't me."

We went to look and sure enough, there it was. What kind of person would do that in another person's cave? He must be a *real* criminal. We cleaned out the cave and vowed that if we ever found out who it was we would kill him. We decided to set up watch. All day we waited in the tall weeds, but no one appeared. The next day we did the same. Finally we gave up, but a couple of weeks later we revisited our cave, and there it was again. We never discovered who defiled our cave, but whoever he was was the worst of all the criminals I ever encountered as a boy in Sheridan, Wyoming.

CHAPTER 8

Bull elk taken by my father and his "meat-gettin'"
30-40 Krag rifle.

"BY THE WAY, I had a little bloody show in my stool the other day," my father said one evening over the phone after we'd been talking along for some time. I waited, the dread sweeping over me. "Doctor says I may have a little tumor in the bowel or something."

"What do you mean 'a little tumor or *something*'?" I couldn't hide the mounting terror. I thought of his lung operation five years before. "Does it have something to do with your lung?"

"No, this is a brand new thing," he said. "Different kind of cell." He was living in Medford, Oregon, in a home Imaging and I had provided. The doctors there thought he should go to the John Wayne Tumor Clinic at UCLA, where Imaging and I met him and Mae, along with my brother Tom and my sister Barbara. Given his history and the suspicious-looking growths on the X rays, the doctors thought he probably had a cancer in his kidney as well. We tried to hide our worry and to keep cheerful. They performed an ultrasound probe of the kidney, and when that proved negative, the doctors began to consider whether they should try to remove the bowel tumor. He was now eighty-eight, with but one old lung left. Besides, he had a history of severe heart attacks, had been hospi-

talized, and survived some ten other incidents of what the doctors call ventric-
ular fibrillation, a condition in which the heart launches into a kind of quivering
St. Vitus' dance from which the victim sometimes dies. The lung specialists
wanted him to convince them he still had minimum lung capacity. They had him
jogging up and down the hall on his old weak legs, after which they tested his
heart. Risky business. His age alone stacked the odds against him, not to mention the other negative factors that would alert prudent medical men that the
likelihood of his surviving the lengthy procedure was in considerable doubt. But
if the cancer went untreated, not only was the prognosis clear, but death would
be tenacious, slow, and painful.

We peered at the tumor through a video colonoscope. You could see the
growth glaring on the screen, red and ugly like the vicious swollen sores old
Hereford range cows sometimes contract, "cancer-eyes" we called them. My father
watched as the screen, reflected in a mirror in full color, revealed the growth.

"Ugly-looking bugger, isn't it?" he said.

"They can get rid of it, and fix you up like new," I said.

He made no reply. Instead he teased the nurses about how he didn't feel as
if the way they were treating him, inspecting his unmentionables and all, was
the way ladies should be treating a fellow. Not real ladies. And he smiled his big
old smile to let the nurses know he was just joshing them, and the nurses
laughed, and everybody loved him.

Soon, once again, we were waiting for the nurses to come haul him off on
that dreadful gurney. And once again he dealt with the danger he knew he faced
like one merely waiting for the waitress to bring on dessert. Once more the family was gathered in his hospital room to spend what would surely be our last
moments with our father. As for him, he was going to enjoy his time with his
family. Although everyone in the room must have been suffering their own kind
of pain and their own brand of fear, the room was again filled with the same
light chit-chat and jokes and laughter. No one prayed. Now no one spoke of
unfinished business, or the "arrangements" that should be made. No one
acknowledged what everyone knew—that he would probably die, if not from
the operation, from the likely postoperative complications.

My father had already signed a "living will," which has nothing to do with
living, but has to do with his right to die in a dignified and economical way. Mae
and we children were designated by our father as the persons to play the role of
God over our father, this mortal who once had been God to us. The magical
cycle by which the child becomes the parent and the parent the child had
occurred. He was, of course, not childish. Yet the infirmities of age impose certain dependencies, and suddenly I realized my father had been born again.
Born to me.

During his employment for the cement company he had secured eleven
patents. He told me once, "I was supposed to get one hundred dollars each for
these, but I never received a cent." Despite the loyal contribution of his best

years to the company, my father needed our economic support in his later years. The pension the company granted him was only a piteous reminder that corporations cannot love, do not love, cannot feel loyalty, and are not loyal to those who have laid it all down for the company. Often I felt ashamed that he should thank me, and I asked him not to. It was a piddling payback for the years of struggle in those hard times that he and my mother had invested to keep things together.

The problem was that my father was in love. And as long as a man is in love, death has to wait. "I could go," he had admitted to me during a moment when we were by ourselves. "But I'm not ready to go, quite yet," he was quick to add. "I don't want to leave Mae alone." And I thought he wanted my reassurance that I would see Mae was taken care of. I told him, "Don't worry about Mae, I'll take care of her," and you could see the peace soften his eyes. Then the nurses came with the damnable gurney, and again we took the long walk with our father down the hall to the operating room. Suddenly I realized no matter how old and how enfeebled he might become, no matter how dependent, no matter how much the child, he would always be my father. Once more he looked up at me and winked.

"Are you afraid?" I asked.

"No," he said. Then he said it again. "There's a lot worse ways for a man to go than on the operating table." As they pushed him through the door I saw him headed into another dark forest, one he had explored before. Once more he was leaving me behind. I was afraid, afraid for him. And I felt my own fear. Suddenly I was convinced I could never live without my father. If he should die, I would shrivel up and perish, as the small spotted fawn left hidden in the tall grass would surely perish after the poacher shot the doe.

"Sickness doesn't seem to worry me much," he'd once said. "I've always had faith in myself." Then just as the door was about to close behind him, he looked back over his shoulder to say one last thing me: "Don't you ever worry about your father, son. I'll be back."

The wait for my father's return from the operating room was a torture of the kind I remembered as a child, when my mother and I waited for this same man to return to us out of another forest. I recalled one occasion when I was old enough to go to hunting camp, and we pitched our tent on Spring Creek in the Big Horns. My father had written a note to my teacher announcing that his son would not be in school for a week or possibly more. He wrote that I was going to hunting camp with his father and mother and, to his way of thinking, I would learn more in the mountains about life than I could learn in school during those same days.

The first day of the season he had taken off on foot in the dark of the early morning. He hunted alone. He said other hunters made too much noise. But the real reason he liked to hunt alone was because alone, an ineffable sense of

being filled his experience. One is keenly aware of every movement, the needles of the lodgepole pine flitting in an errant breeze when all else is still, the
small shadow of a mouse scampering. One sees everything, the eye-drop rust-
colored petals of the kinnikinnick, its berries red, the imprint in the tall forest
grass where an animal has lain, the ferns growing out of a rotten log, proclaiming that life is the fleeting product of death. Alone, one experiences the
total feast, and looks for more, feels for more in the holiness there, in that
sanctuary more perfect than any cathedral. Alone and silent in the forest, one
dissolves into the forest. One would never speak out, never even whisper
there any more than one would stand up on a pew in church and shout.
Walking softly, one looks carefully ahead to spot where each foot will meet the
ground so that no crunch of crumbling twigs or crushing needles will sully the
silence. One steps over the fallen timber with a slow, high step, and carefully,
so as not to permit even the pant leg to brush the side of the log. And one
hears every snap of a twig, the creak of every old tree, the irreverent noisy
chatter of every squirrel who, like Paul Revere, alerts the entire universe to
one's coming. You mouthy little devil! Hush! Who gave you the right to mar
this unspoiled stillness?

Alone in the heavy timber, one's sense of smell takes on the sharpness of the
hunting creature. Many times I have smelled elk in the woods as a dog smells a
rabbit. All the senses become intensified. When one is alone in the deep wilderness, one bursts into an aliveness of another dimension. Alone in the wilderness,
one hears a rhapsody played on the silent strings of the harp of being, to which
one dances in ecstasy with the self.

Notwithstanding my father's assurances that he was quite safe, my mother
was in constant fear that "something might happen to Daddy." She never
expressed her fear quite like that. It was more like, "I wonder where Daddy is?"
But I knew what she meant. He could break a leg out there alone and no one
would find him. And even young men had heart attacks, although my father,
even when he was young, was never a young man to me. And if he had a heart
attack, he would die out there in that fearsome wilderness. Suffused with my
mother's Christian view of the wilderness, I found the wild imponderable and
frightening and dangerous, the antithesis of my father's view of nature. To him,
Mother Nature was a friend, and the wilderness a place of peace, and if there
were a God, which I suspected he privately questioned—at least a God with a
long white beard—God would be in the mountains.

But as all young wild creatures do, I had absorbed my mother's fears.
Whatever would happen to us if our daddy did not come home? What would
happen if he were lost? How could he go out there alone with no map and no
compass and not get lost? I had got lost in the Woolworth store in Denver. And
if I could get lost in Woolworth's, well, how could my father possibly leave camp
in the dark, hunt all day in timber nearly as dark as night, wander over mountain after mountain, all of which looked alike to me, and then find his way home

again? If he were lost out there, I could never find him and no one else could either. How could a boy ever live without a father?

Once in the late morning, my mother and I had walked in the opposite direction from where my father had gone, careful never to stray out of sight of our camp. I was afraid when I was in the woods with her. Perhaps I could see the fear in her eyes. Perhaps, like any small animal, I could smell it. She didn't know how to walk in silence as my father said an Indian walks, the toes, not the heel, softly touching the ground first, the feet caressing the earth, not pounding it. We had picked a basketful of bright red leaves of sumac to take home for the dining room table when, in the distance, way off across the canyon in the direction my father had gone, we could hear the explosions of a hunting rifle. Ka-boom! Ka-boom! Ka-boom! We looked at each other, and then, in violation of the wilderness, she spoke out loud.

"Maybe that's Daddy getting his elk," my mother said.

"That was three shots in a row. That's the SOS signal Daddy taught us," I said. SOS or not, my father would never have spoken in the wilderness. He might have turned around and raised an eyebrow, or smiled, and then I would have walked on behind him trying to keep up, trying not to make any noise, following him like a pup follows an old dog. In small ways I thought my mother permitted herself to enjoy the woods, but, unlike my father, she was not a creature of the wilderness.

"I hope Daddy's got something," she said. "Probably wasn't an emergency at all," she added under her breath. It was already past noon when we returned to camp, and my mother made us a peanut butter and lettuce sandwich, which I washed down with a glass of cold milk from the big two-quart Mason jar she had stored in the creek. We napped on top of our bedrolls, the blankets soaked in the musty smell of old canvas, and in the warm afternoon the only sounds were those of the haughty grasshoppers, snap, snap, snapping their yellow wings in their last earthly flights before the heavy frost would deliver them their come-uppance and silence them forever. Already, at age ten, I had my drawing tablet at hand. I sketched the towering mountains and the shallow creek and the bordering mountain willows, all silverish and purple. I could grow up to be anything I wanted, my mother insisted, even a fine artist like Francis Overton, our watercolorist friend from the church who had earlier that summer given me drawing lessons—twenty-five cents a lesson. "But artists," my mother added quickly, "can never make a living. Poor Francis. We must be sure she gets plenty of fresh meat if Daddy gets his elk."

Then before we knew it, the dark began to rise while the light set in the west. And Daddy was not home. We sat silently together, Mother on a folding camp stool, me on the warm ground, looking, peering, straining our eyes through the dusk in the direction Daddy had gone in the morning.

"Well, he'll surely be along pretty soon," my mother said to break the silence.

"Do you think he's all right?" I asked.

"I'm sure he is," which meant, of course, that she could not be sure.

"Do you think he's hurt?"

"I'm sure he isn't," she said. Her fear was also in the sound of her voice, and in the tightness around the corners of her mouth. Now we strained against the enfolding darkness, and as the sun set, the anxiety set in.

"He likes to hunt in the evening. It's the best time," I tried to comfort myself. "I mean the elk come out of the timber where they been hiding all day, and they edge out into the little meadows up there to eat. He's probably sitting up above someplace where he can get a good look at the clearing."

"I'm sure that's what he's doing," my mother replied.

"He can see in the dark," I said.

"Yes," my mother said. "I suppose so."

And we waited, and the darkness rose all around us.

He had promised to be home before dark so we wouldn't worry. It made no difference that we had gone through this whole anxious exercise before, and that he had always come back after dark. This was now. Finally when we could sit there no longer, Mother said we should get in the car and drive on up the road a little way where we might have a better chance to hear him coming. We drove to a high spot above the camp and Mother parked our '37 Ford, and we rolled down the windows to listen. Nothing. Not even the yapping of a distant coyote. But we kept on listening, straining at the ears. I could hear my mother's shallow breathing. I could hear the occasional rustle in the grass of the scurrying prairie dogs. I thought to myself, Well, if he dies up there, he will die doing something he loves.

Then suddenly I heard it. "Do you hear that?"

"No," my mother said. "What was it?"

"It was like a jingle."

"You are imagining things."

"No. Listen, Mother!" We listened. "Don't you hear it?"

"No," she said.

"Now do you hear it?" It was like a distant tinkling bell.

"Yes," she whispered, "I hear it now."

"What do you think it is?"

"Sounds like a cow bell. Maybe there's an old cow up there with a bell on. Sometimes ranchers put them on the lead cow so he can find his herd in the timber. Your father doesn't carry any bells with him."

We listened. "Do you hear that?" I whispered. "It was a sort of snort."

"I heard it," my mother said. "Those are horses coming down off the mountain in the dark. But your father wasn't on a horse, thank goodness."

"How do they get down off the mountain in the dark?" I asked. She didn't answer. The stars were out, but no moon. I could see the dippers, and the sound of the horses grew closer and closer until finally they were upon us. It was a pack string of about seven horses, all right, and the horses, one with a bell hanging on a collar around its neck, were laden with the quarters of newly slaughtered elk. Then my father walked up to the car.

He had that big grin on his face. He opened the car door on my side. I could see that his hands were bloody, and when he slid into the front seat next to me he brought along the musky smell of elk. Suddenly, as if someone had flipped on the lights, my worry was gone. It was as if I had never worried before, as if the lights had been left always burning, and there had never been darkness, not ever. My father was home. He would always be home. He could walk in the dark. He could never get lost. He could never be hurt. He could see in the dark. He was the king of the mountains. He always had been. He always would be.

"I'm so glad you're down," my mother said. "We were worried. It's past ten o'clock at night, Gerald—way past Gerry's bedtime. What kept you so long? You promised me you'd be home before dark."

"Big kill up on Bull Creek," he said.

"Tell me the story," I begged, which was what I always said when he came home from his hunting. Ah, the stories of my father, the excitement of the stalking, the suspense, the shot, and then what happened, Daddy?

"I'll tell you the story in the morning. Got a lot of elk to get off these horses. Some other hunters coming down behind me. I'll be home soon as we get the work done here."

The next morning at breakfast, I was on him.

"Tell us the story, Daddy."

"Well, all right," he said, without any more urging. "It was like this," he said, as he stopped to stuff a pancake into his mouth. He was the family pancake maker, made pancakes the size of small saucers. You could stuff the whole pancake into your mouth if no one was watching, or, for proper eating, you could cut it into fourths. "I was slippin' through the down timber up on the divide between Spring Creek and Bull Creek," my father continued. "Hadn't come onto any fresh sign all morning. Then at the peak of the divide I came onto where an old bull had been lying. You could tell he was a big old bull by the size of his imprint in the grass. And his feet were as big around as one of those saucers. You remember that old bull I shot last year that had been run out of the herd?"

"Right," I said. The year before my father had told me about how he had come onto the tracks of a bull who had been running. You could see in the snow how he had run and run until at last he fell exhausted, and how he had skidded to the very place where he'd been lying. Then if you looked you could see how the snow had melted around his steamy old body, and how he'd lain there until he got back his strength. Then you could see that he got up and ran some more. But my father, who could walk a deer down in less than a day, got on his trail and stayed on his trail until he caught up with him. And that was the end of that old bull.

"Well," my father said, "this old bull seemed to be another one of those old bulls who'd been run out of the herd by a younger, tougher bull. You could tell because the grass was matted heavy, like he laid there for some time, and then you could see that he took off running again—the tracks a long ways apart, and his prints in the ground deep, and there were those little clods of dirt thrown out behind where his hooves were diggin' in when he ran. But you remember how tough eatin' that old devil was? Well, who wants another one of those to chew on all winter? Man could wear his teeth out on that kind of meat.

"Anyway I figured that old bull was probably over on Hidden Teepee Creek by then. But I wondered if the herd he was run out of might not be around close by someplace. So I start back-tracking the old bull. By now I'm over onto the Bull Creek side of the divide."

"What's it like over there?"

"Just like on Spring Creek, except the timber may be a little thicker. Well, anyway, I'm slipping through the timber backtracking this old bull when suddenly all *hell* breaks loose!"

"Gerald!" my mother said.

"Well, that's the way it was. There was this bunch of hunters who had come up from the other side. Five or six of 'em, and they had dumb-lucked right into the herd and they started shootin'. It was like a war. There were elk falling everywhere and cripples running around. I never raised my gun. I just sat there and watched it."

"How many elk were there?"

"Maybe twenty, twenty-five."

"How come you didn't shoot, Daddy?"

"There was already too many killed for the licenses those fellows had. I figured I'd wait until the smoke cleared and see what was what. There were at least two cows that had been crippled that weren't down yet. And I could see that those fellows weren't the trackin' kind. So I takes after the cripples. First I get on the trail of this one old cow, and I followed her a little ways. She was layin' down behind a big old log, breathin' heavy, and I took careful aim and put her out of her misery. I marked the spot with my bandanna so I could find her easy when I came back to gut her out.

"Then I went back to where they had been shootin' and those fellows were all bunched up laughing and hollering and jumping up and down because they'd made a big kill. Too big a kill, I'll tell ya that. And so I don't say anything. I just slipped around the edge of 'em and picked up the trail of this other old cow they had crippled. I could tell by her tracks that they had shot the front leg off of her. I followed her a little ways. She was stumbling blind from the pain, and she stumbled on up into a crevice in a big granite outcropping, and then she couldn't go any further. And by this time maybe fifty feet behind her. But

I didn't want to shoot her from that angle, cause it would spoil the hindquarters. So I pressed in and I got closer and closer to her. I was about twenty feet away from her when she turned around to face me. She didn't have any place to go except over the top of me. And here she came!"

"Oh, *God!*" I said.

"Gerry!" my mother scolded.

"Here she came, her eyes wild and her one front leg shot nearly off at the knee, her old leg swinging back and forth as she came running to me. At the last minute I lifts up the old Krag, flips her off of safety, took quick aim and let one fly. The old girl came skiddin' in at my feet, dead as a doornail."

"What if she had run over you?"

"She wasn't going to run over me."

"How did you know?"

"Because I had the old Krag. That's why. She's a meat-gettin' son-of-a-gun." He reached over and patted the gun, slipped some sagebrush into the camp stove to keep the fire going, flipped the pancakes, and sat back, his story over.

But I urged him to tell me more. And so he told how he had gutted out the two wounded elk he had shot, and how he had chosen the big dry cow, the one with the leg shot off, for ours. The other wounded elk he shot was a wet cow, but her calf was old enough to wean, he said. Then he had taken one of the other hunters over to where the wet cow lay, marked in the woods by his bandanna, and the man told my father there were several more in their party back at their camp who hadn't gotten their elk, and he was grateful to my father. "Probably the drinkers," my father said to me, "the ones who couldn't get up in the morning for the hunt." And then my father said the other hunters sent one of their party back to camp to bring back the string of pack horses. Because my father helped them gut and quarter their kills and had tracked down the cripples, they hauled his elk down for free. And that was why he was so late getting home.

We broke camp the day following the big kill on Bull Creek. Took two trips in the old Ford to get the camp and the meat back to the house in Sheridan. My father hung up the quartered elk in the garage, skinned the quarters, and left the meat to cure. Then he took a package of steaks to Francis Overton, and he took a couple of roasts to the Sutkas next door. And he took some meat to Pop and Mom Rowe, the town's elderly Boy Scout executive and his wife, who were friends from the church, because Pop Rowe was too old and too fat to "really get out and hunt." And we ate away at the hanging meat like Indians, and when the meat began to turn, my mother canned what was left and we ate canned elk in stew and hash and in sandwiches all winter long.

The surgeon, tall and bony, in his green cap and green surgical pajamas, the mask hanging at his chin, strolled up to us as stone-faced as any Buddha.

"He's quite an old man," the surgeon began. "Never met anybody quite like him. The old boy may make it. The tumor was a well-contained tumor. Got it all. Took a good margin to make sure. Took a good look around while I was in there. Think he's going to be all right."

"I knew he would be all right," Mae said. "He promised me he wasn't going yet, and your father always keeps his promises."

And suddenly we were happy again, as if the lights had been flipped on and there had never been any darkness in the history of the universe. We hurried to the recovery room to be with him. He was conscious and he grinned, not the big grin he could give, but one that said he was all right and that we ought not worry anymore. I sat down beside him.

" 'Member when we shot that big old bull—you and me—that time up on Spring Creek?" His mind was wandering in and out of the anesthetic, and when his mind was free to wander where it pleased it always turned to hunting.

"Yes, I remember," I said. I had his hand in mine. He didn't seem to be in pain.

"Remember how we tracked that old boy through the timber?" his voice nearly inaudible. I had to lean close to hear.

"Yes. I remember. It was a cold son-of-a-bitch, that day," I said.

"Sure was," he whispered. He was gazing at the ceiling, his eyes barely opened, clouded from the shock and the drugs. " 'Member how we had to pack him out?"

"Wore me to a frazzle," I said. I was older then, maybe twelve—old enough to do the heavy work of the elk hunter. He smiled. I had been following my father through the timber. We hadn't gone but a mile or so through the knee-deep snow before we came onto the track of the bull. My father pointed, touched his lips and winked as if to say, "This is a fresh track and a big one!" Now in the hospital bed his eyes were glazed over, but not his mind. He wiggled his finger in a back-and-forth way to suggest that the bull we were tracking was just "lolly-gagging peacefully through the timber, just browsing here and there," as my father would have said if he had spoken. Suddenly he raised the old Krag and shot. There was an explosion up ahead. I had seen nothing.

"Got him!" he whispered. "This is sure a meat-gettin' old son-of-a-gun," he said, giving the rifle a pat. But he still moved cautiously ahead, his gun at the ready. About fifty yards in front, the old bull lay in a heap, the blood running from the fatal wound just above the front elbow where my father always aimed.

"Heart shot," he said. "This old boy never knew what hit him. If you have to go, that's the way to go."

He was drifting off. I reached under my father's gown. I could feel the bandages that covered where the surgeons had opened him up. " 'Member how you gutted that old bull out?" my father whispered. I nodded, but his eyes were closed. My father had handed me his hunting knife, razor sharp. "Want to gut him out?" he asked. He pulled the bull over on his back so that its nose pointed up and the rack, six points on each side, held the animal's belly skyward.

"Yeah," I said, brave-like.

"Well, you start here." He grabbed hold of the bull's testicles. "You cut around here," he motioned, "and then you cut out around the old boy's penis. That makes good food for the Canada jays." Already those precocious light gray birds, larger than a robin, had begun to gather, squawking, waiting. "Slice up the belly between your fingers. That's it. Get your fingers on top of the stomach wall and cut between them so if you're going to cut anything it will be you, not the stomach." I followed his instructions. "We don't want to cut a gut. Spoils the meat." My hands were covered with warm blood. In the cold of the November morning, the animal's warm life steaming out felt good.

"Now you're up to the diaphragm. That's what separates the belly from the lungs and the heart. Let's get the gut cleaned out before we open the diaphragm." We rolled the bull over to his side and lifted out the stomachs. After the stomachs had been removed and dragged away from the carcass, my father took the knife and slit one of the stomachs open. It was full of browse, willows and creek moss the bull had eaten the night before. "Now take this." My father handed me a rock. "We have to split the pelvis. Hammer the knife lightly with this rock. That's the way. Now reach down in there and cut out the anus." I cut around it and pulled it out along with a stream of hot, black elk droppings. Under his direction I cut the liver out, and dumped it into a sack my father had brought along and now held open to receive the meat. "Now we can open the chest cavity," he said. "Let's see where the bullet went."

I sliced away at the pink diaphragm. Once inside I could see that the top of the heart had been nicked by the bullet. The chest cavity was filled with blood. One of the lungs where the bullet exited was half blown away, the other lung pink and airy. I cut the lungs away from their anchors. You could squash the lung tissue between your fingers like whipped Jell-O. Then I cut out the heart and put it in the knapsack along with the liver.

Lunch time. I sat on the carcass, my hands covered with the blood of the fallen elk, blood to the elbows, and I ate my peanut butter and lettuce sandwich, and the white bread turned red on the edges where I held it and I was very proud, for I was a true hunter. True hunters ate with the blood of their kill on their hands.

Pretty soon my father said, "Well, now comes the work. We gotta carry this old boy out." He took the knife from me and with the occasional help from the rock he cut the elk into six pieces. Two hind quarters, two front quarters with half the neck on each quarter, a rib section, and the head with the horns and the cape. Then the terrible trek began.

We each carried a quarter a few hundred yards at most and dropped it. We rested walking back. Then my father loaded me up with another quarter, a lighter front quarter, and he picked up a hind quarter himself, and we lugged them on our shoulders to the place where we had dumped our first load. When we got all six pieces there, we started the next leg and carried all the pieces the next couple of hundred yards. By the time we got the elk to camp I was done in.

"Remember how I had to carry you the last couple of hundred yards up to the camp?" my father whispered, his eyes still glazed over, staring like a dead man's eyes stare at the ceiling.

"I remember," I said.

"It sure was fun, wasn't it?"

"Quite a time," I said. I'd never do it again, with or without my father.

"It was sure some fun," he said again. He closed his eyes and, frightened, I called the nurse. She pointed to the monitor. "He's doing just fine," she said. "Can't believe that father of yours."

Within a couple of weeks he was out in his garden again.

As my father was a hunter, so I became a hunter as well. When I was twelve, I shot my first deer. I shot it as a trespasser on the private property of one of the rich English ranchers, an English remittance man, one of those ne'er-do-wells from a titled British family who was shipped to far-off America where he could no longer embarrass his noble parents, and who, in return, received a yearly remittance from England by which his alleged noble blood was nourished while he chiefly sat on his noble prat. These early remittance men had bought up the choicest land in Sheridan County. They built ranches with their remittances, not earned money, not worked-for-by-the-hard-day money, but soft, easy, noble money that came floating in from England, and they stocked the ranches with fancy horses, some of which were crated in from England as well. They had taken the beautiful stream bottoms at the foot of the Big Horns, and they had erected their mansions there, great houses, some of English style, only a glimpse of which one could get through the trees while driving by. No true Wyoming folks were permitted on their private premises, the rustic locals kept away by fences that bore those fearsome, unfriendly signs NO HUNTING, FISHING OR TRESPASSING. VIOLATORS WILL BE PROSECUTED. Only their own class was welcome, their noble friends with equally noble bottoms who came for cocktails, polo, and fishing. Yet having heard of Sir Patrick Spence, I once had asked my Grandfather Spence about our own ancestry.

"Do we have blue blood in us, Grandpa?"

"No, my boy," my grandfather replied, "the Spences have only good red blood in their veins. Spence means *pantry*. Comes from the word *dispenser*. We were the king's pantry keepers. The only thing we ever inherited from the king was a good appetite." He laughed his soft merry laugh and raised up his big white cup with the happy fat man's face on it and the words in bold at the bottom, I'M NOT GREEDY. I JUST LIKE A LOT. Then he added, "But I will say one thing about the Spences. There hasn't been a felon or a drunk among the lot of us."

Shooting a deer on the private lands of the king's noblemen was like playing Robin Hood, I thought. Like Robin Hood, we had a score to settle with the king's noblemen, and my father was bent on settling it. Our favorite fishing spot was Little Goose Canyon, where a clear mountain stream filled with small rainbow and a few browns came roaring out of the Big Horns, the endless thunder of the rushing stream beating at the ears and the mist from the churning current leaving the body touched with dew. When I was a small child, we often picnicked on Sundays in Little Goose Canyon with our friends, the fathers fishing, the boys playing with their homemade boats and building dams in the tricklets that fed the stream while the mothers watched and gathered wildflowers or sat in the shade and did their embroidering. But one Sunday when we arrived at the mouth of the canyon, we were confronted with a newly constructed barbed wire fence that had been stretched across the road—by the said king's nobleman. Others had turned back. But not my father.

"Why that son-of-a-buck," my father exclaimed. "Does he think he owns the world? This is a county road!"

"What are we going to do, Daddy?"

My father didn't answer for a moment. Then he said, "Get out of the car." My mother began to protest, but she could see that one of those times was upon us when her protests would be useless. We got out of the car and watched, half in awe, half in fear, as my father backed up the old Ford about a hundred feet and revved up the motor until the engine was screaming. Then he let out the clutch, freeing the little beast. I can still see the old car go bouncing down the road at its top speed in second gear. I can still hear the high, sweet sound of its motor, see the dust flying, my father bent over the steering wheel, his nose nearly touching the windshield, his jaw set, his eyes ablaze. He hit the center fence post and down it went, and then the wires, singing like harp strings, snapped one at a time and went flying in every direction. Finally, when the last wire had snapped, he put on the brakes and brought the car to a stop, and backed up to where we waited, stunned and excited.

"Get in," my father hollered.

"What are we going to do now, Daddy?" I asked.

"We're goin' fishing," he said.

That was the last time that the king's nobleman tried to appropriate Little Goose Canyon from the people. My father referred to the road as "Spence Boulevard." "Let's go up to Spence Boulevard," he'd say some Sunday, and off we'd go, and when we drove by where the king's nobleman had built his blockade, my father would smile. "Nice boulevard we have here for the people, right son?"

"Right," I'd reply with pride. "We showed 'em, didn't we Daddy."

At the same time, there in the foothills of the Big Horns, the king's men owned the best deer country in the county. Applying his sense of justice, my father reasoned that since the king's men had tried to steal a whole beautiful canyon from us, it would only be fair that we steal one small deer from them.

Early in the morning on the first day of deer season, my father and I arrived at a beautiful quaking aspen grove, the leaves lately fallen and still yellow and soft underfoot. The early morning sky was gray, the darkness just setting, much too early for the king's man to be awake and about. The air on a fresh fall morning in the mountains of Wyoming is so crisp and chilled one can almost crunch it, and so it was that morning. My father pulled the Ford over to the side of the road, and I took out my own .30-40 Krag, a Spanish-American War model Springfield with its original long barrel, one just like my father's. He had purchased the rifle for me from some mail order house for seventeen dollars, and he had equipped it with an iron peep sight. We eased the car doors shut and slipped quietly through the fence exactly where a NO HUNTING OR TRESPASSING sign greeted us from the fence post. No sooner did we get out of sight of the road than a small herd of does came bouncing, bouncing through the woods. Thump, thump. You could hear their hooves springing to the ground and back up again as they took their long, graceful leaps. My father motioned me to sit down. I did. The deer stopped to look. My father was sitting beside me.

He whispered, "Let's pick out the biggest doe of the bunch, and the fattest. Probably be a dry one," meaning that the doe would probably have no fawn. It was doe season.

"That's the one," I whispered back, so excited I could barely breathe, buck fever already having set in at the premeditation of the murder I was about to commit.

I'd been taught to shoot from a sitting position, using the elbows braced over the spread knees as a tripod. The doe stood looking at me, her big soft eyes without fear, her ears as big across as small watermelons, and pointing at me to hear what only deer could hear, perhaps my breathing, perhaps my beating heart. I knew where to aim, just above and behind the front elbow. "Take your time. Take a deep breath. Squeeze it off nice and slow," my father whispered. I did as I had been taught. I did as my father said. I squeezed the trigger slowly, slowly, and then: *Ka-bam!*

Deer bounded in every direction, all except the old doe. She gave a powerful jump into the air and landed on her back, kicking. We gutted her in a hurry, my father and I, dragged her the small distance to the car and took off, a deer belonging to the king's nobleman, or one he thought he owned, scrunched up in the backseat on a tarp. And as we drove home my father's face was aglow, as if he had just won a war the said nobleman didn't even know had been fought.

The doe was so old she was toothless. She doubtless would have died that winter, and, in his own way, the king's man paid us back, for by my father's code of ethics we were committed to eat her, every bit of her, and we did, rawhide-tough, one bite at a time, the heart, the brains, the tongue, and the liver, too.

My father's sense of justice and the code of ethics by which he was guided were not always in sync with the law. That certain acts were lawful or unlawful did not necessarily make them right or wrong. Right was right, and wrong was wrong, and my father didn't need lawyers or lawmakers to advise him which was which. The deer belonged to all of the people. Therefore, it was not as serious a crime for us to trespass in order to take a deer that we had a legal right to take as it was for the king's man to appropriate whole herds of deer that did not belong to him by putting up his ugly, hostile NO TRESPASSING signs.

Often I have used the Robin Hood metaphor to describe to a jury my intentions in a trial. To the same extent that the deer on the land of the king's nobleman at Sheridan belonged not to him, but to the state, and hence to all of us, so too justice is not a commodity that should be available only to the rich, who by some serendipitous stroke are born with the power of wealth and position and are therefore permitted to fence in justice to the exclusion of all others. The safeguards of the Constitution are legal fences intended to preserve justice for all. Justice, that often elusive quarry, belongs to all who have an honest need for it, even if, sometimes, it must be stolen from the king's noblemen.

Many years later, and after much self-examination and much sport killing in the courtroom, I would come to a simple realization: killing in the courtroom is like killing in the mountains and, like all killing, carries with it the same ethical standards I saw my father live by when I was a child. One does not kill in the courtroom for the sheer sport of killing. One does not kill the opponent simply because one can. Only mad dogs, a few rogue wolves, and trophy hunters with piddling self-esteem who line their walls with the innocent dead kill for pleasure. The killing, the blood on the hands, the hands deep into the entrails of the witness on the witness stand—the whole process known as "the trial"—must not be a mere exercise in killing. Instead, it should be the means by which justice is nourished and by which the rights of ordinary people are, at last, fed.

The courtroom is a place of death. Men die in the courtroom from words that send them to the executioner's gurney or to the gas chamber. They die when their names or their fortunes are taken from them, die as their children are wrenched from them, die when they walk the long walk, in chains, to dark, dank concrete places where living men cannot abide. When I walk into a courtroom, I am the hunter. When I step into the arena, I feel as if I step into eons of history, of bloody duels, of misery and killing. And fear. The king's champion has always been pitted against the poor, the trial by duel—the adversary system, we call it. It is a fair fight, is it not? The king has a champion, as does the poor man. Indeed, there could be no duel in the courtroom, no killing of the poor, unless the poor were defended, so we understand, at last, that providing the poor man with a champion to fight for him may be more to ensure that the duel can occur in the first place than to provide the poor a chance at justice. And the judge who enforces the rules of the fight? Is he not always the king's man? It is, then, in the courtroom that I hunt and I kill, and for the killing to be right, it must be done cleanly, without unnecessary wounding, done with respect, done without waste, done without pleasure. And if the killing is done right, and for the right reasons, the killing, too, is right.

CHAPTER 9

Mae Spence and Gerald M. Spence, age eighty-eight and ninety.

ONE DAY WHEN my father was past ninety he telephoned me. I was in my study in Jackson Hole preparing a case for trial. "Well, Sonny Boy," he said, "your father is no longer a man."

"What do you mean?" I asked.

"I said good-bye to a couple of old friends yesterday."

"Who died?" I asked.

"They cut my nuts out yesterday."

The doctors told him he had prostate cancer. I thought, and competent medicine insists, that such surgery at his age was not indicated. But he had investigated the matter himself and had come to a different conclusion. Taking the testicles wasn't much of an operation, he said. He'd performed the procedure thousands of times on calves. They survived. "Don't need nuts to live," he said. "But prostate cancer can turn into bone cancer, and that's a different story altogether."

"How are you feeling?"

"Nary an ache or a pain."

Many years before I had settled with my father all the issues I could think of, having learned from my mother's death that one should attend to unfinished business while the parent is alive. If you can't say what you have to say, and your parent can't say whatever must be said in return, you may carry the conflict with you in the heart like a time-release poison that never runs out.

It had taken me thirty years to recover from the wounds that had festered in my heart after my mother's death. Yet even today, there are still times when the thick scar tissue is as palpable as shoe leather. So, long before my father died, I had been diligent in settling all the unfinished business I could think of.

I had talked with him about my mother's death many times, talked about it until neither of us could think of another word to say. He was as confounded by her death as I. He had borne the tragedy mostly alone, mostly without help. And mostly without understanding, either his or that of his family and friends.

We had talked about his own dying as well. Was he afraid to die? I needed to know. At ninety my father was out there ahead of me. He had shown me the way through those dense Wyoming forests and now he was headed into a different forest, and I was still following. As usual, he was not afraid. And I was still the child.

"I'm not afraid of dying," he told me. "I'm afraid of pain, but not too afraid of it," he said. "I got a way to take care of pain." He said nothing more, nor did I. But I knew what he meant. "I'm hanging around because of Mae. Don't want to leave Mae alone." By this time he had given up his garden. He was too weak to do much, but I had encouraged him to write another book, which, shortly after his death, I published privately. He had entitled it *The Hunter*, a collection of his favorite hunting stories.

"Remember, Gerry," he said just before he died, "when we cry over the dead, we are not crying over them. We are crying over our own loss. Wherever I go, I'll be all right." He seemed comfortable about death. He was ready for it. His business was finished, his business with himself and his children, but his business with Mae was unresolved. How does a man leave the woman he's in love with?

Did he believe in a life hereafter? "I've had plenty of life already," he said. "More than my share. If there's another life, I'll live it. If there isn't, well, that's all right, too." He had a scientific mind. Things were as they were.

My father had always been a working man, spawned from the most humble beginnings, and he never forgot where he came from, those poor but proud farmers who scraped together the most meager existence from their small, hard dirt farm at the foothills of the Rocky Mountains. Although my father was a chemist by education, at heart his allegiance was with the men who labored in the plants and the mills and the mines, where during his lifetime he too had always labored for the corporate master. He was a Democrat and a union man. He loved Franklin D. Roosevelt and disdained Hoover. He respected those who earned an honest living by hard work, was unafraid of work himself, and would not tolerate the mistreatment of any person. He believed that those who exercised power over others were suspect, for most often power in the hands of the powerful is exercised wrongfully.

My father's friends were the tie hacks who staggered up and down the gangways all day lugging two-hundred-pound ties on their backs, and the workers at the plant who breathed in the toxic fumes from the oil and creosote and who died too early from their cancers. Because the church was the nucleus of my mother's life, he tolerated the menfolk of my mother's church friends, and he tried to be friends with the preachers who came, served their sentences in that far-off community, and soon left for larger, wealthier congregations. But he understood working men. They talked his language. He trusted them and respected them, and fought for them, and was proud that his friends were the workers. He used to say, "A man who's working with his hands hasn't got his hands out for a dole, and he hasn't got his hands in the company till, either."

But the working men died. In those days simple infections were sometimes fatal. Chest colds could easily lead to fatal pneumonia. Mustard plasters and Vicks VapoRub provided the only standard therapy. Ward White, that beautiful, tall, blond, athletic boy, my best friend, his family and ours close friends, came down with polio one day, leaving his right leg shrunken and useless. Even simple fungal infections like athlete's foot often proved to be chronic, painful battles for the victim.

I contracted athlete's foot, the toes raw and cracked, runny and painful. "Those dirty, stinking tennis shoes caused it," my mother said—the kind all kids wore, eighty-nine cents on sale at Penney's. My parents soaked my feet in various medications, but nothing helped. In the morning, the stockings I had worn the day before were hard from the dried infection. Absorbine Jr. was supposed to cure it. Nothing cured it. Soaking the feet in the hot concoctions the doctor prescribed made me cry in pain. It was a dripping, incurable malignancy until I went with my father to see Dr. Inglot.

To my father, Dr. Inglot was the local shaman. A chiropractor, he was a small, squat, dark man with a large head, thick glasses and a heavy French accent. Before my father was forty, his stomach began to pain him. He was in constant agony. Dr. Carr, our family doctor, had already told my father his symptoms were ominous. The doctor suspected cancer. Cancer! My father made an immediate visit to Dr. Inglot, taking me with him. Part of my education. Earlier in the year I'd watched in both horror and amazement when the dentist had pulled all of his teeth, the uppers and lowers, all in the same afternoon.

In his small, dark office, Dr. Inglot instructed my father to lie down on the old leather examining table. Then from a box lined with blue velvet the doctor lifted his small metal divining plumb-bob. Very carefully he held the plumb-bob over various parts of my father's abdomen. At each position the plumb-bob seemed to magically gather energy on its own, and began swinging vigorously back and forth. Sometimes it swung in circles, sometimes not. After each such occasion the doctor would raise one of his bushy eyebrows, clear his throat, and go "Humph!" I waited breathlessly, fearfully for the verdict.

At last the doctor spoke: "You don't have cancer, Mr. Spence. You have an ulcer. I recommend you go to Mayo Clinic and have it removed." Before we left my father asked the doctor about my athlete's foot. Did he have a cure for that? "Of course," the doctor said matter-of-factly. "Take off your shoes." He extract-ed an electric tube, plugged it in, and soon a purplish light began to glow and flicker. The ultraviolet rays let off a smell like the smell of fresh sheets just off the line. "Ozone," my father said. After a few treatments the malady was com-pletely cured. "If I had thought about it," my father said, "we could have cured it ourselves. All we needed to do was lay you down in the backyard with your feet up in the air. Get your toes sunburned, exposed to that ultraviolet light. That would have cured it. Mushrooms are a fungus and they don't grow in the sun, and that fungus on your feet wouldn't either."

Following Dr. Inglot's advice, my father boarded the CB&Q Railroad on his free pass and rode the day coaches the several days and nights it took to get to Rochester, Minnesota. The union medical fund paid the bills. My mother stayed at home with me. She was worried, nearly out of her mind. I could see it on her face. I could see it in her walk, the way she seemed to strangely careen and lurch as if she didn't know for sure where she was or where she was going.

Although my mother did not speak of her fear, I sponged it up. I lay awake at night wondering whatever was happening to our brave father. Were they killing him in some far-off place called Mayo's? The knife! I saw the open belly of the elk and deer I had gutted. But they had more than one stomach, and my father only one. Was he bleeding to death in some hospital room? What would happen to us? The fear was like outhouse lye in the belly. And although I mis-perceived the depth of her inner strength, I knew my mother could not take care of us.

We prayed. We prayed for sweet deliverance. We could not save him. Deliver him from the knife that might transform us into Widow Spence and her small son, Gerry, who, although he bore his father's name, had never been wor-thy of it. Could our father find his way out of these woods this time? But I knew my father was not afraid. He possessed himself, and that was enough. The sur-geons at Mayo's removed half his ulcerous stomach, sewed him up, sent him home on the CB&Q and in two weeks he returned to work.

I used to wonder why this brave man should have suffered from ulcers at such an early age. Although today we can offer speculations made in accordance with the psychology of stress and its known malicious side effects, then I had no idea of the torture this poor native man underwent, captured as he was by the corporate beast, this mountain man who had run untrammeled in the woods and along the streams—how could he have survived it at all? How could he rea-son with "the boss," who knew only how to keep the ledgers straight and how to keep his men in shackles?

I can see my father raging across the supper table to my mother, his arguments bursting with passion and demands for justice. My mother, who had a minor in chemistry, seemed to understand much of what he said. At least she would nod and occasionally comment. I understood none of the scientific issues. Science was boring. Fishing and hunting were not. Chemistry to me was unalive, unrelated to anything important to a boy. But this I understood: The boss did not apply the golden rule. He cared nothing for the plight of the working man. Men were like old rags used to wipe the grease off the machinery. When they were used up they would be discarded. And the boss wouldn't listen to a good man, a just man, a scientific man like my father who made sense and offered humane and logical solutions to the problems at the plant. The boss was a "son-of-a-buck," as my father called him, the worst thing I ever heard him say of a man in front of my mother. But as many arguments as he made, my father lost them all with the boss.

Those were the sparse, sinewy times. Men were on relief, the WPA and before that the PWA. Everyone told ugly jokes about the WPA. I remember one—about how a rich woman called up and asked the WPA office to send a man down to mow her lawn. In a day or two six men appeared in her yard, and they began to dig a hole in the center of her lawn.

"What are you doing?" the woman screamed.

"We're settin' up to mow your lawn, ma'am," the foreman replied.

"Why are you digging that hole in the middle of my yard?" she demanded.

"We're fixin' to put an outhouse here."

"What!" the woman cried. "What in the world for? And what are all of these men doing here?"

"Well, ma'am, we're from the WPA. We're gonna have two comin', two goin', two shittin', and two mowin'." We kids thought the joke was very dirty and very funny.

In those hard times it was shameful for a man to be on relief. Must not be an honest man. An honest man doesn't take relief. There must be something wrong with him that no one will hire him. Francis Overton's husband had to go on relief. My mother talked about it at supper, and I was told never to mention it. The shame of it would hurt the family.

"How would you feel if our daddy had to go on relief?" she would ask. A hundred men, yes, probably a thousand, were lined up to fill my father's position, and to take the jobs of the laboring, sweating tie hacks, and the plant men who gave up their good years to keep food on the table. How could this mountain man, this hillbilly kid, as he saw himself, survive in such a world? He survived, all right. He kept his job and kept food on the table and a roof over our heads, and he sacrificed half his stomach. And later, his heart. And I knew another thing from the earliest times: When I grew up, I didn't want to lose my arguments.

One night our neighbor, Andy Sukta, the Polish policeman, came home badly hurt. He was cut above both eyes. His face was blue from the bruises where he had first been struck many blows and then, while down, kicked, and kicked again until he was nearly dead. He had been beaten up by the gamblers at one of the bars in Sheridan when, single-handed, he had attempted to shut down the saloon's slots and roulette wheels and poker games. He had been foolish, this Andy Sukta, this cop with his wide, warm grin, this one-man police force, this neighbor of ours, and friend.

My father went over to visit Andy. He found out that no one would do anything against the gamblers for their attack on Andy, not even the sheriff. My father said the sheriff was probably taking payoffs—had to be—because the games, illegal in Wyoming, were open and notorious for all to see. No one was ever arrested. The chief of police, as well, made no effort to back up his own officer, and the gambling went right on as if nothing had happened. Something was wrong.

My father, usually a quiet man, was quiet on this occasion as well. He came home from Andy Sukta's house and, without saying anything to us, fashioned himself a pair of homemade fighting knuckles. Taking several thin sheets of lead, he formed the lead to the knuckles of his right hand. Then he wrapped electrician's tape over the lead and around the palm of his hand. My father had been a boxer in college and had acquired some basic skills in the sport. With this homemade weapon adding a terrible power to his otherwise good right hand, one night he went down to the bar where Andy had been beaten up, proceeded to identify the guilty men, and cleaned up the place. I learned of it from the Sukta kids, who retold the story to me that they themselves had heard from their father.

"Your dad sure fixed up those guys who beat up our pa," Andy's youngest son, Floyd, told me. Floyd told how my father had knocked four or five of the gamblers unconscious before they understood what was happening. Then as quietly as he had entered, he left. I asked my father about it, but he refused to discuss the matter with me and forbade me ever to bring the matter up again. "And don't you ever mention this to your mother." My mother never spoke of it either, if indeed she ever knew. But once when I was looking for something in the basement, back up on the east ledge next to the foundation I found his homemade fighting knucks.

"If you get into a fight with another boy, even if he's bigger and stronger than you, and if he knocks you down, well, just get up again and go at him," my father used to tell me. "If he knocks you down again, well, get up again and go at him again. And get up again and again. Finally he will think, 'I can't beat that kid, no matter what, and he'll give up, turn tail and run.' I've done it and it works." He thought any son of his should be tough like that, brave. But I harbored a dreadful secret I forever kept from him. I was a chicken at heart. I was afraid of the bigger kids. Some of the boys my own age were stronger than I. Most were better fighters. Besides, I didn't want to be beaten up and bloodied just to be tough. But worse than the fear of being beaten up was the fear of being revealed to the world for what I was—a dastardly yellow-bellied coward.

My father thought that a true man ought never to walk with his feet out like a duck. "A man shouldn't go paddling through life like a duck paddles, with his toes pointing out." All of my life I have walked with my feet pointing out. You could tell my tracks in the snow, the duck tracks. Even when I consciously attempted to point the toes in, the tracks in the snow still pointed out. "Sissies walk with their feet pointing out." He never quite said it that way, but I knew that was what he meant. Sometimes he would secretly point to the preacher with his fat waddling butt and his duck feet, and I thought, that's the way I am. Besides, I was born with narrower shoulders than most, and I thought I had a big back end like the preacher, and so there it was, as plain as anything: Gerry Spence was a fat-assed sissy. He sure wasn't tough like his father, and although his father never said so, he probably wasn't very proud of such a son. How could he be?

One day when my father was very old, I watched him as he walked about in his garden, quite unconscious of himself. He was checking the tomatoes, nipping off buds here and there, and inspecting the grafts he had made on his apple trees. Suddenly I realized something: It took me aback. This man, this father of mine, was walking with his toes pointing out. Way out.

That same evening we went out to dinner. I watched him alight from the car, talking happily with Mae. As he walked along, I noticed it again. His toes were pointing out, farther than mine. Well, I thought, so be it. This man is ninety years old. It's about time, is it not, that he be permitted to finally walk with his toes pointing out? Then we walked into the restaurant, and I took hold of his arm, and as we followed the hostess to our table, we were two old men who came walking unashamedly through the restaurant in front of fifty people—with our toes pointing out, like a couple of old mallard ducks.

CHAPTER 10

The Bighorn Mountains.

ONE MORNING MAE called. "Your dad is very sick. I think you should come." These are the calls you don't ignore. I asked Glen DeBroder, our pilot, to roll out the plane, and we took off within the hour. A few hours later we arrived in Medford. Mae was there to meet me. She was nearly ninety herself, but she was driving her car as well as most, and better than I. At the house I found my father in bed. His face was badly swollen and he was barely able to talk. I called the doctor.

When the doctor came he sat me down in the living room without examining the old man. "Sit down," he said. "We need to talk."

"What's the matter with Dad?"

"He's going to die. The question is, what heroic action do you want to take to keep him alive? His staying alive isn't his problem. It's yours and his wife's."

"I don't think it's a matter of whose problem it is," I said. "If he's sick and if we can help him, I want to."

"*You* want it," he said.

"Yes, *I* want it."

"Well, what about your *father's* wants?"

"My father says he doesn't want to leave Mae. He's not ready to go."

"Well, he is going to have to leave Mae sometime soon. I see it all the time, Mr. Spence, adult children who are more involved with their own concerns than their parents'."

"What are you saying?"

"I'm saying we ought to let him go."

"Can we save him?"

"What for? If you have a problem with your father, you ought to work it out while you have a chance."

"What do you mean?"

"I mean you are probably driven by your guilt. Why don't you go work your problem out with your father, and then just let him go?"

"Get out of here," I said. I got up, walked past the man to the front door, opened it and waited for him to leave.

"You'll be sorry you did this," he said. "You need help, that's all I have to say."

"I think my father's the one who needs help," I said.

I got back in the plane and flew home. I called Bruce Hayse, a doctor friend in Jackson, and asked him if he could fly back with me and have a look at my father. He agreed.

When I got there with Bruce Hayse, the same doctor had returned. Mae had called him. He still hadn't examined my father. While that doctor sat in the living room, Dr. Hayse went into the bedroom and talked a little while to my father, who was as bright as he ever was, but very weak. In addition to doing a few bedside tests, Dr. Hayse looked him over well and listened to his heart and lungs. A nurse was there. Dr. Hayse asked the woman if she had a catheter, inserted the catheter and emptied the old man's bladder.

"He's suffering from acute urinary retention," he said. "He couldn't pass his water. Things were backing up on him. I think he'll be all right now."

When we came back to the living room, the other doctor said to Dr. Hayse, "Your friend here has a problem."

"I don't think we should be worrying about Mr. Spence's problem, if he has one," Dr. Hayse said, referring to me. "You were called here to help his father. Have you been in to see the old man yet?"

"No," the other doctor said. "I don't believe in heroic action to save a man as old as he."

"Nothing wrong with his father that a simple catheter won't cure. Nothing heroic about that," Dr. Hayse said. "Maybe we should get our priorities in order." Within a few days my father was up again and he and Mae went out to dinner, and nine months later he finished the book he was writing, *The Hunter*.

CHAPTER 11

Ranch buildings at Lembke-Hermburg Ranch.

By THE TIME I was ten, my first job away from home was as a yard boy, for a retired army colonel who was married to a rich eastern woman. The ranch was some twenty miles from Sheridan in the foothills of the Big Horns. My job was trimming the edges of the lawn with a pair of sheep shears, weeding, raking, and hauling off the grass the colonel cut with his power mower. I learned that in the swelter my sweat glands didn't work. I turned red, and I staggered in the heat and remained dry as a fevered child. Desperately I sought the shade whenever I could. What was the matter with me? My father sweat. All men sweat. Even babies sweat.

I thought the colonel had but one life—racing at top speed to keep up with the power mower, and facing the daily horror of his ugly, barrel-bellied shrew of a wife. I thought she hated the man. The colonel's wife changed my viewpoint of marital bliss. We would sit down together for lunch and the first thing I noticed was that no one said the blessing. I felt awkward about that. Eating without praying? Quickly I said my prayers to myself. The colonel sat across from his wife, straight and tall and lean as any soldier, red-faced and silent as the sphinx.

"Well, why don't you say something, you old son-of-a-bitch," she would begin.

Silence.

"What have you been doing all morning? You been down at the creek playing with your prick?" She was already drunk. I'd never seen a woman drunk before.

Silence.

"I am speaking to you, you old bastard." The colonel looked at his plate as if the answer were in the sickly sandwich of white bread and white cheese with white mayonnaise. "I asked you a question!" she shouted.

Silence.

Then she jumped up, grabbed a banana from the fruit bowl in the center of the table, and hit the poor man over the head with it. The banana burst, and she flayed away at him with the ruptured fruit until there was nothing left. Then, with great dignity, he arose from the table, pieces of banana still clinging to his head, and walked out of the room.

I was stricken dumb. Then, to make things worse, the woman began to cry. She sat at the table sobbing and wiping her nose across her fat bare arm, and pretty soon she got up and grabbed my hand and said, "Come with me, son. I want to show you something." Anticipating the worst I followed her into the parlor. All of the shades had been pulled to keep the sun from bleaching the fabrics. The room was cool and musty and spooky. In a niche in the parlor stood an old roll-top desk. She stopped there and sat down, pulled one of its drawers open, withdrew a scrapbook, and turned on the desk lamp. Then she began leafing through the pages slowly, a page at a time, and as I stood above her looking down, she began her narration.

"Here I am, a debutante in Philadelphia, in the year 1912." She stopped at a photograph of a pretty girl with long dark hair. "That was me." In the photo she was wearing a white dress that came down past her knees, and she also wore a sweet, wan smile, her eyes focused on something very far away. "My family was socially prominent in Philadelphia," she said. "That old son-of-a-bitch hasn't the slightest breeding, whatever. Don't you agree, darling?"

"I don't know much about that sort of thing," I said.

"Well, of course, darling," she said. She grabbed hold of my hand and held it, pointing with her other hand to a newspaper clipping yellowed with time, one of a woman with a very serious face and a bottle in her hand standing at a platform built in front of a ship's prow. "And here I am christening one of our ships during the world war," she said. "Too bad that old son-of-a-bitch wasn't killed in the war. It would have saved me the trouble." I could smell the whiskey on her breath, and I turned my head a little and held my own.

"You're not going to kill him, are you?" I asked, alarmed.

"Probably," she said.

That night I worried about the poor colonel. What was my responsibility, bearing, as I did, this terrible knowledge of her murderous intent? Should I seek out the colonel and warn him that his wife was going to kill him?

Stacked on a corner table in the log bunkhouse was a pile of those quarter-inch-thick black discs for the wind-up Victrola. On the opposite side of the room lay rows of old romance novels, their covers battered and threadbare. I turned on the Victrola trying to escape the pestiforous voice demanding that I warn the colonel. Listening to the high, nasal, jumpy singing of a woman, I read about true love in old Kentucky, a love story that peeled back a boy's heart. Finally it got dark in the bunkhouse, and I was all alone. An old owl was hooting up in the cottonwoods, and I was feeling sad for the man in the novel who had lost his true love to another. But try as I might, I could not curb my fear for the colonel. She would probably not only kill the colonel but me as well. I should go find him. But it was too dark out, and the owl was still hooting. I looked out the bunkhouse window. The big house, in the day as massive and white as a marble castle, was enveloped in the trees, and in the night, the lights out, it was a foreboding house of horror. I might stumble over his corpse in the dark, I thought, or she might be waiting for me with a butcher knife right outside the door of the bunkhouse. I locked the door, turned off the light, lay awake for a long time, and finally, when the owl quit hooting, I drifted off to sleep.

The next morning, I ventured over to the main house for breakfast. Perhaps she would demand that I sit down and eat my breakfast with her. And before I could run, she would be on me, first beating me over the head with a banana, and after that who knew what she might do. One way or the other she was probably going to kill me. That much I was pretty sure of.

I slipped quietly onto the back porch, which adjoined the kitchen. I could see that the blinds in the kitchen had been raised and the sun was shining in. Closer, I saw the colonel sitting at the kitchen table eating his bowl of oatmeal, and when he saw me at the door he called to me in a cheerful voice to come in. I walked cautiously into the kitchen. There she stood, this horror of the night before, all smiles, frying up some bacon. She had a fresh cotton dress on.

"Come in, darling." She had the raspy voice of an old sailor. "I have your breakfast cooking." She dumped some crisp bacon on the colonel's waiting plate. "Here, darling," she said, patting him lovingly on the head. "Fresh bacon!" She seemed all peppy and sweet. But I figured either the oatmeal or the bacon was poisoned.

After that first day she got wild and drunk only once in a while, and whenever she did you could tell she was contemplating how she was going to kill the colonel. But I thought the colonel, who had been in the war and had charged over the trenches at the Kaiser's machine guns and still hadn't been killed, probably knew of his wife's intent. Probably slept with his loaded Army .45 Colt automatic under his pillow.

After breakfast I tucked the Kentucky romance novel under my shirt and sneaked it to the shade of the outhouse, and sometimes when I cleaned out the manure from the horse barn, I would sit in the cool of the barn, the hay in the mow insulating the barn from the scorching summer sun, and there I would read a few minutes about love in Kentucky. And sometimes I wished I hadn't been such a coward and that I had kissed Eleanor under the bridge.

During my eleventh summer I worked at the University of Wyoming Experimental Farm south of Sheridan. The resident farmer grew different varieties of wheat and oats and barley, the rows with their little stakes and white tags, all scientific like. And we tended the gardens with their varieties of tomatoes and peppers and cabbages and potatoes. I drove teams of horses, cut the grain with horse-drawn binders, and, by hand, the other hands and I piled the bundles of grain into shocks. After the grain was dried, with three-pronged forks we flung the shocks up onto horse-drawn flatbed wagons. Then the loads were hauled to the thrasher where, with the same three-pronged forks, we threw the bundles into the thrashing machine, which ate them up like a hungry steel dragon.

The workers, some of them older boys, and some weathered men, lived in the bunking quarters above the toolshed. We put up hay and stacked it by hand, and when we came in at night our bodies were black with hay dust, and our skin scratched and raw from the alfalfa stems that hit our naked chests when the hay came plunging down from the top of the stacker. The work was dirty and my young body ached, and already I knew that I didn't want to be a farmer. But my parents thought that hard honest work would cleanse the soul, set the value of work, and, in the end, would make a man of me.

One morning we awoke to discover that a pack of coyotes had attacked the sheep during the night. A dozen ewes lay dead, their throats neatly cut as clean as if with a skinning knife. Only a small amount of the carcasses had been eaten, mainly the bags ripped away and devoured, the milk having been the primary target. I thought perhaps it had been a pack of dogs. "No," the farm manager said. "Dogs can't kill as slick as that. Dogs butcher. Coyotes slice." And I thought of how the county offered a bounty on the coyotes—as much as five dollars for a pair of coyote ears. War. And war in return. Neither coyotes nor their big

University of Wyoming Experimental Farm, Sheridan.

cousins, the wolves, in their natural state, kill for the joy of killing. They kill to survive. But in war, where the killing on both sides is always senseless and vicious, the animals, both coyote and man, become mad, aberrant beasts.

By my twelfth year the chemical, testosterone, had already started its fiendish work. It first attacks the unsuspecting childish brain. In its early stages the cynics called the disease "puppy love." If it is puppy love, I say it is as deep and painful and splendid as the full-blown kind. It is puppyish only because it is innocent. In my freshman year at Sheridan High School I fell in love with Virginia. She was a senior. Why she was interested in me was part of the exciting mystery. She was a popular girl and the president of her class. I could not believe it, but she said she was in love with me—me, this child whose voice was still the voice of a choirboy.

She had the face of a great beauty, and it was obvious to me she was a woman in every way. It must have started as a joke with her. She never told me so. I had walked her home after school, and by winter I had scratched "I love you" with my fingernail in the frost on the glass of the front door of her parents' house. My love for her was deep and divine, and it brought on an enormous happiness that burst from within me. We went to dances at the Canteen, where we played the jukebox and jitterbugged and danced close to songs like "Missed the Saturday Dance," "Deep Purple," "Always," and "It Had to Be You." I saved my money, fifty cents a week, which I earned on my paper route, and bought a new pair of black-and-white wing-tip shoes from the Montgomery Ward catalog. They didn't fit and caused open blisters on the heels, but love is brave and love could endure the pain of blisters to dance all night with Virginia and to walk her home—no limping, only far-off sweetness in my eyes, and her hand in mine, and me flashing my black-and-white wing tips into the night.

In the springtime as the chokecherries came into bloom, Virginia and I walked hand in hand through Kendrick Park, up the hillside at its edge, this woman and this boy, and there, behind the chokecherry bushes, we sat down on the grass. And in that tiny Garden of Eden with the sweet smell of the blooming bushes and the tender grass underneath, we kissed, small, tight-lipped, dry-lipped kisses, the kind Gary Cooper gave, or even Charles Boyer, and then she lay down and looked up at the sky. I lay close to her and gazed down into her face, and we were so close I thought I couldn't breathe. My voice had deserted me, and I felt the excitement pounding, even more excitement than in Buddy Taylor's garage. That she was so beautiful and so wonderful were all the words I could think of. I thought, "Oh, God," who I knew was watching, "how can I think of doing that to such a perfect person, to this person I love so much?" And suddenly I pulled away from her and jumped up.

"What's the matter?" Virginia asked, looking surprised.

"I have to go. Besides," I said, trying to hold back the tears, "I love you too much."

"Too much for what?" she asked, astonished.

I couldn't say anything more. Then I grabbed her hand and we walked down to see the monkeys in the monkey house in the little zoo at the far end of the park.

During the summer of 1943, my father took a job in Laramie with the sponge iron plant, a government experiment to determine if iron, so necessary for the war effort, could be economically extracted from the low-grade iron ores in that area. As a result of his new job we moved to Laramie, the place where I had been born thirteen years before. I would be a sophomore.

That summer the war was raging and most of the qualified men had been drafted. I advertised for summer work in the *Laramie Boomerang,* and got a job right off at a ranch near Medicine Bow. So on the first day of summer vacation my father loaded me into the family's '37 Ford along with a bedroll and a single change of clothes and hauled me off across eighty miles of sagebrush and dirt roads and desolate horizons to the Lembke-Hermburg Ranch. As we pulled out of the yard my mother came running, waving a King James version of the Holy Bible. "Here, Gerry," she said, shoving the book through the open car window. "Read this every night. You'll have time this summer to read every word. As a child one summer I read it from cover to cover myself," and with that she ran back into the house after my brother Tom, then two years old.

In the first part of June the meadow grasses had not yet matured and would not grow to a sea of waist-high blooming brome and timothy for more than a month, when the haying would begin. All ranch work is in competition with nature. And nature always wins. The ditches fill with silt, the fence posts rot and the wire falls to the ground. The corral poles splinter and decay. The barns, the sheds, slapped together from native lumber, degenerate, protesting against having been captured from nature in the first place. The manure piles up in the corrals, and before haying starts, the hands repair the fences, dig the post holes through rock and gravel by hand, and haul the wet, caked reeking manure out of the corrals in old horse-drawn manure spreaders. Ranch work is slow, brutal work. No hurry anyway, no sense of victory over nature, for next spring the work returns. Then one day the men will have grown old or crippled or will have moved on to other hard-bitten, isolated ranches, and other men will have taken their places, and the years will pass on. The years mean nothing to nature, neither the years nor the eons. Nature, with ultimate patience, will win, and the ranches will dissolve into prairies again. Where the meadows once swayed in the green waves of hot summer, the sagebrush and the fescue and other tough prairie grasses will return, and nothing will show for the meadows and the fences and the deep ditches flowing with clear irrigation water, or for the sweat of the men and the dark-night worries of the ranch owners.

I shared the bunkhouse with an entire crew of men, mostly grizzled and gravel-voiced, all rough-talking, Bull Durham–smoking, dirty men. But none was as dirty or as mean-looking, yes, and as mean as Ol' Calsey. He had no teeth in front and didn't give a shit, and his canines were long yellow fangs. He had a gruff voice made as raspy as a chain saw motor by having already drunk a tank car full of cheap whiskey by the time he was fifty.

Ol' Calsey didn't like my pious greenhorn ways, this kid who didn't cuss and didn't smoke, who shied away from the whiskey bottle when it was stuck under his nose, and also had a Bible in his suitcase. He thought I was a fat-ass jerk and that's what he called me—"The Jerk."

"That's not my name," I protested with a threat barely more potent than a pout. He looked at me with disdain. "What the fuck is your name, kid? Don't matter. Ya look like a jerk to me, and ya act like one too. So you must be a jerk." He sneered one of those awful sneers that made you think the man was made deep sick at just the sight of you, and then he turned his back on me. Pretty quick all the hands were calling me "The Jerk," not a friend among them.

The Lembke-Hermburg ranch was a large sheep operation covering thousands of acres, which spread across miles of distant, forsaken prairies, most of which were on the public domain. When, earlier in the spring, the lambing was over, the hands had cut the "dry ewes" from the main herd, these dry ewes being the females that had produced no lambs or had lost their lambs at birth to the scours or other disease or to the marauding coyotes that hung just out of rifle range. Dry ewes are the devil to herd. Having no lambs to contain them, and being driven by the same dark brutish forces that would soon invade my boyish blood, they scattered like flies in a windstorm. No one wanted the job of herding the dry ewes. Even the best Mexican herders would bare their strong, white teeth in polite smiles, shake their heads politely and whisper, "No, señor, por favor."

One night Mr. Hermburg came to the bunkhouse. He was an old German, old to me—past fifty with a powerful, handsome nose and a face ruddied by the sun. He was good with horses and good with the men, who liked him better than his officious partner, Lembke, who looked awkward in the saddle and tried to make up for it by talking loud and tough. Hermburg had a plan. Why not get rid of the Jerk? No one liked the little bastard anyway. Besides, he was a puny sort and couldn't keep up with the other men. Lucky to get a half-day's work out of the kid. But he seemed honest enough and responsible. His solution to the problem seemed perfect. Send the Jerk out to herd the dry ewes.

"Gerry," he began with a heavy German accent that sounded like my Grandpa Pfleeger's, but he smiled when he spoke. "I make you a deal. A herder I need for the dries. If you herd 'em until hayin' starts, ten dollars a month more I pay. Lot more than you're gettin'. When hayin' starts I come up and get ya. Okay?"

"Okay," I said, without knowing what I was agreeing to. Ten dollars was ten dollars. And that was how, at thirteen, I became a sheepherder. By nightfall, bursting with pinfeathers and pimples, I found myself alone, all alone, in the backcountry of Wyoming in charge of a thousand bestial, empty-bellied, empty-sacked, bleating, wild-eyed females—the infamous herd of dry ewes.

Never was gathered on the face of the earth such a filthy, tick-infested, repugnant flock of females: those skinny stick legs, those splayed feet, the hooves curled upward, those bloated bellies—their empty, repulsive bags swinging to and fro with every stride like irrelevant, hanging hide. And the way they darted here and there, looking for what, startled by what, Lord knows, their feet stamping, stamping, like cranky children in tantrums. And those eyes—staring, peering orbs glazed with idiocy—what had I been sentenced to, imprisoned in an endless wasteland with a congregation of imbeciles, all dressed in the same gray and greasy prison suits? Still, as I later thought about it, the dries must have possessed a power greater than our own. Here I was, herding them to their grazing, finding their water, protecting them from every danger. At rutting season they were even furnished the rams to satiate their lust, and at last we saw to their quick and merciful deaths.

I slept in the traditional sheepherder's wagon, a horse-drawn affair that sat on top of a set of old rubber tires with a round canvas roof held up by staves like the covered wagons of old. The wagon was furnished with a wood-burning stove and a fold-down kitchen table. Behind the table lay a bunk with a worn cotton mattress pocked with mice holes, and a gasoline lantern hung overhead from a hook affixed to the roof.

Every morning, long before the meadowlarks began their delirious warbling, even before the sun had once more risen, I was jolted from my slumber by a noise sounding like a long, mournful flatus escaping from the colon of the earth, the first bleating of the dries. Soon other ewes joined in until a thousand discordant gaseous voices provided a chorus befitting the conventions of hell. Still, before the sun rose, the dries, empty-wombed, with nothing tugging at their teats and lusty as pissants in heat, scattered in every direction in search of whatever might cool their passion or satisfy their shameless gluttony. At the first such chorus from the flock, I bounded from bed in my long underwear, the temperature near freezing, bent on my duty to hold the herd together.

In the bunkhouse I had heard Ol' Calsey and the other men exchanging their vulgar tales of certain depraved herders they had known who, they claimed, engaged in the unspeakable "it" with some special ewe in the herd. I can hear their laughter still. But how could a person do such a thing? Once, out of a boy's curiosity, and with a stick, a long stick, I barely touched an old ewe's "pinky," as the older hands called it, and the ewe's tail clamped down on the stick like the shutter valve on a two-cylinder John Deere tractor. And it *was* pink—an awful crusty pink, and the smell of a sheep was revolting to the utmost. Therefore, I gave little credence to such stories. Still, the loneliness was maddening.

Sometimes, there on the prairies, I screamed out loud at the top of my lungs, but the sound of my voice was instantly absorbed in a hundred miles of emptiness. No one answered. No one heard. Occasionally some old ewe, gazing up with dull eyes, and chewing a mouthful of fescue and sage, would bleat a repulsive reply. No sooner had I herded the thousand together than they were off in a cloud of dust running in still every other direction, so that I was soon worn down to a bundle of rags and rattling bones.

All sheep do not look alike. Sheep are individuals, too, identifiable by subtle differences—a spot, a splayed hoof, the tip of an ear frozen off, a missing eye, a stubby nose, a long dewlap—differences apparent to any person with ordinary powers of observation. It's not that we're unable to recognize the difference in sheep or men. Our high-headed arrogance clouds our vision. By summer's end I was able to identify nearly every one of the thousand and, I admit, I began naming them. Wasn't that man's biblical duty, to name all the creatures on the face of the earth? So I named the dries: Abigail, Alice, Arta, Agnes, Annis, Arlene. I named the least revolting ewes, the ones exhibiting the faintest trace of dignity, after women I secretly admired—Helen, my piano teacher, for instance—and I also named a certain very large-bagged ewe for the fat neighbor woman of my childhood.

There was, however, one young ewe who stood out from the herd in the same way that certain comely girls command the eye. She was blond, quite trim, and her tail had escaped the docking knife, and in the presence of her exorbitantly unattractive herdmates she was, indeed, devastatingly beautiful. Of course I called her Heidi. While the others expressed their obvious disdain for me in endless ways, Heidi followed me everywhere I went like a faithful pup, often nibbling at my pants cuff or brushing up against my leg, begging to be petted. If I sat down on the top of a high ridge to watch my flock, she would likely be found lying at my feet. I reciprocated, of course, by offering a friendly word or an occasional approving glance, and as time dragged on, with no one else to talk to, I found myself conversing aloud with Heidi, who I discovered was quite sensible for her age and status in the universe.

"Heidi," I would exclaim at a crisp, clear, endless blue sky in the cool of the morning before the sun rose to scorching heights. "What a nice day we've been given!"

"Yes," she replied without emitting a sound. "Yes, Gerry, yes! It is a miracle! Life is quite itsy."

"Quite itsy?"

"Yes, and also upsy," she cried silently.

"Well, you certainly sound very smart for a blond little ewe who hasn't even had her tail docked yet. So tell me, if you know so much, what is life?"

"Life is a jump, like this—and four footprints in the dust."

"That sounds nice," I said, jumping and landing on all fours. And at that moment I understood and at the moment of understanding I felt afraid.

"Aren't you ever afraid, Heidi?"

"No," she said. "I'm too afraid to be afraid."

"But there are coyotes out here that can eat you. They might even eat me."

"One must keep one's faith on," she said, and went off grazing.

As the kinder light of June began to fade and the hard and glaring light of July arose, my relationship with Heidi grew intimate. I spoke to her as one might speak to a wise and compassionate friend, for, as I began to believe in my loneliness, if one is in the presence of another creature for long periods of time, and if one listens for the universal tongue by which even buttercups and June bugs converse, one can easily learn to converse with an intelligent young ewe.

"I have eaten sheep," I confessed one day out of the blue. "I didn't mean to. But I ate my friend Cousin."

"That is horrible," Heidi replied. "I would never eat you nor your cousin."

"Sheep are better than people," I said, suddenly understanding their superiority.

"Not always," she replied. Then she said nothing more.

So it was that one day Heidi and I were engaged in the serious business of life, that is, jump-jumping and landing on all fours in the dust, this time across Alkali Creek, when, somehow distracted, she fell into a fearsome bog. She struggled vainly to free herself, and as she floundered, her eyes began to bulge with fear.

"Save me!" she cried.

"Keep your faith on," I cried back, but slowly she was sucked down and down until only the tip of her little nose remained above the surface. I had no choice. I jumped in after her. I fought to the surface of the bog and struggled for my footing. Yes, thank God! I could feel the uneven surface of the foundation rocks. I grabbed hold of her ears and pulled her head above the surface and cleared the mud from her nostrils.

"Keep your faith on!" I cried again. Then I threw both arms around her and with every ounce of strength left in my skinny boy's body, I moved her toward the bank, heave at a time. Only when I was able to grab a willow bush on the creek's edge could I predict victory. Utterly exhausted I finally pulled the two of us to safety.

"Upsy daisy dandy," I gasped.

But Heidi didn't reply. "Upsy and itsy," I gasped again. Still Heidi made no reply. We lay there on the grassy bank stuck together, coated with black muck, too spent to move, too weak to separate from each other. How long we lay there I cannot say. I remember the early morning sun was warm and felt good. And life was good. No longer was I alone. But as suddenly, she was up and staggering on her feet, and before long this mud-covered lamb was following me once more, as if it had all been but a dream.

After that, Heidi was never out of my sight. At night she followed me to the sheep wagon, and some nights I lifted her into the wagon and she curled up on my bunk to sleep. Sometimes I awoke in the morning to find an arm thrown carelessly across her body and my head pillowed against her yellow fleece.

Then one day I saw old man Hermburg's pickup coming from forty miles away. I shooed Heidi into the herd.

"Don't worry," I said. "He's only bringing fresh supplies."

"I'm afraid of them," Heidi whispered.

"Keep your faith on," I replied, and then she walked slowly away from me and began grazing with the others, and by the time Mr. Hermburg arrived I had lost sight of her in the flock.

There was another man in the pickup with Mr. Hermburg, a skinny, nasty-looking man with beady black eyes like a lecherous rat.

"Well, Gerry, my boy, I come back like I say. He take over," Mr. Hermburg said, motioning to the man as they stepped out of either side of the truck. "Need ya for hayin' in the mornin'."

"I'll stay on, Mr. Hermburg," I said.

"Romeo, here, don't know how to drive a team a horses. But you do," Hermburg said. Then he laughed and glanced into the sheep wagon. I looked where he was looking. On the floor several telltale small brown pellets were scattered about, left behind by Heidi. "You a *real* sheep man now, I see," Mr. Hermburg said, with an accusing grin on his face. But I was quicker than he expected.

"I've had a time of it with one of the dries," I said, shaking my head and attempting to leave the clear impression, without saying so, that one of the ewes had been sick and I had had to doctor her in the sheep wagon.

"Uh huh," Mr. Hermburg said doubtfully. "I better get ya back to the ranch before it's too late. Them sheeps look nervous." He laughed again.

"Nervous, sir? I've tried to keep 'em calm," I said. "But they scatter like everything. Run my ass right offa me." I wanted to sound like one of the men.

"You know how that old sayin' goes?" he asked in his German accent. " 'Wyomin's where men are men, and the sheep are nervous.' " He threw his head back and laughed a big long laugh.

"Well, these dries sure *are* nervous," I said, innocently. "But I'll stay on, sir!"

"Come on," Mr. Hermburg said. "Let's get your stuff loaded. Hayin's already started. Forty acres down and the sweeps are already goin'. An old team of bays are waitin' for you. I'll be needin' a scatter raker in the fields in the mornin'."

I didn't know what to say. And then Mr. Hermburg put his arm around my shoulder and said, "She'll be okay. Romeo, here, take good care of her. Right, Romeo?" He winked at the Mexican. I had no choice.

Then as Mr. Hermburg started up the truck, Romeo walked up to my side, leaned into the cab and whispered, "Wheech one ees she, boy?" He had the lustful look of a two-peckered billygoat, and his breath was as foul as a brooder house boar's. "They all look alike ta me." Then through tear-filled eyes I searched the herd for one last glimpse of Heidi, and as I left that land of boyish fantasy for the hard world of men, she was lost to me forever.

CHAPTER 12

Wyoming deer herd.

I HAD BEEN sitting with my father at his bedside after Dr. Hayse, with a simple plastic tube, had saved him. Now he was eating well and was up and around a little more every day. It wasn't the first time he had worked his way back to life. To live is work, but my father would have agreed with Emerson: "Give me health and a day, and I will make the pomp of emperors ridiculous."

Nearly forty years before, in 1954, my father had been hunting white-tailed deer in the Black Hills of Wyoming near Sundance. He had taken Barbara and Tom along, both by then in high school. As was his way, he had separated from his children to hunt alone and, probably, to walk down the deer whose misfortune it had been to find my father on his trail. I remember old Charlie Colmer, a tie hack and one of my father's hunting partners, telling me once, "Why, I've seen that dad of yours take out after a deer in good tracking snow, and pretty soon here would come the deer, his old tongue a-hangin' and his head almost to the ground, and right behind him would be your dad, a big grin on his face, hardly broke into a sweat." On this day my father was in his mid-fifties, the deer a lot younger. Suddenly my father was felled by a heart attack. He lay helpless in the deep snow.

"Dad," I said to him, now at his beside those many years later, "tell me the story about the time you had your heart attack." I'd heard parts of the story before, but now I cherished my father's storytelling, and I hoped reminding him of his past victories over "the old man with the scythe," as he referred to death, would urge him to win again.

He sat up in bed a little straighter, the sparkle coming to his old eyes, and a small smile crept over his nearly wrinkle-free face. "Well, I was walking along on this deer's trail. 'Bout ten inches of old snow on the ground. It had melted and then frozen and left a hard crust on top. A fellow could just about get up on the snow when it would break through. Tough walkin' through that stuff. Harder on the deer. He had *four* feet to fall through the snow, not two." He smiled a little at his own joke.

"Well, I hears this buck snort, and he jumps out, a little two-point, and I down him. My shot spooks another little buck, and just as he's goin' over the ridge, I let fire. Got three licenses to fill, mine and the two kids. I dresses the first little buck out, and I walk up to where the second buck was when he disappeared over the ridge and there he was, deader'n a doornail. I dressed him out, and then I starts back for the camp. I was feelin' rotten and every breath was like a dash of cold water inside me, and then I stooped down where the trail went under a tunnel of thick pine bows, and it hit me, just like that, and I fell facedown in the snow.

"Pretty soon I came to and I got up in a sitting position and sat there for quite a while until I got a little strength back. I knew I couldn't get out of there without help, and I knew if I just laid there I'd freeze to death."

"Weren't you scared?" I asked.

"No," he said. "I just kinda scooted myself along until I could get up on a little deadfall under an old pine tree, and there were pine cones and needles there, and I pulled some bark off the tree and found some twigs, and some rotten wood from the deadfall, and a I got a fire goin'. I was shiverin' and the fire felt good. We always had an emergency signal—you remember?" I nodded. "Three quick shots followed by a pause and then three more shots. Tom heard the shots and he started over from where he was huntin', and I kept shootin' volleys of three until Tom found me. Finally he saw the smoke from my fire."

"What then?"

"Well, I couldn't walk. But I knew where the rancher's house was, old Alex Smith's place near where we were hunting, and I told Tom how to get there. Took Tom about forty-five minutes to get up to Smith's place and about that long to get back. Tom told me later that Smith didn't seem too excited. He told Tom, 'Don't worry, son. I've had a couple of them heart attacks myself, and I'm still hangin' around, ain't I?'

"In the meantime I got nice and cozy by the fire and I drifted off to sleep. I was awakened by the sound of shod hooves clattering on the rocky trail above me, and I looked up and there was Tom and old Alex Smith. Smith was looking down at me. I remember he said to Tom, 'He looks sorta puny, don't he?'

"They got me up on the horse Tom had been riding, and I held on with both hands, and they hauled me back to camp. We had camped in an abandoned schoolhouse. Had a good cast iron stove in it, but the flue was plugged with a pack rat's nest and we nearly smoked ourselves out. And it was cold. Good camp, though. Late that afternoon here comes Alex Smith with those two little bucks of mine lashed on a pack horse. He dumped them off in the snow and said, 'See you in the mornin'.' We stayed in the schoolhouse that night, and all night I could hear the wind blowin', and I knew it was blowin' drifts across the road, and we might have a devil of a time getting out with that old Packard I was drivin'.

"Next mornin' I ate some cold meat and some bread. The kids tied the little bucks up on the luggage rack, but they couldn't drive that old Packard through that rutty road and the drifted snow, so I drove out."

"You should have been in a hospital," I said. "Weren't you afraid you were going to die?"

"No," he said. "What's to be afraid of? If you die, you die. Nothin' to be afraid of there. What a man needs to be afraid of is *not living*'." He looked at me as if he'd said something important he wanted me to hear.

"Well," he went on, "on the way out we jumps a bunch of white-tail. We needed one more to fill our licenses. I slid out of the car and shot from the road. Got a nice dry doe. Barb and Tom dressed it out, and put it up on top of the Packard with the two bucks, and on out we went."

"That was a crazy thing to do, Dad," I said.

"What's so crazy about that?" he asked, as if he truly didn't understand. Had he been a piano virtuoso suffering from a ruptured heart, he would likely have struggled to the piano bench to play one last concerto. Most often his innocence protected him, an innocence I have often coveted, but innocence, like virginity, can never be retrieved. Only years later did I begin to understand. He had promised himself to life. And, in the end, a commitment to life, as my father must have known, is the only defense against the fear of death.

He went on with his story. "Eight hours later we were home. Stayed all night at Laramie. Went to the Fort Collins hospital the next day where my insurance was good. The doctor took one listen to my heart and put me in the hospital. I was there a month, with the oxygen tubes up my nose and all that stuff, and then I went home and fiddled around for a month, and then I was back to work, full-time, overtime, all the rest. Well, you know."

And I knew. And after that he had a couple more heart attacks, and he dealt with them in about the same way, as if they were a temporary nuisance, like a sudden rainstorm when you're putting up the hay. The news of his first heart attack came to me, as usual, in one of his periodic telephone calls.

"And by the way," he added to whatever he'd been saying to me on the phone, "I'm in the hospital. Had a little heart attack the other day while I was huntin' white-tails up at Sundance."

My father undoubtedly experienced fear, but he dealt with it differently than I. But the difference in the way my father and I dealt with our fear reflected the way we each perceived death. It was all right with my father that he should die; not a wish, but an acceptance. Life and death were inextricably connected. To live, one must accept the other side of life. My father's acceptance of death freed him to live. I had not arrived at that harmonious juncture. Death was unacceptable. Death, to me, was the ultimate, the ubiquitous fear. And since living brought one closer to death, and since each challenge could end in defeat, which I experienced as something akin to dying, I dared not be defeated. I had not accepted his view—"If one dies, one dies." I had, instead, absorbed my mother's—"Whatever will we do if we miss the train?"

During most of my life, death, or its close relatives, lurked in every breath, and underscored every challenge. Every ache, every pain, every mole, every palpitation of the heart, every phone call, every message to call the office, to call home, any loss in the courtroom could be a harbinger of death, or death's little brothers—defeat or disgrace, injury or infamy, fault or failure.

"Don't be afraid," my father had said to me as a child. But even now I blame myself. I, the great question-asker, should have asked better questions of him. I should have asked: "How can I *not* be afraid?"

Fear to my father was an emotion he understood as a kind of spin-off from the atavistic brotherhood in which both life and death were members. The same forces that cause the lark to fly in fright, the frog to hop in fear and that urge the lion to attack, also out of fear, those emotions that were intended to run free in man and beast alike, were often, by him, held captive. And they attacked where they were imprisoned. They attacked first his belly and then his heart and finally his lung and colon and prostate. I say he never ran from death, for if he did he would be running, as well, from life. He stood his ground, like a gnarled old pine on the crest of the ridge. Like the tree, he took in the wind, and the ice and the thaw, and he soaked up the sun, and his needles grew very green and his massive old trunk grew twisted and bent. Over the years he dropped his cones, and after many more winters came a day when the old tree was taken back into the hard earth, and in its place sprouted a small shoot, its new needles yellow and tender. And I should think, as an old buck came browsing by, its wet black nose close to the ground sniffing here and there for buds, it would have come onto the small sprouting pine, and as if armed with an infinite knowing, it would have stepped carefully aside and browsed on by.

CHAPTER 13

Imaging, Mae, Gerald M. and Gerry Spence.

MY FATHER WAS ninety-two when he died, and it is a wonder that he should have died at all, for he never grew old. His body just shriveled away. His arms grew as thin as a boy's, the skin that covered his old skull seemed tight and very thin, and his cheeks had begun to sink in. The legs that had walked down many deer in the mountains, legs as strong as a mule's, became thin and white, and after a few feet of walking from his bed, quivered under the wasted weight of his body. But he was not old. His mind still bloomed. As he had experienced life with a childlike awe at its unfolding, so too, he anticipated death. He claimed death was a once-in-a-lifetime experience, and he was going to be there to see it through. At the last, a creeping sort of weakness sent him to his bed once more. He was having trouble breathing. His heart, he said. He looked worn out, like something beyond further repair.

"I'd like to go," he whispered. "Time, ya know. But I don't want to leave Mae alone." He had known that his time was short. He said, "I am nearing that long skid into oblivion and I pray—we all pray one way or another—that my death will be quick and painless." But he had fought to be the last to go.

Just before his death, my younger brother Tom, then past fifty, and Dad were recalling some of their early days together, as they often did. And as was his way, my father was thinking not what his death meant to him, but how his death would affect his family. Tom said, "Dad spoke to me in that simple, metaphoric way of his. He said, 'I'm sorry that I can't take your hand and help you cross the creek, little boy. . . . ' "

I arrived at his bedside the morning following his death. Mae had been with him to the last. He lay in their bedroom with his hands over the top of the covers as if he were sleeping. After he was gone, the day nurse, who knew about such things, had closed his eyes. His untouched face appeared peaceful, looked like he was sleeping, but you could tell he was dead. Mae left me with him in the bedroom.

"Daddy," I said. Even now I hoped it was all a mistake, that he would come back as he always had. But this time he had made no promises.

No answer. I saw the shape of his mouth and the dent where the small cancer had been removed from his lower lip. Even in death, his mouth was shaped like mine, I thought. And in life, sometimes he formed his words like I form mine.

"Daddy." I reached over and touched his hand. It was cold. Then I began to cry. I didn't try to fight the tears. People are permitted to cry over their dead fathers. It was my right. And as he had said, the tears were not for him, but for me.

"Daddy," I cried, still a small boy in the woods. "Don't leave me alone out here."

After a while I said, "You were a mighty fine father." And I was glad I had taken the opportunity on many an occasion to tell him so. I doubt that he ever doubted it, as I have so many times doubted my own success as a father. He was as accepting of himself as he was of fate, and of life and of death and of me.

There in the bedroom of his home, the sun shining through the east window, lay my dead father. I could understand death for him, and it was not horrible. I thought the sun might be too hot on his face. I pulled the shades. Then I sat down beside him and held his hand and I thought about his dignity and bravery. Had he been given the chance to pass judgment on the event, he would have been satisfied.

"Were you with him when he died?" (Later, I asked Mae.)

"Yes," she said. She had a distant look on her face and that small sweet smile. I couldn't put the question quite right. "How was it?" I finally asked.

"Well," she said, as if sharing a very great intimacy, "I came into the bedroom, and he was having a hard time breathing. He was just in terrible labor. And I said, 'Honey, I wish you didn't have to struggle so hard.' And he said, 'Honey, I'd go except I don't want to leave you alone.' And I sat down beside him, and I reached over and I took his hand, and I said, 'Honey, you can go,' and he looked up and smiled at me and closed his eyes—and he was gone."

❀   ❀   ❀

After Mr. Hermburg wrenched me from Heidi and drove me down from that herd of dry ewes, he deposited me in the barn behind a team of old plugs who I would hitch to a scatter rake. I had learned to harness and drive a team at the university's experimental farm the summer before, and before that at Grandpa Spence's farm where he'd taught me to drive his team of old mules.

I followed the other teams driven by the men out to the long fields bordering both sides of the mountain stream that fed the meadows and nourished the native grasses into the season's stand of hay. One could wear oneself out tromping through those thick jungles of grass. Even the horses could not run in it, the blooming tassels of brome above their bellies, the grass as dense as fur and deep green, and the smell of it, after the horse-drawn mowers laid it down, sweet and clean. After the mowers came the rakes with their teeth bouncing over the uneven ground, pulling the hay into windrows where the grass would dry in the high, hot sun. After the hay was dry came the horse-drawn sweeps, a powerful draft animal, usually a Percheron, on each side of a scoop crafted of twenty or more oak teeth nearly ten feet long, the driver standing on a small, one-wheeled platform behind, guiding the team down the windrows of hay. And when the sweep was bulging full, the hay piled as high as the driver's head, and higher, the driver turned the horses toward the stacker, drove them up onto the teeth of the stacker and backed them off, "Back now, Johnny, back now Bill," until the load of hay was left behind. Then the man drove the empty sweep back to the field for yet another load.

At the stack, the stacker team took over, usually a kid driving, because all the kid had to do was drive the team straight down the line. The team already knew where to go—been there a thousand times and back. They knew where to stop. And they knew when to back up to the beginning point again, the kid mostly following the horses. As the stacker team pulled, the stacker teeth, loaded with the hay, followed the cable upward, lifted the hay to the top of the slanting, poled affair and, when the hay reached the top, dumped the hay over the top of the stacker onto the stack below. The stackers, who got extra pay, stood back waiting for the hay to fall and the dust to settle. Then they pushed the hay to the four corners and tromped it out to the edges, and they sweat in the dust and drank from the same jug of water. At night they were dirty, and dog-tired. Sometimes they went to the creek to bathe in the cold, clear water, and sometimes after supper they sat around the bunkhouse, drinking cheap whiskey, smoking Bull Durham cigarettes they could roll with one hand, and talking about the whores in the houses in Rawlins.

I drove a scatter rake at first, followed the sweeps and raked up the hay the sweeps, with their large coarse teeth, had missed. Scatter rakers trotted their horses, old gentle horses most any kid could drive. I trotted mine, and I thought it was very fine to be sitting up high on the seat of a rake bouncing along over the fields. And later I became a regular raker, driving a better team of horses and making the windrows, so that when the rake was full, I stomped on the trip.

Then the rake teeth flew up releasing the hay, and then down they fell again, the teeth bouncing over the rough ground until they had filled with hay once more. And so the process would continue, windrow after windrow, the old horses sweating, their tails switching the flies, their heads down, their paces becoming slower and slower until I had to swat them on the butts with the reins again and holler, "Geet up!"

Sometimes I sang. With my cracking, changing voice, I sang "Old Man River," trying to sound like Paul Robeson. Other times I belted out "Waltzing Matilda," and I bounced to the music's rhythm on the iron seat held up like the stem of a

Stacking hay on Wyoming ranch.

toadstool made of spring steel. Sometimes, exhausted by the heat, I sat slumped over, as worn out and empty of energy as the old horses, whose steps, if you didn't holler now and again and slap them with the reins, would get slower and slower until at last they would come to a standstill.

One day in the heat of August that summer of '42, I pulled the team over near a cut bank at the bottom of which seeped a fresh spring of clear, cool water. The redwing blackbirds were singing in the nearby swamp, their song a discordant "sca-wing, sca-wing." I thought I was a better singer of better songs than the blackbirds, but somehow the birds were smarter than I. They sang all day in the marsh, while I was working and sweating behind these old horses.

I got off the rake to get a drink, kept the reins in my hand and stretched down over the bank toward the water. Suddenly the bank caved in. I let out a holler in surprise, jerked the reins as I fell, and the old team bolted, pulled the reins out of my hands, and now I faced my first dreaded runaway. Helplessly I watched as the horses ran, and the faster they ran, the more the rake bounced and the more frightened the horses became. They ran until the rake was broken into pieces, a huge wheel, nearly as tall as I, rolling across the field like a hoop exploding from the hands of a giant, and another wheel bursting off the rake and rolling in the opposite direction as the horses ran in a great circle. At last, exhausted, their bodies covered with sweat, their flanks all foamy, their sides heaving, the team came to a stop at the fence and waited for me to come get them, their old bodies quivering and wet. They stood there ashamed, I thought, looking back at me with plaintive eyes, their traces still attached to what was left of the steel frame of the rake.

Nobody said anything to me at supper. I was now the proven jerk. I had had a "runaway," which was considered the sign of gross incompetence on the part of any driver. Yet, strangely, after my runaway I was somehow elevated in the eyes of the men—not everybody had experienced such a catastrophe, and mine had been one hell of a runaway. Tore the rake all to hell. Kid wasn't hurt.

"Had a runaway, didn't ya, kid?" Ol' Calsey said that evening at the bunkhouse.

"Yeah."

"Lucky bastard, ya didn't get kilt."

"Yeah, I guess."

"Coulda got tied up in that fuckin' rake and you'd a been a piece a fuckin' meat."

Lucky little son-of-a-bitch, that kid. And after that Ol' Calsey took me with him to Elk Mountain, population about ten, a store, a bar, and a dance hall. But Elk Mountain was the place. A creek ran through the town, and the state highway ran through the town, and most of the traffic passed right on through the town as well except on Saturday nights, when folks came from miles around to the dance. The famous country-and-western bands played in Elk Mountain at the Garden Spot Pavilion. Big time. The floor of the dance hall was famous too—built on old truck springs so when the music got wild, the floor jumped up and down to the beat of the song, and the cowboys jumped with the floor, and vice versa. The place was crazy with drunks beating their boots to the music, stomping, grinning and hollering, Ol' Calsey among 'em, swinging and stomping with some scraggly old ranch cook like the two of them were stacking hay.

Garden Spot Pavilion, Elk Mountain.

His old mouth was stained in the corners by tobacco and he was grinning, and slobbering, and hollering, and drunk off his ass, and so was she.

That same night I met a girl there in the dance hall. She was standing over in the corner looking ready, and I gathered up my courage and swaggered up to her, and asked her if she would care to dance.

"Can't dance," she said.

"How come?" I asked.

"Never learned how out here." She had freckles and she wore a tight sweater. She was older than I. At least sixteen, and you could see it in her sweater and everything.

"Wanna learn?" I asked.

"Not here," she said.

"Where ya want to go?"

"I don't know," she said.

"Come on," I said, like a big shot, like Humphrey Bogart without a cigarette, and she followed me out of the dance hall.

We walked down the road toward the saloon, and I walked with my swagger, and I felt very big and very important. When we got into the shadows of some giant old cottonwoods she stopped, and I stopped. And she kissed me, and I kissed her back like Errol Flynn kissed in the movies. And then she sat down under the tree and I sat down, and we kissed a lot more and I said things like, "You are wonderful," and she didn't answer, just kissed back and I felt what was under her sweater, and got all lightheaded, the blood leaving my head and all, and I was breathing very fast, and I said things like, "God Almighty!" and she didn't say anything. And then she got up and said, "I gotta go. My mom's waitin' over at the bar." And she left and that was it.

I went back to the dance hall, like a young stud in heat, and I asked some other girls to dance, but nobody would, because I was too young and I had those pimples, and what self-respecting girl would dance with a skinny kid, whose voice was popping and whose face was also? "Wanna dance?" sounded like a screeching fiddle. Then I thought maybe the girl with the freckles would be over at the bar, and so I went back over there to look for her.

The saloon was one of those old-time rustic rooms—a long pine bar, no stools, the walls of rough-sawed, unpainted boards, sawdust ankle deep on the floors so that the cowboys could spit as they pleased. Ol' Calsey was there. He was trying to make it with a little brown Mexican woman who was round as a post, but who had two big ones all stuck up there high in her uplift bra. She looked more tired than drunk. Ol' Calsey hollered at her: "Hey Nellie, ya 'member me? Come on over here and I'll buy ya a goddamned drink."

"This here woman's drinkin' with me," a stout Mexican wearing an old black leather vest and a dirty, black cowboy hat hollered. He held her back.

"You fuckin' wetbacks ain't even s'posed ta be here," Ol' Calsey shouted. Everybody in the saloon stopped their talking and their drinking to watch the fight comin' on. Good fight every Saturday night at the Elk Mountain Saloon. People looked forward to it. Ol' Calsey walked over and grabbed Nellie by the wrist and started to pull her over to him, and as fast as he did, the knife flashed out, came out of nowhere, came up and out and smashed into Ol' Calsey above the belt, sticking into where the liver lies. Ol' Calsey didn't even blink. Doubt he knew what hit him, but surprise spread over his face, and his eyes got very large, and the blood started to soak up his shirt. Then the Mexican hit him twice more, the last thrust striking a rib, and Ol' Calsey felt that, and by this time his crooked legs began to get weak and he started to fold. Then the Mexican grabbed the woman named Nellie and ran out, and somebody hollered to stop him.

"That goddamned Mexican just stabbed a man," somebody else hollered, but nobody went after him. He had a knife, and he knew how to use it, and he would use it, and outside it was dark.

Ol' Calsey was sitting on the floor in the sawdust, dazed and blubbering like a stuck ox. Red foam was coming out of his mouth, and his one cocked eye was looking up as if he were deep in prayer, and the other was looking down where he had been stabbed.

"I'll get ya to a doctor," I said.

"I been kilt over nothin' but a Mexican whore," he gurgled through the blood. Then he slowly slumped to the floor. "Gotta get him to Rawlins," somebody said. Couple of men pulled him up and hauled him to the yellow pickup Ol' Calsey had borrowed from the ranch. They laid the man out in the pickup bed, and I got in with him and held his head.

"Yer gonna make it, Calsey," I said. I don't know which drunk cowboy was driving. "You're gonna be back stackin' hay in no time at all."

"You ain't no jerk, kid," Calsey said.

He was in the hospital for fourteen days. Then he went east to be with his sister for a while until he got back on his feet again.

From the time I was fourteen my father and mother had been in the process of leaving me. They explained, mostly to themselves, for at that age I was not a good listener, that the child leaving home was like the baby bird leaving its nest. It is frightening for the small bird, but still the bird wants to go, and despite the dangers, the bird will not stay. It is nature's way. The bird is willing. And I had been willing, and my parents, likely relieved to have that noisy, impetuous teenager out of their sight, were also willing.

Fourteen is a fragile age for a boy. That evil potion, *testosterone*, surging unchecked in my veins, caused me, the pubescent male, to present nearly every classic sign and symptom of psychosis yet recorded. Reason had abandoned me. Without provocation I found myself quarreling with authority, any authority, my father, my mother, my teachers. I began to suffer delusions of my perfect wisdom.

My parents, once near deities to me, suddenly turned into strangers. In the developing throes of adolescence, I became obsessed with weird, nonsensical music and, reverting to primitive genes, I perfected the barbaric dance I had already encountered the year before known then and now as the "jitterbug." Ask any father, any mother. If they speak to you forthrightly out of their dismay and grief, they will admit it: Their adolescent sons are, plainly put, quite simply deranged.

That hormone, testosterone, with which Mother Nature cruelly saturates the human male, is to blame. Chinese lords castrated certain male children to keep them safe from the evil stuff and to preserve their sweetness and innocence. An allegedly civilized people neuter their dogs and cats, and the rancher does the same to his bull calves and his horses, for one reason—to save the male of the species from the monstrous mutations brought on by that hideous hormone.

Indeed, the human male, his blood laced with testosterone, is the most dangerous of all creatures occupying space on the earth. That loathsome hormone is responsible for most murders, most child and spousal abuse, most wars and most of the other misery inflicted upon the earth and her inhabitants. If we could drain testosterone from the blood, the brain would suddenly clear, logic would reemerge, the eyes of killers would soften, and kindness and wisdom would prevail. Testosterone is the chemical of male insanity. It is the hormone that transfers all thought from the brained head to the brainless head. By its power, men impregnate every breathing female and then engage in vicious wars to kill off their own offspring. By its power men impregnate every woman in sight and then allow the resulting children to starve in the streets.

In the waning days of that summer, I became the new kid at Laramie High School, the family having moved from Sheridan to Laramie. I wish I could have understood the viciousness of the chemical that hurled me so wild-eyed and so ruthlessly psychotic into puberty. I grieve that I was blinded to the beauty of those two loving, blameless people, my parents, who were helplessly lost in dealing with this teenaged maniac they had spawned. And for me to rediscover thereafter who I was would thereafter occupy the better part of my life to follow. Wiser was I as a child who knew who he was, or, wiser still, who was wise enough never to have thought to ask the question.

Under the consuming influence of testosterone, I began to see my parents as simple, bothersome old fogies whose old-fashioned rules were disgustingly irrelevant to the likes of me. I had no patience for them or their dated, dowdy ideas that, so far as I could tell, were calculated to deprive a person of all life's experiences except Sunday School, church, and study. Everything else was out. I found myself pitying them in a way. They were not, as is said, "hip." They were old-fashioned oddities, the most annoying kind of anachronism.

Yet, I began to feel a power, a sort of heady exuberance, a kind of wonderful recklessness that left me unattached from my acts. Although I heard no voices, I was guided by an overwhelming sense of invincibility, the sense that injury, even death, were ideas that had no application to me. I could take on the world.

I felt trapped living with those strangers, and I wanted out. Yet I was afraid to leave, because I had had no experience in independence. I felt irreconcilably conflicted, in response to which I struck out with sarcasm and scorn at any and all. I was irreverent and irresponsible. In sum, I, like so many spirited youth in the depths of puberty, was entirely mad.

I remember the intense joy I felt in those glorious early fall days on the high Laramie plains, the sky clear, the air crisp as cut crystal, a joy that has since become more measured and—I sorrow over it—less passionate. I could smell the seasons then, and the smells intoxicated me as even today I can smell the seasons, but with less allurement. I roared out with an eternal fervor to get on with life, to bare my soul naked. And who could stop me—me, the new guy beginning his sophomore year at Laramie High?

The great guys in my sophomore class soon made themselves known, and I thought, yes, I will become one of them. They were the football guys, the guys popular with the girls, the ones who ran things while the others played their inconsequential games in the background. The great guys were the ones who wore the best clothes, letter sweaters and cords faded white, rolled up halfway to their knees. They wore their hair in a crewcut, "flat tops" they were called, because the war was still on and the men of war wore their hair cut short and flat on top. Even John Wayne wore his hair that way, and so, too, did I. Soon, I too, was wearing faded cords rolled up almost to my knees. As I saw it, I was a potential power at Laramie High, the rising star, except, of course, I had started sprouting pimples, and my voice hadn't yet begun to change.

"Name's Gerry, huh?"

"Right."

"What's yer gig?"

"What do ya mean?"

"I mean, do you go out for football or anything?"

"I might go out. I'm pretty good at singing, too," I said.

"A regular Bing Crosby? Or a Perry Como, I'll bet? Yer pretty hot, right?"

"Oh, I wouldn't say that," I said, trying to be humble which was not my style.

I was greeted on the second day of school by a couple of the great guys. They both wore flat tops, of course, and the cords and the sweaters, the sleeves pushed up almost to the elbows as if they were getting ready to wash the dishes. Friendly, too, personality guys who laughed at whatever I said and smiled a lot when they were talking, and asked a lot of questions like they were really interested in me. I felt proud, heady, important. The apex of my bounce, that is, the point where you come clear up on your toes at the end of the step, grew still higher. The great guys wanted to meet me after school, walk home with me, get to know me, be my buddies. And that day after school, sure enough, two of them were waiting for me, and they did walk home with me, one of the great guys on each side. Friendly people in Laramie High. When we got to my house one of them asked, incredulity ringing unabated in his voice, "Is *that* where you live?"

"Yeah," I said.

"Oh," the other great guy said. Then the two of them turned and walked back to the part of town where great guys lived, where the bankers and the moneyed people resided, leaving me standing there wondering what was wrong.

The next day my new buddies said "Hi," all right, and nodded as we passed in the hall, but things seemed different. I was confused. One day I had been the newest rave of Laramie High, and the next I had become a forgotten nobody. Nobody walked in the halls with me like before. After class nobody stopped to talk. There was a Thespian Club meeting right after school. But none of the great guys invited me, although everybody knew I was a budding Caruso. I had already told them so.

Several days later I found out what had caused the deterioration in my social standing. "Is it true that you live in a chicken house?" somebody asked me.

"What are ya talkin' about?" I asked back.

"They say you live in a chicken house."

"Well, the hell I do," I said, puffed, proud and haughty. Then somebody else who knew a little Laramie history explained it. I lived in a house that had been added onto. Best house my father could afford when we moved to Laramie, a gray stucco affair, one room upstairs, which was mine, and two bedrooms downstairs, one for my parents and one for my younger brother and sister. My father paid a few thousand cash. It had space in back for chickens and hutches for some white, pink-eyed rabbits I raised, butchered and sold. There was a garden, too, and a small barn. I had purchased a Steeldust mare, a small high-strung two-year-old. Paid ten dollars for her. Named her Madam X because she was a bum, like my lamb, Cousin. I broke the mare to ride, and kept her behind the house in the shed, and staked her out for pasture along the ditch bank, and rode her over the long, flat, endless miles of the Laramie plains. The great guys never rode a horse. And they didn't raise chickens in their backyards, not in the part of town they lived in. Our house wasn't a fancy house but it looked pretty good to me. Yet I found out our house had started as a chicken house, all right, and someone knew that, and they spread the word. "Spence lives in a chicken house."

Madam X, Gerry's Steeldust filly at the Laramie house.

At Laramie High in 1943, you had to come from money or power. Your father had to be a businessman, or a newspaper publisher. If not, you had to be a big-time personality boy or an athlete. I qualified for none of these.

Ignoring my Grandfather Spence's admonition that I didn't have a runner's calf, I thought maybe I should try to become an athlete. I therefore sent my child's white, still soft, hairless body to war. I went out for football. I was shocked at the merciless carnage that ensued under the guise of civilized sport. Soon this body of growing bone and tender tissue was mashed and squashed and reduced to a pulpy mess. A boy's developing muscles were not designed by God for such abuse. Already the boys against whom I competed had that important hair in all the important places. I had none. I was too slow for the backfield. Too slow and too short to play end. Coach Deti, a no-nonsense, jut-chinned, Green Beret type, had no use for me, this hundred-thirty-five-pound, five-foot-seven lump of nothing. I was too small for the line, but he had to put this kid somewhere, so I made the third team. There were only three teams.

"All right, you tough guys, it's a dozen laps. Last one in is a lily-livered sweetheart. Last man in gets a new hair-do and perfume." I always brought up *the* absolute rear. I was embarrassed. Some of the big guys called me "sweet-heart." I no longer feared hell. This *was* hell. When we were ordered to hit the dummies, I was too exhausted to stand. I was the laughingstock of the team.

Dragging myself painfully around like an arthritic old man, I complained to my parents. "You are a year younger than the others," my father said. "Skipped a grade. Besides," he reiterated, "we Spences develop late. Your time is coming."

But teenagers live in the present. They do not live on promises of salvation, and the strongest of all instincts, survival, prevailed. Facing sure extermination, I retained enough native intelligence to quit football halfway through the season. The humiliation and torture I suffered outweighed any possible payoff in acceptance. My father, who had played football in college in the days of the leather helmets and the sparse padding, said, "Well, if you aren't going out for football you better get a job." And I needed a job. I needed the money. You had to have money if you were going to be one of the great guys at Laramie High.

I found work at Friday's Grocery, a store Ed Friday had built in the base-ment of his little white frame house across the street from the high school. You walked down concrete stairs to his dungeon. No windows, the original concrete walls and rafters exposed. Friday was a man past fifty with a large red nose and atrophied patience. He made a modest living selling Coke, candy, and dough-nuts to the high school kids who came flooding to the store at noontime, and he delivered groceries to the households where the wives wanted to do their shop-ping by phone. He did it all—he and I. He bought bull meat by the quarter, hung it up in back of the store, and I sliced it off the bone and ground it into hamburger and mixed it with suet he bought for three cents a pound. And I delivered groceries in his old white Chevy pickup at twenty-five cents an hour.

Life never matched the fantasies of a teenage boy. In my dreams I would knock on the door with the groceries and it would be opened by a beautiful creature in high heels and a black, see-through negligee—sort of like the girls in the Rex Rooms in Sheridan. She would, quite naturally, ask me in.

"Put the groceries over here," she would command, and when, obediently, I set them on the kitchen counter, she would say, "Well, aren't you something special!" And she would come up close to me, and then before I knew what to say, and before I had to say anything, she would take me by the hand, just like that, and lead me to the bedroom. And the matchless wonder of the fantasy is that you can write your own script and cast your own characters. Reality is not so kind. When I knocked on a living housewife's door, it was usually answered by some old crone who hollered, "Leave the groceries inside the porch." That was as exciting as it ever got.

In the years that followed I worked at Garlett's Drugstore downtown stocking shelves and cleaning up, thirty cents an hour, and later as a soda jerk at another drugstore with the old-fashioned marble-topped counters making sundaes, malted milks, and root beer floats. Don't remember ever having received a tip. I worked as a janitor and clean-up boy at Midwest Sporting Goods, which occupied the most important corner in Laramie, the one on Second Street across from the First National Bank. The store was owned by a Jewish family, the first I had ever known. The father, the founder, well into his eighties, stood like a wooden Indian most of the day gazing out of the windows I washed. Sometimes he would hurl outlandish epithets at me, like "Get up and go, Romeo," or "Get the grease goin'." Then he would puff on his old stogie and stare at me with the meanest look on his face, which was never quite mean enough to cover the amusement seeping from underneath.

I was incapable of keeping the glass cases clean enough, the shelves dust-free enough, the floor shining enough. There was no satisfying the family's need for the spic-and-span. I swore that if the room met the standards of a hospital operating room someone would have found an overlooked speck, an errant smudge. My mere presence *ipso facto* seemed to contaminate the place.

Sometimes, to escape their immutable glare, for there were few customers to otherwise occupy their attention, I retreated to the basement toilet. The furnace was down there. I'd shut the door and lock it, and before long I'd break into a sweat. The discomfort was worth it. On the wall hung an old Petty Girl Calendar, featuring those marvelous creatures with the long, full legs, thick ankles, the tiny feet always clad in the highest heels known to man, the fantasy girl with the tiny waist and the bulging breasts that were uncontainable in her thin little frock. The Petty Girl wore that look of sweet, innocent sexuality that was an extraordinary combination of the Madonna and the most licentious vixen of vice. If I looked at her long enough I could hear her speak. She whispered things like, "Gerry, sex is wonderful and sex is good, and I love sex and I love you, and I am a virgin, *or practically a virgin,* and I am in every way yours. Sex is quite okay with me, because I represent nonsinful sex. Don't you understand? I was born for sex. Sex may be sinful with anyone else in the world, but sex with me is divine. It is even required. And I want it, and I want it bad, and I want it now and I want it from you!" And then I would have to run upstairs again before someone came knocking on the bathroom door. "Did you fall in, Gerry? Are you drowning, Gerry? We aren't paying you to sit in there doing whatever you're doing in there. Have you forgotten the windows? And the sidewalk needs sweeping."

But I had money. I made enough to buy a pair of brown-and-white loafers, and so, with my rolled-up cords, I looked like a great guy even if I wasn't one. That's what fashion is about—looking like somebody you really aren't. And I had a little money left to buy my school supplies, and my mother said I must tithe— 10 percent for God, for Christ sakes! It was easier to give it than to argue with her.

"God has his rights as well," my mother said. "He takes care of us and we, in turn, have to help as well."

"Reciprocity" was the word my father liked to use. Big word for a payoff, I thought.

But the pimples bothered me. Why, if I was paying off God, didn't I have a pimple-free complexion like Don Jenson? Why wasn't I able to play at least guard or tackle on the football team like Don Jenson and have a letter sweater that a girl could wear? I had already dated Beverly Caroll a couple of times, and we held hands, although she was a reluctant hand holder. And then this Don Jenson, one of the great guys, came along, and one day I saw her wearing his sweater, and I cried inside, and then I looked her over real good and said to myself, well, hell, he can have her. She ain't so damn hot after all. And I thought, you'll be sorry someday. But why would she be sorry? I mean, she had one of the great guys whose maroon-and-white letter sweater adorned her body and proclaimed to the world that she was the steady of a football hero. Sometimes I secretly hoped the team would lose.

My father said pimples were caused by a fellow doing what he shouldn't be doing with "you know what," as he put it.

"What do you mean?" I asked back with feigned innocence.

"Well, you know if you play a lot with that *thing* it causes pimples. Gets you all excited, and the blood to boiling, and the pimples pop out." And so now I knew. And so did everybody else. Pimples were the exterior manifestation of one's most secret life. Bad enough that God was watching. But to broadcast the secret to the whole world by putting pimples on a person's face—that was a merciful God? I wouldn't do that to my worst enemy. And how was I going to face the world when everyone knew?

I began to look around. A lot of kids must be doing it, I thought. But Don Jenson obviously didn't do it, and most of the other great guys didn't either. Then I began to look for girls who had pimples, realizing, as I did, that having pimples on the face was like wearing a red light on top of one's head that blinked continuously whenever one had engaged in the venal act of "self-abuse," as the *Boy Scout Manual* labeled it. Certain girls must be doing it, too.

I took some comfort in that realization, and from it I formed a daring criminal plan.

I noticed that a certain girl had a few pimples, petite ones on her forehead that she was mostly able to cover with powder. I reasoned as follows: First, it was now clear to me that I could never escape my passion, my mother's expectations to the contrary. Moreover, it was apparent that—shall we call her—"Judy" and I dealt with our passion in approximately the same way. This reasoning seemed to lead to both a logical and merciful conclusion: Perhaps Judy and I could get together, satiate our passions, and rid ourselves of our pimples as well.

I plotted the crime, one detail at a time. I would borrow my father's car and ask Judy out, to a show maybe. *Reciprocity:* that was his word. If I washed the car, raked the leaves and cleaned up the backyard and then asked for the car, maybe he would say yes. I had to have the car before I asked Judy for a date. So I did the work. Then I swaggered up to my father with the proposition.

"Remember reciprocity?" I asked.

"What do you mean?" he asked.

"Well, I washed the car and I cleaned up the yard. Raked the leaves. Could I borrow the car next Saturday night?" I had him. And when I told Judy I had the car and all, and would she like to go to the show with me, she said she'd have to ask her folks, and the next day she said she could go. Then I plotted further. I stole a rubber from the top drawer in the dresser in my parents' bedroom. My father bought them by the dozen. He'd never miss one. But how do you hide a rubber so no one would ever find it? A guy could accidentally leave it in his pants pockets, or it could pop out when you reached in for some change. I saw guys carry rubbers in their billfolds. But when they sat on their billfolds all day in class the rubber left its telltale shape embossed on the leather, and who knows when one's mother might check one's billfold? I mean the crime had to be perfect.

At last I came upon a foolproof plan for hiding the rubber. I took a fountain pen, opened it, removed the bladder and slipped in the rubber. Religiously, I carried my pen with me every day. And, of course, I took it with me on my date with Judy, big-time date, the show, a Coke—and afterward?

Judy was a freckle-faced Irish girl with smallish teeth and a turned-up nose—might have been a little heavy by today's emaciated standards, but I fantasized that naked she would look sort of like those nudes in the old-time paintings—the ones with angels and all—and she had a nice smile and a happy personality. Judy and I got into the old '37 Ford, that rattling wreck, that embarrassment to the automotive world. Its damned fenders flapped like the wings of a wounded bird. It was dented everywhere a car could display a dent. How often my father had proved he could put that old Ford on the top of nearly any mountain in the Big Horns. He was famous for it. I'd heard stories about how some hunter had been trudging all day up a mountain and had suddenly come onto this old Ford already sitting at the top, and he'd ask how the hell that car got up there. My father loved to tell the story.

The great guys had been sired by fathers who had great cars, new four-holer Buicks, mostly. Maybe a Pontiac. Even a Hudson. But no Fords. Worse, the old '37 was a sixty horse, not an eight-five, so that it occupied the very bottom rung of the automotive hierarchy. The only car lower was a Willys. No respectable girl would go out with a fella whose father owned a Willys—that was one thing I knew as an absolute certainty.

So came the night, and there we were, after the show, and after the Coke, Judy and I, in the old '37. A hip guy didn't ask certain questions. If you asked, "Ya wanna go park?" the answer was, "I can't. I gotta go home." But if you drove around acting like a big shot and just happened to drive out on a country road, the girl didn't ask, "Where are we going?" She knew. And if you didn't ask, she wasn't obligated to say she had to go home.

Finally I found a dark spot in the road to park, and Judy and I got to kissing—nice kisses, none of those French kisses, which, so far as Laramie High was concerned, had not yet been invented—and we kissed and got close, and she turned around in the seat with me behind the steering wheel and lay in my arms, but the steering wheel was in the way, of course, and so I said, "Do you want to get in the back?" I shouldn't have asked.

"What for?" she asked.

"So we can be more comfortable," I said.

And she said, "Are you uncomfortable?" and I said, "Yeah, I guess so." And then she said, "Well, okay, if you are *really* that uncomfortable." But the Ford was a two-door, and we had to get out and push the front seats up to get into the back, and it was sort of embarrassing. I knew that the crime of my life was about to take place, this perfect crime I had plotted, diligently, carefully. I felt for my pen. And then it happened, faster than I had even fantasized.

"You have a rubber?" Judy suddenly asked.

"Yeah," I said. I took out the pen and fumbled with it in the dark. I was about to commit this crime, the crime I had dreamed of. I was about to become a "fornicator," as my father called such persons. I had thought of it for weeks, gone to bed at night thinking about it, plotted *its* every move, and now I was going to do *it*, no matter whether God was watching or not. There was no turning back. I plunged ahead, and before I knew it I had become a full-fledged, honest-to-God, complete and unmitigated fornicator. I had actuated my fantasies, but my fantasies had never anticipated guilt. And they never included the possibility that the other person had feelings as well. Fantasies are not about the other person. Moreover, my fantasies had never included the realization that I had lost my innocence, right there in the backseat of the old '37 Ford.

And what of her? What had I done to Judy? When we got to Judy's house I walked her to the door. I didn't know what to say. I felt ashamed. But I wanted to get out of there. I wanted to go home. But what could I say to Judy? Finally I said, "I think you are a very nice person."

She looked down.

"Really," I insisted.

"Do you really think so?" she whispered, her eyes sad in her quick glance upward.

"Yes, I really think so."

"Really?" she said, looking down again.

"You shouldn't feel bad about it. I really think you are a nice person," I said again. Then I couldn't think of anything else to say, and I kissed her lightly on the lips and left. I was almost fifteen.

The next morning I held back coming down the stairs. My parents could surely tell from my face—the eyes shifty, the mouth tight and quivery. "What is the matter with you, son?" my mother would surely ask. How could I say "Nothing?" I would become not only a fornicator but a dirty, *lying* fornicator. Finally about noon I mustered the courage to face the music. My father was there to meet me as I descended the stairs.

He stopped me before I reached the landing. I could see it in his face, all drawn. I had seen it before, when he tried holding back his temper as he always did when he was angry.

"You should be proud of yourself," he said, standing in front of me. My heart started to pound, and I got very lightheaded. For the first time in my life my father was going to hit me.

"Why? What's the matter?" I tried to fake it, but he knew. I knew he knew.

"Your mother is crying. You have almost killed her."

Oh, God, I thought. She knows, too. Maybe Judy told her mother and her mother called my mother. "What's the matter?" I asked as if I didn't know.

"Your mother took the car to Sunday school this morning. She said some of the ladies were looking at the car when they came out of the church, and they were snickering." Then he explained why. The rubber I had thrown out of the backseat window the night before had stuck to the window, and there it hung, the official flag of fornication flying there for all the Sunday school ladies to see. "It humiliated your mother to the point of dying," my father said. "Hope you're real proud of yourself."

The next summer I returned to the Lembke-Hermburg ranch, a regular hand, no longer a jerk. Now I drove a mower with a team of young, powerful broncs, because it took horsepower to turn the gears that drove the sickles through the thick grass. When the broncs got to acting up, you just dropped the sickle bar to the ground and let the cutter go, and that pulled the rowdy team down good. Later I drove the sweeps with the best and strongest geldings, and I stacked hay, and sweat with the best stackers, including Ol' Calsey, who had recovered from the stabbing and had come back to the ranch. My skinny arms grew muscles, and other signs of manhood began to appear, and I felt like a man because, by God, I worked with men and sweat with men, and I could cuss like a man, and

Cozy Rooms. Rawlins, Wyoming.

spit and swagger, and if you saw me from half a mile away you would have thought I *was* a man. Up close the voice was still crackly and the pimples were still popping out like weeds after the first spring rain, and the fuzz on the chin was like pinfeathers on a young rooster.

Now that I was a man, Ol' Calsey invited me to go with him to Rawlins, which was a man's town. I figured that if a man was a man, then he should do what men do. On a Saturday night I rode with Ol' Calsey in the ancient yellow pickup to Rawlins. Once there we headed straight for the Cozy Rooms, which Ol' Calsey called home. It was, of course, a walk-up whorehouse. The stairs were littered with cigarette butts and papers and cinders blown in from the railroad yards. A black woman in a maid's uniform answered the doorbell. When she saw Ol' Calsey she stepped aside without a word, without a change of expression, and I followed him in, like a calf following a bull.

We sat down in the dingy parlor and we waited. The furniture was that over-stuffed cheap plastic kind with cigarette holes burned in the arms. I looked around for cockroaches and rats. The floors were old worn green linoleum. You could see where the board floor underneath pushed up, making parallel ridges across the room. No rugs. Petty Girl Calendar on the wall. I wondered if any of "the girls," as the women were called, would look like her. Pretty soon they came in, three of them all decked out in those short sexy little things, sexier than in any of my fantasies, sparse coverings that could be put on or taken off with the whisk of a zipper or the pull of a single tie. When they walked in, they strutted their stuff, sort of like models on a stage, and they walked up to where I was sitting and called me "Honey," and "Big Boy."

"I bet this guy is a real goer," one said, and then they would laugh and wink at each other. They stood there looking down at me and Ol' Calsey sitting there, and the girls wiggled up and back, and back and forth, while they were talking, and the stringy blonde who was standing in front of me said, "Why don't ya come to the room with me, sweetheart, and we'll have us some fun, huh?" She had a big red mouth, and the wrinkles had begun to form on her upper lip when she puckered up to drag on her cigarette.

Ol' Calsey said, "Now that there is a damn good woman, kid, and she'll treat ya right, I guarantee ya that. Why don'tcha go on with her?" and then she grabbed hold of my arm and pulled me to my feet and I followed her. What else could I do? I was a man. And I was with Ol' Calsey. And this was what men do, real men, not sissy-ass preachers, not the fathers of sons or the husbands of wives, not the fancy men in the banks and the big-time businessmen, but *real* men, like Ol' Calsey, men out in the world sweating and swearing, real men who drove the teams of horses in the fields, who told dirty jokes together and spun tall tales about whorin' and fightin' and who slept together in the bunkhouse. I was one of them.

I followed the woman down the narrow hall to her room. We sat on the bed, side by side, a small bed that sagged in the middle and was covered with a worn, pink chenille bedspread. I wondered if this was where she slept after all the men she had been with had finally gone home.

"Let me see it," she said.

"What do you mean?" I said back.

"You know what I mean. Let me see it." She reached over to unbutton my jeans.

"What for?" I said, pulling her hand away.

"Listen, sweetheart, I am not going to let some punk-ass kid put me out of business with a dose," and I thought, "Oh, God, I can't go through with this." But before I knew it she had unbuttoned my jeans, grabbed it and inspected it in a way such knowledgeable women do, and, satisfied, she glanced over at me. When she saw the look on my face she began to laugh, and her croaking laughter filled the little room.

"This your first time?" she asked, still laughing.

"No," I said.

"Well, it's five dollars for a 'short time,' and if you want a 'French go,' it's ten. A 'round the world' costs ya twenty, and all night is fifty. What will it be?"

I reached into my pocket and gave her a five, and she took it and walked over to the wall and opened a high small cabinet door about the size of a Bible and shoved the money in. I heard a door open on the other side, where I supposed the money was taken out by the madam. Then the woman unzipped her bright red dress with the double ruffles around the bottom. She let the dress fall to the floor, and there she was, as white as death, all hanging down and her stomach pouching out as if she were early pregnant. She had no waist and her legs were thin and looked weak. She quit her laughing and walked naked to the bed. Her flesh jiggled in various ways and places, and she flopped down on the bed and spread her legs and motioned me to come on. She had a haughty look on her face. Maybe it was to cover her shame, I thought, but she didn't look ashamed.

The lights were on. A single bulb hung down from the ceiling. It was glaring and bright in there. I didn't think a man should look at *it*, because it was one thing for a man to commit a sin, but another for him to look at it square in the eye. I held back. Then she sat up and grabbed me by the arm and pulled me to her. I must have closed my eyes. And I closed my mind, held my breath as if I were diving or something, and although I didn't struggle with her, I struggled against the power that dragged me to her. Then I gave in. A man has to finally give in.

"Don't put all of your weight on me like that," she said. "Get up on your elbows."

"Oh, Jesus. I'm sorry. I didn't know." I mean, whoever was supposed ta tell ya not to put all your weight on a woman.

The world swam by, and then I was swimming into the universe, and suddenly out I came to the surface again, and there I was in the bright and the glare. She knew exactly when it was over. I didn't want to get off, and I didn't want to get up, because I didn't want to look at her. And I was all sweaty. And I thanked God that the woman didn't say anything, and I didn't have to say anything.

She gave me a little push. I got up and started for my pants right away, and then I saw her do it, tried not to watch out of respect for the woman, but I saw it. She filled a white wash basin with warm water from the sink, and then in front of me, and without seeming embarrassed, she washed herself and she took a towel from a stack of towels to dry herself, and I thought about many things at once. I thought about Mazie's towel boy up in the Rex Rooms, and I thought that as hard as she was washing I must be very dirty. I felt very dirty. Then she came over to me, and without looking at me, she washed me in the same intense workmanlike manner.

"Want a 'pro'?" she asked.

I didn't know what she meant, but I found out that a "pro" was short for prophylactic. I said I didn't want any, whatever it was, and I pulled up my pants and walked back down the hall into the waiting room.

Ol' Calsey was sitting there drinking a straight shot of Seagram's Seven, and when he saw me come in he started laughing, his evil old cocked eye staring up at the ceiling and his other eye drunk red. "Ya ain't got much stayin' power, do ya, kid?" he said. "These here girls don't have ta work very hard on yer kind." And he hollered and laughed all in one. "They oughta give ya a discount," and he laughed some more, and then I left Ol' Calsey up there in his home away from home. He cashed his checks there. Stayed with the girls all night, drank their booze, dollar a shot, and when it came time for him to go back to the ranch, if he had any money still coming, they gave it to him.

"Damned honest women," he said. "Rather trust them than them bankers. I like the fuckin' I get at the Cozy Rooms a whole lot better'n the fuckin' I got from them bankers one time."

I walked out into the night. I was drained, yet suddenly sane. What had I done? What would God think? I was still saying my prayers, the Lord's Prayer and "Now I lay me down to sleep," and this night I had lain with a whore, and I would probably contract a terrible disease, the "clap" or the "syph" as Ol' Calsey called it, and if my mother knew she would surely die, and if my father knew he would say nothing, but his eyes would turn sad—this son of his now a proven, before God, whoremonger. I was nothing but a whoremonger. I would rather be a jerk.

"Oh, God, forgive me, and please may I not get the clap, and please may I not get the syph, and may my folks never find out. Amen." That was my humble prayer.

By the time I drifted into my senior year at Laramie High I had sung a few frightened solos at school assemblies where I tried to do the Bing Crosby trill, and I had been in a play or two, but never in a leading role. I had never been elected, not even nominated, to a school office, except once when Judy nominated me for class president, and everybody seemed to know why she had nominated me. I was defeated two to one by one of the great guys who was big and blond and played end and had letters to spare. He had a big grin and a big laugh and a loud voice, and everybody thought he was just fuckin' wonderful. Most popular kid in school.

I never got into much trouble. Drugs in any form were unheard of at Laramie High in the mid-1940s. Most of the great guys didn't drink. Drinking was considered sort of dumb. Some of the nobodies got drunk, but the guys who knew what was going on didn't and most didn't smoke. But we did the jitterbug at the school dances. I could dance about as well as anybody, better than most, and some of the girls said I was a smooth dancer on the slow ones. Sometimes I danced with Judy. Still, there weren't any girls mad after me, including Judy.

Although I was devoid of athletic skill, I was a champion show-off. I had developed a peculiar combination of shyness and extroversion. At times my shyness prevailed and I simply withdrew. But usually I jumped in, invited or not, with a sarcastic remark. Sometimes I was the funny guy who managed to fall just short of being funny, the cutup who tried too hard and who was often more obnoxious than amusing. But when you are not a great guy, your options are limited. You can fade into the woodwork or you can be a smart-ass. The show-off part of me seemed endemic to my personality.

In speech class, I loved to argue with our teacher, Velma Linford, a redheaded, busty, ample woman who was as intransigent as a buffalo bull and an ever-replenishing dynamo of energy. But I, too, would never give up the argument. Finally one day I wore her down.

"You get out of here," she hollered. "I'm kicking you out of this class!"

"How do you want me to go?" I asked with a smirk.

"Any way you want. Just get out of here!"

And so I got up from my desk, walked to the window, opened it, crawled out, and walked on down the street with my silly dorky walk. I am told that Miss Linford, who was fond of me, had no sooner kicked me out than she began to miss me, and within the week I was back at my desk, ready to take her on again at the first excuse.

"You ought to be a lawyer," she said once. Perhaps I remembered that. I respected her spirit, her caring, and although she had kicked me out, I felt loved by her. Of all of my teachers she was, perhaps, the one most responsible for my early leaning toward the law.

From the earliest times my mother admonished, "Don't be a smarty. Nobody likes a smarty." But being smart got you more attention than being nothing at all. Still, I always had a friend or two, always did and do now. And I was able to get close to friends, and somehow I knew how to be a friend. I knew something of caring from the beginning, and I was able to show it, and in the end, caring and not being afraid to care have been an important part of who I am.

As for the scholastic aspects of high school, which were the least important to me, I took five "solids" each semester, sometimes six—chemistry, physics, Spanish, literature, trigonometry, all at the insistence of my parents. But I was no natural scholar. When my parents threatened that I couldn't go out unless my grades improved, I got straight A's. I liked literature. I liked drama. Drama fit my personality—stuff about feelings and the miraculous power of words—how could words have such power? I liked poetry, too. Poetry—about feelings and again, the magic of words and sounds. You could make melodies with words. I liked public speaking, I liked to convince people of my way of thinking. But I hated math and I hated science—hated them with a passion. Figures had no personality. You couldn't feel figures. Chemical formulas were dead on the page. They bored me. Listening to my parents discuss chemistry at supper transported me to another world, my own private world of fantasy beyond the oilcloth table covering and the fried elk steak that had been too long in the freezer. Much to the shock of my scientific parents, I almost failed chemistry.

I had grown up to understand from my earliest days that high school was merely the beginning of the educational process. Spences went to college. It had never occurred to me that I might not go to college. I had been saving for college, my earliest dollar, a dollar at a time, for as long as I could remember. But I had to decide what I was going to study before I went to the university so as not to waste a lot of life meandering around the university's educational smorgasbord—no money or time for such luxuries.

By my senior year I had resolved that I should become a lawyer. The decision wasn't hard to come by. The alternatives weren't many or appealing. A scientific career like my father's was out of the question. How could the likes of me

sit all day looking at test tubes and running calculations? I wanted action. I wanted to be on stage, at the center of the universe. I wanted to be president of the
United States. And I wanted to make a million dollars. Being poor was poor
business. Being nobody was worse.

One thing I knew as an absolute certainty. I was never going to do manual
labor for a living. The summer before I graduated from high school I had
worked as a carpenter's helper building the aluminum plant at Laramie, another government project during the war. The idea was to extract precious aluminum, so necessary for the war effort, from the low-grade bauxite that was in
abundance in the nearby Laramie Mountains. The work was mostly making
forms for the concrete pillars and beams that went into the plant, but the work
was heavy and hot and uninteresting. I was not into this so-called manual labor.
It paid poorly. It wrecked the body and overexerted the sweat glands. Manual
labor was mean, messy and miserable. Manual labor was out. Clear out. Nobody
ever got to be president digging ditches. What you got was a crippled back and
beat-up old legs and a starvation pension if you worked long and hard enough.

I'd given some thought to becoming a veterinarian. I liked dogs and horses
especially. I had taken a job with a local veterinarian. I had planned to work as
his assistant, which included helping him with his operations, cleaning up the
place, and feeding the sick animals—the going wage still being twenty-five cents
an hour. I didn't last long. I hated it when he spayed a little bitch pup, cut the
puppy's belly open and cut out this and that and sewed up the helpless little
beast. And he trimmed the ears of boxer pups and Dobermans as well, and he
docked their tails and the tails of spaniels, and off came the nuts of the little
male puppies. I empathized with them. The animals locked up in his pens were
lonely and frightened and yapping in their cages, and there was the constant
stink of animal dung that permeated the walls. No matter how you cleaned and
scrubbed, it still smelled the same. I thought such a life would be intolerable.

I never seriously considered medicine—too many years in school, too many
science courses. Instead, I possessed obvious verbal skills. I could get up in front
of a group of people and sing. I stood up there, my belly churning with fear, my
legs stiff in terror. Yet I covered it with the imperial bearing of, say, a sixteen-
year-old General Patton. People thought I was fearless when often I was nearly
paralyzed with stage fright. Today, psychologists, who claim to know, say that
many people fear standing in front of an audience to give an extemporaneous
speech more than they fear death.

If only I could be brave like my father. Once I heard him speak in church.
He took the pulpit as an expert, a chemist who knew all about the scientific evils
of alcohol. He demonstrated it to the congregation on Temperance Sunday.

"Now here is an ordinary egg," my father said, holding up an egg freshly
plucked from our hen house. He broke the egg into a clear dish for all to see.
"Now in this bowl I am going to pour some pure alcohol." He did as the whole
congregation watched. They, nor I, had ever seen such carryings-on from the

pulpit. "Watch what happens when I pour this egg into this bowl full of alcohol." We all gazed in amazement. The egg began to turn white, as if it were being poached in boiling water. "Now if that is what alcohol will do to an egg, which has a cellular structure similar to the cells found in the human body, think what it will do to your brain! Now just give that a little thought." And that's all there was to his speech, and he sat down. I have often thought of that simple presentation when I employ demonstrations of my own before a jury that make an argument far more powerful than the most eloquent oratory.

It would be years before I understood the relationship between fear and courage. A coward could never muster the courage to risk singing before an audience, to chance criticism or face the possibility he might be humiliated or scorned. A brave man cannot commit brave acts without first being afraid, for to overcome fear and to act in the face of it is the essence of courage. A fool who fearlessly runs headlong into danger is not brave. He is but a fool. But at sixteen I had yet to learn that the seed of all courage is fear.

Despite my fear of the stage I thought perhaps I could one day become a great singer like Paul Robeson. I was attending choir practice every Thursday night, singing in the Methodist church choir every Sunday—except, of course, during hunting season. I began to sing solos with my newly acquired, sometimes irresponsible, baritone voice. I sang at several weddings. Once I forgot the words to the song—the horror of all horrors! But I kept on singing with "La-la, la-la's," until I came to a part in the music where I again remembered the words. Later my father told me he thought it quite remarkable I hadn't fainted or run from the church. "Why, I would have died," he said. I did die. Yet there was something about performing in public that I cherished—likely the short-lived acclaim, the momentary acceptance, the sparse adulation. Maybe I couldn't run with the football, and maybe I didn't live where the great guys lived. Maybe I had pimples and the family car was nothing but a shameful wreck, but I could stand up there and sing. And when I did, I was somebody.

I even considered going into opera. But my mother said that most singers starved to death, and most of the opera stars I had seen in the movies were potbellied old drones who sang to a bunch of fat old ladies with long black eyelashes. And the men strutted around on the stage like stiff-legged robots in silly costumes and the women swooned, only to recover and swoon again. Already I had been taking voice lessons from Professor Gunn at the University of Wyoming, no more than a dozen blocks from home. He had me singing from the diaphragm, not the throat. He taught me how to breathe, and I was running the scales, singing them on the way to school and singing songs like "No, John, No" and "On the Road to Mandalay." Little by little I had been developing a reputation around town as a singer. But I yearned for money and success, and I didn't want to go to New York where I was told the opera stars hung out. I was a hunter. I was an action man. I saw myself as a rough, tough kind of guy who wouldn't like hanging out with those wimpy sorts singing silly songs in German and Italian that I wanted to learn. Besides which, I had already taken two years of Spanish and a year of Latin. Hated conjugating verbs.

True, I could be a schoolteacher, but I had learned the kind of hell mouthy, pushy, rowdy kids like me could deliver to a teacher. Besides, most of the teachers I knew wore old suits and drove old wrecks for cars, and for sure I didn't want to attend Parent Teacher Association meetings where you had to listen to the parents tell you how wonderful their kid was when you knew the little worthless bastard intimately. Teaching was not for me. Besides, I remembered that Grandpa Pfleeger had fled the old country not only because he didn't want to serve in the Kaiser's army but because he didn't want to be a teacher. And if Grandpa Pfleeger didn't want it, I sure didn't either.

Preachers needed the oral skills I believed I possessed, the ability to sway their congregations, to stand up there on the pulpit and carry on. From time to time my mother had hinted at the idea of my taking up the cloth, but I wasn't the kind to be a damn preacher. I loved sin too much, particularly fornication and salacious thoughts about fornication. Preachers weren't supposed to think about that sort of thing, much less do it. Preachers were all prim and pious and prissy. How could the likes of me, a real man, be a preacher? I was wild and arrogant I thought, and how could I be a preacher when I had already violated most of the Ten Commandments? Better be an honest sinner than a hypocritical preacher, I thought, and in fact, I haven't changed my mind much on that.

Once my father invited a certain saggy-jowled, soft-bellied preacher to go antelope hunting with us—trying to be nice, trying to be friendly with the people my mother thought our family should associate with. After the kill and after my father had dressed out the animal, he took out the ceremonial sandwich of white bread and peanut butter, and, as usual, sat there on top of the freshly killed carcass mindless of how others might see it, and began eating his sandwich with his unwashed, bloody hands. If you had asked him about it he would have looked surprised and said, "Why, it's just clean antelope blood." But the preacher got sick to his stomach. At that moment I lost all remaining respect I had for those types who stand up there hanging on to the pulpit, praying and preaching and peering off to the heavens as if they could see God, but who couldn't gut out an antelope like a real man, like a hunter. Besides, preachers were always begging for money. Asking others for money wasn't my style. I wasn't going to beg anyone. I was going to have so much money they'd have to ask me.

So what else could I possibly become but a lawyer?

I had never known a lawyer, never met one, never seen one, even at a distance. No lawyers ever went to the Methodist church so far as I knew. I had never been in a courtroom. I had no idea what lawyers did. I had never heard of Clarence Darrow. But Abraham Lincoln was a lawyer, and he had become president, and so were Jefferson and Madison, and I thought Roosevelt was probably a lawyer too. All great men were lawyers. I had never heard of a doctor or a veterinarian or a teacher or a preacher who became president. Even when my voice was cracking like a one-celled radio at three in the morning, my speech teacher, Miss Velma Linford, insisted that I possessed this wonderful voice, and that some-day I would become a great public speaker. I believed her. Well, lawyers speak in public. They speak to juries and they become politicians and speak to whole crowds of people. So, on analysis, there wasn't any doubt about it: The law was for me.

I walked up to the law school one day on the University of Wyoming cam-pus, not more than half a mile from our house. The law school was fully contained in the upstairs of the old Library Building. I found the dean. He was sitting in the outer office where a secretary should have been sitting, and he greeted me when I came in.

"Who are you looking for, son?"

"Dean Hamilton," I said.

"I'm Dean Hamilton," he said. "What can I do for you?" He got up and shook my hand like he was pumping water. He was a tall straight man, stood as if his back were in a cast, and he was bald as a hen's egg, his skull pure white, and with his thick glasses off, he would probably look quite a bit like Daddy Warbucks in *Little Orphan Annie*. When he talked his mouth muscles moved around the words, caressed them, then he almost bit them as he spit them out. He gave me a smile like they were free and told me to sit down.

"I think I'd like to be a lawyer," I said. I was wearing my dirty faded cords and, for the occasion, I'd rolled them down a notch.

"Well, now isn't that fine?" he replied. "Why?"

"I don't know," I said. "Figured I'd be good at it." I talked to the dean as I talked to the men in the hayfields, straight on and tough.

"That's as good a reason as any," he replied. The entire law school occupied only three classrooms, and the faculty was composed of four professors, includ-ing the dean, who taught contracts. Twenty or thirty kids usually started each fall, about half of whom flunked out the first quarter—I thought mostly because the school didn't have room for any more.

"Do I have to take Latin?" I asked.

"You don't have to take Latin, son. I can teach you all the Latin you need to be a lawyer in about ten minutes. Waste of time. Never have heard a lawyer make an argument in Latin. That's for priests."

"That's good news," I said. "Think I *will* be a lawyer, then," I said. "Do lawyers make a lot of money?"

"Some do and some don't."

"Well, I'll make a lot of money," I said. I was sixteen. He told me I would have to take three years of pre-law at the university and the first year of law school could count as my fourth year in undergraduate school so that I could get a degree called a bachelor of science in law. The same first year in law school would count for one of the three years necessary for my law degree, so that under this great educational bargain you could get two years' credit for one and end up with two degrees, which seemed absolutely perfect. I could get this education business out of the way and move on to important things like money and politics.

Then the dean told me if I wanted, although it wasn't necessary, I could go sit down in the library. He would give me an aptitude test to see if I was mentally and psychologically suited for the profession. I said okay. I saw through the test right away. I answered every question consistent with what I believed were the characteristics of a lawyer—simple questions like:

If there is a matter to be decided would you:
    (a) argue about the issues or
    (b) sit back and let somebody else decide?
Would you rather:
    (a) be alone or
    (b) be with people?

It wasn't hard to figure out the right answers. The dean retrieved my test paper and in a few minutes was back. He seemed very excited, and he had a glorious smile on his face, as if he'd just won the jackpot of all jackpots. He even sputtered before he got into what he wanted to say. "You have just earned the highest score on this aptitude test I have ever witnessed in all my days as dean, and I've given hundreds. Congratulations, son! You are going to become a very great lawyer."

"Thank you," I said.

"I'll see you in a couple of years," the dean hollered after me as I strutted out of the law library and into my life. Yes, law, whatever it was, however you did it, however you got to the top of it, was for me. I was going to be a lawyer. A great lawyer, by God! The greatest!

CHAPTER 14

Gerald M. Spence, age ninety, surrounded by (from left to right) Tom Spence, Barbara Spence, and his grandson, Kent Spence.

TWO MEN IN navy blue business suits came for my father. I didn't follow them into the bedroom. No one went to represent the dead. The dead can take care of themselves. Muffled noises came out of the room, quiet movements, no speaking between the men in blue. Careful not to awaken. Efficient movers, these men. Shortly they came wheeling out a gurney bearing a cleanly pressed, gray corduroy zipper bag. My father. Yet the bag looked so small. The men in blue pushed the gurney past me, without looking up, and went on out the front door.

My youngest son, Kent, was with me. I grabbed his hand and held it like a small child's, this son, already near forty, standing taller than I by several inches. We followed the men and the gurney out the door as I had often followed the gurney down the long hospital corridors from which my father had always returned. He had always come back from the corridors. But this time he would never come back.

The sun shone brightly, the high, white August light, and the men in blue, their coats unbuttoned, their foreheads without sweat, pushed the gurney with the small gray bag up to the back of the white van, the kind plumbers drive.

They lifted their cargo up against the floor of the van and the legs of the gurney folded, obediently, automatically. Only had to open the back right-hand door. Then the man in charge closed the door, slammed it again to make sure it wouldn't open and let the gray bag fall out on the pavement. The man in charge walked around to the driver's side, and the other man got in, and they drove off. I watched them go.

"Just like that," I said to Kent with a slap of the hand. "Just like that."

That's how it ended, my father's ninety-two years on this earth.

Just like that.

It was August 12, 1992.

The lady across the street who had come to see him every day, drove out of her garage on her golf cart as the van pulled away, and got behind the van and waved at it. "Good-bye," she hollered gaily. "Good-bye," as if, on the way to her game, she was seeing her friend off for a short vacation. I think my father would have liked the way it ended. No fuss, no flowers, no fancy show, no wailing. Just a gray bag in the back end of a white van. And after that, life goes on.

I felt alone, my son Kent standing beside me, holding my hand, my wife, Imaging, at home recovering from a serious back operation. My children grown. Grandchildren, already.

Are we not always children?

Now that he was gone, once more I felt the pain of having been abandoned in the woods. It wasn't as if I needed my father to make my way through the forest. I had fought my battles without him. But I needed him. I needed to know he was there. That's all—that he was there. I needed him to love. I needed him to care for. I needed him because he was entwined around the tree of my being, and I around his, and now he had been stripped away and I felt naked and vulnerable. Who would I call on the telephone to brag about my cases, about my victories? For children can brag only to their parents. How important it had been to make a father proud. And he had been proud. He had ended his autobiography by speaking of Mae and his children: "These four extraordinary individuals have taught me how to live and to love. They have stood by me through sickness and health. These beautiful people have made my life full, so full that sometimes I almost burst. I must have done something right." I thought, yes, that was enough for any man.

I remembered how he had spoken about the loss of his own father, Grandpa Spence. "Now, as an older man with a family of my own, I felt that I had lost a protecting shield." He said of his father, "The scourge of his advanced age and high blood pressure felled a giant. To me and many others, he was a giant." A very gentle, loving giant, I thought.

My father's death was like any great injury. One is not likely to feel the full pain of it at the instant of impact. Men who have lost a leg to a machine claim they hardly felt it. A bullet can penetrate the body, and rip a gaping hole out the back, and at first, the person may not know he has been hit. As the days passed the pain

*Gerry and Little Peggy, ages two years, six
months, and nine months.*

of my father's loss came on me in waves. As he said, my grief, was mine, not his. Wherever he was, he was all right. And now I had come upon the ever-moving conveyor belt that would, one day, dump me and, at last, all of us into the eternal swirl from which we began.

As was his life, my father's death was a precious gift. For over ninety years he had fought the battles in front of us, in plain sight, and he showed us how to fight with grace and with compassion. He showed us how to live. Now he had shown us how to die, in peace, perhaps in simple joy. To him death was not framed in terror. Death, was a part of life. The beginning and the end were, to him, symbiotic twins.

After I went home, Imaging put her arms around me and then she said, "Now you will have to be your own father." And I said, "Yes, and I hope I can be as forgiving and accepting of me as my father was of me." And I cried again.

Although I had become the father of my own children, a grandfather, and indeed, the father figure to many, in my father's presence I was still his little boy. But when the men in blue had taken my father away, once more I began to ask: What had ever happened to the child?

Mae handed me the photographs from the family album, shots my father had taken with flash powder and camera of Peggy and me as small children. I stared at the child in his crib standing side by side with that other baby, his sister, both perfect children, innocent, lighted with a radiance and joy. Yet the child standing next to him was dead, long dead. As I stared at the picture, I felt the tears sliding down my face like an unwelcome leak in the roof.

Already I was a man growing old. Watching the mutation from child to man is like trying to watch a tree grow. From day to day one never sees it happen. But suddenly, the photograph in my hand, I saw the child instantly transformed to the adult. I saw the baby face change into the hard, leather face of the cynic. I saw the eyes narrowed, piercing, sharp, the eyes of the steel-souled skeptic. What I saw frightened me!

Still I longed for the child, for at least those precious remnants of the child. And in that search I have written the foregoing chapters, written them with a sense of both joy and deep sorrow, at times with a certain amusement, and often with dismay. But, at last, I have found the child. He had been there all along, disguised in the big voice and the shaggy demeanor. I suppose he never left. He had only hidden behind the frightening mask of the man.

Winter in Laramie was like living in a wind tunnel, the temperature well below zero, the place unfriendly and bitter. The cinders from the railroad yards piled up, turning the snow black, but mostly the snow had already been blown away. When you stepped outside, you felt as if you'd been slapped in the face, the wind that strong and mean, and the people walked with their heads down and their eyes squinted. The merchants at Christmas thought the wind and weather were on their side, the people scurrying into the stores for protection, but I didn't want to stay for Christmas. I wanted the hell out of Laramie.

As a senior at Laramie High, I had enough credits by midterm to graduate, but I had no special standing in the school. I had a few friends, but no girlfriend to speak of. I had dated the happy, effervescent Marilyn Clippinger, an ample, happy blond girl my age, but then she had gotten herself engaged to John Sommers, a wounded war veteran. How does a boy, sixteen, compete with the veterans coming home from the war, all decorated and brave and wounded, real men, who could go to college on the GI Bill and who had money—and who shaved? They also had cars. You had the sense that under their leather aviator jackets with the brown sheepskin collars they were still caked with the blood of the battle. And I? I was too young to have served. But I was tall enough. People probably thought I was a damned draft dodger or 4-F or something.

I felt trapped in Laramie as I later felt trapped in other towns. I had not yet learned that I dragged my trap with me. A certain spirit was constantly making a lot of bothersome noise. Sometimes I heard the spirit say the same things my mother had said: "You can be anything you wish. You can do anything, be anything. You can even be president." Sometimes I thought it was all bullshit. But one thing I knew: I had to get the hell out—out of the house, out from under my folks, out of Laramie. Out. College and law school would come later. Right now I had to escape.

I thought of trudging off to Alaska where I could set up a trap line, sell the hides of mink and otter and beaver. Be rich, I thought. I opened up the Montgomery Ward catalog. You could order Victor traps of various sizes by mail. I made a list of the traps I'd need. I also needed two pairs of heavy boots, boot grease, three pairs of heavy wool socks, a fur-lined coat, two pairs of fur-lined mittens, two pairs of long underwear. And snowshoes. I'd have to have a dog sled and a team of dogs. I didn't know what they'd cost or how to drive them, but already the total was more than I'd saved up in my college fund.

One night about Christmastime when things had gotten testy and the long silences had set in, I announced at the supper table, "I'm gettin' the hell outta here." My parents didn't believe in argument. My father said nothing. Just looked sad, and my little brother and sister sat looking down at their plates, their mouths going slow, like they'd never swallow their food. Why the hell couldn't somebody say something? My mother stared at her hands. This silence. This pain over me—well, living in this trap was a pain in the ass for me, too. Where had these parents whom I had loved so much gone off to? Didn't they understand me anymore? Didn't they realize I was also caught up in the misery of this, whatever it was? My anger spread over my feelings like an evil salve. Nobody was answering any questions, and finally I didn't care. I wanted out, that's all. I could see their hurt, all right, and I felt the guilt for having hurt them, but Jesus Christ!

"I'm sick and tired of school," I hollered across the small kitchen table with its flowered oilcloth covering. "I'm going to go on up to Alaska and set me up a trap line." I stabbed my fork into a hunk of elk steak. It tasted bad, oxidized in the freezer, and the potatoes were white and anemic. I slapped a big gob of butter on the potatoes and smothered the elk meat with catsup. The home-canned string beans had faded in the jar and had an unpleasant, tart taste to them. I poured a lot of salt on the string beans and some catsup for good measure, gulped down my food and pushed back from the table.

As I was getting up my father said, "I could make you some catnip perfume for lynx. Used to make it in the lab at Laramie before you were born. Used to sell it to the trappers. Ran an ad in *Field and Stream.*" He started to explain the chemistry of his catnip perfume as I turned away. "Works real good," he said. "Spray a little on the trap and there isn't a cat in the world that can resist it. Strange thing about cats and catnip." And that was all he said. My mother was still looking into her plate. I wondered why she didn't beg me to stay home. She didn't say a word, just took those small bites and chewed at them a long time like she couldn't swallow them or something. My father wanted to help me catch lynx in Alaska? Never argued that I should stay at home. Never once! Probably wanted to get rid of me.

The next Sunday morning, the wind still blowing, the snow gathering in long snakelike drifts, I announced that I was leaving. The semester was over. Already I had given up the idea of a trap line in Alaska and decided, instead, to hitchhike to San Diego. My buddy, Jim Brown, and I were going to go to sea.

"What about your graduation?" my mother asked, her eyes sad. But except for the first glance when she spoke, she didn't look at me. She had never mentioned that she wanted to attend my graduation ceremony. Never said that getting her son through high school was her day, too.

"They can send me my diploma by mail," I said. "What the hell do I want to line up with a bunch of idiots in a silly cap and gown for?" And I was sure they didn't give a damn either. Who wanted to hear the senior class president stand up there sputtering and standing on one foot and then the other, as he always did? And who wanted to hear the valedictorian saying a bunch of Pollyanna crap about how we loved Laramie High, and how we were going to make our teachers proud because we were going to be great successes, and all the other silly things they say at graduation?

THE MAKING OF A COUNTRY LAWYER

Jim Brown didn't go for that brand of bullshit either. Made him sick, he said. He had arrived in Laramie his junior year, a boy my age, and without parents. His father had died early of a stroke.

"What happened to your mother?" I asked innocently.

"She took the pipe," Jim said.

"Jesus Christ, what do you mean?"

"She killed herself." He said it with no emotion, a fact, like he was reciting a street address or something. I wondered how anybody could stand it if his mother killed herself. The one unforgivable sin. I felt sorry for Jim, but he was tough. He wasn't one to take sympathy or to feel pity for himself. He accepted the deal of life's cards—all in the game—and he was playing the game.

I pressed it. "How did she do it?" I asked.

"Drank a bottle of lye," he said.

"Jesus," I said. He was making me drag it out, one fact at a time, but what do you do? You're into it. And if you drop it it seems like you didn't care or something. "How come she did it?"

"She'd tried it before. She had a boyfriend. Gonna get married or something. It caved in. That's all I know."

"How old was she?"

"Forty-nine."

"And you?"

"Eleven."

Then he'd gone to live with his sister in Laramie, who was married to a local doctor—a psychiatrist, for Christ's sake. And in his senior year his sister had decided he should attend the Brown Military Academy—no relation—with the hope that that institution would help contain the rampant disease of adolescence from which we both suffered. On the other hand, going to Brown would save Jim from his sister, which he said was another story too long to tell. He wasn't into telling long stories.

Well, by God, Jim and I were buddies. I didn't know why, and I asked him why later and he didn't know. I think I liked it that he didn't give a damn when secretly I wished I didn't either. Anyway, I was going to go with Jim Brown, and the two of us would get the hell out of school and seek our fortune. Only one trouble with Jim Brown. He didn't have that nifty gorky walk. He sort of shuffled from side to side, tough-like, but he grinned a lot and smoked big cigars. He was his own man. Read books, too. Poetry by Robert Service, about the "Malamute Saloon," and Dangerous Dan McGrew, "The Face on the Barroom Floor." I hadn't read a book clear through since I was in grade school. This Jim Brown was smart. Smarter than I. But he didn't have a flat top. Wore his hair like a regular person, a little wave in front. Nice-looking kid with kind of pointy teeth who knew what the hell it was all about. And he said he was going to be a lawyer, just like the lawyer in *The Great Mouthpiece*, another book he'd read and I hadn't.

* * *

That Sunday my father had already gotten dressed for church—his old blue suit, his coat hiked up in the back from the hunch in his spine, his white socks showing, the same old shoes he'd worn to church for ten years, no polish, the points on his white collar curled, his tie twisted instead of lying flat, the knot the thin old-fashioned kind, go 'round once, then twice, then up through and down, for Christ's sake. And my mother was wearing her same Sunday dress, the red one, and her straw hat with the feather in it.

My little sister and brother were also dressed up in their Sunday best, Barbara, prettier than any little girl, all decked out in her curls and her new flowered dress my mother had made, the dress with the big white collar, and she wore thin baby blue ribbons holding back her hair on each side. My little brother Tom was wearing a freshly pressed white Sunday shirt and his own clip-on bow tie. The whole family was ready to board that ridiculous old '37 Ford and go flying off to church. By God, I wasn't going with them. My mother tried not to say anything hurtful, but just the pain in her eyes, like an old workhorse that had been beaten, told the story. Made me sick. My father was silent, as usual. I felt like I was on the outside. Didn't belong there anymore.

My mother had let me take the same old black metal suitcase we had lugged to my grandparents' when I was a child. She kissed me good-bye and told me to say my prayers—trying to say something else, I could tell, but she couldn't get it out. I wanted to smile, but it was forced and didn't hang on my face long. I promised I'd write. I was in a hurry to get the misery of leaving over with. I said, "Dad, considering the fact that I won't be driving the car much anymore, I was wondering if you could drive me out to the highway?" He looked at me, surprised, and then he saw my suitcase standing there at the door, and he didn't say anything. He grabbed it and tossed it in the backseat and said, "Come on." Then the drove the old '37 out to U.S. Highway 30 headed west. It was cold, and a high Laramie wind was blowing. At the edge of town my father let me off.

I shook his hand in the way a man shakes the hand of a man. I wasn't sure I could go through with it, but I got out of the car with my bag, and I stood there on the road alone. Then as if he knew, he revved up the old Ford, made a big U-turn in the middle of the highway, and before I could change my mind, headed the car back toward home, me standing there in the wind and the blowing snow on the empty road. I turned to watch, and for the last time I saw the old Ford, saw it disappear down the street, its fenders still flapping. I wanted to cry out, "Come back and get me, Daddy. Don't leave me." But I was a goddamn man, and I didn't cry. I turned my head into the wind and waited for something to throw my thumb at.

"Well, shit, I'm gettin' the hell out," I said aloud. I'd been alone before. I'd been alone in the hayfields behind a couple of horses, and I'd been alone herding sheep, and I'd been alone in the mountains. I knew how to be alone. I had fifteen dollars in my pocket. I wasn't going to starve to death. I could get work. But I was going to freeze my ass off if a car didn't come along and pick me up pretty quick. Then somebody did come. It has always been that way for me. Somebody always came along to save me. It took four days and a dozen rides in old cars with poor folks, with a lonely truck driver, a salesman in a battered Dodge, a rancher or two in rattling pickups, people in cars like my father's old '37 without room in their worn-out rattletraps. They saw me standing there, my thumb asking for a lift, and they gave it to me, all the way to San Diego.

California was a make-believe place, all warm and balmy in the winter, the palm trees—I had never seen a palm tree that I could remember—the soft, wet air—how could there be such a place as this? If I had known, I'd never have stayed in the backwoods of Wyoming so long. And I would never go back. Look at the fancy cars, the convertibles, Chevies, Caddies, and Fords, the windshields cut down low, the tops padded. The hip Mexicans in black zoot suits, black peg-legged pants, long gold chains hanging from their pockets, hair slicked back, shiny varnished hair.

I hoofed it up to Brown's Academy, found out where Jim was holed up in one of those little rooms, and he packed his bags and by God, that was it. We were out of there whether his sister liked it or not. He said he didn't give a good goddamn, he was going, and we went—decided to take in a little "Mexican culture" before we headed out to sea for good, so we thumbed our way to Tijuana. It was night, and you could tell when you crossed the border. Suddenly there weren't any lights. No streetlights. Save the power. Power costs money, man. We walked down the dark streets of the town to the sound of the mariachi bands, the doors of the honky-tonks open, the lights inside dim. But you could see the sailors in their whites lined up at the bar and dancing, some dancing with each other, and hollering and raising all kinds of hell. And on the streets the sailors were shuffling through the dust, three, four abreast, and we had to step aside. Tough guys. If you had a uniform you were somebody, and without one, well, you were probably a fucking draft dodger or something was wrong with you—heart condition, little weakling bastard who didn't amount to a damn. Maybe queer. We never went into the bars, Jim and I. Sure as hell the drunk sailors in there would kick the shit out of us. We walked over on the side of the street. Hung to the shadows. Then a skinny, dirty kid about ten, maybe twelve, came up to us.

"Hey, you guys wanna good time?" He had a child's voice.

"What do you mean," I said, walking on, him following.

"You wanna girl?" he asked. I looked at Jim. He gave me that shit-eating grin of his and shrugged his shoulders. The kid wanted a dollar and I gave it to him, and we followed him into the night, through the dark, dusty back streets rutted from a long-forgotten summer rain. We walked past shacks and sometimes I saw the flicker of a candle, and sometimes the shacks were dark, but you could hear the people inside talking in high Mexican voices. This was the life. But it was dangerous there in the dark. Maybe the kid was leading us into an ambush. Maybe we would be mugged or killed. Well, they'd have to kill both of us. I gave Jim Brown a nudge. He looked at me and I winked, but he didn't wink back, intent on where he was putting his feet down on the dark road in front of us.

Up the street a couple more blocks we came to a hut with a line of sailors standing in front of it. When somebody pulled out his Zippo and lit up, you could see the sailors in their whites, the line ten men long or more, the sailors laughing, jiving each other.

"Cost ya three bucks," the kid said. "Geet in line." Then he disappeared into the darkness.

We stood in line, the only ones without a uniform. Never said anything to each other. Never said anything to anybody else. Didn't want any trouble. When a sailor came out of the shack someone would holler, "Hey, buddy, any good?" And the sailor would holler back, "She was too damn good for you, fuckhead," and everyone would laugh.

After an hour or so the line ahead diminished and other sailors made up the line behind us. Finally we reached the door. I was in front of Jim. The guy in front of me pushed the door open a little with his foot. The room was dimly lit, but I could plainly see a sailor, his trousers down around his knees, pumping away on top of a small Mexican woman, her brown arms relaxed around him, her knees swaying apart easily to his beating rhythm, her bare feet gray and callused from walking shoeless in the dirt. She stared up at the smoke-colored ceiling, no expression on her face, her eyes glazed over, her face the face of the dead. The sailor got off and pulled up his trousers.

"You're next," Jim said.

"Musta left my wallet in my other pants," I said.

"I'll loan ya the three bucks," Jim said.

"Na, I don't wanna," I said.

"Yer chicken shit," he said. "I'll wait here for you."

"I never had any intention of goin' in there in the first place," I said.

"Me neither," he said. "Let's go."

Back at the border the navy military police herded us into a "Pro Station" like cattle, one of those well-lighted places on the American side, the sailors lined up in long lines getting their parts washed and getting their urethras shot up with an antiseptic that was supposed to save you from all venereal diseases known to man.

"I never did anything," I said to the sailor in charge. He was an older guy.

"Don't give me that shit, kid," he said. "They all say that."

"I'm not a sailor. I'm a civilian."

"If you ain't a sailor, ya ain't got no business in Tijuana," he said. He motioned us to the line where the sailors were washing themselves with a thick, brown liquid soap under the scrutiny of an officer. I looked at Jim. He shrugged, and I shrugged, and we went on through the line, navy or not, fresh fornicators or not, washed, scrubbed, and abraded of all external evidence of sin.

The next day we signed on as messmen on the SS *Roanoke,* a derelict old coal burner that had been converted during the war to oil, a tanker owned by the Texas Company. Scummy old tub painted red, black and white, its paint peeling from its rusting sides, a waterline around its middle like the dirty ring in a bathtub. No self-respecting seaman would think of boarding the *Roanoke.* Consequently, it was the only ship offering work to a first-time seaman. Besides, it was going to Russia, and although, according to the shipping board, it was scheduled for Port Arthur, Texas, through the Panama Canal, Jim Brown and I and all the old salts hanging around the hall knew better. The war was just over, and the Russians were hollering for gasoline, but there were still a bunch of German subs in the Atlantic whose captains hadn't yet surrendered, and the Texas Company wasn't about to send one of its top-line tankers to Russia under those circumstances. If they were going to lose a ship, just as well be the old *Roanoke.* It had pretty well seen its last days anyway.

But Jim and I had it figured another way. Suppose there was a German sub captain who was still poking around out there. Would he waste one of his last precious torpedoes on an old wreck of a tub like the SS *Roanoke*? No. He'd be hanging around just under the surface looking for a big old lumbering Victory tanker loaded to the decks. So why not sign on to the *Roanoke* and go to Russia? Besides, we heard the Russian women were big as horses and wild as March hares.

"Them Roosian women can squeeze the guts right out of a man, legs on 'em like a wrestler." That's how the old salts talked. "An' they're hungry as hell for that big Yankee doodle dandy and a package of cigarettes." And they laughed and gave each other the rib with their elbows.

"Man oughta go to Russia," I said.

"Right," Jim said. "Who the fuck wants ta go to Port Arthur, Texas?"

Jim was assigned to the officer's mess and I to the crew's mess. The steward, a fat, rat-faced black-haired Texan of about fifty, was in charge of both dining rooms. He fed his men well. Had to, to get anybody to stay on the *Roanoke.*

The steward laid it out for me the first morning. "Them men tell you what they want, and they get it," he said. "Eggs over easy. Straight up. Bacon. Cakes. Whatever the fuck they want they get. If they want a lollipop for breakfast they get it. And ya keep the fuckin' coffee urn clean. Take the baking soda here and scrub it good and then flush it out again. And if I ever catch you serving these men coffee out of a dirty urn I'll stuff yer head down the son-of-a-bitch and scrub it out with your ears, understand?" I nodded.

"I'll tell ya one thing more," the steward said. "We don't run no union ship here. The union is run by a bunch of Commie cocksuckers. Ship out under the NMU," which was the National Maritime Union, "and you'll find out. They don't get fresh coffee every morning on one of them union ships, and the cooks

are nothing but a bunch of goddamn Baltimore niggers." He puffed his cigarette between sentences, one long inhaled puff after another. "As long as
these men get what they want there ain't no call for a union. So give 'em what
they want."

The steward wanted the wooden benches scrubbed every day. The oilers
would come up from the engine room with their pants covered with grease and
flop their dirty asses down on the raw wooden benches, and I had to scrub the
grease off, three times a day, Bon Ami, scrub and rinse, scrub and rinse, until
"every by God fucking little crack is as clean as your mother's ass," the steward
said. Jim Brown didn't have to scrub benches because the officers had chairs in
their dining room and they didn't drag in dirty asses to the mess hall. So the
steward could go to hell, I thought, and I scrubbed the benches. And they were
clean, and the crew, the deck hands, the engine room hands all got what they
wanted for breakfast, but nobody asked for lollipops.

Before the ship took off for Russia, the steward brought a bottle of rum on
board—trying to be nice—have a little party before we weighed anchor. "Rum
and Coca-Cola," to treat the messmen, the little bastards who worked every day,
no days off until they got to shore again. I'd never tasted liquor before—like my
mother, none of any kind. I saw my mother's sad face. I could hear her distant
voice telling me that liquor had never touched her lips, never. But I was already
a full-blown sinner, a fornicator, a smoker—smoking big old R. G. Dunns with
Jim Brown. And so what was one more sin to such a chronic sinner as me? After
a couple of double shots of rum and a little Coke I got sick. I thought my liver
would come spitting out in little maroon pieces—kept looking for the liver. I
prayed to God that if He would only get me through this I would never drink
again, not ever for as long as I lived.

The next morning I was awakened by a strange rumbling noise, a vibration
that felt like an impending earthquake. I jumped out of my bunk. The old steel
decks were vibrating. I ran out on the poop deck at the aft of the ship to see
what was happening. The deck was shaking. Suddenly I realized: the *Roanoke's*
old engines were thumping away down in the hold. Then I saw the deckhands
working the lines, saw them hauling the gangplank, and I heard the "whoosh,
whoosh, whoosh" of the screw churning the water like the agitator in a giant
washing machine. Finally the old ship eased out backward into San Pedro harbor, and we were sailors, yes sailors, headed for Russia! Jim Brown was standing there on the poop deck gawking at the disappearing land like a kid saying
good-bye to his homeland forever.

"Well, here we go," I said, giving him a pat on the back.

"Right," he said, a big grin on his face, his eyes all distant and squinty. And
that's all he said.

I got along with the cook pretty well. Kissed his ass, just as the steward said I
should. "Kiss the old fart's ass and you'll get along. If you don't he'll get ya, and
he's got a hundred sneaky little ways to do it." The cook was an old balding, skinny

Mexican with a potbelly and slumping shoulders. He stood with his feet spread out. He'd been molded into the stance after a lifetime standing in front of the galley range trying to cook on rolling seas. He spoke a brand of broken English that few could understand, except for the obscenities. The rest of his words were slurred and mixed in with various Spanish phrases, but if you listened carefully, you could get the drift, and I listened. After the tenth day at sea he said, "Baby," which is what he called me. "Baby, you are my son." He had no kids.

"Baby," he began one evening over a hot cup of my freshly brewed coffee poured out of my immaculately clean urn, "Baby, the steward he is no fooking man." He sipped on the edge of the hot cup with his thin yellow lips. I was surprised at his irreverence toward the steward, who was his boss. "That sum-bitch don't know how to fook a womans."

"What do you mean?" I asked.

"Well, that sum-bitch he always wanna fooking rubber. Unnerstand?" I nodded. "You no can fook no womans with no fooking rubber. Unnerstand?" I nodded again. But I didn't understand. "He ees afraid to fook." He shook his head, laughed and took another slow sip, looking into the steam that drifted up around his sallow face as if he were giving the matter further profound thought. He nodded at the cup to tell me the coffee was good. I loved the cook. "I tol' heem, 'Look at that paper there, Steward. The doctor, he test them girls, says so on the paper there. Them girls is okay to fook,' but the steward, he ees afraid. He no fook them girls. Me, I fook them girls. I geet the clap? Who gives a fook? A fooking runnin' deek ees better to get rid of than a fooking running nose! One shot of that pennumcillum, the clap, she dry up. You got a fooking running nose and get a shot of that pennumcillum and you still got a fooking running nose. I tell the steward, 'Steward, you can geet rid of the clap easier than you can geet rid of a cold,' but he no listen. He ees no man."

"Right," I said.

"When we get to Port Arthurs we go to Galveston. Them girls ees better at Galveston. I show you the girls when we geet there, Baby."

"You damn rights," I said, big. Then I asked the real question. "Are we really going to go to Port Arthur?"

"Yeah," the cook said, "but the girls ees better in Galveston." I knew better—I knew we were headed for Russia. Either the cook was putting me on or he had been taken in like the rest of the crew. Then we sailed through the Panama Canal. Why would they send an old tub like this all the way around to the Atlantic side full of gasoline if they didn't intend to send her on over? Tell me that?

I loved the heat, the feel of sweat on my body, the warmth in the low, deep winter sun. I felt like a tomato plant back home that had been confined in the window box, one that had finally been transplanted into the rich hot soil. The countryside was lush and green like the jungles in the movies. From the poop deck it was a paradise out there, little jutting islands that, from a distance, and through the haze of the morning, pushed out of the ocean like green, moss-covered stumps. Everywhere there were palms, and clear, deep, calm water, the natives running about barefooted in short white pants, an old frayed straw hat maybe, nothing else. The place made me feel all steamy and excited.

"Let's jump this tomato can right here," I said to Jim. "This is the place! Look at the women! Look at the jungle out there! Goddamn, ain't that pretty?" Sometimes you could get a glimpse of a girl strolling along the fringes of the canal carrying a basket on her head or herding a couple of goats. They were slender and tiny and brown skinned and they wore ragged cotton dresses.

"You no jump ship here, Jadie," the old cook warned. Sometimes he called me Jadie. "You jump ship here and they throw your fooking ass in a Panama jail an' you die in them fooking jails. Die of the fooking crud. Wait 'til we geet to Galveston. Them womens is better in Galveston anyways."

One morning I was awakened by the silence. The background rumble of the engines had stopped. Nothing but the quiet slush of water against the tub's old iron sides. I stumbled out of the hold where our tiny bunks were hung by steel straps to the sweating steel hull and ran to the poop deck to find the old *Roanoke* docked. Where in the hell were we? This didn't look like Russia to me. Acres of oil tanks, refinery stacks in the distance, the signs along the dock all in English. Ugly place. Barren of greenery, American trucks. And where were the women, big as horses, who would come on board and unload the ship, and, also slip into your bunk and squeeze your guts out with their thighs as big as a wrestler's?

"Where the hell are we, Cookie?" I hollered at the cook.

"Thees here is Port Arthur, Texas. But don' worry, Baby, I take you to Galveston." I felt like I'd been lied to.

That night we got drunk in the first saloon we could find, the steward, Jim and I, and Cookie. Big time we were, smoking R. G. Dunns, and big-time drunk on straight shots of Seagram's Seven with a beer chaser—drunk on the excuse of diluting the disappointment of not seeing Russia.

"Here's to Russia," I said to Jim, raising my glass.

"Right," he said, still grinning. "And here's to the Russian broads who were saved from us," he added.

I didn't get sick this time; maybe whiskey was kinder to a country boy, or maybe it was because my feet were on the boards of this noisy, nasty saloon along the waterfront and not on the swaying deck of the old *Roanoke*. Big room, this saloon, soggy from wall to wall in uproar and racket, with seamen plastered up against the walls and hanging like slabs of beef from the bar. Some were dozing off, and some had already passed out. Some were staggering around and shouting and throwing their fists at the air, and some were dancing by themselves and with each other. They were awful-looking rogues, a hodgepodge of men and muscle, of giants and pygmies, of Mexicans and blacks, of Puerto Ricans and Swedes as big as oxen. But they were mostly old bastards, at least past thirty, with potbellies and feral eyes, a bearded, scraggly, ridiculous-looking bunch in their shore clothes that were wrinkled from having lain in their sea bags for so long. They wore old blue, pin-striped suit vests over long-sleeved underwear, and pointed-toed black shoes, their gray, once-white socks showing from under faded dungarees. Some had vagrant hair slicked down with hair grease, and some wore beads of shell and coral, and most had large black billfolds stuck in their hip pockets chained in front to their wide leather belts with brass and chromium chains. One old man wore a copper bracelet for his rheumatism. A few of the younger men sported white sailor caps with dirty smudges up front marked from the grime of their thumbs when they pulled their caps down low to look tough. But the older salts came out bareheaded or wore blue woolen knit caps pulled down to their ears. If you closed your eyes you couldn't distinguish a word through the roar of the tumult, except once in a while a high shrieked "fuck you too," or "*bull* shit" rose above the din. The noise of the voices blanketed the jukebox. What was playing no one could know. No one gave a good goddamn. The place smelled like a hundred bottles of booze, and sweat and piss and cheap hair grease and the musk of a hundred foul-breathed men.

Through the drunken flood that took over the mind, I thought of how I had broken my vow to God, drinking and smoking and all. I thought of how I had promised I'd never drink again, and how, drunk again, I would surely be punished. You could break your word to a man and your punishment would be self-transformation into a worthless liar but if you lied to God—Yet maybe a man stood an outside chance of being forgiven. But how about standing in a saloon with a shot of whiskey in your hand, already figuring, as you committed the sin, how to get out of it later on by praying? I'd take the chance. It'd be worth it. A man had to live. Live! Then we hailed a cab, the bunch of us, and with the old cook in charge we headed for Galveston.

"You guys lookin' for a good time?" the cabby asked.

"Yeah," I said.

"I got a line on some high yella," the cabby said.

"What's that?" I whispered to the cook who was sitting next to me. He began to laugh. "Thees kid he no know what high yella ees," and then everybody laughed. Jim laughed, too, but I doubted he knew either.

"High yella is one of them women who is mostly white with a little nigger blood throwed in for good fuckin'," the steward said. "Nigger blood makes 'em hot."

"Best they is," the cabby said like he knew.

"We gonna Galveston," the cook said. "We no fook aroun' with no fooking high yellers."

The bawdy houses in Galveston were situated along the waterfront, those kind of walk-up hotels I'd been in Sheridan and Rawlins. The cook led us straight off to "the best fooking house in thees fooking town." The parlor was decked out with red-frocked wallpaper, and everything else was in red—the women all in red, the blondes looking good in that color, and the brunettes too.

Red candle lights burned in the electric candelabras. The ceiling was painted red. The carpet in the parlor was red, and even the sofas were covered with red velvet. The devil wears red, I thought.

The cook and the steward sat back drinking rum and Coke, watching Jim and me, sort of like parents watching the kids at Christmastime, that superior, amused look on their faces. The cook claimed there were a lot of houses in Galveston, and he was going to do a little shopping first. The steward agreed.

"I ain't gonna pop the first pussy that wiggles in front of my face," the steward said, puffing steadily on his cigarette but never taking his eyes off the parading women. "You can look all night and never see two alike." "Take yer time, kid. Look 'em over" was the steward's advice. But kids are not good at soaking up advice in a whorehouse.

And the cook had been right. The steward was no man. Before we left that first house the steward had followed the skinny redhead with the big ones out of the parlor. You could hear the sound of her high heels pounding down the hall on the wooden floors. Made the same sounds as when I used to walk on the concrete sidewalk on those stilts my father made me when I was a boy. I thought of my father. Hurt me to see his innocent face in a whorehouse. And when the redhead was halfway down the hall we all heard her hollering to the madam, "Get me a rubber. This trick wants a rubber."

There in Galveston, when late at night the last traces of the accursed hormone had been drained from our veins, Jim Brown and I retired to the poker houses and played the game with the big boys for the big money—sometimes five bucks a throw. Five card stud and draw poker. We sat at the round green velvet-covered tables in the smoky back rooms, sat there straight-faced looking mean, looking tough, sat there smoking our big cigars, not talking, not looking up. When it was my deal I dealt the first card face up, the card that, according to tradition, should have been the hole card. I dealt the second card down. In the end, it was all the same—one card up and one card down. But the break from tradition alarmed the old hands, and they complained to the houseman: "This kid is dealing different." The houseman, suspicious, eyes continuously darting to pick up any untoward conduct, hissed, "Deal 'em straight, kid." We were winning.

Despite the unwritten law of poker players that prohibits the display of emotion sometimes I couldn't contain my anger at the luck of the draw, and I would slam the cards down on the table in disgust and throw in the hand. At other times, after I'd sneaked a peek and was overjoyed at what I saw, I couldn't help but come out with a joyous "Jesus Christ!" The old hands with those dried-up, brittle psyches thought I was bluffing because no honest-to-God poker player is honest. The bluff is the essence of the game. The empty face. Poker is a game of lies. But to let the truth hang out?

"Tell that kid to shut his mouth," one of the old hands hollered to the houseman, "or you can cash me in."

"Sorry," I said real mean-like. I puffed a big puff of smoke in the guy's face.

He jumped up and Jim jumped up. And I jumped up. The houseman ran over, stood between us. "Get your asses out of here," he said. "I been watching you. You got some kind of slick scam going on. So get the fuck out or I'll call the cops." Not a veteran poker player, not even the houseman understood the confounding power of the truth. Later, in the courtroom, my seasoned opponents would saunter into court in their blue pin-striped suits and their pretty silk ties, those men of great intelligence who were steeped in the sauce of cynicism and soaked in the brine of distrust—but they were no better suited to understand the power of truth than were those tinhorn gamblers in Galveston.

Between us, Jim and I had twenty bucks in winnings. Big night. We vacated the premises, me with my gorky walk and Jim with his nonchalant, tough-guy shuffle. We ambled like big shots into the next joint, and to celebrate our victory Jim bought a couple of Webster Queens, best cigars made, he said. "Hey, kid," he said like a big brother as he lit my cigar. "Next time cool it. I ain't no fighter. I'm a lover." Then he laughed and I laughed too, and, each in our own style, swaggered on down the waterfront, grabbed a cab and headed back to the ship.

CHAPTER 15

*Jim Brown and Gerry Spence fifty years
after their adventure.*

MAE STORED MY father's ashes on top of the dresser in her bedroom. Kept them in the same black plastic urn they had been delivered in, the urn brought to her front door by the man who had taken my father away in that gray corduroy bag. Fair trade in fulfillment of the contract. She made no inquiry about the contents of the urn when the man handed it over with a polite smile. She thanked him, and put the ashes where they would be close to her.

One day I saw the urn sitting on her dresser. I didn't want to look inside—something about not wanting to see your father's ashes. I wanted to remember *him,* not the ash and the pieces of bone and I could still hear his joke—could just as well be the ashes of some old alley cat.

I talked to my brother Tom about the ashes. Maybe we should climb Cloud Peak together where my father fished in the high clear lakes of the Big Horns when I was a young boy. "No," Mae said. "Your father wanted his ashes spread over the Colorado mountains above Grandpa Spence's place. I'll keep them for a while, and when it's my time, you can spread both of our ashes together up there," and she gave me that same sweet smile that my father loved, and that I had learned to love as well.

❋ ❋ ❋

When you are sixteen you don't think about death or ashes or alley cats. You think about the Russian women. You don't think about life. You're in it. You do it. We shipped out of Port Arthur on the Liberty tanker *Christopher Sholes,* Jim Brown and I. The *Christopher Sholes* was one of those prefabricated ships disguised as a Liberty cargo vessel with artificial booms laid down on the deck. But in its hold, tanks carrying hundreds of thousands of gallons of gasoline had been installed. Liberty ships had been designed to carry cargo, not fuel, and near the end of the war they sailed unescorted across the Atlantic because the Nazi subs were saving their scarce torpedoes for tankers. "Run 'em out of gas and you win the war" was the idea. So when the U-boat captain looked out his periscope and saw what looked like a lone Liberty ship slugging along, he saved his torpedo for a tanker he hoped would come by.

The good ship *Christopher Sholes,* like other Liberty ships, was armed with a big howitzer on the bow and a couple of cannons at mid-deck, because sometimes a U-boat would encounter an unarmed Liberty ship, save its torpedoes, and sink it with its deck cannon. Sailors from the U.S. Navy had been assigned to the *Christopher Sholes* to man the big guns, a bunch of lazy bastards who let the guns grow rusty in the salt air while they lounged on the deck, smoked cigarettes and read girlie magazines. The ship's crew would have nothing to do with the navy guys. But one thing Jim and I knew, this time for sure: Although the board had scheduled this ship for Tampico, Mexico, we knew that once the ship was at sea we would be shanghaied for Russia. Why else would they assign a navy gun crew to the ship? We were going to get our chance with those big Russky women after all.

This time both Jim and I had shipped out as ordinary seamen. Somebody else could scrub the damn benches and labor at the coffee urn. We were deck hands. We beat at the thick rust on the iron deck with hammer and chisel and painted the bare spots, first with red lead, and then with ugly gray paint. We hauled the heavy, four-inch-thick hemp lines when the ship docked, manned the winches and stood watch on the bow at night. Being an ordinary seaman was a man's job, all right. The messmen had to wait on you.

The best watch was the "four-to-eight"—four in the morning until eight in the morning, and four in the afternoon until eight at night. At night, the seas were calm, and the seaman on watch stood alone at the bow peering out in the darkness searching for the lights of other ships, for the lights of a buoy, for any lights, and he signaled the location of the light he saw with a ringing of the bell at the bow of the ship, once for port, twice for starboard, three times for dead ahead.

The stars that hung over the sea on a clear night were as bright and boisterous as boys on the Fourth of July—like kids with sparklers, like kids across town lighting sky rockets, the sky aglow and bursting. And the ship, cutting steadily, almost silently through the sea, riled up the phosphorus particles in the water, so there were fireworks in the water too, like fireflies snapping back at the stars. At the bow of the ship, the porpoises cavorted, making tracks through the sea, up and down and up again, like my mother's needle basting the hem of her skirt. And sometimes they rubbed up against the rough steel bow to rid their silky hides of sea grubs, and I thought I could hear them sing.

In the night standing watch, I gazed up at the stars and I thought the serious thoughts of boys. I thought how the stars had been made by God, and then I wondered who made God, and then I wondered who made whoever it was who made God, and I threw up my arms to the stars and talked to the stars. "I don't give a shit who made you," I hollered. "I, myself, was made by the same outfit—whoever or whatever—you and me and the porpoises—we're all in this together. We are partners." And the wind, soft and balmy, blew back in my face like the breath of a hot naked woman in the dark, and her tongue lapped up easy out of the water, and the spray of the water left my face warm and wet.

Sometimes up there on the bow at night I thought about the time I went antelope hunting with the guy across the street, a guy built like a middleweight wrestler, big red nose from all the beer, and when we got home that evening he said, "Well, see ya kid. Guess I'll go on in and fuck the old lady." She was a broad-hipped woman with a pretty face and black eyes and a space between her teeth, and I imagined how it would be. She was a friend of my mother's. God Almighty, I thought. You are a bad son-of-a-bitch, thinking like that, and I tried not to think about it, but at night on the bow of a ship the mind has no boss.

Sometimes the stars were so bright and so low on the black horizon I couldn't tell what were stars and what were the lights of a ship, and I rang the bell so the mate in the wheelhouse was warned—whatever the hell he was doing up there—probably had both hands down his dungarees. So if this was sinful, this kind of life, well, I was for it.

My mother, Esther Sophie Spence, was an expert on sin, a fully committed advocate against the devil. The devil, she said, provided all degrees of sin to tempt mankind. But since God, upon simply request, would forgive any sin, the hierarchical classification of sin seemed to lose its importance. God would forgive murder and he would forgive stealing a cookie before supper and lying about it. The idea wasn't that murder wasn't the worst of sins. But even murder could be forgiven. And since any sin could be forgiven, it seemed to follow that *sin was sin.* Early on I had that figured out.

Moreover, it was as sinful to think about a sinful act as it was to commit it, a cute little quirk in this religious business to nip sin in the bud, because you can't commit a sin without thinking about it first. But I turned the ethical equation back on God. I figured, if it was as sinful to think about it as it was to do it, I might just as well do it, because no matter how I tried I couldn't stop thinking about it.

Yet up there on the bow of the ship at night I thought about my mother—not that I was homesick, nothing like that. She just kept coming to mind, that sweet woman who knew practically nothing, that farm girl who had never once gotten gloriously drunk, who hadn't even tasted liquor, who had never smoked a cigarette, who had never run wild with the men, and had, instead, devoted her life to her family and to God. She was a woman who, for all practical account-ing, was a child who had never lived. I thought of her innocence and how she would die if she knew the sins this son of hers had committed intentionally, pur-posely, happily. I felt the guilt.

"Read the Bible," were the words I heard.

But I wasn't going to read any goddamned Bible. I was going to find out whatever there was to find out for myself. I didn't need Moses laying down all that crap for me to follow. He'd never been on a ship headed for Russia. What the hell would Moses have done with a bunch of Russky women? I was a man now—shaved once a week. I was going to prop the doors of life wide open and walk out into it. That's more than my mother had ever done. She was scared to death of sin. Well, I wasn't afraid of it. Sin had better get the hell out of my way—that's all I had to say.

And my father? Well, my father knew some things, all right, and he wasn't afraid, and he'd take on man or God if he had to. But he'd never been to a whorehouse in Galveston, Texas, or gone to the beach with a naked girl you could pick up in the bars in Aruba, and he'd never played poker with a black crew on a ship headed for Russia. And he'd never seen men stabbed, as Ol' Calsey had been stabbed. My father had fought in the ring, and he was tough, and could walk a deer down, but he'd never got drunk and stolen a rowboat, as Jim and I did that dark night when we rowed down the Mississippi headed to New Orleans. And he'd never slogged through the Mississippi swamps, stag-gering drunk in the night, laughing, the mud up above his ass, as Jim and I had, when we gave up our trip because we had been nearly capsized a dozen times by those big ships and flat-decked barges being pulled by tugboats that couldn't see us in the dark. My father, so brave and tough, knew nothing about the real world, the world I was in.

One night coming in from his watch Jim said it was Father's Day. Didn't know why he cared. His father being dead, and all, but maybe even Jim thought about things out there, although he never said so. Just sort of mentioned it in passing. "Father's Day, pard," he said and went on. I got to thinking about my own father. He would have liked it out there, the sea calm and silent except for the sound of the ship cutting through the water and the flapping of a flying fish landing on the deck. At times like that I used to compose poems, said them to myself until my watch was over, when I wrote them down in a small black loose-leaf notebook.

That night I wrote a poem to my father, and when we got to port, I sent it to him. Over half a century later, one of my mother's friends, with whom my mother had shared the poem, sent me the poem along with my mother's letter from 1945. In her letter to her friend, my mother had written that it was Sun-day and that my father was out fishing alone. "He seldom gets off without the rest of us, but this was my day to tell flannel-graph stories at Sunday School, so it has turned into a good day to write letters." She wrote that she'd been teaching the last two weeks in Vacation Bible School, working with the beginners, and that she had to read my poem to someone so she had called her friend's mother and read it to her, and now she was sending the poem on to her friend. This was the poem, in retrospect, little more than the sentimental thoughts of a sixteen-year-old boy for his father. I had forgotten it until I read it again in the letter.

A Toast to Father

To Father on this Father's Day
From son, a thousand miles away.
To Dad, whose sweat upon the brow
Gave to me what I've got now.

To Father and his old Krag gun
To those dear days when we had fun
To striking trout and streams so clear
To all those things we hold so dear.

To Father in the campfire's light
I see him as I sit tonight
A man whose face reveals his soul
To be like him has been my goal.

To him who gave the solid start
To me, I thank. I'll do my part
To build on it a worthy man
And with his help, I know I can.

To Father on this Father's Day
A toast: Yes, I'm always proud to say
When people ask, that you're my Dad,
The best that any fellow's had.

Try as I did, I could not shed the country boy in me, nor quiet the pesky voice that shamed me. Despite my profligacy, I was not a profligate at the core. Yet I wanted to be. I admit, I tried. I fought hard to release myself of the chains of my childhood teaching, that bothersome morality stuff that often seemed irrelevant to the good life. Nobody had any use for a sweetpea, milquetoast Sunday school punk who wouldn't drink a shot of good whiskey or smoke a fine cigar. Nobody had any use for a sweetheart goody-two-shoes who was too damn uppity to spend a little time with an honest "working girl" when he got ashore.

I now recount with recurring sorrow that as a teenage sailor in those old romantic ports I saw only the bars and the poker houses and the bordellos. But who wanted to visit some decaying old fort when you could see a "high yella" girl with one breast tattooed "sweet" and the other tattooed "sour" and a bumblebee tattooed down near the place? *The* place, baby!

"Come on, baby, let me sting ya!"

When you could hang out in a lively saloon, with wild music and wild women down on the waterfront, who wanted to trudge through some moldering morgue of a museum? I wanted to be bad. Bad was better. Yet, I admit, at night I was still beseeching the Lord to forgive my many trespasses.

We docked, as promised in the shipping orders, in Tampico, that sprawling port on the east coast of Mexico, the dusty streets, the shacks from a distance looking as if a truckload of shoe boxes had been dumped in the middle of a desert. Skinny brown people everywhere in rags and straw hats. After all those days at sea I couldn't believe we were only in Mexico. Who was supplying the fucking Russkies with gasoline? To soothe our sorrow Jim and I headed straight for the whorehouses.

In Tampico the "working girls" occupied tiny, squalid ground-floor rooms that faced out around a dark square. At night the square was teeming with walking, gawking men. Cost nothing to walk and gawk. The men strained to see the women through the bad light, and the men hollered to the women from the sidewalk— too timid, I thought, to walk up close and speak to them in soft kind voices.

"Hey ya, baby, whatcha got?"

The women sat under the dim light of their doorways, too desperate to feel shame, too tired to care, short, hungry-looking women with thick, slumping bodies offering for sale whatever they had. Some already looked old. The women's breasts, hanging down like that, the women trying to hoist them up with those cloth slings that went down and around and up again, and then tied at the back of the neck. The women fed their babies from those breasts, and now the women offered their breasts to the men walking by, the women still trying to feed their babies. I thought of my mother's breasts. They were small, and she kept them to herself. Hardly noticed them at all. Some of the women had tried to brighten themselves with fresh ribbons in their dusty hair, and most had smeared hard mouths with dark red. Some wore cheap rosaries around their necks. Their clothing was flimsy and worn and some stood in old, tight-fitting bathing suits. Even when they were sitting, you could see their stomachs pouching out like they were six months along.

As the men walked by, a woman, skinny as a stick, hollered, "Come on een here, *señor.* I geeve you good time, cheap."

The men laughed and walked on. "I wouldn't fuck her with *your* dick," the sailor in front of us yelled at his mate. And they laughed again.

"Let's get outta here," I said to Jim.

"Okay, pard," he said. And that's all he said, and I was glad.

* * *

That fall Jim Brown and I returned to Laramie. Nothing had changed. My upstairs room was the same. Town the same. The wind, the same. My folks the same, as if they'd been dumped in a crock of water glass for preserving, along with the eggs. They treated me with a little more respect, I thought. Maybe it was a little more distance. I'd been out there, you know, and they hadn't. I'd seen the world and they'd seen nothing.

Jim and I enrolled at the university—pre-law, by God, going to be big-time lawyers, probably criminal lawyers like old G. R. McConnell, who, right there in Laramie, right there in our own hometown, had defended this certain bootlegger in one of Wyoming's most famous cases. The story went that during the trial old G.R. grabbed the evidence, a pint bottle of whiskey, and took a big swig to sort of test it, and, satisfied, he started his opening argument. Then in a little while he took another swig. And before anybody realized it, he had drunk the whole damned bottle, swig at a time, right there in the courtroom in front of God and the judge and the jury. Well, then, as the story went, old G.R. turned to the judge and made his motion:

"I move to dismiss this case, Your Honor."

"On what grounds, Mr. McConnell?"

"On the grounds that the *corpus delicti,* namely the alleged whiskey, has somehow disappeared. The prosecution doesn't have a case without the *corpus delicti,* and I move to dismiss this case right here and now!"

The judge pondered the matter for a moment and then banged his gavel. "Case dismissed," the judge ordered.

We laughed and laughed, Jim and I. "Drank up the *corpus fuckin' delicti.* Wasn't that too goddamned neat?" I hollered. That's what I wanted to be—a damn criminal lawyer. Yessiree, baby! A big-time criminal lawyer like G. R. McConnell. I was seventeen.

Of course my mother knew how this son, her offering, like Isaac, to God, had departed from "the way." I knew she knew. I could feel it. She could probably smell it, the smoke and the booze. She had a nose for sin. Sometimes I could tell she couldn't bear to look at me, and when she did, she looked as if she were going to burst into that sucked-in, almost silent crying of hers. You could see it coming. I knew she didn't know what to say to me, and when she broached the subjects of drinking or smoking, I would get all tight and hostile. "I wish you wouldn't nag at me like that," I'd say. "I can't stand nagging." Or I'd walk out without saying anything at all.

One day I learned the truth about my mother's intentions for me. I'd just come down those short steep stairs from my room, the old stairs creaking, giving my escape away, and there my father stood, waiting for me. He had that look on his face.

"Time we have a little talk, son."

"What now?" I said.

"Your mother has been crying all night."

"Again? What the hell have I done this time?"

"Your mother was driving home from the church the other day and saw you walking down the street with a cigarette in your mouth. You know how she feels about that."

"Oh, for Christ's sake!" I said.

"And that too—your swearing! These days you don't show much respect for your parents, or for what you've been taught. It sure wouldn't hurt you to go to church with your mother once in a while. Make her happy." I followed him into the kitchen. He started flipping his flapjacks. He usually cooked breakfast on Sunday. "Isn't much for you to do for your mother—give her an hour a week, and go to church with her."

"Oh, for Christ's sake!" I whispered under my breath. I stood there watching him turn the cakes. He put a pile of three on a plate and handed it to me. "When Little Peggy died of meningitis your mother made a bargain with God— a lot of little kids were dying of it and you'd been exposed—well, if God would spare you, she agreed to give you to God."

"Oh, for Christ's sakes," I said again.

"And now your mother thinks she's been a failure as a mother—your smoking, and cussing, and whoring around, and not going to church—and she thinks she's broken her bargain with God. Wouldn't hurt you to at least go to church with her today."

So I went to church with her, the old brick church that looked like every other Methodist church in the world, the black-and-white marquee out front advertising the title of the sermon nobody wanted to hear, a squatty, square bell tower with no bell, the cement steps up. The architect must have been yawning when he drew up the plans. And the church housed preachers who were as dull as the bricks in the church, and the congregation, smiling, nodding, going in, mumbling in song and response, and then smiling, nodding, going out. That was it. She didn't say anything to me about the smoking, and I said nothing to her about her having given me to God without my permission. Seemed to me I should have had something to say about that. I got to stewing about it. I made arguments to myself about it. How could my folks love Lincoln for freeing the slaves and then my own mother give her oldest son to God, I mean, just *give* him—like that! Slavery is slavery.

The conflict was pretty plain and pretty ripe. I was going to be a big-time lawyer. If I went along with my mother's scheme I'd end up being one of those fat-assed preachers who wallowed around the church sticking their noses up the you-know-what of those pinched-up old biddies in the Christian Temperance Union, those were dried-up, self-righteous old crones who would, if they could, condemn your soul to hell forever if you took a single swig of good American whiskey. One thing had become very clear to me: Mothers could be a very big pain in the ass. Very big.

✳   ✳   ✳

I was a better poker player than most of the hands at sea. I watched the players more than the cards. I'd won a lot of money playing poker, maybe five or six hundred dollars—more than I'd saved for college over all the rest of my life—and I'd banked these winnings in my college fund, which led me to believe that I was a pretty smart with the cards. There were card rooms down below the bawdy houses on Front Street in Laramie, so, why wouldn't a smart poker player like me go down there and play a little poker with the boys—make something of myself at an early age?

I didn't care much about school, the professors doing their best to drown you in stiff, wearisome pedantics that meant nothing to anyone but them. I got by, all right, but what I cared about most was poker. Every night Jim and I played poker at Hick's Card Room, a dingy hole on Front Street, two or three tables lit by a hang-down, green porcelain shade, the smoke thick as sewer water, and sometimes we won, and sometimes we lost, and after we'd played all night we'd stop at a Chinese joint called the Paris Café for some chop suey. Mah One, the skinny old cardboard-faced Chinese with his thick glasses and perpetual smile, usually ran the place. Sometimes Jim and I went to the kitchen to talk to the old boys working back there. They never ate the stuff they served up front—they ate a kind of garbagey-looking stuff, held the bowls up to their mouths and just shoved it in with their chopsticks. But sometimes a younger Chinese man, chubby little fellow with slicked-down black hair, was up front, and you could see Mah One in the back cooking away. That was when Mah One had lost the café to his partner, Gene Toy, playing a card game called mahjongg, The ownership of the café changed hands several times a year. But the food was the same and nobody except them gave a damn.

"See ya been winning again at mah-jongg," Jim said to Mah One, standing there behind the cash register looking very proud and entrepreneurial.

"Yes, sir. Yes, sir," Mah One said very fast through grinning teeth.

"Well, the chop suey's better now that you're out of the kitchen," Jim said, with his usual grin.

"Yes, sir. Yes, sir," Mah One replied. They knew each other that way.

The old pros, their faces as wrinkled and yellow as old newspapers, gathered at Hick's Card Room like a pack of aging, hungry jackals waiting for some high roller who thought he could play poker, or for some itinerant trucker who was trying to kill a lonely night in a strange town. Sometimes a brakeman on the railroad, waiting for his train to be called, came in, threw his lunch pail up against the wall and bought a stack of chips. The old pros never dreamed that Sister Luck would deliver them some smart-ass country boy fresh from his virgin tour of the sea. The old pros were the kind of men you ran into at every card room, dried-up, emotionless sorts who played their cards close to their chest, never took a flyer, bluffed once a night at most, and then only on a small pot. They were the kind who memorized the cards and played the odds. They were living, breathing poker machines, their mechanisms churning silently, the machine patient, waiting, willing to give up the big pots in exchange for the right to win a little every night. They never smiled, never laughed, never joked. They sat there hour after hour, night after night, year after year, dead-eyed, a cigarette dangling from their mouths, their eyes squinted against the rising smoke, their talk with each other mostly incomprehensible grunts and nods. But they had a nose for a sucker.

One of these old pros sitting at the poker table, guy about fifty, flat-top haircut, glasses, rock faced, humorless, skinny bastard, was my speech professor at the University of Wyoming, his campus classroom up the street less than a mile away. I never made a speech in speech class. The prospect of sitting through hundreds of bumbling, red-faced, stork-legged orators every year must have been too much for him. In class we talked about giving speeches. We studied speeches, but mercifully for both professor and student, we never were required to give one. His classes were as dry as he was. He taught speechmaking like a half-asleep mechanic teaching somebody how to break down a cylinder head. He was a man who, himself, had probably never given an honest-to-God speech in his life, the best effort I ever saw him display being a flat-sounding grunt of apology to the losers as he racked in a small pot from time to time.

The professor acted as if he didn't recognize me as one of his students, and I returned the favor. I didn't give a shit. I was smarter than some old goat of a speech teacher. If he was so damn smart, he wouldn't be teaching school, I thought. I was going to make a big killing at poker and sail though law school and after that I'd own the world. But I was the kind the old jackals longed for, the kind who never retreated, not even on a bad night.

After a couple of months I'd lost my entire college fund, fifty, a hundred dollars a night, and when I didn't have the money for one last stake, I borrowed a fifty from Jim. That night my luck had been running cold and mean, and I was down to my last borrowed twenty-five bucks. The brakeman sitting next to me had dealt a hand of five card stud, low-ball—low hand wins. I drew a sixty-four. Finally my luck had changed. I held cards that should win 90 percent of the time. But my speech professor drew a wheel, in the language of the poker player, a straight from ace to five, the winning hand. With a quick glance he took into account the chips held by each player at the table. He raised his eyebrow, only slightly, then he bet twenty-five dollars, a perfect bet on a cinch hand—not too much to scare off those holding decent hands themselves, "eighty-fives" or lower—and, of course, his bet left me no choice. With a sixty-four I had to call. He didn't even look up before he began to drag in the pot, and not once did he look at me.

"Well," I said like a real big shot as I shoved my chair back from the table, "I'm all tapped out. Guess I'll go get me a little bite and head on home. Got a speech to make tomorrow." I forced a wink at the professor. But he wasn't looking at me. He was stacking his winnings. I learned more at Hick's Card Room than in any book concerning the underlying rules of jurisprudence—namely, that those who run the card game always win. The house never loses. The power structure stays in power, and we are the players.

In the fall of 1946, at seventeen, I was dead broke. I began to look at my life anew. Who was I? What kind of a true jerk had I turned into? What kind of fool? I had lost every dollar I had saved, a dollar at a time: my Grandmother Pfleeger's birthday dollars, one every year, the money I had earned selling sweetpeas, the tourists' dollars, the money I saved working on the ranches behind the old horses in the hot sun. But I had lost more than the money. I had done what I had done because I was bad, and the bad had caught up with me. How could I face my mother? What could I tell my father? I would rather have been adjudicated a thief and a murderer than to admit to my parents that their son, a gambler, and a poor one at that, had lost all of his precious savings, and, in so doing, had lost his college education, his future, yes, his life. Yes, that was it—I had lost my life at a poker table in Hick's Card Room. "Hell of a way to go," I thought.

I could see my dear mother and me back in those desperate Depression days standing in the kitchen together, I at the ironing board, too short to work it in comfort. I could see myself ironing away at the sheets with those old cast-iron irons, earning fifty cents for my college fund by renting my room to the tourists. I could hear the judgments against mother and son descending upon us "You raised a bad one for a son. Couldn't hardly tell him from a criminal. Stealing from himself, stealing his dear mother's dreams. Couldn't hardly tell him from a murderer. Look how he smashed his mother's heart flat."

And I could see the disappointment on the faces of my dear old frail grandparents. How could I ever face old Grandpa Spence, who used to brag that "the Spences never had been famous but there wasn't a drunk or a felon among 'em"? How could that sweet old man bear learning that his grandson had become nothing but a common two-bit gambler—this old man who had told that small boy that some day he would be a great man? I was worse than a felon. I had stolen from myself, from my family, and from that big bank up in the sky where the universe's fund of decency and morality is stored.

I remember Jim coming up to my room at the house that night. He sat down on a suitcase over in the corner. Only place to sit. I was sitting on the bed with my head in my hands, not wanting to look at anybody, especially Jim. He knew I was tapped out, the money all gone. He knew I was feeling pretty low, and all he did was sit there acting like it was nothing.

"I'm going to kill myself," I finally said to Jim. Maybe he'd say something that could ease the pain. One thing I knew: I was too much of a coward to kill myself, which was the one good thing a man could say about being a coward. Moreover, my mother had told me all about suicide. "God will forgive anything you do if you ask Him," she had argued, even murder. "But if you kill *yourself*, how can you ask God's forgiveness? Suicide is the one and only unforgivable sin a person can commit." She had said it so many times, as if it were an issue with her. I understood. Her own uncle, my Grandmother Pfleeger's brother, had killed himself. Swallowed a whole bottle full of Black Leaf 40, a nicotine poison used to kill the beetles in the garden, and she said they found his tortured, twisted body in the barn—horrified my mother, I could see it in her eyes. No, I would never kill myself.

"I'm going to kill myself," I said again to Jim Brown after he'd said nothing in return.

This time Jim took a big puff off his cigar. Then turned and looked at me with pure disgust. "Listen, pal," he said. "Ya win some an' ya lose some. An' don't give me any more of that bullshit. Besides, you better not kill yourself 'til ya pay me back the fifty ya owe me."

PART TWO

THE REBEL

CHAPTER 16

Railroad yards.

MY MOTHER WAS never my pal. As a teenager, or even before, it wouldn't have occurred to either of us to go to the drugstore for a Coke. Once in the spring we picked wildflowers together up Little Goose Canyon. I remember looking at the stars with her and learning about the constellations, about Orion in the winter, and how to find the North Star by following the two pointer stars on the Big Dipper, and how to recognize the Pleiades and Cassiopeia. But we never played together. My mother didn't play. We never shared each other's secrets. Perhaps she had hers. I had mine. But she was my mother. I loved her deeply.

She represented a mysterious force that was connected to life's power. She exuded an ethereal quality, as do most mothers, especially to their sons. By her magic I had been granted life. There was something ineffably sacred there, holy, something deeply miraculous about having burst from her womb, about having suckled her breasts for first nourishment. The Commandments notwithstanding, I respected her even when, as an adolescent caught in the throes of that madness, I often saw her as a timorous scold. Yet always she was surrounded by an angelic aura, and in that mystical realm, she was elevated above my father. He was human to me. My mother was not—not completely. She had that divine connection with the universe that mothers have, bird and beast alike, the spiritual link between man and God. Then my mother left me.

The first fall rain descended on Laramie in a fine drizzle, turning the night pavement into reflecting black mirrors. The red neon lights of the bus depot stretched in long, wavy patterns across the wet street, and the engines in the switch yards whistled and whined in the rain. The cinders, fine as black dust, blown up in piles against the curbs by the unremitting high plains wind, were wetted down so that they no longer stung the face and caught in the eyes. On this night the rain had pushed out the wind, giving the earth at last to water.

I walked alongside my mother in the rain, my small brother and sister in tow, and then we all boarded the Greyhound bus. My mother looked on as the driver stowed their heavy bags in the bus's hatch, including that old black suitcase and a couple of cardboard boxes tied up tight with binder twine. And after the family had taken its seats, my sister and brother on one side, my mother across from them, I kissed that small, frightened child, Barbara, good-bye, her baby face tight with a quivery smile, and I kissed the boy, Tom, good-bye, his eyes like the rabbits we had cornered and shot. I also kissed my mother, just a peck you know, and then I walked off the bus.

Before they boarded, my mother had said, "You know we are not leaving you, Gerry. You are a man now. You can take care of yourself."

"Right," I said. But I was not a man; I knew that, and she knew that. She said it to throw it back in my face—the way I'd been behaving, like a merciless gunman who had held them all hostage in the house. But now I had to face it. I wasn't a man. I was a child with steel plates on my heels that made a lot of noise walking, and I made a lot of noise talking, and my scrawny frame, my skinny arms, my big feet, they hardly added up to a man. I was a boy. And how could a boy live without a mother? I wanted to cry out, "Mother, don't leave me." Once more I was the small lost child, panicked, crying for his mother in Woolworth's. But I didn't cry, of course. I just pulled my chin back, and turned my mouth down a little, tilted my head from side to side, and all the while, inside, I wrestled back the sobs.

How could she say she wasn't leaving me when she was walking out to that bus to leave? "We'll be back in three short years," my mother said. I saw no tears in her eyes. Glad to be rid of me, I thought. Glad she wouldn't have to see me swaggering around, a living reminder of her broken covenant with God. I didn't want to look at her face. I wished the bus would just get the hell out of there. I wished the whole bunch of them would be gone and the pain of their leaving could be over.

"You write often," I said, as they had said to me. "Doesn't cost much to write." I hadn't written often when I was at sea. I'd probably never see any of them again. I turned my head and dammed up the tears.

My father had taken a job in 1946 as a chemist with the Patino Tin Mines in Bolivia, and my mother had seemed excited about the adventure. Said she had always wanted to go to strange places and see new things. She planned to be a missionary to the native people there, those coca-chewing Catholics who scampered barefooted around the barren rocky heights of the Andes. It was God's will—I think that's how she saw it.

The family would be living in a high native village near the mine, a place called Catavi, elevation about fourteen thousand feet, twice the elevation of Laramie. My father had signed a three-year contract with the Bolivian company. If he stayed three years he would receive certain small bonuses, and they would pay his way back to the States. I had never seen my father as happy. He'd always wanted to see the rest of the world, this Colorado country boy. The aluminum plant at Laramie where he had worked had never made aluminum, and now that the war was over, the sponge iron plant was closing down. It was a good time for them to leave.

I remember watching my mother's hands packing her flannel-graph kit, her careful fingers touching the Jesus cutout as if it could feel. She laid Jesus gingerly down on the flannel-covered board, his arms beckoning, and then next to him she packed in the other cutouts—the other biblical characters, the twelve apostles, Mary, baby Moses in the rushes, all of them. Probably figured she'd accomplished all she could with me. Maybe she could convert the natives.

My father had gone to Bolivia ahead of the family to get things set up and safe for them. My mother stayed back, sold the house, and I had to move out. Jim Brown and I took a basement room in a prim, white frame house on the corner of Fourteenth Street and Grand Avenue—twenty-five dollars a month between us. One double bed. We slept together, but in those days nobody thought anything about men sleeping together.

After I kissed my mother and the little kids good-bye, the faint taste of my mother still on my lips, I marched off the bus, big as hell, and walked off into the cold night rain—didn't wait to see the bus pull out. I felt alone, like an orphan at the station who didn't know which train to take. I heard the lonesome whistle of the locomotives down in the yards, the streets deserted, the streetlights glaring, the sound of the rain running in the gutters. I began to sob out loud—no one to hear me—better to let it out, sort of the way throwing up made a person feel better. I walked by Hick's Card Room. The same dried-up old bastards were staring at the table through the smoke, and then I knew that Laramie, Wyoming, was truly a place of the dead. I stopped at the window and looked in at the players. They hardly moved, except to finger their cards. They sat waiting, pondering. Yes, by God, the poker players at Hick's Card Room were dead, all right, but I had escaped.

While the old pros were feasting on the last of my savings down at Hick's Card Room, the fraternities and sororities were conducting what was known as "Rush Week," when they invited certain "interesting" freshman candidates to their houses. There the said rushees were carefully inspected for their style and dress, for their personalities and pedigrees. Did the rushee come from wealthy or prominent parents? Was his father somebody, even in one of those small, no-place towns in Wyoming from which most of the students at the university were recruited? Had his father been a member of the fraternity? Was the rushee an athlete, even a scholar? Was he anything at all? How about a veteran who had fought overseas and was fresh back from the war? The fraternities and sorori-ties didn't rush nobodies—especially those whose only claim to fame was losing their life savings down at Hick's Card Room.

I was a nobody. I knew that in my heart. I would never be rushed, and although during Rush Week I hoped desperately for an invitation to a fraternity, any fraternity, none came. Surely one house would have invited me—just to take a look at me. I made room for the possibility that after they met me they might not like me. I didn't have one of those great personalities. But surely at least one would have looked me over—at least one. There must be some mis-take. Maybe they didn't know where I lived. Or maybe they did know—in a small room in the basement of a plain white house up on Fourteenth Street, a room next to where the landlady did her laundry. I waited another week, and then another. Maybe they'd heard that my family had lived in a converted chicken house. I wished I hadn't been such an insufferable smart-ass. They probably knew. I could hear my mother's warning, "The things ye do, one by one, ye pay for two by two." The great guys in high school—like the ones who walked me home—well, they were all rushed and they all pledged fraternities. Maybe it was the goddamned pimples. Maybe it was because my father was only a chemist who wore working clothes and drove that ugly Ford with its flapping fenders.

Jim didn't get an invite either. "Who gives a shit?" he said. "I wouldn't have joined up with the bastards if they invited me."

"Me neither. Fuck 'em," I replied.

But certain critical problems arose as a consequence of not belonging to a fraternity. Fewer than two thousand students attended the University of Wyoming in those days, the great majority of whom were men. Any breathing, conscious woman stood at a premium. The students congregated for Cokes and coffee at the Union, one of those stately yellow stone buildings on the campus with a lounge and snack bar, or they flocked to the Campus Shop, an old made-over yellow house with a bunch of booths along the sides of the room and tables in the center. There the "chicks" would sit, two, three, sometimes four at a table, laughing, carrying on, saying "hi" in that late adolescent seductive tone to the great guys who walked by or stopped to lay it on 'em. But if a fellow like me wanted in on the action, he had to, uninvited, just brazenly walk up to where the chicks were sitting and come up with some line. He had to come to *them*, and they knew it, and they sat there, usually with small knowing smiles on their faces, waiting to see what this guy's play would be. Sometimes they put on what

Jim Brown called that "come fuck me" look, gave a quick glance in your direction, and then when you moved in, bam!—they had you.

Oh, the pain, the ignominy, the terror of the overt turndown. Or, worse, the humiliation of the slow, silent rotation of the head in the other direction, the bored casting of the eyes into infinity as you stood there, your teeth in your mouth. How I longed to be suave and steely and strong, but what usually came out of my mouth was something lame and weak and stupid. Thank God, most chicks were never brave enough to look a fellow in the eyes to witness the mortification he endured when he made his move and was turned away. You had to keep your swagger. You had to keep the old head up, and walk away like you were saying, "And fuck you, too!" And when you could hear their laughter behind your back, you had to pretend it didn't bother you one fucking bit.

During these early days, I began to notice something: When you made your move, the chick would always scrutinize your chest, and it was not muscle she was looking for. No. She was looking for the *fraternity pin.* And when she was satisfied that no pin was pinned there, she would ask, "Are you affiliated?" to which one was compelled to reply sternly, as if it were a matter of conviction and conscience, "Hell, no. I'm *independent.*" That usually ended it. One was, indeed, independent—independent of stature and standing, independent of prestige and position, independent of acceptance and affirmation. Anyway, how could any chick give a damn about a guy who had no pin with which to pin her?

The social hierarchy was established early on campus. Sorority sisters usually socialized only with fraternity men, a logical solution by which the nobodies were eliminated right away so that a sorority girl didn't have to bother sorting them out for herself. Most of the fraternity boys wouldn't give you the time of day, walk right by you as if your ass were air. It hurt to be nobody, but I never admitted it to anyone, not even to Jim Brown. I mean, who gave a shit?

I didn't know it then, couldn't have known it, but whereas I was unlucky in poker, I had drawn a straight flush in the draw of life. Still, we roam about in our own small worlds. In mine I felt rejected—worse, banished. I didn't yet understand that the world I ached for was mostly superficial, mostly empty. In those days I didn't feel sorry for myself. I felt angry. But my not having been chosen was one of the great gifts of my life. I dare not consider what might have been my lot had I stared at my chest one morning and there discovered the precious fraternity pin. What if playing golf with the president of the local bank had defined the meaning of my life? What if my life was won or lost depending upon the clubs I belonged to or the socialites who invited me to their deadly standup cocktail parties? What if I ended up representing banks who robbed the poor rather than representing the poor, some of whom robbed the banks? What if, after a lifetime, I had no extra chamber in my heart for the widow mopping the toilets and the laboring man coughing in the mines?

Years later I was to make arguments to the jury that bore the fruit of these early snubs. Petty events often reveal large truths. Many times I have reminded a jury how, having experienced small rejections ourselves, we learn something of the origins of crime. "Criminals are not born," I have argued. "See him in the crib, this man who stands charged before you? See his face no larger than my fist, wrinkled against the light? He looks no different than the newborn in the crib next to him. But at the moment of his birth *this* child was branded as a nothing, as a worse-than-nothing."

More than once I have painted word pictures for the jury. "See his tired, half-starved, unwed mother, addicted to crack, bundling him up in a dirty blanket to take him home to a three-story walk-up with the walls caving in and the roof leaking and the floors falling through and the water in the sink dripping, the toilet plugged. Picture, if you will, a dozen other dirty little wretches of all ages and sizes squirming like human worms in three barren rooms, while the drug-crazy neighbors scream all night and shoot each other in the street. At the moment of birth this child was unjustly branded as less than a full citizen because of a blameless draw of the genes that dictated the color of his skin and the character of his parents."

So my mother wanted me to preach? Well, often I preach to the jury. "All of us become angry when we suffer injustice. We become angry at man and God alike. Angry, we are likely to strike at whatever or whoever is handy. When the boy in the ghetto strikes out at those who wield power over him, he is punished and he becomes more angry. The criminal strikes out at the world. The world strikes back. The cycle that began at birth is a cycle of injustice that begets anger, and the cycle reproduces itself like the anarchy of cancer. Do we not understand that, at last, the world has grown to hate its own children?"

Over and over I have argued that our fate is mostly a matter of vision. Most of us try to fulfill our visions. In the ghetto, the unjustly branded child sees little more than a life of crime. "Give me the child born in the ghetto," I have cried. "Let us lift him out of those venal concrete boxes and take him into the wide-open spaces of Wyoming. Let him see the majesty, the beauty of our mountains. Give him another vision. Give him parents, parents like you, who are educated and loving and responsible. Give him an education where his vision can be further expanded—give him another vision and the child will discover another way. Give him another vision and perhaps he will become a compassionate juror, a juror who does not excuse what this man has done, but who understands who this man is. And why."

Then I have walked up closer to the jurors, and I have held them, each of them, for a long time with my eyes, and I have spoken quietly. "This man was punished when he was born—punished and adjudged and labeled and rejected. Shall we punish him again? Reject him again? Might we not show him that there is something left in this world called love? That there are people who care, and that those people sit on this jury? At last cannot love conquer hate?" I thought my mother would have liked the preaching.

The Buffalo Bar was a favorite beer joint for the college kids. It was dark in there, with black back booths where kids crowded up close to each other, where boys could feel the bodies of the undulating girls trying to make room, or pretending they were making room, wiggling and screaming. The noise in the place put you in mind of an insane asylum. You couldn't hear a thing, and the smoke was so thick you had to sort of feel your way through the place. Once in a while at closing time, a bunch of us who'd been hoisting a few would put together a "nooky pool." The "nooky pool guys" were the real men on campus, not those pretty boys from the fraternities who wore perfumed boxer shorts and came in their pants when a sorority girl happened to rub up against them. Each guy threw in a dollar, and then we'd go hollering and laughing and cutting up to 210 Grand, corner of Grand and Front Street, best whorehouse in town, and we'd stomp up the creaking stairs making a lot of noise, and we'd ring on the doorbell until the madam would open up.

"What are you smart-ass kids doing up here anyway?" she'd say, standing there with her hands on her hips looking down at us.

"Got a nooky pool together," the guy at the top of the stairs would answer.

"Well, you have to buy a beer apiece before you can play," and so she'd let us in and we'd go into the parlor, and after we drank our beer—cost a dollar for a fifty-cent bottle of beer—she'd pull out an old deck of cards and everybody would draw one. High cut won. Once I won.

Soon as I was identified as the winner, the madam hollered down the hall, "Hey, girls, any of you got a minute? Won't last long. Bunch a kids up here in a 'nooky pool.'"

A couple of the girls, looking like tired farm girls with their hair peroxided and their high heels, the kind who were willing to make a quick buck, came swinging out into the parlor as if they had finally made it big on a honky-tonk stage.

Soon as the girls came in, one of the guys in the pool said, "We want to watch."

"Oh, no," I said. "That ain't in the deal."

"The hell it ain't," the guy said. "We got a stake in this deal, and we should at least get to watch." Everybody laughed.

Then the youngest-looking of the two girls piped up: "Listen," she said to the guy who was doing all the talking. "When you go to a café and order a steak, you don't get the right to go back to the kitchen and see the cook fry it." And that ended the argument, and off I went following the woman to her little room with the standard single bed and wash basin in the corner. The room smelled of Lysol. She was a dark-haired girl, strong legs under the red ruffles, pleasant face, and a clear strong voice. If you put a robe on her she could have sung in the choir.

When it was over I said to her, "Could I stay a little longer, please?"

"What do you mean? You only paid for a short time and you're all done."

"I know," I said. "But I don't want to go out there so quick. Everybody will know, and all." I must have looked pretty pitiful.

"Well, okay, we can wait five minutes," she said. She sat down on the bed and lit a Pall Mall. "That's all I got to sell is my time, you know."

I sat there and she sat there. Pretty soon I said, "What's your name?"

"You can call me Lilly."

"That's a nice name," I said. "How did you get into this business?"

"Only jerks ask that question," she said.

"Oh," I said. "I didn't mean to be nosy, or anything."

"That's okay," she said.

After a long silence I said, "I'd like to get to know you better."

"No, you wouldn't." She was pretty young, all right.

"I really would," I said.

"I can't date any tricks," she said, " 'gainst the rules."

"Well," I said, real tough, "fuck the rules."

"Get out of here, kid," she said. "You wanna get us both killed? When I get enough money, I'll be gettin' out of here myself. I'll look ya up."

Then the madam came knocking at the door. "You all right in there?" she hollered. "Okay," the girl hollered back. "This guy is a long go." Then she winked at me and I smiled, and I felt very big. Even felt loved—a little.

I got a job as night bellman—no uniform required—at the Connor Hotel, best hotel in town. Thirty cents an hour. Nothing much to do at night except mop those inch-wide white octagonal tiles that made up the marble floor of the lobby. I dusted the old coffee tables with the cigarette burns along the edges and changed the light bulbs in the yellow glass chandeliers, and with a sieve like the one my mother used to use, I cleaned the cigarette butts out of the sand in ash stands. Then I curled up on one of the maroon leather couches in the lobby and I slept. If a customer checked in, the night clerk, also the hotel's book-keeper, would maliciously bang away at the bell until I'd finally pop up from the couch, stagger to the front desk all blurry-eyed, and grab the guy's bags and show him to his room.

The rooms were old plaster, cracked and patched, with high ceilings where the paint liked to curl, the rooms barely large enough to hold a double bed with those iron pipe headboards. Wasn't room for much in there except a folding stand for your suitcase. You got privacy by pulling down the dark green shade, the kind that if you pulled it hard enough and let it go quickly it would recoil all the way up and flap around a couple of extra flaps before it stopped. Some rooms had small toilets, and some only wash basins, the common toilets down the hall.

Sometimes the customer was a traveling salesman. You could tell. Brought in a big black cardboard sample case, and I carried it up for him, usually wore a rumpled suit, the knees bagging from having driven all day, his shirt dirty, a week away from home. Sometimes a trucker wearing his coveralls and those black cowboys boots would come in looking for a place to bed down for the night. But all of them were horny. Once we were alone in the elevator, the guy would sort of whisper, "Hey, kid, where can a man get himself a little piece of ass in this town?"

"Try 210 Grand," I'd say. "Down the street by the railroad on the corner. Ask for Lilly. She'll give ya a good go." And then the guy would say, "Thanks, kid," and give me a tip, maybe a dime, once in a while a quarter. Jim thought my recommending Lilly was very funny. "You pimping for Lilly, right?" he said. "What would your mother think if she knew her son had turned into a common fuckin' pimp?"

"Lilly's a nice girl," I said. "I like her."

"Right," Jim said. "She's a really nice girl. Kind a fella would like to take home to his mother."

"I don't know how she got into the business," I said. "She wouldn't tell me. Probably white slavery or something." I worried about Lilly. Then one night I went back to 210 Grand in another nooky pool, and while I was waiting for the winner to come back from the room, which wasn't very long, I asked the madam about Lilly.

"There ain't no Lilly here."

"There was when I was here the last time."

"Never has been no Lilly here," the madam said, and after that I made myself believe that Lilly had earned enough money to go free, and that she was all right, and that she lived happily ever after.

Later that year I got a job as a switchman for the Union Pacific Railroad—night work down in the yards making up the trains, dangerous work, hanging off the side of a moving car. If you slipped and fell under a car, you came up with stumps. If you jumped off a moving car and fell, you could break your skull, or if you fell head-first under the car, you could get your head cut off, nice and neat. Dirty work, too, down in the yards, the coal burners belching out black smoke and hard, sharp cinders the size of fine sand that the Laramie winds picked up and blasted into your face so you always had a cinder stuck in your eye. In the morning, after a full shift, a fellow came in dirty as old rags and bone-tired, and in the deep winter, the marrow of a fellow's bones was about half-frozen.

I worked in the dark, my switchman's lantern my light. In the dark you could hear the old coal burners gathering up steam, making their speed and then banging into the cars, the connectors slamming closed. And you could hear the sound of steel sucking on steel as the cars rolled over the rails, thirty-nine-foot sections of steel locked together, and you could hear the bumpity-bump of the front wheels and the bumpity-bump of the rear as the wheels passed over the rail connectors. I held on to the boxcar's ladder with one hand, one foot on the lower rung, and the rest of me hung out over the roadbed, my lantern swinging in my free hand. I rode out past the switch blocks, and then, as switchmen do—it took some practice to get onto it—I swooped down onto the ground a little ahead of the moving car so as not to fall when my foot struck the ground. I threw the switch and swung my lantern in a circle, signaling the engineer that the switch had been pulled. Then you could hear the old steam engine let out a series of quick little breaths, like a panting old man, and the train would head down a new set of tracks after yet another car. As the last car on the train went by, I grabbed its ladder and swung up and rode on.

In the winter, the morning light on the high plains country was dancing yellow light. Crazy patterns of track and tie shimmered and sang in the light, and the light on the side of the men's dirty faces transformed them to bronze. In the winter, the early sun reflected on dirty snow and rendered it bright again, and clean. But when the sun rose, the sky turned pale pink, and the men came in stamping their cold feet and sat down at the long dining table in the caboose. They took off their cotton blue-striped, high-crowned brakeman's hats, the goggles in front, their eyes watering from the cold, their hair mussed and standing every which way. Then they wiped their noses on red bandannas, stuffed their bandannas back in their pockets, folded up their ear muffs, and, in those layers of clothes and their long underwear, all worn under their dirty bib overalls, even the skinny men looked fat. At last, the men opened their Thermos bottles, and poured steaming coffee into the lids, and sipped at the coffee, and stared off into space, and some told dirty stories, and most of them laughed. And sometimes they cussed the boss, and sometimes the men felt helpless and small, but they wouldn't admit it and sometimes they grew silent.

A brakeman in soot-black coveralls, his face showing the same color, came in, took off his gloves, blew on his hands and sat down with the rest of us. He opened up his black tin lunch pail, took out his Thermos and poured himself some coffee. Finally he said, "I got my slip." That's all he said. He blew in his coffee.

"How come ya got yer slip, Hank?" another guy asked. I didn't say anything.

"The fuckin' company doctor says I ain't fit ta work. Hell, I feel okay. Little sore in the back but who the fuck ain't? Tell me that."

"Company doctor's sold out to the company. Why ya think they pay him that big salary?"

"Yeah," Hank said. "They lay me off and then they bring in these young punks ta take my job—don't have to pay 'em any benefits, no retirement, nothing. When they start they're the same as scab labor." Then the man looked at me. "See this slip, kid? That means I don't work. And I been workin' here seventeen years already. Got a family ta feed. All you gotta feed is your dick."

I looked into my cup. Didn't want a fight. I felt for the man.

"If this kid quits another'll take his place," the other guy said. "Ain't his fault. Why don'tcha grieve it to the union?"

"Whose gonna pay the rent while I grieve it?" he asked. "Ever been out in the cold with a bunch a sick kids?"

I finished my coffee, put my Thermos back in my lunch bucket, and headed up Ivinson Avenue toward the campus. I felt sick for the man. I argued it with Jim.

"Fuckin' company," I said. "How can they do that? I oughta quit."

"Well, the dude was right," Jim said. "If ya quit, some other sucker will take your place."

"Yeah," I said, "and if Lilly quits some other girl will take her place in the whorehouse, too." Jim looked at me like I wasn't making sense. "I mean, just because another girl will take her place in the whorehouse is no reason for Lilly to stay on being a whore, is it?"

"You really got it bad for her, don't ya, kid?"

"If I quit somebody else'll take my place. You could always argue that. Why, you could argue, 'If I don't sell snake oil to the sick, somebody else will.' You could argue . . . "

"You're off base, kid," Jim said.

In the cold, clear mornings, fresh off the switching trains, I stomped into my eight o'clock class wearing my dirty overalls and my heavy work shoes with the steel toes. Fundamentals of Philosophy was the course, and I learned about man being born with a mind like a blank piece of white paper, which was prepared at birth to be written on by experience. I didn't need John Locke to tell me that. "I already knew that," I said in class, but nobody paid any attention. But I respected Locke's ideas about the right of the individual to life, liberty and property, and the innate right of the individual to revolt when those fundamental rights were usurped by authority. Thought Jefferson and Madison had read him, too. And I thought that Thomas Hobbes understood what government was all about when he claimed that the authority of government came from a delegation of power by the people, which, in turn, created an obligation by government to the people in return.

As I walked into class my face was smeared with soot, and I still carried my switchman's lantern and my lunch pail. I set them under my desk and looked around. Most of the fraternity boys didn't sign up for an eight o'clock, too hung over to get their asses out of the sack that early, and those who stumbled into the class did some gawking and some whispering and some snickering. And I said "Fuck you" to myself, and of course none of the girls in the class looked at me, none of them but one. Her name was Anna Fidelia Wilson, a tall bright bluebell of a girl with blond hair and good stuff in her sweater.

That spring I quit the railroad.

CHAPTER 17

Hunter and Estes Spence, Gerry's uncle and aunt.

AUNT ESTES, THAT tiny prim lady who is breathing proof that longevity is not as much a matter of health as a matter of genes, is the last living member of my father's generation. Two years after my father's death, his youngest brother, my Uncle Hunter, died. Estes, Uncle Hunter's wife of over sixty years, remembered my mother. She said they were close friends.

"Why were you close?" I asked.

"We were both interested in missionary work, and the church and Sunday school, and we were both homemakers. If I had been in better health as a young woman I would have become a missionary myself." This frail little lady had always been in ill health. One couldn't talk to Uncle Hunter more than five minutes without his expressing his powerful concern over Aunt Estes's health.

"Well, you know, Gerry, your Aunt Estes has been under the weather lately. Oh, how that poor girl has suffered!" he would say, his voice filled with compassion. And so she suffered all her life. Now, well past eighty, with two sons growing old, numerous grandchildren and two great-grandchildren, she had lived through those sixty years of marriage as a farm wife in Colorado, had worked many years as a librarian, had outlived Hunter, had buried all the members of her own family, and was, despite her suffering, still going strong. Aunt Estes had succeeded with her children where my mother had not. Her oldest son, John, was an Episcopal priest.

"Tell me," I asked Aunt Estes many years after my mother's death, "did you ever see my mother upset?"

She thought a long time. "No," she said. "I don't believe I ever did."

"Ever see her mad?"

"No, I don't believe I ever did."

"How could that be?" I asked. "We all get upset. We all lose it once in a while."

"She wasn't the kind to get angry. She wasn't the kind to lose it" was all Aunt Estes could say. "She was a wonderful woman. But she wasn't the kind to say much about how she felt. She kept it all bottled up. I'm sort of like that myself."

I, too, had never seen my mother angry, except on that one occasion when she and my father had exchanged those heated words over whether to spend the money to send me to the doctor. I had seen hurt in her eyes, hurt I had often caused. I had seen her cry, but rarely. Occasionally she had threatened me as a child, but corporal punishment, if it was to be meted out, was the duty of the father. "Well, we shall see about this when your father gets home," she would say. But by the time my father got home, whatever my transgressions, they most often had been forgotten.

I don't remember my mother ever having been sick. Up to the time of her death, she had been in good health so far as I knew, except, of course, the chronic pain in her lower back, which was habitually encased in that Spencer corset. But I was to soon discover that her journey into menopause was a journey into hell.

By the winter of 1946, Jim, too, had finally been "tapped out" down at Hick's Card Room. Broke, he dropped out of school and went back to sea. "Gotta get me another stake. Only thing left for a man to do," he said, puffing on an R. G. Dunn, still grinning, ready to fulfill his own vision of what a man should be.

Something irresistible about the sea—the freedom, the peace. You stand your watch, and if you don't like the ship, or the crew, or its new destination, you take another ship. No responsibility, no worry. I wanted to go with Jim, but I wouldn't be had again by that great seductress, the sea. I was going to be a big-time lawyer. I didn't see myself as a hard-assed seaman or a tinhorn poker player. I was going to be a big-time lawyer like G. R. McConnell.

I was still broke and had to borrow money—had to pay in advance at Mom Moore's Boarding House or I couldn't sit down at the table. Once I was so broke I called my Grandmother Pfleeger and borrowed fifty bucks from her to eat on, promising I'd repay the loan in a month, which, of course, I didn't. She died with me still owing the debt. She never forgot it. She forgave it in her will.

I missed old Jim. Now everybody in my life had "flown the coop," as Jim used to say. Then, as it always happened in my life, I was saved. I met a devil-may-care

Irish kid named Keith Ashton who took up Jim's share of the rent and his place
on his side of the bed. He at least had a good walk, I thought, and that speedy
Irish smile, the head cocking back and forth, proudly, his pants rolled up about six
inches above his ankles. About half a foot shorter than I, he had a too-sharp nose
for an Irishman, I thought. Everything on the Irish is supposed to be easygoing,
including easy faces, but Keith was sharp in every way and, as desperate for food
as I, he was a true master at inventing ways to score a meal. The cafeteria was a
room as large as a gymnasium filled with tables. Sometimes we ate a big bowl of
beans there, and a slice of bread. Cheap meal. Once at the student cafeteria Keith
whispered to me, "Load your plate. Pile 'er up big—enough for two days."

"You buying?" I asked.

"I'll take care of it," he said, giving me that look that told me he had come
up with one of his infamous plots. At the end of the line a student added up the
items on your tray and gave you the bill. Then you paid the bill at the single
cashier by the front door when you left.

I loaded my plate. When we'd finished eating I said, "All right, you smart
bastard, how we going to pay for this one?"

"Get out of here," he said. "I told you I'd take care of it." I got up and had
just passed the cashier's desk, nodding back toward Keith as the one who was
paying the check, when I saw Keith jump up and trip over the table leg. He fell
to the floor, the table on top of him, dirty dishes, the sugar bowl, the salt and
pepper shakers, the silverware exploding in every direction. The whole cafeteria was on its feet staring at the sight. Keith lay on the floor squirming, moaning
and groaning, "My back, my back!" I watched, astonished, fascinated. The
cashier and several others ran to him. With their help Keith struggled to his feet,
and after his soulful, pathetic insistence that he was sure he would be all right
if they would only help him out the front door, for which he thanked them pro-
fusely, he limped on down the street, me at his side. When we were out of sight
of the cafeteria he started laughing, slapping his leg and throwing his arms up
in the air. "You can only pull that one off every other year," he cried, and then
we laughed together all the way home to our little basement room, our bellies
full like any wild beast fresh from the kill.

Once we stopped by the Paris Café for a cup of coffee. "Load up," he said
again. "I'm hungry."

"What's the scam this time?" I asked. Mah One was in the kitchen. A young
Caucasian woman was guarding the cash register.

"No scam," he replied. "Just gonna have me a little conversation with the
cashier." I ordered the won ton soup, the egg rolls, the chop suey, the shrimp
fried rice, the sweet and sour pork, pie à la mode and coffee. He ordered likewise. "Now what?" I asked.

"Gimme the check." He sauntered up to the cashier, a youngish, homely
woman wearing thick glasses and clothes that were too small. Then I noticed
her eyes were severely crossed. Keith had already captured her attention with

his cocky little smile and the way he shook his head when he walked up to the counter, like a prancing Shetland pony. By now they had locked eyes, his as severely crossed as hers. I couldn't believe what my own good eyes were seeing. He tipped his head upward as if beseeching her to hear him, his left eye staring at the right wall and his right eye taking in the left, the cashier caught in between. Then he began to talk to her in his excited, open, Irish way. The woman seemed hungry for conversation. He wondered how long she'd been working there, and how glad he was, for a change, to see somebody who was nice to look at behind the cash register, Mah One being in the kitchen and all. He laughed, and she couldn't help but laugh back. She soon became genuinely interested in her new cross-eyed friend. He wanted to know where she was from and what she was doing in Laramie. When a customer stepped up to pay his check, Keith stood aside, and, after the customer had settled up, Keith started right in again where he'd left off, his eyes still locked in their crossed position. My mother used to warn against crossing one's eyes. You might never be able to get them uncrossed, she said. Didn't bother Keith. He went on talking about how hard it was to meet nice people at school, and how he didn't know anybody in Laramie, except me, which wasn't much comfort. When I was leaving I heard him ask her when she get off work. And as I looked back I saw him hold out his hand and she extended hers, and then he took it and he kissed it lightly, and looked at her for a long time, his eyes so beautifully crossed, and finally I heard him say, "Maybe I could drop back when you get off work," and while she was thinking about that one, and before she could answer one way or the other, he walked out too. Small wonder, Keith became a well-known television personality in Salt Lake City.

The thing I liked about Anna Wilson was her air, the way she carried herself, proud as a poodle, kind of prancy, a tall girl who stood up straight. She walked like she knew where she was going, and she had that smile on her face that punched in a dimple, one in either cheek. I knew she had looked me over in that eight o'clock class. She'd seen my smeared face and my dirty overalls, and she'd smiled—not a mocking smile, not a smile of amusement, not a smile of pity, either. It wasn't one of those come-on smiles. It was a nice sort of friendly smile. And I smiled back the best I could. Later I saw her at a school dance sashaying across the floor with some skinny guy, skinnier than I was, and not as good a dancer either. He held her close, and she had that smile on her face. I stood in the background of people hugging the edge of the dance floor, and like a hawk, I waited for the right moment when the guy she was with turned from her. What if he had kept his eye on her, kept close to her, talked to her, had danced all the dances with her, and I, had never moved in to ask her to dance? Every moment leads somewhere. Every act connects. A piddling juncture, a pause to take a breath, a single word, can turn us down long roads.

"Wanna dance?"

"Sure."

The music was slow and sweet, the kind I could handle, a lazy shuffling of the feet, an occasional whirl around. She was tall and I was tall, and I held her hand and extended her arm out with mine, like Fred Astaire when he danced the slow ones with Ginger Rogers. I spoke softly to her in my best and deepest new baritone. We talked as we danced, and when I asked her what she liked to do, she said she was learning to play tennis, and she liked that a lot, and I said, well, I liked to play tennis too, and so we met the following morning at six o'clock at the tennis courts. I had never played the game, but Anna borrowed a racket for me.

Very soon I came to realize that we had not come to play tennis. We had come to carry on where we paused the night before. Then I swung at the ball and missed. I must have looked ridiculous, my arms flailing at empty air, and then I missed again and again, and when I couldn't hit the first ball, I had to do something. I ran to the net and jumped over, and I kissed Anna Fidelia Wilson, and after that there was no turning back.

What senseless little scenes set the irreversible course of our lives. Such *crux moves* are usually innocent enough. Everyone alive makes one or many during a lifetime—an act, a word, a look, a choice that alters his life forever, and alters the lives of the innocent around him. Had I not missed the ball that last time, which impelled me to throw my racket in the air to stop that silly game, who would I be? And, pray tell, where? At that instant I arrived at the invisible crossroads. Suddenly I had made the crux move. To that move I can trace every act, every decision, nearly every agony, every one of my children, most of the compelling forces in my life, indeed, the very metamorphosis of my being.

I can trace to that kiss my growth as a young man, and from it I can also follow my life to the demise of the child who kissed Anna Fidelia Wilson there on the tennis court at 6:10 in the morning. I can also trace to that exact instant the rebirth of the man known as Gerry Spence, the sun just up, the sun all knowing.

How carelessly I jumped across the net. Considering my deftness as an athlete, little wonder I didn't land spread-eagle, facedown on the concrete. Given the inalterable consequences of that simple act—the kiss, as nearly innocent as it was—how strange there came no warning. But in the end, had I the choice, I would have changed nothing.

From that moment, we were inseparable. I could not live without Anna. She introduced me to parts of me I had never known, showed me wondrous things about me I had only taken for granted. She held me up for my own inspection. Where I had felt rejected in my world, Anna found me "different," "exciting," "engaging," "creative"—her words. I thought she was blind. To her I was "handsome and sexy." Still her words, and she loved me. And I did love her. Love is how we feel toward those who show us that which is lovable about ourselves.

She claimed she had never met anyone like me, and she must have met many—for she was a sorority woman. A Kappa Kappa Gamma, no less. She took me to the Kappa house, that huge, intimidating white brick mansion with the green shutters, and she showed me off to all of her sisters in their fancy living room, and there, in front of her tight-sweatered sisters with the long hair and the bobby sox, she played the piano, played it like the great pianist I had heard at the community concerts as a child, played it like Paul Robeson's great accompanist, played it while I sang "On the Road to Mandalay" in my new baritone voice. She played "Claire de Lune" while I wept at its beauty. Sometimes I couldn't think of what to say. You couldn't say, "I feel like that guy from Kentucky in a romance novel I used to read in the outhouse." Instead, I said, "My mother can play the piano, but nothin' like that." And Anna just smiled and nodded and went on playing. Never told her I had taken piano lessons five years and could hardly play a note.

Ah, Anna Fidelia Wilson, that square-faced girl with dimples. She had freckles, too, and she looked crisp and clean, and when she smiled at me the angels sang. She had heavy eyelids which gave her a bewitching blue-eyed Oriental look, and she wore expensive clothes. And, oh, she was stylish! I had never known a really stylish girl—not like her. And I, this nobody, this commoner, this independent, had somehow attracted her? I must be somebody after all. With Anna Fidelia Wilson I *was* somebody. I called her Sugar. Whatever we had together, and we called it love, was a magical potion that had rendered me, the ugly, beautiful.

Anna was the adopted daughter of the H. R. Wilson family. H.R., as he was known, was a solid, balding man in his late fifties built on an egg-shaped frame who displayed a long, narrow nose and who, although he was a strong man, had the right amount of gentleness in him. He was the most wise, decent, and honorable man, next to my father, I have ever known. He operated a statewide heavy equipment business, crawler tractors, road graders and the like. When I first met him he was confined to their home in Cheyenne in a room specially built for him above the garage. Tuberculosis. The only known cure then was unremitting bed rest.

H. R. Wilson had met Maybelle, I never knew where or under what circumstances. All I knew was that he had married her when he was a man past forty, and she was foxy and young. And I knew one other thing: It didn't make any difference who or what she was, if she hung around H. R. Wilson very long she would turn out to be a better woman than she was before. She was tall, wispy, pretty, as showgirls are pretty; henna-haired, blue-eyed, with so much of that black sooty stuff hanging on her eyelashes one wondered that she could lift her lids at all. She and her sisters had helped their widowed mother run a boardinghouse for the iron miners in Hibbing, Minnesota. As for Maybelle, you could hear her coming a mile away in city traffic. She laughed and hollered and screamed and butchered the king's English at a steady level, several hundred decibels above the Cannonball Express.

Maybelle was one of those women who at any moment had the power to make a man feel as if he were the greatest gift to the universe since Clark Gable. She exuded a sort of seductive air about her, but without warning she could cut your heart out, more likely your gonads, as was her habit with her bedridden husband, H.R. So often I had wanted to come to his defense as he lay there helpless, a large, breathing hunk of flesh in the bed, his long sad face reflecting her deep cuts at both his intelligence and his manhood.

To me, Maybelle Wilson represented the ultimate impetuousness. Neither she nor anyone else could predict her mood. Years before she had sought to achieve acceptance in Cheyenne's upper-crust society, but she was not comfortable with the elite and claimed she didn't give a damn for them in the first place. I understood. On the other hand, beyond the family, she was equally uncomfortable with her own roots, the remnants of which she tried to cover with fur coats, fine clothing, and an imperious public air she never quite carried off. She had had little education. Hadn't seemed to need much. She had two closets full of expensive dresses and a hundred pairs of high-heeled shoes. She owned a personal history as well, but after she married H.R. she kept it mostly a secret.

I thought Maybelle Wilson had had a good deal of experience with rejection and abandonment, and that her weapon against both was control. She needed to control everything and everybody, especially H.R. Having been poor, she desperately needed to possess things. Yet as quickly as she possessed something, she would soon grow tired of it. She might bring home a puppy for Anna and within months, even weeks, give it away. Anna, the adopted child, was to learn as a part of the standard family liturgy that, but for Maybelle, Anna would have grown up in an orphanage somewhere. That underlying, unspoken threat during Anna's early years persisted like a horror beating at the door—if Maybelle was displeased with Anna, the child could be given away as easily as the puppies.

But by the time I met Anna she was no longer so easily threatened. She and her mother often faced off, the mother demanding, screaming, struggling by the power of her fury and the volume of her rage to subdue the indomitable child; the child, modeling after the mother, exercising a similar power to resist the mother.

But for reasons I did not understand, Maybelle never screamed at me. Never once did she turn her psychic butcher knife in my direction. Instead, I felt heady in her presence. She would brag about me, "her son," she called me, this great young man about to become a great lawyer. According to Maybelle, I was intelligent beyond words, exquisitely handsome and wonderfully funny. I loved Maybelle Wilson, a woman more exciting, more worldly, more alive, more fully human than my own mother. She smoked long cigarettes and swore like a drill sergeant, and she often drank whiskey of an evening before dinner. Yet she was an immaculate housekeeper, a lot neater than my mother. Her house never smelled of canned corn simmering away in the pressure cooker, or of relishes bubbling on the kitchen stove. Her house smelled of her own perfume, the fancy guest soaps in the bathrooms, and the far-off smell of tobacco.

The living room had thick wall-to-wall carpeting on the floor, while ours was covered with "cheap" Navajo rugs my mother bought from the Indians for practically nothing when she had taught down near Shiprock. And fine furniture! The windows had real drapes that closed when you pulled a single cord, not those pull-down window shades we had at home. And on the walls Maybelle had hung up handsome, stylish prints of old England in gilded frames. I had never seen such a wonderful house—and down in the old rich part of Cheyenne, a house with a real gas log in the fireplace, a house that faced out on a paved street with a paved driveway right up to the back door. The Wilson family owned not one but two cars, and they were new, to boot—a brown DeSoto and a fancy steel blue Oldsmobile that Maybelle herself drove, and they had a double garage as well. Maybelle Wilson bought roast beef, and pork chops that she habitually overcooked. Yet they tasted heavenly to me. I doubted the Wilsons had ever tried wild meat with its palate-sticking fat; Maybelle served expensive frozen vegetables, and bought beautiful pies at the bakery with crusts better than my mother could make. Such opulence I had never before witnessed. And when Maybelle Wilson smiled at me and winked with those heavy lashes, I felt as invincible as Errol Flynn, as cute as Mickey Rooney, and as handsome as Walter Pidgeon.

By the summer of 1947 I had decided to go to Mexico to study Spanish and become a great writer *and* a great lawyer. Everyone knew that the great writers of the time were colonized in Mexico City, not Paris. I could receive credit at my own university for a summertime of Spanish at the University of Mexico. How a summer in far-off, romantic Mexico City appealed to me over another mean season of sweat and dirt and aching muscles working in Wyoming. Maybe I would meet the great young writers of my own blood. Maybe, exhilarated and enriched, I would become a new writer with great verve and machismo like Hemingway in Paris. I grew enraptured with the idea. I could actually write, I thought. I had written verses to Anna which she said were original and quite divine, and I had been urged by my creative writing professor, who thought I had a talent for storytelling, to write short stories, but none that I wrote were even moderately memorable.

And more, a heart on fire had exacerbated the creative itch. I had a mission, a pure and powerful mission in old Mexico. I wrote passionate letters to my parents begging for a couple hundred dollars they could ill afford—an artist must have his patrons—and when they sent the money, I kissed Anna good-bye, kissed her many times, and held on to her until the last moment. Then we promised each other we would write every day—promised on all that was deeply sacred. We would number our letters so we would know if even one of our precious missives was lost in the mail, and, at last, my thumb my ticket to old Mexico, once more I hit the road.

* * *

I was standing on the shoulder of the road somewhere in north Texas, I don't know how far from the border, my throat nearly closed from swollen tonsils. I was sick, feverish, and unable to swallow. The few cars that passed pulled out wide to give the droopy-looking kid on the highway plenty of room. I remembered how the Joads buried Grandpa along the road in *The Grapes of Wrath*, and I thought, yes, this is where I will die, right here on this desolate stretch in this stifling Texas heat. I would die because my parents had been negligent. One's ills are always the fault of one's parents. The doctors had recommended that not only should my tonsils come out, but my adenoids as well—two operations for the price of one. But my parents had let it go, sore throat after sore throat, winter after winter, until now.

I began to spit out pieces of rotted tonsil. I sat on the side of the road alone, except for the heat waves slithering across the horizon like gaseous snakes, waiting for the final throes of death to set in. At last a pickup truck rattled up and stopped.

"Where ya headed, buddy?" the driver asked. Guy without a shirt on, the window rolled down, a beat-up straw cowboy hat pushed back on his head.

I couldn't talk. I motioned to my throat.

"Got a cold, huh?"

I nodded.

"Well, I don't want to catch no goddamned cold. Get in the back." I climbed aboard, kicked the empty beer cans aside and lay down in the back of the truck, and for the next half-day I was bounced and pummeled like milk in a churn. Likely pounded the cold right out of me. The fever left. By the time I reached the border I was feeling better. And now I surely would live to write the great American novel—it was my destiny!

At the border I boarded a bus already filled with Mexican peons who dragged along all their earthly possessions done up in cardboard suitcases and old wooden boxes. They loaded in their bedrolls and their crated chickens and their skinny, inbred mongrel dogs, mostly ears and tails. And the little snot-nosed, big-eyed kids sat on the chicken crates and the chickens clucked and squawked, and the dogs vomited. The little kids did the same, and the mothers hollered, and the fathers drank long slugs of tequila out of Mason jars and curled their upper lips.

The bus careened wildly around the blind curves of the high mountain road, hanging on mostly by faith. Christ, you could look straight down a thousand feet—and who knew what donkey, what staggering drunk Mexican driver in some suicide jalopy, what herd of goats, what cart loaded with twigs or skinny hogs would be occupying the middle of the road at the next blind curve?

By the time I reached Mexico City I had fully recovered. The swelling in my tonsils had either abated, or the tonsils themselves had rotted off. But my affliction of the heart was raging out of control like one of those prairie fires in late August on the high Laramie plains. Although I had dutifully enrolled in the Spanish course at the University of Mexico, I couldn't concentrate. Suddenly I didn't want to learn Spanish. In the harsh light of loneliness my vision of Hemingway in Paris vanished. Hemingway had never been in love, not like me. The great American novel could wait. A man cannot write with a splintered heart. John Locke, claiming that life cannot be honestly confronted except in the loneliness of the heart, was full of pure bullshit. Creativity is the child of passion, I argued, not pain. One creates out of mad exuberance, not abject agony. I had to be with Sugar.

In Mexico, without her, I was a nobody once more. Nobody in Mexico had ever heard of me. Nobody thought I was great or intelligent or funny. Nobody recognized my beauty. Moreover, Anna's letters had never reached me. And not having heard from her for over a week, I became panicked. Had she, too, abandoned me? "Out of sight, out of mind," my mother used to say.

The classes were held off-campus in a quiet part of the city in a two-story residence, an adobe and plaster structure of classical Spanish architecture, with the requisite red tile roof and balconies all suspended on great beams and corbels, the windows protected with hand-wrought iron window guards. The stairways were laid with Moorish tile, the bottoms of the three-tiered fountains in the courtyard the same, and an eight-foot-tall stone fence guarded the property from the barefoot peasants who stood on the outside, some with babies in their arms, a brown dry hand held out, pleading eyes, the whispers for centavos barely heard.

At breaks the students gathered at the tables under the shade of canvas umbrellas, and there they practiced their newly acquired vocabularies and tried to link their newly conjugated verbs. They were all very sincere and all very devoted to the task. But I could say nothing in Spanish, nothing at all, and I could hear nothing, nothing except the sound of my mother's voice as I left her on the bus. "You are a man now."

I wondered how this mere utterance could make a man of me. I had been in Mexico little more than a week, yet overcome by loneliness, the pain became too much. I couldn't bear another day away from Anna. Losing her, I had lost myself. I felt a high, wild panic, a vicious terror associated in obscure but discernible ways with death. I couldn't wait for the morning bus. I couldn't wait another hour. I threw my things together and boarded the midnight bus for Laredo, heading home to Anna and Wyoming.

I spent the rest of the summer back in the hayfields on the old Fred Boice ranch outside of Cheyenne. Anna was working as a secretary for the Cheyenne Chamber of Commerce. I drove a team of strong black broncs with thick bouncy manes behind a mowing machine. I liked the relationship between man and horse. We understood one another—the need to be harnessed, yet to be wild. I longed for both, as did they, those powerful steeds who any instant would run away, for no reason, for the sheer joy of running. Often they nearly escaped me, my skinny arms barely able to hold them back by the reins, these same docile domestic beasts who, when finally held to it, lowered their massive heads to the tugs, hunched down their muscled, foaming flanks and pulled the mower through the high jungles of grass.

Sometimes Anna could borrow her father's DeSoto. She'd come for an evening only, no Sundays off in the hayfields. Blooming brome grass and budding timothy do not respect the Lord's day, but that was all right, because when Anna came to visit she told me she loved me, and I told her the same, and I was somebody.

That fall I went back to school. But Anna had been exiled by her parents to Denver in a last-ditch hope that if they could pry these mating beasts apart perhaps Anna would apply herself to something, anything, even to the business of being a secretary. Maybe she could learn shorthand and bookkeeping and become an expert typist, make something of herself. They had enrolled her in Barnes Business College in Denver, but the plan wasn't working. Anna saved her food allowance to come see me. When she'd saved enough, she'd grab the bus to Laramie. Half sick from starvation and from love, Anna wasn't doing well at Barnes Business College either.

On the night of January 8, 1948, my nineteenth birthday, I broke my leg. Sober as any Methodist minister on Temperance Sunday, I'd caught a ride home on a motorcycle with some guy who'd left the Buffalo Bar at the same time I walked out. I'd stopped by to purchase a bottle of wine for a cheap celebration in that bleak basement room where, miserable and alone, I intended to toast the bare concrete walls. I'd been riding behind this guy on his motorcycle holding on to him with one hand and the wine with the other, and when we got to Fourteenth and Grand I asked him to let me off. He skidded the rear end of the cycle around, as in the movies, and I fell, broke the bottle of wine on the ice and my knee on the curb. He must not have looked back and drove on. I lay in the snow under the corner streetlight for a long time. Once somebody walked by, but they probably thought I was a drunk moaning away in his stupor over his broken bottle of booze. The night was bitter cold.

After a while I began to chill and I realized I'd better do something or I'd freeze to death. When I could, I started to crawl a little through the snow. The landlord found me lying at the front door and called a doctor, who took a quick look and said I'd be all right in the morning—probably smelled the wine. But the next morning I wasn't all right, and I called Anna, and she called her father. "You tell that boy to take the train over here, and we'll take him to a good doctor." The landlord helped me to the depot and onto the train. I'd suffered a broken left femur at the knee, which required a cast from the hip to the toes.

The broken leg ended my school for the year. I had no car to get to the campus, couldn't have driven it anyway, and, once there, no way to get around to my classes. Mrs. Wilson insisted that I stay with them. I needed a mother, I was grateful. She pulled my pants off over my cast at night and helped me pull them on in the morning—wouldn't let Anna near me.

In six weeks the cast came off, and stiff-legged and sore I went to work in Evanston, Wyoming, on a seismograph crew. Started as a jug hustler. My leg was atrophied and weak, and it hurt to walk. But walking is what a jug hustler does, and the knee got better as the months passed. I was one of two jug hustlers, whose job was to lay out the cables with their sensitive sound wave detectors. We laid the cables by hand, dragging them off the great reels that hung from the truck. We pulled the cables down the draws, through the waist-high sagebrush, and up the steep hills. The drillers had already been to the location with their drill, and the shooters had loaded the deep hole with explosives, and when the charge was set off, the vibrations were picked up by the instruments on the cables we had laid out on the ground and recorded on the graphs in the seismograph truck. After that the graphs were taken to company offices in Texas or Oklahoma and then plotted on maps so that the underground terrain thousands of feet below the surface was shown in black and white so geologists could see the structures, and then tell the companies where the oil and gas might be trapped and where to drill their wells. Companies drilled dry holes with or without seismograph information. But no one could criticize the company men for their decision if they relied on the scientific data. Seismograph companies create excuses for dry holes.

That same spring I worked for the company as a driller's helper, drilling deep holes into the skin of the prairies for the explosive charges to be dropped into and detonated. After that I became a shooter's helper, which brought in more money. We handled the explosives, sticks a yard long and three or four inches in diameter. We got used to it, handled them like kindling wood, but a shooter and his helper had to give up smoking. We chewed Pay Day tobacco instead, a big glob in the mouth, looked like old cows chewing a dirty cud, but we were big-time, drinking dynamite men. All the while, I was still consumed with my love for Anna, and already we were talking about getting married.

Mr. Wilson had given up on Anna's education. The chronic effects of the disease, of this love psychosis, were too powerful for any father to combat. He couldn't keep us apart. And Anna couldn't concentrate at school and had come home at the end of the school year and never gone back. She was still working as a secretary.

"They might as well get married," Mr. Wilson said. He had the fears of all parents. His daughter. How does a man protect his daughter? He couldn't. His religious beliefs limited his choices. Only the law could protect her. Once a couple married, the law legitimized the natural course of mating. Outside the law, a father's dreaded vision of his daughter's ruined life could become a reality, the risk of shame too great. And so being a practical man, Mr. Wilson thought that it was all right that we get married. Best thing. And Maybelle, well, I was her boy. She was up for it, way up! There would be a big wedding and all the rest, big social affair, fill the whole damn church. Everybody was happy, and I thought I was happy about it too.

I had written my parents, not often, not every Sunday as my parents did, but I had written telling them that I wanted to marry this Anna Fidelia Wilson, this love of mine who had launched me into another universe. My mother wrote Anna:

> You mention that both of you enjoy music, and poetry, and Gerry tells me that both of you are interested in church and both are Protestant. As you mentioned too, your interests being similar, you should make a good team. I think it is true that one of the secrets of happy married life is having such in common, and I'm sure your parents will agree with me. We have been married for twenty years and our love has grown with the years. As we look back we have so many pleasant memories of past times that we have enjoyed together. And our children, too, have been a part of many of our happy times, picnics, hunting trips and fishing trips. All of us enjoy the out of doors.

As to my father's advice to Anna, he wrote:

> It seems that serious and lasting love is possible in the Spence family, and from the sound of your letter I believe and hope this is it for Gerry. You'll have a big job cut out for yourself, not to change Gerry, for changing is bad, but you can surely busy yourself influencing his future growth. He is a good boy but takes after his father too much.

And Anna had asked in one of her letters to my parents if she could marry their son. My father had answered, "Yes you can marry him—*someday*." We were still both nineteen.

My job with the seismograph crew took me to the backcountry near Rock Springs and Fort Bridger and Farson. I had been transferred to the water trucks, and I rumbled and bounced along in one of the old beasts—bunch of gears up and over—singing, the water slopping in the tank to the rhythm of the road, and the song I mostly sang was "Because," because I was in love, and because I was going to be married to Anna Fidelia Wilson, and because if anyone was going to sing to her at our wedding, by God, it was going to be me— But I could see myself standing there, singing, and all at once I would forget the words, and the whole damned wedding would be ruined. Mrs. Wilson would run out of the church, humiliated, and Anna would be speechless, standing there, her bouquet of pink roses dangling from her hand, the congregation—all her family's friends, of course—mute as glass monkeys, and me, not knowing whether to shit or go blind. And so I sang the song every ten miles, and I sang it, therefore, hundreds of times.

I figured I could get married in my Levi's. But a man, if he was a man, should wear a suit to his wedding, especially if the bride was to make her march on the arm of her father down the long hall of the Methodist church in her white gown, dragging behind her a train of I didn't know how many yards of satin. And so I bought a new blue serge suit, J. C. Penney's, a red silk tie with a painted feather—they threw the tie in with the suit—a white shirt and new black shoes. When it came time to choose the vocalist to sing one of those wedding-type songs before the wedding march, I stood up in the Wilson living room and said, "Well, folks, I'm a singer. And this is my bride, and I'm going to sing to her," and everybody thought that was just too sweet, just too, too very romantic, and they, of course, agreed.

When the time came, I rushed up to the balcony of the Methodist church in Cheyenne to get ready to sing, and I looked down, and below me I could see the back of the heads of half a church full of people sitting there waiting for the music to begin. Almost all of them were on the bride's side, of course. The groom's side was empty except for my Uncle Hunter and his little wife, Aunt Estes. Jim Brown was at sea. I had asked him to stand up with me. On board ship he'd had a long lucky run and was winning big. He wrote:

I'm again wondering how a man can lose at poker. I hope you get some sense in your head and get back in the game. Just put on a clean shirt and a loud cravat, light up a two-bit cigar, go down to the nearest poker game, buy in and tell 'em you're from Santa Fe. You can't lose.

That was Jim Brown all right. He said he figured he'd stay at sea until he was a thousand ahead, and then go back to school. Instead, he returned to Laramie and played poker for ten years.

I married Anna Fidelia Wilson on the twentieth day of June, 1948. I married her because I loved her, and she loved me, and getting married is what people do who are in love. I married her because right off I had promised to marry her, and I meant it, and I was a man of my word. A man's word is his bond, as they say, and as I say too. A man who cannot keep his word is no man at all. He is nothing.

I asked Norm Johnson, another high school friend, if he would stand up with me, and he said he sure would if he could. He'd let me know. He was a good Catholic kid, and he said he'd have to talk to the priest. Catholics weren't supposed to take part in a non-Catholic ceremony, he said. Just before the wedding he told me the priest wouldn't sanction it, and he was sorry. So another friend, Eric Nelson, stood up with me, along with two of Anna's cousins who were also my friends, and that made up the groom's party.

Then the organist began to play "Because." Jesus God, the introduction! I couldn't believe I was standing alone up there in the church balcony, all decked out in that fancy suit, about to sing a song at my own wedding. Then I heard

Gerry and Anna Wilson Spence.
Wedding photograph.

myself asking out loud, "This is actu-ally happening?" No answer. My col-lar was too tight. I ripped at the top button. The shirt itched from the siz-ing. Already the organist had arrived at the measure where I was to come in. "Because you come to me, with naught save laa—oove." But nothing came. Not a sound escaped. I cleared my throat and the organist waited. The people waited. I could hear the nervous coughing below. Probably Mrs. Wilson. Finally the first words came to my mind, and somehow I was able to force some breath, not much, over my quivering cords, and some vocal vibrations were emitted. People turned around and looked up to see what kind of miserable joke was being played. I don't remember ever finishing the song, although I was later assured by several that they thought I did.

I came stumbling down the stairs and rushed up to the altar where I awaited the bridal march. I don't remember repeating the vows. I don't remember kissing the bride or slipping the ring on her finger, or her slipping one on mine. I have no memory of the reception or cutting the cake. I remember nothing at all until all at once I found myself driving through the rain in Mr. Wilson's new DeSoto automobile, which I had borrowed for our honeymoon. And sitting proudly next to me was Anna, my new bride. I was a man, just as my mother had said. I was a man, all right. And those who said a nineteen-year-old was just a kid had never met *me*.

CHAPTER 18

*Twelve years after the honeymoon. Back
(left to right): Anna, Gerry, H. R. Wilson.
Front: Kip, Kent, Kerry—"the kids."
Maybelle Wilson behind Kerry.*

OUR PLAN CALLED for a honeymoon under the stars, in the Snowy Range Mountains a few miles south of Laramie—romantic, and very cheap. We had no money for a cruise or even a weekend in Reno. We didn't have a tent. We were still children, whirling with visions. It was raining, but it didn't matter. We were in love, and the rain would go away, and the rain was not to be seen as a doomful harbinger of our lives together.

We children, Anna and I, scorned adulthood, the traditional price of marriage. We could have it all without burdening ourselves with all those stodgy responsibilities. We exulted in our freedom, we delighted in our freedom to do the things our elders wanted to do, most of which they could not do, or dared not do. To act adult—that was superficial and stifling stuff. The seriousness of adults was dreary, an evil despoiler of joy. We were the power, the joy, the indomitable. Bring on the whole son-of-a-bitch. Bring on life. We were here. And we were ready.

But there was the rain. We possessed only my old sheepherder's bedroll, tarpaulin top and bottom with a couple of my mother's heavy homemade quilts in between. My plan had been to search out a secluded spot by a murmuring stream up in the mountains above Laramie, chop some pine boughs with my hatchet, spread my bedroll gently over the boughs, lay down my love with tenderness and joy, and there, under a splendid sea of stars, and before God, by God, and the universe, launch the matrimonial ship to the heavens. We had brought along some potatoes and some Hershey chocolate bars. We were ready.

But the rain. The rain and the fog. It was as dark as dusk up there, the tops of the lordly firs and the princely spruces severed by the fog. We didn't care. The roadway was flooded, and water was rushing down the barrow pits like new creeks in springtime.

"We could stay in the car," Anna said. She gave me a loving smile.

"Well, hell, yes, Sugar, we could. But who wants to spend his honeymoon in a fucking DeSoto?" Silence. I drove on. Then I saw this small dirt road on the left-hand side of the highway and suddenly, impetuously, as I have taken many a turn in my life, I took it. I say, when the way is not clear, do *something*.

"Where are we going?"

"Who knows?" I replied, the rear wheels of the car spinning, the mud flying. Suddenly the DeSoto was high-centered in mud and stuck. I looked around. Through the mist of the rain I could see, as in the story of Goldilocks, a small cabin in the trees. "Come on," I said. We ran for the cabin and when we got there, half-soaked, the cabin was locked.

"This cabin shouldn't be locked," I said. "That's a violation of the code of the mountains. One does not lock one's cabin against a stranger in distress." We were laughing, huddled under the small stoop at the front door, the rain pouring down. "When I was a kid my father and I rode horses many miles back to a place called Crystal Mountain above my grandfather's farm. There was an old hotel back there, abandoned for years, but the doors were always open." But Anna wasn't listening. She was shivering. "There was always shelter for a cowboy in a storm, and always food. And when the cowboy left, he left a can of beans or a little coffee out of his pack for the next fellow who came along."

I looked around, found a rock and broke out a small pane of glass in the door, reached in and opened the latch from the inside.

"Enter, my princess," I declared. The cabin was a one-room log structure, open wood rafters on the ceiling, a bed in the corner, a potbellied stove in the center of the room. Couple of those oval rag rugs on the floor made of sewed-together braids. Dry kindling was stacked behind the stove. I built a fire, and when the place was warm and the coals were glowing, I threw the potatoes in, after which we feasted on a wedding supper of roasted potatoes and Hershey bars. The bed had been supplied with a feather tick, and, as in the Goldilocks story, the bed was just right. It was all just right.

In the morning we began to make up the bed, my bride on one side and me on the other. Then I found out something I didn't know about some women: They want their beds made in a certain way.

"Make the corners square, like this," she said.

"What for?" I asked. I was standing in my shorts and she in her white shorty nightgown.

"Because that's the way you do it."

"Who said so?" I asked.

"I say so," she said.

"Why should there be square corners?" I asked.

"Because, square corners look good."

"The corners weren't square when we went to bed."

"That doesn't make any difference. The corners *should* be square."

"You can make yours square. I don't like square people and I don't like square corners, and the people who own this place didn't like them either."

"They just didn't know how to make a bed," she said, the argument heating. "They make square corners in a hospital."

"This isn't a fucking hospital," I said. We were starting to holler.

"They make square corners in four-star hotels."

"I suppose this is a four-star hotel," I said.

Suddenly she rushed over to my side of the bed and pushed me aside with her hips to make the corner square herself. "You are a son-of-a-*bitch,*" she hissed through her teeth. As certain benign chemicals blow up when joined, what followed in that innocent cabin was the first of an endless series of spontaneous explosions that the union would suffer, mostly over matters of little more consequence than making corners square. Memories can be kind, and mine has dimmed as dynamite dust settles also. But I remember in its clearing that Anna was crying. Then I went to her and pulled her to me, and I held her, and she wept and I wept, and after that we made the bed corners square.

"I always did like square corners, Sugar," I said. She laughed and I wiped her tears away, and then I put a piece of cardboard over the broken window pane to keep the weather out, and I wrote a note to the owners, and left it on the kitchen table with two dollars to pay for the glass I had broken. The note read as follows.

Dear People, whoever you are: We were stranded on our honeymoon in a rainstorm. We know if you had seen us shivering in the rain and knocking at your door you would have offered us shelter in this wonderful little cabin. In your absence we accepted the offer we know you would have made had you been here. Thank you. The money is for the window.

Gerry and Anna Spence

The rain had stopped, and the day was bright. I jacked up the DeSoto, filled in the ruts under the wheels with rocks, and backed it out to the highway. Then my bride and I headed down the road to Laramie, to life, in all its exuberant abundance.

CHAPTER 19

Gerry Spence and father, with grandson, Kip.
Front: Barbara and Tom Spence, Gerry's brother and sister.

By THE MAGIC of a Methodist preacher, I had been transformed into the state of "husband." I looked the same on the outside—tall, skinny, unmuscled—a juvenile of the species, distinguishable only by a sort of radiating self-confidence that was as fragile as it was arrogant. If I had been a deer I would have been a gawky, flouncing two-point. But the magical words of the shaman having converted me into husband, I was suddenly thrust into the constricting world of the married male, a condition for which I had no prior training. I had watched my married parents, of course, but often watching teaches little. Married, I had little excuse to be lonely. Yet I longed for my parents, and yearned for them to at last appreciate their wayward son, this upright, married man, this *husband*, whatever that meant. Oh, couldn't they just once be proud of their son, despite the fact that both he and the bride he chose smoked Chesterfields and drank a six-pack of beer a month?

I wrote my parents, but not as regularly as they wished. At times, in their letters, my parents cried out for news of me. My mother would write, "It is exactly a month since we got your last letter in which you said you were going antelope hunting. What in the world is wrong? We hope for a letter next mail day, and always the same. Remember, you are always in our minds and our hearts and this silence is terrible. Let us hear. Good news or bad." She signed off, "Your forgotten parents."

Earlier she had written Anna, "Gerry has been very voluminous in his description of you. He has always had very good taste in his choice of girl-friends, so I can visualize you as an adorable and attractive young lady. Perhaps you realize that Gerry is rather impetuous at times, but on the other hand, I'm sure he is capable of great depth of feeling, which is part of love. If your feel-ing for each other is true love and not merely an infatuation, then you may be assured that we are for you. Love is one of the greatest forces of life, and it is very possible that it may be the steadying force that will make possible greater achievements in life for both of you. Time will answer that question." Mothers know. As before, the letter included a monthly stipend of the fifty dollars my parents had scraped together.

The day following our honeymoon I placed a classified ad in the *Laramie Boomerang*, along with our new telephone number, offering my vaunted ser-vices to the world as the "Penny-ante Contractor."

Husband too busy?
We can do anything, build anything,
fix anything. No job too big or too small.

Anna had taken a job as a secretary at the physical education department at the university while I carried on my new business. I bought a dilapidated 1932 Chevrolet roadster, my first car, for twenty-five dollars. The top was gone and two of the fenders as well. I drove it to my job in Centennial, a historical cow town at the foot of the mountains thirty-five miles or so west of Laramie. That old derelict of a car consumed a quart of oil on the way up and another on the way home. I also took along a five-gallon can of water to placate its constant thirst, for it boiled within minutes of starting and I had to stop every few miles to replenish the radiator with fresh water.

The job was for a widow. First I built her a picket fence. Then I sanded her floors with a commercial sander I had rented, filled the floors and refinished them with two coats of varnish. I raised her sagging house—rented the jacks—poured a footing for the support, mixed the concrete by hand and made a net profit of about fifty dollars. The woman was very pleased, and so was I. My mother was right: I could do anything. All a fellow had to do was walk into the lumber company and ask any of the old hands who gathered there every morn-ing how to do whatever it was a man had contracted to do. They were flattered to be asked and happy to teach. "Seek and ye shall find. Ask and it will be given unto you," my mother used to say, quoting, as she often did, from the Bible.

That summer I did a stucco job on a small house in Laramie, and I repaired the plumbing in another—rented the tools. My prices, quoted out of ignorance, didn't give the regular contractors a chance. Later that summer, Mr. Wilson bought me a used wall-cleaning machine, and I cleaned the walls and the ceilings of what were thought to be the most respectable homes in Laramie. I hated the work, standing on a ladder all day mopping the walls with a towel-covered trowel. And when the job was over, the work had just begun. I had to haul the filthy towels home and wash them and hang them out to dry, after which I had to bring them in again and fold them and load them back into that old jalopy. But I was conditioned to such hard work and Anna wasn't afraid of it, and we didn't complain. To the contrary: I thought we were way out ahead of the pack. Together Anna and I earned enough to feed ourselves, pay my tuition, and pay off my debt to the university for the student loans I had incurred after I had gone broke playing poker at Hick's Card Room. My mother had written Anna:

> Gerry has a real task before him in preparing himself to make a good living for a family. That is very important, for it is hard for love to run smooth without the necessary money for the comforts of life. On the other hand, love can really be tested in those years, and you will have a deeper devotion for each other, when the time arrives to journey down life's path together.

For the first time in my life I was devoted to my studies. My undergraduate classes were as boring then as they must be to students now. I remember nothing of economics except the endless droning of the professor and the meaningless words in the textbook. How could the English language be so thoroughly drained of feeling and emotion? Philosophy and logic were interminable tortures. What I do remember is that we could smoke in those classes. That was important for a fellow who had been sneaking two packs a day while he lived with his parents. I remember nothing of American literature, nothing of the writers I have since revered and whose works have enriched my life. I do remember, however, the professor's insistence that I had neither the intellect nor the soul to understand the first thing about writing, and that the B he awarded me in American literature was a gift for which I should be most grateful. Otherwise my grades were excellent.

I even had time to write a novel that my professor, Joseph Langland, thought, although "seriously flawed and overdone" (and equally immature), was "marvelously innovative." Professor Joseph Langland, a wild young poet singing in ecstasy and made for the melody of words, had become my mentor. He held up my novel as an example of modern experimental literature. Experimental literature? I wasn't experimenting. I had tried only to listen to the cadence of the words that came to the mind's ear and to write them. The class studied the novel, dissected it, fussed over it. The novel's principal character was a poor sculptor who had at last found himself making love to the symbolic female

Christ. I shudder at the thought. Professor Langland wrote that she seemed dead. Here is one of the scenes:

No saying can be found, no noises from the throat to speak of the hard, long heavings of the long green mountain when it burst suddenly against the early winter sky. No sounds to paint the red, the deep red, the nearing blackness of the fire that surged out of the mountain top, the terrible rolling lava flooding down to form the hard devil rock filling in and around, so that on the fifth day there were tall growing pines that shed their needles on the ground to make black soil where a tiny violet could have bloomed inside the moistness.

"Joyce, that's who he is. He is Joycean with a twist of Wyoming lemon," I remember some savant crying.

"The stuff is perfectly vague, but then, why should he do our work for us?" another chortled. "I love the elegiacal cadences."

"Innovative, I should say. And there is that peripheral delight in the prose."

The class understood more about what I had written than I. But I was soon to learn that their insights were their own inventions.

I also loved poetry, studied poetry, wrote it. One small poem that survives:

I had planned as a boy to own a house,
Not because houses are important,
Per se,
To men or boys.
Houses are only places to help us find
The people we are looking for.

(It is not that I wished to be placed,
But to be the owner of icicles
That extend from the roof as far down as the ground.)

Encouraged by my professor, I continued to write short stories that were politely and systematically rejected by *Esquire,* and *Harper's,* and other magazines. I would have run off with my love into the woods and become a bard, lived on love, sung back to Dylan Thomas, bowed respectfully to Robert Frost, saluted T. S. Eliot and run wild with Walt Whitman. But I had adopted a different agenda. I was going to make something of myself. Poets and great writers never amounted to anything. Whitman had to sell his own poetry door to door. Even the revered Thoreau could muster little enthusiasm for his work, and eventually had to go back to making pencils. As for me, I was going to be *somebody,* and how could somebody ever be somebody as a starving poet? Instead I became a fire ax salesman.

Anna's father had bought several hundred old fire axes at an auction for twenty-five dollars, and he gave them to me. I loaded them into the old Chevy and peddled them to the hardware stores, to people on the street, to friends, to anyone in sight—dollar apiece. Walked right into the lumber company. "How about making a fortune," I began when I cornered the owner.

"What do you mean?"

"I mean I got fire axes for a dollar. Used a little, but in good shape. Look at the handles! Handle's worth more than a dollar. Think of it! You can sell one of these for five. Five hundred percent profit! I can let you have twenty. No more."

"Who the hell wants fire axes?"

"Great for chopping kindling." I held up the ax for the guy to inspect. "These are rare. You can't buy 'em anywhere!" Then I'd raise my eyebrow and give the guy a knowing little grin. "And they make a hell of a weapon." Sold them all in less than a week.

I labored weekends at the Sponge Iron Plant where my father had worked as a chemical engineer before me. I hired on as a common laborer, hauled off the black cinders by the wheelbarrows full, poked out the clinkers from the kiln, swept the acres of concrete floors—dirty work fighting iron dust for the next breath. I came home at night to our small apartment on Seventeenth Street, its walls of papered-over cardboard, exhausted, my body black with dust, coughing, my lungs caked with the stuff. It didn't matter. I was going to become a lawyer. Big-time lawyer.

My father began writing in his letters that I should be careful and take some time off. "Seems funny to give such advice to that harum-scarum boy whom we left in the States in 1946, but it seems that people change." It only seems that way. Again my parents were feeling forgotten. My father wrote: "It has been about four weeks now since we have heard from you and we are wondering just what is the hitch? If we don't get a letter this week we will mail a letter to the Wilsons in Cheyenne and see if they can tell us what is the matter."

Then he added, "I have been wondering what car I should get when I come back. Been thinking pretty strongly of a Willys. Could you look into it for me?" A Willys, God almighty, just what he'd buy, all right.

My mother wrote in pencil at the bottom of his letter, "I've been feeling miserable at times of late. The doctor at Catavi found my blood pressure a bit high and things blur before my eyes at times. So I came to La Paz to see Dr. Beck. He says this is all due to the menopause, that I need vitamin C and medicine for a sluggish system, but that I can take the altitude OK. I'll be back in Catavi in a week." A few weeks later my father wrote, "Mother is getting along *mas o menos bien* at the present, improving a little all the time but not putting on any weight."

Then, in 1949, my father wrote another long letter describing how the natives at the tin mine had gone out on strike. They were a wretched, desperate bunch, barely more fortunate than slaves. They chewed coca leaves, which rotted their teeth but blunted the pain of their lives. They labored in the dark, deep underground caverns of the tin mines hacking out the ore in passages that extended for miles below the surface, and they sold their lives for pittances to make the owners some of the richest men in the world. When the miners staggered back to the surface, life was just as dark and bleak. Then the government ordered that their native labor leader, a man called Lechine, be deported to Chile. The miners struck.

A small mob captured the gringo supervisors and held them as hostages—the mine superintendent, the assistant mine superintendent, the master mechanic, the mine engineer, and the assistant geologist. The mob hauled their captives to the union hall. My father, a favorite of the miners, was spared. In the meantime the government, as is the wont of governments, was on the side of money and power. The officials called in the army, thus pitting the poor in the army against the poor strikers. The soldiers, my father wrote, did not lend effective assistance.

My father wrote that the mob outside the union hall was howling, and in the melee a miner was shot. "This put the miners into a worse frenzy and they called for gringos to be killed in retaliation. The miners began to beat their hostages, and then they drug them out of the union hall and paraded them in front of the crazed mob where they were further beaten, kicked and stabbed."

His letter went on to describe how, outside, the master electrician, John O'Connor, and his wife, along with the others, faced their tormentors. Mrs. O'Connor, a fierce little Mexican woman, was arguing with the mob when an armed miner forced his way through the crowd and raised his gun to shoot her. John O'Connor pushed the gun aside just as it fired, the bullet hitting another gringo named Huesser. The miner hollered, "That's good, we wanted to kill him anyway." Mrs. O'Connor turned on the gunman like a tigress and tried to wrest the gun away from him. She was being pushed around, of course, and when John, her husband, came to her aid he was shot. The bullet entered the right side of his chest and came out the opposite side of his back, tearing a two-inch-diameter hole which did not kill him immediately—but, my father wrote, he was soon dead from kicks and blows on his head and neck.

"Green, the surface superintendent, was taken out and nearly beaten to death. They put a rope around his neck and dragged him to a flag pole where he lost consciousness. Cook was beaten and badly cut, one ear being nearly severed. Krefting and a Bolivian named Vargas were shot and their bodies left in the drain ditch alongside the union hall."

My father's letter described how the camp was terrorized, the natives throwing dynamite bombs into the union hall where the hostages were held, but some survived. My mother, Barbara and Tom, along with other surviving gringo families, left on the second plane in. My father stayed back to help with the wounded and the dead.

"Monday we got the two bodies cleaned up and dressed and put in metal-lined caskets and soldered the caskets shut. Tuesday a plane came in after a four-hour delay caused by a couple of Patino Mine officials." An angry mob gathered at the airport threatening the plane, but my father, respected by the miners and being among the gringos, the plane was finally allowed to take off with the bodies.

He wrote passionately concerning the condition of the workers. My parents were so far away, the suffering he described so remote. Yet what he wrote hurt me. I felt I should be helping my father and the struggling people. "The laborer lives with his family—as many as six or seven in a one-room, dirt-floored house about ten by twelve feet in size. The house has one window. As of a month ago there were at least three hundred of these little adobe houses in which two families were living. This condition exists because there are not enough houses to go around. Recent estimations of the ore reserves indicate a fourteen-year supply at this mine, but still there is not one house under construction in Catavi. Does the management expect these families to live together for the next fourteen years? Does management expect the people to be contented and happy living in this type of house while the foreign staff live in houses with four to ten times the floor and window space?

"Here the base wage is probably better than any place in Bolivia. However, the wage averages less than 70 cents a day, and many workers draw as little as fifty-six cents a day. Still, bread, rice, macaroni products and potatoes cost about the same as in the U.S. Medical treatment is provided by the company, but the worker is never given sulfa or penicillin—it's too expensive. If the worker doesn't get well by being put to bed he will just have to die, but what of it? There is an abundant labor supply. Doctors don't seem to mind seeing people suffer. Nothing is given for pain.

"These are the conditions that have persisted for the last fifty years and under which the Patino family has become one of the world's richest. When I see a bright tinned can, a piece of babbitt metal or a hunk of solder, I vividly see in my mind the picture of human anguish under which it was produced." Among other suggestions for reform my father wrote: "I feel that through some channel, the U.S. Government, as a tin consumer, and the American public should put enough pressure on the mine operators in Bolivia that they will be forced to initiate some broad social and accompanying economic changes in the mining centers."

Perhaps because of his closeness to the miners, my father wrote: "Collectively we are afraid to sit in our parlors in the evening with the lights on. Someone [presumably on behalf of the mine owners] is liable to push a gun through the window and fix us, as a labor leader in the states was fixed the other day. We are afraid to walk from one house to the other after dark for fear of a bullet." That was the first time I heard my father say he was afraid. I never heard from my mother about all of this. But my brother Tom said she had been on top of things, tough and brave, and helping those who had been wounded and in need of food and shelter. After their contract was up, my parents decided to come on home.

For eight months Anna and I had lived under the conjugal blankets, smothered in the viscous, ever-replenishing lust of the young. One night she bolted up in bed.

"I'm not pregnant," she announced.

"That's nice," I said.

"But what if I can't get pregnant?"

"Why would you worry about that?" I asked. I reached for her. "Come back here."

"Wait a minute," she said, still sitting upright like one just awakening from a nightmare. "Maybe there's something wrong with me."

"How could there be anything wrong with you? You're using that whatcha-ma-jiggy the doctor gave you to wear, aren't you?"

"Well, yes," she said. "But what if I can't have a baby?"

"Jesus, Anna!"

"I'm going to go see Dr. Pugh," she said.

"Okay, I'll go with you. Now c'mere."

The next day we bounced up to the doctor's office, I and my worried wife, still only nineteen years old. Was the birth control device working as designed, we wanted to know. What if, instead, she were barren like her adoptive mother?

"I don't want to be one of those dry does" was the way she tried to explain it to the doctor. He was a kindly man with a red face and a small, pock-scarred nose, his white physician's smock so stiffly starched it crinkled as he moved.

"A what?" he asked incredulously.

I tried to explain her metaphor. "I'm a hunter," I said, "and a good meat hunter looks for the dry doe in the herd. Good meat hunter can spot the dry doe as far as he can see her—kinda fat and glisteny and . . . "

"This isn't a meat-hunting issue, is it?" the doctor asked. The doctor looked concerned. "You're not afraid this man is going to shoot you, are you?"

"No," she said. "I just want to be able to have a baby."

"Oh," the doctor said. "Well then, let's get to it. Are you using what I prescribed the way I told you to?"

"Yes," she said.

"Well, it's working then, isn't it?"

"How do I know if *it's* working or if it's me that isn't?" Anna asked. "Besides, I don't trust that thing."

"How long have you been using it?"

"Eight months already. Maybe there's something wrong with me," she said.

"Well, let's take a look," the doctor said. She followed him to his examining room. Pretty soon he emerged with the verdict, which when translated meant that some women are constructed this way, and some that, but the world seems to remain overpopulated despite these numerous variations on a theme.

"So what's there to worry about?" the doctor asked with long, quiet patience.

"But what if I can't?" she asked.

The doctor shrugged his shoulders and shook his head. Then he turned to me as if for understanding. "If you want to talk about this in hunting terms, it's like messing with a loaded gun. If you push the safety on, and the gun doesn't go off when you pull the trigger, the only way you can tell if the gun is working is to push the safety off again and then pull the trigger. That could be dangerous. Nothing I'd recommend."

"What *is* the best method of birth control?" I asked, trying to put things in perspective.

"Separate housing," the doctor replied. He smiled a little at his own joke. We didn't get it right off.

Life was confusing. You get to talking about dry does and road machinery, all of which seemed ridiculously irrelevant, and the first thing you know you are about to become a father.

"I have good news," she said one night a little over a month later as we snuggled naked under the conjugal covers.

"You must be pregnant," I said.

"How did you know?" she said, bolting up out of the bedcovers like a rocket launched to Mars.

"How can you be pregnant?" I asked.

"I had to find out," she said. Then she threw her arms around me.

"Oh, Gerry, you are about to become a father!" I held on, stunned.

"Aren't you happy?" she asked when she finally let me go.

I was silent for a long time. At last I came out with the only words I could muster. "How can I be a father when I'm still only a child?"

In August of 1949 my family returned from Bolivia. Having sold their home in Laramie before they had gone off to South America, my parents were now homeless, and my father was unemployed. My mother, I was later told, seemed to be marching on the edge of hysteria. Her bleak and gloomy view of the family's condition had them on the brink of disaster—this couple with two young children to raise, she and my father almost fifty, with no job and no place to live. Always she had fought for security—the steady job, a home with a garden and a cellar to store the food, a place to hide when she was afraid, where she could await the return of a loving husband, the strong and protective daddy. Back from the violence and blood of Bolivia, she must have seen herself like a tumbleweed being blown across the Colorado prairies.

And, of course, my mother was right. They were living temporarily at Grandfather Spence's farm, three generations of Spences in that same small, plain farmhouse I had known as a child. But by then, there had been a few improvements. The old back porch had been converted to a bathroom that had a real toilet in it, one Grandma didn't want to flush too often. Wasted water. That porch had been where Grandpa used to hang up his old sweaty hat when he came limping in, and where he stored that crockery water jug, the one we took when we went out to work with the mules.

"Whatever are we going to do?" my mother had asked my father repeatedly. But even he had no answers. "The children have to go to school," she said. "We can't live here with your parents much longer." My mother and father and the two children were occupying one bedroom with two beds. "We can't go on like this."

"Don't worry, it'll be all right," my father had said. Yet she must have felt trapped; no job, no place to escape the high, whiny, bossy voice of Grandma Spence. She had no kitchen of her own where she could immerse herself in the business of homemaking—her canning, her baking of hot, fresh cinnamon rolls, the smell of which could restore life to the dead. Worse, she had no bedroom where she could snuggle in alone with my father, no way to hide from the busybody ways of an old woman—and two small children running wild, annoying the grandparents.

I hardly recognized my mother when the family came to Laramie on a Sunday afternoon in late August of 1949 for their first visit after their return from South America. My mother hadn't changed much on the outside, same out-of-style homemade dress, same black shoes. But her hair had grayed at the temples and she looked thinner. Still, she was not my mother.

When we hugged she seemed stiff and distant. "This is Anna, your new daughter," I said.

"I'm very glad to meet you," my mother replied politely. She held out her hand and gave Anna's a small, formal shake. Perhaps, I thought, she had always been stiff and distant. As a child, perhaps I had grown used to it like a duckling snuggles up to a large wooden decoy in its pen. She had never been one to hold and to cuddle. She was compassionate. She listened and comforted. Sometimes she kissed me as mothers kiss little children.

Yet I had always felt a distance between us, and as I thought back, a certain reserve between my father and her. They were always polite and caring on the surface, but I wondered what was under the hide of their marriage. I had assumed their lives were predictable but comfortable together. If not the blind, ecstatic rapture of young love, there was security and caring there. Mostly, I believe that today. On the outside my mother exhibited a sort of Christ-like bearing, a gentleness, a charity, but I felt no internal passion ever escape from her. I hold no memories of her crushing me close to her, as I have crushed my own children close to me. I have no memory of her squeezing me so tightly I gasped for air, as I have squeezed my children.

How vividly I see my mother standing in the kitchen, Anna standing next to me, her stomach already announcing the generation to come. I patted Anna's stomach lightly. "See here, Mother! This is what happens when you leave!" I laughed. "You're about to become a grandmother! Aren't you excited?" I wanted excitement. I wanted unconfined exuberance. I needed it to cover my own rising anxiety.

My father held back, his hands in his pockets, but he was smiling. My mother remained polite, like a tired ticket-taker at the theater. At last she forced a small, quivery smile. I reached out for her hand. It was limp and unresponsive. She wasn't there. The eyes appeared blank. She was cold as the dead are cold. She spoke in a flat voice, no life in it, the sound little more animated than mumblings from the crypts.

My father, seeing that Anna was preparing a chicken for the oven, tried in his homey way to break the ice. "Well, Anna," he said as if he had known her all of his life, "you want to know how the Bolivians dress their chickens?" He prefaced what he was about to say with his grin to tell us what he was going to say was humorous.

"Yes, Dad," Anna replied.

"Well, I'll tell you," he began, laughing out loud. "They scrub the rectum up good and then they eat the chicken, rectum and all." He laughed again, but he seemed embarrassed when he finally heard his own words. "What do you think of that?" I could tell he wished he hadn't asked.

"Well, I'll be!" Anna said.

"They don't waste a thing," he said, trying to make his meaning clear. My mother looked as if she hadn't heard a word. Where was she? Mother, are you angry with me for having married without your blessing? I thought I had your blessing. What was I to do? You weren't here. And aren't you happy about your new grandchild? And didn't you miss me? And aren't you glad to see me again? Why are you so distant, so dead?

My father laughed again. "Well," he said, "you're a mighty pretty girl. Don't know how a son of mine was able to hook you, but I'm sure glad he did."

My mother was still silent.

Mother, don't you understand that I needed you, that it was *you* who left me? *You* left me here. Sure, I suppose I have a mother in this wife. She mothers me, as all wives sometimes mother their husbands. But you are still my mother. Don't you care that I'm about to enter law school? I'm going to be a good lawyer—a successful lawyer. You'll be proud. But I couldn't say any of that to her. She stood stiff and silent next to the back door. Maybe she smelled the cigarette smoke on me. Probably smelled it in the house all right. Maybe, when Anna pulled the chicken out of the refrigerator, she saw the beer.

I walked ahead of my parents, beckoning them to follow me into our tiny living room. I'd painted it a dark green, the color of a forest in shade. My parents sat down on the couch, my mother and father sitting close together, not knowing quite how to settle in, so uneasy, my brother Tom, eight, and my sister Barbara, ten, huddled up close, staring at me with large blue children's eyes. I smiled back. I brought in kitchen chairs to sit on, Anna and me on this side of the room and them over there. You could feel the tension.

"Sorry, we haven't been able to buy a rug yet," I said for no reason at all except that I felt the embarrassment of the bare floors.

"Don't need any rugs to make a home," my father said.

"Well, I'm glad you're finally home," I said. "We have a lot of catching up to do."

"Right," my father said. "So you're going to be a lawyer, huh?"

"Right. Gonna make a million dollars and be president." I laughed.

"Well, it's about time somebody in the Spence family makes a million dollars. Right, mama?"

She nodded silently, but I wasn't sure she understood him. Suddenly I wanted to rush across the room, to gather my stony mother into my arms, to hold her close to me.

But instead, my mother suddenly got up. "We have to go," she said abruptly.

"Why, do you have to go? You just got here. Can't you stay for supper? Anna is such a great cook."

"No. We have to go. It's quite a drive back to Masonville, and the children are tired. Your father wants to go antelope hunting in the morning." Her politeness cut like a cold sword right through me.

Embarrassed, my father also got up. The kids followed suit. Anna and I got up. "Can't you stay?" I asked again.

"We'll see you soon," my father said quietly. "We just got back. Things aren't quite settled yet." They walked out of the house like people headed for a graveside ceremony, heads mostly bowed, no lift to their gaits. Then suddenly Tom, ten, jumped up, turned a complete circle in the air, like a kid goat who had been cooped up all day, and then he walked on slowly with the rest of them and got into the car.

Within the week I learned that my father had bought an old rundown country store on the edge of Fort Collins in the poor part of town. A small living quarters had been built on the back of the store. The kids could go to school in Fort Collins. My mother could run the store, and he could get an outside job, and they could get their food wholesale. Maybe they could put something aside. At least now they had a plan. Besides, they would be living near the beloved mountains of my father's childhood, and near his parents, who were growing old. My parents were to take possession of the store very soon, and would be moving from Grandpa Spence's place, and then everything would be all right, and they would, so went my father's argument, live happily ever after.

I had given little thought to my parents' decision. It would be years before I saw their well-being as my responsibility. I was too consumed by my own plight, too staggered by the realization that I was soon to father some little stranger I had never met, who wished to take my place as the child of preference to Anna Fidelia Wilson Spence. I had been given no choice in the matter. I had never been consulted.

* * *

Nobody in Laramie had ever talked about going to Harvard or Yale. Most of us didn't know where those schools were—somewhere in the English-speaking world, no doubt, but as remote and fanciful as Nome or Siam. The real world lay right there in Laramie, Wyoming, where the university stood in tall sandstone buildings and stately spruces and sparse flower gardens, where red and purple petunias bloomed in the late summer. The towering cottonwoods made shade for girls who sat on the lawn in their short skirts and brown-and-white loafers, scuffed at the toes, and over which hung, like derelicts at a street corner, the slothful bobby sox.

I ran up two flights of stairs to that dreary space called the law school. There Dean Hamilton still maintained an office, and if one explored those dreary catacombs, one soon came onto three ancient classrooms and four small, poorly lit, tomblike caverns that served as offices for those unfortunates who called themselves professors of law at this, perhaps the most remote, smallest, least prestigious of all university law schools in America. The law library, barely sufficient to meet the requirements of the American Bar Association, took up most of the room, the endless books that nobody cared to read or, in the end, could bear to read. Libraries impress the beholder with a suggestion of scholarliness, with or without scholars. Yet I have come to conclude that if one were to read every word contained in the greatest law libraries in America, one would end up knowing approximately nothing.

The floors in those quarters were old and wooden, oiled and creaky. No pictures hung on the walls. No ornaments or plaques adorned the premises. No drapes, no wood paneling, no carpet, no brass, no stained glass—these walls were as interesting as the interior of a mausoleum, and a constant reminder of the ultimate resting place of a lawyer's most unfortunate clients. The rooms reflected neither care nor repair. The law school stood as the ontological wonder of the University of Wyoming, a place *in being,* yet utterly without charm or character. Its contents and surroundings accurately reflected the law. Nothing in those premises, bulging as they were with books and students, suggested that the law was either englightening, or interesting, alive or growing. I was to discover it was none of these.

On the first day of law school, in September of 1949, the dean spoke to the freshman class, a disparate bunch of thirty-five gawking, grimacing, some grinning, mostly obsessive, lip-chewing types. Most were large-headed the kind with squinty eyes, unmuscled limbs—the cigarette-smoking, thick-glasses-wearing types. Some wore coats and ties and looked like real lawyers from the waist up. But from the waist down they often wore Levi's snugged up tight at their flat bellies with belts that were too long, the ends of which hung down like the tongues of panting dogs. Most had never read a poem. Most had never sung a song or cared to, except when drinking, at which time their voices took on the sound of droning vacuum cleaners, the bags of which begged to be emptied. They were intellectuals, powerful muscleheads who could wrinkle their brows and polish off a final exam with the repose and eloquence of a cow munching daisies in the pasture. There were, of course, a few of the great guys who had somehow made it to law school, but, I thought, they won't be long for this world. A letter sweater and a new Chevy convertible won't get you through this place.

"Look around you," the dean bellowed to the freshman class. "See your fellow students here situated in this room?" He spoke like a lawyer. "When the first quarter is over, those remaining will find half your fellow students have mysteriously disappeared." As he dusted his hands I thought he looked squarely at me. I knew the class was staring. I had nothing to offer, no fraternity connections, no outside connections, no great scholastic record, no father who was a lawyer or businessman, no father who even wore a respectable suit to church. I didn't know a lawyer. I'd never talked to one.

The dean droned on, avowing that law was a science as much as physics and chemistry. I had been a scurrilous failure at science. My God, I thought, why am I here? I should have gone to divinity school. I could at least recite the Beatitudes. But God and I were at odds.

I listened to the dean's initiating speech with mounting anxiety. "The practice of law is a business, nothing more and nothing less. *Real lawyers*," he pulled his long upper lip down over his teeth and spit out the words in a half-whistle, "are not knights riding around on white chargers seeking that Holy Grail called 'justice.' " His eyes blazed through his thick rimless glasses and his bald head glowed wonderfully. "Real lawyers develop sound billing skills, drive four-hole Buick automobiles and maintain the status quo. One, maybe two of you, the best and the brightest, whoever you are—you already probably know who you are, and so do I"—and he didn't look at me—"will be chosen by a major law firm, perhaps in Cheyenne, perhaps in Denver, perhaps even as far east as Kansas City. Such firms represent the heartbeat of this country, the great American corporation, business, government. The rest of you will end up representing the dredges of the system—the poor and the criminals." He made a face like a newborn after its first taste of Pablum. "Indeed, in the end, it will often become difficult to distinguish such lawyers from their impoverished clients. So heed my words, gentlemen"—there were two women in the class—"and learn to *think like lawyers*." Then he cast us his most generous smile, and bestowed on us his first assignment in Contracts. "Brief the first three cases in your casebook," he said, whatever that mysterious word *brief* was supposed to mean.

"Think like lawyers," the dean had said. I wondered how a lawyer was supposed to think. Logically, without passion, I supposed. Think with thoughts unconnected to emotions. Drive out all feeling, for law was a science and science was feelingless. In the years that followed in law school, I was to learn that the professors' world remained insular—arrogant and out of touch—and that justice to them was a sentimental idea that popped into the rhetoric of politicians and invaded stodgy old documents like the Constitution. No one could define *justice*. What was justice to one was injustice to another. Justice was just a phrase—EQUAL JUSTICE FOR ALL—carved over the doors of buildings like the United States Supreme Court. In the science of law one could not abide such subjective concepts as justice any more than one could talk about love as a component in a chemical formula. Law was law. And, like science, law could not be understood by the unscientific mind. I therefore set out to think like a lawyer.

Of those moldy chambers of misery I remember most the sense of fear that permeated the place. An acerbic odor caked the nostrils, a smell oozing out of the woodwork suggesting that the collective spleen of the student body was leaking, and that the place would soon explode in an awful conflagration of terror. What if I failed? What would happen to my family, my wife, the child *en esse,* as my professors called the fetus? How could I bear being relegated to a dreadful life of selling fire axes and laboring in the dust of the cement plant? What would my father say? Nothing, of course. He would only look sad, and say nothing. What would Mr. Wilson say? He was contributing a sum to our budget in an amount equal to the sum he had been paying for Anna's schooling at Barnes Business College, reasoning that the money spent, whether on Anna directly or on us as a couple in school, would help assure Anna's future. I felt that the money was a gift to me, for it was my obligation to support Anna, not his. I owed him, and the only way I knew how to repay the debt was to make him proud.

Once shortly after the wedding, Mr. Wilson and I were talking like father and son. Maybelle was in the kitchen fiddling around, and Anna was helping her, and there were just the two of us men. Mr. Wilson had said, "Gerry, it took me until I was past forty to save my first twenty-five thousand dollars." Mr. Wilson was probably a millionaire—made it all honestly. "What would you do with the money if I gave you twenty-five thousand dollars so you could get an earlier start than I had?" I took it to be an offer if my answer was right. I didn't want Mr. Wilson's money. But I was going to be a millionaire like him.

"Well, if you gave me twenty-five thousand dollars," I said, "I would take your daughter on a world cruise, and we'd play around, and when the money was gone, I would come back and go to school, and become a lawyer, and make my own money. And thanks," I said, and gave him a grateful smile, and I thought Mr. Wilson respected my answer. And now I wanted to prove myself.

But how could I compete for grades in law school with all of the Phi Beta Kappas and the returning veterans, the engineers who already held degrees and were ten years my senior, clever fellows who had passed physics and chemistry and knew how to think scientifically? I could write a poem. Sometimes I could face an audience and sing. I could feel and cry and raise hell, but I was short on logic, short on in-depth reasoning, short on patience, short on all of the scholarly qualities the others were long on. As an undergraduate, my grades were nothing special. I had majored in English. I liked to write. But I never had to learn to think. Who ever heard of learning to think? You don't learn it, you just *think*. And you don't think like somebody else, you think like *you* think. But now I had no alternative. I had to learn to think *like a lawyer*, however in hell one was supposed to achieve that skill.

Until then, I always thought I had studied hard in school. But now, my previous study habits seemed like child's play. Where my fellow students took notes in class, I took the same notes and that evening, with the lecture fresh in mind, meticulously rewrote them in literary style in a bound notebook. While the others shared their briefing chores—"You brief Contracts, I'll brief Torts"—I briefed every case, typed the brief on a tissue insert, and carefully pasted the brief next to the day's lecture in my bound notebook.

Then I took on the task of teaching an older student, Walt Scott, a friend of mine. He had to miss some of his classes because he was a postal employee who, twice a week, rode the railroad and sorted the mail between Laramie and Denver, a job he had to keep in order to support his family. Teaching him taught me. I held on to the lapels of my jacket, paced the floor before him in the style of the professor, and lectured him on every detail of the lesson. I made my student explain the rules and the application of the rules to the facts until I was satisfied he understood, and thereby I, too, had mastered its most esoteric roots and subroots, until I, too, could think like a lawyer.

As my father was a hunter, so was I. I fed my family as my father had fed his, on the wild game of Wyoming. In late September in the elk season, I stole a weekend from my studies and went to the great Hoback Mountains hunting with my closest friend, Jack Hohnholtz, who was to die tragically within the next decade. He was a big, handsome, redheaded country boy who lived and worked on his father's ranch on the Wyoming–Colorado border near Laramie. In his father's four-wheel-drive Dodge Power Wagon we headed for the high rugged country where the elk hid like frightened fugitives. We camped by a small stream. That night it snowed, but we had no tent. We were wet through and through, and began the day already cold and tired.

Before daylight we had trudged up the long mountain, our early morning energy, born of the thrill of the hunt, taking us far back into the timbered country, where, by day, the elk lay low in the jungles of spruce and lodgepole, and at dawn and dusk, sneaked to the edges of the small islands of grass to graze. You can stand within throwing distance of a whole herd, and they can disappear at full speed like ghosts through the dense timber without the snap of a twig or the sound of a hoof on the forest floor.

I remember some years before I had been slipping through the timber, careful foot up, careful foot down, looking, always looking where each foot would touch the earth, heedful of dry snapping twigs, cautious of the crackling needles, seeking silence in the walking, silence even in the breathing. Yet the elk could hear me coming, and, if the wind was right, they could smell me as well.

I had stopped to listen and had been standing for a long time in timber so dense it was half night at noon. Suddenly I heard a slight snap-snapping. Giant spruces emit their own sounds in the silence, high dead limbs rubbing in a vagrant breeze, a small red squirrel scampering. Slowly I turned my head toward the direction of the sound and there, plain to see, were two cow elk as sleek as brown bunnies, a calf following the lead cow, the three ducking to miss a limb here, swaying to avoid a dead log there, their long legs lifting them over the downfall and through the thick tangle in all-but-perfect silence. I froze, not blinking an eye, my breath slow, without motion. The elk were walking at a rapid pace, directly at me. I wore a red hunter's vest, but elk are color-blind, my vest to them merely another shade of gray.

When the lead cow was within a car's length of me she stopped. A soft south wind was blowing in my face, and I could smell her, the good musk of elk, sweet to the nose of the hunter. Almost on me, she stopped, lifted her head, stared straight at me and then took another cautious step forward. She was so close I could see the hairs inside her nostrils, her black, wet, patent leather muzzle wrinkled, testing the air, her eyes reflecting my own still image. Yet as close as she was, she could not recognize the frozen form of man. Suddenly, when she was so near I could have reached out and put my hand on her nose, she caught my odor and exploded, as did the others. I didn't shoot, I was hunting a big bull. Within seconds the elk had disappeared at full speed into the dense timber, once more in perfect silence.

That evening Jack and I had headed back to camp in the dark. The snow at the lower elevations had melted and the trails were muddy, and we knew that in the morning the going would be hard and slow and the elk higher.

"Gotta get higher in the morning," Jack said. "Gotta get an earlier start before the ground thaws. The mud down here is a killer." It had started to rain.

"I know," I said. "There's an outfitter a few miles down. Let's rent a couple of plugs. Ain't much left of me." That night we rode two big large-footed horses to our camp, one a sorrel with a blazed face, and the other a black with a Roman nose. We staked them out, handy for an early start. We built a fire, but except for the ambiance of warmth, it provided little comfort in the rain. We wrapped ourselves in our wet blankets and shivered, and we laughed at our misery and we cursed. We wondered at what fools we were, soaked in the wet and trapped in the endless night. The horses chewed their coarse alfalfa hay and snorted at the smell of bear or at the ghosts that keep all horses nervous in the night. Nor did we sleep. Perhaps we dozed.

Before sunup we were eager for the hunt again, longing for our bodies to warm with the long ride up the mountain. We saddled up, started out in the dark, Jack in the lead, and by daylight, we found ourselves higher than we had gone the day before. There in the high back range it had snowed all night, the new fluff up to the horse's bellies. About noon we came on a small herd of elk that had been bedded down and were spooked by the noisy horses plodding through the timber. Jack, on the sorrel, was still in the lead. When he saw the elk he pulled his horse up and, like the cowboy he was, yanked his .30-30 from his scabbard and tried to get his shot off without dismounting. Cowboys don't like to get down off their horses. I saw the elk milling ahead, still undecided in what direction to run. I hit the ground, my old Krag ready, and had already fired and downed my bull before Jack got his elk in his sights. Then I heard Jack's old Winchester explode, and I heard him say, matter-of-factly, as if speaking practically to no one, "I got 'em."

We tied the horses, dressed our animals and cut their carcasses in neat halves. We lifted half an elk over each of our saddles in the same fashion that a horse can carry a dead man, hitched our lariats to the other half, and led our horses back down to camp, each horse carrying half an elk, dragging the other half behind.

At last, tired and content, we headed out, a winter's supply of meat secure in the truck, the long road home ahead. We bumped slowly over the same trail we'd come in on, the truck in four-wheel drive fighting through the slush and the mud, groaning steadily, rocking over the ruts and stones, pressing me into nodding sleep. Then we rounded a curve through the lodgepoles. There ahead of us, blocking the road, was a pickup truck.

"What the hell is this?" Jack said. I jerked awake—a forest-green pickup, an orange dome light on top.

"Game warden," I said. A uniformed warden got out of the truck.

"What the hell have we done now?" I said to Jack. "We're in an open area, aren't we?" The sun was shining low through the afternoon trees.

"I think I read the map right," Jack said.

"Got yer license?" I asked.

"Right," he said. I checked in my pocket for my own.

"You tag your elk?"

"Yeah," Jack said. "Did you?"

"Yeah," I said.

The warden walked up. "Your name Gerry Spence?" he asked. He was a tough-looker. Big as a skinned grizzly. His Stetson pulled down over his eyes.

"Yes, sir," I replied.

"Your mother is dead," he said, as if he were relating the state of the weather. "Better call this number." He handed me a slip of paper. What he handed me was more than a number. It was my ticket to hell.

CHAPTER 20

Esther Spence, Gerry's mother with Gerry, holding Little Peggy.

MY MOTHER'S GENES never had an opportunity to play themselves all the way out. I missed knowing her as an old woman, seeing the wisdom that comes in old eyes, in the silences when others speak. I missed the graffiti of wrinkles on her face that time leaves with age, a look that says we are all right now, as we once were. I do not think it is too much to say: I wish I could have heard her say, once more, that she loved me. I would not have forced promises, but I wish I had heard her say she would never leave, never think of it, never again, and if the pain came again, I could bear it for her. I would say, "Give it to me, Mother. I will bear it."

When the game warden handed me the paper, I saw that it bore Grandfather Spence's telephone number. Jack Hohnholtz pulled the Power Wagon up to the first public phone we could find—perhaps in Pinedale. My Uncle Hunter answered.

"Better get up here, Gerry," he said. "Your mother's gone."

"How?" I asked.

"Well, Gerry," he said, the hard words coming straight as was his way, "your mother took her own life."

I drove all night. When I arrived my father was with my brother and sister at Grandpa Spence's, little wide-eyed kids, afraid, holding on to him. People weren't talking. My grandmother embraced me with her frail, bony body, without saying anything. My father grabbed hold of me and wept. The sheriff had already been there and gone. The ambulance had taken her body away.

"Why?" I finally asked. "Why?" No note. No warning. Why? The damnable, unanswered question. Why?

"Why?" I asked Uncle Hunter.

"Don't know," he said. "Barbara Jean was sleeping with your mother. Tommy was sleeping in the other bed. Barbara woke up in the middle of the night. Mother was gone. Her clothes were gone, too. The kids were talking, wondering where their mother was, and that woke up the old folks. They went to the bedroom to find out what was going on. Your mother was missing, all right.

"You know, Gerry, on Monday your folks were going to start moving into that store your dad bought. Your dad was over at the store that night doing inventory with the sellers. He'd just taken possession, so he had to stay over because there was no one to watch the place. That's when she did it, while he was gone."

"Why?" I asked again.

"Nobody knows," Uncle Hunter said, a sound of resignation in his voice as if a son should ask no further questions, that things were as they were, that as in life, death was a private matter and that it should be respected.

"Who found her?" I asked.

"I found her," Uncle Hunter said. He and Aunt Estes lived down the road a quarter of a mile. "Grandma called. She told me your mother was missing and Grandma was worried and wanted me to come up and look for her. We called your dad and some of the neighbors, and we all went out looking for her. When your dad got there he found his hunting rifle was missing. By then we were pretty sure what had happened. I found her in the ditch behind the house."

He stopped and took a long serious look at me to see if I wanted the details. I looked back at him. "She put your father's old .30-40 Krag in her mouth, and pulled the trigger. Efficient job of it," he said.

Meat-gettin' old gun. Heard my father say it a hundred times.

Uncle Hunter showed me the place, the ditch under a good apple tree, the ditch grown over with grass. Stood with me, his thumbs hung into his belt, both of us staring at the place the same place where once as a child I had walked beside Grandpa Spence, his old mules out ahead, hunched down, pulling hard on the ditcher, clearing the ditch for water and for life.

Uncle Hunter went on with the story: "Your dad was looking for her up under the hogback where your mother used to walk. You remember the time you and your mother were up there on top and it got dark, and you couldn't get down?" I remembered. We had climbed the hogback for fun, and like children we had lost track of the time, and when it got dark my mother got frightened and began to holler. Uncle Hunter heard us and found us, and from below he showed us the way down. "When I found your mother in the ditch, here, I gave the signal," he said. "Three quick shots with my rifle."

Many years later I talked to my father about that day in October 1949. He said two of his old friends had been called to help hunt for my mother. When my father heard the three shots he said he knew. He was on his way down from the hogback when he met his friends.

"I asked them two questions: 'Is she dead?' 'Yes,' they said. 'Did she suffer?' 'No,' they said."

Then my father, said, "I fell to pieces." He never took his old sad blue eyes from me as he spoke. "Oh, God, I thought, how can I tell Barbara and Tom? I finally got control of myself and a little later I sat down with the kids in the front yard. I told them, 'Mother is gone. She won't be with us anymore.' I let that soak in and then I said, 'She is dead.' We clung to each other. Then Tom burst out with it: 'Oh, Daddy, we are all alone.' "

When Tom was a man past fifty, he still remembered. He told me the remnants of my family had been sitting under a cedar tree in the front yard, a tree Dad had planted as a boy. He had been trying to explain to Barbara and Tom what had happened, and why. He couldn't explain, of course. And he couldn't answer that damnable *Why?*

Then Tom said Dad took him and Barbara for a long walk. They walked from Grandpa's place down the canyon and through its red sandstone walls to the county road. From there they walked up the road a piece to Great Grandmother Smith's, where my father had often played as a child. Buckhorn Creek, where he had fished for trout and snagged trout. They had been happy times. Now he walked with his own children through the old apple orchard, the trees having survived Great Grandmother Smith who lived past ninety-four. Tom said, "Dad stopped at each of the apple trees and identified the different trees for us." Just talking. Just trying to say something when he didn't know what to say. Then Tom said, "Our mother's death was like a nail driven into one of those apple trees. We have grown around it until you can no longer see the nail."

"We're going to have to get through this together," my father had said to his two small children. "There's just the three of us now, like these three fingers on a hand." He held them up to show them, Tom said, the three fingers pushed tightly together.

But I was the fourth finger, and I was on my father's hand as well.

After Uncle Hunter showed me the place I walked alone to the chokecherries below my grandfather's house. Overhead their boughs formed a small cathedral. The blackbirds had gathered to feast on the ripened cherries, and they fluttered in the branches and made their happy noises, mocking noises to me. How could they sing those blackbird songs, those songs of joy in this place of mourning? Perhaps they knew. Blackbirds know many things. But why should they care? I have never mourned the passing of a blackbird. I sat down on the ground, and laid my head between my knees, and I tried to weep.

"How could you do this, Mother?"

In answer, a black cloud enveloped me, and I lost my breath in it. I opened my eyes and looked up to the sky to escape it, and the sun shone down through the chokecherry branches, as if the sun also knew. I looked at the ground, the ants scurrying through their jungle trails carrying loads of grass seed for the winter, and when the ants came to my foot, they detoured around it and went on. My father was attending the children. And I? I, a man, would soon be attending my own child.

"How could you do this, Mother?" I asked out loud, and the black cloud returned. And the blackbirds went on singing.

Your mother did not do this to you, I heard a voice say. It was you who did this to your mother. Then the voice began reading the charges.

Was it not you who had abandoned her teaching, who turned your back on her church, who scorned her wishes—who scorned the mother?

Was it not you whom she had witnessed, the accursed cigarette hanging from your lips?

I reached into my pocket and lit up a Chesterfield and blew the smoke back into the black cloud. I tried to weep silently. I needed to weep. But it is very hard to weep aloud out of doors before singing blackbirds.

I read the rest of the charges: Was it not you who lay with the whores, who drank with the drunks, who desecrated your mother's life, and mocked at her covenant with God? Was it not you who voided her promise to God, for you had rendered her helpless to fulfill her promise? Was it not you, rather than she, who had been in control of your mother's life all along?

I thought of dear Little Peggy in her casket. Once more I could hear my father's sad voice. "You know, Gerry, she made a bargain with God. If God would only save you she would give you into His service." And you, you miserable mocker of mothers, you arrogant lecher, you despicable gambler, you irreverent son, you egregious sinner of sinners, it was you who demanded your mother's love and who gave none in return. It was you, Gerry Spence, who killed her.

"Oh, God, forgive me," I cried. I did not know what else to say.

But God did not answer. All I heard as the voice of God was the singing of the blackbirds in the chokecherry trees.

And my father—how could he forgive me? I had killed his love, his woman, his wife, the mother of his children. Had he not warned me?

My sister? My little innocent brother? How could they forgive me? I had murdered their mother as well.

I was the murderer. I had pulled the trigger. Her blood had not been soaked up in the ditch. Her blood was on me. And the black cloud that was smothering me—it was smothering me in the blood of my mother.

At the mortuary, my father in his old suit, Barbara and Tom all dressed in their Sunday best, and I in my wedding suit entered that small room with the pink-flowered wallpaper and the sweet heavy smell of roses. We came to say good-bye to her. The casket lay open. We had to crowd up close to see in. I stood at my father's left, the children hanging on to him at his right. She lay as silent as any corpse. Corpses sleep like that, their hands crossed, their faces white, almost translucent. The red birthmark on her cheek, the place where the angel had kissed her, had vanished.

I wanted to speak to her.

I was afraid to stare at her. She said nothing.

I wanted to run away, but I was a man and could not run. I was the eldest, her eldest. I was there to comfort my father, to help him with the children. I was there to face the evil I had committed, to behold it, face to face.

Behold your dead mother, you son.

Behold the work of your hand, you son of the mother.

Then my father began to weep. "Oh, Esther, I'm sorry. Oh, I am so sorry," he sobbed. "Why did you do it? Oh, honey, if I had only known! Oh, God, oh, God, oh, God!" he cried out in abject despair. The children grabbed hold of him and wept for his weeping. He was kissing her face, her cheeks, the place where the angels had kissed her lips, the lips that were sewn together and could not kiss back.

The children stared at their father, at the living and the dead, their eyes like frightened rabbits.

My father was the brave one. I could not touch the corpse. I was afraid to touch what surely I had wrought.

I do not remember the service. I could not say who else was there. I cannot remember their taking the casket to the cemetery or how they buried her next to Little Peggy. I cannot remember the hole in the ground. I cannot recall their lowering the casket. I cannot remember leaving.

CHAPTER 21

Gerry Spence, 1953.

ANNA DIDN'T ATTEND the funeral. I didn't ask her why. Instead, as a child, and in a childish way, I considered it as evidence against her. Those long-established feelings of abandonment took over, abandonment both by my own mother and now by my latest mother, that young wife, herself a child. I had never considered that Anna had only wanted to protect her unborn child from the noxious emotional vapors she thought would surely come spewing out of that wretched scene. Years later she told me her own mother had advised her against going. "The baby, Anna, you know."

After the funeral I returned to Laramie, to the little white house with the forest green living room, and to Anna. My mother's suicide was a monster pounding at the door. Locked behind the door, I barred it and shoved the furniture of my life up against it.

I tried to talk about her death to my friends. Talk it out, people had said. I remember talking about it to Bill Thatch, a tall, skinny kid from Lovell, Wyoming—looked like Abe Lincoln. He was a commoner like me and another whom I helped with his studies in law school.

"She'd couldn't face the hard facts of life," I said of my mother. "Been up there in Bolivia. Been at that high altitude, you know. Going through the change, you understand—you know, the menopause. Saw all those people killed up there in that miners' revolution. Friends of hers and all. Couldn't bear it, I guess." But I knew who had killed my mother. Already at twenty, I was a murderer.

And I could think of no defense. And who would defend me against God? I had committed the unforgivable sin of matricide, a crime so horrible that in comparison, all the other crimes of the world were not worth the mention. Like a death row prisoner, I stood alone, bearing my conviction, staggering under the guilt of it, terrified of the punishment, and convinced that to plead for absolution was futile. I needed power. Perhaps my mother's death reinforced my determination to become a lawyer, for lawyers have power.

We had been buried together, my mother and I. Only the murderer survived. The guilty one survived, of course—hard customer, guilt. I had but one escape—the fearsome demands of law school. I plunged into my studies. I lived on a diet of the law's old biscuits spread over with the stale gravy served up by the professors. I grasped at the cases. I bored in on the professors. Buried in the books, I was unresponsive to the students around me. Dead to the living world, I was alive only to the dead law.

I sat at the small table in front of the living room window, my books and papers in disarray as if a maddened hand had besieged them—the incessant wind pounding at the glass, my eyes blind to all around me, deadly fixed on the law. Anna dared not speak to me for fear I would accuse her of severing my concentration. Often I spoke to her only to scold her. "What if, at the precise moment I was about to learn a major legal proposition, you interrupt me? What if I lose the thought and in the exam, I lose the point? What if that point is the one point I need to pass?" Then she would disappear into the bedroom and I would hear nothing of her for the rest of the night. And I, too, became lonely. But I persisted. Our lives, and the life of the child she carried, this child I could feel kicking against my back in bed at night, could depend on that *one* point, that one nasty little digit.

At last, on the day before finals were to begin, I shut the books. Try not to think about the rules and the exceptions to the rules. Try not to call up the names of old, soggy cases or the pedantic prattling of the professors. If you do, you will surely become nothing but a bowl of corn flakes.

I had to clear the mind. I set out on a long walk into the Laramie Mountains, on a trail leading up through the buckbrush lately turned purple in the early winter and through the high granite outcroppings that formed a city of foreboding stone ghosts. Once more I was touching the earth with my feet, breathing deeply of the thin, dry air, peering long into the crystal sky. A small cottontail rabbit hopped out from under a bush. He stopped and stared, his ears laid back. I could have talked to the rabbit. But instead I talked to the God I had disavowed. I prayed for strength, for knowledge, and for sanity. I prayed that I might shed the misery of my fear. And I also knew where God and I stood. And it was not good.

That night, too early, too exhausted, too exhilarated to sleep, I went to bed. When at last I slept, I slept like a child wracked with a high fever, the feverish dreams attacking and withdrawing, dreams without words, without objects, a wild swelling and then a fading away to nothing. In the morning I arose, exhausted. I didn't say good-bye to Anna.

The old library building, University of Wyoming. Law school upstairs, far right end of building.

The final exam in Judicial Remedies, like all exams, was administered in the law library by the professor. The library, one of those old high-ceilinged rooms with long tubes of newly installed fluorescent lighting, took up a wall of many-paned windows, and across from them an equally long wall of books. One took a seat at one of six library tables, four or five other students at a table. The honor system was in effect. If you cheated you were eliminated from the law school, for if you cheated as a student you would likely sooner cheat as a lawyer. I sat at the table next to the long rows of *Pacific Reporters*, books all looking the same except for the numbers on their binding. A kid in my class with a large head and a mop of mousy-looking hair cropped short at the ears, smart kid, all right, smarter than I, was waiting with the rest of us for the exam to begin. Suddenly he jumped up and began rummaging through the *Pacific Reporters*.

"What are you looking for, George?" I asked, hoping I could give him the answer before the exam began, or at least quiet him down.

"I don't know," he said. "I thought it was here somewhere."

"What, George?" I asked.

He looked at me with a blank stare. Then he turned back to the long rows of books with a jerky movement and continued wildly pulling them out, a volume at a time, opening them, pounding through the pages, and, not finding what he was searching for, slamming the book closed only to pull out another.

"George," I said. "Sit down. It's going to be all right." I took him by the arm and pulled his chair out for him. "Here, sit down." He was breathing heavily.

Then Professor Trelease strolled in, and with masterful nonchalance, began handing out our exams. He was youngish looking, probably older than he looked, and tall. He walked with slumped shoulders and wore the usual thick professorial glasses. His mouth was tight and his lips thin and white. His coat hung over his own shoulders two inches on each side. He had no chest. He would get us all, I thought. A person could read his intent in his every move. He shoved the exams to us like a matador thrusting his sword into the hapless bull. When he handed me my exam, I tried to smile at him. He wouldn't look me in the eye.

We placed our secret numbers at the top of our examination papers where we would have put our names, but most of us didn't believe the professors graded our papers blind. George didn't look at the professor or at the exam. He was staring off into space like a condemned man waiting for the guards to come.

We wrote our answers to the exams in essay form, applying the law we'd learned to the facts contained in the question. There were ten questions supported by ten sets of facts demanding ten essays, each designed to demonstrate whether the student not only had learned the law, but also had learned to think like a lawyer. We could write as much as we wished. But our papers would be collected, finished or not, at noon—it was eight in the morning. I felt like throwing up. I read the first question.

By God! I understood enough of the question that a thought came rising up through the terror. I could see that a certain rule might apply from the holding in an obscure case I had briefed and remembered. Justice was not the issue. Never. The issue was, what result did the facts and the law dictate? I began to write. I wrote as if in a trance, trusting the almost unconscious mind to sort it all out, and when the professor called time, I had somehow finished. After that I awoke and found myself walking down the street toward home.

That quarter I faced other exams like the first, exams in Contracts and Torts and Property. I had tried to think like a lawyer, but I could never be sure how a lawyer thought. I could only trust how I thought. I became absorbed in the examinations, lost in a world the facts created and in the result that the law seemed to dictate. I never struggled for logic, for the answers that logic produced often seemed brittle and superficial. I never sought to follow the loud, lawyerlike reasoning that the up-front brain spilled out, for on paper it made little sense. At last I had no choice but to listen to the easy voice of the mind, to give in to it, and to write the exam as it dictated.

Then the dreaded day came. I heard whispering up and down the hall. The faces of the students grew long and gray. Their eyes wild, darting, like sparrows looking for the hawk. The grades had been posted. We were to be judged. The students didn't seem to breathe. Half of us would be cut—thrown back into the miserable world of reality from whence most of us had come. A kid who had dreamed of being a lawyer would become, instead, a plumber's helper, or go back home to his father's grocery store and be consigned to some form of onerous oblivion. I remember the ghastly bulletin board where the grades were posted opposite our secret numbers. I looked around me. Some students approached the board like prisoners snatching their mandate of death from the warden's hand. Others walked up to the board with great nonchalance, glancing at the numbers as one skims yesterday's headlines, and after that some just disappeared.

I was afraid to go look.

"What did you get, Spence?" George asked, his voice all quaking and distant.

"I don't know. I didn't look."

"Me, neither," George replied. Then without saying anything more, we walked over to the bulletin board together, a white piece of paper bearing our fate. So this was it. I looked at my number. Three A's and a B. Wrong number. Surely wrong number. I looked again. In my terror I must have forgotten my number. I was confounded. I turned to George.

"What did you get?" I asked. George didn't answer. He walked away, and that was the last I ever saw of him. True to the dean's prediction, half of the freshman class simply, quietly dissolved into the void from which they had emerged only a few months before.

The next quarter I tutored my friend, Bill Thatch, in our second quarter of Judicial Remedies. He'd had trouble, and when the grades were posted at the end of the quarter Bill got an A and I got a B. By Jesus H. Christ, that wasn't right. Something stank in Denmark, I said. The law school was not going to do that to me.

"How can this be?" I demanded of the professor. "Bill Thatch would have flunked this course if I hadn't tutored him. Now he gets an A and I get a B. What's going on here?"

"You are a better teacher than a student," the professor said, an amused smirk on his face.

"I'd like to look at my paper."

"That's against the law school policy."

"Why should it be? I wrote it. It belongs to me."

"It belongs to the law school," the professor said.

"Show me where it says any of this in the law school policies," I said, verbally pushing the man to the wall. He glared at me, silent as he made up his mind how he was going to handle this pushy kid.

"I don't have to show you a damn thing."

"Why should you be afraid to show me?" There's a place where you go over the edge. I pounded the table. "I'll bet there isn't a policy to that effect," I shouted. I'd gone over.

"You calling me a liar?"

"Show me the policy."

"Get out!" he shouted.

I left, of course. But it wasn't over for me. I went to the dean—my first appeal. "I want to know, Dean, is there a written set of law school policies that govern what goes on up here?"

"We don't need things in writing here. We are all gentlemen," he said. "We trust each other. Be a good thing if you learned to be a little more trusting, too." He gave me that look that told me the conversation was ended.

I thought about taking the matter to the university board of directors, but fortunately the pressure of my classes intervened. Most of my fellow students who heard about it thought I was an ingrate or a smart-ass. Looking the gift horse in the mouth. Several came up to me: "Hell, Spence, I'd be happy with a C in that course." But I wouldn't choose a lawyer to fight for me who wouldn't first fight for himself.

Nearly broke, I took on the delivery of the *Sunday Denver Post,* a miserable job, requiring me to stagger out of bed at four on Sunday morning, try to start my car, which was always problematical, and drive down slippery streets to the Greyhound bus depot. There I picked up the bundles of papers, large as large suitcases, and hauled them home again. On the living room floor, Anna and I untied the bundles, rolled the papers into tubes, slipped a rubber band over each tube and loaded the papers back into the car. Then I drove from customer to customer through the neat rows of small houses along old streets, blizzard or no, delivering the citizens of Laramie, Wyoming, news from the mighty city of Denver. Starting and stopping the car, and walking up to the front door of each subscriber took a lot of time and more energy. I decided to take on a partner, my friend Bill Thatch.

I wired a big box to the front bumper of the '37 Ford coupe Anna and I had bought for a hundred dollars when the old Chevy finally expired. Then I dumped a load of the papers into the box on the bumper and Bill drove down the streets slowly, getting as close to the customer's house as he could while I sat on the fender heaving the papers toward the customer's front door. Sometimes I got close. Suddenly there was a huge crash—wild pitch—*Sunday Denver Post* through a front picture window.

I satisfied the folks, nice people, who forgave "a poor kid just trying to work his way through college." I put in a new window for them. But I had to give up throwing the papers from the car. Once a month I went back over the route collecting from my customers. I earned about thirty dollars a month. Good business. I wasn't studying at four in the morning on a Sunday anyway.

In December of 1949, three months after my mother's death, Kip Tyler Spence, weighing ten pounds, was born. I was twenty. We had scoured all the books of names. I thought the name "Gerald" should end with me. Never liked it. I wasn't a makeover of my father. I was an original person. Why hadn't my parents given me an original name, like Sebastian or Lorenzo, or if they couldn't be original, why hadn't they named me after my grandfather, John Henry Spence? That had a ring to it. But *Gerald?* We gave our son an original name, all right. Named him Kip. If he didn't like the name he could call himself K. Tyler Spence. Sounded pretty good, we thought.

The baby's grandmother Maybelle was at the hospital when he was born. We looked at him together through the nursery window, his head wrinkled and red and pushed out of shape, his eyes shut, squinting against the light.

"My God!" Maybelle exclaimed. "He's a moose!"

A few days later I stood at the nursery door waiting for the nurse to deliver my new son to me. When she came with the bundle I held out my arms to receive it, and when she let loose of the bundle I was holding my son in my arms. He was mine, and, once mine, he would always be mine. His head was covered against the cold, but I could feel him inside, wiggling and strong. I carried the baby down to the '37 Ford, Anna at my side, and then I handed the child to Anna, and proudly drove my wife and new son home, Anna all smiles, her dimples as deep as I'd ever seen them. And cooing to this baby.

Not a sound from the child lying over there on the couch all wrapped up in flannel. Didn't understand what all that fuss of parenthood was about. Not much to it. Anna was in the kitchen mixing up some formula on the stove.

"Aren't you going to nurse old Kippy here?" I asked.

"No," Anna said. "I wish I could."

"Why don'tcha then?"

"Doctor said I probably wouldn't have enough."

"How come? Mother Nature sure as hell gave you ample containers. Why wouldn't she see that they were filled?"

"The doctor says the formula they make nowadays is better than mother's milk."

"Oh," I said. I didn't know enough to ask obvious questions such as, Why would the baby be better nourished by artificial milk manufactured and sold by one of America's major corporations than by the mother herself? Was it the child or the corporation being served by such wisdom? And how did the doctor know? All he knew was what the manufacturer's rep told him. And all the rep knew was what the marketing people told him. So my son's diet was being selected by marketing people whose principal interest was sales and profit, not the growth and health of my son. Had I not been so intimidated by the prevailing view that a doctor's knowledge was unassailable, I could have told the doctor myself that mother's milk was the food of choice. If Mother Nature had intended a child to suckle the corporate tit, our son would have been born with his umbilical cord attached to a corporate test tube.

I had been taught to believe that a child knows what it needs. But the doctor said no. Would you put the wisdom of a day-old baby up against the medical profession? The child should eat when he was told to eat because the medical profession had worked out the proper feeding regimen. He should be relegated to a strict schedule of bottle feedings. He should sleep when he was put down to sleep. As it often is, the medical profession was at odds with Mother Nature.

Predictably, Kippy rebelled. Once he began to cry, he cried without ceasing. He refused to sleep, nor could we. I couldn't concentrate on my studies. I awoke, exhausted. Anna needed help. I helped her wash the diapers. I waded through the drifts of snow in the backyard, hung the baby's laundry out to dry on the line where it immediately froze in Laramie's bitter mountain cold. At over seven thousand feet, the temperature was often below zero. A relentless wind blew without mercy. I can still see the frozen diapers, stiff as boards, paddling in the gale without oarsmen. At last, despite the cold, they froze dry. Then out again I ventured, braced and swaying against the wind. That which had been pinned up had now to be unpinned, despite the frozen fingers, the chill through the ribs. I hauled in massive armloads of the diapers and nighties and stockings and bibs, baby stuff that required folding, stacks of it. And the eternal source of it was a single bundle of wailing who could engage half an army to keep him dry and clean and quiet, this first son of ours, Kip Tyler Spence.

I cuddled the child, kept him warm and close to me. We fed him as and when we were told to feed him, fed him the nasty powdered stuff we dutifully bought while Anna's breasts bulged to overflowing and her milk soaked through her undergarments and dresses. We fed him by the book, the doctor's book. In desperation we called the doctor, but he assured us nothing was wrong with our son. "Some babies are like that," he said. The doctor didn't have to listen to him. We were at our wits' end, the child crying, Anna crying. Finally I was crying too.

One night I'd been walking the floor with Kippy, jiggling him until his poor little head would surely come loose at the socket. Then I rocked him, sang to him, talked to him, cooed to him, told him stories. Still he cried. I was exhausted. At last, all else having failed, I decided he was simply being obstinate. Nothing was wrong with this child. The doctor had said so. Suddenly I knew what to do. Spare the rod and spoil the child. I slipped his diaper down and gave this three-week-old baby the tiniest spat on the bottom. Maybe he would associate crying with that small spat and stop—conditioning, like Pavlov's dog. He cried all the harder. He cried until finally, hours later, he was cried out. Exhausted, he slept, but we were awakened by the damnable alarm clock, had to awaken him for his bottle—the book, you know.

At the end of my freshman year in the spring of 1950, I was at the top of my class. I had stumbled onto an easier way to score high grades than exercising the under-brain. I learned that a person didn't have to explain the law to the professors, not really. A fellow didn't even have to think like a lawyer. All he had to do was merely think like the professor—tell him what he wanted to hear, play back his top-ten legal tunes, laud his most precious jurisprudential scenarios. He was not interested in original thought, in a student's creativity, in legal insight or judicial wisdom. He appreciated those who appreciated him, who grasped his deepest meanings, revered his most profound pontifications and stored them for eternity in the infinite folds of our cerebral cortex. Those who could only quote the law got C's, but those who could quote the professor—ah, what exquisite intellects, what eloquent words on the page! Those were the few, the rare, the A students, and I was one of them.

* * *

The summer between my first and second years in law school, I was employed by the Wyoming Public Service Commission as its sole summertime inspector.

On "easy time payments" as they were called, Anna and I bought from the local Plymouth dealer, a light brown Plymouth coupe, '47 model, ugly car, that I drove that summer the width and breadth of the state snooping into the trucking companies' archives. Never had I experienced such power before. To have them call you *Mister* Spence, to send them scurrying into the vaults for their records, to demand answers and to have them stutter as you waited, perhaps absently tapping your foot. Before the time of my plastic badge I couldn't get the waitress to pour me a second cup of coffee. Now the company people wanted to take me to dinner. Not on your life! I was untouchable. Ah, it was heady business. I loved being a paper-work cop. The power! I even wore a tie.

So I was driving along in my '47 tan Plymouth coupe between Rawlins and Rock Springs on that lonely stretch of highway that traverses the entire width of southern part of the state, then U.S. Highway 30. More than a hundred miles of plains populated only by harvester ants, coyotes, antelope and prairie dogs and a few high country rattle snakes separated those nearly empty, lonely settlements along the Union Pacific Railroad. There, a tough, proud people held on year after year, generation after generation, fighting against being blown the hell out of the country in the summer, and hanging on against the same bitter winds in the winter that would freeze-dry a lizard. Ahead of me a rig half a block long, an eighteen wheeler and pup, was barreling down the highway at eighty miles an hour. The speed limit was sixty-five. The Public Service Regulations provided in black and white that all common carriers must also obey the traffic laws of the state, and since I was an inspector charged with enforcing those regulations, I reasoned that I had the authority to stop that speeding eighteen wheeler.

It took me several miles to get my Plymouth up along side of the tractor, and finally when I got even with the rig, I had trouble keeping up with it. All the time I was vigorously motioning the driver to pull over. I wore no uniform, of course. My Plymouth coupe displayed no official identification. Besides, a cop would never drive a tan Plymouth coupe, much less a '47 model. The driver must have thought I was some nut and drove right on. But no jack-leg truck jockey was going to ignore *me,* the duly appointed, constituted and fully authorized inspector for the PSC who could, as quick as a fast-draw gunman, pull his plastic covered badge from his billfold and slap it in front of the face of any suspected offender of the law. And don't forget, I was now twenty-one years old and, legally, a man.

After five miles or so I was able to gradually nurse the old Plymouth a few feet ahead of the eighteen wheeler. Then I started forcing the rig over toward the edge of the highway. Wonder he didn't run me through like a Brahma bull over a yapping hound dog. Gradually, he slowed down, pulled over, and stopped.

"What the fuck do you want?" he yelled down from the cab window.

"How fast were you going?" I demanded adopting the standard line of a highway cop, hoping for an on-the-spot confession.

"What the fuck's it to you?" he hollered. I was standing there in my white shirt and my bright red necktie. He probably would have killed me but for the shirt and necktie. Highway robbers do not wear white shirts and neckties. Anybody knew that.

I pulled out my badge, climbed the several steps up to the tractor's running board, and stuck the hunk of plastic in his face. "I am the inspector for the Public Service Commission. You were doing eighty."

"So fuckin' what? There ain't another vehicle on this fuckin' road for a hundred fuckin' miles in either direction. Who the fuck cares?"

"I care. The law is the law."

"Well, what the fuck you gonna do about it?" Suddenly I wondered what the fuck I *was* going to do about it. I had no authority to give anybody a ticket, and I had no ticket to give.

"You want a ticket?" I asked.

He didn't answer. Just glared down at me.

"Okay," I said. "Slow down, buddy, or you're likely to get one." I stepped off the truck and strutted back to my car, and after that I followed him all the way into Rock Springs. He kept his eighteen-wheeler at exactly sixty-five miles an hour. Oh, the marvelous power of power. And those with power use it, usually all of it. And those with the least of it usually use the little they have to the absolute utmost.

Anna and I worked hard at rearing our family, always struggling for money, always fighting to make it through one more year of school. But we fought. We fought whatever was in our way, but we mostly fought each other. Fighting had become an obsessive, everyday experience. At last it grew into an expectation. After that an excuse. Why would one avoid a fight when it helped relieve the building pressure? I could holler at Anna when I couldn't holler at a professor. She could holler at me when she couldn't whip a child. Free to fight each other, we could scream out at our respective ghosts and strike out at our respective goblins. Yet not having witnessed marital war in my own family, I suspected at times that something was wrong with me, and that something was surely wrong with Anna. Married people, especially people in love, shouldn't fight. I had little insight into the cause of our battles. Wisdom is a rare luxury and, for most of us, a late arrival to the party of life.

As the fresh wounds of my mother's death began to heal, I found myself an angry, rebellious, juvenile man, caught in an eternal struggle against authority—authority anywhere. I had no respect for the adults around me. None for my father, for my professors, for the elders of the community. I was not to be intimidated by authority. I was sometimes out of control, and usually uncontrollable.

I found it hard to trust. Trust them and they lie down in a ditch someplace and put a gun in their mouth.

At twenty I understood little about such dynamics. I exploded easily, often, but I was as unaware of the source of this angry force as Old Faithful understood the geological causes of its regular eruptions. The geyser just blew. I blamed it on the inherent nature of my personality, my genetic composition. Anna, for her part, had not yet suffered the inhibiting opiate of adulthood, and was as likely to contest me with her own wild and unscheduled eruptions. Both of us were yet to learn that anger covers hurt, that it is always easier to be angry than to feel pain, easier to explode than to weep, to attack than to ask for love.

All men need mothers, even old men clawing from the edge of the grave. The healthy adult becomes his own mother, and when mother's love is demanded, loves and comforts himself. I made Anna my mother and in the process I remained this unabashed adolescent this wild, impetuous, untameable male child, this married man who was no more able to conform to the demands of husband-hood than a wild colt could plod along hitched to the milk wagon.

We fought about anything brought before the house. Each issue, issue or not, became an issue of life and death. I hated most convention, while Anna usually respected it. I fought against manners, while Anna found them important. I despised polite talk, while Anna expected that I at least not insult the innocent who happened by. Like a child who wanted to show off, I delighted in shocking friends and strangers alike. I fought against all remnants of parental authority while Anna, from the beginning, and fulfilling our mutual needs, took on her assigned role of the mother. She insisted on proper ways, demanded common manners. She knew all about how to set a table, what fork to use, and when and where the napkins and the glasses should be placed, and she possessed the important social graces. On the other hand, I, the volatile teenager, didn't give a damn. I wouldn't be told, corrected or directed. Try to change me and you were in for a fight. And we fought. Yet, in some ways, the fighting made us stronger.

Even now I struggle to put that marriage in perspective. There was always the touch of the mystical about Anna. Sometimes she seemed connected to a universe I could not penetrate, and when we fought, she retreated there and took on a dimension where logic could not enter and reason was not permissible. She became a native of that foreign realm, and she knew it empowered her. Still, Anna devoted her life to me and to Kip, and later to our other children. She became the mother who she was by nature, and who I unwittingly insisted she be to me. But she also stood as the mother against whom I revolted. She, too, was caught in a dilemma that defied solution. The more I sought her mothering the more I fought against her authority. I demanded a wife, a lover. I wanted a mate, a companion. She tried to be all things to me, this woman, herself then but a child, this mother of child and husband alike.

I lived in an ever-replenishing anger. I was angry at God, at my own dear dead mother. But I missed her beyond the telling. I grieved for her. I tried to strike her from my memory and my life, but she spoke to me every day, not with an hallucinatory voice, but with her silent presence, her ever-watchful, judging eye. I was angry at the unjust charges that had been leveled against me—by me—angry at both the murderer and the murdered.

I longed to be the kind of man who would have pleased both her and my living father. But I came to realize that they were as conflicted as I, that their views of the world were as different from each other's as mine from theirs. I could not please anyone. Nor could I please myself. Unable to understand the clashing dynamics that were to mold me, I blamed Anna. I blamed the mystical "them" out there. Blinded by an inner conflagration, often I could only emote, only scream out in rage like a pitiful pig caught in the said gate. I attacked with words, and as soon felt the resulting pain of guilt. Remorse was as much a part of my life as anger. I was sorry, always sorry, but I seemed unable to elude the next explosion. Horrified by the tears I caused, I lived in a perpetual cycle of mounting anger, explosion, remorse and self-hate. I seemed helpless to stop the cycle. At last, I hung on to one goal that kept me lashed to reality: to get out of law school and become a lawyer.

These injured children, Anna and me, gripped together by the vise of wed-lock, had become divinely suited for the endless wars that followed. Anna, the adopted daughter, the child who feared her mother might at any moment give her away, hauled those fears into the marriage by the truckload. Repelled by me, she hung on to me. Rejected by me, she fought all the harder to possess me. The more she demanded, the more she clung, the more she sought control, the more I revolted, fought her off, struggled, as if drowning, to be free of her. Yet my need for her was as desperate as hers for me, as desperate as my need for my mother, and in this mud pit of rage and confusion we wrestled as if the win-ner should take all.

Sometimes the face of my dead mother came to me in my dreams. She would be lying in the coffin. In my dreams she would not accept the fact that she was dead, crying in the coffin, pleading against the shutting of the coffin lid. She could not be reasoned with.

"Mother, you are dead. Don't you understand? You have to be buried."

"Nooo, noooo," she would cry. "Pleeease! Pleease!" she would beg.

Sometimes she appeared in my dreams quite alive, having previously left us for mysterious reasons that somehow seemed connected with a secret she could not bear to share with us.

"Why did you leave us, Mother?" I would ask.

She was sweet, yet distant and cold, and to my question she remained silent. That she would not answer made no difference. I was filled with elation. My mother had come back. The abandonment was over. But she would not listen when I told her that I loved her. She could not hear me tell of my aching at the marrow. Always she remained impassive, as steely and unresponsive in my dreams as she had been that last time I saw her in our little house with the forest green living room. Counseling in those days was mostly unheard of in Wyoming, and in any case was shamefully reserved for the mentally infirm. Men were tough, and women bore their miseries silently, as my mother had borne hers. Anna and I tried to transcend the demons that plagued us—some recognized, most not.

I came to loathe law school even more. In class the people in the cases never seemed real—faceless names, people with labels like "plaintiff," "defendant," "appellant," "appellee." The facts were usually some judge's summary of the evidence provided him by his clerk, a kid fresh out of law school who had earned top grades, but who had likely never in his life come face to face with a poor person trapped in the law, and whose principal life's experience qualifying him for personhood was that he had survived three years of law school at his parents' expense.

Our casebooks were jammed with reported cases, some old, some recent, but none described the anguish or fear or the anger of human beings seeking justice. None addressed the notion of justice or how, through the functioning of the legal system, justice had triumphed. Instead, the cases became the intellectual playpens of the judges, where they toyed with archaic language and juggled stodgy reasoning to achieve vague, sometimes fanciful conclusions that usually left the door open for more of the same. To this moment I have never read a case in which, say, a parent's agony over the death of a child killed by a drunk was communicated to us through the words of a judge. Never yet have I come across a reported case in which the judge takes us to the bed of the dying worker and attempts to describe for us the injuries he suffered as a result of the company's short-shrifted safety. We never learned from the cases what it must feel like to be an innocent accused, or even a guilty man whose rights to a fair trial were stolen by the prosecutor. In the cases I read in law school and since, passion was treated like some crazy step-sister locked in the closet, As if passion were shameful and feelings a crime, the judges wrote their antiseptic opinions. The law had no relationship to living, suffering persons. Law was business. And business was served by the law. Law was a science, and I hated science, and I hated the law. I wanted out of that prison guarded by those morticians of the law, the professors. And the only way I knew how to escape was to graduate.

I had a couple of good friends among my classmates, but I was not a popular person. No one looked to me for leadership. I was the youngest in the class. The others, being older, more worldly, less passionate, were also, I thought, more intelligent. I wasn't good at a party. To this day I have never learned how to sit down and fill the air with empty palaver. When I tried to be funny, I wasn't. When I tried to be socially darling, I failed. The few who could bear me did so, I think, mostly because they knew I cared about them.

Despite my disdain for the formal study of law, I ended up feeling close to most of my professors. These men who had done little lawyering themselves tried hard to make lawyers of us. I admired the easy, gentlemanly style of my property teacher, Gene Kuntz—a tall, handsome, dark, articulate man who was both benevolent and funny. He had compassionate black eyes and became a role model for the quintessential gentleman a lawyer should be. Despite his enslavement to the casebook method of teaching and to the highly conservative bent of law school, Frank Trelease, our torts professor, was one who cared more about the plight of the poor and the injured than about the logic and reasoning of the judges whose decisions usually deprived them of justice. His unconventional view of the law held that the law was purposeless unless it provided justice for the people. Our criminal law professor, John Rames, had probably never tried a criminal case in his life, and had probably never even met a criminal. Yet he was as sweet and naive as a first-year monk, and although we learned little about the meanness of criminal law, it hardly mattered. We all adored him, and he taught us how to be gentlemen by his example.

In law school we never met a criminal, never drew the simplest complaint, never drafted the most rudimentary contract—never saw one—never authored the most perfunctory sort of will—never saw one of those either—and we knew nothing about domestic relations, including our own. We never met a client. Yet we were soon to be lawyers who would represent living clients.

I did experience one actual trial in law school. One day, late for class, I was driving along a little faster than prudent and collided at an intersection with another law student, one of the two women in the law school. She was also late. I had no insurance to pay her bill, but she had a policy, and her company sued me—in her name, of course, as insurance companies always do—to recover the cost they had paid in repairing her car, some ninety-seven dollars. The suit was filed in the Albany County Justice of the Peace Court before Justice of the Peace Vernon Bentley. The local prosecutor, Gordon Davis, a former FBI agent looking for an extra dollar, took on the case for the insurance company. In those days public prosecutors were allowed to conduct a private practice to supplement the income the county paid them. Without money to pay the damages the insurance company sought against me, and unable to hire a lawyer to defend me, I decided to defend myself. Somewhere I had heard that the best defense was a good offense. I countersued. Frantically I sought advice from my professors, but none that I could discover had ever been in court themselves, not even in a justice of the peace court.

My defense was that the other driver was going too fast, that I had entered the intersection first, and therefore I had the right of way. I revisited the accident scene and measured the distance that the mud from under her fender had flown after the impact. Then I tromped over to the physics department and found a graduate student who was willing to apply the simple laws of inertia to determine her speed. I carefully prepared my case, and at the trial I cross-examined the plaintiff, who claimed she had entered the intersection first.

"How fast were you going, madam?" I asked my fellow student.

"Fifteen miles an hour."

"Preposterous," I shouted. "You had to be going forty. Maybe fifty."

"Objection!" her lawyer, Gordon Davis, screamed. "He can't make comments like that."

"I *can* make comments like that. I was there!"

"He cannot!" Davis hollered back. "He isn't acting as a witness. He's acting as a lawyer. He is cross-examining my client."

"I know what he's doing, Mr. Davis," Judge Bentley said. "Sustained."

"I have a right to ask her questions," I protested.

"He can ask questions if he wants, but he cannot make comments like 'Preposterous,' " Davis said.

"I'll rule as to what he can or cannot do," the judge said, "and I will decide what is or is not preposterous, Mr. Spence."

"How can you do that? You haven't even heard the evidence," I shot back at the judge. "I want to testify."

"If you do I'll cross-examine you," Davis warned.

"How can you cross-examine me?" I retorted. "I'm the lawyer. I want to cross-examine *you*."

"You can't examine me. I'm the lawyer," the lawyer said.

"That's what I said," I said.

"He's not a lawyer. He's just a law student," the woman law student piped up. "If you want to know the truth, he never will be a lawyer. He is a liar of the first water. I may have been going twenty, but not a second faster. Besides, my car won't go forty."

"Who asked you?" I shouted. "You tell her to quit that," I ordered the judge.

"Quit what?" the judge asked.

"Quit saying how fast her car will or will not go. I never asked her that."

"Well, I told him," she said.

"You know better than that," I said to the woman. "We took civil procedure together in the same class. Besides, my expert will testify differently, Your Honor. Her speed is a matter of absolute science. You cannot change the law of physics."

"How fast were you going, Mr. Spence?" Judge Bentley asked.

"I thought I was asking the questions of this witness," I said. "Are you going to represent the plaintiff, too?"

"The court can ask questions," the judge said.

"Well, of course," I replied. "But it is not considered good judicial etiquette. I can cite you the case."

"This is the justice of the peace court," the judge said. "How fast were you going?"

"Well, doesn't the justice of the peace court practice good etiquette?" I demanded. "In the meantime, reminding the plaintiff that she is under oath, I want to know if the plaintiff wants to change her testimony again. She has already told us she was going fifteen and now she tells us twenty. Do you want to change your testimony again?"

"I could have been going twenty-five," she said.

"Well, the speed limit's twenty!" I hollered, slamming my first down on the lectern.

"Order!" the judge shouted.

"Who said the speed limit is twenty?" Davis shouted. "That's his unsupported testimony again. I'm getting tired of this!"

"It says right there on the sign," I said.

"There you are testifying again. What sign?"

"Don't try to cross-examine me," I said. "I am here as a lawyer. The truth will out!"

"The truth can be heard without the shouting," the judge said.

Then lawyer Davis offered the repair bill into evidence, and I contested that as well.

"I want the repairman to come to court. I want to cross-examine him. I want the insurance company to prove that it paid the bill. I want the insurance executive from Denver who wrote the check in payment of the bill to come to Laramie to testify."

Then I put my physics student on the stand and qualified him as an expert concerning the law of inertia.

"Did you measure the distance the mud flew from the point of impact?" I asked.

"I did," he said.

"Applying the law of inertia, how fast was she going?"

"Forty-one and a half miles per hour, according to my calculations."

"Aha!" I exclaimed.

"I rest my case," I said.

"Let's get out of here," Davis said to the insurance adjuster sitting next to him. He got up and started to leave the courtroom. "I have better things to do than spend the rest of my life with this crazy over ninety-seven bucks."

"Don't you want my decision?" Judge Bentley asked as they headed for the door.

"Okay," the lawyer said, stopping in his tracks in the doorway. "What is your decision?"

"I am more confused than amused," the judge said.

"Is that a legal decision?" the lawyer asked.

"Why not?" the judge said. "It's the truth. "I find that both parties were negligent and therefore neither can recover from the other."

"Really!" I exclaimed. "I haven't even testified."

"Case is closed," the judge said. "I have a golf game."

"I'm going to appeal," I said.

"I hope so," Judge Bentley said. "The district judge deserves you."

I didn't appeal, of course—didn't have the time or the filing fee of ten dollars. That was my first case, and, as the saying goes, I had a fool for a client.

So the district judge deserved me? Well, he got me. The district judge was Glen Parker, white-haired, stately, beautiful to behold, a man who could wrinkle his forehead, all right, and raise his right eyebrow almost to his hairline. He was an abundantly serious man who looked as every judge should. A thoroughly practical sort, he had no patience for nonsense of any kind. He taught trial procedure at the law school and conducted the moot court trials that were to follow. To my knowledge, before he took the bench, his reputation as a trial lawyer was nonexistent.

Each of the students was assigned a teammate, the student with the highest and lowest grades being joined as a team. If grades are any criterion for trial skills, which they are not and never have been, that should make it fair. We were provided a set of facts that were played by witnesses from the drama department of the university. We took this moot court business very seriously. An actual fistfight appeared imminent when a member of the opposing team refused to allow us to interview his witness. My teammate was the toughest man at the University of Wyoming, a stocky, barrel-chested sort, short neck, small head, big smile, good guy we all adored when he was sober, but drunk or sober, tough. Fought and won the heavyweight boxing championship. Everybody knew that, and the threatened fight turned out to be little more than my partner slamming our opponent up against the wall. We got the facts. But the trial was a disaster.

I attacked every witness in sight. I shouted and pounded the podium. I was uncontrollable, unruly, unmanageable, like a pet raccoon running wild in the parlor. I raised such a ruckus the judge threatened to throw us out of his courtroom. But he couldn't throw me in jail. I remembered that. This was only *moot* court. The opposition wasn't able to ask a question without my objection, my argument on the judge's ruling on the objection, my argument on the judge's threats of contempt, my arguments *ad infinitum,* as I had now learned to say at every opportunity. At the conclusion of the case the judge raised his eyebrow very high, peered down at me from the bench, his pure white collar outlining his pure black robe, and, like Moses about to judge an unrelenting sinner, rendered his critique.

"You will never become a trial lawyer, Mr. Spence. You may just as well face that fact now. I am doing you a favor by being brutally honest with you. I offer you not the slightest encouragement. You have absolutely no native ability whatever to size up a situation and to act upon it appropriately. You are severely lacking in judgment. If you must stay in the law, and I recommend that you don't, you should confine yourself to office work. The trial of cases requires not only skill and judgment but grace and subtlety. You have none of these attributes.

"In sum," Judge Parker said, "your performance here today was disgusting." He slammed down the gavel and stomped off the bench. I was devastated. How could one ever doubt the likes of Judge Parker, a man revered by all, and one who later became the Chief Justice of the Wyoming Supreme Court? I knew that underneath all the noise and the ego that had paraded up and down the courtroom the judge was right. I didn't have the stuff of a trial lawyer. But I couldn't quit the law now unless I wanted to go back to selling axes. The moot trial counted one third of our grade. The written exam must have saved me. I scored a *B*. I admit: I was out of balance.

But things in balance never go anywhere.

CHAPTER 22

Laramie, Wyoming.

IN THE SPRING of 1950, following my mother's death, Anna and I drove to
Sheridan, just the two of us. In my mind's eye the vision of my mother's face had
vanished, and I could not call it back. Perhaps in Little Goose Canyon, where
we had been happy, my father fishing, my mother laughing her tight little laugh,
talking easily with her friends, crocheting a doily, perhaps there I might see her
face once more. If I could find the exact limber pine where we sat, perhaps I
could look at its shaggy bark, see its twisted limbs, feel the same ground moist
in the springtime, and from renewed memories my mother's face would return.

Perhaps there I could once more hear the sound of her voice in my mind's
ear, for since her death, her voice had remained as silent as still air. Perhaps now
as I lay on the ground I could hear her scold, "Don't lie down on the ground like
that, Gerry. You'll catch cold."

Anna and I drove up to Little Goose Canyon in the light brown '46 Plymouth, past the ranches of the rich English heirs, past the ranch of the one who
had once blocked the road with his barbed-wire. We drove farther up toward
the head of the canyon where we had spent many a Sunday fishing, the small

rainbows and browns fresh and slick from my father's grass-lined creel. He'd send us off to gather wood, and he'd challenge me to build a fire with one match. "You might find yourself out in the woods sometime with only one match. Can't waste matches in the woods," he said. Besides, we had to learn to build a fire with one match and no paper for Boy Scouts.

When the fire was right and the grease in the pan smoking, he dipped the fish in cornmeal and flour and tossed them in the frying pan. The fish, so fresh, curled in protest, and the smoke got in our eyes, and we would cough and make a big fuss and scurry to another side of the campfire, and Mother would say, "Smoke follows beauty," and sure enough the smoke followed us wherever we went, which was the only confirmation I'd ever had that I was beautiful.

Shortly my father would pull the fish from the fire and toss them on our plates, and we would begin stripping the tender morsels from the bones with a fork, starting at the tail, easing the meat from the bones down one side and then the other until only the skeleton, the head attached, remained in our fingers. Then we tossed the skeleton aside for the magpies and Canada jays and began our feast. The meat was so hot it burned our lips, and so tender and sweet my father would exclaim, "Heaven hasn't got anything on us. I'll bet they don't feed a fella like this up there." He'd smack his lips and throw another six-inch trout on our tin plates. "Here. Eat that!" he'd order. We loved his kind of bossing at fish-eating time.

Anna and I parked the car and walked down toward the creek. We were silent as we walked, and then I stopped at a great spreading limber pine above the creek, and I touched the bark and sat down on the ground. I looked around but I could not see her. But suddenly I could hear her calling to me as a small boy.

"This is Sunday, Gerry. We mustn't forget the Lord's day. Sit over here by me." And I had protested. I was a wild fawn. Wild fawns do not read the Bible. "Let us read a psalm together and then you can play." I wanted to run with my pal, Ward White. I wanted to sail the boat I had whittled from a stick. "Psalm 118:24 is a poem. It was written to praise the Lord for such a day as this," my mother had said. And I sat down, and quickly read the psalm to her:

"This is the day the Lord hath made. Let us rejoice and be glad in it."

My mother listened reverently, as if she had never heard it before. Then, finished, I handed the Bible back to her, and my mother seemed very happy. Then I jumped up and ran to the creek to throw rocks and to float boat sticks. On the way back to the camp again, I shot all of the Indians who were hiding behind the granite boulders left ten thousand years ago by the receding glaciers.

For Anna and me the flowers that spring, as far as the eye could see, danced and waved gaily in the pretty breezes, laughing and cheering like a great stadium brimming with precocious children. Mountain bluebells, blue as old blue bottles, wildly pink geraniums, long-stemmed buttercups, dainty fuchsia shooting stars—outrageous pink, their tiny pointed noses trimmed in gold—all bloomed wildly, sang silently, shamelessly, all showing off across those ten thousand acres of mountain meadow. The blue harebells, the deeper yellow *Balsamhoriza*—black-eyed with daisy petals—the whole stadium, the whole wild mob, flung out their arms and danced up from their roots and out of their stems.

That morning, reverently, carefully I picked a large bouquet of flowers in memory of my mother. I held them close to my skinny chest, pressed them to me. Anna caught my contagious tears.

"What are you going to do with the flowers?" she asked.

The Whites had moved away. But Pop and Mom Rowe, the white-haired tubby old Boy Scout executive, still lived with his wife in Sheridan. Mom Rowe had been close to my mother. They had labored for church causes together in Ladies' Aid and fought the endless battle against "demon alcohol," as it was called then by members of the Women's Christian Temperance Union. "I'm going to take these flowers to Mom Rowe," I said, "in memory of my mother. She'll appreciate them, especially coming from Little Goose Canyon where we used to have our Sunday picnics together."

Shortly after the time that church was over, I knocked at the Rowes' front door. Anna sat in the car. I waited. At last Pop Rowe came to the door. He had always looked old, his red face and round nose, his white hair, his stomach, his thick, arthritic waddle. I expected his happy smile to greet me.

"Yes?" he asked as if he were speaking to a stranger. He hadn't seen me since I was a boy of twelve.

"You probably don't recognize me, Pop," I said. "It's been a lot of years. I'm Gerry Spence." I was clutching the bouquet of flowers.

"Yes, I know," he said. Of course, he hadn't forgotten me. As a child, I had tromped through snow over my knees lugging an elk he'd shot down the mountain, a quarter at a time. He was with my father and me the day I shot my first antelope near Pumpkin Buttes. And I shot a buck for Pop Rowe that day as well, shot both bucks with the very gun my mother had taken with her to the ditch. I'd gone to scout camp in the summer with this man. He and his wife had been to our home scores of times.

"You remember me, Pop?" I asked still in disbelief. "My folks . . ."

"I know about your folks. I know about your mother." He made no offer for me to come in. His face was without expression, like a poor portrait.

"I was up Little Goose Canyon this morning where we used to go on picnics, remember? And I brought these flowers down for Mom Rowe. Is she home?"

"Just a minute," he said. He shut the door, left me standing there, but shortly he came back. "She doesn't want your flowers."

I couldn't believe the words. "What do you mean?" I was finally able to ask. "I picked them for her."

"She said that if it hadn't been for you, your mother would be alive today." Then he shut the door.

I stood there for a moment too stunned to move. Finally I turned and walked away. I dropped the flowers on the sidewalk, not by design.

Back in the car Anna asked, "What's the matter, honey?"

I couldn't speak. I didn't speak. It was a long time before I was able to find any words to speak.

Law school had its moments, as there must be breathers in hell, else how could hell be hell without some relief from the pain against which to compare it? Traditionally the homecoming queen was delivered to the law students to escort to her appearances in Cheyenne and Casper. The same tradition held that the engineering students would try to kidnap her so they could have the honor of presenting her at the halftime ceremonies of the homecoming football game. A married couple was usually among those designated as chaperones, and Anna and I were chosen.

In Cheyenne, Miss Homecoming had just made her appearance before the Cheyenne Chamber of Commerce. She was all duded up in her cowboy hat and boots and her leather skirt with the fringe, her big homecoming queen smile glued to her face. And as she was leaving the Plains Hotel, closely guarded by us, out of nowhere the engineers appeared and attacked.

"We got her!" I heard somebody shout. I turned around to see a couple of big guys starting to drag off the queen. She wasn't struggling. Then all hell broke loose: It was Anna.

"You bastards, turn her loose," she hollered, swinging her purse, laden with only she knew what. I saw the surprised look on the faces of the would-be kidnappers. I saw her purse hit an engineer square on the side of the head. His knees buckled. "Let loose of her," Anna hollered again. Again her fearsome weapon swung out, and again she was square with her aim.

"Jesus Christ!" the engineer hollered, half to his knees. "Get this bitch off of me!" Anna was still swinging on him.

"Let loose of the queen," she hollered.

"I did let loose of her," the engineer hollered back, holding both hands up in front of him for Anna to see.

"Here's one for good measure," Anna yelled. Then, as if she had conquered the Romans single-handed, and I have made room for the possibility that she could have, she escorted the queen out the front door past the dumbfounded engineers, their mouths gaping at such unremitting fierceness. Just as Anna was about to load her into the car, she turned to the queen, who wasn't quite sure whether she was going to bolt or not, and said, pointing her finger at the girl, "and you behave yourself." Nobody fiddled with Anna Fidelia Spence.

◊   ◊   ◊

Despite such moments, nothing could silence the relentless, implacable demons that charged me with my mother's suicide. Moreover, an elder of the tribe, the venerable Mom Rowe, my mother's dear friend, had become a witness against me and had confirmed the charges. Perhaps my mother had written her from Bolivia, grieved in her letters about my drinking and smoking, about my rebellious attitude against all she had taught. Perhaps she had written of her pain at having broken her covenant with God.

No doubt remained. I was guilty as charged. God had taken the case against me and had laid out the irrefutable evidence perfectly. The charge against me was murder, and I could marshal no defense. Day by day her death rotted on me.

Inevitably I asked my father about it. I knew that he too had been wounded like a deer shot in the entrails. And I knew that somehow he had survived, only because now he had taken on the role of both mother and father to Barbara and Tom. You could see the pain leaking out from behind the eyes and hear it in the flatness of his voice. The easy smile was replaced by a forced, jerky grin, and he plastered us with attempts at humor.

After her death I hadn't gone to see him often enough. He must have felt as if I blamed him, and, I admit it. I tried not to, but now I had ambivalent feelings about him. Justice or not, the horrors of my mother's death required an explanation. The horror demanded blame. "Why, Dad?" I asked. Not once but many times I asked why, hoping that a fact, a clue not before revealed might surface. What secret was he holding back? Why hadn't he taken better care of my mother? I had entrusted her to him. Those kinds of thoughts were never said, but likely he felt them in the subtle intonations of my voice, the unskillful choice of language, or the silence when easy talking should suffice.

"Why, Dad?"

"Don't know. Can't figure it out, son. She never hinted to me she was going to do anything like that. She was going through the change. I took her to the doctor."

"What did the doctor tell her?" My father wanted to blame the doctor.

"Well, she told the doctor she was having a lot of trouble sleeping and she was having trouble concentrating. Told him she was afraid about taking on the store and all, that she didn't think she could handle facing all of those people."

"What did the doctor say?"

"He just said she'd get through it. 'Every woman your age goes through it,' he said. Said, 'You'll be all right as soon as you adjust to your hormonal deficiency.' He didn't give it much heed at all. Then he said, 'Your trouble, Mrs. Spence, is all in your head.' " With that my father seemed agitated, his voice got higher, his face tight. "The doctor said, 'Things have been happening too fast, and your financial situation has been too dubious. Now that Mr. Spence has a job, and you have a place to live and a little store to run, I'm sure you will be okay in no time.' That cost five dollars," my father said. "And when the doctor said, 'It's all in your head,' I saw your mother's body stiffen and it worried me. The son-of-a-buck!" he said, shaking his head. "He never gave her any heed."

Then in a little while he said, "You know her father, Grandpa Pfleeger, lost his mind at the last. Had a stroke. Fell off the roof. Had to put him in a home, and she was afraid she was going to lose it like him. If I had only known how much she was suffering I would have done something different."

"What?" I asked.

"Would have gotten her to a better doctor. Would have found a doctor who would do more than just shrug her off like nothing!" After a while he said, "Your mother wasn't one to talk about things that were bothering her. The real things. I just didn't know . . ." and then he would begin weeping quietly and that would stop the questioning.

"Grin and bear it" was a familiar cliché in our family, a remnant of the hard pioneer mentality that dominated the West. Another was "Which way the wind doth blow, that way is best." I had heard my mother say it many times. Yet I knew that she had worried about my father's return from Bolivia after she and the kids had been sent home ahead of him and he had stayed on to help the wounded and the dead.

Aunt Estes remembered too. "Oh, how your mother worried over your father, and how delighted she was when he called from Miami to say he was back in the States."

"Why did she do it?" I asked, hoping Aunt Estes could provide facts that might lead to my acquittal.

"Nobody knows. Nobody had any idea she was so sick. Nobody has been able to figure it out, except, of course, she must have been out of her mind to do such a thing."

And there was her uncle who had killed himself. Aunt Estes went on with her diagnosis. "She was probably suffering from a condition we now call 'depression.' " She spoke as if she were explaining it to a child. Perhaps she could only remember me as a little boy who came to visit Grandpa. "It's a chemical imbalance in the brain, you know. They can treat it with drugs nowadays."

"How did my grandparents take her death?" I asked.

"Well," Aunt Estes said, "as you know, we aren't the kind who talk much about things like that. Your Grandmother Spence always believed that suicide was the one unforgivable sin." That same sick logic about how you can't be forgiven if you aren't alive to ask for it. Logic, not love.

Aunt Estes went on to tell me that my dear old Grandfather Spence sat down on the red flagstone steps to the front door of his house, put his head in his hands and wept uncontrollably over the death of his daughter-in-law. Only time she had ever seen him cry like that. She was the daughter he had never had. My grandmother, too, was governed by love. "Your grandmother," Aunt Estes continued, "said that your mother was such a perfect Christian woman that the Lord would surely make an exception for her. She said she knew your mother's soul rested peacefully with God in heaven." Then Aunt Estes didn't say anything for a while, as if to let the idea filter through the pain. "There, now," she said. "Does that make you feel any better?"

Once more I could hear Grandmother Spence confessing to me, a child, "I wish I were as good a Christian woman as your mother." And I knew my grandmother was right. I had never known a woman, even my Grandmother Spence, who seemed as sinless as she. Sinners were sinners, but they were first to be understood and always to be forgiven. Anger was a stranger to her lips. She must have felt it, for having failed to feel anger, how could she feel love?

Yet the Christ she had embraced was not a person I would have found attractive, nor do I think he existed. The Christ she emulated was a man who administered a kind of intellectual love—*agape,* the Greeks called it. But the Christ I could have loved would have been a compassionate man, a man who felt to the marrow, whose feeling was not calculated up in the safe, steely reaches of the mind. This at-a-distance, intellectual love provided a means by which Christians might avoid those unchristian passions—anger, hatred, revenge, and the raging passions of the body.

Sometimes I thought my mother, like the sort of Christ she adulated, loved only with the mind. She shared that universal Christian love, *agape,* with the world at large, with her neighbors, with the enemy, with the killers being executed, and with us. Sometimes I thought she loved us all the same. I remember thinking that Buddy Taylor's mother loved him more than my mother loved me. Buddy Taylor's mother would fight for him. My mother would as likely take the side of the other child against me. "Remember, Gerry, he is a poor boy whose parents don't go to church except on Christmas and Easter. He doesn't know any better."

Yet what emanated from such love and compassion was an overriding sense of justice in this farm girl—this daughter of a most bigoted father who could hate without reason, judge without basis and condemn without fault. Grandpa Pfleeger was a man prejudiced to the core, a man who disdained the poor, although he had mostly been poor, who despised the weak, and who detested the Jews despite the fact that he followed the major tenets of the Jewish religion. He hated blacks and Indians and every other minority. He loathed Catholics and mocked the Mormons. He could not abide those who had a better education than he and those whom he thought his intellectual inferiors. Perhaps in her heart my mother hated him—I couldn't say—this Christ-like woman had never said, and would never have said. She was, in most ways, like my Grandmother Pfleeger, one who quietly suffered, and who tried to bring the old man's meanness into balance by her own kindness.

Love of any kind was foreign to Leonard Pfleeger. He had relegated love to the weak. Love was a useless emotion that only created endless obstacles. To him, justice and power were synonymous. But to my mother, justice meant that the poor should be fed as Christ fed the multitudes. It meant that all persons, especially the wretched, should be adorned with love. She would have been a revolutionary had she lived today, as is Mother Teresa.

But a child wants his mother's love to be his private possession, not a resource for everyone else. In those dreadful days of the Depression, when the whole family was shy of new clothes, she could always find an extra dollar to help clothe a poor child. We too were poor, but to her we were never poor, for she could always point to those in greater need. How often my parents, at my mother's urging, took baskets of food to the townspeople in need, fresh cuts of wild meat, vegetables from the garden, a freshly canned quart of peaches, usually delivered in stealth so as not to embarrass the recipients.

Years later, still struggling to comprehend her life and her death, I spoke with my sister Barbara about her. Barbara told me how one day a black woman came to our house, a new person in a strange white community. Few blacks lived in Laramie. The woman brought with her a small boy about Barbara's age. And after the black woman left, my mother took Barbara aside.

"This little boy will be in your class, Barbara. The other children will likely be unkind to him. You must be sure to be good to him and see that he is treated fairly."

Then Barbara began to softly sing to me the same sweet tune that I too remembered as a child.

> Red and yellow, black and white
> All are perfect in his sight
> Jesus loves the little children of the world.

I found myself, the grown man, the seasoned trial lawyer, singing the words along with her.

According to Barbara, before our mother's return from South America, she was deeply involved in missionary work—not just the proselytizing, but the feeding of the famished and the care of the malnourished and the dying. "She must have felt very alive," Barbara said, "as I felt when we marched at Selma. And then she came back to the States, and to what? Who knows what she came home to? I doubt that Dad knew. And they had their secrets. Whatever they were she would not complain. She would, like Christ, only endure." And then she could endure no longer.

Barbara said, "I remember in Laramie before we left for South America that I had been sleeping with Dad when Mother crawled into the bed. Dad was holding her and she was crying. She was crying over you." I heard the old demons laughing and jeering in my ears, and I saw them pointing their filthy fingers at me.

"That stabs me with that same old guilt," I said to Barbara.

"I didn't mean to make you feel guilty," Barbara said. "I only meant to tell you how they kept things from us. The next morning I asked Dad why Mother had been crying. He said, 'She wasn't crying. You must have dreamed it.' But I know I didn't dream it.

"Their whole lives were secrets," Barbara said. "They must have lived secret lives from themselves, and each other and from us. They didn't talk about things. They made things go away by refusing to admit they were there. Dad smoked all those years we grew up. Yet we never knew he smoked until after Mother died, and he began smoking at home. They never let us know they fought. But they fought. I remember they had a fight one day over an old stove in the house at Laramie. Mother wanted to get rid of it and to get another stove. 'Why were you fighting?' I asked Dad the next day. He said, 'We weren't fighting.' 'Are you going to get a divorce?' I asked. 'Of course not. We weren't fighting, honey,' "

I told Barbara how Mother had been at the last, cold and distant, as if she were already dead. "I think she was always cold and distant," Barbara said. "I don't remember ever having heard her laugh. She took care of us. But she never played with us. She never teased us or had fun with us. She would see that my hair was combed and that my dress was tied in the back and that we were fed the proper diet, three wholesome meals a day. But she loved others as much as she loved us." It was startling to hear Barbara say that. "I think," Barbara said, "that she was seriously depressed for a very long time."

But I remembered her when she was a much younger. I remembered her held-back laughter. I remembered a young, happy woman in those days when I was happy too.

Anne and I had moved to cheaper quarters, into those long rows of prefabricated huts hastily slapped up along dirt streets to house the returning veterans and their families, a place called "Vets' Village," an on-campus ghetto of apartments constructed of composition board on the outside and plywood floors on the inside. If you dared to jump up and down on the floors, your neighbors four apartments down could feel it. Seventeen dollars a month rent ate at our budget, but not like the twenty-five dollars a month we'd been paying. The place had two bedrooms—at last, one for the baby—but the walls were so thin we could hear the last intimate detail of our neighbors diddling to the beat of "Deep Purple." The whole apartment, bedrooms and all, heated with one converted wood-burning stove, a single gas pipe up the middle that when fired up roared like a V-2 rocket lately launched by the Third Reich. There at the kitchen table I began my study for the bar examination.

I had graduated the top man of my class, but I refused to attend the graduation ceremonies. They could send me my diploma. Graduation was silly, senseless stuff for a man who had but one goal in life, "to earn a living for my family." Besides, I couldn't afford the cost of renting the gown, and, underneath, I knew that I was a phony. I didn't know the law. I wasn't as intelligent as those with lower grade averages. I had simply been able to outsmart the professors, and thereby I had cheated some deserving student with a great legal mind out of his chance to proudly stand in my place. And I didn't want to make some silly-ass speech as the valedictorian of twenty law graduates, most of whom hadn't the first idea about how they were going to make a living, who were as desperate and scared as I about being evicted from the nest of the law school.

Wyoming, in 1952, was not a place of great opportunity for graduating lawyers. Untrained for any useful purpose, we were being unloaded into a world that had no need for us. Why would anyone need us? Suing was not the way good neighbors settled differences in Wyoming. "A man's word was his bond." Most lawyers merely read real estate abstracts to make sure the titles were without serious flaws, and drafted simple wills, deeds and the like. Sometimes domestic problems brought one party or the other to the back door of the lawyer's office so as to avoid town gossip. Such cases were usually settled between the parties out of court, the lawyer acting for both, and, if he was unable to achieve a rec-onciliation, which was his ethical duty to attempt, then he took one of the parties to the judge for a quiet default divorce. People didn't want to "wash their dirty linen in public." Mostly, people didn't need lawyers, because people were peace-ful and law-abiding and too busy minding their own business to sue anyone. America had not yet transmogrified itself into the wolfish world we live in today. So how were any of us going to scratch out a living?

One day, as the fear of being expelled into the real world had escalated to a new high, one of the more audacious graduates from the class ahead of mine returned to make a quick visit to the law school. We seniors, about to take the bar, gathered admiringly around this hero, lately returned from the wars of "the young lawyer's life out there." Braver than any of us ever hoped to be, he had opened an office on his own in Casper. He hadn't been a top student, but he was a loud-talking guy glazed with more than a generous patina of conceit. "Do you have any clients?" I asked right off.

"Hell, yes," he said. "I already drafted a will and I got a lady a divorce." He'd been out there six months.

"How did you draft a will?" I asked, amazed.

"Book company came around and sold me a set of form books. Fifteen dol-lars a month."

"Jesus!" another kid exclaimed. "You actually drafted a will?"

"Damn right!" he said.

"What did they pay you for it?" another kid asked.

"Fifty bucks."

"You got fifty bucks for copying a will out of a form book?"

"Yeah. But you have to listen to 'em tell you all about their cute grandkids and their family problems, and you have to figure out what form to use."

"But fifty bucks!"

"What did you get for the divorce?" I asked.

"Hundred fifty, uncontested."

"Hundred fifty! Jesus, how did you have the nerve to ask that much for a divorce?"

"Gotta ask that much. Gotta charge what the bar sets. Uniform minimum fee schedule. Everybody has to charge at least that much."

"You mean the bar sets the fees and everybody charges the same?"

"You bet," he said, as if we should have known. "You're not supposed to be competing with each other like a bunch of used car salesmen." He seemed very haughty and very proud. "The law is a *profession*. People don't compete in a profession. The bar sets the minimum fees. Can't go below 'em. You can always go above 'em," he said and laughed. And we laughed, too.

"How did you figure out how to do a divorce?"

"Ya go down to the courthouse and ya get real friendly with the clerk of court. Then you get her to tell ya who the best divorce lawyers are, and you ask her to let you see one of their case files. You can check it out, just like you check out a book from the library, and you can take it back to your office and copy the papers."

"God almighty, I never thought of that," somebody said.

"They don't teach ya nothin' here," he said.

"Where do ya get the clients?" someone else asked.

"They come. Somebody looking for a cheap deal thinks he can get it from a starting lawyer. Don't know about the minimum fee schedule. Somebody sends a friend to you. Meet 'em in the bar. I met this lady client in the bar."

"Well, I'll be!" We were staggered at his boldness and his courage. We could never do that.

Earlier in the year I had been contacted by a lawyer in Worland, a smallish farm town in north-central Wyoming where the farmers raised sugar beets and fed the tops and the pulp to cattle in the feed lots. The feed lots stank up the town. When the wind was right you could smell them ten miles away. This lawyer was a nervous sort with prematurely white hair, and he smoked cigarettes as fast as was humanly possible, smashed one out and grabbed another. Although he was a fast-talking, hardworking, slam-bang fellow, he said he still couldn't keep up with the work. I couldn't believe it. And in Worland! Farmers up there must be a lot different from any I had ever met. This fellow had a proposition for the top man of our graduating class. He would provide that man with a free office, and that young lawyer would have the privilege of sorting through whatever work this lawyer didn't want—his overflow. Sort of like giving you a free seat by the garbage can so far as lucrative paying legal work was concerned. I would probably get an occasional small collection, a hard-to-win fender-bender intersection case involving damages of less than a hundred bucks, a five-dollar power of attorney, that sort of thing. But who cared? I wanted to be a lawyer and I needed to start somewhere—just as well be at the bottom. I was grateful for the chance.

By Christmas of 1951, Anna and I were well into this parent business. Kippy was starting to toddle around, huge baby, tall as a kid twice his age. We had cut down a Christmas tree, stole it right out of the national forest—thieves we were—and Kippy was pulling himself up by the tree limbs and jerking the tinsel off as fast as we could put it on. Anna and I were giving each other presents that we needed, like socks and underwear, and light bulbs for the reading lamp that we wrapped up pretty. I kept track of every penny we spent in a small notebook I carried with me, a skill Mr. Wilson taught me—said you had to know where your money went, or you could never keep any of it. I knew it didn't take much for us to get by on, and that we could make it in Worland. But I wanted a reaffirmation of the arrangement the lawyer had proposed to me. I had this family to feed. I hadn't heard from him since May, so I wrote:

> . . . as I understood, you felt that there was a need in your office for a younger attorney to relieve you of certain minor work that was taking your time away from more major activities, and since you felt that one of your chief assets was promptness, you deemed it wise to bring in someone to relieve you of otherwise time consuming cases. In return you were willing to offer an office and the use of your library, and such initial legal assistance as might be necessary. . . .
>
> . . . I feel that I am at the crossroads, and having never before traveled without a road map, I am anxious that the right route be chosen. May I hear from you? With my best personal regards to you and your family, and wishing all of you a very Merry Christmas, I remain, Sincerely.

I studied endlessly, tirelessly for the bar examination, most often at the law library where I could escape family diversions. I often studied in the stacks, as those endless rows of ceiling-high bookshelves were called. Nobody visited the stacks because nobody wanted to read the books. There were thousands of lonely books back there that had never been read, not once, books that had never been touched by a human hand after they had once been assigned their place in the shelves. And in the far reaches of these stacks, I would pull up a chair under a light, take out my old notebooks from the courses of three years before, and refresh my memory concerning the finer but more unmemorable aspects of the law. I ate a nickel Snickers bar for lunch, carried a Thermos of coffee, and all I was likely to digest the rest of the day was pure, no-calorie law. I was consumed by study. I slept little. When I did, I dreamed of the law. I was married to the law, imprisoned by it. Nothing resembling a normal, healthy human male of twenty-three was left of me. I was a walking legal machine. My brain had become a jumble of legal propositions. I knew every rule, and every exception to every rule. I was run-down, frazzled, fatigued, done in. I had no wife. No child. Anna, already pregnant with our second child, Kerry, did not exist. Nothing existed but the law.

No bar refresher courses were given in those days. None were in existence. Today, young, deserving kids scratch the bottom of their financial resources, and their parents mortgage their own future with school loans to get their children through law school, and after having graduated from law school, most still have not yet learned enough to pass the bar. Now, they must take a bar refresher course, and those can be costly. As for the success rate at passing the bar, it is often not which law school you graduated from but which bar refresher course you took. In my day, nobody offered us a clue on how to study for the bar. Nobody knew. No Multistate Bar Exam, as is presently fashioned by the American Bar Association, existed. Nobody knew what the bar exam would include since it was recomposed each year by a committee of old-time practicing Wyoming lawyers. Our job was to convince the examiners that we knew the entire body of the law, or at least enough to satisfy them that we wouldn't bring the bar itself into disrepute. The examination took all day.

I didn't sleep the night before. I tossed and groaned and pummeled the pillow all night in that small dark closet of a bedroom. In the morning I was aching, exhausted and numb. The examination was given in a barren room on campus somewhere—I can no longer remember the precise place or the questions on the examination. I have no memory of the lawyer who was in charge. But after I had turned in my paper, I knew I had failed. I knew I couldn't fool the real lawyers as I had fooled the professors all of these years.

And I was right. I became the first valedictorian in the history of the Wyoming Law School to fail the bar. The real lawyers had caught me at last.

CHAPTER 23

*Law School library, Dean Hamilton (center) and entire faculty and
student body about 1948.*

THE NOTICE, COLD as the law itself, so impersonal it was hateful, read:

> The State Board of Law Examiners has filed a report stating that you
> failed to pass the bar examination and recommending that you be
> given a second examination if applied for within the time provided by
> the statute, which is one year.

That ugly dispatch was hand-typed by the clerk of the Wyoming Supreme
Court on half a sheet of official stationery containing the names of the supreme
court judges, Fred H. Blume, William A. Riner, and Harry P. Ilsley, those three
wizened yellowed corpses who had sat propped up on the high bench in their
black robes from nearly the beginning of time. I had once made a law school
visit to the court. The judges, all of them, slept through the argument. Nobody
knew for sure how old they were. Occasionally, as if to dispute the suspicion that
they were dead, one would shake a shaggy jowl to dislodge a fly, or an eye would
pop open as if one of the mortician's disc, used to make sure the eyes of the
corpse stay closed, had suddenly failed.

Flunking the bar was more than a personal defeat. It was something more on the order of irreversible shame. It meant you couldn't measure up to the standard of a lawyer in Wyoming. Lord knows how you could ever pass the bar in a real state, like Nebraska or even South Dakota. It meant that you were inferior, probably a borderline imbecile, and that somebody had finally caught you. Moreover, they had proof of it, right there in black and white on the exam paper. And they had no choice but to reject you. Indeed, it was their solemn duty to do so. It meant more than that. It meant terrible things about your overall fitness to be alive. It meant that you were a fraud, a phony, and that Ol' Calsey had been smarter than all of the law professors put together. It meant Gerry Spence had been a jerk all along. At least that's what it meant to me.

Today, a bar examination failure or two is often standard. Then it was a sort of blight on one's record, a stigma. So devastated I couldn't study further, so confused I didn't know what to study anymore, so ashamed for having failed, I never wanted to think about the law again. How could I have ever thought the law was for me? Judge Parker had said I should get out. Now the bar examiners had concurred.

"Nothin' but a bunch of stuffy shysters anyway who don't want real competition," I would argue one minute to Anna, and the next I would be saying, "I knew it all along. I was never cut out for this work. I'm not smart enough to be a lawyer. You remember that English professor who said my IQ was too measly to get an *A* in his class? Well, he knew, too."

"Well, what about the fact that you were top man in your class?" Anna would argue back.

"I just knew how to write a paper that tickled their asses. Doesn't mean I knew a damned thing about the law."

"Well, what about the fact that the dean said you had the highest aptitude test for being a lawyer he ever saw?"

"Probably bullshittin' me. Probably low on enrollment that year."

"You couldn't have fooled all the professors," Anna argued back.

"What do you mean I couldn't," I hollered. "I did!"

Finally, the following August, to quiet Anna and to satisfy Mr. Wilson, I trudged up to the university, too ashamed to look anybody in the face, and took the bar a second time, this time without having cracked a book or reviewed a note. I hated the law. Couldn't stand to look at a case or read another paragraph in another old stale notebook. I took the bar to satisfy them. I took it to prove that there had been no mistake the first time. I took it as further punishment for my having failed the bar in the first place, for my having fooled the professors all those years. That's why I took it.

In the meantime I had gone to work at the cement plant in Laramie to earn a living for my family. The cement dust in the sacking room was so thick a man couldn't see his hand in front of him. We laborers didn't wear respirators. Couldn't breathe with them on, the dust too thick. We coughed and held our breaths, gasped for air, shoveled into our wheelbarrows the knee-deep, flour-fine dust that covered the entire floor and we hauled the dust, load after load, to the outside where the air was minimally better. By night my face was black, my eyelids coated with dust, my lips sticking with cement mud, my lungs caked. I coughed up cement mud all night, but in the morning I headed out once more for the cement plant. Eighty cents an hour.

I was one of the laborers. They were my kind. They were hardworking, hard-talking poor men who had but one asset to cash in for their living—their muscle. Their bodies. They didn't give a shit that I had failed the bar. They didn't even know what the hell it was. A man was respected if he did his share of the work and didn't complain and didn't jerk off the boss. We cheated a little once in a while. If the boss was on another job, a guy might sit down in a warm place in the kiln room and bullshit. Getting by was part of the game. Sometimes I tried to talk about my life, but to be a man you had to be tough. I was complaining to one of my brother workers one night about the problems I was having in my marriage. He was an old boy who'd just moved in from Arkansas.

"Shit, I'll tell ya how ya treat yer old lady," he said. He spit his tobacco in a careless stream. "Ya do like I do. When you're in bed of a night with the old lady, you gets yerself a big mouthful of chewin' tobacco, and ya get a good wad a-goin', and then when it's time to spit, you give an elbow inta the ribs a the old lady an' ya holler, 'Duck yer head unner the covers, I'm gonna spit straight up!' and when she gets her head unner there fer protection ya let go one a them big ones—'bout three foot long. That there teaches 'em respec', and ya never have no more trouble with 'em, after that," and then he laughed and everybody laughed.

Dean Hamilton had commiserated with me. In the same plain office where I had first met the man as a graduating high school student, he propped his feet up on the desk, his suit coat off, his starched white shirt as pure and stiff as his intent, and tried to explain why I, his top student, had failed the bar. He had some explaining to do.

"Not your fault, my fault," he said, jabbing a finger into his chest. "I've been in a knock-down, drag-out confrontation with the Wyoming bar for a long time. They want to tell us how to run this law school, and I'm not letting the god-damned bar run this law school, you can bet your biffy on that." He was talking loud so anybody who might be hanging around on the fringes could hear him. "I've been campaigning to eliminate the bar examination altogether. If a kid gets through our school, he's ready to go. He shouldn't have to be tested by anybody. We've tested that kid for three years. What more do they want?"

"My boy," he leaned toward me like a doctor about to pronounce my terminal illness, and the softness of his eyes surprised me. "You got caught in the middle of our argument. They showed us *they* had the power. They flunked our top grad. Doesn't make sense—the only two they flunk—our top grad and our bottom one! Who are they trying to kid?"

"The exams were numbered with our secret number," I said.

"They know!" he shouted. "Who the hell do you think had the numbering key!"

I had asked the bar examiners to let me review my paper, but they refused. Policy, you know. "No use making a fuss about it," the dean said. "Only further enrage them. Gotta remember—they do have the power. All of it, you know. Isn't like it was up here. You could do your fussing and hollering and we would forgive you, because you were one of our kids, but you don't belong to them. So just back off. Man needs to know when to kinda hunker down and take it."

Secretly I thought that the bar examiners had probably heard about me—probably talked to Judge Bentley, the justice of the peace, about the way I defended that case, and they probably talked to Judge Parker, who must have told them I was an insufferable mouthy bastard who should never be permitted to get near a client, much less enter a courtroom.

"Why the chairman of the bar examiners is the biggest ignoramus in the state of Wyoming," the dean hollered. "He never went to law school a day of his life. Read law. And he can't read." He laughed. "That's all he ever did, that and represent the Union Pacific Railroad, and because the Union Pacific runs the state he thinks he can tell me how to run this law school!"

Weeks after I had taken the bar the second time I got a call from the chairman of the bar examiners himself. "I want to be the first to tell you, Mr. Spence: You passed the bar this time with flying colors. Best paper we've ever had the privilege to read. Congratulations!"

I couldn't reply for a long time. My God, maybe it was a cruel joke. How could I pass the bar without studying when I had failed the bar after cramming three months solid for it? How could I write the best paper they had "the privilege to read" and be the same stupid shit who dredged the bottom before? Must be a miserable joke, but I thought, if it isn't, I better say thank you before he changes his mind. "Thank you," I whispered, and then I started to cry. Suddenly I realized it was true, and I went hollering for Anna. And sure enough, in the next afternoon's mail, I received the written notice on the official stationery of the Wyoming Supreme Court. I had passed, all right. Finally, I had fooled the real lawyers, too.

PART THREE
THE COUNTRY LAWYER

CHAPTER 24

—

Franklin B. Sheldon.

I KISSED ANNA and Kippy good-bye, jumped in the car and drove westward toward the Wind River Mountains. That August of 1952, I was a man who needed the mountains, their lulling streams, the trout, the wild game. I needed the mountains as a boy needs a home. Maybe somewhere at the foot of the great Wind Rivers, somewhere behind their wild, fingered pinnacles and their high, brooding peaks, there would be a small spot waiting for a country lawyer to seed and to take root. I was wearing my gettin'-married suit, the same white shirt and the red tie with the big painted feather.

Later I stood on a sidewalk in Lander talking to Ernest Newton, who was guarding the doorway to his walk-up law office as a prairie dog guards his hole. He was a large, lean, stoop-shouldered man past fifty with sallow skin and quick eyes, the dark bags hanging below them—put a person in mind of Franklin Roosevelt's in the last days of his presidency. I'd met Newton in law school when he was a senior and I was a freshman.

A genial sort, with a loud, easily triggered leather-lunged laugh, Newton had worn himself out publishing the town's only paper, a weekly called the *Lander State Journal,* sold the paper, left publishing behind and went to law school.

Riverton, Wyoming. Masonic Temple Building, left.

Now Newton put his arm around my shoulder like a father to a son. He gave me a friendly smile. "You ought to go talk to Franklin Sheldon. He's the big lawyer in Riverton. Represents the bank and the Midvale Irrigation District. He's got most of the business, the farmers, too. Riverton's a good town. They got 'The Project' over there, you know," Newton said, referring to the Riverton Project, a federal irrigation project that over the past decade had attracted several hundred homesteaders. "I hear Sheldon needs somebody."

I looked up and down the main street of this small cowtown, huddled at the foot of the Wind River Range. Nothing of mention had happened in Lander in the last fifty years. People died, and those who lived paid their taxes and minded their own business. I liked the looks of the old town. Its buildings, their false fronts fooling no one, had been stacked up out of yellow sandstone blocks quarried from a nearby canyon. The Popo Agie, a clear mountain stream, couple of car lengths wide, and clean enough for the baby to drink, tumbled down over rocks too cold to grow moss. The streets were mostly empty. The few people hanging around looked like the kind you could stop, ask them the time of day, and they'd give you an honest answer.

"Any law business here?" I asked Newton. It was late August of 1952. After I failed the bar I had never heard from the lawyer in Worland again. Probably didn't want any bar-flunking punk hanging around his office sorting through his leftovers.

"Not much," Newton said. His big laugh. "Frank Hays represents the town and Bill Smith is the county attorney. They're partners. Got it sewed up pretty good. Old Art Oeland's here. He's not too healthy, and Jack Crofts has been hanging around for Lord knows how long. They get what's left. Then there's old John Spriggs. Must be near eighty. He represents the criminals and the drunk Indians. I'm the justice of the peace. I'm getting by—barely." He laughed again. "But Riverton—now that town is something else again."

I drove to Riverton the same afternoon and found Franklin Sheldon's office, the front office on the second floor of the Masonic Temple Building where his wife, Elsie, kept watch over him. She was a blonde in her mid-forties, a smiling but haughty sort with a cigarette hanging from her mouth, her eyes squinted against the smoke, her tumbling fingers on the typewriter never stopping while she talked.

"I came to see Mr. Sheldon," I answered when she asked me my business.

"What about?"

"I'm looking for a job. I just passed the bar. I'm a lawyer."

"You're a lawyer?" She looked me up and down and then laughed.

"Well, yes, I am," I said.

"You look more like a Mormon missionary," she said. She puffed on her cigarette. "Well, I'll see if he's in, but I don't think he wants to hire any Mormon missionaries." She laughed again.

Franklin B. Sheldon, an ordinary-sized man in his early fifties, had a flat belly, a large hawk nose, and a mouth full of crooked teeth. He kept a package of Pall Malls in his freshly ironed shirt pocket. You could see the cigarette package and his summer underwear through the thin cotton. I thought he was a very neat-looking person. He was bald all the way around his head and down to the tips of his big ears. The size of a man's ears had meaning. Grandfather Spence used to say, "You can always tell a man's intelligence by the size of his ears. You'll never see a really top-rate man with little ears. All the great men had big ears. Look at Lincoln's ears. Look at Roosevelt's." I thought Grandpa made that argument because he had big ears himself. So did I.

"Come on in, son," Sheldon said, giving me his big toothy smile. Standing in front of his desk I could look down on Main Street. Lot of farmers down there, bustling around, their pickups loaded with fence posts and bailing wire and dogs, some with sacks of seed and machine parts. Some pulled used farm equipment behind their trucks and some pulled horse trailers. No parking meters. The streets intersecting Main Street were unpaved. The building directly across the street was of brick, a general mercantile store; the sign on the building said it had been erected in 1906. Down the street I could see a Gamble's store, and across the street in the other direction a drugstore. The farmers on the street wore cheap cowboy hats, their shape lost long ago in the first sudden summer rain, and they wore Levi's with their denim shirts open at the neck. Some wore their cowboy boots to town, J. C. Penney's kind, machine stitched, none of those fancy hand-tooled tops, and some came into town still wearing their everyday round-toed, lace-up work boots. The Indians in Riverton had given up looking like Indians. They all wore cowboy outfits, old hats, boots and western shirts, and once in a while an Indian would came staggering out of Tony's Bar next to the drugstore and head down the street, taking up both sides of the sidewalk.

Franklin B. Sheldon shook my hand, nothing vigorous, his hands as soft as a lady's, the skin thin and shiny, the nails perfectly groomed. Then he sat back down, propped shiny loafers up on his gray metal desk, aimed his big nose in my direction, sighted down it and looked me over good. I smiled back.

"So you're looking for work?" he asked, still smiling, more amused than friendly, I thought.

"Well, yes, I am. I just got the results of the bar examination yesterday. Drove up here from Laramie this morning."

"How did you do in school?" he asked, pulling out a Pall Mall, beating it on the desktop and lighting it with a Zippo. Snapped the Zippo shut and blew the smoke in my direction.

"First in my class, sir," I said, proudly. Didn't tell him I also had achieved that other honor—the first honor graduate from the University of Wyoming Law School ever to have failed the bar.

"Just a minute here," Franklin Sheldon said to me. He picked up the phone and dialed. Then I heard him ask for Dean Hamilton. I sat, amazed, listening to Frank Sheldon's side of the conversation.

"Can he think on his feet?" Sheldon asked. Can he think on his feet? A lawyer must not only think like a lawyer, but be able to do so on his feet as well? I had never thought of thinking on my feet. "You say he's as fast on his feet as they come? First in his class? Good enough." Sheldon hung up the phone and turned to me. "I'll pay you two hundred dollars a month. But you can't use my wife for your secretary. Have to do your own typing."

"Deal!" I shouted before he could change his mind. I grabbed his hand and pumped it hard. Something suspect about this man Sheldon to hire me—just like that. But this world was crazy too, up and down, me hanging on. Still I was in it and I was for it, and I was going to be a lawyer—maybe not a big-time lawyer, but a lawyer. I was going to do what lawyers do, whatever the hell that was, and I wasn't going to waste any time getting to it.

Before I drove back to Laramie that evening, Elsie Sheldon escorted me around the little town of Riverton, helping me look for an apartment. I settled on the first place we looked at, a set of basement rooms on North Second Street under a log house belonging to a Swedish log house builder named Joe Hagstrom. I liked the neighborhood, and one of those pale green weeping willows spread its lacy limbs in the front yard. There was even a lawn where Kippy could play. The basement apartment consisted of a small dark kitchen, a darker living room furnished with cheap lawn furniture, and two tiny unlit bedrooms. The floors were unfinished cement. What little natural light illuminated the place seeped through eye-level basement windows.

"This place will be just perfect!" I exclaimed to Mrs. Sheldon. "Wonderful!" Twenty-five dollars a month.

That same night I drove back to Laramie. Then Anna and I stuffed our small closet of clothes along with a stack of diapers, my hunting rifles and fishing pole, a few books—that was about it—into the back of an old broken-down black and yellow DeSoto station wagon—looked like a stepped-on bee, a car we had traded for after Kippy was born. And with Kippy on her lap, we headed into our new lives.

The *Riverton Guide* announced in a small front-page paragraph the news that Gerry Spence, fresh out of law school, had come to Riverton to practice law with Franklin B. Sheldon. It mentioned that Spence had a wife and a child. That was it—after which the Wyoming State Bar wrote Sheldon a firm letter of reprimand. His permitting such a story to run in the local paper was a form of advertising and was to be severely censured. Sheldon wrote back. He agreed that lawyers ought not advertise. It had not been his intention to advertise the arrival of his young associate. He simply could not control the free press of Riverton, Wyoming, which published the article as news—First Amendment rights, as the bar should know. If they didn't, he suggested they review the clear language of the Constitution of the United States for guidance in the future.

Franklin B. Sheldon was a perfectionist. Professional in work and in appearance, meticulous in the drafting of documents, he made sure that competence and honest representation were a given in his office. He had no respect for indolence or a muddy mind. He thought the other lawyers in town were, simply put, a detriment to the profession. He listed them off like St. Peter taking an inventory of those knocking at the gate. There was the old tubby boy down the hall who coughed and harrumphed better than he could talk, and who Sheldon claimed couldn't write a contract anyone could read or understand. Robert Moran, a retired schoolteacher, who late in life went to law school, was nothing more than a wearisome blowhard who, according to Sheldon, possessed neither judgment nor credibility. Then there was that "simpering, gutless old fool who was drunk most of the time" and who officed next to the old tubby guy, all of the town's lawyers then being housed in the upstairs of the Masonic Temple Building. None could enter the kingdom of jurisprudence so far as Frank Sheldon was concerned. He treated his fellow lawyers with respect, but he always dealt with them at arm's length.

As for me, he sat me down in his other office, his smallish library that consumed only part of one wall, and laid a stack of abstracts in front of me.

"What are these?" I asked.

"My God!" he said, slapping his forehead. "You've never seen an abstract? What do they teach you in law school these days?"

An abstract of title was a summary of the documents recorded in the courthouse that pertained to the land one's client was in the process of purchasing. A lawyer examined an abstract of title to assure the purchaser that he was receiving "merchantable title." The lawyer could not examine an abstract of title without knowing a good deal about the law of the state—about the correct form of deeds and mortgages and releases, and whether the recording statutes had been properly met. One had to know the law concerning heirship and estates, the law of remainders, of partnerships, how a partnership was formed and thereafter dissolved. One needed to know who could sign deeds for a corporation and evidence of corporate authority to execute the instruments must appear of record. One had to know how corporations were formed and dissolved, who were the trustees of the corporate assets of a dissolved corporation, how quiet title suits were brought and the defendants served and what proof of their service must appear of record. One had to know the statutes of limitations, the lien laws, and how bankruptcy affects the title to property. In short, one could not examine an abstract if one was not a thoroughly knowledgeable lawyer. But in law school we had never heard of an abstract.

After a lawyer had examined the abstract, he was required to write a title opinion for which the lawyer was fully liable.

"What do you think happens if you approve a title, the purchaser builds a million-dollar building on it, and the title is defective?" Sheldon asked. "Who is going to pay? I'll tell you who will pay." He didn't need to tell me. For such service bearing such exposure, Franklin B. Sheldon charged $25 for his title opinion. He got $5 for a deed, $5 for a mortgage. His fee was $150 for a quiet title suit. He had several going at the same time. He got $5 for a farm lease. Minimum fee schedule of the bar.

One day the American Bar Association delegate for Wyoming, the Honorable Edward Murane of Casper, Wyoming's largest city, population then about twenty-five thousand windblown souls, came to visit us members of the Fremont County Bar. His job. We had a luncheon in his honor at the Noble Hotel in Lander, one of those old, dark, cut-up, redone places that looked like an old woman who had suffered through fifteen face-lifts. After lunch, Mr. Murane, as bald as Sheldon himself, stood up to address the ten lawyers there assembled. The table was silent, the lawyers gazing up into the face of the bar leader, their own faces radiant with respect.

"We of the bar are duty bound to do something about our public image," he said. I listened in awe. This was *the* ABA delegate speaking to us small-town lawyers, in person! "The ABA is going to solicit moneys from across the land. We are going to put on a national program, a blitz, so to speak, creating a new image for lawyers! You in Fremont County will have the opportunity to contribute to our effort. We plan to assess each member of the Wyoming bar twenty-five dollars for this crucial campaign." Twenty-five dollars, I thought. That's the price of an abstract examination. Took me several days to examine an abstract and write the title opinion.

Suddenly I found myself standing up in that long, dark windowless room illuminated only by small lamps on the table and the enlightened rhetoric of our leader. Standing there facing my peers, I felt suddenly afraid. Once up, I wished I could sit down again. One does not ask questions of the delegate of the ABA. But there I stood. Edward Murane peered through his glasses at me like one encountering a half-fried larva in his hamburger. "I was just wondering," I said, "if we lawyers have such a bad image, and we want to change our image, why don't we just do a better job?"

Edward Murane didn't bother to answer the question, an obvious incoherency escaping the lips of some upstart not yet dry behind the ears, one of those know-it-all kids who had no understanding of the problems of the profession. He probably knew I flunked the bar. He left me standing there and went right on reporting on the numerous programs of the House of Delegates of the ABA, which had nothing to do with anything so far as I could see, and he told us how we could all be proud of the University of Wyoming's extensive law library which, along with certain other requirements, continued to qualify the law school for ABA approval. Finally I sat down. He never noticed.

I labored nine months in the office of Franklin B. Sheldon, mostly over abstracts and title opinions and other standard legal papers. He represented Riverton's only bank, and for every loan the bank made there were all those legal documents to be drawn. He took me to court several times, where I was allowed to argue what was called a "demurrer," a pleading by which one lawyer tested the legal adequacy of the complaint filed by his opponent. I thought it splendid stuff.

The pretrial process went like this: First, the plaintiff filed a petition, which set forth in detail why this aggrieved party had come to court and why he was suing that certain rascal named in the petition as "the defendant." "The said defendant then and there and at such time and place, and in the manner aforesaid, having negligently driven his motor vehicle into the motor vehicle driven by the plaintiff . . . " language like that. Then the defendant hired a lawyer who, after several extensions of time granted by the plaintiff's lawyer out of professional courtesy, filed his demurrer. As to the language of the petition above, the opposing lawyer might argue to the judge, "This petition, on its face, is fatally defective for its failure to allege that the motor vehicle driven by the plaintiff was owned by the plaintiff, for, as it must be apparent to the court, we cannot proceed in this case if the ownership of the said motor vehicle is not in the plaintiff since the cause of action may be vested in another. . . ." Or the defendant might file a motion to strike, claiming that the plaintiff's lawyer alleged too many facts, and that the surplus should be stricken from the petition. If the court after hearing the arguments agreed, the lawyer who filed such a defective petition in the first place then filed his amended petition correcting the error, or if the necessary facts could not be alleged in good faith the case would be dismissed. After the amended petition was filed, the defendant's lawyer might file another motion to strike, or another demurrer, or both. The process continued, month after month, sometimes year after year, sometimes requiring the fourth or fifth amended petition until, at last, the judge was satisfied that the petition stated a proper cause of action in the proper language.

The lawyers argued their motions and demurrers, citing cases that went back to the Magna Carta. The question was never "What is the problem between these parties?" The question was, instead, "How does one state what the problem is in an acceptable way according to the case law of the state?" Wyoming was blessed with scores of cases authored by the three deacons of the dead, Blume, Riner, and Ilsley, and their equally anesthetized predecessors, setting out in obscure and erudite phrases what a petition should or shouldn't contain and what issues could or could not be raised by a demurrer. It was all a game, unattached to any search for justice, a game designed for lawyers and judges to play. Although today, the demurrer has evolved into a motion for summary judgment, the game is still essentially the same—how do you get past all of the legal gamesmanship so you can finally present your client's case to the jury?

Justice Blume loved to cite Roman law, although Wyoming claimed to be an English common law state. Why shouldn't he cite the Justinian codes? No one else had a copy. And he had cornered an audience. If we wanted to keep current and be seen as competent lawyers, we had to read his decisions. More-over, his reference to the Justinian codes gave his decisions an elegant touch, a sort of ethereal literacy. Many Wyoming lawyers and judges treated his deci-sions as if they were teetering on the brink of the divine. As for me, I couldn't understand them. I don't think anyone else could either.

Justice Blume, his face the face of a hanging-down hound dog, already past eighty, tottered to his office every day, his big old German shepherd bringing up the rear on a slack leash. When the two entered the judge's chambers, the dog plopped down at the judge's feet where he slept all day, and one was hard pressed to distinguish which was the snore of the dog and which the man. Some of the more erudite court observers had long ago concluded that Justice Blume was in better communication with his sleeping dog than the demands of justice. Yet the other two justices always concurred with whatever he wrote, and that, I suspect, was because if one of his fellow justices considered writing a dissenting opinion, before he could write it he would have to understand what Judge Blume had written in the first place.

The following May, in 1953, Franklin B. Sheldon called me into his office. He had a big smile on his face. He had been a member of the Wyoming legis-lature, and, as I already knew, had been instrumental in convincing that body to create a new judgeship for Fremont County. Casper was 120 miles away, and he had argued to the legislature that the visiting judge from Casper couldn't travel to Fremont County often enough to hear the lawyers' arguments on their motions and demurrers and to sign the decrees of quiet title and to grant the default divorces that were piling up. A new judge residing in Lander, the county seat, would cure this problem. The legislature having agreed, Franklin B. Shel-don had called me in to tell me "the good news." He had just been appointed by the governor to fill the new judgeship, the one he himself had created. He would be closing his office within the month.

I was struck dumb. I didn't know how to try a real case in front of a real judge. I didn't know much of anything else, either. I had no clients. Then shortly after the governor announced that he had appointed Franklin Sheldon to the bench, the bank took its business down the hall to a more mature lawyer, one C. J. Mur-phy, Robert Moran's partner. Murphy was six feet seven inches tall, a dark, quiet man who smiled a lot, and it was also said that he could read an abstract.

"Well, Gerry," Franklin B. Sheldon said as he put on his small-brimmed sil-ver beaver Stetson. "I'm leaving a lifetime of practice to you." He gave me that toothy grin.

"Thanks," I said. And after he walked out the door of his office for the last time I looked at the filing cabinets I had purchased. But for a case-file or two, they were empty.

CHAPTER 25

Fourth of July parade, Riverton.

AFTER FRANK SHELDON left and I began the solo practice of law, I didn't know how to file the simplest case in the justice of the peace court, not even a suit to collect twenty dollars for the Riverton Credit Bureau. The justice of the peace court in Riverton was housed in the front of Judge Shorty Anderson's wool shed. Judge Anderson, a crusty old curmudgeon with a round red nose like one of Snow White's dwarfs, was a dwarf himself. He had been crippled with polio, and his legs were withered and useless, but he got around on crutches, and he bought wool from the project farmers and stored it in his long tin warehouse down by the railroad where he held court.

On a cold day, you could walk in the door of his courtroom, the wool bags six feet long, hanging in rows from the ceiling, his old wood-burning stove having heated up the place until the wool grease began dripping from the burlap bags. The wool grease stank the place up so bad that even the dogs preferred the cold outside to fighting the stench inside. Everybody breathed through their mouth to avoid being knocked over. But it was the justice of the peace court, and we all respected Judge Anderson and his court, stench or not.

"Why, you get used to it, Gerry," the judge said. And he'd get that amused look on his face, and sit back with his thumbs in his wide elastic green suspenders. "And the stink in here ain't near so bad as the justice most folks get." He was the philosophical kind, who liked to point out that his court was a court of common sense. Law didn't matter much. In his court what was right was what counted. And it was Judge Anderson who, seeing the look on my face, pulled out the forms for me to fill out—the summons, the petition, the return of service—so I could file my first lawsuit in his court. "Don't know what they teach you in law school," he said.

A small boy, together with his playmates, was playing in the backcountry town of Shoshoni, Wyoming, down at the railroad station, when they came onto an empty wooden cable spool, six feet or more in diameter. There, in that web of steel tracks crossing the prairie, the children climbed up on the spool and rode the thing like circus performers. Day after day they played on the rolling spool until one day the boy fell off, was slammed up against the tracks and broke both legs. The legs didn't heal, and the child, in agony, underwent countless operations at the hands of the country surgeons, and the surgeons bungled the surgery. The child was in constant misery. His single mother was near exhaustion attempting to care for the little fellow. She, a maid, was deeply in debt and without funds to pay the doctor and hospital bills. The case for her child was one that Franklin Sheldon had left behind when he ascended to the bench. When the judge set the case for trial, the mother, not knowing any better, asked me to take the case to court for her.

The suit had been filed against the Chicago and Northwestern Railroad—an "attractive nuisance" case, which meant in the law that if the railroad knew, or should have known, that children were attracted to the railroad's premises and that the device or condition that attracted them was dangerous, the owner, in our case the railroad, could be held responsible for the child's resulting injuries. The railroad was represented by the dean of Wyoming trial lawyers, the dry, droll, and deadly William Werhli of Casper. Werhli looked a good deal like Clarence Darrow, but he was a more straightforward, no-nonsense, no-drama, no-oratory kind of fellow. I doubt that he ever made a stand-up-and-come-to-Jesus speech in his life. Things were as they were with Bill Werhli. He was a reasonable, unemotional straight shooter, and he expected everyone else, the jury included, to see things that way as well—his way. Judge Smoky Lewis presided, a crusty good-natured old devil—Judge Sheldon, of course, having disqualified himself to hear the case.

I climbed the creaky stairs to the courtroom on the second floor. I was twenty-four years old. A person wouldn't want to jump too hard on the floor up there for fear he might land in the assessor's office below. The jury, penned off behind one of those old Victorian spindled railings, sat in old oak swivel chairs with black leather backs, and the judge sat on the bench, mostly staring up at the high empty ceiling hoping his torture in the case would soon end.

Fremont County Court House, Lander, Wyo.

Courthouse. Lander, Wyoming.

I had showed up at the courthouse in my wedding suit, the obligatory white shirt and the red tie with the painted feather. We chose the jury, people who simply affirmed they could be fair. I didn't know the questions trial lawyers asked prospective jurors trying to get a feel for who the jurors were. Nobody ever taught us that. I didn't know how to condition the jury to my case. No one had ever heard of a jury consultant. If the juror said he or she could be fair, that was good enough for me. It was good enough for Bill Werhli, too. He didn't have much faith in the business of jury selection anyway. People were people. His defense was reasonable. He figured the jury was reasonable. He would just as soon take the first twelve out of the box. Besides, the plaintiff's attorney had to convince all twelve people to his case to win, and he knew that this was the kid's first case.

I wanted the jury to care about this little boy. But as Bill Werhli saw it, kids get injured. It wasn't the railroad's fault, it was the mother's. Everybody cares about kids, Bill Werhli included. "But that's why God put mothers on this earth—to take care of their kids," he argued in a kind of tight, high drone that put you in mind of an errant French horn. The railroad was not and could not be expected to become the baby-sitter for the mothers in Shoshoni, Wyoming. I knew I had the burden to prove the railroad's negligence, and I also had to show that the mother had no knowledge that her child was playing in the railroad yards. I put her on the stand at the beginning of the case.

"Sammy is your son, right?"

"Objected to as leading," Werhli said.

"Sustained," Judge Smoky Lewis ruled.

I couldn't think of how to ask the question. I stood there, rocking from foot to foot, embarrassed that I couldn't get the first question right. Finally the judge came to my rescue. "Why don't you ask the lady, 'What relationship, if any, does Sammy Smith hold to you?'" I asked the question exactly as the judge suggested. Then came my next question.

"You didn't know Sammy was playing at the railroad, right?"

"Objected to as leading," Werhli said.

"Sustained," the judge ruled.

Again I stood mute, stricken with terror. Standing there, the jury staring, and again I couldn't think of how to modify the question. Once more the judge came to my rescue. "Why not inquire about it in this fashion, Mr. Spence: 'What knowledge did you have concerning the whereabouts of your son on the day in question?'"

I asked the question exactly as the judge had suggested.

Werhli jumped up. "I object to that question. It assumes a fact not in evidence, namely, that she had *any* knowledge concerning the whereabouts of her child on the day in question."

"Sustained," the judge ruled.

"But Your Honor, that was *your* question."

"It was a bad question," the judge said. The jury laughed. My face got red. My mind went blank.

Finally I turned to the judge. "Well, Your Honor, if you can't ask the question right, how do you expect me to?"

"That's enough out of you, Mr. Spence," the judge said in a voice conceived in a gravel pit and scowling down at me through glasses that made him look like a malicious hoot owl.

I stood speechless. The jury seemed amused. "Let me help you, Mr. Spence," Werhli offered in a kindly tone of voice. "Ask it this way: 'What knowledge, *if any,* did you have concerning the whereabouts of your son on the day in question?'"

"Thank you," I said. "What knowledge, *if any,* did you have concerning the whereabouts of your son on the day in question?"

"Are you going to object to that question?" the judge asked.

"Yes," Werhli replied, "if the Court please. The 'day in question' has not been established."

"Sustained," Judge Smoky Lewis ruled. "Can you figure that one out by yourself, Mr. Spence?" the judge asked, hiding a smirk.

"I don't think so, but I'll try," I said. "What knowledge, *if any,* did you have concerning the whereabouts of your son, Sammy Smith, on the day in question, *October 12, 1951?*"

"That's objected to," Werhli said. "October 12, 1951, has not yet been established as 'the day in question.'"

"Sustained," the judge ruled.

I rushed in to establish the foundation for the question. "Did your son get hurt on October 12, 1951?"

"Objected to, Your Honor," Werhli said, exasperated. "Leading."

"Sustained," the judge ruled. "Mr. Spence, start your next question with the word 'What'"

"What day did your son get hurt?" I asked.

"Objected to. That is irrelevant unless it can be established that he was hurt on the defendant's premises."

"Sustained," the judge said.

"I'm confused, Your Honor," I said.

"So am I," the judge replied. "But our confusion does not convert improper questions into proper ones. Try it this way: 'Was your son hurt on premises belonging to the railroad?'"

"I object to that question on the grounds that the ownership of the premises has not been established," Werhli said.

"Well, I'll have to sustain that objection," the judge said. "But, in the interest of getting this trial over with before Christmas, could you agree that the railroad owns the yards where this boy was hurt?"

"Of course," Mr. Werhli said. "I would be most happy to stipulate to that fact if such a stipulation were requested by my learned colleague."

"I request it," I said.

"You request what?" Werhli asked.

I couldn't remember.

"I stipulate that the railroad yards where the boy was injured belong to the railroad," Werhli said, coming to my rescue.

It was a long day, with several long days following. When the evidence was in the judge instructed the jury as follows:

> The negligence of the mother, if any, in failing to exercise due care for
> the safety of her child, prevents the mother from recovering any sum
> from the defendant for the child's injuries, despite the fact that you
> may also find the railroad was negligent. If you find the mother's neg-
> ligence contributed to the accident you will return a verdict for the
> railroad.

The jury was out about ten minutes and returned a verdict for the railroad. A nice motherly woman hurried up to me.

"Mr. Spence," she said. She began to weep. "We didn't have any choice." She was sobbing now. "The judge told us to return a verdict for the railroad if the mother was negligent. That mother should have been watching her child. And," she added, wiping her nose, "it might not hurt if you learned how to ask a simple question. I could have done better." Before I could think of what to say, she turned and ran away with those fast little steps women used to take in the days of four-inch-high spiked heels.

Then I watched the mother help her small boy get settled into his crutches,

Gerry Spence and Frank Hill.

and I watched the child hobble out of the courtroom, his mother in her cheap cotton dress holding on to him. She never looked at me. She never said an unkind word to me. She just went on out through the door. The sight still bites at my heart. I had lost my first case—lost it because I was not a good lawyer. Judge Parker was right. My shadow should never have fallen across the door of a courthouse.

Frank Hill, a returning air force pilot from the Korean War, was as tall as I, but broader chested with a square, handsome face and blue eyes and a full head of thick black hair. He was nearly fifteen years my senior. Every woman who ever met Frank Hill loved him. But he wasn't a lady's man. Every mother wanted him for a son. Every child would have loved to have him as a father. He dropped by the office one day. Said he was canvassing the state looking for a place to practice and wondered if I needed a partner.

He had grown up in Wheatland, Wyoming, had graduated from the University of Wyoming Law School in 1947, and after the war had been recalled to the air force, where he had served again, this time as a member of the judge-advocate staff at Maxwell Air Force Base in Alabama. There he married a southern belle with a viscous southern accent, Katherine, and by this time they had two boys, Frank Parker, eight, and William, five. I didn't know if we could make a living for the whole bunch of us or not. I was having trouble making ends meet, and our oldest daughter, Kerry, had been born on September 24, 1952, a month after we moved to Riverton. Who could predict whether two Wyoming lawyers could muster a living for their families in that way-off cowtown where men were men and most didn't need lawyers?

I have never known a man like Frank Hill, who could win your confidence in ten minutes and never betray it for a lifetime. I didn't need a partner—but I needed somebody to talk to. It was getting pretty lonely up there in the old offices of Franklin B. Sheldon. We formed the partnership of Spence and Hill on Thursday, August 27, 1953, almost a year to the day after I had come to Riverton as the $200-a-month wet-eared employee of Franklin B. Sheldon. But at least I knew one thing: I knew how to examine an abstract.

Making a living didn't prove to be easy. We billed our clients in accordance

with the Fremont County Bar Minimum Fee Schedule. Once in a while a
nobody in town would get a divorce. Anybody who was anybody had a happy
marriage—the same being a requirement for admission into even the outer
fringes of Riverton society—so mostly you couldn't tell who really had the good
marriages and who didn't. Occasionally we examined an abstract or two. I got a
fifty-dollar-a-month retainer from Midvale Irrigation District, the one steady
client I inherited from Frank Sheldon. Frank Hill got a job as city attorney and
dumped his meager salary into the partnership. We were able to glean a few
dollars from the collections we made for the Credit Bureau, and picked up
twenty-five or thirty dollars now and again from an insurance subrogation case,
collecting back from the party at fault the monies the company had paid its own
insured in one of those hundred-dollar fender benders. Got a third of what we
collected.

One day I came to court to try a case against a well-known slicker in the
county, who had bought my client's hay and fed it to his sheep, but, as promised,
had refused to pay my client, an old homesteader, when the slicker sold his
sheep. When we came to court the slicker, of course, claimed the hay was defective. The farmer, an old man with crooked legs and a bent back, took the stand
to testify about how good his hay was. He was wearing a clean pair of bib overalls, a denim shirt buttoned up at the collar, and his farmer shoes, newly shined.

Judge Sheldon, already on the bench, waited patiently for the farmer to get
settled in the witness stand before he attacked. "Get that man off the witness
stand," he yelled down at me.

"Why?" I asked, astounded. "What's the matter?"

"Don't you ask why! You get him off of there!" Sheldon's face was the color
of a taillight at midnight.

"What's wrong Your Honor?" I asked again.

"You know this court's rule. It's posted out there on the bulletin board. 'It is
the *attorney's* duty to properly dress his witnesses before they take the stand.'
This witness does not comply with my court rule that proper court attire
includes a *coat*."

"I ain't got no problem with that," the farmer said, stepping down. In a few
minutes he returned wearing a heavy winter sheepskin coat. The coat had been
lying in the back of his pickup for an emergency, but mostly for his old dog to
lie on. He took the stand—it was the middle of July and ungodly hot in that old
uninsulated upstairs courtroom.

The judge, who in the meantime had retired to chambers, took the bench
once more, and looked down to see that his court rule had, at last, been com-
plied with. The coat was a disgrace, covered with dirt and grease and dog hair.
Again the judge turned every shade. His bounced up out of his chair, on the
brink of apoplexy.

"What kind of unethical skulduggery is this?" he cried.

"It's yer damn rule, Yer Honor," the farmer said. The judge was taken aback

by the willingness of the farmer to confront him. A long silence ensued while
the judge decided whether he wanted to take on the petulant old devil or not. I
was concerned for His Honor's well-being—this could turn into a cerebral hem-
orrhage or something. Finally the judge said in a very feeble voice, "Proceed."

I started the testimony: "The weather was hot and dry when you put up the
hay, wasn't it?" I asked.

"Leading," R. Lauren Moran, the slicker's lawyer, objected.

"Sustained," the judge ruled.

"Well, you were there, weren't you? You put the hay up, didn't you?"

"Leading!" Moran hollered in his deeply dramatic baritone, while he
grasped his lapels as if, were he to let them loose, he would go flying up through
the courthouse ceiling.

"Mr. Spence, I am sick and tired of your leading questions. If I hear one
more, you know what I'm going to do?"

"No, I don't know, Your Honor."

"Well, maybe you don't want to know," the judge replied, looking very
mean. I was stumped. Frank Hill, my partner, was sitting next to me. "Ask him
what the weather was like on the day he put the hay up."

"What was the weather like the day you put up your hay?"

" 'Putting up hay,' as Mr. Spence wants to call it, is a collective verb," Moran
said. "Putting up hay, as the jurors know," Moran turned and flashed them a
very evil smile, which was his best smile, "includes cutting the hay, raking it, cur-
ing it, bailing it, and stacking it. The question is too broad."

"Sustained," the judge ruled. The judge gave me another of his hard looks.
I would never be a trial lawyer. I wanted to run out of the courtroom. The trial
went on for a week and nothing much improved. I was constantly on the edge
of disaster with the judge. He thought I was being contentious and stubborn,
whereas I was really frightened and incompetent, but too proud to admit it.
Men, when they are afraid, cover their fear in whatever way they can. Some
men run. Some become impertinent or evasive. I became defiant and often
attacked where retreat would have served me better.

The second jury trial confirmed it: There was no hope for me as a trial
lawyer. No hope whatever. The work was too painful, and, with a judge like
Judge Sheldon, too dangerous. I'd be better off, safer, and making more money
shoveling clinker under the kiln at the cement plant in Laramie. Work eight
hours, take home better pay, and no one would be threatening to throw me in
the slammer.

Frank Hill and I sat on the concrete foundation supporting an old ball-
shooting cannon that adorned the front lawn of the courthouse in Lander, a relic
of the Civil War to remind people that we Americans are more famous for wars
than justice. Why not decorate the courthouse lawn with plows and baby cra-
dles? I was saying things like that when suddenly I blurted, "We are going to
lose this case."

Frank was silent. I knew he agreed. "You did the best you could," he said. "I couldn't have done any better." He himself had had little experience to begin with, and he didn't like to try cases. There wasn't a mean streak in the man anywhere, and you had to have a little meanness, an eagerness to battle at least, an ability to move in for the kill and to make the kill, and Frank Hill wasn't a killer. In the end he did more for his clients out of court through his kindness and his reason than most lawyers ever dreamed of accomplishing through the hurt and misery of a down and dirty trial.

"Well, I'm going to quit if we don't win this one," I said to Frank Hill.

"I never figured you for a quitter," Frank said. He gave me a pat on the back, and covered his own anxiety with that little chuckle of his.

In a few hours the jury returned its verdict. It was against our client, all right. The farmer trudged down to his pickup and patted the old dog, threw his sheepskin in the back, and the old dog lay down on it.

"Never figured on winning it, son. Don't worry none. But I wasn't gonna let that cheatin' son-of-a-bitch get away without a fight." Never saw the farmer again, probably couldn't make his bank payment that fall. And we were having trouble meeting our own bills, too. Both cases I'd lost were on a contingency—if I didn't win and collect for my client I didn't get paid. Yet I would have gladly forfeited any fee if only I had been a better lawyer and my clients could have won even a little justice.

Despite my unbroken record of losses in court, I attracted yet another old farmer client whose complaint was that the wild Canada geese were eating up his corn crop. My client was an old man too crippled to make it up the stairs to my office. Men get hurt on those farms. So I'd come down to the street level, sit in his pickup parked there on the side street of the Masonic Temple Building, and listen at close range to his ear-splitting rage.

"The damnable 'gob-ment,'" as he called the state, "oughta feed their own damn geese. I feed my chickens. I feed my cows. I take care of my livestock. The state oughta take care a theirs." He was shouting at the top of his lungs. Seemed to be some logic in his argument. The state sold licenses to hunters and made a fair profit on the business, but the Wyoming Game and Fish Commission wouldn't pay the old boy anything, claimed geese were migratory birds, that geese came under federal jurisdiction, and that therefore my client would have to sue the United States of America if he wanted compensation.

I sued the Wyoming Game and Fish Commission anyway. I argued that these were not migratory geese, these were local fellas born and raised in Fremont County. Besides, Wyoming undertook to regulate goose hunting, which prevented the state from claiming it had no responsibility. If the state had no jurisdiction, then the goose seasons the state had set all these years were void, and half the male population in Fremont County, who were avid goose hunters, had violated federal law by killing geese out of season. After consulting *Corpus Juris Secundum,* and after I had read all of Justice Blume's decisions, I'd gotten

so I could argue the various demurrers and motions pretty well. The court set
the case for trial, and just before trial the Game and Fish Commission caved in.
The state's lawyers didn't know I still hadn't learned how to ask a simple question. Probably they hadn't either.

Wyoming paid my client five hundred dollars, enough in those days to buy
corn for half the goose population of the entire state of Wyoming. I charged my
client fifty dollars. He was outraged. I was a jack-legged, no-good robbing shyster like all of those other lawyers. I was taking a crippled old man—fifty dollars
for typing up a few papers and filing them in the court, and then standing
there—and all I did was talk! Why, an honest laboring man putting in an honest day's work only got paid a dollar an hour. No jack-legged lawyer was worth
a dollar an hour, much less fifty dollars for just that paper filing and talking. Said
he was going to report me to the bar. But he didn't.

The principal thing I'd inherited from Franklin B. Sheldon was the obligation to pay the rent, and my accompanying agreement to pay him twenty-five
dollars a month for his brown, plastic-covered *Wyoming Statutes,* and his blue,
plastic-covered set of *Corpus Juris Secundum.* Frank Hill and I needed a regular income, one that would smooth out the hills and the valleys that left us desperate to pay our bills one month and with a dollar or two to spare the next. I
had a plan.

One afternoon I drove the twenty-five miles to Lander to proposition the
Honorable William A. Smith for a job. He was the county and prosecuting attorney for Fremont County. I could make a good case that he needed me. As I
drove through the Wind River Reservation heading for Lander, I practiced my
speech. I drove past the small Indian shacks, a single rusted stove pipe pro-
tuding from a tarpaper roof, a half dozen old wrecked cars sitting in front. You
could drive through the reservation and understand the Indian's function in
Fremont County. It was his purpose in life, so far as the white man was concerned, to buy up all of the old junker cars the local used-car peddlers would
have otherwise had to haul off to the junkyard themselves, and to pledge the
Indians' allotment checks, month after month, to pay for them.

I drove on through the quaint old coal mining town of Hudson, now abandoned to three businesses, all bars, and as I drove on I practiced my speech
aloud.

"Mr. Smith, you are a very important and busy man. You shouldn't be
required to drive all the way to Riverton a couple of times a week to take care
of the county's legal business. You have many more important things to do
than that." I thought his interest would perk right up with that "important and
busy man" approach. I'd let the suspense gather with a few seconds' silence.
Then I'd continue. "What I propose, Mr. Smith, is a perfect solution. Since
the largest part of the county's population is at the Riverton end of the county,
you could hire me as your deputy. I could take care of things in Riverton for
you, and you could cover Lander, and all the citizens in the county would be

fully served, justice would be done, and the people would be happy"—and, of course, I didn't intend to add that I, Gerry Spence, would have a steady income.

Beyond Hudson the green alfalfa meadows and the harvested fields of golden oat stubble, and after that, the sagebrush and rolling hills dotted with Hereford cattle, made a rumpled bed quilt of the land. At the edge of the quilt, the Popo Agie came rolling down the valley in no special hurry. The river ran past dilapidated corrals and grayed barns, their roofs sunken like old sway-backed horses. Towering narrow-leafed cottonwoods bordered the stream, their yellow freshly fallen leaves the shape of squinting cat's eyes. As I approached the town of Lander, the front range of the Wind Rivers lunged up, so close, so blue, so long, so endless that although you could see for sixty miles in either direction, you could detect neither their beginning nor their end, nor see the mighty, jagged, snow-covered peaks shielded from view by the mountains in the foreground. The highway sign at the edge of town read ELEVATION 5,357 FEET, POPULATION 4,623.

William A. Smith had long aligned himself with power, big power. From the first he had joined up with Harry Harnsberger, who had been the most famous and fearsome of trial attorneys in the County's history. If you were in trouble or wanted to scare off your enemies, you hired Harry Harnsberger. His hair was antiseptically white, his translucent baby skin revealing the tiny vascular red rivulets often observed in the antediluvian male. He was erudite to the extreme and unctuous and dangerous as grease on the floor. He even had Franklin B. Sheldon cowed.

Before Harnsberger had been appointed as the attorney general of the State of Wyoming, Harnsberger and Smith had been partners, and they had had it pretty much their own way. In fact, they ran Fremont County. Following Smith's election as the county and prosecuting attorney, Harnsberger owned a part of the First National bank, and after Harnsberger, Smith continued to represent the bank, the Fremont County government, its commissioners and all of its elected officers. As the prosecutor, he had the power to bring down the entire force of the state on any citizen's head. Add to that the merciless power of money in representing the biggest bank in town and you could easily and rightly conclude that Will Smith ran the county. He thought so, too. And he did so with a kind of negligent arrogance. You could pick up on it right away, the way some folks look down on you as if you were an uncouth aborigine who had nothing intelligent to say nor any right to say it. Perhaps he inherited insolent poses from Harry Harnsberger. He was the master of patronization. When you were around him, you felt like a six-year-old who had just been patted on the head by the teacher.

Smith's offices, like Sheldon's, looked down on the Main Street of Lander, where the Native Americans from the Shoshoni side of the reservation came to town to do their business—in those days, mostly to drink up as much dollar-a-bottle wine as they could find dollars for. "Got a dollar. Gimme bottle a tokay. Okay?"

Cowboys from miles around in old battered pickups, also came to Lander, their dogs chained by training to the back of the truck, their rifles slung across the pickup's rear window. Nobody locked the doors of his truck or his house. From Smith's office you could see the newpaper office, the old Fremont Hotel with its false front, the bar next door where the cowboys hung out, a couple of more bars down the street, and if you got up close and looked out the window to the far right, you could see the Lander State Bank. On the opposite end of Main Street the feed store with its corrugated steel elevator rose up as the highest structure in town.

I headed up the stairs, my heart pounding, my belly spasming in sympathy. To cut the squeaking of the stairs in half, I took two steps at a time. The offices up there smelled like a hundred years of connivance and trickery. The black, hand-painted letters on the door read: SMITH AND HAYS, ATTORNEYS AND COUN-SELORS AT LAW.

I strolled big as you please into Mr. William A. Smith's office wearing my said wedding suit, the said white shirt and the red tie with the painted feather. I walked right up to Smith's petite blond secretary and told her I had private business with Mr. Smith. She thumbed through her appointment book like a maître d' with a room full of empty tables.

Was he expecting you? No, he wasn't. After an hour's wait—and no one had emerged from his office—she finally ushered me in. Smith got up from behind a large walnut desk—plate glass saving the top from the careless scratches of clients. A neat pile of papers lay close to his right hand, a marble pen holder with twin gold pens in their holsters stood up front, all the more handy for the client to sign on the dotted line. Picture of his smiling wife. His diplomas, all the way back to high school, including one certifying he was a member of the Lander Chamber of Commerce, provided an impressive array on the wall. The carpet was thick, shaggy and red. You could tell a lot about a lawyer by what he put on his floor. Judge Sheldon had plain worn linoleum on his. Said he didn't want to scare the farmers away. "They see carpet, they figure they're going to pay big fees. They see linoleum, they feel right at home."

Smith shook my hand—soft, no conviction there. He offered me a chair and a cigarette. I took the chair, skipped the cigarette—Old Golds, I think. I was smoking long Chesterfields in those days—got more for your money, I thought. He lit his cigarette and let the smoke drift out and then upward through his nose, for a second take on the same drag. Nose looked sort of like George Washington's.

"Well, what's on your mind?" he asked, getting right to the point, a busy man, soft, portly fellow in his early forties with prematurely graying hair and reddish, chunky cheeks, the kind, if they were on a boy, a spinster aunt would want to pinch. He offered a habitual smile, one that always looked the same whether in response to amusement, joy or rancor, not a friendly smile. I gave him back my own best, the widest I could muster. His stayed the same.

My head awhirl, I launched into my speech, almost perfectly. Thank God I'd practiced it. When I'd finished, he smashed out his cigarette and said, "Not interested." Same smile. "Already hired Jack Nicholas, one of your classmates, I believe. Thanks anyway," and with nothing more William A. Smith stood up, and I had to stand up, too, and then he politely showed me the door. I took the steps down to the street one step at a time. Jack Nicholas. He'd hired Jack Nicholas. Well, he'd passed the bar the first time. I should have known better. I could never work for the likes of William A. Smith. I didn't have the style or the breeding. I hadn't belonged to a fraternity. I didn't have the social graces. I didn't know how to be charming up front, to carry on clever, entertaining conversation and underneath, be thinking whatever such minds were always plotting.

During those years of the early 1950s, rumblings among the citizenry occasionally bubbled up from the great pool of voter apathy concerning the proliferation of "crime and corruption" in the county, as the broad spectrum of unlawful carryings-on in Fremont County were collectively referred to. Everybody knew of the "cat house" in Hudson above the El Toro nightclub; the "Little Yellow House" in Riverton, a long-established institution of harlotry there, and the Blue Goose Cafe in Shoshoni, where the "girls" were waitresses by day and available for amatory pleasures by night. Gambling was openly carried on in that wide spot in the road at the other end of the county, a one-horse cowtown called Dubois—crap tables, slots, poker games, you name it. As for serving liquor to minors—if the bartender could detect a sprouting whisker and a dollar in a kid's pocket, he could drink with the best of them. Sunday closings and legal hours set by law were mostly ignored. In short, Fremont County was wide open.

At the urging of practically no one, I decided I was going to run for county and prosecuting attorney. Just as well. Frank Hill and I didn't have much of anything else to do. He'd run the office. I'd run the politics. I joined the Kiwanis Club, where we pledged allegiance to the flag every Thursday, sang "Ka-ka-ka-kawanis" and other songs out of the *Kiwanis Song Book,* and we listened to dry speeches, mostly about local politics, and although the avowed purpose of the organization was community service, the real purpose was more about business among its members than altruism for the "people out there." I spoke at the Flag Day Ceremony at the Town Park on behalf of Elks Lodge No. 1693. I cochaired the Boy Scout Fund Drive and got my picture on the front page of *The Riverton Ranger.* On June 22, 1954, at age twenty-five, I announced my candidacy for county and prosecuting attorney in the Republican primary against Mr. William A. Smith. I made one promise: to clean up the county.

Things had settled down in Fremont County, the Korean War being over, the baby boom bursting from the bedrooms of the nation, couples just settling down, making a family, and making something of themselves. The South East

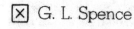

Ad for Spence's first campaign for county attorney.

Asia Treaty Organization that would drag us into Vietnam had been established, but with Eisenhower at the reins, the coach of state was trotting right along. My own campaign was naively conceived. I knocked on every door in every town in the county, beginning in Riverton, then in Lander, and after that in Dubois, eighty miles to the west. I knocked on every door in Shoshoni, twenty miles to the east. On the maps of the town (you could find one in front of the telephone directory), I marked off each city block as I finished knocking on the doors in that block. If no one answered the door, I left a handwritten note on my campaign literature. The note read, "Sorry I missed you. Hope you'll vote for me." I signed the note, stuck it in the door and went on. But before I left I also stuck a check in the door. The check was drawn on the Bank of Good Government and read, "Good for four years of honest service to the people."

I drove out to the Wind River Reservation that adjoined the town of Riverton. The Arapahoes lived on the Riverton end of the reservation, where their allotment consumed the empty plains and high dry lands. No tipis anymore, of course; the rusted tin-sided shacks and raggedy tents marred the barren landscape. Whenever I saw any sign of life—an old plug swishing flies tied to a tree, chickens running loose, a skinny hound lying in the shade, a dirty-faced kid, his bare behind saluting the sun—I'd stop, a couple of Spence checks in my hands as my only weapons.

Day after day, I engaged in the infamous political sport known as "tipi tapping," which, in the parlance of the times, meant that I knocked at the doors on the little wooden shacks and lean-tos and stuck my head into the tents to ask the Native Americans I found there to be sure and go to the polls and vote for their pal, Gerry Spence. Most of the Indians had never met a politician who gave a damn about their vote, the conventional wisdom in 1954 being that the Indians were ignorant lumpens, too lazy to go to the polls, and if they did go the only way you could get them there was to first butcher and barbecue a steer, boil up a couple of washtubs full of beans, haul the Indians to the feed trough and immediately afterward haul them to the polls in the back of pickup trucks. Christ could feed the masses with his bread and fishes for his campaign, and in the same way, the big-time politicians fed the Indians beef and beans for theirs. I had nothing to feed them except a little honest attention.

One day in the heat of August I walked up to the door of an Indian shack, where I could make out the image of an old man sitting on the dirt floor in the dark. He was wrapped up in a blanket like one of those Indian dolls, his big old broken handle of a nose protruding, his eyes staring off into space, and in his right hand he held a large knife with which he was absently whittling at a piece of wood. I gave a timid knock.

Gerry Spence and old chief.

"I'm Gerry Spence. I'm here campaigning for the job of county attorney," I said.

"Jesus H. Christ!" he cried. "Ya scared me plumb outta my hide. Never do that to a man. I mighta throwed this knife right through ya like I done to Custer's men." The old man struggled to his feet. "Ain't ya got no respec' fer a ol' man's meditation?" It was Sunday afternoon. "What ya say yer name was?"

"Gerry Spence."

"Never heerd of ya." The ceiling and the walls of the shack were black with soot and the room smelled like the den of a dozen grizzlies fresh out of hibernation. The old man gave a kick at a couple of yellow hounds lying on a blanket covered with dog hair and dirt. "Ya can sit down here beside me," he said. I sat down. He rolled a cigarette with gnarled shaking hands and handed me the Zig-Zag papers and his sack of Bull Durham. Then he turned to me with sagging old eyes, and while he watched me he lit up.

"I was wanting you to vote for me for county and prosecuting attorney," I said.

"What for?" he asked, lipping his cigarette. "Don't need no prosecuting attorney. When I was a boy we just shot them white-eyed sons-a-bitches." I struggled with the paper and tobacco. "Here, gimme that, boy," he said, whereupon he proceeded to roll one for me. He opened his wet, toothless old mouth and licked the paper closed, stroked it a couple of times between his dirty thumb and first three fingers, and handed it to me with the matches. I closed my eyes, put the wet cigarette in my mouth and lit up. On election day I carried every precinct on the reservation. The old man turned out to be the chief of the Arapahoes.

        ❖   ❖   ❖

The Riverton Ranger proudly announced the election results.

> Riverton Attorney, G. L. Spence, staged the upset of the day Tuesday
> when he won the Republican nomination for Fremont County and
> Prosecuting Attorney in a landslide vote, defeating incumbent William
> A. Smith by more than 500 votes. Young Spence was the favorite of
> the election, winning Riverton with a resounding majority and coming
> within an ace of beating Smith in Lander where he trailed Smith by
> only 12 votes.

I was opposed in the general election by Bud Spriggs, son of the venerable
old lawyer, John Spriggs, who represented the criminals and the Indians of Fremont County. If you were represented by John Spriggs, it meant to most that
you were a criminal, a drunk, an Indian, or all three. But the old man cared
about poor people, and he didn't give the first damn about the finer points of
the law. Only interested in the Constitution. Every defense, every case, was a
pure constitutional issue. He hand-typed his own pleadings, single spaced with
a lot of cross-outs, and provided you the fifth carbon copy, so fuzzy and faint you
couldn't read it anyway. And he had the foolish idea, then held in universal dis-
favor in Fremont County, that Indians had rights the same as white people. I
watched him many a time standing there jabbing his old crooked finger up at
the judge, pacing the floor like an ancient street preacher, hollering about the
rights of "this fellow," as he called his client, having forgotten his name, under
the United States Constitution. I saw his hoary old head tremble and heard his
blistery old voice crack under the strain as he staggered across the courtroom
floor, nearly exhausted from the fight. And I saw people smile at him in amusement, but in their hearts, I knew they admired John Spriggs. Judges spurned
him, and Harry Harnsberger despised him because the old man claimed Harnsberger stole a gold mine from him, and he had fought Harnsberger all the way
to the Supreme Court and back I don't know how many times. But the old man
had his principles, one of which was he would never give up, not so long as you
hadn't cut his head off yet. You couldn't buy him. And you couldn't get rid of
him. And although he was rustic and not too rooted in the latest law books, he
would fight for his client. The judges and the lawyers knew that too, although
publicly they would not speak out for old John Spriggs.

Young Bud Spriggs had moved back to Lander just in time to run for county
and prosecuting attorney against me. Like his father, he was a Democrat. In
1954 the Republicans ruled the country and, as they usually did, owned
Wyoming as well. Fremont County went every which way—depending on who
was running. Peewee McDougall, the sheriff, always won as a Democrat. The
county occasionally sent a Democrat to the legislature, but all things being
equal, Fremont County usually joined the rest of the state on the Republican
side.

A few days before the election, I took out a large ad in the Riverton paper proclaiming that, while both my opponent and I were native sons, I was the only candidate who could claim he was Wyoming educated, the only one who was a practicing Fremont County attorney, the only candidate professionally listed as a Wyoming lawyer, the only continuous resident of the county, the only parent and homeowner and civic leader, and I was experienced in the law. I was, in short, one of the folks while my opponent was, I implied, a mere carpetbagger who had moved into the county for the sole purpose of running for political office.

I won the general election by a landslide. Led the ticket. And, at twenty-five, I became the youngest prosecutor in Wyoming's history. I had asked for the job. But, as the saying goes, a person should be careful what he asks for—lest he get it.

Prosecutor to Push Clean-Up

Spence Asserts Attempt on Life Hastens Action

Gunshot Misses County Attorney Probing Liquor

LANDER, Wyo., March 28 (P) —A county prosecuting attorney today said he escaped death when a revolver bullet shattered the window of his car after he was forced off the road by a dark sedan.

The attorney, G. L. Spence, said he has received three threatening telephone calls within the last two weeks warn-

LANDER (P)—A young county attorney pledged Tuesday to continue to crack down on liquor violators in Fremont County despite a mobster-like attempt on his life.

Prosecuting Atty. G. L. Spence told Monday how he escaped death when a revolver bullet shattered the window of his car last Friday night after he was forced to the road by a dark sedan.

The attempt on the 28-year-old crusading attorney's life came after he had received three phone calls within two weeks. The calls warned him to halt prosecution of Fremont county liquor dealers.

Spence said the shooting incident has only increased "my determination to take care of the situation if I can."

TWO CLUBS CLOSED

Two clubs in the county have been shut down recently for selling liquor to minors and on Sunday.

Spence said details of the ab-

they thought the calls were made by cranks.

Spence was elected county prosecutor last fall on a campaign pledge to clean up illegal sales of liquor. Since then the District Court has ordered the closure of two bars in the county.

The Red Rocks Lodge at Dubois was shut down after being charged with more than 30 counts of selling liquor to minors.

The Union Bar in Riverton was closed after being charged with 40 counts of selling liquor to minors and Sunday sales.

G. L. SPENCE

Spence's "clean-up the county" campaign.

NO ONE SPEAKS so vociferously, so adamantly and with such conviction as the freshly reformed. I had promised to clean up the county and, by damn, I was going to keep my promise! Moreover, few had a more intimate, inside knowledge of the carryings-on of gamblers and prostitutes as did I.

Yet an inner voice argued against me: "How can you be such a magnificent hypocrite, such a Pharisee, such a champion of demagoguery? You, the whoremonger and gambler, now the double-faced pettifogger, how are you going to clean up gambling and prostitution? You're like a repenting whore who joins the church, and wants to lead the choir the very first day. You make Elmer Gantry look saintly. One thing: You better hope nobody finds out who you really are."

"Look. I was only a kid then," I fought back. "It's not who I *was*, but who I *am*. And a little firsthand experience with sin ought to come in handy to those who sincerely want to clean it up." I made even better arguments: "Who is the better physician—the one who has contracted the disease he treats and knows its pain, or the one who has never been sick in his life? I think there's a lot to be said for electing public servants who have experienced the flip side of virtue, who know something of the frailties of the species. How can they who have never walked in the shadow judge those who have?"

And so I argued, "If experience in the art of sinning qualifies the reformer, you are exquisitely qualified." Perhaps, I thought, that is what true atonement is about. Still, Fremont County should beware of a reformed sinner, especially one with newfound power and not much experience in wielding it. Nothing is more awesome to behold than he who has sinned casting the first stone.

My days as a whoremonger, drunk, and preeminent scoundrel came to an unheralded end when I married Anna. For me, that tawdry life was over. I was one of the leading citizens of the town—in my eyes, *the* leading citizen now that I had been cloaked with the power of the state. My juvenile past was irrelevant. A man grows up—that's how I saw it. In the early winter of 1955, shortly after I took office, I sent letters to all the bar owners in the county directing them to comply with the liquor and gambling laws of the state. I intended to strictly enforce those laws I told them. Following my letter I met with Peewee McDougall, the sheriff, who had been reelected at the same time I had won my office. He'd been the sheriff during those prior years when William A. Smith had been the county attorney. This had been their county. I was as wary of McDougall as he was of me.

"What about all of the whorehouses and the gambling?" I asked. "And the kids in the bars?"

"They ain't hurtin' nothin', Gerry," he said. He was short and stocky with a little potbelly that he tried to hold in. But he also possessed a tough streak that nobody wanted to mess with. He had the face of a guy who'd been in a fight with a grizzly and won, a wry smile, and a quiet humor. "They was here before I came. Kind of a tradition in the county, Gerry." To Peewee I was nothing but a tight-ass whipper-snapper. "I never go lookin' fer trouble." I knew he and Smith, although on opposite sides of the ticket, had been good friends. Peewee had a way of getting along.

"I'll tell you how it's gonna be," I said, trying to look tough myself. "They are gonna clean up or clear out. You know 'em. You tell 'em if they aren't squeaky clean in thirty days I'm moving in." Just like in the movies.

"I wouldn't get too tough too soon," Peewee said, "that is, if you are looking for a little advice." Peewee didn't come up much past my shoulder, but his big hat and cowboy boots helped some.

"That's how its gonna be, Peewee," I said. And I left.

Thirty days later things were unchanged. I was getting embarrassed. People were asking questions: "When's this big-time cleanup of yours gonna happen?" I went to see Peewee again, and the conversation was practically the same. "Look," I said. "If you're on the take, you shouldn't be. If you're not, people will think you are anyway. If you're honest, there's nothing in it for you except trouble. I want this county closed down. If you don't want to do it I'll call a grand jury."

He thought that one over. "Well, if that's the way you want it," he finally said.

"Why don't you go close down the Union Bar at Hudson for starters?" I said. "I drove through Hudson last Sunday and they were wide open."

He shrugged. "I'll look into it," he said. A couple of weeks later nothing had changed. When I asked him about it he said, "I tried to pull a little raid at Hudson the other night. But somebody tipped 'em off 'fore I got there with my men."

I expected as much. "Well, let's do something different, then," I said. "We'll raid 'em next Sunday afternoon. Just you and I know that, right?"

"Right," he said, already seeing where I was going.

"And if anybody tips them off it will have to be either you or me, right?"

"I guess so," he said.

"We'll meet at three in the afternoon next Sunday. You call your two most trusted deputies and tell them to meet us at the edge of town. Don't tell them what we have in mind. When we walk into the Union Bar, still nobody but you and me will know what we're up to until we're there, right?" That time it worked.

The saloon was situated in an old brick building fronting on the main street of Hudson, which was merely the highway passing through. Inside the bar, one of those old, hand-carved wooden affairs, took up most of the length of the building. The ceiling was covered with ancient tin-embossed panels, long ago painted over and dimmed with smoke.

On the back bar and in front of a cracked mirror stood a long row of various whiskeys, all standing mute and straight as sober soldiers, and behind them a row of gins and vodkas, a few cheap wines, and a liqueur or two. A couple of punch boards sat within easy reach of the bartender. And above the bottles and up against the mirror hung a Schlitz Beer sign in yellow neon, giving off the holy light of Sunday and reminding the congregation that Schlitz was the sacrament of choice.

A dozen locals snuggled up to the bar, some slouching over it. Most were drinking Coors. A few old boys wearing their cowboy hats drank Hamm's. I walked in with Peewee and his deputies. The customers hardly paid us any attention until Peewee began to apologize as he and his deputies took down their names. The lawmen moved slowly down the bar and, following my direction, picked up the beer bottles, capped them with old caps, and labeled them for evidence. The next morning I drove to Lander, met with Judge Sheldon, and he signed an order temporarily suspending the license of the Union Bar until a hearing could be had, and when the hearing was finally held a month or so later Judge Sheldon didn't hesitate. He ordered the license of the Union Bar suspended, permanently. "That oughta teach the liquor dealers we mean business," I said to Peewee.

He didn't say anything back right away. After a long hard pause he said,

"Kinda tough for just a little Sunday drinking, don't ya think, Gerry? Take a man's livelihood away. Those folks have a hard time making it."

"Maybe," I said. "But maybe the rest of the county will get the message."

Long accustomed to Peewee's laissez-faire version of the law, I was perceived as a wild-eyed firebrand. But they were going to get the message or I'd know the reason why. I closed the bar at the Red Rocks Lodge on thirty-five counts of liquor law violations—mostly selling to minors. I closed the Sky Club at the airport in Riverton on another of those secret raids by Peewee and his deputies where they found the bar open early Sunday morning, an unlicensed bar operating in the basement and a twenty-one table in operation in violation of the gambling laws of the state. The gamblers and the pimps in Fremont County were as obdurate as a mule headed home, and about as smart. They hadn't reckoned with the simple idea that this twenty-five-year-old pipsqueak of a prosecutor had made promises, and thought he should keep them.

I was determined to shut down the county's whorehouses. A man who doesn't keep his word is no man—the issue was that simple. And I ought to give myself credit: I tried to do my duty in a way that any gentleman would under the circumstances. I went personally to talk to the madam at the Blue Goose, man to man, as it were. The café in Shoshoni, occupied the ground floor space where the bus stopped, and the "girls" lived and worked upstairs.

The Greyhound bus from Casper stopped at the joint twice a day: once on its way to Riverton, to allow the passengers to relieve themselves and grab a bite and a cup of coffee after the long hundred-mile haul across the empty prairies; and once on the way back to Casper again, to allow the passengers to prepare for the long, nonstop trip in the other direction. The café was indistinguishable from most roadside truck stops, the tin Coca-Cola sign out front swinging to and fro in the wind, big store windows in front a reminder that the room had once housed a retail business, now long gone. The walls were papered-over plaster covering most of the cracks, the high spots bulging through. The high ceilings were those old tin-embossed panels, and the long U-shaped counter was covered with marble patterned linoleum worn through in places where it had been scrubbed to the wood. The oiled wooden floors needed sweeping, and on the counter sat a jar collecting itinerant change for the Girl Scouts.

The place smelled of stale grease, cheap perfume and cigarette smoke. Suddenly, as if the show had begun, the noise erupted in the Blue Goose when the bus came through. The driver hollered out to each of the girls as if each were his best friend. "Hey, Minnie, baby, how's my Minnie baby? And June Bug. If you aren't the cutest punkins a man ever laid eyes on! Gimme a cup a coffee. Black like I like my women!"

"How ya doin' Roy," the woman said, the one with the black hair, the one reading the newspaper and getting up. "Missed ya a lot, honey." She poured him a cup of coffee.

Three other women came charging down the stairs, immediately transforming themselves into swishing waitresses, all standing behind the counter, too many for the six passengers who got off the bus, not including the driver. They hustled here and there doing practically nothing, wiggling, hollering. They stuck their faces with their powdered cheeks and bright red painted mouths into the faces of the customers, all men, demanding to know, in their double-entendre clear to all, "Whatcha want, Mac?" "What'll it be, big boy. Huh? Speak up there, honey. I ain't gonna bite ya, ya know. Ha. Ha." They were there to sell you more than mother's apple pie.

The girls didn't know me that afternoon. Never paid me any attention after I ordered my coffee. All men start looking alike after a while, they say, and I looked like the rest of them, except I was skinnier than most, younger than most, and I wore a suit coat, a white shirt and a tie. Probably a traveling salesman.

The madam wasn't your usual worn-out working girl turned whorehouse mother. She was more the grandmotherly type, past sixty I supposed, a woman who would have been more comfortable in a front porch rocking chair with her knitting, her fat legs covered by a nice white apron and her hair all done up in a respectable bun, rather than herding around a bunch of frazzled prostitutes who had been rejected in the better houses along the Union Pacific and who, like old movie stars, were taking the best jobs they could find in their waning years.

The madam motioned me over to her table, where she sat smoking a ciga-rette. She knew who I was, and she probably knew why I was there. She made a checkmark with her head to one of the girls who came over with the round Pyrex pot and poured us both a cup of old coffee. I dumped in the sugar and the cream and stirred it for a long while before I looked up at her. Then I said, "Minnie, I came to ask you to close your house down."

"What house?" she said in mock offense. "I run a respectable restaurant here. Can't ya see?"

"I'm not here to ask you to close your restaurant," I said.

"This is America," she said.

"Right, and this is Fremont County, America, and it's against the law to run a whorehouse in Fremont County, America."

"You got nothin' on me," she said. "Ask any of my customers here. Hey, Roy," she hollered to the bus driver, "is this a respectable restaurant or ain't it?"

"Damn right," Roy said. He grabbed the bill of his official Greyhound cap, pulled it down low to look tough and stood up. "You need a little backup there, Minnie?"

"I don't need no backup," she said. Then she saw things were getting tight and she laughed, the kind that sounded like distant, broken thunder. "Listen, Spence, here at my restaurant I got bankers for customers, and I got preachers for customers. I was here before you was even thought of. Now you're a big fish in a little puddle. You don't want to get too big for your puddle. So if you'd take a little advice from an old lady," the bus driver was making our conversation his business, "why don't you go home to your wife and your kids and mind your own business?"

"I recognize you're an institution in Shoshoni, Minnie," I said. "But everything has a life of its own. It's time we shut the doors on this one."

"Is there something I could do to help?" she asked.

"Yes, you can give these girls of yours a little separation pay and send 'em on their way."

"You didn't get my meaning," she said. She could raise an eyebrow.

"I got your meaning," I said.

"Well, if you're interested in these girls," she said, "most of them can't get a job anywhere else."

"They'll find a way," I said. Then she laid her big rap on me about how she was serving the community, that this was the sheep-raising end of the county, and that she serviced the sheepherders and the cowboys, that if she wasn't there with her girls, the Mexican herders would come to town and rape the townspeople's women, and I would have to answer to them for having shut down the Blue Goose. She was an honest-to-God public servant. Every county attorney before me, every sheriff, and even the mayor of Shoshoni recognized that she and her girls performed a good and proper service, and therefore, by God, she was not going to close down the house.

"Well, we shall see, Minnie," I said, getting up. "Don't forget, I came in here like a gentleman and gave you fair warning."

"You can talk to my attorney," she hollered at me as I left the café. "You can't prove a thing!"

As I walked out, I nudged the bus driver with an elbow. "Greyhound's gonna love knowin' that its Casper-to-Shoshoni driver is pimpin' for Minnie." Then I walked on out into one hell of a Wyoming blizzard, the snow blowing across the road and piling up drifts in long graceful lines like dunes in the desert.

I took the problem to bed with me. Minnie had it figured out, all right. She'd given a lot more thought to her business than I had. How was I going to prove she was running a house? Who would testify against her? She counted among her steady customers some of the community leaders in the rough little cowtown of Shoshoni as well as some of the old pillars of power in Riverton. I knew about the banker and the preacher she mentioned. She probably had a little trick or two going with the Shoshoni deputies.

Then along about morning when the mind is easy, and on the outskirts of consciousness, a plan came to me. The whores in Shoshoni weren't my problem. They were the mayor's problem. The next week I invited the mayor of Shoshoni to my house for supper. Beefsteak and all. He knew something was up, all the polite talk, and just the two of us and my family there. He was nervous. Picked at his food as if he thought it might be poisoned. Hardly ate a thing.

When the kids were off to bed and Anna, knowing what was on my agenda, had disappeared, I said, "Mayor, I want the Blue Goose shut down."

He gave me a friendly smile, relieved to know it was something he thought he could handle. Bald-headed little guy, face like it had been taken in both hands, pulled down and pinched together. He'd been the town's plumber and handyman for twenty years. Wore a cowboy hat, like everybody else, and those old boots shined up for the occasion, but I doubt he'd ever been on a horse.

"Why, Gerry," he looked so innocent and sweet. "How can we do that? That house has been there a hunnert years. Why, it's just like Mount Rushmore or somethin'. And," he laughed, "it's the only industry Shoshoni has. Minnie—you know Minnie—is always a big contributor to the Girl Scouts and about anything else that comes along. Kids all go there and get a hell of a handout on Halloween. And who is going to take care of all them Mexican sheepherders that come to town?"

"Time to close it down," I said. "You're the mayor. I want to give you the chance to do it first."

He looked concerned. Then he tested me, his mouth barely large enough to form the words. "Let's face it. You couldn't close it anyway," he said. "Who would testify they'd ever been upstairs in the Blue Goose?"

"I'll tell you how I'm going to do it, because I know you're an honest man." He folded his arms tight across his chest against that preamble. "For the last months I've had a sheriff's deputy out there taking the license numbers of every car that's been parked anywhere near the Blue Goose between midnight and five in the morning. Think that one over for a minute." I gave him some thinking time. Then I went on. "Now, Mayor, there's a lot of interesting names on that list." The long, knowing look from me to him. "It's going to be an easy case to prove. All I have to do is call a grand jury, subpoena every person on that list as a witness, and we'll have a real big party. You could probably guess who the first witness is going to be." I let him think about that one, too. "How much time do you want to close her down?"

He didn't answer.

"In ten days, I'm going to call the grand jury."

Within the week the Blue Goose became a relic of the past. I never learned what the mayor said to Minnie, how he talked her into leaving town or where the "girls" found further employment. All I know is that one day there was a CLOSED sign on the café door.

The proprietors of the house in Hudson and the "Little Yellow House" in Riverton, both of which claimed grandfather rights for their operations, also warned me that rape by the randy cowboys and horny miners would become epidemic if their services were withdrawn. Nevertheless, at my similar urgings, both houses soon closed their doors.

People, like coins, have two sides, and the bottom side is not necessarily always down. Although I'd been elected on the promise that I'd clean up the county, now that their infamous institutions were closed, many folks didn't like it.

"How come you closed down our Little Yellow House?" some leading citizen would ask me. It was *their* Little Yellow House.

"Didn't you want it closed?"

"Who's going to take care of the sheepherders?"

"Prostitution is against the law. I'm doing my job."

"A little good clean playtime like that ain't no sin. Never hurt anybody. Besides, Doc Hamm"—he was the local chiropractor—"checks those girls out."

"Right," I said. Even Doc Hamm would have been hard pressed to explain how a chiropractor, a bone buncher, could run a test for venereal disease on "the girls." Doc Hamm had never been in a medical lab in his life. Probably inspected the girls, all right. At least that's what his handwritten certificate pinned up on the wall said:

This is to certify, that I, Doc Hamm, have inspected these girls and
they are free from all venereal disease whatsoever.
Signed: *Doc Henry E. Hamm*

Even the mothers at the Parent and Teachers Association meetings took the issue up.

"I know how evil that sort of thing is, and I definitely am not for prostitution in any shape, kind or form. But we have to balance which is the worst evil—a place for the cowboys to go, or the safety of our children." That was the speech from the town's leading mother.

I tried to combat the growing sentiment in support of the town's Little Yellow House. I gave a speech at the Kiwanis Club quoting statistics from the National Prosecutors Association to the effect that rape and prostitution were as irrelevant, one to the other, as robbery and bingo. I tried to explain that men rape, not out of uncontrollable passion, but out of a need to rape. The townfolk didn't understand the pathology of rape—that rape was the acted-out hostility of certain males of the species expressing their compulsive need, not for sex, but to injure females of their own species. People didn't understand such subtle arguments then. Men were men, concupiscent beasts that were likely to immediately attack anything female, from sheep to little girls, if they couldn't find a place to douse their passions in living adult female flesh.

When I was introduced by a citizen to a stranger in the county, I was as often introduced as "the man who closed down *our* Little Yellow House." Even today, if you go to Riverton these many years later and ask the trivia question, Who closed down Riverton's Little Yellow House?, 90 percent of the townspeople old enough to remember would be able to identify the miscreant. Everywhere I went people came up to me complaining about my closing down *their* Little Yellow House. That little joint next to the depot in Riverton turned out to be their furtive pride. And when the people jumped Peewee about closing their Little Yellow House, his stock reply was "Don't talk to me about it. Talk to

Spence. You know how things were before he come along." Peewee was a good politician and a regular sort who didn't get all bound up in those soul-searching philosophical questions of right and wrong. He left such questions to the preachers and the church ladies.

I could have debated the issue on behalf of prostitution from another stance: When there are no victims of crime, what about our freedom? Do we need the pious do-gooders telling us what is or isn't sin, to tell us what to do or not to do? I thought of my own revolt against my mother. Now, ironically, I found myself imposing her morals, her values, her religious views on a whole community of miners and cowboys and toughs. I was telling the bankers and cops and business-men and preachers, who sneaked in the back door of the Little Yellow House, what they should do with their out-of-hand libidos, or at least what they couldn't do with them. And the biblical verse came oozing up out of my past—you can't escape your own history, especially the early stuff: "Even so ye also outwardly appear righteous unto men, but within ye are full of hypocrisy and iniquity."

So I was a hypocrite. I could either be a hypocrite or violate my oath of office to enforce the law. I'd promised the voters. And I knew if I didn't enforce the law the next thing I'd hear would be, "Spence is on the take. The Little Yel-low House is running wide open and so is the house at Hudson." Didn't seem to me that an honest man had any choice. The Little Yellow House stayed closed. So did the house in Hudson. In the end, I pretty much cleaned up the county whether the good citizens liked it that way or not.

But I kept getting these threats, which I ignored. I received several anony-mous calls, one, a male voice, telling me, "We're gonna burn yer fuckin' ass good if ya don't lay off." Things like that. I hung up. I thought the warnings were from cranks or some old boy who wanted to drink his beer on Sunday afternoons at the Union Bar. I always maintained you're safest when you're get-ting threats. It's when you're not that you need to watch out. People don't usu-ally warn you if they're going to kill you. A woman who worked in one of the bars—didn't know her, didn't recognize the name—had called me several days earlier, tearfully imploring me to be careful, that she had heard that someone was going to kill me. She wouldn't say who it was. I thought her call was a clumsy attempt by the saloon keepers, through a barmaid on their payroll, to intimidate me.

Then on a dark, snowy March night in 1955, I was driving home from Lan-der, having spent the day in court, when a car pulled up behind me and began blinking its lights and blowing its horn. As I slowed down, the car wheeled around me, cut in front of me, and forced me to take the barrow pit. Just as my car came to a stop, someone in the car fired at me. The bullet entered the left rear window at an angle, missed me by a good foot. The car—I couldn't iden-tify it in the dark—sped away.

The bullet made a three-quarter-inch hole in the window as it passed through. Pieces of glass and lead showered my neck and head and were scat-

Assassin's bullet hole through Spence's rear left window.

tered throughout the car. I later recovered the spent bullet in the backseat, gave it to Peewee, and he sent it off to the FBI for identification.

One day Peewee came by my office to talk about some cases. When he got up to leave he said, "By the way, do you own a pistol?"

"Why, yeah," I said.

"What caliber?"

"A .357 Magnum. Smith and Wesson. Why?"

"Oh, nothing."

"What do you mean, 'nothing'?" I demanded.

"Oh," he said, "it was a .38 caliber that was shot into your car. A .357 is a .38 caliber."

"So what?" I demanded.

"Nothin'," he said. "Don't mean nothin' by it at all. Just curious."

Within a few days I was hearing the rumor around the county that I had shot the hole in my car for the publicity—as if I needed more. Peewee never solved the case. But I never blamed him for that. There wasn't much to go on except a mangled .38 caliber bullet that even the FBI couldn't match with anything. When Peewee questioned the woman who had warned me, she told him she couldn't say who the men were she had overheard that night. Drifters, maybe, she said, and after that night she never saw them again. I thought she knew more, but what was in it for her to spill it? People have to make a living.

The Thermopolis town paper from the adjoining county of Hot Springs lauded me mightily for cleaning up my county. "Lack of enforcement of liquor and gambling laws in that county has been a shameful violation of decency for many years," the paper editorialized. "There were a number of places in the county that had no respect for laws and some of them were mighty close to Hot Springs County which we felt was an intolerable situation." In the meantime, Thermopolis's own infamous house of ill repute was in full and wondrous operation and had been for many years. The Hot Springs County prosecutor, I was told, sometimes played the piano in the Thermopolis bawdy house, got drunk with the girls, and had a glorious time up there for many years to come.

As the county's prosecutor I began to try more cases, but I never perfected the skill of asking a simple, lucid question. Over the years, compassionate judges have come to accept my deficiency, and they make room for it. Opposing attorneys have learned that to continually object to my questioning usually results in the jury's rejection of them. Some students of trial technique theorize that mine is an innovative style in which direct and cross-examination, and leading and direct questions are somehow deftly blended into an effective interrogation of a witness. But in truth, I have always been more interested in telling a story to the jury through the witnesses than in demonstrating a flawless ability to comply with sterile rules of evidence.

As soon as I had taken the oath of office as the county's new prosecuter, the down-and-out came flooding into my office to see if they could wrest a better kind of justice from me than they had received from my predecessor. Most couldn't afford a lawyer, or the lawyer they could afford provided little effective assistance. Justice, therefore, often lay in the hands of the county attorney himself. Would he prosecute? What would the charges be? What punishment would he recommend to the judge?

One of the first cases that came to me as the county's new prosecutor involved a "breed," as Indians who lived on the reservation but looked white were called in those days. The man had been charged with writing a bad check. A Fremont County jury of all whites had convicted Howey, and he'd been sentenced to the penitentiary. He lived with his family on a small allotment, and his sister, a woman as slothful and filthy as Howey was simple, came to see me.

"Won't you please help us?" Her words came slowly and hard, her eyes as dull as mud. I felt sorry for her. "That Bill Smith fella put Howey in the pen and who is gonna put up the hay this summer and feed the cattle this winter?" she asked, as if it were my job to supply the answer. She looked down. I could see she was pregnant. "Howey, he's a good boy. He just has a bad habit, which is gamblin'."

"What do you mean, gambling?" I asked. I knew something about gambling, all right.

"Well, Howey wrote that check to pay off a gambling debt up at the Sky Club," she said. Smith's office had prosecuted Howey. But the *Wyoming Statutes* provided a complete defense against a charge of writing a bad check if the check had been given to pay, in whole or part, any gambling debt. I called in the local deputy, Frank Slagle, to investigate. Slagle was an avuncular kind who had never been caught breathing without a cigarette hanging from his lips, the smoke drifting upward where, over the years, it had stained the underside of his white Stetson a rich brown.

I expected an answer from Slagle that afternoon, but it was a couple of weeks before he got around to reporting. The check had been given to pay a gambling debt, all right. Howey's court-appointed lawyers, who in Fremont County worked *pro bono,* were apparently ignorant of the gambling defense. They had never raised it but instead pled him guilty and Howey was sentenced to the penitentiary. I moved to have the case dismissed. Judge Sheldon granted my motion.

I was becoming a nuisance to Peewee McDougall, who stuck his old lower lip out at me and scowled and then looked away. He didn't have to say anything, his petulance growing out of his putting them in the penitentiary and my getting them out. We were supposed to be on the same side. Now he had to drive all the way over the mountains and across the long, barren, snowswept plains to Rawlins, where the penitentiary was located, to fetch "that damn breed" and bring him back home again where he'd continue causing a lot of trouble. Peewee had the view of most law enforcement officers. Some criminal types you couldn't help. Lawmen called them "pukes," saw them as pathogens who had to be separated from society or they'd keep on spreading their disease.

"We'll have him back in the pen on something else," Peewee said. "Last time I had him up on his sister's complaint for beating the shit out her. Put her in the hospital."

"The same sister who came to me to get him out of the pen?"

"Right," Peewee said. "Wouldn't hurt fer ya to talk to me about stuff like this before ya go running to the judge. I been around here quite a while." He'd grown up in Lander and knew most of the people in the county.

"Well, the law's the law," I said. "If you want to put him in the pen, you gotta do it right."

Peewee just grunted. "We'll see," he said, looking at me askance.

A couple of years later, the judge sent Howey back to the pen all right, that monstrous edifice of stone and steel on the outside, its fancy old French front belying the malignant misery that awaited within. Howey, that poor ignorant waif of a man, was tossed back into that hell hole, his crime a series of forgeries which had been little more than a game between the saloon keepers and the Indians. Drunk Indians were good business. An Indian rarely left the bar until his money was gone and he had to be carried out like you carry out a dead man. I've seen the floors of saloons littered with drunken Indians lying still as death in their own vomit, the bartender serving up the drinks as fast as those who were still on their feet could write their checks. The saloon keepers would take a third party check from the Indian without the first question, even though they knew the check was likely a forgery. When the check was returned from the bank, the bar owner would charge down to my office, all put out, noisily demanding justice. He wanted that "fuckin' no-good check-forgin' redskin" prosecuted, all the while knowing I would likely force the Indian to make restitution to the saloon keeper rather than send him to prison. Howey and another drunk Indian had forged not one, but a dozen or more such checks. The newspaper called it "a crude forgery ring."

In those days alcoholism among the Native Americans was considered a disease from which there was no deliverance. Native American alcoholics could not then and cannot now afford a stint at Betty Ford's, and often they are not provided the family support required for successful treatment. In the end, having exhausted all other alternatives, I had sent Howey back to the pen.

One day I was driving home from Lander after a long day in court and stopped by a crossroads tavern for a beer. There was Howey, fresh out of the pen and already hoisting a few.

"Well, if it ain't my old buddy, Spence," he said, staggering up to me and looking up into my face from about two inches away. "I just got out of the pen. And I'm celebratin'. I wanna buy ya a drink." What do you do?

"Well, Howey, this isn't the way you ought to be celebrating," I said.

"The hell it ain't!" he said. Then he turned and hollered to the bartender. "Georgie, buy my pal Spence a drink."

Georgie slid a Coors in front of me. "Better settle up," Georgie said to Howey. "Ya already owe me five."

"Okay," Howey said. "Gimme a check."

The bartender tossed him a tablet of blank checks without even asking him which bank he wanted to write the check on. I got the hell out of there. Couple of days later the bartender dropped the check by my office. Howey had signed *my* name to it. I paid the bartender his money. He was happy, Howey was happy, and under the circumstances, I was happy too. Never did tell Peewee.

A county prosecutor in the back counties of Wyoming gets plenty of courtroom experience. I'd try an aggravated assault and battery case one day and a first-degree murder case the next. One of the former such cases involved a fellow by the name of Arden Coad. Coad was carpenter, plumber, contractor, hunter, fire chief and self-appointed protector of the small cowtown of Dubois. He was one of the most authoritative, opinionated, self-righteous men I'd ever met. He wore one of those small mustaches, like those fancy-pants movie stars, but you'd be advised not to let that mislead you. As my adversary, I grew to respect him. He put his convictions where his mouth was, out in front. He cared about people and about justice, and you didn't have to egg him into a fight for a friend or a cause— he'd take you on with his words or his fists, take your choice.

Arden defended himself. Didn't want any damned shyster standing up for him. Couldn't afford one anyway. Said some time previously the local game warden had hit Arden when the two got into it as to how a fire should be put out at the warden's house. Arden was the town's volunteer fire chief. To make matters worse, the warden had insulted Arden's friend, and it was when the warden came to Arden's house and hassled Arden about the incident that Arden hit him.

"Sure I hit him first," Arden admitted on my cross-examination. "I probably hit him four or five times. He had it comin'. He come to my house lookin' fer trouble and I gave it to him."

The jury was out all that afternoon and late into the night before it returned its verdict. Under the judge's instructions the jury had no choice—that a citizen "had it coming" is no defense to aggravated assault and battery. Judge Sheldon sentenced Arden to a year in the state penitentiary, suspended the sentence, put him on parole for a year and fined him four hundred dollars. Peewee told me that Arden couldn't raise the fine money. I went down to see him.

Arden was sitting in a small, plain cell looking pretty glum. It was cold in there, the cement floors, the steel bars, the sound of steel hitting steel as the prisoners were locked up. I could smell the antelope meat the prisoners were being fed for supper. The county commissioners gave Peewee an allowance, so many cents a prisoner per meal, and he fed them twice a day, as they do in most jails. The game wardens, all friends of Peewee's, brought Peewee confiscated game animals, which he fed to the prisoners. I knew the smell. Didn't like it. But it was good, healthy food. His wife, Gladys, cooked it.

I asked Peewee to let me in to see Arden.

"What do ya wanna see him for? He's pretty mad, Gerry. I wouldn't go in there lookin' fer trouble if I was you."

"It'll be all right," I said. Peewee gave me that look of his, let me in and stood outside the cell for a minute, watching to make sure.

I went over and sat down on the steel bunk by Arden. Just a mattress. No covers. I gave him a slap on the leg. "I'm sorry you're in here, Arden," I said. "You put up a good fight, better than if you had a lawyer."

"Ain't no justice in that verdict," he said. He looked tired, and beaten.

"I'll help you raise the money for your fine," I said.

Suddenly he came to life, ready for the fight again. "Don't you worry none about me, Gerry," Arden said. "Our national guard company spent twenty-nine months in Adolf Hitler's prison camp. A night in your jail ain't gonna hurt me." The next day Arden gathered up the fine money and got out of jail on his own. A man has his pride. Arden and I have been friends now for nearly forty years.

At about the same time as the affray between Coad and the game warden, I'd been called to the Barquin Ranch early on a Sunday morning. "We've had a murder out here." It was Jimmy Barquin. "Ya better get out here, Gerry." The Barquins ran sheep both on and off the reservation.

I called Peewee, met him on the way, and we drove out to the ranch together. The ranch lay on the high sagebrush flatlands, the frame buildings stuck there, tentative, waiting for the certain wind to blow them off. When we got to the ranch Jimmy Barquin met us. He was the heir of the clan, dark, Basque by blood, with the aloof mannerism of a Spanish don, his dark hair shining. He led us to the bunkhouse to view the *corpus delicti*. The suspect was Joe Cruz Martinez, one of Barquin's herders. He was hanging around in the background, scowling, all gilded with malice and meanness.

"What happened?" I asked Martinez.

"Me and Ramon was in Lander, and we had a fight with them Indians and they run us off the road, and then they come to the bunkhouse later and I was under the bed hiding, and they come in and shot ol' Ramon there in the head."

The deceased, Ramon Gonzales, another Mexican herder, was lying faceup in his bed. He looked peaceful enough. He had obviously caught a bullet between the eyes. Never moved a muscle, his hands resting just outside the blankets of his bedroll like a man in deep slumber. Not much blood. We took some photographs, and then Peewee asked Martinez if he'd mind coming along with the sheriff to help the sheriff find the true killers. Joe Cruz Martinez said he would be only too happy to help, whereupon Peewee "offered him lodging for two nights in the county jail," as Peewee was later to put it, while the murder was being investigated. A .22 caliber rifle from the ranch was missing. The following day the rifle was found under the granary at the ranch.

Peewee pulled Martinez out of his cell and led him into the sheriff's office. Peewee told Martinez that he'd found the rifle, that Martinez's fingerprints were on the gun, that they had matched the .22 bullet to the rifle, and, he added, it would be very kind of Martinez if he would now confess. At least that's how Peewee told it. Martinez signed a confession.

Those were the days before *Miranda,* long before you had to tell a frightened suspect that if he said a word it could be used against him. Mexicans then had no rights—none in Mexico and few in the United States. He had no lawyer to advise him. He was very poor. In truth, no fingerprints had been lifted from the gun and none had been matched to Martinez. I don't think Peewee even took Martinez's prints. But people believed Peewee. He looked straight at you and said things straight, like "I know you killed him, and you know you killed him, so let's get this down on paper so as we all can go home." Except Martinez didn't go home.

The confession said that Joe Cruz Martinez and the dead man, Gonzales, had been fighting over a certain woman. Gonzales had called Martinez a foul name, which, imprecisely translated, meant he had a sexual affinity for his mother. Gonzales, Martinez insisted, asked Martinez to stop the car. He wanted to get out and fight Martinez, but Martinez said he was too drunk and sick to fight. When they got to the bunkhouse, they went to bed, and after the lights were turned off Martinez said to Gonzales, "Happy dreams," to which Gonzales responded by calling Martinez the same name as before. This, Martinez asserted, caused him great fear. He said, "I thought he would get up and cut my throat off, and I wasn't going to take any chances." He got up, got dressed, walked to the Barquin house, took the rifle off the front porch, checked to see if it was loaded, returned to the bunkhouse where Gonzales was sleeping, and shot Gonzales in the head.

At the trial Joe Cruz Martinez took the stand in his own defense. His lawyer, Jack Crofts, a tall, blinking Ichabod, as skinny as a stick, was a man thirty years my senior whom everybody liked. Crofts never held himself out as a trial lawyer. In those days, the members of the Wyoming bar represented the indigent as part of their duties to the justice system. Judge Sheldon had appointed Crofts to represent the accused, and he was going to defend him the best he could.

Crofts had Martinez recount all of the drinks at all of the saloons he had visited the night of the killing. Then he let the accused tell how he and the deceased had fallen into a brawl, how they had fought for the gun, and how in the melee the gun had discharged, thus killing the deceased.

"I suppose," I said on cross-examination, "that as soon as the bullet went between Ramon Gonzales' eyes, he marched right over, opened up his bedroll, climbed in, went to sleep, and died, is that right?"

"Objected to as a compound question," Jack Crofts cried.

"Sustained," Judge Sheldon ruled. I had already learned that the question, not the answer, most often sends the important argument to the jury.

"Well, let's show the jury how the fight between you and Ramon Gonzales went," I said. I handed Martinez the .22 rifle. "If you would, please, step down off the stand and demonstrate for us how this happened."

Martinez hadn't been prepared for the question or the demonstration. The poor foolish frightened man: Suddenly he grabbed the rifle and launched into a wrestling match with the ghost of the deceased. "He grab me here, and I grab back, and he have the gun on me, and I push it up like this, and then, we are fightin' fer the gun and a-fightin', and then the gun, she goes off and he is dead."

"I see," I said. I looked over at the jury, raised an eyebrow, and said nothing. I handed the jury the photo of the deceased in slumber where obviously he had been shot. Then I went to the blackboard and had Martinez list the bars he had visited that night, and at each bar I had him account for the number of drinks he had consumed. As he answered me, I wrote them down on the board. By the time I added them up, he claimed he had drunk something like fifty-three shots of whiskey, and I don't know how many beers.

I had just arrived at the grand total when one of the jurors piped up. "You forgot a shot there, Mr. Spence. That makes fifty-four."

I thanked the juror. "Not too good with figures," I said. I took after the defendant on a dozen other issues that exposed him as a clumsy liar. There are more men in prison who are there because the jury thought they were lying about the murder than there are men in prison because they committed the murder. We can understand the human frailties that lead to crime. But we cannot forgive the liar who cheats us of the truth. The accused, even when he's innocent, under the relentless ripping of cross-examination, can rarely avoid lying or, even when he's telling the truth, creating the appearance that he is lying.

During a recess Judge Sheldon called me into his chambers. "Gerry," he said. "It's all right to kill a witness once with your cross-examination. You can even kill him twice. But you've killed Martinez at least twenty times. Kill him once more and the jury is liable to resurrect him." I rested my case.

The jury was out fifteen minutes, found the defendant guilty of first-degree murder, as charged, "without special qualification," which under the law then in force meant that the defendant would be put to death. I thought of Arden Coad's case which I had tried a couple of days before. It took the jury most of the day and half of the night to find Arden guilty of assault, but it took another jury from the same county of citizens only fifteen minutes to find the Mexican, Martinez, guilty of murder and to take his life.

Suddenly the full impact of power came slamming home to me. I could actually kill with my power as a prosecutor. What had once been a lawyer's game against a frightened, poorly prepared, poorly educated, not too bright Mexican sheepherder had been converted into his death warrant. I had just killed a man in the courtroom with power. Words had been my weapon and it had not been a fair fight. Joe Cruz Martinez was not as good with words. He could only speak the language in a few fractured syllables, and his words came stained with the deep accent of his native tongue. Now a man would die because I had been better with words than he. I talked to Judge Sheldon about it.

"I'm not sure I did the right thing," I said.

"What do you mean? You did your job. The guy killed the other guy. The law is the law." But I remembered my mother's quiet preachings that Christians must exchange love for hate, that Christians must turn the other cheek. Christians must try to bring peace to the world by compassion. I tried to cast off her ideas. Yet they hung on to me like a mob of small children grabbing at my knees.

Sheldon lit up a cigarette, held it with long fingers brown from the stain of smoke and then dragged on it fastidiously. "I remember old Judge Cromer," he said. "He'd snivel and cry about having to pronounce a death sentence on a defendant. I'll tell you one thing: You won't see me sniveling about this one."

"Won't it bother you?" I asked.

The judge looked at me as if I were a milksop. "Not in the slightest," he said. "I asked for the job. I'll do it."

When it came time for the sentencing, Peewee brought Martinez up from the jail, led him into the courtroom in cuffs and shackles. He was in the same dirty pants he was wearing the day he killed Gonzales. Judge Sheldon took the bench and looked down at the defendant. I thought of a hawk on a high perch, ready, waiting. The courtroom was nearly empty. The clerk was there, of course, and Crofts, Martinez's attorney. If the deceased had relatives they were absent. I was the only representative of the dead. Otherwise, nobody cared about the case.

"All rise," the clerk intoned.

Jack Crofts, half as big around as his client, and twice as tall, stood next to the little Mexican.

The clerk read the title of the case, the formalities, of course. The black robe of the judge. The few people there, standing, looking up, as if to the king, and the judge looking down as if on his subjects, about to pronounce his sentence, as unimpassioned as a pot pouring out lukewarm tea.

"Does the defendant have anything to say before the court pronounces its sentence?" Judge Sheldon asked.

"I ain't got nothin'," Martinez said. He stood with his head up, not looking down like a man ashamed. His hands were in front of him, cuffed. His old cowboy boots were turned over at the heels. To the system, Martinez was nothing. No influential parents, no wealthy family, no powerful friends. He was an object about to be disposed of. The clerk looked bored. Crofts stood by his client on stork's legs staring at the judge, his eyes perpetually blinking their slow, out-of-sync blink, his nose lifting slightly when the lids came down.

Judge Sheldon began to read, and, finding that the jury had not qualified its verdict, the judge, stumbling on a word here and there, and going back to pick them up, ended with the hard part of the sentence. His voice was steady, but not once did he look up from his reading. "Accordingly, the court does hereby remand you to the custody of the sheriff of Fremont County, Wyoming, to deliver you forthwith to the warden of the Wyoming State Penitentiary at Rawlins, Wyoming, who shall, in accordance with the mandate of this court, subject you to lethal gas in the gas chamber at said penitentiary until you are dead. God save your soul."

The judge, without a glance at the defendant, got up and swooped out of the courtroom, leaving the defendant and his lawyer standing alone in front of the bench. Martinez didn't know where to go. Then Peewee stepped toward him and motioned with his head for Martinez to come to him, motioned him like a dog. And before Crofts could say any last good-byes, the man turned and shuffled toward the sheriff, his chains rattling as they dragged between his steps. Crofts stood there for a moment, started to follow his client, and then, changing his mind, turned and left the courtroom. When he walked by me he nodded without a smile, as people nod to each other at funerals.

In those days all death penalty cases were automatically appealed to the Wyoming Supreme Court. Months later, when the briefs had been filed and the case called up for argument, I drove to Cheyenne to represent the state's side of the case. Full day's drive down and a full day's drive back. The question before the court, reduced to its simplest form: Should Joe Cruz Martinez be put to death?

William A. Smith had now joined Jack Crofts for the defendant, the seriousness of the death penalty prompting the court to appoint yet another attorney for the defendant. And two new justices had finally taken the bench: the former district judge, Glen Parker, who in law school had warned me against staying in the law; and Harry Harnsberger, Smith's former partner, who had been recently elevated from attorney general to the Supreme Court of Wyoming. Judge Blume, venerable, and as much loved as ever, was still toddling around up there.

Smith argued the appeal before his old partner, Harry Harnsberger. How could I complain? I'd tried the same case to my former employer, Judge Sheldon. I can see Smith standing there looking up, hear him clearing his throat like a nervous choirboy about to sing his solo, see him smiling, none of the judges smiling back, hear him clearing his throat again, and finally getting into his argument.

"This was just a drunken herder. He was so drunk, may the court please, he couldn't form the requisite intent to kill." He argued on for an hour, and when he sat down, the judges took a recess, and like bored priests waiting for the response of the congregation, they turned to me for mine.

"Your Honors," I began. "I agree with the defense. This man was too drunk to form the specific intent to kill." I asked the judges to reduce the sentence of Joe Cruz Martinez to second-degree murder—twenty years to life imprisonment.

Judge Parker leaned over the bench and peered down at me as if he had never seen me before. "Counsel, are you the prosecutor who tried this case?" My name was on the title page of the record in front of him.

"Yes, Your Honor."

"Well, this is a first up here." He turned to Justice Blume for confirmation. The old judge wasn't listening. "Never before have we had a prosecutor admit in court that he made a mistake."

"He doesn't admit he made a mistake. He's arguing that he did too good a job—he was *too* brilliant," Judge Harnsberger remarked with splendid insouciance. Judge Blume must have heard the comment. His laugh sounded like an errant gurgle out of the throat of the dead.

"I'm arguing that the defendant shouldn't be put to death. He was drunk," I replied.

"Well, that means that inebriation is a sure cure for murder," Justice Parker remarked. "Under your theory, Mr. Spence, all you have to do to make sure you don't go to the gas chamber is to get drunk before you commit the murder, isn't that true?"

"No sir, if Your Honor will permit me," I replied. "The proposition you have just argued presupposes that the defendant formed the requisite intent *before* he got drunk. I argue that this defendant, because he was drunk, never, at any time, before or after his drunkenness, formed the requisite intent to kill."

"Well, if he hadn't formed the requisite intent to kill, how did he just happen to shoot the decedent between the eyes so neatly?"

"That is a rational question, Your Honor . . ."

"I should hope so," Judge Parker interrupted.

"Yes, it is a rational question, Your Honor, but drunk men do rational things. That is why the law recognizes that a man may be so drunk that he is able to kill, neatly, as you point out, yet he may be unable to premeditate the murder with malice, as is required for murder in the first degree."

"I see," Judge Parker said. But I didn't think he saw the point. He cast me a look as if I were the world's champion mollycoddler, this prosecutor caving in to the defense. Then the justices marched off the bench to consider their opinion.

"You are a pansy," Peewee said. "How the hell could he not have premeditated it, going to the house for the gun and all? If the Supreme Court turns him loose he'll just go out and get drunk and kill somebody else."

"Maybe," I said. "But if we're ever going to stop killing in this country, the state has to stop killing first."

"If you're so damn solid against the death penalty, maybe you shouldn't be in this job."

"Do there always have to be killers on both sides?"

He didn't answer. The scowl. Peewee wasn't a man to hang on to a philosophical question. He was a man of simple solutions.

Months later the court's unanimous decision was handed down. Justice Parker authored the opinion. The fact that I had requested that the court lower the sentence to second-degree murder was never mentioned. Judge Parker held that the confession was the only substantial evidence of the defendant's guilt and that therefore one must look to the confession for the requisite intent of premeditation. However, he wrote, "the confession introduced uncontraverted factors which negatived [sic] premeditated malice . . ." which, as Judge Parker held, turned out to be the facts surrounding his drinking and "carousing"—the judge's word—the night before. The judges reduced the sentence to second-degree murder. Joe Cruz Martinez spent several years in the Wyoming Penitentiary. He was released without any fanfare, after which he was never heard from again.

CHAPTER 27

Campaign wagon during Spence's run for reelection as county attorney.

ONE DAY I was driving down the Main Street of Riverton with my father, who had come for a visit. He wasn't much for compliments in those days, and I was trying my best to impress him. As we drove by the stores I pointed out one after another the local businesses that Frank Hill and I represented.

"Now there's the Ben Franklin Store, Dad," I said. "I represent old Tom House, who owns that store. Hell of a fisherman, too."

"Uh-huh," he said.

"And there's the Gamble's store. Owned by a fellow named Jim Hill. I represent him and we do a lot of goose hunting together, went to Canada once."

"Uh-huh," he said.

And on down the street we drove past the Rexall Pharmacy, owned by Andy Anderson, and over on Federal Boulevard, Sam Stanbury's Riverton Tire. Stanbury was my hunting partner and close friend—hell of a man with a fly rod up there on the Dinwoody, too. I didn't think my father knew what to say to this son of his, this loquacious twerp who wasn't dry behind the ears, who had already joined the establishment. So far as he was concerned, I'd gone over to the other side, a side for which he held little charity. All his life he'd been one of the flock who went into the stores to get fleeced, a little at a time. Never had been on the side of those who were doing the shearing. That day he never got around to saying he was proud of me.

In the years that followed, the firm of Spence and Hill began to gather momentum. We didn't represent a bank and we didn't represent the oil and mining companies—that's where the big money was—but we represented many of the local folks, state law providing that the county attorney could take on private cases so long as they weren't in conflict with his official duties.

Already I was transferring the skills I had been learning as a prosecutor to the civil side of the law. I began trying any decent case that came along. I needed the experience, and Frank Hill and I could use the money—our families, like nests full of squawking baby birds, their mouths open and waiting.

Among the early civil cases that I took was one for LaVeta Wempen, a solid-boned, motherly woman who had been fired from her job as school cook. She had a contract with the school board for the nine-month school term at a salary of $151.11 per month. It was her contract, and when the school board fired her she had three months to go on it, and they had fired her without cause, she said. She came to see me. "I want you to sue those devils," she said. "Sue 'em good." She was so mad she was crying.

She'd performed her duties well—that was undisputed. She made great chili and pumpkin pie with real whipped cream, and the kids loved her. Even the board members seemed to visit the school, when, just by chance, lunch happened to be served. But she fell into an altercation with a truculent superintendent, the kind who runs a rural school of less than a hundred kids and thinks he runs the world. Leroy, Mrs. Wempen's ten-year-old, had caused some damage to school property—about a dollar's worth. At the behest of another boy he'd cut off the round rubber tip of a folding chair, and the other boy had tossed the rubber tip up on the stage during a school program. The superintendent hauled Leroy in. Leroy, a wide-eyed, scared farm boy, had never been confronted with anything more ferocious than a barnyard rooster. He was terrified out of his new bib overalls.

The next day Mrs. Wempen met the superintendent in the lunch room and offered a silver dollar—they were still in general circulation in Wyoming in those days—to pay the damage caused by Leroy's mischief.

"I want Leroy to pay for this, not you," the superintendent said in a loud voice so everybody could hear it. He shoved her dollar back.

"Leroy doesn't have any money," Mrs. Wempen said.

"He can pay it out of his allowance," the superintendent shot back.

"Leroy doesn't get an allowance."

"Well, doesn't he do any work around the house?"

"He does the chores at home and all, but we don't pay him nothin'." She shoved the dollar back. I have no doubt the dollar was exchanged several more times, along with words heating up in the lunch room in front of a gawking audience of teachers and kids. Mrs. Wempen said the man finally jumped up and pounded the table.

"You come into my office and we'll get this settled!"

"It is settled. Here's the dollar." She shoved it back at the superintendent.

"Are you coming to my office or not?"

"I'm not going anyplace," she said. "My job's in the kitchen."

"We'll see about that," the superintendent said, storming off.

The superintendent took his complaint against Mrs. Wempen to the school board, and, at a special meeting, without notice to her and without hearing her side of it, the school board fired her.

I filed her case, one for breach of contract, and asked for damages of $453.33, the balance due under her contract. Not much of a case, I suppose you could say, but money never measures the value of human dignity. The Wempens had no money to pay a lawyer. Every nickel they could get their hands on was mortgaged to the government. A farmer out there on the project just about had to beg the federal government's Farmers Home Administration for permission to buy a new pair of shoes for his kid. I took the case on the bar's standard contingency fee. I'd get a third of whatever I recovered for Mrs. Wempen, but if the case was appealed, then I'd get half.

The school board was represented by the tenacious thespian R. Lauren Moran, a man who possessed the unrivaled ability to infuriate Judge Sheldon and who exercised his talent with considerable glee. Moran, an articulate but borderline insolent sort, would purposely hold a magnificent Napoleonic pose in front of the judge, his hand grasping the lapel of his suit coat. Throwing back his head he would orate in his deep, splenetic baritone, choosing his words with care and style so that they came out with the syntax perfect, the lines fully punctuated, the meaning pointed and precise. I thought he would have been better appreciated as a villain, like Iago, on a Shakespearean stage. To all who observed, including the judge, it became clear that he placed His Honor, who glared down at him, barely above the level of some blinking bumpkin fresh from the sticks. As he paced the floor he spoke down to everyone—to the judge, to me, and at last, to the jury as well.

Moreover, what Moran lacked in circumspection, he made up for in unfettered bullheadedness. Not inhibited one bit by the judicial robe, he would argue with Judge Sheldon on any point. He had argued with Sheldon as a lawyer about everything and anything whether the points were arguable or not, and the mere fact that Sheldon had taken the bench, through no fault of Moran's, was no reason, as Moran saw it, for Moran to stop arguing with the man now. Once during the trial, then twice, finally a third time, Judge Sheldon warned the man to sit down.

"You're merely harassing this witness with your groundless objections," Sheldon ruled.

Moran argued back. "I have an absolute right to make the record and I intend to do so, Your Honor."

Sheldon excused the jury. Then he turned to Moran. "You can make any record you want, but you are not going to continue this harangue in my court."

"I am not continuing a harangue. I am making proper objections."

"I am warning you, Mr. Moran."

"I'll not be intimidated," Moran replied, trying to stare down the judge.

"You're about to find yourself in a free room in the county hotel, Mr. Moran," the judge warned, everyone understanding he was referring to the jail in the basement.

"You're the judge. You have your job. I have my client to represent."

"Are you inviting contempt, Mr. Moran?"

"I invite nothing, I only intend to represent my client," Moran replied.

"Do I have your assurance then that you will desist from your groundless objections?"

"I can assure the court of nothing," Moran said.

"Very well," Judge Sheldon shouted, turning his usual neon red. "I hereby find your conduct contemptuous. You are given over to the custody of the sheriff of Fremont County, Wyoming, until you purge yourself of said contempt. Call the sheriff," the judge said to the clerk, and he stormed off the bench.

A few minutes later the sheriff came for his prisoner. And a few minutes after that I stepped into the county law library to find Moran and his partner, Murphy, busily beating the books. They were reading furiously from the appropriate blue volumes of *Corpus Juris Secundum*.

"I thought the judge ordered Moran to jail," I said to Peewee.

"Well, he did," Peewee said. "But Moran's my trustee." He gave me that little knowing grin of his.

Then I joined Moran and Murphy in the library in an attempt to find a way out of jail for my opponent.

"Gotta have due process," I said. "Judge can't throw you in jail without a hearing."

"Yes," Moran said. "But while I'm in jail, who am I going to argue that to? Sheldon?" Sheldon was the only judge in the county.

"We'll have to go to the Supreme Court in Cheyenne," I said. But I thought it would be a good move for both Moran and me to go to the judge and suggest a compromise. Moran would give up the contempt hearing to which he was entitled and would apologize if the judge would lift the contempt order.

"I wouldn't think of it," Moran said. "I shall never apologize for representing my client."

"This is just a four-hundred-dollar case, remember?"

"I haven't forgotten. Neither have you. We are prisoners of our principles," Moran said, with all the drama of a great stage actor. I had to admire him.

"All right," I said. "How about if I go to the judge and tell him I, personally, would appreciate it if he would lift the contempt order so we can continue the trial? I can't finish the trial with you in jail."

"You can do as you please," Moran said. "I do not control your conduct nor your conscience," he said.

"I couldn't sleep tonight if you were in jail," I said. So I went to the judge, and, on my request, he lifted his order. The next morning we completed the case, and the jury returned its verdict for my client in the full amount of her claim, namely, $453.33.

After the verdict, the school board, still represented by R. Lauren Moran, appealed the jury's verdict to the Wyoming Supreme Court. No plain Jane farmer's wife was going to take R. Lauren Moran, or the school board, to court and beat them. Months later after the record and all of the briefs had been filed in the Supreme Court, I again traveled to Cheyenne, and again I appeared before the court to argue the case. Months after that Justice Harry Harnsberger rendered the opinion of the court:

> Before the school board was entitled to take that drastic action [the
> firing], it was necessary that the employee be apprised of charges pre-
> ferred against her; that notice of hearing upon those charges be given
> her; that at such hearing she be permitted full opportunity to offer
> such explanation, excuse, justification or refutation as might be avail-
> able to her. . . . The board was not entitled to act arbitrarily in an *ex
> parte* proceeding, solely upon the representations of the superinten-
> dent, which, in the nature of things, were possible to be colored from
> his interested position.

Judge Harnsberger wrote on for many pages. As I read the decision, I thought how lovely that ordinary people, poor people, who claimed they were owed as little as $453.33, could have their cases heard, considered and deter-mined by the highest court in the state and only after a careful and thorough review of the law. By contrast, most often I have found that justice is like caviar—rotten, fishy, and usually only the rich can afford it.

When I delivered the school board's check to Mrs Wempen you would have thought she had been vindicated by a proclamation from heaven. I had never seen such a face so fully lit by the great incandescent beam of justice. She grabbed hold of me and hugged me until she was breathless, and so was I. Although it won't pay the rent, that is good pay for any lawyer.

Since it took an appeal to win the case my fee was half the recovery— $226.67. She would have given me all the money.

But money wasn't the whole issue—not for me, not for Mrs. Wempen, and not for the school board either. What is justice and what is pride, what is honor and what is vengeance gets thrown into the stew pot of a trial. What comes out for one may be the gravy of justice, and for the other, the burned leavings at the bottom of the kettle. But it's the search for *Justice* that excites the fiber of every trial lawyer worth a pinch. I believed then as I believe now—a trial lawyer isn't a trial lawyer without a good case in his file to fire up his smoldering zeal.

When it came time to make my decision as to whether or not to run for reelection as county and prosecuting attorney, I had pretty much decided against it. Four years seemed enough. I was constantly at odds with the demands of my job as a prosecutor, on the one hand, and my natural compassion for the wretched souls I had to prosecute on the other. Native Americans made up the largest ethnic numbers against whom I brought criminal charges. Poverty and crime are hateful brothers. As for the Native American, that so-called heathen, usually his only real crime was that he had become addicted to the white man's fire water. The white man, on the other hand, worshiped an evil god—his money god called Mammon. The Indians felt deep resentment at the white man's cruelty, which was plainly evidenced when the white culture attempted to force the Indian into the slavery of the white man's work ethic. The Native Americans knew nothing of white man's work, the idea being foreign to the aborigine. Work was the invention of civilization. It was not work to roam the prairies and hunt for buffalo. It was not work to gather chokecherries and to pound them into jerky to make pemmican. Hunters and gatherers do not work. Hunters and gatherers had not yet left the Garden, and would not until they were forced out by cultivation and commerce. As Smohalla, a Nez Percé chief, said when asked why his "lazy" tribesmen refused to work, especially the young braves with strong bodies well suited for manual labor: "My young men shall never work. Men who work cannot dream, and wisdom comes to us in dreams."

During my first term in office I had sought and obtained the revocation of four liquor licenses against saloon keepers who had served intoxicants to minors, and I took the licenses of three others for gambling and Sunday infractions. I had tried many cases, from spousal abuse to murder. Never lost a case as a prosecutor. I was learning how to survive in the courtroom. I thought I had made a difference. Frank Hill and I would be able to make it in our private practice, and I was ready to pass the responsibilities on to some other lawyer. The office had served me well. It had established me as this respected citizen, as a man with his feet solidly tamped into the ground like a good cedar fence post. I no longer inhabited the ephemeral world of fantasy where, during my adolescence, I had flown, like a space cadet, right up to the presidency of the United States. I had set goals I could accomplish. I thought I might be able to buy some property some day, maybe a little ranch. I could advance in politics, not big-time politics, but maybe I could go to the Wyoming legislature as Frank Sheldon had. Over the years I had tried to bury the devastation of my mother's suicide. I thought I was as happy as reality permitted. I was beginning to feel like a successful lawyer. I believed I was a good parent. The early years in Riverton were years when I grew from late childhood to early manhood, and the town, like a brooder house for young chicks, had provided a sheltered place for my maturation.

But when the last day for filing was at hand, and when I saw the lawyers who were running for my office, both on the Republican and Democratic tickets, I decided I'd better run one more time to make sure that what I had planted grew. I was proud of what I'd accomplished in the county, made it a better place I thought, and what had been hard to accomplish could be lost overnight if the wrong prosecutor got into office.

As election time grew near, *The Riverton Ranger* editorialized: "The record in office compiled by Mr. Spence in the last four years is a record of conscientious service for the whole of the community."

This time around I didn't have time for a door-to-door campaign. I was still the prosecutor, and I had a full load of cases to try. Instead, I hired an old farmer along with his team of horses and his wagon. The horses pulled the wagon through every street in both Riverton and Lander with a loudspeaker blaring out patriotic marches. People rushed to the door to see what in the world all the commotion was about. There in front of their house they saw the old wagon with Gerry Spence aboard, and a large sign hanging down on both sides of the wagon reading, "We're Pulling for G. L. Spence for County Attorney."

Spence campaign poster for his run for reelection as county attorney.

I spoke to the women's clubs in the county, shook hands with the people wherever I went, made speeches at the service clubs, the Kiwanis, the Lions Club, and Rotary. Always I was greeted with "And this is the man who closed down our Little Yellow House." Sometimes people laughed and sometimes they booed. But whether they thought I had been right or wrong, they likely suspected I was honest. In November I was the only Riverton candidate who survived both the primary and the general election. Reelected for another term, I would end up ruing the day.

I had no sooner taken office in my second term when a group of Indians came to see me. They were a solemn lot—only the men, of course, the women not permitted to take part in the important business of the tribe. They took off their cowboy hats and set them on their laps, crossed their arms, and waited for their spokesman to break the silence, their faces as communicative as gravestones. Finally the oldest among them, a man with long gray braids and a beaded bolo tie, spoke up.

"Them peyotes. They should be prosecuted."

"What do you mean?" I asked.

His voice, as flat as a board, said it again. "Them peyotes is takin' drugs and callin' it religion."

Then another man, a younger brave with a fatter face and smooth brown skin, said, "Them peyotes bring a bad name ta us. You should put them peyotes in jail."

The peyotes they referred to were members of the controversial Native American Church, a religious sect on the Wind River Reservation known among its enemies as "peyote eaters." Peyote is the root of a cactus plant that contains the drug mescaline, which, when taken in sufficient quantities, creates a hallucinatory high. People under its influence were said to experience visions, and at times to transcend their bodies and enter into another realm. The "nonpeyotes" wanted me to prosecute the peyote eaters for violation of the criminal laws governing the possession and use of such drugs.

But the peyotes claimed that their use of the cactus root was incidental to their religion and, therefore, that precious constitutional investiture known as freedom of religion protected them. I told the group that came to see me that I would look into the matter personally. I knew one of the alleged peyote eaters, a youngish Indian brave, a tall, straight man and handsome but for the fact that he was missing half his left ear. I told him I wanted to see for myself what they were up to out there. He immediately invited me to come to one of their ceremonies. "And bring your wife," he said, almost as an afterthought.

Anna and I drove to the heart of the reservation on a dark, early winter night, the countryside frozen still and stiff, the tiny lights from the Indian shacks like pin holes through a cold, black screen. The temperature outside was twenty below, the snow, thigh deep, piled up and pushed in around the base of the tent where the Indians had gathered for their service.

Inside we took our places on the ground joining the others, all Indians, all wrapped in their blankets, all shy, none meeting us with their eyes, the group of about ten forming a large oval around the outer perimeters of the old white army tent held up by one long ridge pole and a pole at each end. A small iron wood stove at the far end of the tent threw out its heat, those nearest the tent flaps nearly frozen, those nearest the stove sweltering. A small gasoline lantern hung from the ceiling, humming along as they do. The occupants were all men except for a gaunt old woman who sat near the chief, her old bones separated from the cold ground by only the thickness of her hide. She wore a heavy wearing robe, a blanket of mostly black and gray Indian designs, her straight gray hair was braided on either side, her feet protruding from the blanket clad in beaded moccasins with rawhide soles. She didn't look at either Anna or me, but stared straight ahead as if she could see through the tent, out through the gathering storm, and on into the infinite nothing, the eternal everything.

The warmth of the stove had already reached Anna and me. Soon the men began to beat their drums, rawhide stretched over hollowed-out cottonwood logs. The sound of the drums, the wild beating, the *ta*-da, *ta*-da, *ta*-da, went on as if the men were bent on breaking the rawhide, bent on splitting their drums beneath, set on sending the sound of their beat out to rupture the frozen sky and to stab down to the core of Mother Earth. Then the drummers began to sing—not the songs of civilization but the feral, primal songs that scream out of the throat of the loon, that are joined by the cry of the coyote and the high, eerie howl of the wolf. The pitched wild crying of the men released the sounds of the earth, and the sounds out of ourselves, and we became the beating and the singing.

The old chief, too, was wrapped in his red wearing blanket. Carefully, reverently, he removed a scoop of ashes from the stove with a small square shovel, for ashes were the sacred symbol of their ancestors. The old chief spread the ashes on the dirt floor in front of him, and as the peyote, ground into a fine powder, was passed from person to person, the old chief spread the ashes into precise, parallel lines. When the peyote came to me, I took the plastic spoon, dipped out a spoonful, and when the young brave with half a left ear, like a priest, offered the peyote tea to wash it down, I drank of it as well. So did Anna. It bore a nasty, bitter taste.

Soon a mystical presence grew out of the chanting and hung over the tent hot and womblike. I transcended the moment. I began to traverse the earth into

another land. I would have felt it even without the peyote. I would have felt it from the drums, from the nascent reverberations, from the singing.

In his quivery old voice the chief prayed for the young man in the tribe with the broken leg. He prayed for the woman sick in bed with the demon eating at her belly. He prayed for their ancestors, for their souls, and he prayed for the Mother Earth. And in the Indians' one-toned voice he prayed for me,

Native Americans beating their drums and singing.

the first syllable at the same tonal level as the next. "And may the county attorney have long life and much wisdom," he said.

About midnight I began to feel very strange. Already Anna was leaning over, whispering to me that we should go home.

"We can't leave," I whispered back. "We promised to stay with them until sunup." The young brave had told me that if we left sooner the meeting would be ruined and of no account.

After a while she whispered to me again. "We have to get out of here. People are crawling in under the tent."

I looked. I could see no one. Besides, the snow was piled up outside. But how did I know? I was hovering above myself, looking down on this man known as Gerry Spence, his earthly body an irrelevancy, a mere curiosity.

"If you don't leave with me, I'll leave by myself," Anna said. She got up and I got up with her. I apologized to the old chief. I told him we were not feeling well and that we must leave. He was gracious. He said he would pray for us.

I drove home very slowly; the roads icy, we the first to break through the blowing drifts. I hunkered down over the steering wheel, my eyes up close to the windshield trying to see the way. What was road and what was drift was hard to distinguish. Anna watched out the side window. "You're getting too close over here," she'd say, and I'd ease back. Bad night to be caught on the road. High on peyote, no other life there on that white, frozen, shifting moonscape.

By some nameless power we were transported home that night. Later I found myself in bed, staring up at the dark ceiling to behold this same man staring down at the prone body of the man lying there, staring up. Sleep was frightened away. In our warm bed I was cold and I shivered. And I did not find sleep until well into the middle of the following morning.

If anything, I thought the experience must be religious. It had certainly not been a hedonistic outing for us. The Native Americans' use of the cactus button was limited to their ceremonies, and I wouldn't wonder that they used it from time to time for medicine. It was strong medicine. I thought its use exempted under the Constitution. Who was I, one who himself had never found a satisfactory way to worship, to tell the Indians how?

When I had returned to the land called "the real world," I thought that instead of prosecuting the members of the Native American Church, I should prosecute the white man, who by the sale of his abominable swill had robbed the Indian of his dignity, his sacred heritage, his pride, his life, and the lives of his children. I thought, if the Indian were to kill our children, a little at a time, before our eyes, if he were to degrade us and humiliate us and rob us of our land and our fortunes, we would lock him away for the very safety of society. But the white man, by his power, has bestowed upon himself the lawful right to destroy the lives of the American Native for the white man's profit. The white man's poison takes the Indian on a different excursion from the one I had taken with the peyote eaters. His drink does not raise the Indian above himself. The white man's poison casts native man into a dungeon of drunkenness and a hell from which he and his family can rarely escape.

Black Elk observed that everything the Indian does is done in a circle. "That is because the power of the world always works in a circle. The sky is round, and the earth. The wind, in its greatest power, whirls. The sun comes forth and goes down in a circle. . . . The bird makes its nest in a circle, for theirs is the same religion as ours. Our tipis are round like the nests of birds. . . . "

We too in the white world speak of the circle. We say, "What goes around comes around." Life can be defined in cycles, which are, at last, circles. My life in Riverton began with Ernest Newton, the man who directed me to Judge Sheldon in the first place. He now returned to my life. It was a bitter reentry for both of us.

I received a call one day from the governor of Wyoming, Milward Simpson. He was concerned about the expense accounts of Ernest Newton, who had been employed as the secretary of the Legislative Interim Committee—something about a desk that Newton allegedly had absconded with. Shortly I got a call from the Wyoming attorney general, Thomas Miller. Since I was an arm of state law enforcement, and he was the attorney general, I had the duty to do as ordered: investigate this man Newton.

As the facts came to be known, the officials were accusing Newton of appropriating a desk to his private use, a desk that had cost the state $369.90. As I saw it, the case, if there was one, didn't amount to much. Newton was probably crossways with some of the politicians at Cheyenne. From the beginning, the case carried with it those putrid odors of politics.

I dragged my feet. Finally I got another call from Attorney General Miller. "Are you going to prosecute Newton or not?"

"On a $369.90 desk?"

"In Wyoming if the property is worth more than twenty-five dollars it's a felony. If the guy's a thief, he's a thief. Doesn't make any difference if it's twenty-five dollars or twenty-five thousand dollars. Now isn't that so, Mr. Spence?" Miller asked in a high, sarcastic voice.

"Well, I can't get the justices of the peace to take the case. Shorty Anderson in Riverton says he's disqualified. Says I represent his son, which I do. The other justices in the county never tried a big case with a lot of lawyers. And Bill Smith is representing Newton."

"Those aren't my problems, Mr. Spence. You are, of course, aware of the statute that makes it a crime for the prosecuting attorney to fail to prosecute crimes within his jurisdiction that are properly called to his attention?" Miller said darkly.

"Are you threatening me?" I asked.

"I'm trying to educate you," he shot back.

In the meantime Newton himself had gone to see Attorney General Miller in an attempt to explain what had happened. According to Miller, Newton had confessed the crime. Whether he did or not I do not confirm. But by asserting he had, the attorney general had made himself a material witness. I could no longer ignore the matter.

Then more rumors began to fly—that Newton hadn't properly remitted the fines he had collected as justice of the peace. I examined his books. I checked the fines he said he'd levied and collected against the remittances he'd made to the county. Then I went to the people, mostly Native Americans who had been fined for various misdemeanors, assaults and batteries, public drunkenness, bad checks and the like, to see if they had paid larger fines than the ones reported or had paid fines he hadn't reported. The fines in question ranged from $4 to $100 and totaled $213. Petty bookkeeping errors, Newton said. Then someone brought me the information that Newton had represented someone in a divorce case and had allegedly counterfeited a decree of the court.

Since I couldn't settle on a justice of the peace to sit for the preliminary hearing required by law, I decided to call a grand jury, present the evidence to the grand jury, obtain the grand jury's indictment and thereby avoid the problem. No one had ever called a grand jury in the county before, or so far as I knew, in the state. No one knew how. There were no forms, no precedents, no case law, nothing. I opened up the statute books and devised a procedure, prepared the forms, had the court sign an order convening the grand jury, had the clerk draw the names of the citizens to serve on it—all of which is old hat these days. Then I presented what evidence I had to the eighteen citizens, good and true, who deliberated and brought in their indictment.

Immediately Bill Smith asked for a change of venue on behalf of his client. Judge Sheldon gladly transferred the case to Washakie County, where the town of Worland was the county seat, and he assigned the case to Judge Joseph Spangler for trial. Then Smith filed a motion to quash the indictment.

He stood before the judge looking up and sounding irate. "This man," he said, referring to me, "has had the temerity to file an indictment against my client without including the absolutely imperative concluding language in the indictment: 'against the peace and dignity of the State of Wyoming.' Not only that," Smith now sounded shocked, "*women* sat on this grand jury and women are constitutionally prohibited from sitting on grand juries in this state. The Constitution provides clearly that the grand jury will be composed of not less than eighteen *men*."

Judge Spangler granted Smith's motion to quash, which now required me to go back to the same grand jury and obtain a new indictment. This time the jury returned an amended indictment that concluded, "against the peace and dignity of the State of Wyoming."

When it came time for the trial, Miller had suddenly gone on vacation to Mexico. He had known full well that the trial was coming up, this man who had been so insistent that I bring the charges against Newton in the first place. And he knew he was the crucial witness in what was otherwise a hard case to prove. Now, in Mexico, beyond the subpoena power of the state, he refused to return. I finally tracked him down and talked to him on the phone.

"I need your testimony," I said. "It's absolutely critical."

"Well, I'm on vacation."

"I know," I said, "but you were the one who forced this case to trial in the first place. You told me he confessed."

"Well," he said, "I'm sorry. You'll have to do the best you can without me."

"Well, I'll subpoena you," I sputtered.

He knew I couldn't. "Have fun," he said. "Bye." And he hung up. Perhaps I should have dismissed the case right then. With more experience I probably would have done exactly that or sought a continuance. But for me, it was too late. Too much had been invested in pain and preparation. Nobody cared about the case in Worland. People were interested in their sugar beet checks and the price of steers. People had never heard of me or Ernest Newton. Smith was known by no one. The judge was from Cody. The courtroom was empty right up until the time of the verdict.

Smith, with his two partners at his side, defended Newton every inch of the way, against every question, every move. I couldn't cough without an objection. Newton sat silently bellicose, often striking out at me with his hard stares. I didn't blame him. The witnesses I presented on the charges concerning the fine monies he had collected as justice of the peace were mostly uneducated Native Americans who found themselves sitting in a witness chair in the white man's court, the judge peering down at them, a hostile jury staring. Who would believe Billy Red Horse, who had been fined for drunkenness? Who would give any credibility to Rosy Lou Whiteplumes, who had been fined for disturbing the peace? My witnesses were not convincing to the all-white jury. And as for the desk, there was testimony that exonerated Newton's use of it in his office. Some of Newton's friends from the legislature, important men in the state, came to testify on his behalf. They passed me by in the halls, politicians with watches tucked into their suit vests at the end of gold chains, important-looking men with gray hair. The trial dragged on for several weeks. I felt bad for the man, Ernest Newton. I hurt for myself. Sometimes the charges seemed no more important than the carping of some petulant politician. I hated prosecuting the case. I hated being caught in the cross fire of politicians who didn't have the courage, perhaps not even the facts, to stand up and be counted. I thought of Miller lying on a Mexican beach somewhere, amused by it all.

I never felt the jury was any more friendly to my case than I had been. I thought they probably saw me as an ambitious young punk trying to make a name for himself. At last the jury returned its verdict. The judge handed the verdict to the clerk to read. The courtroom, nearly empty, was silent as a sepulchre.

The clerk, a friendly sort, a permanent smile cut into his face, droned on as if he were reading the funny papers to sleeping children. "We, the jury, duly impaneled and sworn to try the above entitled cause, do find as follows:

"Count one, Not guilty." The count about the desk.

"Count two, Not guilty." Allegations concerning his accounting for the monies collected as justice of the peace.

"Count three, Not guilty," More allegations about his justice of the peace accounting.

"Count four, Not guilty." And more.

"Count five, Not guilty." And more.

"Count six, Not guilty." I couldn't breathe. I had failed.

"Count seven, Not guilty." It was I who began to feel guilty. How could I have brought the case?

I was frozen, the blood rushing from me. I saw the politicians in Cheyenne chortling. The clerk continued his reading. I turned away to look at Ernest Newton. Relief was flooding his face. In a way, I felt relief as well.

"Count eight, Not guilty.

"Count nine, Not guilty.

"Count ten, Not guilty." The last count was yet to be read. The clerk cleared his throat and looked over at Newton.

"Count eleven. *Guilty.*" Guilty of forging the judge's signature on a decree.

Everyone was stunned. A dreadful silence followed. I heard a small sob. I shoved my papers in my briefcase and headed for the door, sad, at last, for having won at all. No one had won. Newton stood convicted of a felony on a single count.

As I walked out Newton said, "Well, Gerry, I hope you're satisfied." It wasn't anger I heard. It was as if he were saying, *You have killed me.*

I didn't answer. No answer would have served up well.

Smith appealed the case for Newton, a new attorney general argued the case for the state, and months later the decision of the court was handed down, Smith's old partner, Harry Harnsberger, delivering the opinion of the court.

The judges weren't sure that the amended indictment properly charged a forgery, the count on which Newton was convicted. But one thing they were sure of: When the grand jury amended the indictment, the jurisdiction of the case went back to Fremont County. For the Washakie County District Court to obtain jurisdiction, a new assignment of the case by the judge in Fremont County to the judge in Washakie County was necessary. Failing such assignment, the jurisdiction in the case remained with Fremont County, not Washakie County. The trial had been before a court without jurisdiction and was therefore a nullity.

The capacity of high courts to render frivolous, flighty, featherbrained decisions clothed in high-sounding language is often astounding. Remembering that it was Newton who, in the first place, wanted the venue in the case changed to Washakie County, Justice Harnsberger now opined with ambitious language that, even so, Newton might have later changed his mind and decided to try the case in Fremont County. Therefore, taking the case to Washakie County without the defendant having first requested the second change of venue deprived the defendant of the right to be tried at home. I thought Newton's submission to the trial without objection, his plea of "not guilty" before the court, his motion to have the case sent to Washakie County in the first place probably provided the court with jurisdiction or estopped Newton from asserting such a defense.

Perhaps I could have brought the case anew. If there was no jurisdiction, jeopardy probably hadn't attached. But I had no stomach for the case, and on February 25, 1960, Ernest Newton withdrew his membership in the Wyoming bar and moved to Nevada. After that no one seemed interested in the case. But I never got over it. Nor, likely, did he. The power of every prosecutor is immense, a power that can destroy both the guilty and the innocent. Guilty or not, the pain of seeing that man endure that trial and the lengthy proceedings that led up to it inevitably brought me the full circle of which Black Elk spoke. I had begun my legal career in Fremont County as a result of Ernest Newton. It was Newton who had directed me to Franklin Sheldon in the first place. Now I decided to end my career as a prosecutor in that county as a result of the prosecution of the same man. I thought of how Newton, too, must have seen it. Newton had been responsible for helping establish in Fremont County the very man who would later bring about the end of his career there. "The power of the world always works in a circle," Black Elk said.

I finished my second term having tried many more cases, none of which I lost, not that such a record stands for much. With all the power prosecutors possess, they ought not lose cases. The wrong case, the unjust case should be rejected in the prosecutor's office before he seeks an indictment. When other competent attorneys announced they would run for the job of county and prosecuting attorney, I decided it was time for me to move on. I had learned how to talk to a jury and to try a case. I was still young, just past thirty.

One rare day when Judge Sheldon was sitting in his plain office, his feet up on his gray steel desk, a cigarette held lightly between his brown fingers, he leaned back and took a good look at me. Here was this kid who as a wide-eyed puppy had started in his office, and who then didn't even know what an abstract looked like. The judge gave me a toothy smile, and I accepted the rare gift.

"Gerry, you have what it takes to become a great trial lawyer."

I didn't know what to say. "What do you mean?"

"That's all I gotta say," he said, puffing on his cigarette and looking at me as if I should heed those words. And his words created a vision. Such visions, if honestly imparted, are the greatest gift one person can bestow upon another. I held Judge Sheldon's vision of me in contrast with the one imposed by Judge Parker. I could still hear his exasperated admonishment: "You will never become a trial lawyer, Mr. Spence. . . . I am doing you a favor by being brutally honest with you. I offer you not the slightest encouragement."

To be a trial lawyer: that had become the ambition of my life—to be what Judge Parker said I would never be, to be what Judge Sheldon said I could be. I began to limit my practice to the trial of cases; no more abstracts, no divorces, no contracts. My ambition to try cases consumed me. I can remember driving the barren road to the courthouse in Lander. Sometimes, as I drove, I practiced my closing arguments—the powerful rising of the voice, the crescendos, the hushed whispers. Sometimes I watched my performance in the rearview mirror. And had any old cow dared drift onto the highway at that precise moment, she would, indeed, have been sacrificed to the reverie of a young and restive country lawyer.

CHAPTER 28

GERRY SPENCE believes:

"Federal welfare is the great narcotic of men's souls."

let's pull for

A MAN WHO WON'T STRADDLE THE FENCE . . . .

GERRY SPENCE

for Congress—Republican

Spence for Cong. Comm.; Tom Spence, Sec'y.

Ad in Spence's congressional race.

IN 1962 I came to the curious conclusion, beclouded in the fog of ego, that Wyoming deserved me, a young, aggressive, skilled trial lawyer who would charge out of the vacant spaces of the West and take Washington by storm. I would fight for the people, there make a name for myself, and perhaps become president of the United States. Why not? I was thirty-three years old. My second term as a prosecutor was coming to a close. Convinced as I was that merely prosecuting the poor, who robbed back, and the forgotten, who struck back, the despised, who hated back, did not fulfill my predestined role in the universe, I decided it was time to burst into the big time. Moreover, something felt stifling to me in that small town of Riverton, like a child who had outgrown his playpen. I felt trapped in the town. But more, I felt the need to bloom, *to become.* I had read and absorbed Paul Tillich's masterwork, *The Courage to Be,* and I told myself in those monologues in the shower and on the lonely drives to the county seat in Lander that surely I possessed such courage.

Wyoming's political stage starred a nondescript, extremely bland fellow by the name of William Henry Harrison—named after his grandfather, the ninth president of the United States, back in the 1840s. He was also the first president to die in office, after having served but one month. I thought the tendency ran in the family. William Henry Harrison, his grandson, had been in the House of Representatives for three terms and displayed every indication of having been dead from the first day he was elected. The grandson had emigrated from Indiana to Sheridan, Wyoming, had taken up a ranch there among the wealthy, donned a silver belly Stetson with a small brim, one of those businessman kinds of cowboy hats, and had run for the United States Congress on the Republican ticket. Wyoming was easy pickings for a person with politics in his marrow, especially with a name like William Henry Harrison. The people of the state were isolated and provincial, with a frontiersman mentality. They did whatever needed to be done for themselves. They suffered quietly if they had to. They were used to it. They made do. They paid their taxes. Their word was their bond. Independence was their dominant characteristic, honesty their most appreciated virtue. The electorate in the state had not congealed into a single political mind through the pervasive influence of any media. The people in Buffalo, Wyoming, had little awareness of what the people in Newcastle or Rock Springs were thinking. Most didn't care. No statewide newspaper had the power to form attitudes. No television station created a collective Wyoming conscience. People were more a tribe than a community, and, at last, more a family than a tribe. The rancher in Meeteetse was unconnected with the rancher at Bosler Junction. The railroad man in Moorcroft had no connection with the laborer in Ucross. But there was one thing that finally connected them—a name, one familiar to all, and that name was William Henry Harrison.

People, including me, knew nothing about the grandfather, William Henry Harrison. Perhaps in their history books they had heard about "Tippecanoe and Tyler too," which was the slogan that elected him after his defeat of the Shawnees at the battle of the same name. The president's grandson, as I saw it, had little to offer the people of the state save his marvelously propitious name and his stability—which, upon the most generous analysis, was grounded in doing nothing. In short, this man did one thing in Washington, and one thing only: He filled a chair. I sat down with Bob Peck, my old friend at *The Riverton Ranger,* to discuss the idea that was bursting out of my belly.

While my parents were "Rooseveltians," as it were, for Franklin Roosevelt to the core, I was a Republican; probably had something to do with my pounding determination to be as different from my parents as I could. The kind of success I had in mind didn't seem consistent with the simple, folksy, love-your-neighbor, care-for-the-poor, be-poor-yourself, it's-okay-if-you're-honest kind of philosophy that drove my parents. Such ideas had not led them down the road to the big time and were, therefore, incompatible with my own heady ambitions. Besides, I liked to tell the story about when I was thrown overboard in New York Harbor because I wouldn't join the union—trying to save the money to go to college, I argued, but the goons weren't buying it, threw me overboard and dumped a ton of garbage down on me, almost smothered to death. The first

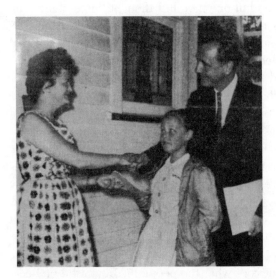

*Spence in his door-to-door campaign
for Congress.*

*William Henry Harrison, Spence's
Congressional opponent.*

thing I saw when I could get my eyes cleared of the coffee grounds and toilet paper was the Statute of Liberty. Then, just before I drowned, they pulled me on board, but by that time I had already become a rock-ribbed Republican, standing as far right as William Henry Harrison's grandfather himself.

I turned to Bob Peck, waiting for his reply. "What do you think, Bob?"

"Probably can't beat him in the primary," he finally replied.

"Why not?" I could do anything. "Everybody knows he's never done a damn thing in his life but run on his grandfather's name." Peck looked at me in that sad, patient way of his. "He at least has a name."

I wouldn't be discouraged. "I can beat him. You know why? Because he's a lazy old drone. He's as exciting as mumps. I'll get out and knock on every door in the state of Wyoming. By the time he realizes what's up and gets off his petrified duff it'll be too late. I'll have the election won."

"Maybe so," Bob said. "That's the only way you can beat him." He was silent a long time. I waited. Finally he said, "If that's what you want to do, and you do it, I'll support you."

The next day I filed for Congress on the Republican ticket. I thought the electorate would appreciate a little original rhetoric. My letter to the state chairman of the Republican party, published in *The Riverton Ranger* and the other state papers, read in part:

> When a young man contemplates his destiny, he must discover first the path on which his state and nation proceed, for on such path he and his children must also follow. When I did this I could not avoid the frightful spectacle of a runaway nation tumbling uncontrollably down a pre-greased road to socialism, and as the monster hurtled by, it squashed each individual who stood in its path.

A "pre-greased road to socialism," indeed! Already I was looking at the world through the eyes of my opponent. I promised I would seek people of the same mind "in every city and town, in every farm and ranch, in every mine and oil patch, in the sheep wagons, the cow camps and roadside stops—and together the people of Wyoming will be heard and our force will be felt in Washington." Franklin Delano Roosevelt couldn't have found more grandiose-sounding prose.

Yet nobody but me was impressed with my rhetoric. Nobody gave a damn about this alleged "pre-greased road to socialism," whatever that was supposed to mean. If I had listened I could have heard the folks ask, "What kind of high-falutin perfumed horse puckey is that?" It had nothing to do with the price of cattle at Omaha, where the ranchers shipped their steers in the fall. It sounded good, all right, but good to whom? Good to me. I was lathered before the race began, and amazed that people weren't as excited as I about the prospect of electing this young, aggressive fighter to Congress so that "together the people of Wyoming could be heard." My announcement, carried in all the newspapers in the state, created not a ripple. "Gerry Spence? Who the hell is Gerry Spence?"

Bob Peck tried to create a little stir over my candidacy. I give him credit. I had been the youngest prosecutor in the state's history, reminiscent of Tom Dewey, who had cleaned up New York. But in the end, I was the only person in the state who was really excited over my campaign. Undaunted, I set out to fulfill my promise. Again I got out the telephone books with their maps of the towns in the front. I'd done it before, and I'd do it again. I'd knock on every door in the state, and I'd beat old William Henry Harrison. Beat him good. And the people of the state would be heard in the hallowed halls of Congress through the voice of their new champion, Gerry Spence.

I knew as much about running a statewide political campaign as a cowboy knows about the tax code. I knew you needed an organization, so I organized. I knew you needed money, so I solicited my friends to chip in. I had a finance chairman—a guy who liked money but who also didn't like the work of raising money. I traveled around the state and appointed county chairpersons in nearly

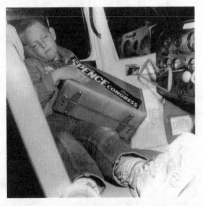

Kent on the campaign trail with his dad.

The Spence family as used on the campaign literature.

Worn out shoes of Gerry and Tom Spence campaigning.

every county. People liked to be chairpersons. But they didn't like the work. They liked the title, the respect. I had an overall chairman, a friend of mine who grinned a lot and whom everybody liked but who also didn't like the gritty, tiring work of running a campaign, and when he couldn't keep up the pace, I brought in my brother Tom, then just twenty, to help me run this thing I had spawned.

Sometimes Tom and I arose before dawn and pounded posters to the telephone poles up and down Main Street in whatever town we happened to be in at the time. You had to get up before the cops rolled out. It was against many town ordinances to deface telephone and light poles with posters. Then, as soon as it was marginally decent to do so, we began knocking on the doors, a block at a time. Sometimes Anna came along with the kids—made a hell of an impression if anybody looked, family man and all.

By this time in my life, I had purchased an old Cessna single-engine tricycle-geared airplane, and I was flying around the state trying to create the image of a candidate who was at least alive, of somebody who could walk, talk, and even fly—*a lot more than William Henry Harrison could do* was the implied message.

When I flew into town, Tom, my brother, would have already driven there the night before. He'd call up the local newspaper in the little town and announce, excitedly, "Gerry Spence is flying in tomorrow!" The guy who answered the phone was usually the owner, who wrote the stories, set the type, and printed the paper.

"Who's that?" the guy would ask.

"Why, he's running for Congress, and he'll be at the airport at two this afternoon. Come on down and meet him!"

"Right!" the guy would say. "I'll stop what I'm doin'—quit setting the type on the want ads, and I'll junk the front-page story on how the county commissioners refused to extend the county road to Mrs. Hollingsworth's ranch and how she is pissed, and the paper will be late, and I'll lose half of my customers, all so I can have the pleasure of meeting this guy. What's his name again?"

When we got to Casper, Tom called the *Casper Star Tribune*, the state's largest and most powerful newspaper. Had to have its support. At least its interest. At least its tolerance.

"Gerry Spence is flying in this afternoon," Tom said, with all the enthusiasm he could muster to Phil McCauley, editor in chief.

"So what?" McCauley asked.

"Don't you want to come out to the airport and meet him?"

"What for?" McCauley asked.

I took photographs showing little Kent, then five, sleeping in the cockpit of his daddy's airplane with an "I'm with Spence for Congress" bumper sticker stuck to his suitcase. Cute. One or two of the over twenty papers in the state ran it.

My campaign literature showed me with the smiling Anna and the four smiling kids and the smiling candidate. What else did they want? I was the right kind—plenty conservative, a family man, obviously virile, a former prosecutor—an energetic man who was deliriously dedicated to almost everything and who was totally opposed to the do-nothing stance of my opponent.

I stood against all the things Wyoming people fought against—Medicare, federal aid to education, and foreign aid. Harrison thought that the school lunch program was a sin, the severity of which was exceeded only by outright communism itself. That's the way I saw it. Moreover, the elderly didn't want help. Wyoming people were self-reliant. I made speeches flaying at "the approaching welfare state." I was "appalled and heartsick at the pathetic specter of a once-proud republic, now reverting to the intolerable days of the WPA." I said that freedom was a "flag-waving, patriotic, all-day, everyday task." The sound of my voice and the cadence of my speeches were reminiscent of Franklin Roosevelt, but I struck out at the New Frontier with words that would have brought gasps of abounding admiration today from the likes of Newt Gingrich, and that would have caused the far right to swoon in fathomless joy.

I would have bet the election on the proposition that Harrison had never given birth to an original idea in his entire life. But Wyoming folks mostly liked what he stood for. If the truth were known, it was perfectly acceptable to the voters that he go to Washington, that he do nothing and say nothing, and that thereafter he leave the people of Wyoming the hell alone.

As for me, I seemed a slight bit shy of original ideas myself. But nobody asked. Nobody cared. I hadn't studied politics or government. At thirty-three I had yet to undertake an in-depth study of myself. I was still in revolt. My father, an old-line Democrat, must have been shocked at my platform. If he was he remained silent. He was patient, as usual, and willing to let his son find his own way—that was always his great gift to me.

On the campaign trail I never missed a chance for exposure—any exposure. I spoke at the Pinedale High School graduating class—I think there were fifteen graduating seniors. But remember, most had two parents in attendance—sometimes a grandparent or an aunt. Relentlessly I knocked on the doors in the summer's heat, believing, as I did, that the next door I knocked on might well house the winning vote. One day both Tom and I caved in from the summer heat. At Lusk, after campaigning for several days and having knocked on every door in town, I decided to take a poll. Couldn't afford a professional pollster, so one evening I randomly picked out twenty names in the phone book and called the numbers myself.

"Sir, we are taking a poll. In the U.S. House race, who do you favor, William Henry Harrison or Gerry Spence?"

"Harrison or who?"

"Gerry Spence, you know, the young dynamic candidate from Riverton." I'd been at that very house the day before.

"Oh, I guess I'll vote for Harrison, if I vote."

"Why?" I asked.

"I dunno."

The next number— the same. Never heard of Gerry Spence. How could the *Evanston Herald* have once claimed in its editorial that Spence is "the owner of a striking personality. He is brilliant. He is courageous and energetic and has plenty of zip and go. He is a campaigner deluxe"?

Goshen county attorney, Stan Hathaway, is shown above as he met G. L. Spence, Fremont county attorney and Republican Congressional candidate at the court house here Tuesday.

Spence and Stan Hathaway at Torrington during congressional campaign.

I must not be too damn "striking." I should have changed my name to Abraham Lincoln if name recognition was the only issue.

Yet periodic bright spots seeped through the gloom, and my setback in the poll only intensified my determination to win. I received encouragement from the most up-and-coming young politician in the state, the cigar-smoking, perpetually grinning, earthy Stanley K. Hathaway of Torrington, a man who was soon to become governor.

"I'll support you all the way," Stan Hathaway said, and his big smile made me happy too. "Win or lose, Gerry, I'm your friend." I felt it. Believed it. I was standing there with the photographer, and so when I asked him, he bravely stepped up and let the photographer take his photograph with me, these two Young Turks, he older than I, and the photograph was published right there in his hometown paper. His wife even had me to his house for a tea, but William Henry Harrison was also there, just happened by, I suppose, which only made it fair. Stanley K. Hathaway was a fair man. Fair to everybody. But, I thought, one thing you had to admire about Stanley K. Hathaway. He wasn't afraid to buck the party. I loved Stanley Hathaway. He wasn't your ordinary politician. He had courage.

I continued to knock on the doors and to shake hands with the customers at the grocery stores, and to set my posters in the store windows by day, which I observed were often removed within the hour following my departure. By night I wrote press releases for every newspaper in the state on every conceivable subject, from "the unconscious conspiracy to enslave America" to essays concerning my alliance with agriculture. "There's a lot more farmers and ranchers in Wyoming than lawyers, thank the Lord," I wrote.

And Harrison's seniority in the House was no great asset to the people of the state, either. If I defeated him the people would lose nothing in seniority benefits that the old pros were always hollering about. Despite his three terms in Congress, I pointed out that on one committee he was fourth from the bottom in a committee of thirty-four, and on another committee, third from the bottom out of twenty-five. I argued that I had wielded that much national power when I was a member of the Sheridan Boy Scouts. By night I also authored small statewide ads to run in the various papers. My picture, which gave the appearance of a semicomatose high schooler, was published in the ads along with scripts like:

Abe Lincoln said: "Even if you're on the right track . . . you'll get run over if you just stand there." Let's MOVE with a young WYOMING man.

and

Speak out for a man who won't straddle the fence.

and

Stand up for the man who will stand up for you.

Heady, deeply moving, big-time stuff. I couldn't understand why the voters weren't simply staggered by it all.

By late July I had completed my door-to-door campaign in every town and I began writing open letters to the people, thanking them, and saying things in agricultural areas like:

I pledge myself to the task of getting government off agriculture's back so Wyoming farmers and ranchers can get back in. We don't need more government. We need more liberty. Ours is the heritage of a free frontier. Let's keep it that way.

Finally I closed the campaign with an ad that read:

The man you can count on is counting on you.

The night of the election I was home with my family and some of my friends. Tom was there. Some friends in Riverton came over at our invitation. They seemed somber, like people who had been appointed to witness an execution. In my heart I also knew I had lost the election. You can't beat an old war horse by hollering at it. People vote the names they know. If the name stays unstained, the people will vote for it even when the bearer is dead and buried, like that congressman I'd heard about who got elected even though he'd been in the grave six weeks. My hands weren't muddy from throwing mud, but I hadn't won. Yet as I waited for the returns I had vague hopes. The first precinct to report was always from the town of Bill, Wyoming.

We were glued to the radio. "Folks," the announcer interrupted the country music, "the first return of the primary election has just come in. From Bill, Wyoming, as usual." He read off the returns starting with the senate race, then the governor's, then the U.S. House. "For the U.S. House of Representatives: Gerry Spence, two, William Henry Harrison, one." Two to one! The kitchen, where we were all huddled around the radio, erupted.

"Congratulations!" they hollered, and they pounded my back, and I was all smiles, and my heart sang. I had won Bill, Wyoming. That was the real poll! The people in Bill knew what this was all about. They wanted to be heard and to put Wyoming on the map. And then the next return came in from Wheatland, and the news wasn't quite that good. Harrison won by a comfortable margin. But I'd campaigned in Wheatland early, and hadn't been back—likely just an aberration. "Remember Bill, Wyoming" was the new slogan in the kitchen. Anna was serving up little bits of this and that on a tray, and the kids were running around not paying attention to what was going on.

In the end that's what we did—remember Bill, Wyoming. Never again was I ahead. Our house turned into a morgue; the party became a funeral. Some of our guests slipped away, saying nothing. Others came by to say goodnight, sad faced, not knowing what to say.

The next day the Associated Press reported that Gerry Spence, Fremont County Attorney, was "drubbed decisively." I wasn't beaten, I was *drubbed*— something like twenty-six thousand votes for Harrison to sixteen-thousand for me. I carried my own county. For that I was marginally grateful.

I was crushed. How could I have lost? Didn't the person who worked the hardest and cared the most always win? Wasn't that the credo of the American ethic? I felt betrayed. And the hurt turned to anger, for it is always easier to be angry and rage than to be hurt and cry. Looking back, as hard as it is to reconcile that campaign with my political philosophy today, I must have deeply believed what I said. I had taken on the role of the fighting frontier politician, the incorruptible hope of all those who wanted to be represented in Washington. Still in all, my campaign was nothing more than a lively copy of my opponent's.

Today, given the same choice as the voters in Wyoming were given in 1962, I would probably have to vote for William Henry Harrison. He was at least quiet about his emptyheadedness. Sometimes I am staggered when I realize that the brittle tenets of the conservative Republican haven't changed in over three decades. Thirty years ago I was raising hell with the Supreme Court for banning prayer in the schools. Thirty years ago I was tooting that same old tinny horn about how "dependence on government destroys self-reliance," and at the same time, I was totally unaware of the fact that in this country hundreds of thousands of kids go to bed every night hungry. Perhaps I could be forgiven.

Wyoming was a poor state, but we were uniformly poor. There wasn't a million-aire in Riverton that I knew of. The so-called wealthy were the small business-people and the ranchers who drove their beat-up pickups to town and stomped down to the local saloon to hoist one with the rest of the folks. But people had jobs, and people weren't hungry, and their kids weren't hungry. I'd never been in a big-city ghetto. I'd never seen kids crowded up in decaying old traps full of disease and rats and drugs.

I got a few condolences, including one from Stanley K. Hathaway. He was sorry I'd been defeated. "Great loss to the state," he said. The state needed, more than anything else, young men with courage and talent and foresight, and I was such a man. But he would always be my friend. That meant a lot to me. Yet I felt like the bull elk in my father's story, the one driven from the heard by the bigger, stronger bull. Defeated, the bull ran from the herd and he ran until he fell exhausted in the snow, only to stagger to his feet to run even farther. He ran until at last he could find a new herd. I felt banished, hated, beaten. I felt like running. I had laid it all down in the campaign—the total me. And the total me had been cast aside like something tainted in the slaughterhouse.

But I was trapped. I couldn't run. Down where you really know things, I realized my run for Congress had been about escaping Riverton. Now I wanted to be free of everything that seemed to snare me—my marriage, my parents' teachings, my mother's deeply religious expectations, my partnership, even good manners. Within a few weeks I sat down with my old friend and part-ner, Frank Hill. I wanted to end the partnership. And I thought that Frank needed to be free of me. Somehow Frank Hill, who had always understood, still understood.

Frank kept our building. I decided to build a new office across the street. There I opened my solo practice devoted to the specialty of trials. If I couldn't be a lawyer for the whole state in Congress, I was going to be a trial lawyer in private practice. Examining abstracts, representing irrigation districts, drawing up farm leases and handling default divorces was no longer for me.

My new office would become a sanctuary where people could drag in their ponderous problems, and, in front of a roaring fire in the red stone fireplace, reminiscent of the red stone canyon of Grandpa Spence's hogback, I would lis-ten to my clients' pain. I was a person who knew about disappointment and how it was to feel beaten and lost. In this office I would have no desk, because desks say, "I am the lawyer who, on this side of the desk, knows. You, on the other side, do not know." It said, "I will also never need to get close to you because the desk separates us and keeps me free of you."

In the center of the room I set a large, round oak table with oak captain's chairs. I would sit down with my client in a chair just like his, no big fancy over-stuffed leather affair. I could reach over and touch my client, and without a desk separating us, we could talk, like people, like friends. Sometimes I'd pour a cup of coffee. Then we'd get into the misery and fear and the anger that always brings people to trial lawyers, as a pain in the belly brings people to their surgeon.

Inside the small courtyard off my private office I built a small waterfall that came tumbling down over the red stone, and the sound of the water soothed me. My isolation protected me and let me begin to heal. I hired Cleo Arguello, the Mexican-American wife of Manuel, my quadriplegic client. By her gentleness and quiet compassion I was comforted. I grew a single tomato plant inside the office and wrote poetry about the need of the plant to be pollinated. I was the lonely tomato plant. No other plants like it grew in its world, my office, and alone the tomato plant could not bear fruit. It bloomed, all right, and, failing to bear fruit, it bloomed and bloomed again, and then, long after the season, the disappointed blossoms finally dried up and fell off.

I built a bar inside my private office, and the sour mash whiskey also soothed me, or I thought it did, and of an evening my friends and I drank and laughed and spoke of ribald matters. We were a cynical lot, and my new, deep cynicism sometimes soothed me, or I thought it did. Often we laughed at the sacred. Debauchery became virtue, depravity the best balm for pain. I struggled to make sense out of my life, but, except for my work, life seemed empty and fatuous.

One day I hollered for Cleo. "Cleo, come take a letter."

She traipsed into the office, sat down at the round table and waited her kindly, patient wait. I began to dictate:

"To the *American Bar Association Journal*. Want Ads. Please insert the following ad under 'Employment Wanted': Best trial lawyer in America needs work.

"Put our phone number down," I said.

"Is that all?" she asked.

"Yeah, that's all."

"You don't need work," she said. "You need to get to work."

"Well, I'm going to go to work on this great new case." Then I told her about the murder case I had taken in Rawlins. "Mexican fella shot his wife in front of a bunch of witnesses."

Cleo appeared suddenly sad and serious. "Why did he do that?" she asked.

"Because he wanted to," I said. His name was Joe Esquibel. I later wrote a book about the case.° I had taken the hopeless defense of a vicious murderer, a man who murdered his wife in the presence of eight eyewitnesses. But why not take the case? I doubt I exactly understood my motives. I was angry. Perhaps I only needed tangible work to latch on to, to keep from drowning in murky waters. Yet I could argue my taking the case on another ground: A real trial lawyer without a good murder case is not a trial lawyer—I said things like that. The defendant, of course, was penniless.

°See *Of Murder and Madness*, Doubleday, 1983 (hardcover), and St. Martin's Press, 1995 (paperback).

Joe Esquibel during his sanity trial.

I tried the case three times
before a jury, twice on the question
of his ability to stand trial, and, after
the United States Supreme Court
had thrown out the death penalty, I
tried the case again, the last time
pleading insanity as a defense, and
again the jury acquitted. My friend
Raymond Whitaker, who saw things
through a cynic's eyes like my own,
and a young law student who would
himself later become a great trial
lawyer, John Ackerman, helped me
in the case.

The *American Bar Association
Journal* sent my letter and my check
back with a terse, snooty note. The
editors would not think of running
the ad. It violated certain "obvious ethical standards" of the publication.

The trap grew more oppressive. I couldn't escape from that small town law
practice that no longer challenged me nor from the provincial politics of many
of the townsfolk that especially, after the election, often offended me. I felt
trapped by a marriage that had become a war with a roof over it. I was trapped
all right, and frantic. But search as I did, I saw no way out. I was a married man,
the father of four, a man with responsibility, a lawyer with duties to his clients.
I had to work to make a living, to feed the family, to pay the bills. Surely I would
perish here. I found small solace at the little bar in my office where the Old
Cabin Still flowed. With those friends who could drink as much and as long as
I, I often carried my fight against the trapping demons on into the night.

"You're late for dinner as usual," Anna would say.

And then the fight would begin anew. She'd been at home all day, working,
taking care of kids, keeping a house. She'd prepared dinner, and for whom? For
a man who didn't care enough or respect her enough to come home at supper
time. Dinner was spoiled. Third time this week. And what does a trapped man
say back to his wife? We had no counseling. We had little insight into the
dynamics of our lives. As for me, I was a tangled mass of pain and anger. And
Anna was as trapped as I, trapped with a wild, wounded animal and four kids.
Sometimes I would forgo supper, and the attendant pain of the harsh words and
bitter feelings. Sometimes I'd just have another drink and stumble into bed.
Sometimes Anna would drink with me, and at times that was better, and at times
worse, and sometimes I couldn't remember, and sometimes I didn't care.

In the night I saw my dead mother in her casket, her translucent face, those
tightly sewed lips. In my dreams she was dead, but crying, begging me not to

bury her. When I awakened I was sweating, horrified, weeping. Desperate, I drank more. Often, after a night's drinking, I couldn't sleep and lay wide-eyed, staring up at the empty void, drunk, agitated, and on the cusp of crazy.

At the office, my friends and I, during an evening's drinking, often argued over what constituted insanity. Perhaps we were all insane. The world was insane. The universe was a hodgepodge of insanity, without order, without purpose. It was insane to demand meaning and purpose from life.

But there was saneness in the bottle. Look inside. You can see sanity down there, floating around, all amber and pretty and pure. I poured the liquid into the glass, and then I put an ice cube in the palm of my hand, smacked the cube smartly with a tablespoon, and the ice cracked and I dumped it into the glass. Then I poured the fizz-water over it all and held the glass up to the light to see what I could see.

"Here's to sanity," I said, lifting my glass again. And my friends, laughing, thinking this was all too dreadfully funny, dutifully drank to sanity. They would have as quickly drunk to the opposite.

A sense of futility set in. I thought of how it would be to die, but I was afraid to die. I began to comprehend what must have been my mother's hopeless entanglement with a misery from which she could not escape. My God, had I inherited my mother's propensity to self destruction? Could the son of the mother also put the gun to his mouth? I thought of the cold evilness of it, the curved, accursed steel beckoning the finger, imploring, holding out the promise of eternal peace. And why should we be against it? Why not escape life at the first opportunity? Was not life merely the initiation fee one must pay for timeless silence? Anna thought I should see a shrink. This time I didn't argue with her.

I made an appointment with a well-known psychiatrist in Denver. He was a short, gray-haired elf of a man with a large reputation, past seventy, a man who seemed more suited to selling kids' cereal on television than treating the mentally ill.

He wanted to know if I was going to kill myself.

"Yes, I probably will," I said.

"Have you thought of it much?"

"How much is much?"

"Have you thought of it this week?"

"Well, yes, but dying is not such a big fucking deal, is it? I mean, everybody can do it." He wasn't there to answer questions, he said. He puffed on his pipe and stared. I thought Sigmund Freud must be his role model. Already I didn't like the little bastard.

"You need to be tested, Mr. Spence," he said. He sat behind a big walnut desk in a dark walnut-paneled room. A person could hardly see in the place. "When you try a case, Mr. Spence, you need the facts. When I diagnose a patient, I need them, too."

"Don't humor me," I said. "If you want to test me, test me."

I'd go along with the man—at least for a while, at least until he tried to get me over there on the couch. On the other hand I was paying good money to the man, more money per hour than I made. Better get my money's worth. Besides, I decided to test the shrink while he was testing me. Never did have much respect for shrinks.

But before I could launch my attack he introduced me to his psychologist. "This is Miss Bradley," he said. She had powerful breasts, and was a woman twice his size. The psychologist wore a bright, tight, red sweater. You could tell she was proud of what she had—a little plump, all right, but you noticed the sweater. She knew it. She, also had a large mouth that was wet with bright red viscous lipstick, and she had that long red hair to match. Her hips were large and pushed out against her tightly pleated black and white plaid skirt, and she wore high-heeled black shoes, and black stockings. Suddenly she stuck a card in my face with an inkblot on it and asked me what I saw, and suddenly, I felt afraid.

"You want me to *really* tell you what I see?" I asked, all wide-eyed and innocent acting.

"Oh, yes," she said. "That's exactly what I want you to tell me."

"You don't care what I say, I mean, whatever I see there I should tell you, right?"

"Yes, that's what the test is all about." Holding the card, she leaned over closer to me, her bosom almost in my face. She licked her red lips. "The testing is very important, and you must tell me exactly what you see."

"Exactly?"

"Exactly."

"Hold nothing back, Miss Bradley?"

"Nothing."

"Well, I feel like something is coming over me," I said, setting her up. "I actually feel it."

She leaned closer, her eyes full of light and anticipation. "Tell me what you see." Her voice was suddenly soft and seductive, excited, you know.

"I don't always feel this way," I said, "but I feel this coming over me now."

"Tell me," she begged.

"I'm embarrassed," I said. "All right, I will tell you." I blurted it out. "I see big, beautiful, luscious tits with pretty pink nipples."

She didn't seem surprised. She held up another card. "And what do you see here?" She leaned even closer.

"This may not seem right to you, but you still want me to tell you the complete truth?"

"Yes," she said.

"I see the same thing—big, wonderful, luscious tits." Pretty soon she left, and when she came back she said that the doctor would see me now, and as she walked away, she swung her big hips across the room as if she were clearing the way through the crowd for a parade of tanks.

"I've made arrangements for you to be admitted to a local psychiatric hospital here in Denver. "Wonderful place. Wonderful people," he said, like a travel agent selling me on a resort in Palm Springs. He told me about the grounds, the gardens, the good eating at the mess hall, and how I would be with other folks who were suffering from similar disorders, that I would no longer be alone, and that I could be cured if I submitted to treatment right away. He puffed on his pipe to emphasize his points.

"What's wrong with me? What kind of treatments?"

"I am going to recommend electric shock therapy," he said, as if he had just suggested the BLT sandwich on the menu.

"What's that?" I asked. "Like being strapped in the electric chair or something?"

"Well, not exactly," he said, still puffing in quick little puffs on his pipe. "But you are obviously suffering from a deep psychotic episode, and electric shock therapy will change all of that for you."

"What do you mean, 'deep psychotic episode'? What do you mean it will change all of *that*?" I'd heard about shock treatments. In those days they strapped you—often without anesthesia—to a table and attached a bunch of electrodes to your skull. Then they turned the juice to you, and you screamed and fought against the straps and suffered unspeakable pain and horror as every cell in your brain was slammed with electricity and thereby rearranged.

"Electric shock is known to modify personality," he said, still puffing in faster puffs, and when he couldn't get any more smoke he grabbed for a box of kitchen matches sitting on his desk, struck a match to flame and puffed in the fire.

"It's as if your brain is a sack of marbles of different colors," I said, "and the marbles make up your personality, and if you don't like your personality, all you have to do is shake up the marbles and dump them out and, presto, you have a new personality, right?"

"No cause to be cynical, Mr. Spence. But then deep cynicism is a form of paranoia and is, of course, part of the described syndrome. But I am warning you, Mr. Spence, that you are not to take this lightly. You are presently a danger to yourself and to others."

I recognized the classic words that, when spoken in court by such as he, permitted the medical profession to incarcerate a respondent, sane or insane. A cold chill played up my ribs and made the hackles on the back of my neck tingle. My head got light. I was going to be committed as a lunatic. But I fought back. I had to keep calm and in control.

"I have always been a danger to myself and others," I said. "And so are you. Especially you." I gave him a long look and let him think about that. Paranoid, he probably thought. "Tell me Doctor, what kind of a new personality are you about to give me? Will I be sweet and gentle? Will I be friendly and compliant? Will people like me? Will I give up masturbation and thus save my eyesight?"

"Don't be absurd, Mr. Spence," he said. "Your tests reveal a man who is severely disoriented. You need help. I am here to help you."

"Can you predict the personality that I'll come out with? I mean if I go to a plastic surgeon to get my nose fixed he can tell me how I'll look after the operation. What will I be like? That's all I want to know. Will I be a bowl of corn flakes? Will my wife like the new me? Maybe she should have the same shock treatments so when we come out we will be utterly compatible."

"You insist on making light of this, Mr. Spence. But I shouldn't wonder in your condition." After that he wrote a letter to me emphasizing that I was a very real suicide risk, that I should immediately submit to treatment without which he would not, absolutely not, bear any responsibility whatsoever for the ensuing consequences, which he predicted would be dire.

"I'm crazy," I said to Anna when we got back to the hotel. She wouldn't even agree with me on that.

"You are not crazy," she argued. "You may be a little nuts sometimes. You may be mixed up. You may be hurt. But you are not crazy."

But the shrink had left me in a state of deep panic. Even though I knew I had fiddled with Miss Bradley, how was I to know that such conduct wasn't, itself, a symptom of insanity? As usual, I had outsmarted myself. And the shrink said I was about to do myself in. Maybe he knew and I didn't. Maybe my mother didn't know she was actually going to do it. Maybe she had just been testing herself to see how it felt, and before she realized what happened, she had pulled the trigger. Maybe I was a danger to myself and to others and didn't recognize it. Maybe Anna was in danger. What about the kids? What if I were insane? Insane people don't know they are insane. That's the very definition of insanity.

Already I could hear the lawyers arguing whether "the respondent," as I would be called, had "lost contact with reality." Yes, but then all the sane people in the world must really be insane, because the so-called sane people don't think they are insane and the whole world is indeed insane. At least, I reasoned, I could reason. And people who could reason were not insane. Unless, of course, the reasoning was insane reasoning. But even so, there was, I sanely reasoned, plenty of insane reasoning going around—starting with those who reasoned you out of heaven when you committed suicide, right on down the list to the voters of Wyoming who had just reelected William Henry Harrison. And the ABA people were also insane. What did they know about ethics? How could it be unethical to want to practice your skill some other place than in Riverton, Wyoming? And so, probably, was God insane. He put this whole crazy mess together. He was the author of the paranoid schizo and the creator of all the crazy things man invented to deal with insanity, including that crazy fucking machine that shocked insane people into a different form of insanity.

On the other hand, maybe both the shrink and Miss Bradley were themselves insane, and were judging sane people against their own insanity. Maybe my own thought that *they* were insane was paranoid. Maybe I was a monster and didn't know it. Do monsters know they are monsters? No. On the other hand, if I were this monster who must be strapped down and zapped in order for the world to be safe, I had a responsibility to surrender the monster to the shrink. And don't forget, I kept arguing to myself, as if in a morbid refrain, my mother killed herself. The propensity for suicide was probably bubbling away unchecked in my genes. But in the end I was more terrified of the prescribed electric shock therapy.

"I gotta have a second opinion," I said to Anna, "and I'm not leaving Denver until I get one."

"I think you should, too," she said.

We found another shrink, one recommended over the phone by my friend John Johnson in Lander, the local mental health director, and we hurried off to see this new psychiatrist. He was a tall guy and skinny, with a nose on him like a chicken's beak. But his eyes appeared friendly and he didn't smoke a pipe. He put his feet up on the desk while we talked. Sometimes he laughed at what I said. Good affect, I thought. I had more confidence in him. I told him all about what was hurting me, about my mother, about my dreams, about the humiliating election, about how I felt rejected and betrayed, and then I told him about what the pipe puffer wanted to do to me.

"He wants to do that to all of his patients," he said. "Easy way out for him. You have some problems, all right, Gerry, but you don't need electric shock, and you aren't insane. What you need is some rest. You could use some counseling. You could be a little more friendly to yourself. You can, one of these days when you've had enough, quit flagellating yourself for all of the sins you've charged yourself with. You need a good friend. Start with yourself." I was still confused, but one thing I had gotten straight. I wasn't going to let that little pipe-puffing psychiatrist put my marbles in a sack, shake them up and pour them out again.

At home once more, I sat with my friends at the office drinking, arguing to the bottom of the bottles. I argued that the world—not Gerry Spence, not the lately defeated candidate for the United States House of Representatives, not the greatest trial lawyer in America—was insane.

"I will tell you one thing," I shouted, and early in the evening before the whiskey had settled in, my friends listened. "Only an insane nation would build bombs to destroy the world, in order to save it."

"You want to let the Commies have it?" a veteran buddy of mine asked. He had never been known to smile. Came home from the war and had refused to go back to work.

"Only an insane nation would blow millions of people to hell to preserve the right of the moneyed class to hoard their money."

"This, gentlemen, was our Republican candidate," my beanpole fly fishing partner, Sam, said. He laughed. "Let's drink to him."

"Money is not the test of worth," I shouted.

"I'll tell you one thing: You ain't worth a shit without it." He shoved his empty glass over. "I'll take mine on the rocks."

"Only an insane society cherishes money over all other virtues, including life." No one answered to that one. Some were looking into the fire. Others were talking in small groups. "Only an insane society would celebrate the rich as they became richer over the broken bodies of laboring men," I said.

"That's bullshit," the little guy with the big voice from the radio station said. "This is a free country."

"Only an insane system would permit the powerful to gather money as a means of merely 'keeping score,' while millions of babies the world over die of starvation."

"That's bullshit too, Spence. That's straight out of Karl Marx."

"You never read Karl Marx," I said.

"Right," he said. "Don't have to."

We argued on into the night, the fire raging and snapping in the hearth, the yellow ghosts dancing on the ceiling with the flames, the cacophony of drunken voices laughing, yelling, drowning out the arguments as soon as they were born.

"The law which protects the rich while it puts people in prison, mostly because they are poor, is insane," I said.

Once, in the corner, alone, I began to weep. Doubtless I had driven Anna mad. The whole world was mad. I slumped into a captain's chair at the round oak table. I listened to the others talking, about hunting and business and women, mostly about women. Suddenly I jumped up and stood on the seat of the chair. Above my drinking friends I shouted, "The human species itself is *ipso facto* insane!"

"You are *ipso facto* full of shit," the drunken lawyer stretched out on the couch said.

"If we are not insane at birth we are taught insanity. Religion is insanity taught to the masses."

"Get a load of this guy," somebody laughed. "Get down off of there. Give him another drink."

I went on like that for a long time. What was wrong with insanity? The great Nietzsche was insane. Most geniuses were. Van Gogh was insane. Christ, who thought men could love one another, must have been insane. And Marx and Freud were obviously insane, too.

"Here's to insanity," I shouted.

"I'll drink to that," somebody else hollered.

"Here's to pussy," the guy with the thick glasses said, and everybody laughed, and later some staggered home early, and a few stayed on with me until the whiskey was gone.

When the office was empty again, and the fire was in embers, glowing and sad, and the awful silence smothered the room, I was startled to hear my own voice, the words exploding in the silence. "What if I get up in the middle of the night as my mother did, and I take my .30-40 Krag, and I stick the barrel in my mouth?"

CHAPTER 29

Kent and Katy, Spence's two youngest children.

IF, WHEN I WAS an adolescent, my parents had suffered my revolt, so, in my manhood, the town of Riverton suffered my insurrection. I stomped capriciously, conspicuously, carelessly up and down the ribs of the town. But I was feared in the courtroom, and there alone I commanded the people's respect. More than once I heard a patient citizen's sigh: "He's an insufferable son-of-a-bitch. But he's *our* son-of-a-bitch."

If someone was in trouble, he came to me for advice. He knew nothing would shock me, for, indeed, I'd probably been down the same hard road myself. If a man was injured on the job, he came to me to fight for him against his employer. If a person was charged with a crime, he or she knew I would defend them. I fought for all of them. I held the so-called "lowliest" people up in the faces of the petty politicians. I shoved the poor and the powerless down their throats, for my clients' vengeance, and for my own. If there was an unpopular case, I took it. I fought the battles of the pariahs because they were my battles. I was their anger, their voice.

As for my growing reputation as a trial lawyer, I knew what accounted for it: the consuming work, the meticulous preparing of every move, every detail, every question. I had become the hunter in the courtroom. Winning was the product of creating and caring—mostly caring, for my client, and for me. Every case could be won, *every case,* and since the case could be won, my duty was easy to define. If only I had wiser eyes. If only I were better in this courtroom craft called trial lawyering. If only I weren't so afraid. And when people found it hard to understand why I didn't seem overjoyed when I won, I tried to explain: It wasn't joy I felt, but relief, like the gladiator who staggered from the arena bloodied, saved to fight another war the next day, the next week.

I took the cases as they came. I remember the rancher—more a squatter— who lived on a few high rocky acres and ran his stock on government land. When they charged him with stealing his neighbor's hay he just stood there in front of the judge and said he was guilty, scared out of his country skin, and the judge sent the poor bastard to the penitentiary—first offense. His brother came knocking at my door in the middle of the night, his face as long and drawn as a whipped mule's. Would I please help? "He's a dumb fucker," his brother said. "Never was smart in school. Never been off the ranch."

When Peewee brought the man back from that dank hole of a place at Rawlins called the penitentiary, the man's red hair was standing on end, his jaw slack. He looked dead. His cattle were starving, he said. How could a man watch his cattle starve in one of those wild winters that come out of the other end of hell and will freeze you dry in that high, desolate country? I petitioned the court to set aside the man's guilty plea, argued that the plea had been given under duress, by a simple man who couldn't feed his cattle, much less hire a lawyer for himself. And when the judge set his plea aside I took his case to the jury. I cross-examined the sheriff. He couldn't match the hay he'd seized from the defendant with the hay from the stack where the defendant had allegedly stolen the hay, and the jury, shaking their heads, returned the rancher to his forlorn acres in the cold backcountry where he belonged. The jury knew. The man was scared so bad he'd never steal again, not that man, not after he'd looked into the eyes of the law and seen the devil.

I took the case of a paraplegic who, lying helplessly paralyzed on his bed, had accepted a few thousand from an insurance company adjuster in full set-tlement of his case. The money wouldn't buy the diapers he had to wear the rest of his life. The adjuster sat there on the stand, trying to make the jury believe that it was all fair and proper—but the jury knew otherwise. The son-of-a-bitch got a commendation from the company for all the money he saved it. "You get commendations for cheating the helpless?" Questions like that the insurance lawyer objected to, the judge pounding his gavel, pointing his finger at me and threatening. I didn't care. Nor did the jury. They set the release aside. Then I settled the case and got enough out of the company to take care of the man.

I won a case for a drunk Indian who was injured by the negligence of a sober truck driver. There he was, weaving across the street, half his brain chopped out by the cheap wine, staggering in that thick drunken fog where he couldn't see his hand in front of him. Insurance company lawyer said he wasn't going to pay some drunk Indian a penny.

I never tried to say the Indian wasn't drunk. You tell the truth to juries. They know it. "If he's drunk, you can run over him, right?" I asked the truck driver. The objections again. "Let me put it another way," I said. "There's something in the Constitution that says, if you are drunk, you lose your rights as a citizen, and people can run you down, right?" More objections. The judge going crazy up there. "Can't we at least agree that a drunk needs more protection than a sober man? A sober man can take care of himself. A drunk can't." The truck driver was getting mad. "Ain't my job to watch after every drunk Indian in the street," the truck driver said. That's when I saw a head or two on the jury starting to nod with me.

My scrapbooks are full, those yellowed clippings of cases I had once anguished over, some I've now forgotten, yet in those days each case was a final confrontation between life and death for me. But in the throes of a trial my demons faded into legal briefs, the face of my mother dissolved into the faces of mothers clutching their dead children, mothers left penniless by delinquent husbands and beaten senseless by drunken spouses. In the heat of a trial, the tangled stuff within that left me twisted and wild was replaced with an indomitable anger that must have bewildered many an opponent. Still I was always afraid. But my fear was of losing, for losing and betrayal, losing and failure, losing and dying had started to feel the same.

I defended a postal clerk charged in the United States District Court in Cheyenne with larceny from the mail. Stealing mail orders, they said, and money. The man's son, a friend of my own son Kent, sat at our supper table, the boy's small soft face already pale and frightened. In the dark of the night I could see in my mind's eye the jury filing in, their hard faces not looking at the defendant. Then I saw the father being hauled off, the boy hushed in shame.

The postmaster, the man's boss, came off like a big-bellied, loud-mouthed politician. You need to have a hero and a villain in any drama. My job in the courtroom was to convert the accused into the hero. I attacked the postmaster. "You got your job by scratching the backs and filling the pockets of the politicians, didn't you?" "Well, how much money did you give the party?" The objections again. The judge sustaining. The jury watching, knowing. "And this little clerk sitting over here all shivering and scared stood up to you that once, didn't he? You had a hollering match right there in front of all the other clerks. And you were going to show him." The postmaster tried to laugh it off, but the jury did not laugh back. I called it "the case of the postmaster's revenge."

I didn't call the defendant to the stand to testify. Most lawyers put their clients up there to squirm like a live chicken on a spit. The United States attorney, anticipating that I'd call the clerk to the stand, held back his best witnesses for rebuttal, but when I put on no defense, his witnesses sat muted in the courtroom while I argued the holes in the government's case to the jury.

The clerk had promised to pay me a thousand-dollar fee. I needed the money. But he paid me only with promises, and they weren't any good. Yet I always figured that if he'd stolen very much he would have had the money to pay a lawyer. I don't remember that after the trial he even thanked me when the jury brought back an acquittal. But there's pay in walking out of the courtroom with your client, both of you free men, and there's pay in seeing the boy grab his father's hand and watching the two of them walk on home together.

I wasn't always on the just side of a case. I only say there's justice on both sides of every case. It's the lawyer's duty to show the jury the justice on his client's side of things, a justice that always lies hidden behind the hard-sounding charges in the indictment. It's the lawyer's duty to discover the human frailty of his client that every juror knows in his own human belly. I believed that if I could understand my client's infirmities as my own, if I could understand his fear as the fear in my belly, I could make the jury understand him as well.

I argue that before a man is convicted of a crime the jury has to know him. How can a jury, without knowing that gaunt, frightened man in the shackles over there, pass judgment on him? I saw them, so young, their innocent faces, their lives a sickness, a deep blemish on them. The prisoner is not an apple or a bolt. He cannot be classified. Like us, he is not identical to any other human being in the history of the world. He was custom-made by God, I argued. And we must custom-make a justice that will fit the man.

I defended a young working man for the murder of his wife in a case the newspapers called "The Love Triangle Murder Case." He shot his wife with a hunting rifle when he found her hosting another man overnight in their home.

"They oughta hang me," he said.

"You want to be hung?"

"Yeah," he said. "I wanna be hung." His voice was flat, his eyes like holes. And the prosecutor wanted to hang him, too. Good politics, being tough on crime. But prosecutors cannot hang my clients.

I led the state's attorney through a maze of wearisome legal entanglements. He got lost in the jungle of motions and side issues. I wore him down, and my own client as well, and I brought the two together. Where they had agreed before that the man should hang, now both my client and the prosecutor settled on a nolo contendere plea to second-degree murder. My client wanted punishment. Well, he could feel it in those long days and empty nights behind the concrete and the steel. I was told he was a model prisoner. Eventually he was released on parole, and perhaps—I never knew—some of his life had been saved. Some small good, I hoped, out of the death and the hatred and the agony.

I represented mostly the working men who came to court in new jeans and faces raw from the sun. Sometimes I thought, God Almighty, there I am—that's me. Sometimes I thought it was only a matter of luck in the genes I drew, in the decent parents I had, in the life that was dealt out to me, lucky I thought that I'd never been driven back into some desperate corner like some of them had.

Were they guilty? Guilty of what was always my question. Guilty of violating the law? Sometimes. Guilty of being human? You could argue about that all day.

One day I stood up in court for an old man whom the prosecutor wanted to store away in the insane asylum. Among other reasons, he was out in the middle of the streets of Lander filling in the potholes with a shovel. He was a damned nuisance; everybody admitted that. I happened to walk into court during the competency hearing, and there he was standing alone trying to defend himself. I listened to him for a minute. Then I walked up to the bar. "If the court please, I'm here to represent this man." The judge looked at me askance. I had never met the man before. But he looked tired and he looked alone up there, and he seemed confused. Why were they bringing him here to this unfriendly place?

"If you want to represent him you can," the judge said, "assuming the respondent agrees."

"Why sure," the old man said. "I can use all the help I can get." I walked over and stood beside him. "I was only tryin' to help," he said to me. "That ain't crazy, is it?"

"It is for some folks," I said. "What's the matter with an old man filling in the potholes of our streets?" I asked the court. "We all ought to be out there helping him. God knows, the streets need it."

The county attorney jumped up and claimed the old man stole a horse, but before I could stop him he was speaking to the judge. "Why, I never stole no horse. Why, that poor old horse was standing out in the sun—and it was hot as Hades, Your Honor. Why, I was just movin' the ol' boy into the shade and along comes the sheriff and says I am stealin' the horse. How come, Your Honor, they don't haul that horse's owner up here to face you? Why, I'll bet you would give him a good goin' over for leaving a poor animal like that out in the sun."

Then the prosecutor said he had stolen a wheelbarrow, too.

"What do you say about that?" I asked the old man.

"Why, I was just a-borrowing it. I never owned a wheelbarrow. And, ya see, that lot over there was full of trash, and it made me plum ashamed to be a citizen of Lander, Wyoming, U.S. of A, with a trashy lot like that right there on the main street. So I borrows the wheelbarrow to haul off the trash and along comes the sheriff again. Must be a pretty peaceful county we live in," he said.

"Why do you say that?" I asked.

"Well, if there was any real criminals out there, I bet ya old Peewee would be out lookin' for 'em. Must be plum outta criminals or he wouldn't be follerin' me aroun' all the time."

"Good point, don't you think, Your Honor?"

The judge mumbled, "Proceed."

People complained that the old boy was always preaching about the Constitution—made a hell of a racket—preached to the people in the cafés, in the bars, on the streets, anywhere he could collar somebody. I said he was only lonely. Needed to talk to folks. Anyway, I told the judge, "It wouldn't hurt us to listen to an old man once in a while. We all need to have our constitutional batteries recharged, this case being a good example of our need to be sensitive to the rights of a citizen, even an old lonely man."

Besides filling in potholes, the old fella spent the few dollars he had bailing poor people out of jail. He loved his old horse and rode it proudly in the Fourth of July parade, even though the horse plugged along, his nose nearly dragging the pavement. The horse was thirty-three years old. "Think a that!" the old boy said, looking up to the judge with a tear in his eye. He wiped it away. "Why, if he was a human bein' he'd be about two hunnert years old!"

The prosecutor called a local doctor to inquire about whether the old man was a danger to himself and to others, and when, under my cross-examination, the doctor started hedging his answers, the judge turned the old man loose. Later I saw him still patching up the streets of Lander and hollering to the people about the Constitution of the United States, and the people just nodded and rolled their eyes. But I thought I knew how the old man felt. He was one of a kind, and too different from the rest of the world. He cared too much. And that's a hard way to be.

It wasn't long before I began to set record verdicts for those times—piddling verdicts compared to those we get today, but the press was always shocked at the size of the awards, and often the judges were as well. Most judges were men who had never gotten a decent verdict for their own clients, never in their lives, and when they took the bench, they judged justice by their own history.

Sometimes a lawyer would sidle up to me and want to know how a fellow got a verdict like that. There was no magic to it, I'd tell him. "Ask, and it shall be given unto you," the Good Book says. I asked the juries for the money. They gave it to me. Times were tough, and the people were tough, but they acted like they didn't know it, their teeth clenched against the weather, the "piss poor cattle prices—just as well give your cattle away as take what the buyers will give ya these days." If you wanted to know how things were, go down to the sale barn when a man's calves were being run through the ring, and look at his face. Those were the people who sat on my juries.

I took the case of the grieving parents of a three-year-old child, run over in the street by a speeding drunk. The jury awarded fifteen thousand dollars to the parents. The insurance company attorney was outraged. Fifteen thousand dollars for a kid! The lawyer, one of those tight-assed religious misanthropists, polled every clerk of court in the state to prove to the judge that the verdict was so large that, as he argued, "on its face it's the abominable product of prejudice and passion." His research showed that the largest sum then ever awarded in Wyoming for the death of any child of any age had been five thousand dollars. He demanded that the court reduce the verdict.

"This child had no monetary value," he argued. That has always been their argument of the insurance companies. "This child contributed nothing to her parents of a pecuniary nature," he shouted in his high, squeezed-up voice. The case was all about money—not about grieving parents, not about retribution, but about money. Today the same case might result in a verdict of half a million dollars or more. Then in the early 1960s, the sleeping conscience of American juries was only slowly awakening. Gradually lawyers were beginning to understand that it was all right to ask a jury for money. In a civil suit for damages, money was the only justice the jury could deliver to the parents of the little girl. It's hard for lawyers to equate a dead child with dollars—it makes the dollars seem dirty, and makes the lawyers look like a money-grubbing shysters. Nothing has changed. The insurance companies love it, play on it.

I tried to argue about justice to the judge. "If these folks could have their baby for just one more hour, they'd give every penny of this verdict back to that insurance company."

"Your idea of justice is not the issue here, Mr. Spence," Judge Sheldon said. "The law is the issue. You know the law, Mr. Spence. The law does not permit the jury to return money for grief. Grief is not a recognized element of damage."

"Yes, of course," I said. "A drunk can go speeding blindly down the street in the broad daylight, run over your child, and the law ignores the grief of these parents? It's something free the drunk gets for killing the child. The law only wants to know, 'What did it cost to bury the child? What doctor and hospital bills were incurred as the child lay dying?' The law, as someone said, is an ass, but even as ass has more compassion than the law."

"I've heard enough of that," the judge said. Sometimes he growled like an old dog lying in front of the door.

Then the insurance company lawyer chimed in. "Anticipating your thought, Your Honor, the law does allow a reasonable sum for the loss of care, comfort, advice and society of the deceased child. But, pray tell, what advice can a three-year-old child give to her parents? What care?"

"She can give comfort," I said. "Ask any parent. Ask yourself, Your Honor. You have daughters."

"Children *require* comforting," the lawyer argued back. "No, the law does not permit a recovery for the parent's loss of the child's comfort. It's the other way around." The lawyer thought his argument very smart and looked up with that cynical smirk on his face, inviting the court to join him in the sport of his intellectual exercises.

"I agree with the lawyer for the insurance company," I said. "The law is not interested in justice. Instead, the law, concerned only with money, holds that the drunk did these parents a lovely favor when he ran over their child. He saved the parents the financial burden of rearing and educating the child. The parents owe him."

"Enough of that, Mr. Spence," the judge mumbled. I thought I was getting to him, all right.

"Well, why not face it," I said. "If the law is not interested in justice, and Your Honor is bound by the law, and if Your Honor is not able to discover how

Gerry Spence and antelope.

Gerry Spence, a duck hunt.

Gerry Spence, string of mountain trout.

Gerry Spence and his horse, Charlie.

the law can be applied to give relief where justice demands it, then ought we not all run off and play polo?"

"The legislature makes the laws, Mr. Spence. You know that. I only administer it." The judge was beginning to sound apologetic.

"I agree," I said. "But as you are a just and intelligent man, I trust you can administer the law in such manner as will cause the least carnage." And I let my argument go at that. I thought he would find a way to sustain the verdict.

Suddenly the judge said, "I've heard all the arguments I want to hear. I find that the verdict of the jury is just and that it is sustained by the evidence. While the jury is not permitted to award any sum for loss of care and comfort, it can provide a reasonable sum for the parent's loss of the child's *society*. I find that under the circumstances of this case, the sum of fifteen thousand dollars does not 'shock the court's conscience,'"—the test—"and the jury's award will therefore stand."

I was still a hunter, both in and out of the courtroom, and fed my family the wild game I killed. Shortly after that verdict, I drove over South Pass, where the scant remains of that old ghost town stood against the high mountain winds, where the timbers of the abandoned gold mines rotted in the dankness, where once ten thousand men lived in a tent town, all grubbing in the granite searching for gold. I drove through the dead of winter, through the blizzard beating at the land with long, whipping ropes of wind and ice. I traveled on across a hundred miles of white frozen plains to Evanston, where, in those far, bleak reaches, Wyoming stored its insane, as distant from civilization, it was alleged, as the state's territorial legislature could find. There I tried a case against Ford Motor Company for injuries it had caused to Manuel Arguello, a Mexican-American oil field worker. The Ford he'd been riding in had been manufactured with a defective rivet in the wheel, the rivet gave way, and the tubeless tire deflated through the rivet hole. The flat tire caused the car to careen off the road, roll, and burst into pieces. Manuel was thrown from the car, his back broken and his spinal cord ripped, leaving him permanently paralyzed from the waist down.

Vincent Vehar, a big, gruff, pigeon-toed bear of a lawyer whose barrel chest was barely large enough to encase his mammoth heart, sat at my side at the counsel table. Said he couldn't try a case. Got too upset. Got too mad. Wanted to throw some of the lying bastards out of the courthouse window, he said. He could have. But he never stepped on a grasshopper.

The courtroom was on the second floor of the old courthouse, the Victorian woodwork, the wooden floors creaking as the lawyers paced in front of the jury. Every day Vince would grab one side of Manuel's wheelchair, and I the other, and we'd hoist Manuel up the stairs, one stair at a time. Manuel was no lightweight. Before the trial was over, some of the men on the jury began to spell us as we struggled up the stairs. And Manuel would lay his big smile on them, his long front teeth shining, and he'd thank them, and we thanked them. Things were different then.

Ford Motor Company, of course, brought in its fancy lawyers from a large firm in nearby Salt Lake City. The jurors had no degrees hanging on their walls, but the carpenter, there in the front row, and the telephone company employee sitting next to him understood what the case was about. It was about money. What would happen if the damn car you were driving to work fell to pieces, and after that, you couldn't wiggle a toe, and somebody had to put diapers on you like a baby? And what about his kids? Who was going to take care of them? Those big shots from the city come into court with their pretty pressed pin-striped suits, and the do-dads flopping on their patent leather loafers, and they smile at you like you're about to buy a new Caddy from 'em. But if you watched the jury you could tell—they didn't smile back, or, embarrassed, they looked away when the lawyers shot them their quick smiles. Jurors don't want to be messed with like that.

It's a hard fight to win justice for regular people. They have to win against the boundless money, the infinite power of the American corporation. Ford brought in its experts from the big universities, impressive men with long strings of degrees behind their names, men who wrote articles for all of the important scientific publications, men with sober faces and big words who said as a mat-ter of scientific fact that the rivet in the wheel had broken *in* the accident. Wanted to blame the driver. They always do. They put those charts up there in front of the jury and showed the jury their X rays, and of course, I attacked them—I, that skinny kid standing there with his blond hair slicked back and his shirttail hanging out from under his cheap sport coat.

"What does Ford pay you to come here? How much did you get in the last case you testified in for Ford?" The Ford lawyers were objecting to every one of my questions. "Where is the lab tech you claim had this rivet in his hand and supposedly took these X rays? When did you last talk to Ford's attorney—over there for breakfast, you say? Last night up in his hotel room? Could you give the jury your honest testimony without the lawyers helping you?" It was a standard attack, but the jury wanted the fight evened up, wanted this blond kid-of-a-lawyer to win for the Mexican kid sitting over there in his wheelchair, this kid who never whimpered or complained, who sat there with a smile that stayed fixed when other men would have been crying.

But a jury of hardworking Wyoming people are not the peers of a corpora-tion. Bring in the dead law for the corporations. Corporations love the dead law. Bring in the judges. Corporations feel more comfortable pleading to judges. But don't let in a human being who can feel pain, who holds on to the pride he earned in a lifetime of mean, hard work—don't bring in those people with gnarled fingers and callused hands to judge the corporation. I looked over at the jury. Manuel was looking at them, too. I thought the jurors saw past the pasted-on smiles, and that they could sense the natural corporate animosity toward them—something in the way the lawyers crossed their arms and turned their backs; something in the uncomfortable way they sat at the counsel table, little things the jurors couldn't put to words.

After the long day in court, Vince and I went to the bar to *re*-lax. Man has to *re*-lax. Every bone in his body aches. The head pounds. "Gimme a Coors and a double shot of Jack Daniel's, green. I like the green better'n the black. We kicked the shit out of 'em today, Vince."

"Right," Vince said. "Ya better go easy on that Jack." He was twenty years older than I was. Liked to give me advice.

"Give us another round," I said. I kept watching the door into the restaurant, and when I couldn't see the door anymore, I knew it was time to eat. We ate those thick, greasy steaks because I thought a guy had to have red meat in him to fight, to keep the blood up. Then you hit the sack about ten and were up by six, preparing the next day's cross-examination.

I was right up in their faces the next morning. Hung over, I suppose, but I never noticed it. I could make it through to five, until the Coors and double shots came on again. Adrenaline keeps you going. And I never backed up. It wasn't bravery. It was the kind of fighting men do in the trenches. Not a pretty fight, but a fight to survive, and when you're fighting to survive, you are not brave.

"We gonna win?" Manuel asked, still smiling.

"Yeah," I said. "We are gonna win. They can't beat you."

"How come?" Manuel said.

"On account of the fact that they have to kill me first, and they can't kill me."

"Yeah?" And then he laughed, but it was a good-natured laugh, an innocent kind of laugh.

In those days I set my opponent up for the final argument. Sort of like Rocky in the movies. You want the underdog to win. You want the kid standing there, the fighting kid, to win against those slick big-city lawyers. You want the kid from Riverton to win against the motherfuckers who are smiling at you all the time. And jurors in small towns know things you don't know. "I seen them company lawyers down in the café last night with their noses up against their star witness, giving him the music."

The verdict for Manuel was $108,000, then the largest personal injury verdict in the state's history. The award astounded the lawyers around the state. They never congratulated me. Never even mentioned it. But you got it second-hand, talk about how Spence got that big verdict, and he got it down there in Evanston, too, like Siberia, the most conservative town on the face of the earth. Of course the guy has to win in the Supreme Court—they said things like that, but around me they acted like I was nobody.

Of course, Ford appealed the jury's verdict to the Wyoming Supreme Court. The justice writing the opinion for the court, a big, tall, slump-shouldered guy with slicked-down black hair, former attorney general, was one of those rare, old-line Democrats by the name of Tiny Gray. No one knows how he'd gotten to the Supreme Court of Wyoming. And he affirmed the jury's verdict. In one opinion he changed the price we put on people's destroyed lives: $108,000! And the price for every other kind of injury went up, too.

Manuel took some of the money and learned the watch repair business. He was good with his hands. I hired Manuel's wife, Cleo, as my secretary. And, of course, as most folks in Wyoming know, old Vince was later murdered and I prosecuted the murderer as a special prosecutor. Had nothing to do with the Ford case. Wrote about it in another book.° I had to ask for the death penalty and I hated the death penalty, always have. But the jury imposed it in that case, because it was the law, and then, afterwards I fought against the execution of the man, beseeched the governor to commute it. I tried to forgive, tried not to let the hatred poison me. For ten years I sat stuck in the miserable mud of the moral dilemma created by the death penalty—this smart bastard who had killed four innocent human beings, Vince and his darling, devoted, brown-eyed wife, Beverly, and their fifteen-year-old son, as well as the torture death of Jeff Green, our witness, those decent small town people who had clung to everything that was right. The smart bastard ought to be killed for the killing. Yet the death penalty tormented me, the deep, senseless wrong of it. That story, many years out of time, does not belong here. But I couldn't pass the mention of it. Old Vince would have liked it that I didn't.

I tried a wide range of cases in those days, nearly always before a jury, and nearly always each verdict exceeding the last. It wasn't long before I was regularly getting more for a sprained neck than I had previously gotten for a baby who had died. Within a year, I had doubled the size of the verdicts juries were bringing back in a child's death case, and within a few more years juries were returning verdicts for my clients in whiplash cases for nearly as much as I had received for Manuel Arguello's record award.

I told the juries the story of my case in the language of working people. I had learned storytelling from my father. A true trial lawyer is a storyteller. Storytelling, and listening to stories, is in our genes. We hear stories and we're moved by them. Human beings do not respond to abstractions, to that empty pedantry spangled in dull legalisms. Storytelling is the means by which man, from the time he came swinging out of the trees, passed down his history, his wisdom, his religion. If I were to choose but one skill from the grab-bag of skills necessary for the successful trial lawyer, it would be the skill of storytelling.

About that time I had a couple of clients, two older women, who had been riding along in their car minding their own business when they were rear-ended

°See *Gunning for Justice,* Doubleday, 1982.

by an automobile insured against liability by one of the nation's largest insurance companies. At the trial, the company's lawyer hauled their investigator's movies into court—surveillance movies they're called. Included was a scene in which the ladies drove up to a liquor store to buy a six-pack of beer. Now the company had them! What Wyoming jury would return a verdict for women who had the temerity to buy a six-pack of beer, and in broad daylight, and then claim they were injured!

I learned of the movies, I subpoenaed them, and after identifying them to the jury as "the defendant's *spy* movies," I presented them in my own case before the defendant's attorney had a chance to show them in his. I put our orthopedic surgeon on the stand to comment on what he saw as the movies were being played.

"Yes, there! Stop it. Play it back," the doctor said. "See how stiffly she reaches for the beer? Look there! That is quite an abnormal movement for a woman her age."

She looked healthy enough to the defense attorney, and he attacked the doctor on cross-examination, but the doctor held firm.

"You can't *see* pain, counsel," our doctor said. "This woman was in pain. And it is not uncommon for people in pain to try to assuage their misery through alcohol. Alcohol has proven to be one of the best analgesics known to man. We must not attempt to discredit someone simply because they are brave and bear up to their misery."

When I called my client to the stand—you always call your client in a civil case—I asked her about her activities during the time the surveillance movies had been taken.

"You went to the liquor store?"

"Yes."

"They took movies of that?"

"I guess so."

"Where else did you go during those weeks?"

"I went to church every day."

"Did they take movies of you going to church?"

"Not that I know of."

"And where else did you go?"

"I went to the grocery store."

"How did you get your groceries out?"

"The boy carried them out for me."

"Did they take movies of that?"

"No."

The jury knew. The surveillance movies were taken by the hired spy of the insurance company, who had invaded the women's privacy, and after that had edited the film to prejudice the jurors. If you could have listened in the jury room you probably would have heard some juror saying, "Tell ya one thing: If you and I did that the law would be all over our asses. Telling only part of the truth is a form of lyin'." The jury's verdict for the whiplash injuries suffered by the women was $123,000. I wouldn't mind being judged by God, if God were a jury of twelve good, hardworking Wyoming citizens.

The *Casper Star Tribune* hollered about the size of the verdict as if the insurance company's money were its own. Those crazy juries were at it again—"The largest amounts ever given in Wyoming for a rear-ender," they cried in headlines. Everybody was shocked, or said they were shocked. A little rear-ender and you have to pay $123,000! What's the world coming to? But of course, the people who read the newspaper never heard the testimony or saw this company spy with his stash of secret movies.

The trial judge, an old gentleman we all revered a lot, Judge Ewing B. Kerr, also thought this jury had gone too far. He was from the old school of Wyoming pioneers, had been a politician himself, and the Republican state chairman, a man steeped in sweet and simple conservatism. People live on this earth, they get hurt, they suffer, they die, and they bear up to it until then. He did. His parents did. Everybody should. You don't go spreading the money of insurance companies around just because they have a lot of it. If juries can spread insurance company money around like that they can spread yours. You give justice, all right, but too much justice is injustice.

The verdict, Judge Kerr said, "shocked the conscience of the court," and he promptly reduced the judgment to $43,000. Who knows how he arrived at that figure? I can see him all hooked up to God, a transmission line going out into the firmament though which he received the word: *$43,000 is justice*. Not $42,000? Not $44,000? No, exactly $43,000!

The lawyer who represented the insurance company in that case was a fellow by the name of Clarence Brimmer, from that small penitentiary town of Rawlins. A few years later Brimmer ran for governor on the Republican ticket, and after he was defeated in the Republican primary by none other than my friend, Stanley K. Hathaway, he was appointed to the federal judgeship. Before he was appointed to the federal bench—that is, before we began to address him as "Your Honor"—everybody used to call him Bud, just plain old Bud. Strange thing: This Bud Brimmer turned out to be a damned good judge. Once in a while that happens. Not often. Tried many a case to him after that.

In that same year I took a case against Continental Motor Company for the injuries my client, Tony Jolly, suffered when the airplane he was flying crashed into a mountain—engine failure. Tony was an old-time pilot, one of the best. Everybody in the business knew him, admired him, even modeled after him. But he was smashed up in the crash, his brain damaged, his body ruined. He was in constant pain and needed help.

I tried to settle the case with the old stalwart, Edward Murane, still dean of the insurance company lawyers and then the head of the state's largest law firm, Murane and Bostwick of Casper. I knew the case would be difficult. Tony needed medical attention, and he and his wife were on the verge of bankruptcy. I didn't want to risk a trial. I went to see Eddie Murane, hat in hand. That's how you always went to see Eddie.

"Eddie, I need the money for my client," I said. "He's gotta have help. Needs doctors. He can't work. It's an honest case, Eddie. I can settle it for half what the jury will bring in if you'll settle it now. Give me fifty thousand. I'll go home, my client can get some medical help, and your company can save a lot of money."

"You still don't get it, do you kid?" Murane said. His old jowls hung down over his jawbones. "I told you once before." And he had. He walked over to his filing cabinet and pulled open one of the drawers. "Like I told you, every one of these cases is a new Cadillac automobile for me." The file drawer was full of cases. He scowled at me. "I'm not giving you a new Cadillac automobile." Then he got up and showed me the door. "I'll beat you anyway."

It was one of those long trials with a lot of paper, records about the plane, manufacturing data, specifications on the design, a parade of witnesses who testified about how the engines should have been adjusted—the usual know-it-all experts with their impressive portfolios. And I attacked them as usual. Our evidence showed an improper magneto setting that caused preignition and finally the engine failure. I thought the jurors had a hard time warming up to Eddie Murane. They were only out for a few hours before they returned their verdict for $310,000, a verdict that today would have stood in the millions.

I talked to a couple of the jurors after the trial. An oil field worker told me how he and his fellow juror in the next seat, a farmer, saw the case.

"Why, this case was simple," he said. "An old pilot like that knows what he's doin'. You finally have to decide whether you trust the pilot or you trust the big companies. I know them big companies. I work for one. They will cheat you out of five minutes of your lunch hour if they can."

"Right," I said.

When the jury left the courthouse, I walked over to where Eddie was shoving his papers into his briefcase. I shook his hand.

"Good trial, kid." He shook my hand. "But we're just starting in this case. See you in court." He meant the Wyoming Supreme Court, and he was right. The case had just started. Murane's appeal was to a supreme court that had grown even more conservative with the appointment of new judges. Murane knew where to try his cases. He tried them where corporate America tries its cases: to its own juries, to the appellate court judges who are mostly appointed by the politicians the corporations support. Of course, the appellate court judges are required to follow the law. But the appellate court judges *make* the law.

Eddie Murane was a member of the bar's social elite; had been for years. Most of the insurance company lawyers were. Most judges and Wyoming's topflight lawyers do not hobnob with the riffraff who take contingency cases. Few of the people's lawyers are ever officers in the state bar. Eddie Murane had been Wyoming's representative to the American Bar Association for a decade or longer. As for me, I only joined the ABA so I could holler at it.

I knew that the judges who now sat on the court were unfriendly to the big claims of injured people like Tony Jolly. You knew that before they took the bench. You knew it by the politicians who appointed them. You knew it from their past practice, from the clients they represented as lawyers—the banks, the insurance companies, the railroads. You knew it from the way they talked, and by the people they played golf with. You knew it because their best friends were bank presidents or lawyers who represented the oil companies. You knew it from their past decisions on the court, which revealed a sort of exalted intellectual ordinariness. You could see it in their frozen faces and hear it in their polite, cold language. Sometimes I thought you could smell it, as you can smell the mold in a church basement.

I wanted to save what I could of Tony Jolly's verdict before those judges up there started hacking at it from that lofty safe place called the Wyoming Supreme Court. Once more I traveled to Casper to try to make a deal with Eddie Murane, and I did. He was marginally more amiable this time.

"Want to gamble?" he asked, looking at me with that unhappy come-on smile of his.

"What do you have in mind?"

"Continental Motor Company will pay your client $80,000 now. Now that's more than you offered to settle the case for way back then. And if you win in the Supreme Court, which is doubtful, we'll pay you another $100,000. Total, $180,000. If we win on the appeal, you keep the eighty, and you get nothing more."

I talked to Tony and his wife about it. I worried over it. Tony needed more than the $310,000 the jury had given him to make it the rest of the way. But a majority on the court were those conservatives whose souls were as dried up as last night's pizza, and Tony would probably lose it all. It hurt me. But Tony had to make the deal. How could an injured man gamble when he was in need of medical attention and his creditors were beating at the door?

"Why do we have to give up what the jury gave us?" Tony's wife asked.

"Because we are afraid of our own judges," I said.

Justice McIntyre on the high court took twelve pages of fine print to analyze the evidence on behalf of Continental Motor. Under the law the judge was required to examine the entire record and afford Mr. Jolly all of the favorable inferences that arose from the whole of the evidence. Instead, he substituted his own factual findings for those of the jury, set their verdict aside and ordered the case reversed. Tony, under that decision, would have gotten nothing. No one was surprised. Justice McEwan, a maverick on the court, held in his dissent that there had been sufficient facts presented to the jury to allow the verdict to stand. But the justices didn't listen to him. He didn't belong to their club, and never had.

Judge Parker, whom I remembered from law school, joined Judge McIntyre in setting the verdict aside. In Wyoming, to win for a severely crippled man you had to first convince twelve jurors and get a *unanimous* verdict, and then on appeal you had to win a majority of the judges on the high court. For Continental to win—well, that corporation was only required to win once: to capture two out of the three judges up there. Eddie Murane knew that, and he was right. He did beat me, he and two justices on the Supreme Court, and they beat the jury and they beat Tony Jolly, and they beat justice. No contest, really. Just took one quick vote in their chambers, ten minutes—less, probably—and it was all over. I suppose Tony was glad I'd made the deal for him, glad through his tears, his wife by him, forcing a smile, still trying to understand.

Sometimes I resorted to courtroom "special effects" to win a case. In 1966, I filed suit against a company that had manufactured a defective rock drill. My client was a hardworking man trying to make an honest living in a dangerous place, a road job where they had to drill through rock formations a hundred feet thick. When the drill broke, it fell pulverizing his leg, and later the leg had to be amputated. I ordered the surgeons to deliver the amputated limb to the local undertaker, had the undertaker embalm it and place it in a small wooden box shaped like a casket. Then I lugged the casket, leg and all, into court.

During the long trial I never made mention of any kind to that small casket that sat every day in plain sight on my table. When it came my time to argue the case the defense attorney, another of those lawyers from the big insurance firms, rose to address the court.

Suddenly, and without warning, he said, "I demand that Mr. Spence advise us as to the contents of that box." Took everybody by surprise.

"It's nothing that belongs to counsel," I said. The box must have been bothering him all along.

"What is in the box, Mr. Spence?" the judge asked, himself curious.

"I admit, Your Honor, that the box contains something that shouldn't be there."

"I demand, then, that he be ordered to open the box," counsel hollered.

"I resist," I said. "The box is my client's business, and none of counsel's."

"What's in the box, Mr. Spence?" The judge was becoming more interested.

"I'd rather not say."

"I demand that he tell us," the attorney shouted. The jury was watching.

"All right, Mr. Spence, what's in the box?" the judge asked for the third time.

I hauled the box over to the attorney's table and sat it in front of him. "Here," I said. "You open the box. It contains my client's amputated leg." The lawyer shied back, his mouth open, speechless. Then, before he could recover, I began my final argument.

"Ladies and gentlemen: A leg should be on a man, not in a box." I walked over to my client, and asked him to remove his artificial limb. Embarrassed, he unstrapped the leg and handed it to me. Then I walked over to the closest juror and handed the thing to him. "Won't you give this man justice? Give him, in dollars, the difference between the value of his once perfect leg, now in that box, and the piece of plastic and steel you hold in your hand." I turned to my client. "George, could you please stand up?" He struggled up on his one good leg, his pant leg empty, swaying, lifeless, like wash on the line. "This man stood up for you. Now can't you stand up for him?"

The verdict was for $242,000.

But of course, I knew what the final jury, the appeals court, would likely do to the verdict. I settled the case for half the amount of the jury's award. Today, as in those days, we read in the papers about the large verdicts occasionally given to injured people. But we never see what the injured person finally takes home after settlements are made that slice the verdicts to a fraction of their original size, because the injured person can never trust the appeals court judges to respect the jury's findings.

By 1966 I was beginning to break records I had set previously. Later that year, a jury of eight men and four women awarded my client $60,000 for the death of a high school boy, then the largest verdict ever rendered in the state for the death of a child. Such an award would be considered nothing today. The largest award in Park County history had been $10,000, but in 1966, a Park County jury in the town of Cody returned the largest libel verdict in the state's history, a verdict of $100,000. A local publication had attacked the man, an ex-con, with a blast of vile name-calling after he had been arrested for an alleged assault on a Cody teenager. But my client had been later cleared of the crime. Yet again we had to settle for slim pickin's, faced, as we were, with the miserly minds on the Wyoming Supreme Court.

A year later, in the same little town of Cody, another jury awarded my client a million dollars when she was infected with gonorrhea by a wealthy local playboy. He had induced her to go with him across the country on a spree, promised to marry her when they got home, met her family and all the rest, infected her with gonorrhea on the way, and then, when the trip—and his use for her—was over, he laughed. "Marry you? Can't you take a joke? And by the way, you better go see a doctor. I think you may have the clap. I do."

The disease left her sterile. A million dollars seemed right, the jury said. We wouldn't trade places with her for a million. Justice is justice. You can't treat people like that around here, not in Cody, Wyoming.

But the Wyoming Supreme Court, not much attuned to women's rights, thought the verdict outrageous. And they'd figured out how to beat the woman. How could she prove she got infected *in Wyoming?* She was probably infected in one of the other dozen or more states they'd traveled through on their trip, and the statute of limitations had run in the other states. So too bad. Clever holding, all right, that you can give a woman the clap if you're on the move, because when it comes time to go to court she won't be able to prove where she was when she got it. The court set the million-dollar verdict aside. The woman got nothing.

Their decision was easy for me to interpret behind their pedagogical legalese. No woman was worth a million, much less an unmarried female with a dose of clap. Besides, she had done the "unchristian thing." She had bedded down in interstate lechery, and she deserved what she got. I suspect that the same court today, under the pressure of women's rights groups, would have lauded the verdict and become the darling of the media. The law is never the law. The law, if it were ever otherwise, has become a feather which men with power use to tickle their private whimsies.

Although I hadn't lost a jury trial of any kind in over ten years and despite my long, unbroken string of record verdicts, I was constantly plagued by the secret, nagging suspicion that I was a mountebank who had gained his reputation mostly by luck. I had worked hard, I admitted that, and I was prepared to the teeth, always prepared. But my successes, I thought, were attributable to the fact that my opponents were mostly mediocre regional lawyers like me who hadn't worked as hard and who didn't care as much. In the same way that the "real lawyers" had exposed me at the bar examination, so, too, I would eventually be found out by the real trial lawyers—those from the big cities like Denver and Chicago and New York. Eventually they would show me up for what I was—a frightened man who compensated for his fear with an abundance of gall, a man with but modest talent, a loud voice, a somewhat imposing demeanor, and great luck, and a man who, for many years, had been guilty of the tepid crime of over-achieving.

CHAPTER 30

*Three generations of Spences on a rabbit hunt:
Brother Tom, Kip, Kent, and Grandpa Spence.*

WE MIGHT HAVE been dysfunctional, but we remained a family, although sometimes just barely. The father still came home at night, but with too much Old Cabin Still in him. The supper was cold, the mother angry, left out, the children hanging on, caught up in the turmoil, sometimes accepting it, sometimes indifferent, focused as they were on their own lives. Nobody offered a class at the universities called Successful Parenhood, 101. Nobody offered a class in school on how to be a successful child to one's parents.

At times I didn't want to be a husband or a father. I was in my third decade of life and never claimed I was wise. I never claimed I made the right decisions. Yet Anna and I were parents, and we were a family. I compared myself to an old grizzly. I roamed my woods and pursued my own life, but let something, anything, threaten one of my cubs, and the instinctual attack came and there were no other priorities.

I thought of my father, and I remembered the old biblical saw about how the sins of the father are visited on the child. But then so were my father's gifts to me bestowed by me on my children. I taught them how to make chokecherry whistles, and kites, and how to make fire by flint and steel. I taught them how to hunt and to gut out an antelope and catch a high mountain trout on a spinner. We raised a garden in the backyard, and I sent the kids to Scouts and to Brownies. But my father was a different man from me. I never thought he had any goals. I thought he had traps, all right, and maybe the traps wiped out his visions. I had different traps, and different ambitions and my kids were also in my traps.

Gerry's first son, Kip, dressing out a freshly downed antelope.

My mother? Her legacy was indisputable. We sent the kids to Sunday school at the Methodist church in Riverton, and sometimes we went to church ourselves where Bob Peck, that near saint, gave his wonderously plain voice to the choir. And mine? I felt ashamed to hold it back, but I wasn't going to sing in any choir. I drank and I smoked and I raised hell. Tell me about religion. Tell me about Jesus H. Christ. I'll tell you one thing: I wasn't going to parade around all puffed up with pretty piety. But you send your kids to church anyway. And if the kids grow up confused, well why should they rate a different fate from anybody else?

Sometimes I felt the need to defend myself as a father. Well, I put the food on the table, didn't I? I paid the bills on time. And the kids grew

Kip, Kerry, and Kent — home from fishing.

up thinking they were rich, for Christ's sakes, while some years we were living from case to case. The kids thought they were members of Riverton's royalty. I never knew where they got such an idea. Other kids, I suppose. "Your old man drives a new Pontiac," which I knew to be a two-tone piece of shit, mortgaged, green and cream. "Your old man is a big-shot attorney," but the town fathers thought I was an enigmatic renegade, maybe a madman. "You live in a big house," but, in fact, it only had three small bedrooms, all upstairs. I suppose it was a big house to kids who lived in trailer parks and in those stiff, square little bungalows that stood at strict attention along the streets of River-

Kerry, Spence's oldest daughter,
family skiing trip.

Kent with his horse on a pack trip.

ton. My parents never thought they were poor. They knew what poor was. On the other hand, I thought I grew up poor, and, as a father, I never intended to raise rich kids.

One thing: We were honest. Honest about who we were, and what we believed, and how we felt. Nothing hidden, no secret parental agendas, no plotting to turn some kid into a preacher. No lying to the kids about how Anna and I got along. Ugly as it might have been, as it was from time to time, it was all laid out there plain to look at. Once in a while I took the belt out, which I admit was wrong. But I also hugged my kids, and squeezed them till they hollered and I wrestled with them, and I yelled at them and I loved them right out of their baggy little pants. And they knew that I loved them.

They also knew I was nuts, and they forgave me and loved me back. When I'd later confess to them that I wasn't worth a damn as a father, they would protest. "You were a good father," they'd say. Then they'd make excuses for me. "You were only twenty when Kippy was born. You had three kids by the time you were twenty-five. You were too young." "Well," I'd say back, "you think I was a good father because I was the only father you ever had. Good thing you didn't have a good father to compare me with." We went on like that.

In the 1960s, the whole country was in revolt, and in Riverton, Wyoming, a few of the kids started to smoke grass. People in Wyoming had hardly heard of it before. Now the boys were letting their hair grow long, like those Beatles, and it scared the townspeople—all that long hair on the boys, the wild music and the marijuana. If you had long hair, well, you must be one of *them.* It was a kind of prejudice, like racial prejudice.

Kip's hair was so long he could almost sit on it. The superintendent at the

Katy, Spence's youngest daughter.

Bear looking into window on family trip to Yellowstone.

Katy Spence.

Kerry Spence.

Kip on the family horse, Misty. In the back country.

high school thought long hair was scurrilous and dangerous. He told Kip, and the other boys, to cut their hair or get their asses out.

"I'll tell you one thing," I said. "They are not going to kick your ass out without a fight."

"Who do they think they are?" Kip asked. "What right does he have to tell me how to wear my hair? This is a free country, you know. I got the right to wear my hair any way I please, you know." He nodded his head up and down the way the hippies talked, talking and nodding, nodding and talking. "I'll fight 'em, you know."

"We'll take this up in a proper and lawful way," I said. "We'll demand a hearing before the full board." The school board's attorney, seeing possible legal trouble brewing, advised the board to grant the hearing. I thought that Kip should speak for himself.

Kip got up before a packed house, the board members sitting at a table in front of the room, their arms crossed, those straight, self-appointed town fathers, their anal orifices spasmed, some still wearing their World War II vintage crew cuts, their own dress, thrift-store stylish. The kid got up, tall as a budding NBA star, already over six feet five, and in his slow, easygoing way, he began his argument:

"I am told that a rule without a reason is no rule at all. This rule about hair length is a rule without a reason. It is a matter of *your* taste, not a matter of reason," he said. As he spoke, his long blond hair, freshly laundered, glowed under the ceiling's fluorescent tubes. "You were elected to see to our education. You were not elected to pass judgment on style. For me, I am offended by the style of your short-clipped haircuts. I wouldn't be caught dead in a haircut like that. It reflects the kind of men you are. And some of you have no hair at all. You're the ones who are probably the strongest against us. If I had the power to give you a full head of hair like mine in exchange for my freedom to wear mine as I wish, you would probably accept the bargain in a minute—and there'd be no fight here at all."

I thought he was his father's son. I also thought he was going too far.

"You are forcing your rule on me because you have the power. I will tell you what your rule tells the students of this school. It tells them that you are more interested in style than in education. You are more concerned with your power than with my freedom. That's all I have to say." He sat down. Nobody said anything. I heard some throats being cleared.

Finally I stood up. "I am, as you know, Kip's father. He has made a better argument to you than I could have made, and I endorse everything he has said, and I laud the courage he has demonstrated in saying it. I'm not particularly wild about his hairstyle myself. But I hear you say more. I hear you say you find my son's hair offensive. Yet it is clean. It is combed. How could it offend you? I have not chosen his hairstyle for myself. But I have been free to choose my style of hair. I find it meddlesome for elected public officials to invade the homes of their constituents and dictate such basic things as style for the child. Is that not the parent's prerogative? What right do you have to meet my child at the breakfast table and tell him how he must wear his hair before he can attend school today? So you are offended by his hair? I am offended by your impertinence. And that's all I have to say."

We had not couched our arguments in language that was likely to win. We chose words that served our anger instead. After the hearing the school board went into executive session a few minutes and came back to give us their verdict: They were not going to let a bunch of hippy-looking kids run up and down the halls of their high school. "When people look bad they tend to act bad," the school board president said. "People with no respect for themselves usually show no respect for others. That's what's wrong with America: People show no respect. The public schools are failing because there's no discipline, and the Riverton High School is going to enforce its dress code." They were saying, if Kip Spence or his parents didn't like it, they could go elsewhere.

"Well, Kip, what do you think now?" I asked him when we got home. His reply taught me something of the dynamics of justice. To be heard can be as important as to win.

"We told 'em," he said. "I just didn't want to get my hair cut without tellin' 'em."

I built a studio in the rear of the house from logs and blocks and glass, and I began to paint. I had no prior training in art except those few drawing lessons as a child. At first my paintings were tightly constructed. I struggled with the mixing of colors, the stretching of canvas, the creation of form. Studiously I copied from photographs I had taken of mountains and people. I realized I needed to learn about painting and about painters, lest I become redundant and banal. I needed to know what art was already out there. I began to read art history, and art criticism. I studied the Fauves and the Impressionists, and I became intimate with Picasso and the Cubists. I flew with Chagall. I wept with Van Gogh, read his lonely, despairing letters to Theo, his brother, and I perceived that that wild, desperate, rejected man and I were brothers. Sometimes in the night I talked to Van Gogh.

One day I came upon a book of fine reproductions of the works of Monet, containing his cathedrals, the haystacks, his water lilies. Having finished the book, I sat holding it to my heart, and I wept. How could one weep over a book of paintings? The immense impact of an entire work viewed in the span of few minutes was overwhelming, and I thought that surely painting was a way out of my trap. Soon my escape became my feral brush, my creations in oil as haunting and tortured as Van Gogh's. Self-portraits, paintings of wounded birds, of crows caught in the snow, paintings of withered bird carcasses, human carcasses, paintings that reflected pain, not joy, agony, not redemption.

Sometimes I painted rapaciously, into the night. Sometimes I painted drunk. Sometimes I slept in the studio. Sometimes I raged at the impudence of the rising sun that awakened me. How dare it throw itself in front of my face? I raged and I wept, and I asked for my mother to come to me in the night, and sometimes she came, her ghost, her unforgiving, unrelenting ghost, and sometimes I was frightened. I was ensnared by guilt. But by day my power returned, my twisted senses unraveled, and I found solace in the courtroom.

My marriage, too, was tortured. Still, I thought the marriage could never be worn away. It could absorb the madness, take whatever was thrown at it, whatever injury, whatever insult, whatever infidelity, whatever horror. The marriage could withstand the drinking and the screaming into the night, take it like the rocks at the bottom of a pounding waterfall. Yet we shared times of joy, Anna and I, which, at last, represented the wild, schizoid swings of that confused and turbulent arrangement.

In 1968, for the first time, a collection of my paintings was exhibited to the public in a one-man show held in the lobby of the American National Bank at Riverton, my own bank, The First National, too conservative, too proper for such extravagances. I entitled the show "Of, By and For the Birds." To the thoughtful viewer, the paintings must have revealed the painter in deep psychic misery.

The Riverton Ranger reported that the show was "a shock to a stalwart citizen buzzing into the bank with money orders on the mind only to be seized by the imposing 'Self Portrait,' a scowling Spence adorned with nothing more than a scowling crow." The painting was of the nude Spence, all right, his face drawn in pain, a raven perched on his arm where a falcon might have been tethered, the raucous bird squawking in his face. There was also a large painting of a bright red nude, her posterior blaring with the words brushed in at the bottom of the painting, "Please be quiet and listen." The paintings clung to the sanity of the bank's walls: a crow lost in a blinding snowstorm, a crippled parrot, another painting of a wounded owl, and still another of a monster with birdlike claws.

"Why the prevalence of birds in your paintings?" the reporter had asked.

"I see birds as symbols of freedom," I said. Some of the paintings frightened me. Sometimes at night I was afraid to carry a finished painting to the house. I told the reporter, "I am both beautiful and ugly. I paint the way I am." Then I laughed. "I would like to see their faces when they see this show," I said. "But perhaps they will be tolerant. The people of Riverton have grown to be tolerant of me."

For me, painting was not a Sunday afternoon diversion. As with everything, I painted with a fervor. Sometimes I physically attacked the canvas with the brush. Sometimes I shot holes through the paintings with a pistol. Often I painted until I was exhausted.

LOCAL ARTIST—Gerry Spence, lawyer, artist and controversial citizen, has a one-man show at the American National Bank. He calls his show of paintings "Of, By and For the Birds."
—Photo by Bill Hunsucker

Spence at one-man show.

I saw symbolic meaning in the process. "It is frightening to approach a blank canvas. It's like life," I told the reporter. "The first stroke spoils the virgin white. From that moment on the painting is your responsibility. Every stroke cries out for yet another stroke. Stroke on stroke. Like life, you cannot blame the painting on anyone but yourself. You must have the courage to lay the first stroke on the canvas, and you must also have the wisdom to know when the painting is finished. One stroke too many can destroy it. One must see the painting, but one must also listen to it. It will speak to you."

I hadn't realized the paintings were religious until I saw the whole of them hung in one room. "Look over there at the wounded owl. The fate of that poor creature is the fate of man. His wings are broken, and even if he could move, he'd be trapped in the barbed wire. Look at the dilemma he's in. See his faint black tears?"

"And look at this painting"—one I had called "God Is a Great Green Owl." "You can look into God's eye and ponder—and this one called 'Green Goddess.' I equate muted colors with peace and happiness. It may mean, on the other hand, that God is but a great green grinning glob."

"Would you ever leave the courtroom to devote your life to art?" the reporter asked.

"That is highly unlikely," I replied. "A man makes a mistake delivering his whole being to one activity. I wouldn't want to be known as Gerry Spence, lawyer, or Gerry Spence, artist. I would like to be known simply as Gerry Spence, the whole man."

That was only a wish. I would never be whole. I would never escape with my life from that prison on the prairies, called Riverton, Wyoming.

Anna and I became pseudo-hippies ourselves. I began to further test the values that had been plastered on me as a child, and the plaster was cracking. Maybe work wasn't what life was all about. Maybe you could escape your traps in the mountains, in deep talk with nature, and with yourself in poetry and painting. I began to take the summers off. Took the family to that little ranch on the reservation that I had bought for about $25,000, a hundred-twenty acres on Dry Creek, a clear mountain stream that came roaring out of a box canyon and through a high meadow that waved in native timothy and brome grass. The place was surrounded by mountains on every side, a small spot on the Forest Service topographical map called Hidden Valley.

To get to the ranch, you drove west out of Riverton about fifty miles and then you took an hour's Jeep drive on a trail that had been originally cut by horses and wagons—two ruts, that's all—up over the rocks and down into the washes, and then up the steep mountain slope, a slow, hard, rough grind through stone and sagebrush to the ranch. When you popped over the last ridge you suddenly found yourself under those audacious peaks of the Wind River Range, the glaciers glistening in the clear high air, the creek rushing by misnamed, for it had never been dry, this beautiful fly stream filled with brook trout and lined with mountain willows.

Nothing to do up there but paint and fish and irrigate the pasture, write poetry, and build a tower. Kent, then a boy of twelve, and I built it.

"Why are you building that tower?" people would ask.

"Because," we would say. Good answer.

And when we were up on the tower, building it higher and higher until at the very top there was room for but a single chair, someone would come along and look up and see us building away, they would holler, "What the hell are you doing up there?" And we would holler down out of that paradoxical existential wisdom, or folly, "What the hell are you doing down there?"

Once, leaning out over the edge of the tower to nail on a brace, I lost my balance and began to fall. Kent saw my fall starting just in time and reached out and pulled me back, and saved himself a father. Sometimes when we got into arguments Kent would say, "Okay now, Dad. Remember, I saved you." And that usually ended it.

Some summers we stayed hidden in Hidden Valley without coming down once. If someone really needed to see me, they could fight their way up the mountain. We named the ranch "Fingolia," and Anna, our Wyoming Betsy Ross, sewed us up a large flag that we designed and flew from the flagpole at the top of the tower. The flag was composed of a blue field with a single white hand in the center, its long third finger extended to the world. Kerry, then an early teenager, rode old Molly the mule up the side of the mountain, and there she explored the bat caves and the Indian petroglyphs, and Katy, past toddling was like a butterfly, testing new yellow wings in the wind.

The flower children were in revolt. The flower children were my children, and the flower children were Anna and I. We were all in revolt. We revolted against authority, against custom, against historical wisdom, against religion. Especially religion. We were in revolt against each other. We loved each other, but love in the war zone is a hard crop to grow.

We all longed for our freedom, but we were inextricably tied to each other. We embraced the ideas of the new culture that people ought to be free, that their lives should not be governed by meaningless convention, that there was more wisdom within than without, that politics and government were ludicrous, corrupt, and too boring to pay much attention to. The spiritual themes in nature, and beyond nature, in the universe, were important to us, and we tried to tune into them. Yet we remained wedded to hard work. A person had to earn his way. A man had a duty to be productive, to contribute to the earth and to the people on the earth. It wasn't enough to occupy space and bob your head up and down and murmur, "Cool, man, cool." The hippy movement was no excuse to slack off.

Most often I felt alone. I felt like Job. Often I thought of his story about how God told Job to gather up His children, known as "the remnant."

"And how, Lord," Job asked, "will I know Your children?"

And God answered, "They will make themselves known unto you." I longed to find the remnant—not God's, but my own. I was searching out there for the one soul who could hear me, who could hear whatever I had to say and who could feel whatever I felt.

I cried out: "Make yourself known to me. I am waiting. I am here."

But all that answered were the ravens, the black and noisy ravens.

CHAPTER 31

Kerry and Kent with Indian children at Sun Dance.

I WAS DRINKING a lot of whiskey in those days, and doing things that have no place in a public confession, things most people want to do, and the closest some can connect with their desires is to point their long condemnatory fingers at those who take the desperate, mindless risks. Yet if you feel as if you're in a trap, it's hard to sit there all proper and polite like a kid in church who's just taken his Sunday bath.

Then one day a claims man for St. Paul Insurance Company came to visit, one of those nice, smiling fellows who laughed at whatever a person said.

"We've been watching you a long time, Gerry," this guy said. "Frankly, we're tired of having you shove our cases up our ass." He laughed, offered the peace-making cigarette. "If we can't beat you, we'll join you. What do you say?" The glad hand.

"Well, this certainly is a surprise to me," I said, trying to remain calm, my mind awhirl, being propositioned by the enemy like that.

"There's a lot of young lawyers out there. We look 'em over pretty good. Watch 'em over the years. Then we pick the winners. You're a winner." Like the rich man with a stable of young colts, I thought. They let the colts race and keep the ones who finish in the money. "Got a whole raft of cases here." He opened his briefcase, bulging with files. "Some pretty big ones." I remembered Eddie Murane and his file drawer full of Cadillacs. "We'd like you to join our team."

You can claim to believe this or that, pray, preach, strut, and tremble in righteous rage. But when you hit the *here and now* and slam your principles up against a shot at money or power, something happens. Watch principle fade into a haze of rationalizations. "I'll just do it once" becomes the refrain. A man hates the rich, then falls into it—makes a pile of money. Guy says all politicians are crooks, and he'd rather shovel shit in Singapore than be one. Then they appoint him to the city council and he runs for mayor. I know people who go to church every Sunday and pray, then cheat their customers half an ounce at a time on the scales the rest of the week. Principle in the abstract has a hard time surviving when faced with a corrupted reality.

"Yield not to temptation." I remember my mother saying it over and over, preaching from the pulpit of the supper table. And I was tempted by the insurance company's rep, all right. What's wrong with making a little money? You can make an honest living representing the insurance company. The best lawyers around did. You don't have to be a soulless shyster to represent insurance companies.

I went home to brag about it to Anna, to sort of bounce it off of her. "Well, I've finally made it as a lawyer," I said for starters. She waited for the news. "I've been asked by St. Paul Insurance Company to represent them."

"An insurance company? How could you do that?" she asked. "I thought you hated insurance companies."

"I know," I said. "But the big lawyers in the state, the really *big* lawyers everywhere represent the insurance companies and the banks—big money. You never heard of a big-time lawyer who didn't represent the companies."

"How about Melvin Belli?" she asked.

"Who else?" She couldn't think of anyone else.

"Look at Bill Brown, and Eddie Murane, and those guys. Look at Dick Bostwick. They represent the insurance companies and they've made it big. They're the bar leaders. They run things. They get respect." I remembered Bill Werhli, who had beaten me in that first case, the old dean of the bar. Everybody thought Bill Werhli was the lawyer's lawyer. "And a guy gets paid whether he wins or loses. The insurance guy says I can bill the company every month. We won't be silly rich one month and dumb poor the next."

"What about the poor people you'll be up against?" Anna asked.

"Jesus Christ," I said. "You don't get it, do you? I've finally made it as a lawyer and you're asking about the poor people? How about *us*? How about Eddie Murane with a file drawer full of Cadillacs, and some days we're scraping to make the fucking car payment? A lawyer should be able to represent either side in any case and win." That's the way the system works. Poor people don't drive Cadillacs.

Under the angry arguments that bore my frustration, and my guilt, something else was burning through. I wanted to be the great trial lawyer and I wanted a way out of Riverton. I argued to myself that I had the courage *to be,* even if I had to back off of principle a little, make a little concession. Nobody would condemn me but me. The other lawyers around would be envious. They'd give me respect. They and the judges always respect the lawyers who represent money.

There's two sides to every case, I argued. The injured and the poor, the workman, the ordinary citizen weren't always right. Somebody had to defend the other side or there wouldn't be a lawsuit. Nobody from the insurance companies ever came to see Judge Sheldon when he was practicing law. Nobody from the insurance companies ever came to see Harry Harnsberger when he was a big-shot lawyer in the county. The insurance companies didn't come knocking at their doors because the lawyers in Fremont County had never made it to the big time as I was about to do.

"And, remember one thing," I said to Anna, "The poor people never gave a damn about me. Where were the people I've been fighting my ass off for all these years when I was running for Congress? They said, 'We don't want that loudmouth in Congress.' That's what they said."

I took a case for the company. Then a couple. It's easy to slip into it. You get hardened to what you do, and it gets to be okay after a while. Doctors become inured to cutting people up, seeing them falter and die because the doctor's knife slipped, or maybe he was playing golf when he should have been putting his patient on oxygen. Doctors see a man in terrible pain, and he isn't John Jones, a man who is suffering, but "another gall bladder."

"Where ya headed, Doctor?"

"Oh, I got a gall bladder up at the hospital."

You get hardened to such things. The mortician flops the corpses around in his preparation room like so many slabs of beef. Grieving family never knows. The guy in the slaughterhouse knocks the little lambs in the head, a thousand a day, and never thinks a thing about it. The rancher cuts the nuts off of the calves and burns huge blisters on the poor animal's hide, an inhumane torture, and we eat the beef.

It's dangerous, this getting hardened to things. You argue yourself out of your humanity, your soul leaks away. But it leaks one small drip at a time. You hardly notice it. You plaster it up with arguments like "Somebody has to do it, just as well be me." But I'd heard arguments like that before. You could be Lilly up in the whorehouse and use that argument. Pretty soon you don't have any time for arguments. The case for the insurance company has been called up for trial. You have to win the case. You're a fighter. You fight for whoever hires you. Doctors don't examine the souls of their patients before they try to save them. You never hear a doctor say, "I can't take your case. It's against my principles to treat a crook like you. You'll have to find another doctor or die." Doctors are doctors and lawyers are lawyers—that's how I argued it.

Then I went to court and fought another case for the company. My job. That's where true principle lay—representing your client honestly, with all you had.

So the word got around. Spence was working for the insurance companies. Spence was a winner. Other insurance companies began sending their claims men to see me, and I had new cases to defend. Then one December day just before Christmas, a claims man representing a major insurance company called me. "Emergency," he said. "I'm flying up from Denver to see you this afternoon."

When he got to the office he told me about a case he was supervising in Colorado. The company's insured driver was a drunk who had run into the back end of a car carrying a family coming home from church. The car, with the family in it, had crashed, caught fire, and the passengers—father, mother, couple of kids—were burned to death. The drunk, their insured, who rear-ended the car, didn't stop. He ran.

"The estate of the dead family wanted a couple million dollars. We figured we owe 'em all right," the claims man said, "but not a couple of million. So we were in trial, and the little kid who got thrown out of the car when it crashed was on the stand. And he's telling the jury how he reaches into the burning car to try to pull his mother out, and all he pulls out is her burned-off arm. The jury can't stand it. Everybody's crying. One woman on the jury runs out of the jury box. And the clerk of court—I mean, she's heard it all before—well, she breaks up and runs out of the courtroom. And then *our* lawyer folds—actually folds, I'm telling you the truth. *He has a heart attack!*"

"You're telling me a story," I said in disbelief.

"No, I'm not telling you a story. We tried to get the judge to continue the case. The judge wouldn't. Gave us five days to get another lawyer. You're it."

"Settle the case," I said.

"Can't. They know they got us over the barrel. They want five million now."

"Who's representing the family's estate?"

He told me. A lawyer with a reputation for big verdicts. An explosive, aggressive man from a big Denver firm whom everybody was afraid of. "You have to go to Denver and finish the trial for us. Hold the verdict down the best you can."

"Why me? You got plenty of lawyers in Denver."

"You're the right one" was all he would say.

When I walked into the courtroom five days later the lawyer on the other side was waiting for me. Beautiful navy blue silk suit, tiniest stripe. Few years older than I. Sultry complexion. Thick black hair slicked back, and shiny. Looked like he'd just stepped out of *GQ*.

"Who, Your Honor, is this supposed to be?" The plaintiff's lawyer motioned toward me. "This man, whoever he is, has no standing in this court. He's not a member of the Colorado bar. Who are they bringing up here, anyway? We object to his admission."

"He can come in on motion," the judge said. The insurance representative had brought a Denver lawyer to court to present me to the judge. "You want to finish the trial, don't you?" the judge asked. "Somebody has to represent the defendant."

"They can get a Colorado lawyer," the opposing lawyer shouted.

"Maybe a Colorado lawyer wouldn't take the case," the judge said, raising an eyebrow. Then he ordered me into the case.

I told the jury I had come from the small town of Riverton, Wyoming, to defend this fellow. Intimated he was my friend. He needed help—they could surely see that. He was in terrible trouble. I was quiet in my cross-examinations, respectful of the grieving family. I showed opposing counsel great deference.

Later I put the defendant on the stand, this drunk who had hit, and killed, and run as innocent people burned. With quiet questions, with soft sounds in the courtroom that the people had to strain to hear, I had him admit he was wrong. He was afraid. He made no cheap excuses. He wept.

On cross, the opposing lawyer, teeth bared, attacked. He was merciless, relentless. And in response, there was only the man's weeping and the hard but honest admission that he was wrong—afraid, but wrong; horrified, but wrong; sick at heart, but wrong.

In his final arguments the lawyer's attack was even more chilling. He was imperious, mean. He assaulted the drunk, assailed me, and demanded millions. Clamorous, infuriated, his anger bounced from every wall in the courtroom. The jury shied back. He picked up a piece of the car, a fender that had been an exhibit, lifted it up above his head and smashed it onto the floor the way a professional wrestler slams down his opponent. The jury jumped. "This is what I want you to do with the defense of that drunk murderer," he hollered.

I held back. I argued for the plaintiffs, argued their case, asked for justice for them, that innocent grieving family. But my client had already been punished. He wanted to pay what was right, what he could, what was fair—the jury never knowing, and, as always under the law, never permitted to know, that the drunk owned a big insurance policy, and that I was the insurance company's lawyer.

"What about this hot wind that blows in from Wyoming?" the lawyer cried, pointing at me. I looked over at the jury, then I looked down.

The jury returned a verdict—for $12,000.

"Twelve thousand dollars? I can't believe it!" The insurance rep laughed. "Twelve grand for a million-dollar case? What did you do? What kind of a magician are you? Jesus! The home office will shit their pants."

I didn't know how I felt. I'd won. But what did I win? I saw the family walk out of the courtroom, stunned, their lawyers too dumbfounded to speak. Then, like the hunter, the one ingredient that every trial lawyer must have—the will to kill—took over. The hunter kills in the forest, the lawyer in the courtroom.

You are there to fight for your side, to kill for your side. And you lay it all down. The morality is not in the killing, not in whom or what you kill, but how you kill. We all agree it is immoral to win even the most just case by, say, bribing a juror. On the other hand, lawyers find nothing immoral about winning an unjust case if they do it by honest lawyering. That's why decent men and women can go into court and with their trial skills cheat honest folks out of their justice, and then go home at night and sleep like an old dog in the shade.

Later the insurance company rep came to the office. He wanted to pay the family $100,000 to settle the case, to prevent the family's appeal and to close the file.

"You wanted me to hold down the verdict," I said. "Now you're telling me I held it too far down?"

"If we can get out for a hundred, the home office will be ecstatic."

Then I heard the words come oozing out of a newly hardened soul. I heard the words, and I never once winced. "I wouldn't pay them a penny more than the twelve grand the jury gave them. Appeals courts never reverse when the verdicts are too small. They only reverse when they're too big. That verdict will stand."

"We have to pay 'em a little, Gerry," the insurance rep said, hanging out his sympathetic voice. "Besides, the appeal and all will cost the hundred thousand anyway. We can't lose on a hundred." And that's how he settled the case. There's a place at the bedrock of a man, where his footings stand, and there I must have realized I was on the wrong side. I must have fought off the guilt, but I had become an expert at sloughing off guilt. Honorable men and women represent big money and big corporations. Yet I must have known that representing insurance companies against injured people was a waste of my life. In the end, I must have known: Power is the bastard child of money.

But there is no power like the power of justice.

CHAPTER 32

John C. Johnson.

I MET THIS kind of ordinary-looking fellow, John C. Johnson was his name, a man a couple inches shorter than I. For as smart as he was, I thought he had a small head. He was a guy who got up close to your face when he talked, and when you backed up, he followed you, and got his face right up there again, held you with his eyes like a lemur hanging from a limb peering at you, held you deeply and quizzically, trying to look you through. When he walked, he threw his legs out to the side with each step, as if to get around huge hanging gonads. He grew a beard later on, and then he looked very handsome, I thought. Big bushy beard and bushy eyebrows to go along with it. His glasses put you in mind of a great sage, and he was. He liked to play with words and to make jokes with them, the kind that made you cringe and say, "Jesus, John!" And then he'd laugh. He'd been educated by the nuns, and he liked to quote Thomas Aquinas, but he called himself a recovering Catholic. He was a wise man, although I was not wise enough to know that when I first met him. Wisdom is something I believe that you are born with, but experience is what wears away the coatings that cover it so that the wisdom can make its appearance. And as the years went on, John C. Johnson faced death many times, sometimes all of the time, and his wisdom emerged accordingly. For many years he was my best friend, and I loved him as much as any man can love a man.

When I first met Johnson, he was working at the Fremont County Mental Health Clinic at what he had been trained to do—as a psychiatric social worker. In furtherance of the county's mental health, Johnson traveled once a week from Lander, where he lived, to Riverton, where he set up what was known in those days as "an encounter group." I was searching. So was Anna.

Our group consisted of ten or twelve disparate souls, men and women with troubled marriages, with emotional pain, curious people, lonely and confused— in short, ordinary people with problems. We wanted to learn more about who we were, and that was to be accomplished by a simple technique Johnson told us about: telling the truth and requiring that everybody else one encountered in the group do likewise. "How do you feel?" was the key to an epiphany.

This new experience of "encounter grouping" seemed radical. To those who observed it from the outside, it was "that touchy, feely stuff," as if there were something ugly, repulsive and occultish going on. Often when the subject came up, those who had never encountered "encountering" put on their fanciest sneers and acted as if they were above it. Reminded me of one of my boys when I tried to get him to eat eggplant. "I don't like it," he said, "haven't tried it."

But the idea of encountering was simple and right: to become a person, one had to first become acquainted with oneself, and that required one to become aware of one's feelings. And after that, to become a person one had to develop the elusive skill of sharing one's feelings with others. When the notion of those simple propositions sank through, it struck me like salvation staggers the born-again.

Before, I had felt, all right, and deeply. Before, I had been only too aware of my feelings. But mostly, I fought them back like a person on the verge of retching. Feeling caused pain. And, like the draft horses in the hayfields of my youth, when I let loose of the reins the team stampeded. Feelings were dangerous, the enemy in fact. If one could contain one's feelings, perhaps one could survive in this world, for the world was rendered crazy with the crazy feelings of its crazy occupants. I thought that. But now, suddenly, feelings were *it*. And to tell the truth about one's feelings was also *it*.

We talked with a new jargon in the groups. We talked about "crawling into the hide of others." We talked about not judging, but being, not thinking, but feeling. The new paradigm was becoming aware of oneself and accepting what one encountered there. In the group, I became the predominant protagonist. Often I became too powerful, too unrelenting, too aggressive, too oppressive. I had those bursting insights, *gestalts* they were called, and I would permit no one to escape them. To some I became a sort of shaman. Yet, of course, I could not heal myself. To others, I was a frightening ogre. Yet, of course, I had not learned much about gentleness.

One day John Johnson took me aside. "The Episcopal clergy and their wives are going to have a couples' group. You and Anna oughta go."

"What is it? Group sex?" I had a smart mouth.

"You and Anna might learn something about yourselves that you don't know," he said. The group leader was also an Episcopal priest who had brought along his wife.

"I don't want to hang out with a bunch of fuckin' preachers," I said.

"They're the kind you need to hang with," John said. "They're probably as screwed-up as you are." But Anna wanted to go. She knew our marriage was in trouble, and so did I, but it had been in trouble so long I thought that was how a marriage was supposed to be. I had never thought of leaving her. People who got divorces were weak, immoral, stupid.

In the late winter of 1968 we met—six Episcopal priests, their wives, and Anna and I, the only couple outside the clergy. The meeting, three days long, was held at Trail Lake Lodge, a mountain retreat east of Dubois. I was hostile and arrogant, as usual, and more disturbed than I knew.

I looked around the large log meeting room. We sat in a big circle, some of the preachers sitting there with that saintly I've-just-seen-Jesus look on their faces. But the group leader was a skinny, crusty cynic with a high nasal voice. His eyes were animated, and he had energy like a striking cobra.

"Well, what are you doing here and why?" he began. He waited. The silence in the room grew uncomfortable. Then the silence became oppressive and after a while somebody who couldn't take it any longer broke it, saying, "I'm fighting through a decision about whether to stay in the clergy." He looked down at his hands as if, in the morning, he'd be charged with heresy and stoned.

"We are having difficulty communicating in our marriage," a preacher's wife said. She was all stuffed into a tight sweater, but her voice was one of those high-pitched whiny voices that makes you want to run out and slam the door. "I would like to understand my husband better." I looked at her. The bitch wasn't telling the truth, I thought. I glanced over at her husband—sitting there looking as pious as a fat pope. Already I understood. How could she give a damn about a simpering yes-man to a congregation of hypocrites.

When it came my turn I looked right at the woman in the sweater, mean, I suppose, angry. I hated preachers. "I've come here, brothers and sisters, to fuck your wives," I said in a mocking voice. The woman in the tight sweater never blinked.

My hostility was there to diffuse the pain. My mother was there, of course. Couldn't get rid of her. One late night before I had joined the group, I had retreated to the studio and painted her ghost, and I'd brought the painting, as if to bring her along in an earthly form so she could be seen and touched, and therefore dealt with. During the second day I stood before the group and held up the painting.

"I am God," I said, still mocking the clergy. "I've made my mother in my own image." They stared at the haunting canvas, a ghostlike form glistening through layers of glazes. My voice was taunting, and my hostility seeped into the room like noxious fumes. Yet as belligerent as I was, I knew these were decent people with whom I shared a common island. They had wanted to do something with their lives and were disappointed. Disillusioned, most of them eventually left the church. Later, one became a stock broker and made so much money he could have bought the whole damn town of Riverton.

Suddenly the group leader struck out at me. "Let's get rid of the ghost of your mother. Let's burn her up." There was a fire in the fireplace.

"Yes," I said. "You fuckers have always been for burning." I thought of the witches.

"Let's burn the witch of your mother," he said. "Throw her in the fire!"

I stood there, suddenly unable to speak. At last I began to weep. I was ashamed of the weeping, me, the arrogant tough, there in front of all those preachers.

The leader struck again. "Are you afraid to burn the witch?"

A preacher came over and quietly put his arm around me. "You don't have to burn your mother. You only need to burn the ghost that haunts you," he said. His voice was kind. His face, too.

I stood there, the tears flowing, my nose running, sobbing, humiliated.

Then the others came around me, and stood with me, and suddenly I threw the painting in the fire. And we watched it burn. I watched the flames suck up the paint and the glaze, and I saw the face become the fire. And I was horrified, for once again I had destroyed my mother. Yet somehow I was relieved.

But ghosts are not so easily destroyed.

Later that same spring John Johnson suggested I go to Bethel, Maine, to attend the National Training Laboratories for advanced group work. And, of course, the relentless ghost of my mother followed me.

There, in another group, I spoke to the ghost. "Why don't you leave?" And when the ghost did not retreat I asked the same eternal question: "Why did you do it, Mother? Why?" I was afraid of the answer.

The trainer, an older woman with a placid face and deep-set eyes, pale blue like an early sky, took off her watch and put it on the floor. She pointed at the watch. "This is your mother," she said. "Talk to your mother."

I stared at the watch. Finally I said to it, "Why did you leave us, Mother?"

The watch was silent.

"Your mother can speak through you," the trainer said.

The silence went on for a long time. "I had to go," I finally heard my mother answer.

"Why?"

My mother's whisper from my lips. "I couldn't stand the pain."

Again, I began to cry. For several minutes I couldn't speak.

At last I heard my mother's surrogate voice. "No, it was not you. It was my own pain from my own life." And I saw the ghost rise up out of the watch, and I spoke with the ghost.

"But I loved you." The small child sobbing there, some in the group weeping in a silent chorus.

"How, if you loved me, how could you hurt me so?" I asked.

Then I heard the voice whisper back. "It was you who hurt you."

When I returned to Riverton I began working with a group on my own. The people met at my office once a week in the evening. There we were free to feel and to say what we felt, to experiment and to learn. Once we did the blind man's trust walk—took a partner who was sworn to blindness, and we, responsible for our partner, led him, introduced him silently to such things as the rough bark of a tree and the softness of a flower petal. We took him down the curbs and up the steps. Each, in our turn, we learned to trust and to be trustworthy, to put ourselves into the hands of another, to relinquish control—that is an important lesson, and in turn we learned to exercise control responsibly, and that is caring. Over time, people changed. I think it was more like growing than changing. I learned how to listen, and how to hear. There is a difference, of course, and you know it when you have been heard. You are not so lonely. And when you hear another, you are not so lonely, like Robinson Crusoe who, to his delight, discovered another living being inhabiting the same island.

I had been afraid that if I explored down there at the bottom, where the ugly stuff was hidden, I would be repulsed. I discovered something different. I found a fragile man, a man who was afraid and had always been afraid. But I discovered nothing there to be afraid of. I learned something very hard to learn—that it was all right to love oneself. You learn that and you forget it, and you have to learn it again. Over and over. My God, why is it so difficult? Why do we beat ourselves so unmercifully, yet strike out at anyone who drops a passing insult at us? Why am I not, instead, an open territory of love, where I and everyone else might enter? What is so wrong about love? I thought of flowers in growth, and I asked questions, like What flower in growth does not love itself? And I thought of my mother. How could she have loved so many without first having loved herself?

Of course the local deputy sheriff, who spent a lifetime driving up and down the streets, nodding at the cars as he drove by, had gotten wind of our meetings—something going on there. He didn't get it, people leading people up and down the street, people feeling trees, hugging trees, touching flowers to their faces. Very strange. Narcotics or something. He spent a lot of time looking into this strange cult of "touchy-feelies." Maybe a new witch cult, devil worshipers— he'd heard of them. Had we known of his interest we would have invited him to join us. Might have changed his life. But he spread the word: Spence has lost it. Better keep your eye on him.

In the meantime I began to incorporate what I had learned in the groups into my trial work, by now half of which was for insurance companies. I began to better understand the witnesses, the judges, the juries. I was better able to hear both what was said and what was not said. People reported that a new sort of aura surrounded me, a power they did not fully understand which followed me into the courtroom. People wondered about the new power. And, in one of my cases, a leading Cheyenne attorney went so far as to address the federal judge about it.

"I've studied this man. Nobody could have won as many cases as he has without something going on. I've been watching him. You watch him, too, Your Honor. You will see that he waves his pencil slowly back and forth before the jurors' faces. You can hear the sound in his voice. I say he is hypnotizing the jury. And that is unprofessional!" He was livid.

The judge was amused at the attorney's argument. "Do you confess, Mr. Spence?"

"Of course, Your Honor."

"Aha! As I suspected!" the defendant's attorney bellowed.

"Very well, then," the judge ruled, "you are hereby ordered not to wave your pencil at the jury, Mr. Spence." After that the attorney focused on me throughout the trial, trying to hold me down, objecting. He never understood that by being consumed with me, he gave me his power, and when the jury brought in a verdict for my client, he was heard to say, "You never can predict what those simple shits on a jury are going to do." But in his heart I thought he believed I possessed some evil, magical power.

I had discovered that the courtroom is a place where lawyers are often impotent, for no matter how much power they exhibit, the jury can reject it. And the lawyer's power is usually met by the power of his opponent, and it is neutralized. The more powerful the lawyer seems, the more he rages, raises hell, hollers, attacks, the more power he loses. The judge has power. But the more powerful he becomes, the more he threatens, intimidates, belittles, the more his power is perverted, the more fear he engenders, the more hate and contempt for the law is born, and the less justice is found in his courtroom.

And I had learned that the lawyer does not always have to destroy the witness. He can hear the witness, and because the witness knows he has been heard, the witness begins to hear the lawyer. Often my opponent's witnesses ended up supporting my case before they stepped down from the stand. Nor must the lawyer always contest the judge. The lawyer with power is the one who can hear beyond the judge's ranting, who can hear what he does not say—that with all of his power, the judge feels powerless, that alone he cannot bring on justice, that the lawyers do not help, that they wade through the waters of justice and muddy it. The lawyer who can admit to the frailties of his case can enjoy immense credibility with the judge, and that becomes power.

I learned that great power grew out of listening and hearing. And I realized that something happened in a courtroom when the lawyer could feel. If I could feel my own fear, feel my own sense of weakness and powerlessness, I could recognize it in others. If I could speak of my feeling in a straight way, others could hear me—the judge, the jurors—it was as if people in the court-room suddenly became members of a brotherhood. To admit to being a person—and to admit that others are persons as well—that becomes power in a courtroom.

The courtroom is a lonely place. It is lonely for the juror sitting there next to other jurors, people the juror did not choose to be with, strangers he has never met, whom he has no reason to trust. It is lonely for the client sitting next to his lawyer, a man who is there for the money, who goes home to a comfort-able house and a martini, a family, while the client, alone, goes back to his cell, the cold steel bench, a bare mattress. The judge is lonely up there as well, even with all of his apparent power, his is the loneliest place in the courtroom, for no one can speak to the judge, not as a person. But when there is one human being in the courtroom who cares for his client, who speaks of his feelings, who admits his fear, his confusion, we are not so lonely. Such a person becomes a metaphor for all of us, and there is great power in that. That kind of power could not be turned away by the stale legal teachings of trickery and technique. It was a power that demanded simple honesty. It was a very great power, and John John-son had introduced me to it.

Often John Johnson and I painted together, drank Old Cabin Still into the night together, staggered and laughed and raged together. Sometimes we spoke of philosophy, and the meaning of life and of religion. Once I told him I thought that Christ and the apostles had probably been an encounter group.

"And one thing for sure," I said. "If Christ came back for a visit he'd have raised hell about all the pomp and power the church promulgates in his name."

"Right," John said.

"All of the ritual and dogma, all the hatred and the killing done in the name of a man whose simple message was 'Love one another.' " We saw things the same, John and I. I said that Christ would have run the priests out of the cathe-drals and thrown open the doors of the churches to the homeless. Neither of us were any longer Christians if the organized church stood for Christianity.

We laughed a lot and drank a lot but underneath we knew there was some-thing important we had learned from our religious childhoods, something that was endearing to both of us. It had to do with the messages that had touched Christ and Gandhi and Martin Luther King alike, for that matter, my mother as well. It had to do with the dignity of people. It had to do with the longing of people for justice. I remember the beatitudes as a child: "Blessed are the meek, for they shall inherit the earth. Blessed are they who hunger and thirst after righteousness, for they shall be filled."

Once I said, "Nowhere in the Bible does it ever say anything about Jesus ever smiling, or laughing. You know why?" I asked.

"Why?"

"Because being the son of God is a serious business that does not cater to smiling and laughing."

"No, that isn't why," John said. "If he was laughing, he might have lost his balance while he was walking on the water. It never said anything in the Bible about Jesus being able to swim, either." John was like that. And when we talked about power, I said I thought that Christ had it figured out. In a world where the Jews were powerless, love became a powerful weapon, their only weapon, and later I was to discover that love, indeed, was a powerful weapon in the courtroom as well.

One January day in 1968, during a scorching white blizzard, we had just skied down Rendezvous Peak, in the Tetons, a sheer rock slope covered with that deep, blowing, high-altitude snow, the mountain so steep that looking down you wanted to turn around and back down, step at a time, and it was slippery, the trail, moguled and cut, and mostly concealed in the storm. I fought the mountain all the way, lost all the way, fell and rolled, got up, stiffened and determined, headed down again and fell again, until at last, having fallen down the steepest part of the peak, and nearly exhausted, I was able, by reverting to the snow plow, to ski the rest of the way down. At the bottom we took off our boards and limped into the Alpenhof for lunch. Then I saw her.

I have spoken of the event many times, the Rubicon of my life. Verdi called it *La Forza del Destino*. But what did Verdi know about this woman, this force, who came bursting into that small restaurant like an avalanche? Meeting Jesus in a rainstorm on the roof garden of the Space Needle would have been infinitely more likely. I mean to say, had I not gone skiing with John Johnson that very day,

had I not skied down the mountain—*fallen* down, let us say it correctly,

had I not survived, after which,

had we, John Johnson and I, not ventured into the Alpenhof for lunch at that precise moment,

had we, instead, stood in line at the cafeteria, as John had suggested, but who wanted the fucking chili dogs? And

had I not hollered out across the room to that preposterously beautiful phantasm—could it be a woman?—the one with the raven hair and the wild blue cat eyes who, when she walked in, caused every woman to turn from her, and made every man stare. No. It was not possible. And

had it not been for my insolence in speaking out to the entire restaurant— she knew I was speaking to her—"How do you get down off that Rendezvous Peak? By God, it scares the hell out of me!" I had said, as if the two of us were the only two in the room, and

had she not answered, her husband sitting there, politely amused, "You put a hot little skier in front of you who says, 'Come on, baby,' "—she was beckoning with her finger—"and you follow her down"—that's what she said back, smart like, and she also said it as if we were the only two in that room. But when we spoke to each other, the room fell silent, and then I said to the man with her "May I borrow your wife for a run?" and he did not answer, as if he did not hear me.

Had all that not taken place, then and there, in the realm of a tangible, earthly reality, and in that order, and at that precise moment, I cannot venture what other course my life would have taken.

Seeing the woman was proof of something. Call it preordination if you wish. Call it the hand of Providence. I have a hunch that I've been touched by it many times. Had these events not occurred, perhaps I would be moldering in a grave, my liver rotted out. Perhaps the bud of the man would have dried up on the stem like the lonely tomato plant in my office. Perhaps I would never have realized even a small part of the dreams of a young man bouncing blithely down the road, hollering out his boyish fantasies about one day becoming a great trial lawyer.

To behold that woman, that day, at that place—it was like Creation. It was the creation of a new life for me. Nature works in that way, the elements in the sea, all the proteins in exact order, the lightning, the first stroke of life as unexpected as when she walked into the restaurant. When I saw the woman, I poked John Johnson with an elbow and nodded over in her direction.

"You see that black bitch, over there, the one with the eyes?" Like all the rest, he had already seen her, and when he looked at me, he knew what I had in my mind. And that was when I began to holler to the whole restaurant about how does a fellow get down from the mountain.

I did not speak to her again that day. She had gone off skiing somewhere with her husband, and John and I had struggled down Rendezvous Peak once more, to prove to the mountain that we were fools, but not cowards. Then months later I had gone to Casper to try a case in the district court, and the forces came into line a second time. The gods—they were dancing with me.

Had I not seen and spoken to her before, for by now I was installed in her memory, and she in mine, and

had I not taken that case, the one the judge set for trial in Casper, and

had the judge not set the trial for *that* day, the judge surely a conspirator with the gods, and

had I not gone to the Ramada for lunch, not to any of the other dozen or more possible restaurants, but to the Ramada, and

had she not been sitting in that same restaurant with her friend Sally, at that precise moment, that same inexcusably, shockingly beautiful woman, and not knowing she was there,

had I not gotten up from my own table in the front of the restaurant, and happened, just happened, to walk through the rear of the bar for a reason that now escapes me, and

had the two of them not been sitting there, the gods still playing around, she at a booth having lunch, at that precise place, at that second, and

had she taken Sally's seat instead, and Sally hers, so when I walked in I could not have seen her—I mean, she was just sitting there, facing me, her face as naked and beautiful as a blaring brass band would be deafening, and

had all that not transpired in that order on that day, in that way against odds that make winning the lottery look like a certainty, my life on this planet in space—life as I know it, this unpredictable, this incorrigible, this wild and beautiful life—would not exist. It was as if my life was born there at that moment, but it was no less mysterious than the life that was bestowed upon the first cell in a lifeless ocean eons ago—I have no doubt—it was that same mysterious process.

Seeing her, I felt like an idiot. Not knowing what I was going to say to her, I was on the verge of a stammer. Then I sat down next to her. The booth was small, and I was large. I pushed her over a little with my hips to make room, kind of snuggled into the booth next to her. I said nothing at first, just looked at her. Then I said, "Give me a bite of your steak."

"Oh, I remember you." She seemed amused. "You're the one who couldn't get down off of Rendezvous Peak. I see you made it." She cut a piece of steak and fed me like a child.

"You talk essentially out of the left side of your mouth," I said, staring at her lips—the ample, luxuriant kind. Her girlfriend was angry.

"Who is this jerk, anyway? Who invited you to the party?"

I ignored the other woman, my eyes locked on this woman with the face, the high bones at the cheeks; I, having to fight back primitive compulsions, and she in control, amused, still toying with me, I thought. For Christ's sake, the closer you got to the woman, the more beautiful she was, like burying your own face in a field of wild iris.

Later, when they got up to leave I followed them out the door, and at the door I caught her. Stepped in front of her.

"How about your phone number? Friends could give each other phone numbers. We are already friends, aren't we?"

"I haven't any time for that," she said. "I've been through all of that before." When she left, I watched her drive off in a new Thunderbird. But I knew people in the bar who knew her. "Who is that black-headed bitch with the blue eyes, you know, the one who staggers your ass when you look at her?" They knew who I meant.

In court that afternoon the other lawyer was up, ranting about something, the judge's eyes glazed over, the jury half asleep, and I saw the woman, her eyes slightly mocking that way, the mouth. She was burned into the retina. I saw her everywhere I looked. I called her that evening after a couple of shots of Jack Daniel's and a Bud chaser.

"No, you can't come up here. What's the matter with you?"

"Why? Is your husband home?"

"I don't want to see you," she said.

"I have to see you. How do I get to your place?" She hung up.

I got out the phone book and from the map in the front of the book I tried to locate where she lived. Then I ran to my car and began to drive. But I couldn't find the street. I found a pay phone. I called again.

"I'm lost," I said. "I'm just a country boy." I told her the name of the street I was on. "Where's your place from here?"

"You must be crazy," she said. "Go away." She hung up again. But there was something in the voice—not the disgust, not the alarm.

Still lost, I drove around until I found another phone, and I called her the third time. This time she didn't answer. Then I started driving up and down the streets, and suddenly I recognized her Thunderbird in front of a house. The gods still playing with me. What was I supposed to do? Turn around and drive home? Not with the gods watching.

I walked up to the door and rang the bell. I rang again. After a while the door opened a crack, the chain securely in place.

"Hi," I said, a big smile on my face.

"How did you get here?" It was she all right. The voice clear and strong.

"Let me in," I said.

"Get out of here," she said. She shut the door.

I knocked on the door again. Once more she opened it a crack. "Shhh, you'll wake up my kids!"

"If you don't let me in, I'm going to serenade you out here in the street and I'll wake up the whole neighborhood." I pulled up my most powerful baritone and began singing, like Ezio Pinza. "With a song in my heart, I behold your adorable face . . ."

"Jesus!" she cried. "Stop it! My kids are going to be wide awake."

I went on with the song, my legs braced apart like the great opera singers, one hand on the heart, the other extended toward her, my voice this time a little louder. "With a song in my heart . . . "

"All right," she said. "You win." She was laughing. "But you have to promise—just for a moment."

"Of course, I promise," I said.

The door opened.

We did not understand what happened, she no more than I. We were children toddling on the brink, not knowing where we were, delighted by the sound of the falls, the mist and the spray in the face. We knew there was danger there, the power mostly, you could feel it and be terrorized by it. I had no deep abiding convictions against friendly coitus, against the "zipless fuck," as Erica Jong characterized it, a mark of the times. But this?

I was thirty-nine years old, sane, allegedly, on the edge of sanity at least, and this insane thing?

We were both frightened. But we would be safe enough if we never fell in love. Love was the danger. You could eat mushrooms, but not the deadly poisonous *Amanita*. You could safely eat the *Psilocybe*, which brought on those delicious hallucinations, but who could tell the difference? We made our vows. That was the best we could do.

"We will never do that thing," I said. She was next to me.

"What thing?"

"That *thing*, you know, that falling in love thing."

But was not pleasure a part of life? Should we only pass by the grapes, ripe and succulent, and toil on in the dust? No, pick the grapes. But the wine? We knew we were consumed by the power of this thing, else why did we have to fight it so? Why was there only one thought running wild in my brain—the woman, one picture, the woman, one smell, the smell of the woman. I could not eradicate her.

"Are you in love with me?"

"Of course not," she said.

"Why do you lie to me already?" I asked.

From that first night on we met in secret places, in old Arminto, for one, at a derelict hotel some twenty miles off the desolate Casper–Riverton highway. Nothing remained of the town of Arminto but that dreary white-framed, two-story, hip-roofed hotel with the bar downstairs and the post office up front. Across from the hotel at the railroad, the corrals rotted away where half a century before the ranchers had herded their livestock for shipment to their eastern markets. Beyond that lay an endless string of dirt road curled out into empty spaces, which, if you followed it far enough, led over the Big Horn Mountains and ended up in Sheridan.

We called the Riverton–Casper highway the "Manic-depressive Highway"—an eruption of manic coming to meet each other, a deep pool of depression, perhaps of guilt leaving each other once more.

"This is not for love, right?" I asked.

"Yes. I don't believe in love," she said, as she snuggled in close to me.

"Promise you will never fall in love with me," I said.

"I promise," she said. "Now *you* promise," and I looked into her eyes, and with the words brushing her lips I said, "I promise I will never fall in love with you." I could easily make the promise. I had already fallen.

One night we were together in a small motel in Lander, the Popo Agie Creek gurgling by like a lunatic whose party we had joined, a springtime storm having lately descended upon the land, the mountains fresh and white, the earth anew with snow.

I dreamed her name and woke up laughing. She was startled—this large, loud man next to her laughing in the night.

"What is it?" she asked, turning on the light, her eyes large and purple.

"I just dreamed a poem."

"What are you saying? Tell me the poem." And I recited the poem while it was still fresh in my mind:

An untoothed crow
Came Imaging *around*
And mocked right up
To mockery town

Said he, some think I'm just a clown
But to me, I'm a drowned dog
And that's what I've maintained
All a-log.

I sat up in bed and laughed some more. "Your name is Imaging Crow," I said. And that has been her name ever since. One day she named me Adam, the first man, the first for her. And, for her and her two boys, that has been my name.

In the morning I said to Imaging, "Let's walk out of this place backwards." And then we walked backwards in the snow, laughing.

"What if people see us walking backwards in the snow?"

"They will know we are insane," I said. "And they will be jealous of our insanity. And, after we leave, if anyone is out there gathering up evidence against us, they will find only our tracks entering this small shrine of ours, and no tracks coming out again, and they will therefore be required to conclude that these tracks were the tracks of ghosts." And later I wrote a poem about April spooks who walked backwards in the snow.

This time there was no escaping. I had fallen. And the landing left me wounded and delirious. We both knew it, and finally we both confessed it.

"We are insane," she said to me as we lay in one of the upper rooms of the Arminto Hotel, a single bulb hanging from the ceiling, an old calendar with a picture of Christ staring at us, the American flag on the post office flagpole whipping and popping in the wind by the window.

"I know," I said. "And I know what the cure for insanity is."

"What is it?" she asked.

"Love—a lot of love."

She was gazing up at the ceiling, the two of us staring simultaneously as if to behold the apocryphal image that would make its appearance there. Then she nestled up close to me, and put her head on my shoulder, and I felt the wetness of a tear on my neck.

But falling in love when one is indentured by law, by responsibility, by wife, by children—this is a hideous thing.

I was a husband, in love with another.

I was a father of four who was in love with the mother of another man's children.

She had those two small boys, handsome boys, Brents about eight and Christopher not yet three. By this time she had already divorced their father once, a good man, a businessman. But in a desperate concern over their first son, she had remarried her husband and promised to devote herself to her children, now including the second child, Christopher, who was born of the second marriage. She was twenty-eight. I was ten years older—not wiser, not more mature, both of us children. Sometimes when we met she wore a blond wig so people wouldn't know who she was. And sometimes people she knew would stop her and say, "Puddy"—her childhood nickname—"what are you doing wearing that silly blond wig?"

I remained busy in my office. By this time I was making good money, steady money. I had acquired those insurance company clients and I billed them by the hour—the way insurance company lawyers make their money. Sometimes the bills included entries such as:

—Thinking about the case in the shower . . . 15 minutes
—Wake up at 2 A.M. worrying, planning strategy . . . 2 hours

The claims men said nobody but me got away with that kind of billing. They paid. Insurance companies don't squint too long at the bills of winning lawyers. Lose? That's another story. Insurance companies don't stick by losers. No such thing as a loyal insurance company. Although I won, I grew unhappy in my work. I felt empty. Drank more whiskey. Thought it helped. Drank it even though I knew it didn't. I found myself arranging my days around the time when I could have a drink. Just as well arrange your days around the bottle as anything, I thought. Big-time trial lawyers were supposed to be heavy drinkers. Most were. It was the professional disease. Just as well be proud of it as hide it.

The mother demon was still there. I had never been able to quiet her down, always intruding as mothers do, dead or alive. Sometimes I could hear her.

"What are you doing with your life? You are nearly forty years old. Do something better. Be something better. Remember how we took care of the Sutkas? Remember how we had Mrs. Sutka help in the house when we couldn't afford it, and we gave them wild meat, and your father fought for Andy, the cop? Remember?"

"Mother," I said back, "why don't you listen to me once? I have four kids to feed, to take care of and to put through college. For Christ's sakes, that's service to mankind." The older kids were running headlong into hippyhood. Kip had left home and was out somewhere in California picking strawberries. Kerry had run off. She didn't say where. It was a full-time job just trying to keep up with them.

"You are unhappy," the voice of the ghost said.

For Christ's sakes, we are not supposed to be happy. Happiness gurgles from the lips of idiots. Happiness is for people who are delirious in their idiocy. Happiness is a myth. A double shot of Old Cabin Still on the rocks is happiness.

I saw where my mother had written in her cookbook:

Christian Happiness . . .
God wants us to live and to be glad this day
   I thank thee just for life
   The chance to live
   To be alive, so great thy gift
   If thou doest nothing give
   Beside, it is enough
   To breathe thy air
   To walk this mountain sod
   To feel the play of mighty winds
   To look thee in the face
   And call thee God.

That is happiness? *"I thank thee just for life, the chance to live. To be alive. So great thy gift!"* The .30-40 Krag was her gift. So great the pain.

"Becoming who you are is happiness," I said.

"Being of service is happiness," the voice said back.

Yes, I thought. I could see her placing figures of Jesus and the little children of the various races on her flannel-graph board. I could hear her talking about how Jesus loved the little children, all the children of the world. Red and yellow, black and white . . . And you, Mother, you had two little kids of your own at home. And you got up and left them in their bed, and you walked out to the ditch Grandpa and I cleaned with the mules. Did you forget that, Mother? Don't preach to me.

"I see the light through the clouds," she had written in her cookbook.

I saw no light.

Later she wrote:

THE ART OF HAPPINESS

   Happiness they say is the reward of right adjustment to your many jobs—your wage job, your family job, your friendship job, your citizenship job.

   Happiness does not come from constant fighting to have your own way, from head-on human collisions, from trying to change folks over into duplicates of ourselves or from raving against fate.

   The art of happiness is the art of adjusting to life as we find it. It is the art of illuminating discord and creating human harmony. When the gears of human adjustment fail to mesh, happiness goes out of the window.

Then she had written:

See some beauty each day.

And at the bottom of the page:

If you have a faith, preach it; If you have doubts, bury them; If you have joy, share it; If you have sorrow, bear it. Find the bright side of things and help others to find it also. This is the surest and only way to be cheerful and happy.

One day the good news came: Through the tireless efforts of Robert Peck and others, Riverton would soon have a junior college. It would provide an oasis of culture for that hard-bitten, culture-free little town. Up there on the hill on the edge of town a flame of enlightenment, albeit faint, would begin to burn. New people would come—artists, writers, philosophers. I could join them. We could establish a small community of our own. I could find new friends, people to listen to my poems, to see my paintings, to hear me, as I would listen to them.

I watched with anticipation as every building went up. Then one day the college opened its doors for the first time. The board had hired a president and teachers. I was eager to meet the president. He would surely be an inquiring, creative, worldly person who would cherish academic freedom and promote the arts, and, here in this isolated Mecca, with the junior college as the community's new nucleus, I would no longer need to escape, for we could all grow and bloom and live happily ever after.

Very soon I got to know some of the newly hired instructors. But already they were complaining. The college was being run like a high school, they said. Discipline was more important than learning. Rules, not creativity, were God. Experiment and inquiry gave way to hierarchy and convention. Several of the instructors had already resigned. Several came to my office seeking legal redress for their grievances. But I didn't give up. I thought, I will run for the junior college board. Perhaps I could influence the attitude of the administration and some of it would trickle down.

I talked around town about my newest ambition. Then one day an old friend, the former mayor of the town, came by to see me. He was a straight talker. Came right out with what was on his mind.

"Hear you are thinking about runnin' for the junior college board."

"I was thinking about it," I said.

"Well, I've decided to run for that vacancy myself."

To my knowledge, the man had never seen the inside of a college. I doubted that he had ever read a book from cover to cover. I thought the closest he ever got to literature was the *Readers' Digest*. He was a good and decent sort, an outspoken, crusty old curmudgeon whom people trusted, and whom I trusted. He had a practical, common sense approach to life—from work ethic to art. Things had to be in plain English and he had to understand them. Things had to be useful and cost effective. Things had to fit within the mores of the townsfolk, or they had to go. He'd fit right in with the administration, I thought.

But he was popular with the townspeople. He was their kind, their champion. He'd be their guardian on the board so that no hocus-pocus artsy bullshit would take over that junior college. He'd make sure of that. The college was a business. Education had a monetary value. That college was going to be a place to send your kids to get an education so they could go out in the world and earn an honest living. Nothing complicated about education, so far as he could see.

"Go ahead and run for the board, if you want," he said. "But I'll tell you one thing: I'm not withdrawing." He gave me that look of his, like he'd give a fellow for making a pass at his wife.

I knew I couldn't beat him in the election, and he knew it, too. I'd been too long the controversial citizen who claimed he didn't give a damn what people thought. The townsfolk were not going to put the education of their children in the hands of my kind, even though I might be the best trial lawyer in the state. The door of escape had been locked again.

Over the years the junior college proved to serve the community well. I thought it brought hope to many, to the housewife abandoned by her husband who desperately needed a new career, to the farmer who wanted more education in the business of agriculture, to the Native American who had been shunned and forgotten. I thought that Bob Peck, as usual, had a better grip on things than I. He was seen by many as the father of the community. That's how I saw him as well, and he knew better than I what his community needed. But for me, at last, there was no escaping into a more enlightened world through the Riverton Junior College.

Main Street in Riverton seemed frozen in place—like a Hopper painting. Five blocks of businesses on one street, the same stores, shoes all looked alike, the suits in J. C. Penney the same every year. People knew your wardrobe. If you got a new tie for Christmas, people knew. Everything was as it had always been. The same Gamble's store—had been there for twenty years or more, the Rexall Pharmacy where you whispered to the pharmacist out of the side of your mouth that you wanted a dozen Trojans, and the electric store, where bunches of fancy-looking chandeliers hung down from the ceiling, and, of course, Hay's General Store, in business since 1909, said so right up on the front of the building.

I walked into the Teton Hotel Coffee Shop, a big plain room with those old high ceilings with peeling paint, plastic-covered booths along the wall, and tables out in the middle. The city fathers had gathered, as on every morning, to pass the current gossip, to proclaim the prevailing wisdom that would be handed down to the townsfolk. They sat at a long table by the window where they could watch the same people walk by. When I stepped into the room the talking stopped.

The mayor was there, always was, the city engineer, too, the chief of police, the old boy who ran the local shoe store, the local Coors distributor, the owner of the electrical supply house, the owner of the local lumber company—they were the town fathers. I knew them all, knew their kids, their wives, their customers, their competitors, their enemies, their cousins, for Christ's sakes; knew them, and had known them for all those years.

When they saw me walk in, they looked silently away. Not one invited me to join them. I was a pariah, all right. Always had been. We fulfill our visions of ourselves. I looked over at that frieze of leading citizens at the coffee table. Suddenly I understood. I had sued some of them, or some member of their family, some of the lawsuits so long ago I had nearly forgotten. But they hadn't forgotten. One of the old boys I had challenged in a divorce case, and I had taken criminal cases against the chief of police. When you take a case in a small town, you pay. The person you sue never forgets. His family never forgets, and his friends become your enemies. Even your own clients can turn on you. You didn't get as much money for them as they wanted. Your fee was too high. You can walk away from a case with everyone in it despising you, even when you've won. I'd lived in Riverton, Wyoming, those seventeen years, and I'd been successful in alienating nearly every living soul in that small, forgiving community.

I used to visit old Orville Griffey up there on Griffey Hill by the airport. He was a recluse who lived with his herd of goats on that barren sagebrush-covered rise looking down on the town, his skinny house bursting out of the empty prairie like an oversized two-story outhouse. The siding on the house was of unpainted lumber, the wood darkened into a beautiful umber, the shingles on the roof mostly gone, gray and scaly like an old elephant's hide.

I liked to paint that ramshackle old house of Orville's sitting up there all alone like it was lost. Sometimes Orville would come over where I was painting away, and we would talk. He was lonely. You could tell that. Once he had been in love, he said, and something had happened, and he never got over it. I thought of that. I thought if I ever lost Imaging I would end up like Orville Griffey. Everything inside of the man had been mashed. People like Orville Griffey grew old and alone in strange ways. I understood the man.

When the wind whipped across the top of Griffey Hill and you couldn't see through the blizzard, Orville brought his goats into the house with him. Over the years, the goat manure had piled up because Orville didn't shovel it out. He didn't care. And when it got too high around him, he lifted his bed on top of the manure, and, as the years went by, the pile grew higher and higher until his bed was nearly touching the ceiling. I was like old Orville Griffey, I thought. I had fouled my nest, this town of Riverton, until at last I had to leave.

One morning I decided to go to Laramie, see the dean at the law school. Maybe I could teach. At my old alma mater I hunted up Frank Trelease, who was now the dean. He had been an important person in my life. He taught Torts and Judicial Remedies and he stood out in my mind as the one professor who, more than any, cared about the rights of human beings.

"If your client is even one percent negligent and the other party is ninety-nine percent negligent, under the law your client cannot recover," he once raged. The law of contributory negligence. "No one is ever totally free of negligence, except, perhaps, the baby in the cradle," Trelease said. "And even then, the negligence of the parent is imputed to the child." He paced up and down the floor as he talked. "The law is designed to deprive the people of justice. It is designed to protect the manufacturer, the employer, the banker and the businessman. It is designed to protect the rich and powerful. To hell with the ordinary citizen!" I didn't know what had gotten into the man. Tears came to his eyes. Tears in a professor's eyes? Some of the students made fun of him afterward.

Now I had a proposition for Dean Frank Trelease. We sat down in the corner of the library to talk. Some of the students were staring in our direction.

"Dean, it's time for me to make a change in my life. I've been a prosecutor. Never lost a case. I've defended criminals from petty thieves to murderers. Never lost a case. I hold every record verdict in this state in almost every area of damage law, and I've defended the insurance companies as well. Dean," I was laying a good argument on him, "I am your own *cum laude* graduate. I am the product of this law school. I think I know more about the trial of lawsuits in Wyoming than about anybody out there. I want to give something back. I'd like you to hire me as a professor. I can teach Torts and Criminal Law and Evidence and Procedure. I can teach whatever you want. And I can teach it from the standpoint of a man who's been there, who's done it. I can teach the kids how the real law works."

He looked at me and smiled sadly, as if I were still his innocent student. "You've done pretty well, Gerry," he said. "I'll give you that. Never had a doubt in my mind that you would."

"Don't remember you ever telling me so," I said, smiling back.

"But you don't understand this business," he said. "We have to be concerned about what the American Bar Association thinks of us. We don't get any Brownie points for hiring our own graduates. That's considered inbreeding. We get the nod from the ABA when we hire some top grad out of Harvard or Yale or Michigan who has practiced a year or two in a big firm back East and who then comes to us."

"But what the hell does a back East pointyhead know about practicing law in Wyoming?"

"That isn't the point. We're in a different game." Then he wanted to talk about fishing. How was the fishing up in Fremont County? And then he said he had a class in five minutes, and stood up and offered his hand. "You hang in there," he said. "You're doing all right. You made a hell of a lot more money last year than I did."

☼ ☼ ☼

By the spring of 1969, there was but one last avenue left open for my escape. Judge Sheldon had retired from the bench. If I successfully sought the judge-ship he was vacating I could become a judicial monk. I could live quietly in that small town in which I was inextricably trapped, give myself to selfless service, to the law and to the people. I would render justice in the court as I had longed to have it rendered in my cases. I would bring dignity back to my name, and to my family. Anna deserved no less. My children deserved no less. They had been patient with their father. Time for me to grow up. Yet I was still in love with Imaging. But in the same way that one fell into such traps, one must spring them, one trap at a time.

I set out with a fervor to obtain the required endorsements of the bar asso-ciations of both Natrona County—the county in which Casper, Wyoming's largest town, is situated—and the endorsement of my own home county of Fre-mont, both counties making up the judicial district where Sheldon's judgeship had been vacated. I met with the bar in Casper one noon. After lunch I made a moving speech about service to the bar, about how the members of the Natrona County Bar should endorse a trial lawyer who understood what it was to be a trial lawyer. Too many judges, before they became judges, had been helpless ninnies in a courtroom. "But," I argued, "when elevated to the bench, these judges now presume to tell us how to represent our clients and how to try our cases." I was gathering steam. "Too many mediocre lawyers who couldn't make a living trying cases if the other side defaulted have taken the bench." There was applause. I knew how to stir up an audience.

I saved the best reason for their endorsement for last: "Now you can get rid of me—permanently." They laughed, but their laugh only confirmed the truth. I had tried cases against many of them. I had been a "thorn in their side," as someone said in a separate speech on my behalf. By increasing my representa-tion of insurance companies, I was cutting into the business of the old insurance defense firms in that city. But, as judge, I would "ascend," as it is said, and traipse off to Fremont County, never to be encountered again by them, either as an adversary or a competitor.

I also had friends in the Natrona County Bar, men against whom I had tried many cases and won. And when the cases were over, we could sit down and have a drink together. Friendships grow out of respect. Several of the bar leaders—the venerable Bill Brown, then the respected dean of the bar; and Bill Barton, his partner; Joe Cardine, later Chief Justice of the Wyoming Supreme Court; Robert Rose, soon to become one of my closest friends, and later also to become the Chief Justice of the Wyoming Supreme Court; Raymond Whitaker, who had helped me try the now-famous Esquibel murder case; Tom Fagen, dean of the state's criminal defense lawyers—all of them rose to speak on my behalf. They could trust me, they said. They spoke kindly, reverently.

Bill Brown stood up. Everybody listened when Bill Brown stood up. "This guy will kill you in the courtroom," he said, his thin hair greased and slicked straight back, "but you don't have to watch your blind side with the man. I say, let's endorse him, let's put a great trial lawyer on the bench, and I agree—let's get rid of him." The applause was followed by a motion to endorse me to the new governor, Stanley K. Hathaway, and the motion unanimously carried. I felt loved.

But it wasn't love, although respect is sometimes better than love. I was endorsed by Fremont County as well, and Stanley K. Hathaway, the governor, was my friend. My appointment was a cinch. I began to plan my new life.

I was going to be a judicial monk, but what about Imaging? I could never give her up. Not once, however, had we spoken of marriage. How could we? We spoke fervently about love, and ardently of our longing when we were apart. We spoke about being with each other—always—about our dreams that someday, "when things worked out," whatever that meant, we might live with each other. But we never spoke about marriage. Now we didn't talk about what would happen after I became the judge. Things would work out. We knew that, trusted it. Had to.

With the announcement that Spence was seeking the district judgeship, my home county exploded into controversy. Gerry Spence a judge? The lawyers had endorsed him? Not on your life, some said! *The Riverton Ranger* was besieged with an organized letter campaign instigated by my enemies. One woman wrote,

> I am much opposed to the appointment of Gerry Spence, "square" as my opinions might be, I still maintain we need a strong, firm hand guiding our misguided youth. I don't think Mr. Spence is the man qualified to do this.

Others supported me, like a high school boy who wrote:

> . . . I have heard comments of other students and faculty members. I have come to the conclusion that many people in this area are blinded by prejudice and will believe anything they hear. . . .
>
> We definitely need more lawyers like Spence who are open-minded and individualistic in their work and their lives. I believe we need some sort of change, and Mr. Spence will give it to us.
>
> People of the community, please tell me why you are against Gerry Spence.

The Riverton Ranger editorialized without mentioning my name. Bob Peck, true to his friend, as always, wrote on my behalf:

> There is evidence that some chose the route of malicious gossip to try to get their way . . . Learned Hand, who observed that a community was already in the process of dissolution where " . . . non-conformity

is a mark of disaffection, where denunciation without specification takes the place of evidence."

Then one day, my friend Governor Hathaway called and asked that I come to see him in Cheyenne. I flew down, a sense of desolation having enveloped me. I knew what he wanted to tell me. He wasn't going to appoint me to the judgeship. I trudged up the steps of the state's Capitol Building, to receive the final word, face to face, from my old friend. He met me with his usual smile, puffing on the usual cigar. I sat opposite him, the massive official desk of the governor separating us, the American flag on one side and the flag of the great State of Wyoming buttressing him on the other.

"They put on quite a campaign against you," he started, smiling.

"Who?" I asked.

"You wouldn't want to know, Gerry."

"I do want to know."

"I have a stack of letters this high." He raised his hand off his desk a couple of feet.

"Could I see them?"

"I'll save you the pain." He sounded ominous. "I'm doing you a favor, Gerry. You could never be successful as a judge of others with so many judging you—and so harshly. You would be doomed to start with. You could never get reelected. Frankly, Gerry, I never saw such a grassroots uprising as your candidacy for judge has created. You are a great lawyer. Go try your cases. What a waste to put you on the bench." He got up, put out his hand, and I shook it.

"Remember," he said. "I will always be your friend." Then I went home to Anna.

That April, in the year of 1969, Governor Hathaway appointed a longtime resident of Lander as judge. He was an attorney I had known for years. He had defended Joe Cruz Martinez—a lawyer who by everyone's account, including mine, was as bland as oatmeal and as uncontroversial as chicken soup. Yet you had to like the tall, toothpick, blinking Jack Crofts. Everybody did. I did. The people did. That's the way of a free society, I tried to argue to myself. The people of Fremont County had spoken and I had heard them.

But I had yet to make my last remark.

CHAPTER 33

Imaging and Gerry and Christopher.

AT FIRST I had lied to Anna. I lacked the courage to injure her further. I could, of course, find fault with Anna. I don't paint her without it, but when I did point a finger trying to lessen my pain, the finger was always directed toward me.

That I grew weary of the guilt I bore over my mother's death never decreased its capacity to cause pain. A whip always cuts better with use. And having become an expert at dancing with guilt, I took on the guilt of my betrayal of Anna and held it close to me. Having killed my mother, I should now kill, as well, this woman, this early love, this mother of my children, and of me. No. I lied. Lied for as long as I could. But the voice betrays, the words too, the hesitation before the words stumble out. And that whistle-blowing body double-crosses you the way it jerks when it should be still, stiffens when it should be easy, the way the hands drop things and the eyes try to escape. A woman knows, and at last, she came onto us together.

I could no more erase Imaging than I could wash the spilled ink from the front of my white Sunday shirt. To love someone who loves you—men have killed for it, kings have renounced their thrones, and bloody wars have been fought for it. I was no different from any of those pathetic, stricken fools. Yet my wife and I had built this nest. Maybe it was ramshackle and hanging by small threads from a limb. Maybe it was swaying wildly in the wind, but it was the nest we had built, and we were both in it along with our kids. I had created a classic dilemma, of course. I could not give up Imaging, but I could not leave Anna.

Often I didn't sleep. I worried about Anna. Maybe she would be stunted in her heart like Orville Griffey. Once I broke the silence of the night with a loud cry, "Nooo!," and the sound in the silence startled me, and I was afraid.

Like a lawyer, I tried to put the issue on paper, in black and white, the small things I understood. Over and over, the word *trapped* kept appearing. But the trap was of my own making—I knew that. I was trapped as long as I was afraid to walk out of the trap. And Anna was trapped with me. I felt her hanging on, as a small animal clutches to the hide of its mother. To those who drank with me, I argued that I might do Anna a great kindness if only I had the courage to break free from her, "for in so doing" I said, "I would release her." But I knew it was only a lawyer's argument.

One time I saw a male robin who, against the laws of nature, had taken two nests. I saw the robin fly from one nest to the other, skinny as a flying snake, his eyes bulging, his squawks piteous. The robin was wrong. No, society was wrong. I could point the long, white, accusatory finger at society—this Christian dogma that decreed I could have but one love when I had been loosed on the world fully equipped to love two. It was Christ's fault, the church's fault, the fault of the compliant dullards who forced their mindless, puritanical mores on us. It was not my fault that I had simply followed the music and was being pummeled against the rocks. But this was not about fault.

And the kids. The old argument: A dysfunctional marriage is not good for the children. Better that parents have the courage to be divorced. How could children be healthy, I argued, living in a kitchen where the hurling of wild angry words provided the fodder for supper, and the endless screaming matches of wounded parents filtered through the floor registers to their rooms in lieu of bedtime lullabies? We must have the courage to destroy this rotting bed, I said, for the sake of the kids.

"That's bullshit," Anna said. "And you know it. 'The worst marriage is better than the best divorce.' I've heard you say it a thousand times yourself."

"I was wrong."

"You weren't wrong. You're wrong now," she said. "And what about your duty to me and to your children?"

"I thought you said you loved me. Love isn't duty."

"If the love is gone," she pointed her own long finger, "you took it away, and gave it to her."

I could no longer sleep in our bed, my back to her. I could no longer eat at our table, my eyes unable to look up from my plate. You fool. You are not that idiot robin. You can no longer hop from one woman to another. When I announced to Anna that I was moving out of the house, she walked up to me very quietly and asked, "Why are you leaving?"

"Because I have to," I said.

She began to cry, and she cried for a long time.

Then after a while her pain was replaced with anger, and I was glad for that. I could deal with the anger. Like screaming primates in the zoo, we raged at each other. And I wondered how the ape in the monkey house could survive outside his cage. Nonetheless, my stuff was packed. And I knew that all I had to do was walk out the door. Yet like a zoo-raised beast, when the door to the cage had been opened, I was afraid to leave. I had lived all my adult life with Anna. I had never left home, never considered it.

But I moved into a small, three-bedroom house on the other side of town. I asked the children to help me move. Perhaps, I thought, I could convince them I hadn't abandoned them, even in my leaving. I remember the innocent child, Kent, and that small blond angel, Katy, then only six. I remember their eyes, wide and hurt, as they helped me unload my things from the car. I thought if God were kind, he would cause me to disappear at this moment into the fog. I could remember my own fear when, as a child, I witnessed that one quarrel between my parents. I had whimpered to my father, "Are you going to get a divorce, Daddy?" I could remember his quiet reassurance, which I could not now give to my own children.

After I moved, I called Imaging, who, newly divorced, was still living in Casper. Sometimes she spent afternoons helping me make the stark rooms comfortable. She had been an interior decorator for some time—one, I soon learned, of great talent—and she knew how to do such things without all the money. She sewed up large fluffy pillows, and I brought along a grotesque statue of an armless woman sculpted by my brother, Tom, one Anna had stored in the garage. Then, I had a carpenter friend build a large, round table, and I set the statue in the middle of it. Imaging made a red corduroy doughnut-shaped pillow the size of the table so people could sit around it. I hung a porch swing from the ceiling, painted it bright yellow, and she lined the swing with more pillows.

One day, as Imaging was working at the house, we heard a knock at the door and there stood Kent and Katy. They had come for a visit. They looked at Imaging and pointed their baby fingers at the strange woman.

"Who is she?" Katy asked in her high child's voice.

"This is the pillow lady," I said.

"Yes," Imaging said, "you may call me Pillow," and after that they called her Pillow, and there were those special times when I, too, forgot and called her Pillow.

I tore down the wall between the two small unused bedrooms and set up my painting studio. There, among other tortured paintings, I painted the nude Imaging, the crow woman. She sat on the ground, her arms uplifted to the crows, the sky swarming with crows, crows fluttering down to her, cawing, crying, screaming at her peaceful, placid face. And one of the crows, perhaps the largest, the blackest, the loudest, was surely I.

I had to grow up. I thought if, at forty, I could finally grow up, everything would work out. Such a spoiled, frightened, child. I was no more capable of living

Painting of Imaging by Gerry Spence.

on my own than the featherless bird could fly. I set about trying to learn the art of independence. I wrote long letters to myself attempting to understand this monster child, with whom I was imprisoned. I wrote:

> As babies, we are selfish and live in a state of narcissistic love. As we grow older, we begin to lose our self-love and depend upon the love of others for our self-worth. But the healthy adult is one who gains his own self-worth and can live independent of the love of others.

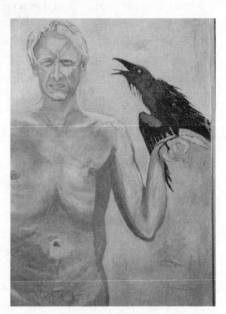

At night, in bed, in the dark, in this strange little house without the reassuring noises of children, in that tomb of

Self-portrait by Gerry Spence.

silence, I often put my arms around myself, held on to myself, trying to comfort this child, trying to become my own father and my own mother, and to thereby escape the larva of my past.

Invited or not, I received constant advice from my friends. One friend was Charles Hamilton, a Riverton lawyer, whose father had been the dean of the Wyoming Law School, a man who had been important in helping me make my early decisions. The younger Hamilton rented space from me in my new small

office building. One day he sat down with me to convince me that I should go
home to Anna. He listed all the reasons why.

"This falling in love is bullshit," Hamilton said. "You are thinking with your
dick. When your dick goes down, this love thing will wear off, but maybe it'll be
too late. Maybe you'll go home, and Anna and the kids won't be there anymore."
He began writing on a napkin the reasons why I should stay with Anna. I already
knew them.

> Anna is the mother of your children.
> She's a good woman.
> You will never get over the guilt.
> You have never lived a day with Imaging—how do you know it will
>   work?
> You will hurt your children beyond repair.
> Statistically, second marriages don't work.
> You are crazy. (How can a crazy man make an intelligent decision that
>   will irrevocably affect the lives of his wife and his four kids?)
> You are not sure. (If you were sure, you wouldn't be in such a
>   miserable quandary.)
> Besides, going home is the *right* thing to do.

I continued to live alone in that strange small house. Months passed. The
loneliness grew like thistles. When Imaging came to Riverton, my loneliness
disappeared like a whimsical storm, only to return when she left again. I longed
too much for her. I missed my children too much. I was too guilty over Anna.
At night I saw their faces. Once more at night I heard Kerry, my second child,
almost a young woman, crying, "It's about time you become a father to us,
Daddy!" I heard her agony and felt her anger. And I heard Kip saying in
response, "Maybe it's time we were children to him." I wept. More and more I
fell into the extravagant phases of manic depression. With Imaging I was wildly
happy. Without her I wallowed in the deepest abyss. Often I wondered about
my mother. Was this the pain she had experienced?

If I could escape the town perhaps I could heal and go home again. Perhaps I
would see Anna differently. Maybe there would be peace outside the trap. I also
felt trapped by my possessions. I was trapped by a home, by even that small paradise called Hidden Valley, where I had been happy. My developing plan was simple: I would sell everything, leave Riverton, abandon the entwining practice, leave
my friends, my history, and I would run, run even from Imaging, and perhaps I
could be free.

I found myself watching myself as I carried out the plan. Anna was in agree-
ment. I rented the vacant Western Auto Store building in downtown Riverton.
I took a full-page ad in *The Riverton Ranger.* I called the sale "Spence's Last
Remark!" The sale would be on June 6th, 1969. The ad read in part:

This is a complete sale, without reservation, of all of our personal belongings, my paintings, art works, our china, antiques, furnishings, knick-knacks, junk, extravagances . . . all of those things we have collected or created with love and sometimes foolishness in our past 17 years here.

I sold my guns, my archery equipment, the paintings other painters had given me, my own paintings, scores of them, Tom's paintings, his etchings, the pillows Imaging had made, our old clothes, new clothes, bikes, skates, fishing poles—it was all part of the trap, and I wanted rid of it all.

The ad went on:

Ad announcing the sale of Spence's property as they left Riverton.

Paintings are priced at $5.00, $10.00, $15.00; a few higher so that anyone who wants a Spence painting can have one. Some will sell for less than the cost of the paint and canvas . . . to any who have wanted a Spence painting, they are yours, almost for the asking—if you, indeed, want them.

All of the paintings were sold. For twenty dollars I sold the mounted hide of a young bear I had shot with a pistol far back in the Wind Rivers in a rainstorm one drunken morning. I sold the pistol. We sold our books, the piano. Every item one takes for granted in one's home was sold, down to the boxes of junk and the kitchen clock. The mounted trophies of the wild game I had shot I sold for a few dollars, and one that my father had given me, the first buck he had bagged as a boy, I sold for seventy-five dollars. We sold our home. I sold the beautiful Hidden Valley on the reservation. I sold my hideaway office building. I sold everything, right down to the extra toothbrush.

Already I had presented a portfolio of my artwork to San Francisco State, and although I had never taken a painting lesson, the art school, one of the best in the country, admitted me into its master's program in fine art based on my portfolio. I would still be useful, I thought. I had learned much about life from painting. I would give up the law. The law was not an instrument by which justice could be delivered to the people. I had witnessed its failures for almost twenty years. Rarely did the law hunker down and, like Grandpa Spence's old mules, pull for justice. I was sick of the deceit, the deviousness, the lawyer games, of the judges pretending to be the guardians of justice when they were the obsequious handmaidens of the rich. Charles Evans Hughes once remarked, undoubtedly with a smirk, "We are under a constitution, but the constitution is what we judges say it is." The judges had owned the law from the beginning. But they knew little of justice and, I thought, they also cared little for it. Dickens's Mr. Bumble was right. The law was "an ass."

The law had served me well, and I it. We were even. For me, the law had become a weapon. You could kill with the law. Like a pistol, if you possessed the courtroom skills, you could kill wherever you pointed it. I said it made me sick. Some said I was sick of myself. Some Freudian dilettantes made their unsolicited diagnosis of my condition. The sale of everything—down to the last spoon—my rejection of the law, of my career, of the town, of the townspeople, and finally, of my family, was only a subtle form of suicide. All right. I agreed. But I could not reject Imaging. In that one last place I still wanted life.

I remember the night I told Imaging I was going back to Anna. Had to make one last honest try, I told her. If I didn't try I would live in an eternal doubt, and one cannot live in such doubt. My words fell out of my mouth in horrid splatters, and I couldn't look at her, and I couldn't touch her to comfort her.

Serial killer.

Fiend.

I ran out into the night, but not after Imaging. She had already gone. The next morning, on a gray drizzling day, the heavens weeping, I left with Anna and the children for Mill Valley, California.

Anna and I leased a house in the tall dank redwoods, the sodden sun not often visible. The people passed me by like another stray dog on the street, another lost soul in cutoffs and sandals, another of the kind who slouched in the doorways, peering into the fog, the long, dirty faces under stringy hair looking for Nirvana, an olfactory halo of marijuana around them. I walked on by, the gorky walk only a bounce in the memory. I was looking for a pay phone to call Imaging. I found one at the filling station.

"Stay on your spot, darling," I said.

"It's you!" I could hear the joy. "What spot?"

"The spot right there. That black spot. Look down. Do you see it?"

"Yes," she said. "Of course, I see it."

"Stay on that spot. Stay there, exactly there, every minute, so I know where you are."

"Are you all right?"

"I'm in a well. And when I get out of this well I'm coming after you," I said. And when I called her, sometimes every hour, I would ask, "Are you on your spot?"

"Yes, darling, I'm on my spot," she would say.

It was strange to walk on those streets. Where once I had been somebody, admired, despised, but somebody to everybody, here I was a mere digit on the census count. I felt as if I had died and no one knew. I felt as if I were an unrecognized name in the obituary columns, that I was only a job for an undertaker. The amateur psychologists were right. I had killed myself. I lay in the bottom of this well I had described to Imaging, and the bottom of the well had become my sepulchre. I learned what the blues were like. I wrote a blues song about the well.

Falling in love when you're tied to another,
Yeah, falling in love when you're tied to another,
Is like falling to the bottom of the well, my brother.

Falling in love when you're tied to another,
Yeah baby, fallin' in love when you're tied to another,
Is like fallin' in a well where ya drown and ya smother.

And the sides of the well are all covered with ooze,
Yeah, the sides of the well are all covered with ooze,
And there's no way out but a bottle of booze.

Lookin' up from the well, there ain't much light,
Lookin' up from the well, there ain't much light,
'cept you, baby, far off in the night.

I'm crawlin' out, baby, crawlin' out for you,
I'm crawlin' out, baby, crawlin' out for you,
I may die in the tryin' but that's all I can do.

When I get out of this cold, deep well, baby,
Yeah, when I get out of this cold, deep well,
I'm gonna run to you baby, freed from this trap in hell.

I enrolled in the art school. The professors at San Francisco State were young, cocky, and as brittlely articulate as any graduate of Harvard Business School. They could talk a great painting, and they painted crisp canvases of junkyard cars, and of bicycles lined up in long racks, painted so precisely one thought an unfortunate photograph had been snapped, and hung in a blind man's room—"photo realism" they called it. They viewed me, politely, as this rustic refugee from the sticks, this curious winter bird blown in from Wyoming. I told them I wanted to learn something of life from painting, to teach it, to pass it on. How charming, they said with straight faces. But I would soon learn that painting was for painting, just as, I supposed, masturbation was for itself. Within a few days, disillusioned, disappointed, I dropped out.

Gerry Spence, the artist. 1969.

Imaging said she never left the house. Afraid to, she said. Afraid I would call and she would miss the call, those calls that came crying like the lost loon in the night.

"Are you on your spot, honey?"

"Yes, Adam, I'm on my spot." Yet I couldn't climb out of the well to come to her; the walls were too slippery, the well too deep. At last, terminally hopeless, I abandoned my disdain for psychiatry and sought a therapist recommended to me by a trainer I had known at Bethel, a man whom I trusted and who, by chance, was also a professor at San Francisco State. The psychiatrist he recommended was an austere, humorless fellow. Thin, pale and cadaverous, he looked like an undertaker—one who had spent a lifetime embalming the souls of the dead. Yet his distance, his refusal to join me in my panic, at last seemed kind. A distilled sort of caring seeped through his stodgy professional stance.

"I want to hire you," I said. "I need you to help me escape from my trap."

"Your trap?"

"Yes, my marriage."

"You carry your trap with you wherever you go," he said.

"All right," I said. "I want to hire you to help me get out of my portable trap."

"Fair enough," he said.

I called him "Shrink" to try to loosen him up. But he never loosened up. I drove into the city to see him several times a week. I tried to explain how I saw the trap—the well. I described the mossy, slippery sides, how I struggled up the sides, fighting to hold against the slippery sides. Sometimes, I barely got my head above the surface of the ground, and just when I was about to pull myself out, I went sliding back to the bottom again, exhausted.

"I am a backslider," I said. "Sort of like Sisyphus in a cistern."

He didn't laugh.

As soon as a session was over I would call Imaging. She was on her spot. Waiting. At times my friend John Ackerman got on the phone. He and my other friends were with her. They reported she was drinking too much. John Ackerman said he was afraid for her. And I grew afraid. Then, less than two months after I had fled to Mill Valley with my family, I called her to tell her the news.

"I'm coming back," I heard myself say.

Silence. As if she didn't hear me.

"I'm coming back," I said.

"When?"

"I'm leaving this afternoon."

"Are you coming back for good?"

"Yes," I said. "Are you on your spot?"

"Yes, I'm on my spot," she said, and her voice was very soft and the sound of her voice seemed very weak. I turned and walked down the street toward the house. When I came in the front door Anna was waiting. She looked at me. I didn't have to tell her.

My heart was racing, as if I were about to commit a fiendish crime.

"Where are you going?" she asked. I began packing my bags.

"Back to Wyoming," I said. "I belong in Wyoming."

Anna stood silent, watching. We had said it all, said it until the words were frayed and soiled.

Then I said good-bye to little Katy, kissed her, held her until I felt my footing at the edge of the well begin to give way, and the green ooze on the sides of the well began to envelop me. I whispered to Katy that I loved her and that I would never leave her, that I was leaving Mill Valley, not her. And there were no tears, just a child seeing her father leave. I thought I saw relief on her small face.

Then I was outside in the front yard. I was afraid to look back. The sides of the well began to surround me once more. I threw my bag in the trunk of the car and ran for the car door.

"You left your boots, Daddy," Katy said, running to me.

I looked down. I was barefooted.

Anna had followed me out to the car. "Can't you come back in and sit down and say good-bye?" she asked, her face deeply maimed by sorrow. "After all of these years, can't you say good-bye to me?" It was August 2, 1969, my father's birthday.

In panic, I turned from her, slammed the car door and drove off down the road barefooted, my boots still standing in the living room.

CHAPTER 34

Gerry and Imaging, wedding picture. 1969.

AT FIRST LIGHT the wind became silent and knelt with the rest of the world for those early morning rites to the sun. I had known for a long time that without the singing of robins in the springtime, the sun would never rise. Then the first flat yellow rays of the sun broke into the bedroom, like muted, dancing children, and when they bounced up on the bed, they lit the mountains of covers. And at the core of the earth I could feel her toe with my toe, and I carressed her foot with my foot, but I didn't look at her.

The bed was a magical bed, I have no doubt of that. I have thought, if any were so fortunate as to have slept in that bed, they could not but experience its benevolent power, and the magic of it would surely change their lives. A fine walnut Mallard bed of the Victorian period, its tall headboard dominated the room, and its stately face was defined with symmetrical posts and moldings and finely carved inlays. The bed had belonged to Imaging's Aunt Flo, who, even during Mississippi's hardest days, had lived a long and prosperous life. And she had grown to be a very wise old woman, the magic of the bed quite likely having accounted for it.

The bedroom, the bed butting up against its east wall, was on the second floor of one of those old English-style houses on Durbin Street in Casper with the twelve-foot-high ceilings on the first floor and ten-foot ceilings on the second. The wallpaper in the bedroom consisted of stripes and flowers—you could hardly notice the pattern, but the colors, the rich browns, the terra cotta, the gold and creams and grays, warmed the room, even before the sun had arrived. Facing the foot of the bed was a small love seat covered with gold velvet where I sat in the morning to put on my boots and stockings, and where the black Labrador pup, Old Sam, came bursting into the room to pull a stocking off of my foot before the boots went on, hiding it and himself under the bed.

Before the first rays of the sun had broken into the room, I had already made the coffee and brought our cups to the bed. At first we sat quietly, propped up against our pillows, peering into the rising steam from the coffee as if to see through to our future. It was a good time of the day, the kids still in their bedrooms below, and it was in the bed, that magic bed, where our lives took root and began to grow and bloom.

My divorce from Anna had been one of those default affairs in an empty courtroom, all the property and custody issues having been previously worked out by the lawyers, the assets split down the middle. When my case was called up, I sat there on the witness stand in an empty courtroom with Bob Rose, by then my partner, asking the questions, the judge looking down, nobody else giving a damn. In Wyoming you had to establish fault—"intolerable indignities" was the test. You took the oath, and then you testified to something against your spouse, the indignities of which had supposedly rendered the marriage intolerable.

"What has happened in your marriage that has made it intolerable?" Rose asked the standard question. I thought for a long time. The judge waited.

Falling in love when you're tied to another,
Yeah baby, fallin' in love when you're tied to another,
Is like fallin' to the bottom of a well, my brother.

I thought of jumping up and hollering, "I've fallen in love with another woman, Your Honor. And that renders the marriage intolerable for everybody. You have been there yourself, Your Honor," and he had. I thought of saying, "What is intolerable is watching Anna fight to hold on to her family. You cannot imagine the pain—for both of us." Nothing would come. Then I wept. And after a while the judge broke through it.

"You want a divorce?" the judge finally asked.

I nodded. I couldn't look up.

"Divorce granted," he said, and he walked off the bench.

That was in 1969, and within days after my divorce, Imaging and I had run off to Tahoe to get married. I used to laugh about it—just as well—that I've been unmarried only nine days in my entire adult life. The Sunday morning shrinks would have said I had escaped one trap only to fall into another. But a trap of love is not a trap. It's heaven with a fence around it. Imaging changed my life.

In bed, Imaging and I talked quietly about the war we were fighting. We were committed to stick together—no matter what we faced. Lot of enemies out there, waiting. We knew that. And the first enemy we had to whip was the booze. It could beat us if we didn't beat it first.

We were a new entity with six kids now. "My God," I said. "It's like inheriting a whole orphanage."

"Yes," Imaging said, "and all the kids in it are ours."

We had Christopher, her four-year-old, and Brents, nine. Sometimes Kent and Kerry were with us. Sometimes Katy, eight. Sometimes my kids were with Anna, and sometimes the kids, from two torn families, were thrown together.

We had to grow up ourselves. Parents growing up with their kids. Called for every brain cell we could muster. And we had to tap to the bottom of our reserve to keep from collapsing under the stress, the ripping apart of two marriages, the kids left confused, hurt more than they knew, more than they said. Mostly, the kids loved us back, but they also struck back in predictible ways, and at times there was no peace. And all of that hurt, the hurt of abandoned spouses, too, had to stand for something more than their sacrifice to some hedonistic orgy.

"We gotta make this thing work, Imaging," I said. "If we don't we've screwed ourselves good."

"And everybody else," she said. If love meant anything it had to be responsible—we said things like that. I knew the booze was in the way. She knew it, too. The booze was dangerous. It had to go.

I remember how, after we were married by the Justice of the Peace outdoors at Tahoe, those tall pines gawking down as witnesses, we had hurried back to San Francisco to be with my kids, and before we broke the news to them, we celebrated our marriage with a couple of hot fudge sundaes at Zim's.

"Here's to us," I said. I held up a dripping spoonful of ice-cream and chocolate.

"I'll eat to that," Imaging said holding up her own dripping spoon, And then we gave each other one of those hot chocolate kisses, and the people in there watched and thought we were the nuts for the topping.

Our morning sessions in the magical bed, became our daily meeting of Alcoholics Anonymous. In that magical bed we talked about living without the booze. "Strange life without the booze, like losing an old friend," I said.

"We have to find new friends. If you aren't drunk with your old friends you can't stand 'em anymore," Imaging said. "Sometimes I look in the bars now," she said. "You know, when you walk by from the dining room and see in, and you see all the losers lined up at the bar."

"I used to hang in the bars with all the losers. I was a loser," I said.

"Our old friends don't come around anymore," Imaging handed me her empty cup.

"They think we left them," I got us another cup of coffee.

"Sometimes I feel as if we left everybody," she said.

"We never left each other. And we aren't ever going to."

"Don't forget. No promises," she said. Then she didn't say anything more, just squeezed my hand.

And most mornings we talked about my "mother thing," as we called it. The same old hang-up, the guilt. And always the question, *Why?* I tried to use anger to get over it. It was a craven thing to do, to sneak out of bed, leave a note to nobody, blow your head off, and leave everybody sick and lost like that. But the anger didn't help. I remained guilty over Anna as well. The people you hurt always think there must be something wrong with them. But you did the hurting, and you feel the guilt. You can't pull something apart without hurting both ends.

You can't deal with all of these thoughts coming in from every direction unless you're stone-ass sober, as Imaging and I now were. We beat the booze, and we began to win most of the wars. I was learning as well in that magical bed how to deal with that whip called guilt.

I used to say to a friend who was laying the guilt on himself that guilt was the handiest self-flagellater I knew. "You wouldn't whip a friend like you whip yourself," I'd say. "But when it's you, you flog yourself unmercifully with the guilt whip, and you suffer. Then one day you've whipped yourself enough, and you know it. May take years, but one day you wake up and out of the blue you say, 'I've had enough. I've punished myself enough. This atonement is over. You, Guilt, get your ass out of here!'" And one day that's what I said. I said, "Guilt, get your ass out of here. I've had enough of you." And I had. But once in a while the demon snuck back in.

One morning shortly after we were married, Imaging and I were sitting in bed propped up on our pillows, and I was sipping at my coffee, looking through the steam and thinking about the trial I had won for the insurance company the day before. I recalled standing in a courtroom, a longtime friend on the other side of the case. In his way Ernest Wilkerson, my friend who was representing an old man, was as innocent as my father. Wilkerson's client had been injured in a car wreck, one caused by a drunk, the woman insured by the company we represented. I thought of the huckster at the carnival at Sheridan who had taken my father, an innocent farm boy, in a shell game, and there had been no money left for me to ride the bumper cars or the Ferris wheel. Now, over thirty years later, in another sort of shell game, we had taken the old man, and we had laughed about the trick. Bob Rose and I, by then my partner, called the drunk we now defended, "Apple Annie," and we had dressed the woman for court in a funny old hat and poor clothes. We had created a pitiful picture, with her sitting there while our friend Wilkerson was accusing her, with all due style and vehemence, of being drunk. We had trained the woman to sit quietly, her hands folded, and to look down in shame. As usual, the jury never knew about her insurance, and that if the old man got justice, not a penny of it would come out of the pocket of Apple Annie.

Ernest Wilkerson called his client to the stand. The old man had worked all of his life at the refinery at Casper. He was about to retire when he was hit by the drunk, this Apple Annie sitting there in court in that floppy hat. You could hardly see her face. The man had been badly hurt. He would never get well—his back, his legs, the old joints—the pain that never went away. He had looked to retirement, worked all of his good days in that noisy, smelly, poisonous hell hole, gave up the best part of his life to make a living for his family there, and all those years he had waited for his payback—his retirement. Big plans. Planned to go fishing with his grandchildren, spend balmy days in the mountains with his wife, take the pickup camper to the coast like old Jake in the warehouse had. But that was before our drunk had run into him, before the long months of hospitalization that followed and the final medical report that said he would never get any better, never be able to hit the stream with a good fly. It was over for him, all over, except the pain. Once invited, pain hangs on like a unemployed cousin.

When the old man took the stand, I didn't think of Grandpa Spence. Only later did I see the likeness between them, the sparse white hair, the limp, the old faded blue eyes. In the courtroom I sat a good distance from the man, focused on the words he spoke in a proud, matter-of-fact way, no whine in the voice, no underlying plea for sympathy. In the courtroom I am the hunter, and I saw the witness merely as the game. Had I seen him as a metaphor for my grandfather, I could not have made the kill.

I got up and began the cross-examination.

You cannot attack an old man. The jury would not stand for such bullying. The trick, instead, is to subtlely undermine his credibility, to politely dismember the old man, even with an unstated apology, to pull out a support here and one there until he begins to collapse and attacks you. Then, as the hunter, you have him cornered, and it is soon over.

I found the inconsistencies in what the old man had said to the jury a few minutes earlier and what he had said in his deposition months before. I mentioned them, a line at a time from the deposition, almost as if I were embarrassed for him. Then I found the contradictions between what the old man had just said to the jury and what the doctor said the old man told him in the hospital. In the eyes of the jury the doctor is always right. The doctor's not supposed to have a stake in the case, and therefore he records accurately what his patient told him. We trust doctors. We don't trust old men looking for a lot of money from an Apple Annie sitting over there looking as poor as old newspapers.

The jury watched. Listening, testing.

To me he was only a witness. He was not a man. He was not my grandfather, of course, and I did not know his grandchildren. As the cross-examination grew tighter, the old man became frustrated. I did not seem to understand his answers, and I asked the question again, but I was kind about it. I seem to care about the pain he claimed, but I insisted politely on putting him in nice corners. Then his frustrations broke out. That was the time when the witness began to lose the case, the pinch of frustration turning to anger, the anger breaking loose in small chunks, the edge of the voice tinged with hostility.

Still, I was kind to the old man. I pushed, but only gently, so that the jury was put off not by me, but by the witness who snapped back, his voiced gilded in anger. And angry faces are usually not pretty, especially on old men. He was controlling it, everyone could see that. But everyone knew that underneath, the man was seething, and we do not like angry people, not when the other person is being kind.

Now I backed off and I smiled sadly—compassion, you know. But the witness knew what was happening to him. He was caught between what he had said to the jury and what was being pushed in his face, the deposition pages that I showed to him, in black and white, which was where he said what he did not mean to say, which was where he said something different from what he now wants to tell the jury. He tried to explain. But explaining is for a man who is caught. I let him explain. His words were not careful words. They became tangled. The old man was not used to such a fight. He was like the wounded elk, trapped in the rock crevice, who could no longer run from the hunter, and at last the elk had no choice. It turned and charged, running at the hunter only to escape. The man was afraid, of course, but in the charge the fear came off as anger. But the hunter was not angry. The hunter was calm, his rifle ready, and the elk's eyes were red, its nostrils like gaping holes, and when the charge was over, the animal has been mortally wounded and fell dead at the hunter's feet. The witness was also injured. He struggled. And charged again. The anger of the beast, caught and helpless, was not good to see.

When I was finished with my cross-examination, the case was over, and justice for the old man was over, too.

After the jury returned its verdict for Apple Annie, Imaging and I had gone to Safeway to gather the fixings for a feast—the celebration. I would have invited our old friend, Ernest Wilkerson, but I knew he was too hurt over having lost the case. He had been a friend to both Imaging and me even before Imaging and I had met, and he had represented Imaging in her last divorce.

We had filled our grocery cart, and I was carrying on in the store, making a big scene, playing. I had grabbed a large green cucumber and had just completed a mock attack with it against Imaging when we rolled our cart up to the check-out line. An old man was standing in front of us. Hearing our voices behind him, the old man slowly, painfully, turned around. For the first time I was up close to him. He looked tired and sick. Up close I saw that his eyes were pale blue and watery, like Grandpa Spence's. I didn't know what to say.

"I'm sorry the way your case came out," I finally said. I saw the marks of pain on his face. Pain leaves a different track than age. I heard his labored breathing. Before, he had been "the adversary," the person the law gave me the right to kill in the courtroom, the person from whom I could steal justice, legally.

"You don't need to be sorry, Mr. Spence," the old man said. His voice was weary and soft. "You were just doing your job." Then he said it again, as if to convince himself. "You were just doing your job, Mr. Spence." He gave me a small smile.

I helped the old man out with his sack of groceries, and he thanked me, and Imaging and I went home—young, healthy, powerful, in love—the two of us off to celebrate having beaten an old hurt man.

It was that following morning, of course, that Imaging and I were sipping our coffee in the magical bed. I held the cup to my mouth and peered through the steam rising up from the coffee, and through it I began to hear the black leopards in the night, their words frightening my mother, my father, his back already tired, willing to lay more down for the insurance to protect my mother and "little Gerry" when there wasn't more for him to give. Suddenly I broke the morning's silence.

"Imaging, is that my job?"

"What, Adam?"

"Is it my job to cheat old men out of justice?"

But Imaging was silent.

She is a wise one, one who knows how to make great points with silence. Through the steam I could still see the old man's weary face. I thought of my Grandfather Spence, and how he had labored away his life behind a team of mules, drowned in his own sweat on that small farm, and I saw my old Grandfather Pfleeger fighting the dust and the jackrabbits, and I could hear my spindly little Grandmother Spence confessing to me, "Gerry, I wish I could be as good a Christian as your mother."

I saw my parents, that gentle fearless father coming down from the mountain, the blood of the elk on his hands, and that angel mother happily canning the corn, the old pressure cooker singing. I saw the hope that reflected in their eyes when they looked at me. Even as a child I saw it. I was the product of the toil of those generations. I was their blood, their history. I was their immortality, as our children are ours. Surely they hoped that the devotion of their genes would do something more than work to the profit of the insurance companies. Surely they had hoped for something better than my cheating poor old men out of their justice.

Once more I heard the leopards in the night, and suddenly I jumped out of bed, beat the Labrador pup to my socks, threw on my clothes and ran out the door.

"Where are you going?" Imaging asked.

"Gotta do something," I said.

I drove to the office. "Gotta talk to you," I hollered to my partner, Bob Rose. When I had returned from Mill Valley, he had made room for me in his practice in Casper. And, as soon as the companies discovered that I had returned, as if I had never left, they swarmed back like old vultures on new carrion.

"I mean, Jesus Christ, Bob, how can we do this for the rest of our lives?" I told him about the night before and the old man at Safeway. "How can we do this and walk down the street and call ourselves lawyers?"

"I been thinking about it a long time myself," he said. "Makes you sort of sick."

"The money?"

"We can make it," he said.

I thought about Lilly in the whorehouse in Laramie. If she wasn't lying with the college boys for five dollars a go, some other pretty girl with her flesh still firm and her eyes still clear would lie down on her small bed and take her place. It was the old argument. If Lilly didn't, somebody else would. Somebody was always in line. But when I had asked for Lilly, she was gone. Lilly had made her choice, both to start and to stop. Decent enough men and women make their own arguments for what they do for the insurance companies and banks. I had made them myself. But once you take a room in the house, it's hard to get out again. Yet Lilly had.

I composed a letter to all of the insurance companies and other corporations Rose and I represented. They would please send their representatives to pick up their files. We would no longer represent them—not any of the "non-breathers," as I liked to call them.

I could still hear my father saying that the company treated its people like old rags, and when they were used up, the company tossed them out. My father never had a choice. Those corporations with ink for eyes and digits for souls could go on staring at their financial statements without me.

So that morning in that magical bed drinking coffee with Imaging, I made my choice. And after that I refused to represent any insurance companies and any banks and any more of those invisible creatures called corporations, those fictional entities created by man that permit men to do against each other what they would not do in their own names. And, unless there was an overriding public issue in the case, I refused to represent the rich and the powerful. There are plenty of lawyers for the rich. I represented only the people, people like the old man in the Safeway Store. After that I represented the lost and the forgotten. And the hated. I took on the cases of the people against the powerful, and I did not do it for points in heaven or out of any generosity of the heart, for my motive was wholly selfish. I was still a pleasure-seeking man, and there wasn't much pleasure taking on the fight for the non-breathers against the ordinary person struggling for justice. And, too, I never had a corporation hug me out of gratitude for having won its case.

Over the years my decision seemed to somewhat muffle the demons. As for my mother, she began to hang out in the shadows and became a more silent observer. And sometimes, through the dim light of the early morning, when I was bringing our coffee back to bed, and when the first beams of the sun danced over the mountains of covers, I thought, at last, I saw my mother smile.

EPILOGUE

Esther Sophie Spence, mother of Gerry Spence.

WHY HAD MY mother, that angel, who had never exhibited the first suggestion of violence, not to me, not to a bug on the floor, turned the ultimate human violence on herself? How could my mother, who was as sinless as any saint, have committed that one unforgiveable sin? The ghostly finger continued to point itself at me, and although as the years flew by, the ghost more often stood in the shadows, still the "why" of my mother's suicide remained a persistent pain at my core. I dreamed of her often.

As I began to write this book, I read anew my father's autobiography, *The Evolution of a Hillbilly Kid.* Perhaps during all of those painful years I hadn't wanted to look closer at my mother's last days for fear that what I might see would magnify my pain. In his book my father wrote along in his sparse sort of way:

> Esther worked quite closely with this Bolivian fellow, Pastor Meneses.
> He was at our house frequently and at all hours. We got word that
> Pastor Meneses had been killed by the Indians—stoned to death. It

really shook Esther up. Every time we talked about it tears filled her eyes. Had she fallen in love with Pastor Meneses?

My father wrote on:

Esther was having trouble sleeping. Several times I was awakened by her crying. I would ask her what the trouble was and she would reply. "I don't know. I just can't sleep." I would roll over and hold her close and she would quiet down.

In my dream, when the music stopped, my mother and I walked from the dance floor to the edge of the crowd. I thought that we should get the matter settled between us.

"Why did you leave us, Mother?" I looked straight into her eyes.

"I never left," she said.

"Where have you been, then, all of these years?"

She turned away from me as if to go. I reached out for her hand.

"I couldn't sleep," she said. She was looking off into the distance. "I grew old without sleeping."

And then I saw the natives circling around the man, and I heard them chanting and jeering. He was a smallish Bolivian with a moustache, and he had both arms over his head and was stooped over trying to fend off the rocks the mob was hurling at him. The mob, all in rags and bare feet was screaming.

And the stones, some larger than baseballs landed on the man, and the stones struck his arms where he protected his head, and the stones hit his back with a terrible thud of rock on flesh, and soon the man fell, and he took the fetal position, his arms still over his head.

Then the mob moved in close to him, and at the edge of the crowd I saw my mother. She was horror stricken and her hands were at her face. I heard her crying, and after that the mob made quick work of the missionary, and his skull was crushed in. And in the distance, I saw my mother running, and after that I never saw her again.

AFTERWORD

1996

ANNA STAYED IN Mill Valley, bought a nice home. She liked it there. She was a good and handsome woman and found friends and loves of her own and has devoted much of her life to their spiritual uplifting. She was always there for the children, and she helped many people. I thought of her as a tree struck in an early storm that took on a grace and dignity that set the tree apart from the forest.

We tried to share the children, Anna and I, to make safe havens for them at both ends, but the kids were confused, like baby birds dumped out of their nests, and they were hurt, and although they said they were glad the anguish was over, it wasn't over. You don't turn the hurt on or off like an alarm clock. And the kids, trying to escape the hurt—some of which grew out of their own growing up—were not easy, not with themselves or with any of us. It was as if a new war had begun, a wild free-for-all in the orphanage. If one wasn't up with a problem or causing one, another took over, like in tag team wrestling. Imaging's boys became mine and my children hers. Where she had had two, mostly peaceful younger sons, Brents and Christopher, she now had six swinging prehensiles, one of every age, one in every stage of development: dependence, revolt, aggression, you name the psychic poison. We needed all of the new power that sobriety had provided. I felt like one of those old hens in grandpa's barnyard, the chicks running in every direction and the coyotes after me.

Our children, despite the resulting trauma of our divorces, all magically succeeded. Kip took a graduate degree in fine art from the San Francisco Art Institute and is married with two daughters. He is a fine craftsman in finish carpentry. Kerry has her own paralegal practice of many years, is devoted to helping the poor, and is also married, a model mother with two children. Kent practices law with me and has turned into a fine trial lawyer. He, too, is married and sports a new baby daughter. Katy has taken a graduate degree in psychology, is licensed as a family counselor, and is presently building her own practice. Brents is a successful businessman, and has his own climbing gym in Jackson. He is married with a baby son on the way. Christopher established his private law practice in Jackson, is married and has one son and another child coming soon. The children that our children married are also our children, as are our six grandchildren. We are fast approaching the dilemma of the Old Lady in the Shoe.

ABOUT THE AUTHOR

Gerry Spence, the Country Lawyer. 1995.

IN THE YEARS that followed, Gerry Spence went on to try the renowned Karen Silkwood case, which elevated him into national prominence, a case in which the jury awarded his client a verdict in excess of ten million dollars. After that he obtained a series of multimillion-dollar verdicts including a fifty-two million dollar verdict against McDonald's for a small bankrupt ice cream company, a twenty-six million dollar verdict against *Penthouse Magazine* for Miss Wyoming, and a settlement in excess of forty million dollars for the workers against U.S. Steel. He won a verdict in excess of forty-five million against Aetna Insurance Company for a severely injured client who alleged fraud against the company, and numerous other multimillion-dollar verdicts. During the more than twenty years that followed the time frame of this book, his court work has changed the face of trial law in America. He has successfully defended numerous first-degree murder cases, obtained acquittals for Imelda Marcos and Randy Weaver of Ruby Ridge, and has not lost a jury trial since 1969. He has never lost a criminal case either as a prosecutor or as a defense attorney. For over twenty-five years he has refused to represent banks, insurance companies, big business, big

corporations, and, unless, as in the Imelda Marcos case, there are overshadow-
ing public issues, he also refuses to represent the rich and famous.

Spence is the author of seven books, is an accomplished photographer,
painter, and television host and commentator. He is the founder of Trial
Lawyer's College, a nonprofit school, where he and the nation's leading trial
lawyers teach young trial lawyers how to win against government and large corporations on behalf of the individual. He is also the founder of Lawyers and
Advocates for Wyoming, a public interest law firm devoted to public interest
cases. His agenda: to promote justice in America for the "little guy" and to make
the American justice system work for the "average citizen."

LIST OF PHOTOGRAPHS
AND ILLUSTRATIONS

Front cover: Spence as a boy with gun: Photo by Spence's father, G. M. Spence

Spence as a man: Photo by D. J. Bassett

Back cover: Spence as a baby in his father's arms (c. 1930). Photographer: unknown

All drawings by Tom Spence, Gerry's brother

I am deeply indebted to *The Riverton Ranger* and my friend of many years, Bob Peck, for the historical photographs supplied for this book.

—*Gerry Spence*

INDEX